Facets of Social Geography
International and Indian Perspectives

Edited by

Ashok K. Dutt, Vandana Wadhwa, Baleshwar Thakur,
Frank J. Costa

FOUNDATION®
BOOKS

Delhi • Bengaluru • Mumbai • Kolkata • Chennai • Hyderabad • Pune

Published by
Cambridge University Press India Pvt. Ltd.
under the imprint of Foundation Books
Cambridge House, 4381/4 Ansari Road, Daryaganj, **New Delhi** 110 002

Cambridge University Press India Pvt. Ltd.
C-22, C-Block, Brigade M.M., K.R. Road, Jayanagar, **Bengaluru** 560 070
Plot No. 80, Service Industries, Shirvane, Sector-1, Nerul, **Navi Mumbai** 400 706
10 Raja Subodh Mullick Square, 2nd Floor, **Kolkata** 700 013
21/1 (New No. 49), 1st Floor, Model School Road, Thousand Lights, **Chennai** 600 006
House No. 3-5-874/6/4, (Near Apollo Hospital), Hyderguda, **Hyderabad** 500 029
Agarwal Pride, 'A' Wing, 1308 Kasba Peth, Near Surya Hospital, **Pune** 411 011

First Published 2012

ISBN 978-81-7596-801-1

Published by Manas Saikia for Cambridge University Press India Pvt. Ltd.
Printed at India Binding House, Noida

Allen G. Noble
Distinguished Professor Emeritus of Geography and Planning,
The University of Akron, USA

Contents

Foreword

It has been more than thirty years since I first met Allen Noble. I was a first-year graduate student who had just entered the MA program in geography at the University of Akron. Allen was Head of the Department. One of my earliest memories of those graduate school days was a day-long field trip around Akron and its environs, an annual event which Allen always led for new students. It began early in the morning and went well into the evening. By day's end the group was completely exhausted save one. Allen ended the day as fresh, enthusiastic, and energetic as he began it.

Throughout my graduate days at Akron I saw that same enthusiasm and energy exhibited over and over again. I saw it in the classes I took from Allen, in the mentoring he provided as my thesis advisor, and in his informal interactions with faculty, staff, and students. Ultimately, I too entered academe and over the years have worked with Allen on various projects. And, yes, he always approached our collaborations with the same enthusiasm that I experienced in my early graduate school days.

Those who know Allen are quick to realize that this enthusiasm springs from his passion for all things geographical. It is a passion that spans Geography's spectrum – physical, cultural, social, regional, urban, etc. He brings a distinct intellectual curiosity to virtually every sub-field of the discipline. It is fitting, then, that this particular volume has been assembled in his honour. Like Allen's own research, the works presented here span a range of topics and regions (e.g., ethnic newspapers in the US, regional development in China, minority groups in Israel, urban sprawl in Nepal, and crime patterns in India). That said, the book's emphasis on South Asia is entirely appropriate given Allen's love of that region and his own work there. Further, the breadth and depth herein neatly parallels the considerable breadth and depth of Allen's own work which has been defined by a keen interest in cultures and the regions they have shaped.

Allen's geographical acumen has caused others to look to him for leadership and guidance and he has provided much of that over the years. His many contributions to the field, both as a scholar and as a teacher, will impact the discipline for generations to come. One can learn about many of these contributions in the first three chapters of this work. From there the reader can continue on and explore a multiplicity of themes which will surely serve to expand her or his geographical horizons.

Brian Coffey
Professor and Director
Urban Studies
The University of Washington Tacoma

Preface

> I claim that human mind or human society is not divided into water-tight compartments called social, political and religious. All act and react upon one another.
>
> Mohandas Karamchand Gandhi

Although it may be possible to distinguish the various streams that comprise Social Geography, these fluid currents flow together to create a vast body of inter-and-intra-disciplinary study. This book attempts to capture the holistic essence of this field as well as highlight its rich thematic and areal diversity. Organized society and its institutions and characteristics over space go back to prehistoric times. It is no surprise then, that the field of social geography presents a full panoply of subjects of study.

Since its establishment as a recognized sub-field of geography in the twentieth century, Social Geography has continuously evolved to reflect the changing socioeconomic and political climate. Thus, the birth of radical geographies of feminism, the increased volume of alternate voices of transnationalism, postcolonialism and emerging geographies, the embracing of postmodernist methodologies and tools of interpretivism, the adoption of Geographic Information Systems (GIS) and remote sensing techniques to tackle social themes of study and so on. Such rapid changes necessitate the need for revisiting the state of the field every so often, while maintaining a connection with its traditional roots and themes.

Therein lies the significance of this book. The current work presents a number of contributions that provide an overview of the works that laid the foundation for Social Geography, or themselves address some of the traditional themes in Social Geography, such as art and culture, urbanism and crime, and social institutions of caste, class, and religion. It includes contributions that reflect the changes in the field over the latter half of the twentieth century, presenting chapters on the geographies of gender, disability and activism, and works that use newer methods and methodologies. All in all, it is a fitting tribute to Dr. Allen G. Noble's scholarly contributions in this field. Noble, a Distinguished Professor Emeritus of Geography and Planning at the University of Akron, and a recipient of multiple awards from the Association of American Geographers (AAG) and Asian Urban Research Association (AURA), is a world class social geographer and has worked on various facets of social geography in India and the United States. Thus, book is a joint product of scholars primarily from these countries. Of the 42 contributors, 27 are from the United States, 13 from India, and one each from Nepal and Israel. Of the 27 contributors from the United States, about half are of Indian origin; thus, in the mould of Noble, each contributor is deeply engaged with the region of their study. All authors are familiar with Noble's scholarship, and most of them have been associated with him academically.

The book's subject matter represents both conceptual and empirical approaches. Noble's significant contributions to studies on South Asia and China have been specifically elaborated upon. In keeping with the rich complexity of the field of social geography, this book covers a range of themes, geographies, scales of study, and methodologies. The book's conceptual section is universally relevant to the student or scholar of this field, regardless of their own geographical placement. This section is valuable due to its inclusion of both traditional and emergent social geography themes and methodologies. Additionally, international comparisons and perspectives have been included for topics as diverse as social planning, enterprise zones, social and economic inequities, and thematic and methodological developments in Social Geography. A majority of the chapters of the book are on India, three on the United States, and one each on China, Israel and Nepal. The book thus has a primary focus on India, though it provides a view of social geography from an international perspective.

The chapters on India relate to Noble's contributions on Indian social geography, socio-cultural groups of Indian society, its religion and linguistic identities, folk arts and dance, its hierarchical social structures of caste, gender, and class, and social issues pertaining to crime, and rural human resource development, among others. The book specifically deals with regional, state, and city-scale social geographical aspects of India, covering topics such as the human–environment relationship, health and healthcare, the geography of sacred places, dynamics of urban growth and its consequences, and analyses of city and society based on literature. India's social structure, based on centuries old principles of *Karma* and a four-level caste system is specifically dealt with in this book in order to help unravel the country's unique social geography. Thus, this book provides a comprehensive understanding of India's social structures and offers an analytical framework to understand this using various methods such as statistical analyses, GI Sciences (GIS and Remote Sensing), and literary and qualitative analyses.

The book chapters contain research by both established and emerging scholars. Since this book provides a breadth of information on the nature, scope, history and evolution of Social Geography, along with a good representation of approaches and techniques used in the field, it is specifically meant for library acquisitions in various countries of the world. The contents would be of interest to students, researchers and those interested in social geography.

Ashok K. Dutt
Vandana Wadhwa
Baleshwar Thakur
Frank J. Costa

Acknowledgements

We extend our appreciation to the faculty and staff of the Department of Geography and Planning, University of Akron. We especially thank former Head Professor Robert Kent, who now heads the Department of Geography at California State University, Northridge. We also extend our thanks to Professor Charles Monroe, who was former and Interim Head of the Department and Associate Dean of the College of Arts and Science when this book was undertaken. Many thanks are also due to Marlene Harmon, Department Secretary, Dr Kevin Butler, Computer Services Director, Graduate Assistants Thomas J. Young, Joseph Boateng, Jinnan Zhang, and Qing Shi for their valuable assistance and diligent work in preparation of this manuscript. We are also deeply indebted to the entire Cambridge University Press India Pvt. Ltd. team who have patiently and tirelessly worked with us to bring this volume to fruition.

Additionally, I (Ashok K. Dutt) am personally indebted to Allen for a long association of forty-two years at the University of Akron where we were colleagues and organizers of several projects all over the world. My association with him resulted in benefits to my scholarly intake and enriched my academic credentials. I also acknowledge the contributions in this book by Allen's former students from the Akron Geography and Planning Department, such as (alphabetically) Satish Davgun, Ramesh Dhussa, Rajrani Kalra, Chandra Khan, Chadralekha Sangwan, Sudhir Thakur, Samuel Thompson, and Vandana Wadhwa. They have all benefited from Allen's guidance in the advancement of their scholarship. I am also deeply thankful to my wife Dr Hiran Dutta, Professor Emeritus, Kent State University, for her encouragement and constant help during the four year period of the planning and editing of this book.

I (Vandana Wadhwa) would like to acknowledge Dr Noble's contribution to my personal and professional growth – starting from my first encounter with him, he has always provided encouragement, constructive critique for scholarship, and a wonderful sense of humour to every situation. I would also like to take this opportunity to thank all three of my coeditors in this venture; Dr Dutt for being a wonderful mentor and father-figure who has shaped my life greatly, Dr Costa, whose constant faith in me and immense enthusiasm for good scholarship have left a lasting impression on every piece of research I undertake, and Dr Thakur, whose help and encouragement in many projects has been absolutely invaluable. My thanks also to Dr Hiran Dutta ('mommy'), who is an inspirational figure, both as a scholar and a person. Finally, thanks as always to the two constant sources of love and encouragement in my life: my husband Vikram and my sister Meenakshi.

List of Contributors

1. **Rais Akhtar**, Professor (retired) of Geography, University of Kashmir, Srinagar, J&K, India, and current National Fellow, Indian Council of Social Science Research, New Delhi, India.
2. **John E. Benhart**, Professor (retired) of Geography, Shippensburg University, Shippensburg PA, USA.
3. **R. B. Bhagat**, Professor, Department of Migration and Urban Studies, International Institute for Population Sciences, Mumbai, India.
4. **Manjusri Chaki-Sircar** (Deceased), former Faculty, Columbia University, New York, USA.
5. **Meera Chatterjee**, Visiting Assistant Professor, Department of Geography and Planning, University of Akron, Akron OH, USA.
6. **Frank J. Costa**, Professor Emeritus of Geography, Planning, Urban Studies and Urban Affairs, University of Akron, Akron OH, USA.
7. **Anindita Datta**, Senior Lecturer, Department of Geography, Delhi School of Economics, University of Delhi, Delhi, India.
8. **Satish K. Davgun**, Chair and Professor, Geography Department, Bemidji State University, Bemidji MN, USA.
9. **Aparajita De**, Assistant Professor, Department of Geography, Delhi School of Economics, University of Delhi, Delhi, India.
10. **Ramesh C. Dhussa**, Associate Professor, Department of Geography, Drake University, Des Moines IA, USA.
11. **Ashok K. Dutt**, Professor Emeritus of Geography, Planning, and Urban Studies, The University of Akron, Akron OH, USA.
12. **Elisha Efrat**, Professor Emeritus of Geography, Tel Aviv University, Tel Aviv, Israel.
13. **Maura E. Huntz**, Technical Training Manager, Commercial Systems Group, Sunnyvale CA, USA.

14. **Nilofar Izhar**, Academy for the Study of Environment and Social Wellbeing, Aligarh Muslim University, Aligarh, UP, India.
15. **Thomas R. Jordan**, Associate Director, CRMS, Department of Geography, University of Georgia, Athens GA, USA.
16. **Chi Kin Leung**, Professor, Department of Geography, California State University, Fresno CA, USA.
17. **Rajrani Kalra**, Assistant Professor, Department of Geography and Environmental Studies, California State University, San Bernardino CA, USA.
18. **Surya Kant**, Professor, Department of Geography, Panjab University, Chandigarh, India.
19. **Pradyumna P. Karan**, Distinguished Professor, Department of Geography, University of Kentucky, Lexington, KY, USA.
20. **Sya Buryn Kedzior**, Lecturer, Geography Department, Humboldt State University (a CSU campus), Arcata CA, USA.
21. **Robert B. Kent**, Professor and Chair, Department of Urban Studies and Planning, California State University, Northridge CA, USA.
22. **Chandrakanta C. Khan**, Professor, School of Critical Studies, California Institute of the Arts, Valencia CA, USA.
23. **V. Vijay Kumar**, Ph.D. Scholar, Department of Geography, Osmania University, Hyderabad, AP, India.
24. **Chi Kin Leung**, Professor, Department of Geography, California State University, Fresno CA, USA.
25. **Lawrence J. C. Ma**, Professor Emeritus of Geography and Planning, University of Akron, Akron OH, USA.
26. **Kalpana Markandey**, Professor, Department of Geography, Osmania University, Hyderabad, AP, India.
27. **E. Cotton Mather** (Deceased), former Professor of Geography, University of Minnesota, Minneapolis-St. Paul MA, USA.
28. **Chandana Mitra**, Ph.D. Candidate, Department of Geography, University of Georgia, Athens GA, USA.
29. **Debnath Mookherjee**, Professor, Department of Environmental Studies, Western Washington University, Bellingham, WA, USA.
30. **A. B. Mukerji**, Professor (retired) of Geography, Panjab University, Chandigarh, India.
31. **Harry 'Bud' Pilarski**, City Planner, Collier County, Naples FL, USA.

32. **Krishna Prasad Poudel**, Reader in Geography Education, Tribhuvan University, Kirtipur, Kathmandu, Nepal.
33. **B. K. Roy**, Director (retired), National Atlas and Thematic Mapping Organization, New Delhi, India.
34. **Chandralekha Sangwan**, Dayton OH, USA.
35. **J. Marshall Shepherd**, Associate Professor, Department of Geography, University of Georgia, Athens, GA, USA.
36. **Rana P. B. Singh**, Professor of Geography, Banaras Hindu University, Varanasi, UP, India.
37. **B. R. K. Sinha**, Professor, Department of Geography, Banaras Hindu University, Varanasi, UP, India.
38. **Parbati K. Sircar** (Deceased), former Professor of Geography, State University of New York, New Paltz NY, USA.
39. **Baleshwar Thakur**, Professor (retired), Department of Geography, Delhi School of Economics, Delhi University, Delhi, India.
40. **Sudhir K. Thakur**, Assistant Professor, College of Business Administration, California State University, Sacramento CA, USA.
41. **Samuel Thompson**, Associate Professor and Chair, Department of Geography, Western Illinois University, Macomb IL, USA.
42. **Kavita Toran**, Project Associate, Department of Geography, Osmania University, Hyderabad, AP, India.
43. **Vandana Wadhwa**, Visiting Scholar, Department of Geography and Environment, Boston University, Boston MA, USA.
44. **Yehua Dennis Wei**, Professor, Department of Geography, University of Utah, Salt Lake City UT, USA.
45. **Mukesh Yadav**, Manager, Development & Management Group, Delhi, India.

I

Introductory Framework: Allen G. Noble's Contribution to Social Geography

1

Allen G. Noble: The Making of a Scholar

Ashok K. Dutt, Vandana Wadhwa,
Frank J. Costa and Baleshwar Thakur

Allen G. Noble, born in New York City and raised in central New York State, received his undergraduate degree from Utica College of Syracuse University in 1951. From there he went on to the University of Maryland to complete an MA in Geography in 1953. He undertook doctoral work at the University of Illinois where he was awarded a PhD in Geography in 1957. After completing his PhD, Allen joined the United States diplomatic service. He held consular positions in India and Brazil and was also posted at the State Department in Washington, D.C. Allen's international experience and consequent interest in diverse geographic settings became the foundation for his future research work in geography. Through his international exposure, he came to appreciate diverse political and geographic issues and conditions. Initially an observer, Allen progressed towards detailed study and research into different cultures and their constituent elements. He, thus, was establishing the basis for his career as a cultural geographer. Among the diverse settings to which Allen has applied his research skills and attention are India, China, Sri Lanka, Pakistan, Bangladesh, Nepal, Indo-China, Saudi Arabia, Israel, Finland, Spain, Greece, Italy, Poland and Brazil.

After more than six years in the diplomatic service, Allen decided to seek a teaching position in USA. His first appointment was in the Department of Geography at California State College in Pennsylvania (1963–64). Allen then moved on to the University of Akron where he has spent the rest of his career as Professor, Head of the Department of Geography and Planning, Distinguished University Professor and, currently, Professor Emeritus.

Noble Emerges as a Distinguished Cultural Geographer

As with many scholars, Noble's work has progressed through several stages. The late 1960s and early 1970s make up the first stage during which Noble established a professional niche for his future research. During this period he worked on the physical geography of Latin America, but eventually gravitated towards cultural geography. His early work in cultural geography relates primarily to the built environment and includes topics such as fence patterns, houses, cottages, silos and barns. Fortunately, he discovered an associate with whom he could collaborate. This was Margaret Geib, staff cartographer at the Department of Geography and Planning of the University of Akron. Margaret, now deceased, was raised on a farm and continued to live in her family's rural homestead until the end of her life. Noble and Geib worked together on seven papers published between 1974 and 1976. Margaret brought to the works her knowledge of farming and farming techniques, along with her outstanding ability as a cartographer. Her artwork greatly enhanced Noble's text and this collaboration greatly encouraged his interest in the rural built environment.

Noble's work has had a lasting influence on cultural geography. Apart from his work on the built environment and material culture, he has also published extensively in the field of non-material culture. His primary research focus in material culture has been on the United States. He has published on a vast array of topics including barns, silos, house types, greenhouses, windmills, building materials, small town design and morphology, and preservation of historical structures and places. In his work he has traced the evolution of built-form materials and patterns from more traditional forms to recent innovations using metallic and polymer products. An important milestone in Noble's research career was reached with the publication of three books on material culture. These are *Wood, Brick and Stone: The North American Settlement Landscape* (Volumes 1 and 2) in 1984 and *The Old Barn Book: A Field Guide to North American Barns and Other Farm Structure* in 1995. These books are now classics and standard reference materials. They are found in most major libraries of the world.

In her review of *Wood, Brick and Stone* in the *New York Times Book Review*, Sara Ferrell wrote:

> The richness of American folk architecture, in both its original and evolved forms, is enough to make your head spin, and Mr Noble does

> it full justice. To give only a few examples of his subjects – which range from the earliest dwelling on this continent to the California bungalows of the 1920s – there are the saddlebag houses, double-pen houses and dogtrot houses (all derived from the log cabin) of the Southeast, the cornbelt cubes (descended from the western bungalows and German–Russian houses of the great plains) of the Midwest, the indigenous hogans and Ramadas of the Southwest and the Spanish-Mexican Monterey house of California. Mr Noble tells us anything we might ever need to know about them–what they are built of, how they were built, why they are where they are. His arguments are further served by a good selection of slightly muddy black-and-white photographs and clear maps, floor plans and detailed drawing by M. Margaret Geib. The second volume, *Barns and Farm Structures*, is every bit as good, which is saying quite a lot. No architectural taxonomist should be without them. (Ferrell, 1985, p. 22)

Noble has utilized modern geographic research techniques including Geographic Positioning System (GPS) in mapping material culture. In the area of non-material culture, Noble focused on ethnic settlement patterns, migration, and crime patterns. His work on ethnicity in Utica, New York and Dumka, India and his studies of immigrant experiences in the United States have been noteworthy. Noble has also published extensively in the areas of tourism and sustainable development in tourism.

Noble is an internationally recognized cultural geographer. His studies of rural building types and the material composition of settlements and settlement patterns are classics. His most recent contribution in this field is *Traditional Building: A Global Survey of Structural Forms and Cultural Functions,* published in 2007. This work is already recognized as a major resource in the field of cultural geography. Consisting of 14 chapters, the book provides a comprehensive and in-depth analysis of traditional building forms across the globe and is the culmination of a lifetime of fieldwork and research. An important theme of the book is that form does not always follow function. He calls attention to numerous discontinuities between form and function primarily due to the force of traditional customs associated with the religious and socio-political aspects of human settlements. To cite one example of Toda dwellings in the Nilgiri Hills of India:

> Even though function remains inflexible, the form is quite variable. Houses may be excavated or erected, or partly both. They may rise to a single story or several. Their floor plans are square, round, oval, or combinations of such figures. Roof forms are equally diverse and depend

> more upon climate and available local materials than function. (Noble, 2007, p. 18)

The preceding observation was based on Noble's fieldwork in 1976 when he found that the arched roof of the dwellings of the Todas had small doors for reasons of security – an example of human adaptation to environmental concerns.

While dealing with 'ceremonies and decorations' Noble found that graceful geometrical symbols called *rangoli* were carefully marked in front of the entrances of other Indian structures for good fortune on festive occasions (*also see* Hakansson 1977, p. 84). He also found that houses in the hilly regions in Assam are supported on stilts with the cattle being tethered on the ground floor below the house platform. This ground floor was also used for general storage (Scherman, 1915).

While dealing with 'coverings and climate' Noble considers that variation in roof forms occurs, but there are some forms that have worldwide applicability. Nonetheless they are all largely influenced by climate, building material availability and the evolution of the structural system. They are also culturally controlled:

> The roofs found on Chinese structures do not appear outside East Asia, but some Chinese roofs do have a superficial resemblance to roofs elsewhere. (Noble, 2007, p. 147)

In the concluding chapter on 'change versus constancy', Noble argues that traditional domestic architecture holds onto established methods, material and forms but can change to adjust to new situations and a changing physical environment. Traditional societies prefer to live in housing consonant with their cultural heritage, but will make accommodations for new techniques and political circumstances.

Noble's Contribution to Asian Cultural Geography

Noble co-edited the book *Cultural Patterns of India* with Ashok Dutt. This book is considered a valuable contribution to the field of cultural geography, especially in India where it has been frequently used as a resource by other geographers. Following is an extract dealing with the morphology of South Indian cities as distinct from other Indian cities.

> A basic morphological pattern can be found in South Indian cities, although significant variations occur in the specific cities. Generally, the

> main business or a business-cum-residential quarters and congested residential houses with narrow lanes form the central core of the town. This zone is surrounded by an intermediate zone where residential houses occur, interspersed with supplementary shopping areas, parks, clubs and hospitals and administrative units. Finally, along the peripheral tracts of the urban place, industrial areas and cultivated and vacant lands are located.
>
> Sample studies of certain cities show the variety associated with the origin, growth and functional morphology of South Indian urban places. Madurai grew around the temple and the morphology of the town is completely controlled by the location of this temple. In Coimbatore double nuclei (temple and fort) played an important role in the origin and development process. Hyderabad has grown out of several nuclei, each functioning during different historical periods. Madras grew as a composite of a number of loosely linked, self-contained villages, which subsequently have coalesced into the most significant urban place in South India. (Ramesh and Noble, 1978, p. 63)

In *Cultural Patterns of India*, Noble and Dhussa studied the Bengali neighbourhoods of Dumka and Bhagalpur. Both are in the state of Bihar where Hindi is the state's dominant language. Bengali migrants called *probashis* formed their own distinctive neighbourhoods (*para* or *tola*). Worship of *Kali* and *Durga* had been common to these *para*. The temples of these migrants are devoted to these goddesses, although the locals did not commonly worship these. With acculturation, worship of *Kali* and *Durga* have become common among the locals in Bihar. Distinct characteristics of the Bengali *tolas* in Bihar are described as:

> A Bengali school, i.e. an institution to provide instruction in the Bengali medium, and a library of Bengali language books and periodicals are the two most characteristic features of the Bengali *tola*. Both institutions perpetuate Bengali culture and both are usually highly visible landmarks. Each facility confirms the significance of the cultural dimension of the *tola*.
>
> Other social institutions occur which provide further evidence of the cohesiveness of the *tola*. A Bengali social club organized to support sports, recreational activities and to provide a vehicle for cultural events, such as dramas in the Bengali language, is almost as typical of the *tola* as a school or library. . . . Somewhat less often encountered is an *akhara* or *vyayamsala* which functions as a platform for wrestling and body building exercises, an especially popular Bengali recreation.

> Finally, found only in the largest settlements are the offices which print Bengali newspapers, pamphlets and books.
>
> In addition to cultural facilities, a range of shops and commercial establishments identifies the Bengali *tola.* Of these, the most usually encountered are the restaurant serving Bengali types of food and the sweetmeat shop specializing in distinctive Bengali confections. (Noble and Dhussa, 1982, p. 98).

Allen Noble's work on Asia is noteworthy. He is probably the only geographer who has undertaken fieldwork and published articles and books on all the major regions in Asia. Gaile and Wilmott (1989, p. 534) stated that fewer than 25 American geographers had published on Asia. Noble has covered all major regions of the continent.

> Geographers having expertise in languages that would be useful in the field research requiring personal interviews and the recording of oral traditions are still fewer. Almost none (A. G. Noble is an exception) have done field research in all of the major regions of Asia. An increasingly large proportion of the contemporary scholarly American literature on South and East Asia is by geographers native of these regions who now live in North America. (Gaile and Willmott, 1989, p. 534)

Much of Noble's work has been done in collaboration with Asians belonging to different regions and countries as well as Asia experts. Noble has collaborated with Elisha Efrat, Frank J. Costa, and Ahmed Moustapha for his Middle Eastern research; Larry Ma, Yichun Xie and A. K. Dutt are his collaborators on China studies. He also collaborated with Dutt for his Southeast Asia study. As for South Asia, he has collaborated with a large number of scholars. They include Surinder Aggarwal, Frank J. Costa, Gerardine D'Sa, Satish K. Davgan, Ashok K. Dutt, Ramesh C. Dhussa, Zeenat Hassan, Abdulla Khan, M. T. Khan, Rahman, Pandit Ratni, K. K. Sharma, Sitasaran Singh and Gopalan Venugopal. He is possibly the only geographer who has worked on Middle East geography both with Jewish and Muslim scholars.

Noble and Dutt edited a book on Indian planning in 1978 which reviewed Indian planning from various points of view. It included contributions on national, regional and city planning. The book is considered a classic.

> This collection of materials on the process of urbanization in India and on the planning process … contains several important articles by leading authorities. (Howad Spodek, 1979, p. 815).

This overview of Allen Noble's professional and scholarly work in various branches of geography can only allude to a few of his accomplishments. Noble has had an exceptionally productive academic career which places him in the ranks of the top American geographers. Subsequent chapters in this book offer additional background and assessment of his remarkable abilities as a teacher and scholar. (See Appendix A for a comprehensive listing of Noble's publications.)

Overview of the Book Chapters

The scope of social geography is so wide as to almost defy listing, let alone be captured in a single volume. While this book aims to capture a large breadth of content of the field, there are many areas that will remain untouched, such as emergent sub-fields on sexuality, transnationalism, the body as a social construct, and geographies of media, or of conflict; the list goes on. What the contributors have accomplished, however, is to give us a veritable kaleidoscope of studies in social geography, utilizing a range of methodologies and techniques, from descriptive and theoretical accounts to positivistic statistical analyses, Geographic Information Systems (GIS) and remote sensing techniques, interpretivism and qualitative research. This spectrum of topics, methods and tools is representative enough as to provide the reader with a sense of the richness and depth of this field.

Introductory Framework and Conceptual Bases for the Book

The book is divided into five sections. Section I provides an introduction within which Noble's contributions to several fields of research are discussed. Chapter 2 by Debnath Mookherjee provides an account of Noble's contributions to South Asian cultural geography, while Chapter 3 by LAwrence J.C. Ma does the same for his contributions to the field of Chinese geography. Both chapters are invaluable in highlighting Noble's prolific contributions to the field, and also in establishing how relevant these works remain in understanding these rich and complex societies.

Section II is a compilation of works that discuss some of the conceptual bases, theoretical traditions, epistemologies and methodological aspects of social geography. B. K. Roy in Chapter 4 explores the history and evolving nature of social geography. He mentions the works of Vidal de la Blache and Jean Brunhes as trend setting, although it was only in the twentieth century that the field broadened its scope from accounts of physical environmental influences on human activities to a range of other themes, primarily: (a) ethnologies, (b) role of the spatial dimension, (c) temporal dimensions in social systems, and (d) social aspects of geography.

A comprehensive look at the methodological developments in this vast field is provided by Sudhir K. Thakur in Chapter 5, where usefulness and application of different statistical techniques have been analysed in the field of social geography. In line with emergent epistemological and methodological trends in social geography, Vandana Wadhwa examines the notions of 'impairment' and 'disability' disabilities within the context of social geography and cultural differences in Chapter 6.

A. B. Mukerji in Chapter 7 presents the traditional social geographic exploration into the 'personality' of a region. The history of this sub-field is presented, revealing that it evolved from the three fields of geography, archaeology and folk studies almost simultaneously. Throughout the chapter, Mukerji makes particular references to the Indian context, valuable to students and scholars of Asian studies. Mukerji elaborates on the significant contributions of scholars such as Vidal de la Blache (France) and Herbert Fleure (England) in the early twentieth century, followed by others such as Carl Sauer and E. E. Evans. Blache and Fleure in particular maintained that personality studies reached excellence only with the comprehensive treatment of all aspects of a cultural region.

Any work on social geography would, of course, embrace a discussion of the field of planning for the fundamental reason that the latter inherently plays out in social and spatial contexts. Frank J. Costa in Chapter 8 indicates exactly this concern of social geography with planning in general, and social planning in particular. Since the breadth of social planning is immense, Costa focuses on the spatial dimensions of selected issues as situated within an urban context. He points out that most social planning concerns such as racism and sexism, crime, economic and housing issues, among others, have a spatial component. He also mentions architectural or physical determinism as a dominant theme in social planning, which posits that built form can influence human behavioural patterns.

Section III, a global perspective, presents specific aspects of social geography at various scales of analysis from around the world. The diversity of topics reflects the richness of the discipline. In Chapter 9, Maura Huntz and Robert Kent examine the spatial patterns of Spanish language papers in the United States over a century-and-a-half, spanning the years 1842 to 1992, focusing on the historical evolution of these papers in each of the several regions identified for analysis, particularly addressing issues of longevity and publication frequency.

Samuel Thomson and Ashok K. Dutt in Chapter 10 explore the role of enterprise zones as a means of stimulating economic development in depressed regions, providing overviews of the experiences in Hong Kong, Great Britain, The Netherlands, China, India and the United States, with specific focus on case studies from the last. It is a logical and informative follow-up to the subsequent chapter.

Chapter 11 by Yehua Dennis Wei and Chi Kin Leung addresses regional disparities, an area of immense concern to social policy and planning academicians and practitioners. The authors investigate various facets of such inequality in post-Mao China, particularly in the context of globalization and the attendant foreign economic policy and Foreign Direct Investments (FDI) in the country through 1994–99. Wei and Leung make the case that the restructuring of China's economy and economic policy has been gradual, and spatially uneven. For example, all four of its incentivised Special Economic Zones (SEZs) established in 1980 were located in South China in Guangdong and Fujian, in order to attract investment from Hong Kong and overseas Chinese.

Chapter 12 by Elisha Efrat concentrates on the experiences of a particular demographic (the minority, mostly Arab population in Israel) within an unique social structure. However, despite their significant presence in areas such as Galilee and the eastern coastal plain by 1991, Efrat points out that they have not been provided with advantages similar to those afforded to the Jewish populations that reside in the central part of the nation.

Krishna Poudel in Chapter 13 focuses on the phenomena of urban sprawl and socioeconomic change in the Kathmandu Valley region of Nepal. While the valley has been inhabited since ancient times and was well established by the medieval period, it has experienced tremendous increase in population due to natural growth and inmigration leading to multiple socio-economic and environmental issues. In Chapter 14, John Benhart and Harry Pilaski examine the development of a new town in Florida established on the basis of religion, where the central focus is on the social and cultural role of the Catholic Church. Ave Maria, a new town-like planned community of high income elites in Florida, USA mostly attracts migrants to this 'Sunshine State' from other parts of USA that experience harsh winters.

Section IV exemplifies the diversity of topics within social geography by examining specific aspects of the field, with a special focus on India.

These are national level studies, each investigating a distinct social aspect or structural piece of Indian society.

In Chapter 15, Surya Kant traces the establishment and evolution of socio-cultural regions in India in prehistoric and historic eras. Acknowledging and enumerating the challenges presented by such an exercise, Kant still attempts this comprehensive task through an orderly discussion wherein the origin and development of socio-cultural regions have been traced for the prehistoric or preliterate era (4000–2500 BC), the protohistoric times (2500–600 BC) and historic or literate eras (600 BC onwards to medieval times).

Ashok Dutt, Satish Davgun, Chandrakanta Khan, and Chandralekha Sangwan in Chapter 16 explore the impact of religion and language in identifying regional cultures. The chapter explores the religious pattern and its impact in the first part. It examines the pattern of diffusion and regional cultural development common to major religions such as Hinduism, Islam, Christianity, Sikhism, Buddhism and Jainism. Religion distribution maps are presented, based on 2001 district level data. In the second section the diffusion and impact made by the languages of India have been examined; followed by a historic and contemporary analysis of origin and distributional characteristics of major Indian languages. It is interesting to note that after 1971, the census never published district-wise figures because it was considered divisive.

In Chapter 17, Rajrani Kalra examines changes in linguistic diversity for the years 1971–2001 for Indian states and union territories; natural continuation to the preceding chapter. The major conclusion is that highly developed states have greater diversity than less developed states because their economic prosperity attracts migrants from diverse linguistic backgrounds.

Chapter 18 by Cotton Mather and Pradyumna P. Karan explores the geography of Indian folk art, an intrinsic element of regional personality. They find that its regional patterns are largely congruent to the major Indian cultural zones as delineated by Spate (1961). The authors assert that vernacular art is one of the most telling aspects of a region's culture and history, since it reflects the values, and socio-economic, cultural and physical contexts of the people. In the case of India, folk art is immensely varied and reflective of local contexts, despite cultural exchanges and information transmissions across regions.

Continuing the focus on art forms, Manjusri Chaki-Sircar and Parbati K. Sircar in Chapter 19 examine the traditions of Indian dance and dance theatre in a regional context. Using the popular Radha-Krishna theme as an exemplar, they show how various local folk styles have amalgamated into the more 'elite' classical traditions to render unique regional patterns of dance and dance drama. The authors enumerate and expand on the four major schools of classical dance, namely, Kathak, Manipuri, Kathakali and Bharatanatyam, and how they have been influenced in their thematic content due to their physical and cultural environments.

Chapter 20 by Anindita Datta examines the question of gender disparities in shaping social well-being, as defined by education and health, utilizing (social) space and region as an explanatory context. This qualitative study is based on two Indian villages, each from two contrasting socio-physical environments – the Awadh plain and the Uttarakhand region.

Touching upon an elemental aspect of Indian society, in Chapter 21, Aparajita De takes up the discussion of caste and how it still thrives in public imagination and discourse. De attempts this through a qualitative methodology, analyzing written and verbally expressed views on reservations and quotas for 'backward castes', and the issues concerning such definitions. In essence, De explores how the concept of caste is viewed, understood and constructed by society, and finds that the issue of reservations and quotas is often understood as promoting underperformance over merit.

Crime is an almost universal social condition usually displaying distinct spatial patterns. As such, it is an intrinsic part of social geography. Vandana Wadhwa and Ashok K. Dutt in Chapter 22 present a review of major studies of crime in India, covering a variety of approaches (descriptive, inductive and deductive) and scales (micro, meso and macro). In a way, this work is a descriptive counterpart of a statistical meta-analysis. Among city-scale studies, the crime ecologies of Kolkata (erstwhile Calcutta), Chennai (erstwhile Madras), Ajmer and Delhi, and comparative studies of a number of other cities are included.

While population pressure presents its own problems, it can have an upside – a large wealth of human resource. However, in Chapter 23, B.R.K. Sinha finds that in the case of India, and rural India in particular, human resources are more often than not underdeveloped, undeveloped, unutilized, under-utilized, and over utilized, as well as poor in quality and efficiency.

In the same vein as the preceding section, Section V, the last of this book, looks at the particularities of Indian social geography, but at state/regional and urban scales. R. B. Bhagat in Chapter 24 assesses (i) health and family welfare services that are provided at India's Primary Health Centres (PHCs) and Sub-Centres (SCs), and (ii) clients' views of the availability and delivery of these services, in the context of six districts of the state of Uttar Pradesh, which has particularly high fertility rates. PHCs and SCs cater to prenatal, neonatal and postnatal health needs along with family planning issues.

In a nation where patriarchal systems often result in the deprivation of educational rights of women, female employment and related potential empowerment suffers. It has been indicated that the status of women in academic and/or other high positions does not reflect the situation faced by the average Indian woman. In Chapter 25, Nilofer Izhar contends that this might well be the case, but women in such positions also face discrimination and other problems. Izhar examines the status of women employed by the Aligarh Muslim University at Aligarh, finding gender differentials in appointment processes, representation on various councils and committees, and their health situation.

In Chapter 26, Sya Buryn Kedzior examines an early protest movement in India where rural people attempted to protect their forest resources through organized social protest that lasted for four decades in the newly formed state of Uttarakhand. This chapter explores the power of collective action in influencing policy.

Rana P. B. Singh in Chapter 27 explores the sacred geography of the Hindu holy city of Gaya. Looking at the elements of sacredscape (place-divinity relationships) and manscapes (place-ancestral spirit relationships), he constructs a map of the city in relation to the sacred functions and powers, as told in mythology and Hindu scriptures.

A suitable follow-up is Chapter 28, where Meera Chatterjee and Askok K. Dutt look at the holy city of Madurai and the role of the famous Meenakshi temple in the city's form and function. Madurai's influence has been felt on South Indian culture and civilization as a centre not only for religion and culture, but also for education, commerce and industry. As a background, the authors provide an account of the city's origin – which dates back at least two millennia – and its history through the early Christian era to modern times.

In Chapter 29, Chandana Mitra, Marshall Shepherd and Thomas R. Jordan trace the spatial spread of the Kolkata megalopolis over an approximate span of 300 years, beginning from 1735. They provide a literature survey of the use of GIS for studying urban growth and sprawl and make a case for their use of historical maps and satellite images for delineating the extent of urban growth in Kolkata. They have buttressed their historically-traced physical observations of growth by providing explanatory factors.

Kalpana Markandey and Kavita Taran in Chapter 30 emphasize that most rapidly growing cities in the developing world face the unpleasant consequences of such a fast rise in population; and that Hyderabad is no exception. Slum creation is one of these consequences, and the rapidly developing city of Hyderabad is seeing its share of growth in slums. The author points to the multi-dimensional nature of slums, namely, their structural, demographic, social, locational, economic, political, and behavioural dimensions.

Exploring a rich trove of literature in the form of poetry and letters of the great Urdu poet Mirza Ghalib, Nilofar Izhar and Rais Akhtar reveal dimensions of social geography in the latter half of the nineteenth century in Chapter 31. The socio-cultural, political, environmental and even health and healthcare situations prevalent at his time have been unveiled through the use of literary geography. Ghalib was witness to the last days of the crumbling Mughal Empire and the consolidation of the British Empire after the historic revolt of 1857.

A seamless continuation to the above methodology is Ramesh Dhussa's geographical imagery of Old Delhi (Shahjahanabad) through literature, presented in Chapter 32. Using both English and Hindi literature from major Indian writers, he explores the centuries old world of Old Delhi, which has been referred to as an 'idea with physical boundaries'. Through immersing himself in narratives that use Old Delhi as a backdrop, Dhussa is able to extract the cultural and social ethos of the city, as well as descriptions of its physical environments.

Chapter 33 by Baleshwar Thakur and Mukesh Yadav investigates changes in the levels of elite residential colonies in Delhi between the period of 1982–2004. The study reveals that number, size, distribution and functional characteristics of elite colonies have variations across the city, reflecting stability at the core and instability at the periphery. It also demonstrates the process of peripheralization and suburbanization in the location of elite colonies due to the city's evolution, policy decisions and migration.

Conclusion

At the annual meeting of the Association of American Geographers in Pittsburgh, PA, a special session was held to honor him on the occasion of his retirement from the University of Akron. It is appropriate to conclude this overview of Allen G. Noble's career as a scholar with a verbatim transcript of his comments at this session. More than anything else, these remarks reveal his remarkably varied experiences, the breadth of his scholarly interests and his never failing sense of humour – prerequisites for a scholar who takes his research much more seriously than himself.

> As I stand here I can hear again in my mind those richly pronounced words of Winston Churchill, speaking to supporters during his last political campaign. What he said was, "I am, as I am reminded, an old man and all the dreams of my youth have been accomplished." Here today, I reflect on my own much more modest life and career in Geography and in Foreign Service but have much the same feeling. What opportunities there have been and what experiences! I have participated in sessions with Indira Gandhi and President Nasser, met, exchanged greetings, or shaken hands with Prince Phillip, the author John DosPassos, the opera singer Blanche Thiebom, John Foster Dulles, Dean Atcheson, Mrs Bandarinaike, Prime Minister of Sri Lanka, and most memorably, Harry Truman. The list of those famous personalities I have seen at close quarters includes two Presidents of India, the President of Colombia, President Galo Plaza of Ecuador and Kubicheik of Brazil, former US President Herbert Hoover and future Presidents Eisenhower, Johnson and Nixon, Prime Ministers Nehru, Thatcher, and for the long and short of it, 6'4" Charles DeGalle and 4'11" Haile Selassie. What opportunities! I look back on unparalleled instances of travel and field work overseas, long periods of residence in India and Brazil and much shorter residences in Uganda, Sri Lanka, Israel and Finland. In my mind's eye I see again the Taj Mahal in moonlight, Mount St Michel in pouring rain, Fatehpur Sikri in heat and blazing sun, the magnificent Buddhist and Hindu caves of Ellora and Ajanta, the overwhelming mass of the Rock of Gibraltar, the cloud bedecked slopes of Machu Picchu, the tortuous, smelly, congested lanes of Fez or Banaras, the opulence of the Forbidden

City and the Summer Palace, and the aura of Petra, "the rose red city half as old as time". As a geographer I have stood in awe before the peaks and valleys, the slopes and plains across the world – atop the Peak in Hong Kong listening to the hum of the city, on the plains of Tanzania gazing at mist-capped Kilimanjaro, before the scattered Bedouin fires in the blackness of the Sahara Desert night, the carefree wildness of Carnival in Rio de Janeiro, and absorbing the historical associations of the Ridge in Delhi, the Valley of the Kings in Egypt, the Alhambra in Spain, the Marco Polo bridge near Beijing, where World War II really began, the Bodhi tree in Bodh Gaya where Buddha received enlightenment. I wonder at the chances I have had to see and experience the Nile in flood; Lipari Island volcano, as well as that of White Island, New Zealand, both in quiet eruption; earthquakes in Caracas, the African rift and, perhaps near where mankind began, Ngorongoro Crater; afternoon thunderstorms which come every day at the mouth of the Amazon where I lived for a year, and the break of the monsoon as low clouds come scudding out of the Arabian Sea from the southwest bringing sheets of driving rain to Mumbai, where I also lived for two years. I have been able to stay in houseboats in Kashmir, to visit bamboo huts near sea level in the rain forest of Ecuador and near 10,000 feet on the wind swept plateaus of Ethopia and to accept welcome in Berber encampments in the Atlas Mountains and shepherds' makeshift hutments in the Carpathians of Poland. I have seen women with bound feet in China, the blue bodies of the Tuareg in Morocco, lepers in India, and also in China, old persons being carried in sedan chairs by coolie retainers. I have touched the Wailing Wall in Israel, walked along the Great Wall in China, gazed through the mists at Hadrian's Wall in Britain, and even experienced the drug store in Wall, South Dakota. What opportunities and experiences! How fortunate I have been to have parents, relatives, and teachers who encouraged an interest in the outside world. I have learned much from colleagues – both diplomats and academics – who I now count as valuable friends. I hope I have been able to pass some of my interests and enthusiasms on to generations of my students. To close these few words I'd like to share a few from Eric Sevareid, one of my heroes. He wrote, "As far as knowledge and conscious reason go, we should follow resolutely their austere guidance, careful always to seek for truth and not just for our own emotional satisfaction, remembering above all to walk gently in a world where the lights are dim and the very stars wander."[1]

Note

1. A number of references cited in this chapter have been included in Chapter 2.

References

Noble, Allen G. *Traditional Buildings, A Global Survey of Structural Forms and Cultural Functions*, London: I B Tauris, 2007.

Ferrell, Sarah. '*House and Barns', The New York Times Book Review*, January 27, 1985, p. 22.

Gaile, Gary L. and Cort J. Willmott (eds.), *Geography in America*, Columbus: Merrill Publishing Co., 1989, p. 534.

Hakansson, Tore, 'House Decoration among South Asian People', in Paul Oliver (ed.). *Shelter, Sign and Symbol*, Woodstock, NY: Overlook Press, 1980, pp. 84–94.

Howad, Spodek. 'Review of Indian Urbanization and Planning: Vehicles of Modernization', *Journal of Asia Studies*, Vol. xxxviii, 1, 1979, pp. 815–816.

Levin, Micheal D. 'House Form and Social Structure in Bakosi', in Paul Oliver (ed.). *Shelter in Africa*, London: Barre and Jenkins, 1971, pp. 143–152.

Lowenthal, David. 'Past time, present place: Landscape and memory', *Geographical Review*, Vol. 65, No. 1, 1975, pp. 1–36.

Scherman, L. 'Wohnhaustttypen in Birma and Assam', *Archiv fur Anthropologie*, Vol. 42, 1915, pp. 203–234 + 10pp. of plates.

Appendix A

Allen G. Noble's additional list of publications not included in Chapters 1, 2 and 3.

Authored Books

An Ethnic Geography of Early Utica, New York: Time, Space and Community, Lewiston, NY: Edwin Mellen Press, 1999.

The Old Barn Book: A Field Guide to North American Barns and Other Farm Structures, (with Richard K. Cleek), Brunswick, NJ: Rutgers University Press, 1995.

'Wood, Brick and Stone: The North American Settlement Landscape', *Barns and Farm Structures*, Amherst: University of Massachusetts Press, 1984, Vol. 2, p. 186.

'Wood, Brick and Stone: The North American Settlement Landscape', *Houses*, Amherst: University of Massachusetts Press, 1984, Vol. 1, p. 160.

Ohio: An American Heartland, (with Albert Korsok), Ohio Division of Geological Survey, Columbus, 1975, p. 230.

Edited Books

Thakur, Baleshwar, A. B. Mukerji, Allen G. Noble and Frank J. Costa (eds.), *Geographic and Planning Research Themes for The New Millennium*, Delhi: Vikas Publishing House Pvt. Ltd., 2000.

Noble, Allen G., and Frank J. Costa (eds.), *Preserving the Legacy: Concepts in Support of Sustainability,* Lanham, MD: Lexington Books, 1999.

Noble, Allen G., Frank J. Costa, Ashok K. Dutt and Robert B. Kent (eds.), *Regional Development and Planning for the 21st Century: New Priorities, New Philosophies*, Aldershot, UK: Ashgate Publishing Ltd., 1998.

Noble, Allen G., and Hubert G. Wilhelm (eds.), *Barns of the Midwest*, Athens: Ohio University Press, 1995.

Dutt, Ashok K., Frank J. Costa, Allen G. Noble and Surinder Aggarwal (eds.), *The Asian City: Processes of Development, Characteristics and Planning*, Dordrecht, The Netherlands: Kluwer Academic Publishers, 1994.

Noble, Allen G. (ed.), *To Build in a New Land*, Baltimore: Johns Hopkins University Press, 1992, p. 455.

Costa, Frank J., Ashok K. Dutt, Laurence J. C. Ma and Allen G. Noble (eds.), *Urbanization in Asia*, Honolulu: University of Hawaii Press, 1989, p. 412.

Costa, Frank J., Ashok K. Dutt, Laurence J. C. Ma, and Allen G. Noble (eds.), *Asian Urbanization: Problems and Processes*, Stuttgart: Verlag Gebruder Borntraeger, 1988, p. 165.

Dutt, Ashok K., and Allen G. Noble (eds.), *Proceedings of the Rural–Urban Change in India Faculty Seminar*, Patna, India: University of Patna and Regional Council for International Education, University of Pittsburgh, 1975, p. 188.

Book Chapters – Sole Authored

'The Development of Indian Geography', in Kashi Grover and Neelam Nath Singh (eds.), *Cultural Geography: Form and Process* (essays in honour of A. B. Mukerji), New Delhi, India: Concept Publishing Co., 2004, pp. 14–21.

'Patterns and Relationships of Indian Houses', in Ronald Knapp (ed.), *Asia's Dwellings: Tradition, Resilience, and Change*, New York: Oxford University Press, 2003.

'The Character and Composition of Rural Ethnic Islands', in Jesse O. McKee (ed.), *Ethnicity in Contemporary America*, 2nd edition, Lanham, MD: Rowman and Littlefield, 2000, pp. 349–373.

'Ohio Small Towns', in Leonard Peacefull (ed.), *Geography of Ohio*, Kent, OH: Kent State University Press, 1996, pp. 211–221.

'The Physical Environment', in Ashok K. Dutt (ed.), *Southeast Asia: A Ten Nation Region*, Dordrecht, The Netherlands: Kluwer Academic Publishers, 1996, pp. 41–56.

'The Immigrant Experience in the 19th Century and Afterwards', in Allen G. Noble (ed.), *To Build in a New Land*, Baltimore: Johns Hopkins University Press, 1992, pp. 399–406.

'The German-Russian Mennonites in Manitoba', in Allen G. Noble (ed.), *To Build in a New Land*, Baltimore: Johns Hopkins University Press, 1992, pp. 268–284.

'Nineteenth Century Migration to North America', in Allen G. Noble (ed.), *To Build in a New Land*. Baltimore: Johns Hopkins University Press, 1992, pp. 3–25.

'Public Approaches to Historic Preservation in the United States', in Stanislaus Otok (ed.), *Environment in the Social Policy of the State*, Warsaw: University of Warsaw Press, 1990, pp. 101–110.

'Small Towns', in Leonard Peacefull (ed.), *The Changing Heartland–A Geography of Ohio*. Needham Heights, Mass.: Ginn Press, 1990, pp. 191–200.

'The Countryside and Small Town in Ohio', in Stanislaus Otok (ed.), *Research Approach to Social Geography*, Warsaw: University of Warsaw, 1988, pp. 69–110.

'Rural Ethnic Islands', in Jesse McKee (ed.), *Ethnicity in Contemporary America*, Dubuque, Iowa: Kendall Hunt Publishing Company, 1985, pp. 241–257.

'The Physical Environment', in Ashok K. Dutt', (ed.), Southeast *Asia: Realm of Contrasts*, Boulder: Westview Press, 1985, pp. 36–52.

'The Emergence and Evolution of Malgudi: An Interpretation of South Indian Townscapes from the Fictional Writings of R. K. Narayan', *Proceedings of the Association of American Geographers*, 1976 Vol. 8, pp. 106–110.

'The Green Revolution in India: Unfulfilled Promise', *Proceedings of the Southwest Conference on Asian Studies*, Austin: University of Texas, 1975, pp. 36–42.

'The Physical Environment', in Ashok K. Dutt (ed.), *Southeast Asia: Realm of Contrasts*, Dubuque, Iowa: Kendall/Hunt Publishing Company, 1974, pp. 17–33.

'Physical Basis of Resources', in Ashok K. Dutt (ed.), *India: Resources, Potentialities, and Planning*, Dubuque, Iowa: Kendall/Hunt Publishing Company, 1972, Revised Edition, 1973; Indian Edition pp. 13–37.

Book Chapters – Co-Authored

'Challenges to Asian Urbanization: An Introduction', (with Ashok K. Dutt), in Ashok K. Dutt, Allen G. Noble, and G. Venugopal (eds.), *Challenges to Asian Urbanization*, Dordrecht: Kluwer Academic Publishers, 2003.

'Colombo and the Pattern of South Asian and Port City Models', (with B. L. Panditharatne), in Ashok K. Dutt, Allen G. Noble and G. Venugopal (eds.), *Challenges to Asian Urbanization*, Dordrecht: Kluwer Academic Publishers, 2003.

'Recent Planning Strategies in Jerusalem', (with Elisha Effrat), in, Ashok K. Dutt, Allen G. Noble, and G. Venugopal (eds.), *Challenges to Asian Urbanization*, Dordrecht: Kluwer Academic Publishers, 2003.

'Urban Development of South Asia', (with Ashok K. Dutt), in Ashok K. Dutt, Allen G. Noble and G. Venugopal, (eds.), *Challenges to Asian Urbanization*, Dordrecht: Kluwer Academic Publishers, 2003.

'Professor Ashok Dutt: A Retrospective of Career and Contributions', (with A. B. Mukerji, B. Thakur and Frank J. Costa), in B. Thakur, A. B. Mukerji, Allen G. Noble and Frank J. Costa (eds.), *Geographic and Planning Research Themes for the New Millennium*, Delhi: Vikas Publishing, 2000, pp. 1–15.

'Conservation and the Emergence of the Sustainability Concept', (with Frank J. Costa), in Allen G. Noble and Frank J. Costa (eds.), *Preserving the Legacy: Concepts in Support of Sustainability*, Lanham, MD: Lexington Books, 1999, pp. 3–17.

'Sustainability in an Urban Environment' (with Timothy J. Peterson and Frank J. Costa), in Allen G. Noble and Frank J. Costa (eds.), *Preserving the Legacy: Concepts in Support of Sustainability*, Lanham, MD: Lexington Books, 1999, pp. 97–104.

'Sustainable Tourism: An Overview', (with Frank J. Costa), in Allen G. Noble and Frank J. Costa (eds.), *Preserving the Legacy: Concepts in Support of Sustainability*, Lanham, MD: Lexington Books, 1999, pp. 159–170.

'Untapped Resources for Sustainable Tourism in Western India', (with Frank J. Costa), in Allen G. Noble and Frank J. Costa (eds.), *Preserving the Legacy: Concepts in Support of Sustainability*, Lanham, MD: Lexington Books, 1999, pp. 171–188.

'Currents of Change: Urban Planning and Regional Development', (with Frank J. Costa, Ashok K. Dutt and Robert B. Kent), in Allen G. Noble *et al.* (eds.), *Regional Development and Planning for the 21st Century*, Aldershot, UK: Ashgate, 1998, pp. 1–17.

'Finnish and American Planning: A Comparative Analysis', (with Frank J. Costa), in Allen G. Noble, *et al.* (eds.), *Regional Development and Planning for the 21st Century*, Aldershot, UK: Ashgate, 1998, pp. 19–34.

'Cities in Ohio', (with Leonard Peacefull), in Leonard Peacefull (ed.), *A Geography of Ohio*, Kent, OH: Kent State University Press, 1996, pp. 146–158.

'Ohio's Settlement Landscape', (with Hubert Wilhelm), in Leonard Peacefull (ed.), *A Geography of Ohio*, Kent, OH: Kent State University Press, 1996, pp. 80–109.

'Urbanization Trends in Asia', (with Ashok K. Dutt and Yichun Xie), *Proceedings: Fourth Asian Urbanization Conference*, Taipei: National Taiwan University and Michigan State University, Center for Asian Studies, 1996, pp. 1–14.

'Reflections', (with H. Wilhelm), in Allen G. Noble and Hubert G. H. Wilhelm (eds.), *Barns of the Midwest*, Athens: Ohio University Press, 1995, pp. 284–291.

'The Farm Barns of the American Midwest', (with Hubert G. H. Wilhelm), in Allen G. Noble and Hubert G. H. Wilhelm (eds.), *Barns of the Midwest*, Athens: Ohio University Press, 1995, pp. 1–23.

'Spatial Pattern of Commercial Establishments in two South Asian City Centers: Rajshahi and Madurai', (with Ashok Dutt and Zeenat Hasan), in Ashok Dutt, Frank Costa, Surinder Aggarwal and Allen Noble (eds.), *The Asian City: Processes of Development, Characteristics and Planning*, Dordrecht, Netherlands: Kluwer Academic Publishers, 1994, pp. 99–118.

'An Introduction to the Asian City', (with Ashok K. Dutt, Frank J. Costa and Surinder Aggarwal), in Ashok K. Dutt, Frank J. Costa, Surinder Aggarwal and Allen G. Noble (eds.), *The Asian City: Processes of Development, Characteristics and Planning*, Dordrecht, The Netherlands: Kluwer Academic Publishers, 1994, pp. 1–11.

'Planning in a Rapid Growth Center: The Case of Riyadh, Saudi Arabia', (with Saud Al-Oteibi and Frank J. Costa), in Dutt, Costa, Aggarwal and Noble (eds.), *The Asian City: Processes of Development, Characteristics and Planning,* Dordrecht, The Netherlands: Kluwer Academic Publishers, 1994, pp. 265–278.

'Religious Diversity Patterns: Rajasthan and India', (with Ashok K. Dutt), in R. N. P. Sinha (ed.), *Environment and Human Response*, New Delhi: Concept Publishing Co., 1990, pp. 207–220.

'Buildings on the Landscape', (with Hugh Wilhelm), in Leonard Peacefull (ed.), *The Changing Heartland–A Geography of Ohio*, Needham Heights, Mass.: Ginn Press, 1990, pp. 97–103.

'Trends and Prospects', (with Frank J. Costa, Ashok K. Dutt and Laurence J. C. Ma), in Frank J. Costa, Ashok K. Dutt, Laurence J. C. Ma and Allen G. Noble (eds.), *Urbanization in Asia*, Honolulu: University of Hawaii Press, 1989, pp. 3–17.

'Here Today, Gone Tomorrow: Determining the Disappearance Rate of Agricultural Structures in Pike County, Ohio', (with Deborah P. King), in Robert E. Walls (ed.), *The Old Traditional Way of Life: Essays in Honor of Warren E. Roberts*, Bloomington: Trickster Press, Indiana University Folklore Institute, 1989, pp. 272–282.

'Social Planning: A Conceptual Overview', (with Frank J. Costa and Ashok K. Dutt), in Stanislaus Otok (ed.), *Research Approach to Social Geography*, Warsaw: University of Warsaw, 1988, pp. 173–188.

'The Morphology of a Temple Town Center: Madurai, India, 1975', (with Ashok K. Dutt and Charles B. Monroe), in Frank J. Costa, Ashok K. Dutt, Laurence J. C. Ma and Allen G. Noble (eds.), *Asian Urbanization: Problems and Processes*, Stuttgart: Verlag Gebruder Borntraeger, 1988, pp. 143–164.

'Trends in Urbanization and Urban Development in Sri Lanka', (with B. L. Panditharatne), in Frank J. Costa, Ashok K. Dutt, Laurence J. C. Ma and Allen G. Noble (eds.), *Asian Urbanization: Problems and Processes*, Stuttgart: Verlag Gebruder Borntraeger, 1988, pp. 47–62.

'The Gemeinschaft/Gesellschaft Approach: A Conceptual Framework for Planning and Designing Arab Towns', (with Frank J. Costa), in Frank J. Costa, Ashok K. Dutt, Laurence J. C. Ma and Allen G. Noble (eds.), *Asian Urbanization: Problems and Processes*, Stuttgart: Verlag Gebruder Borntraeger, 1988, pp. 93–102.

'Divergent Paths and Policy Responses in Asian Urbanization and Planning', (with Frank J. Costa, Ashok K. Dutt and Laurence J. C. Ma), in Frank J. Costa, Ashok K. Dutt, Laurence J. C. Ma and Allen G. Noble (eds.), *Asian Urbanization: Problems and Processes*, Stuttgart: Verlag Gebruder Borntraeger, 1988, pp. 1–8.

'Daily and Diurnal Fluctuation in the Attendance Patterns of the Meenakshi Temple, Madurai, India', (with Ashok K. Dutt), in V. S. Datye *et al.* (eds.), *Exploration in the Tropics*, Pune, India: PKRDFVC, 1987, pp. 290–294.

'Function Based Hierarchy of Settlements in Kohat District, Pakistan', (with M. T. Khan and Ashok K. Dutt), *Muslim World: Geography and Development*, Washington: University Press of America, 1987, pp. 121–130.

'Creating Arab Islamic Cities through Application of Modern Building Codes', (with A. F. Moustapha and Frank J. Costa), *Muslim World: Geography and Development*, Washington: University Press of America, 1987, pp. 101–120.

'Bengal: A Search for Regional Identity', (with Ashok K. Dutt and Abdullah A. Khan), *Focus*, Vol. 34, No. 5, 1984, pp. 1–12.

'The Cultural Geography of India in Perspective', (with Ashok K. Dutt), in Allen G. Noble and Ashok K. Dutt (eds.), *India: Cultural Patterns and Processes*, Boulder: Westview Press, 1982, pp. 367–373.

'Ethnic Neighborhoods in Indian Cities: The Paras of Dumka and the Bengali Tola of Bhagalpur', (with Ramesh Dhussa), in Allen G. Noble and Ashok K. Dutt (eds.), *India: Cultural Patterns and Processes*, Boulder: Westview Press, 1982, pp. 81–103.

'The Culture of India in Spatial Perspective: An Introduction', (with Ashok K. Dutt), in Allen G. Noble and Ashok K. Dutt (eds.), *India: Cultural Patterns and Processes*, Boulder: Westview Press, 1982, pp. 1–28.

'Toward a Model for Monitoring Community Noise', (with Vern R. Harnapp), in Laurence J. C. Ma and Allen G. Noble (eds.), *The Environment: Chinese and American Views*, New York: Methuen, 1981, pp. 275–288.

'Language Patterns in a North Indian Town', (with Ramesh Dhussa), in L. R. Singh (ed.), *New Perspectives in Geography*, Allahabad, India: Thinkers Library 1981, pp. 162–168.

'Religious Pattern in Rajasthan', (with Ashok K. Dutt and Satish Davgun), *Environment, Man and Society, Volumes in Honor of S. P. Chatterjee, Asian Economic and Social Review*, Vol. 4, Nos. 3 and 4, 1979.

'Land Values and Land Use: Spatial Relations in Madras, India', (with Ashok K. Dutt and G. Venugopal), *Proceedings of the East Lakes Division, Association of American Geographers*, Akron, Ohio: Department of Geography, University of Akron, 1979, pp. 45–52.

'Pattern and Process in South Indian Cities', (with Attur Ramesh), in Allen G. Noble and Ashok K. Dutt (eds.), *Indian Urbanization and Planning: Vehicles of Modernization*, New Delhi: Tata-McGraw Hill Publishing Company, 1977, pp. 41–63.

'Modernization and Urbanization: An Introduction', (with Ashok K. Dutt), in Allen G. Noble and Ashok K. Dutt (eds.), *Indian Urbanization and Planning: Vehicles of Modernization*, New Delhi: Tata-McGraw Hill Publishing Company, 1977, pp. 1–10.

'The Nature of Rural-Urban Change in India', (with Ashok K. Dutt), in Ashok K. Dutt and Allen G. Noble (eds.), *Proceedings of The Rural–Urban Change in India Faculty Seminar*, Patna, India: University of Patna and Regional Council for International Education (Pittsburgh), 1975, pp. 2–14.

Technical Reports

Report VI, Minerals, Northwest Ohio Water Development Plan, George E. Wilson Company, Akron, 1966.

Report V, Geology, Northwest Ohio Water Development Plan, George E. Wilson Company, Akron, 1966.

Articles in Refereed Journals

'Ethnic Tourism and Commercial Landscape Evolution: the Example of the Amish in Holmes County, Ohio', (with Brian Coffey), *Small Towns*, (accepted).

'Tale of the Trail: Material Culture Elements Along Ridge Road', *Voices: The Journal of New York Folklore*, Vol. 27, Nos. 1–2, Spring–Summer 2001, pp 39–43.

'The Changing Occupational Structure of the Amish of the Holmes County, Ohio Settlement', (with Sean Lowery), *The Great Lakes Geographer*, Vol. 7, No. 1, 2000, pp. 26–37.

'Patterns of Building Material as Revealed in the Farm Housing Survey of 1934', *Material Culture*, Vol. 32, No. 1, Spring 2000, pp. 57–77.

'South Asian Sacred Places', *Journal of Cultural Geography*, Vol. 17, No. 2, Spring–Summer 1998, pp. 1–3.

'Using Descriptive Models to Understand South Asian Cities', *Education About Asia*, Vol. 3, No. 3, Winter 1998, pp. 24–29.

'Use of GPS Technology in Material Culture Studies', (with Thomas M. Besch), *Material Culture*, Vol. 30, No. 2, Summer 1998, pp. 33–41.

'Mid-Nineteenth Century Housing in Buffalo, New York', (with Brian Coffey), *Material Culture*, Vol. 28, No. 3, Fall 1996, pp. 1–16.

'Reply to Hart', (with Richard K. Cleek), *Material Culture*, Vol. 27, No. 1, Spring 1995, pp. 25–30.

'Greenhouse Horticulture and Economic Transition', (with Mauri Palomaki), *Geographical Review*, Vol. 85, No. 2, April 1995, pp. 173–184.

'Sorting out the Nomenclature for English Barns', (with Richard K. Cleek), *Material Culture*, Vol. 26, No. 1, Spring 1994, pp. 49–63.

'Barn Entry Porches, Pent Roofs and Decorated Doors of the Eastern Midwest', *Journal of Cultural Geography*, Vol. 14, No. 1 Fall–Winter 1993, pp. 21–34.

'Floor Area Ratio (FAR) as an Urban Development Tool', (with Matthew A. Noble and Frank J. Costa), *Land Use Policy*, Vol. 10, No. 2, April 1993, pp. 127–139.

'European Urbanization–Special Issue', (with John E. Mulhauser, Frank J. Costa and Ashok K. Dutt), *Landscape and Urban Planning*, Vol. 22, Nos. 2–4, November 1992.

'Windmills in American Agriculture', *Material Culture*, Vol. 24, No. 1, Spring 1992, pp. 1–12.

'Measuring Vernacular Buildings: A Field Course Unit', *Material Culture*, Vol. 23, No. 1, Spring 1991, pp. 1–14.

'The Geography of the Intifada', (with Elisha Efrat), *The Geographical Review*, Vol. 80, No. 3, July 1990, pp. 288–307.

'The Growth of Metro Systems in Madrid, Rome and Athens', (with Frank J. Costa), *Cities: The International Quarterly on Urban Policy*, Vol. 7, No. 3, August 1990, pp. 224–229.

'Image and Substance: A Review of Literary Geography', (with Ramesh Dhussa), *Journal of Cultural Geography*, Vol. 10, No. 2, Spring–Summer 1990, pp. 49–65.

'Landscape of the Future: The Art Deco and Streamlined Styles in Akron, Ohio, 1920–1940', (with Jill Schuler), *The East Lakes Geographer*, Vol. 24, 1989, pp. 13–33.

'Residential Building Materials in New York State, 1855–1875', (with Brian Coffey) *Material Culture*, Vol. 21, No. 1, Spring 1989, pp. 3–21.

'Problems of Reunified Jerusalem', (with Elisha Efrat), *Cities: The International Quarterly on Urban Policy*, Vol. 5, No. 4 November 1988, pp. 326–332.

'Planning Jerusalem', (with Elisha Efrat), *The Geographical Review*, Vol. 78, No. 4, October 1988, pp. 387–404.

'Crib Death: The Demise of Elevated Corn Cribs in Pike County, Ohio', *The East Lakes Geographer*, Vol. 23, 1988, pp. 27–36.

'Landscape of Piety/Landscape of Profit: The Amish–Mennonite and Derived Landscapes of Northeastern Ohio', *The East Lakes Geographer*, Vol. 21, 1986, pp. 34–48.

'Planning Arabic Towns', (with Frank J. Costa), *The Geographical Review*, Vol. 76, No. 2, April 1986, pp. 160–172.

'The Hay Barrack: Form and Function of a Relic Landscape Feature', *Journal of Cultural Geography*, Vol. 5, No. 2, Spring–Summer 1985, pp. 107–116.

'Cultural Geography', in 'Material Culture Studies: A Symposium', *Material Culture*, Vol. 17, Nos. 2 and 3, Summer-Fall 1985, pp. 95–98.

'Variations in Noise Generation – Bangalore, India', (with Ashok K. Dutt and G. Venugopal), *Geografiska Annaler*, Ser. B, Vol. 67, No. 1, 1985, pp. 15–19.

'Urban Development in Saudi Arabia', (with A. F. Moustapha and Frank J. Costa), *Cities: The International Quarterly on Urban Policy*, Vol. 2, No. 2, May 1985, pp. 140–148.

'The Finnish Landscape of the Upper Great Lakes', *The East Lakes Geographer*, Vol. 18, 1983, pp. 14–24.

'Building Mormon Houses: A Preliminary Typology', *Pioneer America*, Vol. 15, No. 2, July 1983, pp. 55–66.

'Distribution of Barn Types in Northeastern United States', (with Gayle Seymour), *The Geographical Review*, Vol. 72, No. 2, April 1982, pp. 155–170.

'The Farm Silo: An Annotated Bibliography', *Journal of Cultural Geography*, Vol. 1, No. 2, Spring–Summer 1981, pp. 118–126.

'The Diffusion of Silos', *Landscape*, Vol. 25, No. 1, 1981, pp. 11–14.

'Socio-Economic Factors Affecting Marriage Distance in Two Sikh Villages of Punjab', (with Ashok K. Dutt and Satish Davgun), *Journal of Cultural Geography*, Vol. 2, No. 1, Fall–Winter 1981, pp. 13–25.

'Sod Houses and Similar Structures: A Brief Evaluation of the Literature', *Pioneer America*, Vol. 13, No. 2, September 1981, pp. 61–66.

'The Evolution of American Farm Silos', *Journal of Cultural Geography*, Vol. 1, No. 1, Fall–Winter 1980, pp. 138–148.

'Village of Tranquility: Shakertown at Pleasant Hill, Kentucky', *Pioneer America*, Vol. 10, No. 1, June 1978, pp. 117–123.

'Diffusion of Hinduism in Southeast Asia with Special Reference to Indo-China', (with Ashok K. Dutt), *National Geographical Journal of India*, Vol. 23, Nos. 1 and 2, March–June 1977, pp. 86–94.

'Barn Variations in Columbiana County, Ohio', (with Albert J. Korsok), *The East Lakes Geographer*, Vol. 12, 1977, pp. 98–111.

'Barns as Elements of the Settlement Landscape of Rural Ohio', *Pioneer America*, Vol. 9, No. 1, July 1977, pp. 62–79.

'A Method for Estimating Distribution of Barn Styles: Indiana as a Case Study', (with Victoria Hosler), *Geographical Survey*, Vol. 6, No. 3, July 1977, pp. 14–31.

'Regional Variation in the Evolution of Housing in Eastern North America', *The Indian Geographical Journal*, Vol. 51, No. 2, December 1976, pp. 1–16.

'Some Notes on Himalayan Mapping', (with Richard Palmieri), *Journal of Asian Studies*, Vol. XXXIV, No. 3, May 1975, pp. 795–797.

'The Evolution and Classification of Nineteenth Century Housing in Ohio', *Journal of Geography*, Vol. 74, No. 5, May 1975, pp. 285–302.

'Barns and Square Silos in Northeast Ohio', *Pioneer America*, Vol. VI, No. 2, July 1974, pp. 12–21.

Articles in Non-Refereed Journals

'The Evolution of a Professional Journal: The First Thirty Years of *Pioneer America/Material Culture*', *P.A.S.T.—Pioneer America Society Transactions*, Vol. 24, 2001.

'Filling Up the Land: Amish Settlement in and around Holmes County, Ohio', (with Sean Lowery), *P.A.S.T.—Pioneer America Society Transactions*, Vol. 22, 1999, pp. 15–26.

'Introducing the Dutch Landscape of Southwestern Michigan', *P.A.S.T.—Pioneer America Society Transactions*, Vol. 19, 1996, pp. 11–18.

'The Last Ropewalk in America', *P.A.S.T.–Pioneer America Society Transactions*, Vol. 16, 1993, pp. 13–23.

'The Impact of Planning on Growth and Development in Riyadh, Saudi Arabia, 1970–1990', (with Saud Al-Oteibi and Frank J. Costa), GeoJournal, Vol. 24, No. 2, February 1993, pp. 163–170.

Urban Issues and Urbanization Characteristics of Asia, Special issue of *GeoJournal*, A. K. Dutt, S. Aggarwal, F. J. Costa and A. G. Noble (eds.), Vol. 29, No. 2, February 1993.

Old Trends and New Impulses in Europe's Urban Affairs, in Special issue of *GeoJournal*, Allen G. Noble, Frank J. Costa and Ashok K. Dutt (eds.), Vol. 24, No. 3, July 1991.

'House Types in Blota, Poland and a Source for North American I-Houses', *P.A.S.T.–Pioneer America Society Transactions*, Vol. 14, 1991, pp. 1–9.

'Evolving Planning Systems in Madrid, Rome and Athens', (with Frank J. Costa and Glenna Pendleton), *GeoJournal*, Vol. 24, No. 3, July 1991, pp. 293–303.

'Perception of Housing and Community Conditions in a Suburban Settlement of Warsaw, Poland', (with Anna Achmatowicz-Otok), *Papers and Proceedings of the Applied Geography Conference*, Vol. 13, 1990, pp. 227–232.

'Foreword', Iqbal Mohiuddin, *Political Geography of India*, Delhi: Adam Publishers, 1987, pp. v and vi.

'Noise Pollution', (with Vern R. Harnapp), *GeoJournal*, Vol. 14, No. 2, March 1987, pp. 217–226.

'The Use of Cobblestones as a Folk Building Material', (with Brian Coffey), *P.A.S.T.–Pioneer America Society Transactions*, Vol. 9, 1986, pp. 45–51.

'Variation of the Spatial Patterns of Crime in Ajmer, India', (with Ashok K. Dutt and K. K. Sharma), *Indian Journal of Criminology*, Vol. 13, No. 1, January 1985, pp. 57–72.

'Identifying Ethnic Regions in Ohio', *Ohio Geographers: Recent Research Themes*, Vol. 12, 1984, pp. 18–29.

'The Evolution of the Corn Crib, With Special Reference to Putnam County, Illinois', (with James R. Schimmer), *P.A.S.T.–Pioneer America Society Transactions*, Vol. 7, 1984, pp. 21–33.

'The Literature on Fences, Walls and Hedges as Cultural Landscape Features', (with Jean M. Danis), *Pennsylvania Folklife*, Vol. 33, No. 1, Autumn 1983, pp. 41–47.

'Building Mormon Houses: A Preliminary Typology', *Pioneer America*, Vol. 15, No. 2, July 1983, pp. 55–66.

'Retrospect on Fifty Years of Geography in the Ohio Academy of Science', (with Vern R. Harnapp), *Ohio Journal of Science*, Vol. 83, No. 4, September 1983, pp. 161–167.

'Time Variations in Urban Traffic Noise: A Case Study in Akron, Ohio', (with Vern R. Harnapp), *Sound and Vibration*, Vol. 16, No. 12, December 1982, pp. 20–22.

'Navajo Housing: Example of Environmental Adjustments', *Ohio Geographers: Recent Research Themes*, Vol. 9, 1981, pp. 17–26.

'Pioneer Settlement on the Plains: Sod Dugouts and Sod Houses', *P.A.S.T.–Pioneer America Society Transactions*, Vol. 4, 1981, pp. 11–19.

'Variance in Floor Plans of Dutch Houses of the Colonial Period', *P.A.S.T.–Pioneer America Society Transactions*, Vol. 3, 1980, pp. 46–56.

'New Research Institute on South Asia Established in China', *Asian Studies Newsletter*, Vol. 25, No. 2, November 1979, pp. 5–6.

'A Tentative Classification of Dutch Colonial Rural Houses in New York and New Jersey', *Ohio Geographers: Recent Research Themes*, Vol. 7, 1979, pp. 31–40.

Studies of the American Settlement Landscape, Akron, Ohio: Department of Geography, University of Akron, 1978; Third edition, 1979.

'The Octagon House', (with M. Margaret Geib), *Places*, Vol. III, No. 2, July 1976, p. 47.

'A Preliminary Annotated Bibliography on Silos', *Historic Schaefferstown Record*, Vol. 10, No. 1, January 1976, pp. 2–12.

'The Silo in the Eastern Midwest: Patterns of Evolution and Distribution', *Ohio Geographers: Recent Research Themes*, Vol. 4, 1976, pp. 9–22.

'The Navajo Hogan', (with M. Margaret Geib), *Places*, Vol. 3, No. 1, March 1976, p. 35.

'The Quaker Plan House', (with M. Margaret Geib), *Places*, Vol. 2, No. 3, November 1975, pp. 22–23.

'Barn Style Variations in Southern Ontario: A Technique for Rapid Survey' (Abstract), *Visible Landscapes of the Past*, Quebec: Special Session of the Canadian Association of Geographers, 1975, p. 2.

'The Dog Trot Cabin', (with M. Margaret Geib), *Places*, Vol. 2, No. 2, July 1975, p. 19.

'The Gothic Revival Cottage', (with M. Margaret Geib), *Places*, Vol. 1, No. 4, December 1974, p. 7.

'Barn and Silo Types in Pennsylvania', (with Brian Coffey), *The Pennsylvania Geographer*, Vol. 12, No. 3, November 1974, pp. 20–29.

'The One-and-a-half New England Cottage', (with M. Margaret Geib), *Places*, Vol. 1, No. 3, October 1974, p. 14.

'Geographic Aspects of the Agriculture of Santa Catarina State, Brazil' (Abstract), *World Agricultural Economics and Rural Sociology Abstracts*, Vol. 11, No. 4, December 1969, p. 574.

'Geographic Aspects of the Agriculture of Santa Catarina State, Brazil', *Ohio Journal of Science*, Vol. 67, No. 5, September 1967, pp. 257–273.

'Computing Coal Costs', *Industrial Development Magazine*, July 1958, pp. 49–50.

Encyclopaedia

'Mid-West and Lakes', *Encyclopedia of Vernacular Architecture of the World*, Oxford: Blackwell Publishing, 1998.

'Dutch in the Mid-West', *Encyclopedia of Vernacular Architecture of the World*, Oxford: Blackwell Publishing, 1998.

'English in the Mid-West', *Encyclopedia of Vernacular Architecture of the World*, Oxford: Blackwell Publishing, 1998.

'Welsh in the Mid-West', *Encyclopedia of Vernacular Architecture of the World*, Oxford: Blackwell Publishing, 1998.

'Silos', *Encyclopedia of Vernacular Architecture of the World*, Oxford: Blackwell Publishing, 1998.

'Cleveland', *Microsoft Encarta*, 1997.

'Columbus', *Microsoft Encarta*, 1997.

'Cincinnati', *Microsoft Encarta*, 1997.

2

Perspectives on Allen G. Noble's Contributions to Cultural Geography in South Asia

DEBNATH MOOKHERJEE

Introduction

I thank the editors of this volume for the opportunity to contribute this essay to honour Dr Allen G. Noble, a cultural geographer, who retired from the University of Akron, Ohio, as Professor Emeritus after a long and distinguished career. I first met Allen at one of the annual conferences of the Association of American Geographers in the early 1970s. The meeting marked the beginning of an enriching professional relationship that has spanned three decades.

The South Asian region is 'set apart from the rest of the globe' (Norton, 1997) for its diversity of peoples, plurality of cultures and distinctive landscapes. The region has been a reservoir of rich cultural heritage from the very dawn of civilization. While many aspects of the geography of the region are well recorded in historical contexts, its cultural geographical phenomena, reflecting the spatial patterns of people, places, and societies have received much less attention from geographers. Statements made in the context of India, the core country of the region, are also equally applicable to the other South Asian regions:

> The rich tapestry of Indian culture provides a frame within which a myriad of topics may be pursued. . . . But this luxuriant fabric lies as yet little disturbed by scholarly inquiry. (Noble and Dutt, 1982, Preface p. xi)

In a similar vein, on the progress of geography in India, it is noted that:

> Interest in the regional variations in material culture has been totally ignored. Indian cultural geography continues to be ignorant of its epistemological needs. The geographical implications of cultural pluralism have not been properly evaluated. (Ahmad, 1996, p. 7)

The study of cultural geography, like other sub-fields of geography, is multifaceted. Because socio-cultural processes intricately affect all aspects of spatial development, geographical perspectives in the identification and analysis of unique socio-cultural elements are especially important in the context of contemporary issues. Recent events in the Asian subcontinent – religious conflicts, assertions of ethnic identity and terrorism – once again reiterate the need for research and study of the cultural constructs and processes that shape the socio-spatial phenomena of the Asian region. Noble, an American geographer in the forefront of socio-cultural geographic research, anticipated this important research frontier, and strove to fill the void. With his colleagues and students at Akron, he has explored a variety of cultural textures of the South Asian region for over three decades.

The two sets of collected articles co-edited by Noble and Dutt in *Indian Urbanization and Planning: Vehicles of Modernization* (1977) and *Cultural Patterns and Processes* (1982) are excellent examples of the 'State-of-the-Art' of Indian cultural geography during the post-independence period. By masterfully maintaining an interdisciplinary research focus, Noble has shown how cultural traits are manifested in spatial forms, both in the context of urban and rural environments.

These two edited volumes are Noble's landmark contributions and have added to his status as one of the most distinguished contemporary cultural geographers in the country. Many of the papers provide excellent examples of how cultural elements are spatially manifested in the creation of distinctive regional patterns. These volumes ought to be on the reading list of anyone interested in the spatial implications of regional culture and the modernization processes of South Asian societies.

Noble's research is an amalgam of empirical and conceptual contributions that transcends political and disciplinary boundaries. A comprehensive review, or even brief notations, of his vast contributions would be a daunting task and would go beyond the scope of this paper. Two broad themes run through most of Noble's South Asian work (Fig. 2.1). The first deals with the cultural elements that relate to the formation of urban structures. The second is his characterization of rural socio-cultural patterns. The confluence of these two – as reflected in his work – reveals a complex regional cultural mosaic, an understanding of which is essential in mitigating many of the current regional problems in South Asia.

SOUTH ASIA: ALLEN NOBLE'S RESEARCH AREAS (SELECTED)

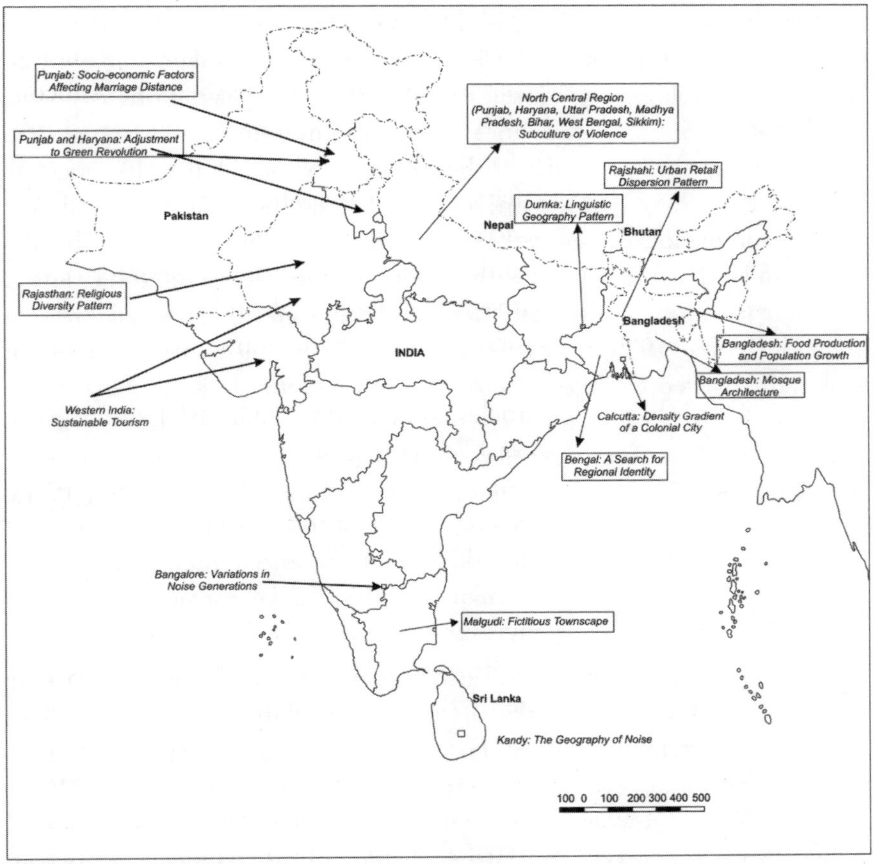

Fig. 2.1 Allen G. Noble's research areas in South Asia.

The Urban Paradigm

Noble's exploration of cultural elements in the identification and interpretation of the urban spatial patterns has not only added to our knowledge, but has also provided valuable insights into the non-Western cultural influences on those patterns. In his descriptive model of South Asian cities (Noble, 1998), his characterization of spatial 'symbolism' is a powerful tool in conceptualizing the evolution of urban landscapes. He presents two graphic models, which are indeed a major contribution to the study of the morphology of Asian cities. In a society where 'tradition coexists with modernity', Noble has captured the changing structural complexities.

The density gradient of the city of Calcutta portrays a 'dual structure' – the consequence of European colonial rule in co-existence with the modern Indian society (Dutt, Noble and D'Sa, 1985). He has identified neighbourhood boundaries based on patterns of spoken and written languages (Noble and Dhussa, 1983) and assessed variations of noise generation in South Asian cities based on environmental features and socio-economic characteristics of the residents (Noble, Dutt and Venugopal, 1985; Noble, 1986). In addition, he has explored the influence of historic processes in the location of retail and service establishments and in shaping the urban land use structures within a city (Hasan, Dutt and Noble, 1992). His interpretation of novelist R. K. Narayan's imaginary small town of Malgudi (Noble, 1980) is noteworthy. In short, he shows that a variety of tools can be used to depict the dynamics of cultural phenomena in the urban landscape. I must note here that in my own field of interest – urban developmental studies – Noble's work has made me rethink my own approaches towards an understanding of urbanization in multi-cultural contexts.

The Rural Paradigm

Noble and his colleagues have also pursued much thought-provoking research into the cultural realm of the predominantly rural South Asian societies in a variety of scales. His research on spatial aspects of marriages, for example, revealed a pattern analogous to the 'crater effect.' The use of the Green Revolution as a technique in rural development showed higher disposable income for farmers, which in turn induced changes in the consumption of food, use of household utensils and transportation, and in the expansion of the marriage field (Dutt, Noble and Davgun, 1981; Dutt, Noble and Aggarwal, 1978). In addition to portraying socio-cultural changes at the village level, such studies also led us to ponder over the cultural and spatial complexities of rural societies.

Regional ethnic unrest and religious tensions are far too common in South Asia. Is there a spatial manifestation of the subculture of violence? An analysis of the north-central region of India yielded a plausible explanation of the regional patterns of invasion from the west, and the subsequent absorption of divergent cultural groups (Dutt, Noble and Singh 1979). Such studies point to the complexities of socio-cultural patterns in space and highlight areas for further research. Similarly, the discovery of religious, linguistic, and architectural patterns (Dutt and Noble, 1985; Dutt, Khan and Noble, 1984; Islam and Noble, 1998) signifies myriad cultural identities, acculturation processes and conflicts in context of the societies of the region.

Noble's analysis of population growth and food production in one of the most impoverished countries of the region clearly indicates the need for firm population control policies and programmes (Noble, Dutt and Rahman, 1980). His research focus on the cultural artifacts in western India – the 'painted walls' and 'murals'-and his plea for preservation and sustainable development of these resources of 'inestimable value' has also brought clarity to our views on cultural preservation (Noble and Costa, 1999).

Geography's syncretic approach makes it a key discipline for regional studies. Drawing on a variety of approaches (qualitative to quantitative), at varying scales (city to metropolis, village to state) and based on wide-ranging data (field research to census), Noble has highlighted 'cogent avenues of research' towards the understanding of regional patterns. His research focus underscores the importance of socio-cultural elements in the study of South Asian societies.

Conclusion

Let me conclude my brief remarks on Noble's work by borrowing from a renowned geographer. In his editorial comment 'Why are you a geographer?' Yi-Fu Tuan wrote, ". . . [How] can it be otherwise if geography is for me more than just a way of earning a living, . . . it is how I make the long and difficult process of understanding the world – cities and rural landscapes . . . ." I feel that, like Professor Tuan, Professor Allen Noble has also not been in the profession of geography for merely 'earning a living'. His insightful work in cultural geography reveals a profound passion for research that has extended our horizons and enriched our understanding of the sub-field of cultural geography. Like a masterful painter, Noble has portrayed complex cultural landscapes in a simple spatial framework. Noble's unique contribution to the literature on South Asian geography is like the monsoon showers nourishing the field for future generations of cultural geographers who will sow seeds of inquiry and harvest cross-cultural understanding.

Author's Note

The selected references used in this essay reflect Noble's collaborative works as author or co-author of research articles, books and book chapters.

References

Ahmad, Aijazuddin, *Progress in Indian Geography: 1992–1996*, New Delhi: Indian National Science Academy, 1996.

Noble, Allen G. and Frank J. Costa, 'Sustainable Tourism: Resources and Strategies for Western India and the Case of the Shekhawati Painted Walls', in Graham P. Chapman, Ashok K. Dutt and Robert W. Bradnock (eds.), *Urban Growth and Development in Asia: Making the Cities*, Aldershot: Ashgate, 1999, pp. 185–199.

Noble, Allen G., 'Using Descriptive Models to Understand South Asian Cities', *Education About Asia*, Vol. 3, No. 3, 1998, pp. 24–29.

Noble, Allen G., 'The Geography of Noise in the South Asian City: A Case Study of Kandy, Sri Lanka', in Mohammed Shaft and Mehdi Raz (eds.), *Spectrum of Modern Geography: Essays in Memory of Professor Mohammed Anas*, 1986, pp. 437–446.

Noble, Allen G., Ashok K. Dutt and G. Venugopal, 'Variations in Noise Generations: Bangalore, India', *Geografiska Annaler*, Vol. 67, No. 1, 1985, pp. 15–19.

Noble, Allen G. and Ramesh C. Dhussa, 'The Linguistic Geography of Dumka, Bihar, India', *Journal of Cultural Geography*, Vol. 3, No. 2, 1983, pp. 73–81.

Noble, Allen G. and Ashok K. Dutt, *India: Cultural Patterns and Processes*, Boulder: Westview Press, 1982.

Noble, Allen G., 'Malgudi: The South Indian Townscape of R. K. Narayan', *The Deccan Geographer*, Vol. 18, No. 1, 1980, pp. 803–811.

Noble, Allen G., Ashok K. Dutt and Abu Rahman, 'Food Production and Population Growth in Bangladesh', *Asian Profile*, Vol. 8, No. 1, 1980, pp. 53–77.

Noble, Allen G. and Ashok K. Dutt, *Indian Urbanization and Planning: Vehicles of Modernization*, New Delhi: Tata-McGraw Hill, 1977.

Dutt, Ashok K. and Allen G. Noble, 'Religious Diversity Patterns of Rajasthan within an Indian Framework', *Asian Geographer*, Vol. 4, No. 2, pp. 136–146.

Dutt, Ashok K., Allen G. Noble and Gerardine D'Sa, 'A Historical View of the Density Gradient of Calcutta, A Colonial City', *National Geographical Journal of India*, Vol. 31, No. 4, 1985, pp. 269–279.

Dutt, Ashok K., Abdullah A. Khan and Allen G. Noble, 'Bengal: A Search for Regional Identity', *Focus on Geography*, Vol. 34, No. 5, 1984, pp. 1–12.

Dutt, Ashok K., Allen G. Noble and Satish K. Davgun, 'Socio-Economic Factors Affecting Marriage Distance in Two Sikh Villages of Punjab', *Journal of Cultural Geography*, Vol. 2, No. 1, 1981, pp. 13–25.

Dutt, Ashok K., Allen G. Noble and Sitasaran Singh, 'Is There a North-Central Sub-Culture of Violence in India?', *National Geographical Journal of India*, Vol. 25, No. 2, 1979, pp. 101–111.

Dutt, Ashok K., Allen G. Noble and Surinder Aggarwal, 'Village Level Adjustment to the Green Revolution in India', *Geographical Bulletin of India*, December 1978, pp. 1–15.

Dutt, Ashok K., Allen G. Noble, 'Growing and Changing of Cities and the Spread of Urbanization in South Asia,' in Ashok K. Dutt, H. N. Mishra and Meera Chatterjee (eds.) *Explorations in Applied Geography*, Prentice Hall India, New Delhi, 2008.

Norton, H. K. James, *India and South Asia*, Guilford: Dushkin / McGraw Hill, 1997.

Islam, Ishrat and Allen G. Noble, 'Mosque Architecture in Bangladesh: The Archetype and Its Changing Morphology', *Journal of Cultural Geography*, Vol. 17, No. 2, 1998, pp. 5–25.

Hasan, Zeenat F., Ashok K. Dutt and Allen G. Noble, 'Spatial Pattern of Retail and Service Establishments of the Central Bazar of Rajshahi, Bangladesh', *Journal of Scientific Research*, Vol. 42, 1992, pp. 45–68.

3

Allen G. Noble's Contributions to the Field of Chinese Geography

LAWRENCE J. C. MA

Colleagues and friends of Dr Allen G. Noble have long been amazed by how much he could write while being deeply involved in several different activities at the same time. A prolific writer in diverse fields, a leading scholar in settlement landscapes, cultural geography and South Asia, a superb department head, a highly respected leader in campus affairs and an active member in several professional organizations, Allen's multiple talents are truly remarkable. During the time when he was at the helm, the Department of Geography at the University of Akron grew into a leading centre for the study of Asian geography, especially Asian urbanization. His prolific writings, insistence on research, exemplary work ethic and superb administrative skills also gave rise to a very healthy academic environment for faculty to pursue their own research interests.

Apart from the fact that he has been widely recognized as one of the leading scholars in settlement landscapes in North America, Noble has also made major contributions to such diverse areas of scholarship as the geography of South Asia, especially India, urban planning, sustainable development, noise pollution, tourism, and urban development in India, Sri Lanka, Bangladesh, China, Poland, Italy, Israel, Saudi Arabia and many towns in the Arab world. I am yet to meet another scholar who has published so much in so many different areas of study. Contributors to this volume have discussed many of his achievements. The purpose of this chapter is to document the contributions that Noble has made in the area of the geography of China, an area I have been involved in for more than three decades. The story needs to be told as Noble's work has had a long-term impact on the field of Chinese geography in the United States.

Perceptive Foresight and Early Action

Allen played a key role in initiating the earliest scholarly contact between American and Chinese geographers. The success of this endeavour was due largely to his perceptive foresight and early action. The development of the field of Chinese geography had been severely constrained before China adopted the 'reform and open-door' policy in 1978. It was almost impossible for Americans to visit China as there was no official diplomatic relationship between the two countries until January 1, 1979. China's contact with foreign countries was severely limited during the three decades after the founding of the Communist state in 1949. During the Cultural Revolution (1966–76), a chaotic decade of ultra-leftist political turbulence and factionalism, all schools and universities were closed and all academic work ceased. China's isolation from the outside world, especially the US, was almost complete. Tourism was non-existent, and few foreign visitors were allowed to visit China for any reason. Fieldwork by social scientists was out of the question. Social science in general was severely constrained by Marxism–Leninism–Maoism, and few Chinese scholars were exposed to western scholarship. There was little information coming out of China that was not propaganda, which was of little use to Western scholars who wished to understand Chinese society. Scholars on China had to rely on the news media or interviews given by refugees in Hong Kong to gather information. I used to comb through the *People's Daily*, China's official newspaper that was available overseas, but too often I could not find a single line of useful information for days. It was often stated at the time that Westerners knew more about the moon than about China.

Dramatic changes occurred in China with the death of Chairman Mao Zedong in September 1976. A month after Mao's death, the 'Gang of Four,' a group of ultra-leftist top-level leaders led by Mao's wife Jiang Qing that had been mainly responsible for the national political turmoil and large-scale persecution of cadres, was arrested. Shortly after that, Allen asked me casually one day: "When are we going to China?" As I saw few signs at the time suggesting that China was about to open its doors to the outside world, I thought it was premature to explore any possibilities of going there. I did not pay heed to Allen's sensitive and suggestive inquiry. Despite getting little reaction from me, Allen did not give up. A few days later he asked me again: "When are we going to China? This is the time to get the ball rolling." Knowing that he would never say anything without careful thought, I decided to take his cue seriously and began to find a way to visit China, which I had not seen since 1949 when I was a sixth grader. As a scholar on China, I had longed to return to see what socialism had done to my native land, that was nothing more exciting and important than seeing the place that I had studied about for nearly a decade in the library as a graduate student and a young instructor.

In the days that followed, Allen would periodically ask me "When are we going to China?" at coffee breaks, sometimes just to get conversations started. In 1977, a few US–China scholarly exchange programmes in the natural sciences had been established. Such programmes were structured and carried out almost exclusively under the auspices of the Chinese Academy of Sciences (CAS) and the Committee on Scholarly Communications with the People's Republic of China (CSCPRC), the latter being a quasi-official US agency at the national level. Knowing that the chances for individual social scientists to visit China were slim, I suggested to Allen that a group of geographers could visit China. After several conversations, we decided to write to the CAS in November 1976 suggesting that we would like to organize such a group visit. We approached the CAS instead of any university because the CAS had been the only Chinese agency involved in official international academic exchanges with the US and because, following the Soviet model of structuring scientific disciplines, geography was an integral part of the CAS. It employed a large number of geographers in its Institute of Geography and the Commission on the Comprehensive Investigation of Natural Resources.

We did not really expect that the CAS would respond to a letter from two American human geographers requesting a visit to China because geography was not a science that had dominated the limited number of US–China scholarly exchange programmes and because we had no ties with the CSCPRC. The programmes under the aegis of the CAS and CSCPRC were deemed 'official' by the Chinese side because the CAS considered the CSCPRC its counterpart. Such programmes were typically two-way exchanges with both sides sending an equal number of delegations to the other side, often for a three-week period. Each side would pay for its own international travel but once a delegation arrived, the host country would cover all local expenses. With scholarly exchange being so highly regulated and limited to the hard sciences, I felt a trip to China at that time was a long shot.

Scholarly Exchanges with Chinese Geographers, 1977–1979

For almost six months we heard nothing from China. But one day in April 1977, out of the blue, a short letter came from the CAS addressed to Allen. We were greatly but very happily surprised that the CAS not only accepted our request for a visit to China, but it also suggested an exchange programme for the discipline of geography. The CAS proposed that each side would send a group of geographers to the other country for a three-week visit, with the American group going to China in 1977 and a Chinese delegation coming to the US for a return visit in 1978. Following the established model of official exchanges, we had to structure a program and find financial support to host the Chinese group. This exchange programme was the first outside the 'official' channel between the CAS and the CSCPRC. As the only possible time for us to visit China was during the summer, we immediately got to work to form a group of geographers for the visit.

To put together a group of American geographers to visit China, we needed to find a professional organization that would be willing to serve as the group's official sponsor. We naturally approached our professional society, the Association of American Geographers (AAG), for sponsorship. Allen and I drove to Washington, DC, to discuss the matter with the Executive Director of the AAG. Unfortunately, he showed no interest in the matter, even though the sponsorship would not entail any financial responsibility. We were certain that members of the group would be more than willing to grab the opportunity to visit China and pay for their own travel. The rejection by the Executive Director of the AAG was quite a surprise and disappointment to us and we have never quite understood the reasons for it. Allen then suggested that the Ohio Academy of Sciences might be an appropriate and willing sponsor for our group. We approached its Executive Officer, Mr Lynn Elfner, who graciously agreed to support us. Thus, seven of the ten members of the group were recruited from Ohio, with Allen serving as the leader of the delegation.[1]

The group flew to Hong Kong and entered China at Luohu. Mr Su Fenlin of the Bureau of Foreign Affairs of the CAS, who would accompany us for the entire three-week trip, greeted us. It was the first time that the other members of the group saw China. I was especially excited because I had longed for such a chance to see my homeland after I had emigrated to Taiwan in 1949 just before the Communist Party took over the country. I still had vivid memories of the country in the 1940s and was eager to see what changes had occurred during the 28-year period of socialist rule since 1949.

We visited such cities as Guangzhou, Guilin, Changsha, Shaoshan (Mao's birth place), Xi'an, Beijing and Shanghai. Aside from the usual tourist sites, we visited a number of geography institutes and departments and met many geographers. Everywhere we went, we were warmly welcomed. We held discussions with our Chinese colleagues on the development of geography in the US and China. It was Allen who would answer most of the questions for us. Allen also gave several lectures in packed rooms on the status of American geography, and these lectures gave our Chinese colleagues the first glimpse of geographic research in a non-communist society.

In 1978, we hosted a ten-member delegation of Chinese geographers organized by the CAS for a return visit to the US.[2] We were fortunate in having some financial support from the National Science Foundation, the Ford Foundation, the Johnson Foundation and the University of Akron, but it was the remarkably warm hospitality extended to our guests by a large number of geography departments and government agencies in the US that greatly surprised us. We originally scheduled the group for a three-week visit, but the number of universities and government units that wished to host the Chinese delegation was so large that the visit was extended to 40 days. To accommodate as many requests for hosting the group as possible and to give the visitors a chance to see as many places as possible, each stop was allocated no more than four days. It was Allen who not only provided guidance in structuring the programme of the return visit but also actively took part in the planning of a detailed itinerary. He also made the initial contact with many geography departments to see if they would be willing to receive the delegation. I was fortunate to have the opportunity to accompany the group for the entire trip in the fall of 1978.[3] The requests for hosting and meeting with the Chinese visitors were so numerous that we had to arrange not only dinner and evening events but also lunch and breakfast meetings.

The highlight of the visit was a bi-national academic symposium supported generously by the Johnson Foundation and held at its picturesque Wingspread Conference centre in Racine, Wisconsin, on October 13–14, 1978. The symposium was attended by the Chinese guests and 20 carefully selected leading American geographers who were well established in their own areas of expertise. This included several members of the original American delegation. The symposium was the first US–China scholarly meeting at which scholarly papers were presented from both sides. The papers were subsequently published in a volume titled *The Environment: Chinese and American Views* (Ma and Noble, 1981).

It should be pointed out that the geography exchange programme, in which Allen was involved from the very beginning, was the first outside of the CAS–CSCPRC organizational framework. I was told a couple of years later in China that the success of the exchange programme convinced the CAS that it constituted a new model for expanded scholarly exchanges between Chinese and American scholars. For the discipline of geography, the exchange programme was the first bridge, a strong and successful one, ever built linking the field across the Pacific. It opened up numerous doors for geographers of both countries to engage in various academic interactions in the future.

In the summer of 1979, the CAS invited Allen and I and our families to China for a lecturing tour. It was an immensely enjoyable trip during which Allen lectured on American geographical research, including urban geography, a field which was just beginning to emerge in China. Since 1979, numerous academic programmes in geography have been developed and a large number of geographers and students have come to the US, many as a result of the initial contacts made during the 1977–79 exchanges.

Contributions to the Field of Chinese Geography

Although not a specialist on China, Allen has made significant contributions to the study of Chinese geography. First, he has edited a volume of papers on the Chinese and American environment. The book contained nine scholarly contributions dealing with China's agricultural landscape, agricultural potential, the relationship between forest cover and rainfall runoff in the Loess Plateau, non-Hortonian runoff generation in the humid regions of South China, China's marshes, debris flows on the Tibetan plateau, the development of small towns, the application of Landsat imagery to the interpretation of buried faults in Shanxi, and the digital and writing system at the Institute of Geography of the CAS. These papers represent the earliest works by leading Chinese geographers published in English in the West. They also point to the major areas of geographic concern at the end of the 1970s. The papers by American contributors provided our Chinese colleagues with a good sample of what American geographers were interested in at that time.

After the 1978 return visit, Allen informed American scholars about the status of Chinese geography and geographic research in two papers (Noble and Ma, 1978 and 1979). These papers provided the first glimpses of China's geography and geographic research, which at the time was dominated heavily by the study of physical and agricultural geographies and oriented towards the solution of practical problems of production. The emphasis on physical geography was natural, as the Chinese had followed the Soviet system of structuring geographic knowledge to emphasize physical geography. Geomorphology, climatology, hydrology, pedology, medical geography (especially local diseases) and cartography were very well developed, and remote sensing was quickly emerging as an important field of study. Chinese geographers had also spent a great deal of time and energy to identify China's natural resources, to understand the potential of the land for agricultural production and to increase food production to feed the growing population. Economic geography employed a much smaller number of geographers who nonetheless were actively involved in the nation's economic development by providing field-based information in such areas as transportation planning, water supply, and industrial location. As China had been isolated from the West, Chinese geographers were neither affected by the quantitative and theoretical revolutions taking place in the West in the late 1950s and the 1960s nor aware of the developments in Western economic, urban and human geography.

While in China, Allen conducted research on noise pollution in several cities. He would find time from his busy schedule to measure the levels of noise on the street and, at meetings with Chinese geographers, would discuss their research on the subject. His paper (Noble, 1980) on the noise levels in Chinese cities is perhaps the earliest on the subject published in the West.

As noted earlier, Allen has written extensively on urban development in various countries. In 1985, the first International Conference on Asian Urbanization was held at the University of Akron in which a large number of high-quality papers on Asian cities were delivered. A selected number of papers on China were published in a special issue on Chinese cities in *Urban Geography*. In that issue, we co-authored a paper on the status of Chinese urban geography and proposed an agenda for further research (Ma and Noble, 1986). The paper has been well received and widely quoted.

Aside from scholarly work, Allen in his capacity as the head of the Department of Geography at the University of Akron played a crucial role in attracting a number of high-quality Chinese geographers to the campus for long and short-term stays. The first visiting professor to the US was Professor Chun-fen Lee of Shanghai Normal University who taught a semester at Akron in the early 1980s. Professor Lee was the first recipient of PhD on Chinese geography at the University of Toronto. Long-term visiting scholars at Akron in subsequent years included Professor Changming Liu of the Institute of Geography, CAS, who is now an academician (*yuanshi*) at the CAS and Vice-President of the International Geographical Union; Professor Jianzhong Tang of Shanghai Normal University; and Professor Gonghao Cui of Nanjing University, one of the top urban geographers in China.

Allen was always interested in getting the best graduate students from China. Over the years, the geography department at the University of Akron attracted some of the most talented graduate students in the field of Chinese geography. Some of these students went on to pursue their PhDs in major universities after they had earned their Master's degree from Akron, and a few of them have since become highly productive scholars and dominant figures in their own areas of expertise. Among the most active are George C. S. Lin (PhD, University of British Columbia), a specialist on the Pearl River delta and economic geography; Yehua Wei of the University of Utah at Salt Lake City (PhD, UCLA), a specialist on China's regional development; Yichun Xie of Eastern Michigan University (PhD, SUNY Buffalo), a GIS specialist; Ge Lin of the University of West Virginia (PhD, SUNY Buffalo), a population expert; and Yifei Sun of California State University, Northridge (PhD, SUNY Buffalo) who is one of the very few geographers working on the geography of research and innovation at the national, regional, local and enterprise levels using China as an example. Through teaching and publications, these visitors and former students have all made significant contributions to the study of Chinese geography. Their experiences at Akron and their impact on the fields of their expertise were closely related to the active role that Allen played in bringing them to the United States.

A Personal Note of Appreciation

Life is a series of planned and accidental encounters. Allen G. Noble has immensely affected my life. I was fortunate enough to be Allen's colleague at the University of Akron for nearly three decades. In the spring of

1971, while busily finishing my doctoral dissertation and desperately trying to find a job, I was luckily 'discovered' by Allen who was recruiting a geographer who could teach eastern civilizations, a general studies course. I was thrilled to have a job because the job market was extremely tight and almost excluded regional geographers specializing in the non-Western world, because regional geography was equated with descriptive work and was viewed with disdain at the time. I must thank Allen for offering me the job at Akron as few jobs were available at the time, and even these were mostly reserved for 'quantitative geography.'

I must also thank Allen for providing a congenial, free and stimulating academic environment in the Department of Geography at Akron that emphasized research and other scholarly activities and that gave faculty sufficient financial support for their research work. As a productive researcher, Allen set the tone for the department and was a model for colleagues to emulate. I am immensely grateful to Allen for his strong support of my work on China and for his kind collaboration in structuring the (1977–1978) exchange programme, which I deem one of the most important events in my professional life since it enabled me to establish wide contacts with geographers in China and conduct fieldwork there.

Notes

1. Members of the delegation, all professional geographers, were Allen G. Noble (delegation leader), Lawrence J. C. Ma and Lathardus Goggins of the University of Akron, Akron, Ohio; Jordan Hodgkins of Kent State University, Kent, Ohio; Lawrence Hoffman and Donald W. Lewis of the University of Toledo, Toledo, Ohio; James Osborn of the University of Chicago, Chicago, Illinois; Clifton W. Pannell of the University of Georgia, Athens, Georgia; Christopher L. Salter of the University of California, Los Angeles, and Jack F. Williams of Michigan State University, East Lansing, Michigan. Ma, Pannell, Salter and Williams are specialists of Chinese geography.
2. The delegation was led by Professor Huang Bingwei, a leading physical geographer specializing in agricultural land potential, Director of the Institute of Geography, CAS, and Director of the Chinese Geographical Society. The deputy leader of the group was Professor Wu Chuanjun, China's top economic geographer and Deputy Director of the Institute of Geography, CAS, and Deputy Director of the Chinese Geographical Society. Other members included Mr Huang Xichou of the Changchun Institute of Geography, CAS, a marshland specialist; Mr Yang Shiren of the Institute of Geography, CAS, a remote sensing specialist; Mr Cheng Jicheng of the Department of Geography, Beijing University, another remote sensing specialist; Mr Liu Changming of the Institute of Geography, CAS, a hydrologist;

Mr Tang Bangxing of the Chengdu Institute of Geography, CAS, a geomorphologist specializing in debris flows; Mr Shen Canxin of Zhongshan University, a hydrologist; Mr Yao Shimou of Nanjing Institute of Geography, CAS, an urban geographer; and Mr Wang Renquan of the Bureau of Foreign Affairs, CAS.

3. The group visited a large number of university geography departments, including the Universities of Akron, Johns Hopkins, Georgia, Chicago, Michigan State, Minnesota, Indiana State, Southern Illinois, Colorado, Arizona, Arizona State, UCLA, Cal State at Fullerton and Hawai'i. The delegation also visited various federal and state research and planning agencies, including USGS and Ohio Department of Natural Resources.

References

Ma, L. J. C. and Allen G. Noble, 'Recent Development in Chinese Geographical Research', *The Geographical Review*, Vol. 69, 1979, pp. 63–78.

Ma, L. J. C. and Allen G. Noble, *The Environment: Chinese and American Views*, New York: Methuen and Co. Ltd., 1981.

Ma, L. J. C. and Allen G. Noble, 'Chinese Cities: A Research Agenda', *Urban Geography*, Vol. 7, 1986, pp. 279–290.

Noble, Allen G. and L. J. C. Ma, 'Some Observations on Geographic Research in China', *Ohio Journal of Science*, Vol. 78, 1978, pp. 239–244.

Noble, Allen G. and L. J. C. Ma, 'Noise Pollution in Selected Chinese and American Cities', *GeoJournal*, Vol. 4, 1980, pp. 573–575.

II
Conceptual and Theoretical Basis of Social Geography

4

Social Geography: History, Structure and Reflections, with Special Reference to India

B. K. Roy

The field of social geography is inherent to the study of societies, their way of life, customs and traditions. The historical dispersal of social geography has undergone change through many different stages due to new scientific development. Explorations of various time periods had great bearing on the exposition of routes, civilizations, and economics of lands and people, which brought the societies to limelight and established contemporary trends. In geography, the contributions of Vidal de la Blache (1845–1918) paved a distinctive role to relate the qualities of environment to societies, and Jean Brunhes (1869–1930) emphasized the assessment of communities by their background and economic resources. The contributions of de la Blache and Brunhes, along with those who followed their lead, initiated a particular study of causative social geography throughout the world. Their studies were actually related to human adjustments to climate, physical bases, transports, economic activities, houses, dwellings and cultivation of environment. Before World War II, the scope and objectives in the study of social geography were confined to physical geographic influences on human societies. As far as the American and the European views on the structure of social geography are concerned, the ideas of Hartshorne and Houston respectively are the most characteristic and parallel in alignment as noted below. Their ideas, in a way, satisfied universal appeal. Thus, this chapter is centred on these parameters with reference to important literature on their subject.

Generalities were brought into the study of macro systems of man and land[1] relations; gradually, it shifted to diagnose microscopic patterns of this relationship (Taylor, 1957). Here lie the cut-off divisions of general geography and social geography. The geographical use of the term 'social' has become prevalent in the recent years but with various meanings. In this regard, Hartshorne's (1939) idea of systematic sciences interfacing with geography and radiating in regional geography, brought out a stream of social elements in geography concerning ethnology, economics, political science and sociology. This infused geography of ethnology, economic geography, political and social geography as specialities in the subject.

On account of various dimensions of possibilism and, presently, by the advances of ideas on behaviourism, the structure of social geography in Europe included a gamut of geographical basis of ethnology, sociology, human ecology, racial aspects of synthesis and demography, mostly distributional aspects of population and structure (Houston, 1953). Is it that the subject geography encroaches upon other disciplines or other disciplines encroach upon geography to create a specific realm of social geography? Their question is debatable. The value of history, in addition, helps to measure temporal trends in them with varying degree to streamline geographical studies on topical issues.

Taking clues from the above views and the objective to deal with history, structure and reflections on social geography, it is proposed to highlight the development from the selected contributions on the issues of (i) ethnologies, (ii) sociology *vis-à-vis* human ecology, (iii) temporal dimensions in social systems, and finally, (iv) a consideration on an outlook of emergence in social aspects of Geography. In fact, the trends are discussed in a limited way, as to make one understand that the fabric of social geography is intricate.

Ethnologies

Ethnological studies on specific issues have been written abundantly and recorded by explorers, administrators, sailors and sociologists at various times in many parts of the world. Immediate attention goes to Forde's (1938) work, *Habitat, Economy and Society*. His masterly treatment in this study of food-gatherers, cultivators, and pastoral nomads and their habitats and economy is still considered as a basic literature in their studies. According to the author, 'the studies are incomplete,' yet no attempt has been made to take up the unfinished work and connect them with the present situations by any school of social thought at one place in the format of the above-mentioned work. Casual updates, however, have been attempted in geographic encyclopedia of certain continents and regions on these societies by the Library Larousse, Paris and others.

A great deal on the scenario of United States, particularly aboriginal culture and ethno-history are published by the Bureau of American Ethnology of the Smithsonian Institute (1946–1979). These are arranged chronologically into American native-groups by the states with short description and summary on tribes. A large number of books and magazines have presented issues on aboriginal population of America residing in the north of Mexico. Estimates of their population at the time of European contacts are available on cultural diversity among aboriginal American Indians and their ethno-historical sequences.

In Europe, the long glacier epoch limited human activities to tools of chipped stones or bone which gave rise to reindeer hunting and the tillage of land in north Europe. It took centuries to organize human activities to develop rye cultivation. Gradual processes led the role of the sea to come into play, explorations started and industrial and cultural revolutions marked a special effect on the life and society of people in specific areas. The impact of these can be noticed clearly in the social systems of these areas.

Asia also saw the change of events gradually. The prehistoric events remained a mark over the modern events of human culture and society. It is true that the ethnological studies by anthropologists formed a strong base to develop the urge to study the social system background in geography. This was contributed by borrowing the concepts of other allied disciplines which strengthened the conceptualization in geography in general and social geography in particular.

Indian Scenario in Ethnologies

The ethnological studies became prominent in academic deliberations on account of the pre-independence Indian censuses, which grew mostly on the field-notes of the census commissioners, starting especially from 1901. It was the efforts of Hodson (1937), who organized the census ethnographies particularly in relation to house-types, caste and occupations, races and languages, marriage-institutions, family systems, religious pursuits and tribalism. A special mention can be cited of J. H. Hutton (1931) who elaborated the field-notes along with the works of a large number of foreign and Indian scholars and created a systematic analysis of tribal life, social conditions and geography of localities of tribes and castes in India. In addition, the District Gazetteers which were taken up for preparation and publication during 1860–1940s by the Collectors and other British officers in India also helped to understand ethnologies in a socioeconomic setting of districts.

Geographers in India, in general, could not do much to integrate and elaborate ethnological studies in its inter-relationship of physical, cultural and regional set-up due to lack of training in geography as against sociology and anthropology. Nonetheless, the work on the Himalayan Beas Basin by Kayastha (1964) drew a lot of research interest, especially in the narration of seasonal migration study of 'Gaddis' and semi-pastoralists of the Himachal Himalaya. Such studies to unravel the inter-relationship between geography and society were not carried out for other parts of India.

Since its inception, the Census of India has greatly contributed to the assessment of the life and economy of people as base-line studies from Risley, the former Census Director, to Mitra, the Director in the 1950s and 1960s (Census 1978). The former created a sound base of classification for both physical and socio-cultural aspects; while the latter infused a frame to develop a contemporary understanding of castes and tribes in view of the census population data. Accordingly, one may find a profile of details in relation to: (i) social structure and cultural reorientation, (ii) traditional rights, (iii) social mobility, and (iv) to some extent compared data of the earlier censuses with the post-independence ones for a number of castes and tribes. It is mentioned that the Census of India prepared ethnographic studies on 225 communities, including separate full-length monographs on 30 communities by social scientists, sociologists and their teams. The monograph on *Siddi* (1969) is a full-length study on a Negroid tribe living in India. Studies on tribes like *Kadar* (1965) and *Toda* (1966) present a diachronic perspective of change among these communities. Likewise, studies on *Gond* (1970) and *Chenchu* (1972) provide time-series data. For castes, important studies are on *Pasi* (1972), *Tiyar* (1974), and *Parhaiya* (1977).

During the latter part of 1990s, a project called the *People of India*, dealing with social-anthropology, history and contemporary data on castes and tribes/sub-groups was brought out in several volumes. This gigantic compilation of source materials gave a great feedback on the needs of socio-political platforms of the changing situations in the societal scenario of India (Singh, 1992–1995). The project identified 4,635 Indian communities or castes out of which 16 per cent were scheduled castes, 14 per cent scheduled tribes and 23 per cent other backward communities (OBC). However, this exercise does not attempt to study how far these communities have benefited from the programmes of development in various planned phases of the country. During the past 50 years a great deal of conflict has ensued, especially in the real transition in geographical habitat, language and way of living (Roy, 1983).

Social Sciences vis-a-vis Social Geography

The greater number of phenomena are related spatially and microscopically in the sector of social sciences. In this process, it is challenging to portray space values. More challenging is to depict values and compare them over time and space. The crux, thus, is a matter of establishing relationship with factors in societal issues in social sciences in general, and social geography in particular. But, the concepts in dealing with the issues are varying, precisely different and sometimes overlapping in the typical treatment of sociologists, economists and geographers. In addition, aims and objectives to detect co-variance in studies of course are different with regard to tools utilized. In these pretexts, sociologists, economists, anthropologists and geographers interpret dimensional social perspectives in human- and area-specific realms, dominated by their theoretical concepts respectively. Standard and nature of work, thus, are different when a theme of common interest is dealt with.

Geographers, in particular, have spatial view and employ a strong tool of mapping and diagrammatic exposition. However, in its basic constitution, the social scientists, particularly sociologists and economists test the concepts and theoretical derivations in evaluation of the problems and their solutions. This basic difference in approach matters a lot for appeal and strategy in decision making on different issues. Some Indian studies in this regard are referred to here. The 1960s witnessed great attempts to study the village as a social unit. Geographers and sociologists have done a great deal of research on this. Dube (1955) introduced the concept of an Indian village from the point of view of how he perceived the village in its microscopic organism or social entity and identity. Following this, he also spelled out India's changing villages in the background of community development, a system which projected the country's thinking to reorient the preceding socioeconomic and humanistic thinking of pre-independent India (Dube, 1960). Further, it is interesting to note that Beteille (1991, 317) postulated that there was a need for an individual to loosen his allegiance to his village, his sub-caste and his lineage. The individual was being drawn into networks of interpersonal relation which are right across the boundaries of the village, sub-caste and lineage. It is further noted that the post-1950 community programmes focused mostly on the part of the Central and State Governments for social welfare (Sachchidananda, 1964). These are all based on village oriented studies and evaluations of sociologists.

Studies of the villages by geographers have also enriched the literature in social evaluation, distribution of castes or tribes, interconnecting land use synthesis and mapping to depict changes in societies and farm-economy leading to a branch of rural geography concerned with settlements and their morphology, histogenesis, shapes and sizes, house types, physical response to sites and situations, and the ecology of smaller areas. It is clear that the village studies conducted by socioeconomists and anthropologists gave a substantial background to politicians in India to develop policies in improving and judging social problems. On the other hand, the works of geographers, who conducted village level case studies and recorded trend patterns in land use, settlements, and ecology were greatly helped by the introduction of Remote sensing and geographic information system (GIS). Many honours and graduate level Geography curricula in India introduced fieldwork based village study in their required course work. The earlier recorded patterns provided a great deal of information for reconstructing synchronous database in understanding the missing link of records to study recent trends in landscape and societies. Geographers' work came late for recognition.

Temporal Dimensions

'Man-and-land' have been interactive in moulding societies. Blache was very much concerned with the numerical distribution and associated density patterns, while Trewartha (1953) was concerned with the activities of man in time dimensions. These philosophies, thus, evoked many facets of evaluation of societies over the globe. The techniques of assessment have been various and numerous to deal with the structure and process at macro levels. The canvas, field of examination and interest multiplied on topics and areas. This provided an enlargement of the nature and scope of social geography during the post-1940s period. The following discussions, thus, may deal with selected issues dealt with by geographers. They are: (i) man and land matters, (ii) urban issues, and (iii) demography and population (social purpose). It is in these fields that substantial work has been carried out both for nations and regions.

Man and Land Matters

Man and land have been closely associated in generating social values and environment. Yates (1987) observed that the societal demands upon their members or the opportunities societies present to their members provide the basis for a materialistic explanation by different groups. He emphasized that there was also a physical environment factor that reduces or enlarges the gaps of societies living in a particular environment. Sometimes any statistical explanation may not project clearly the correlation in assessing the quality of human life in an area. It requires perception-based thinking besides statistical measures on a large number of factors of society, land, men and women and attributes (Roy, 1987). It also requires a rigorous pursuance of the causative factors in social studies to develop such subjects for shaping and changing societies. Geographers should engage themselves in such topical interest to generate awareness in social systems.

Man and land being basic and compelling, a large sector of social geography is dominated by the studies of land use as an indicator of social concern. The well-known work of land use survey in Britain (Stamp, 1948) paved grounds to geographers of many other countries to deal with the classification of land into various categories. It helped identification of urgent need of farm and non-farm utilities and their reorientation. Indian geographers, during 1950s and through 1970s, conducted a large number of area studies. This remained mostly an academic exercise as against the rigorous competition of statistical exercise by economists and agricultural scientists for perspective evaluations, to decide the country's social change. Lately, due to being partly political and partly compulsion, the land waste assessment in the land use mosaics caught the imagination of social scientists and the non-governmental agencies (NGO) in India. Maps generated by remote sensing technique also helped to settle a matching proposal to populations suffering from lack of land and struggling for survival. However, it remains to be seen whether land-waste studies in the mosaic of land utilization are the last hope of the poor for development by helping to reduce the imbalance of landed and landless households of rural societies.

Urban Issues

Urban geographers face intense competition from sociologists and planners. However, their works provide a great feedback on the geographical problems of the urban landscape. It is true that urban populations performing non-primary pursuits in its zones are better-off, but the ethos and pains of various profiles of the internal population from rich to poor have long remained a valid issue for consideration. Geographers in this competition feel depressed because their works and concepts do not provide deep insights; rather, studies on settlement patterns, and histogenesis alike have given stimulous and support to the works of other social scientists.

Rurban, ribbon developments, umlands, conurbations, internal structure assessments, and classifications of rural and urban areas were not concepts new to developing societies. The credit, however, goes to the geographers like B. J. L. Berry (USA), R. L. Singh (India) and others, to bring about such forms to the limelight and explanations in view of the growth of urban system. No doubt, a temporal dimension could not be projected successfully in space considerations over time. On the contrary, the works of non-geographers used statistical measures and projections, showing the alarming nature of expansion, congestion and the ills of urban society. These were very convincing to policy makers and drew their attention to the subject.

The consensus on urban gradient to measure social and sectoral profiles in Chicago city in five concentric zones arranged by sociologist E. W. Burgess in 1920s gave a great impetus specially to the geographers who tested and followed case studies on many towns all over the world. After the 1980s, delineation of colonial urban cores in cities in selected areas and their influences in building up further growth of such cities also inspired the geographers significantly to carry out studies in Asia (Dutt, 1985). Dutt (1983, 1993, 1994, 2000) presented descriptive models for traditional bazaar and colonial based cities of South Asia in successive studies.

In the international scenario, the classical works and studies on the urbanized seaboard of the USA, particularly Gottmann's *Megalopolis* (1961) and Dickinson's (1951), *The West European City* guided geographers to examine the problems of social reconstruction in cities. In addition, the social purpose, overpowered by the functional transformation and reorientation, were also taken over for studies by the non-geographers for small areas.

There are numerous interludes in the initiatives to create awareness on social problems in urban areas at par with the works of various other thinkers now. The cities in developing countries provide a good forum and field for investigations of a contemporary nature. Studies on crime, urban morphology, and health and hazard management are some of the key areas of social interest. Studies by Dutt (USA) on crime and urban geography, and by Akhtar and Dutt on medical and health infrastructure of South Asia (India), to name a few, provide good models to be followed up by young geographers. It is interesting to note that during the 1970s and through the 1980s, research by the Indian scholars on social problems have appeared in important geographic journals of India, showing an encouraging trend. It is also significant to note that such articles published in the *Annals of the Association of American Geographers* constituted a high 40 per cent of all articles on social sector problems in 1977, and 23 per cent in 1987. During the same period, trend on urban research of general nature has declined (Stoddard, 1992). In this context, it is interesting to find paradigm changes in Indian geography and the future challenges (Karan, 1992) which outline the specific cluster of social geographic researches during the 1920s and 1980s. During this period, the nature and vision of this subject changed from deterministic to nomothetic and humanistic concerns.

Events, in comparative study of towns, have taken many forms and concepts; the important one has been on the functional classifications followed up in various ways (Harris, 1943). Demographers developed a distaste for this tool especially in India after the 1981 census. Data responsible for testing the functional classification of towns or cities were abandoned.

The institutional concern to project new data and statistical materials for the development of society by the census organizations are commendable and timely. The USA's concept of SMSAs and Britain's concept of large statistical area (conurbation), such as London, West-Midlands, West-Yorkshire, Merseyside, Tyneside and central Clydeside served as models to the developing countries to project data in these frames for socioeconomic development. The 1971 Indian census also introduced Standard Urban Areas (SUA) numbering 324 for the country as a whole in order to prepare metro plans.

The 2001 Indian census abandoned the exercise of projecting data on SUAs that was so useful for 1971, 1981 and 1991 censuses; the reasons being that some typical socioeconomic inconsistencies resulted from such data. It was concerned with increasing speculation of land, unplanned build-up and habitation of illegal migrants, unhygienic conditions, and degradation of environment alike. In a sense, spreading of ills of larger towns or cities have been shifting in these SUAs. Studies are awaited on these issues for such areas.

Demographic and Applied Population Concerns (Social Purpose)

The issues of demography and applied population geography in the investigation of social purpose have a strong bearing as a tool of synthesis. There is a need to apply these methods of demographic analysis in population study in geographic training. Panjab University at Chandigarh has been known as the 'home of population geography' in India due to its nurturing of the field since the Geography Department's establishment in 1960. Jawaharlal Nehru University (JNU), Delhi also introduced a course on population study during the 1970s; it is still an integral part of the higher graduate program. A course on population studies has also been introduced at the International Institute of Population Studies (IIPS), Mumbai. It is a broad-based curriculum which trains a limited number of geographers. However, the study of population in the field of Geography is not carried out from the base level or pre-degree curriculum in real terms. Additionally Geography is a subject for the entrance examinations for the Indian Administrative Services (IAS), but Demography as a subject has not been included by the Union Public Service Commission (UPSC), the federal agency responsible for such examinations and recruitment of the civil services. Geography as a subject lies basically in the graduate and masters' level courses at the Indian universities in general perspective and standard. It is high time for geographers to train students and introduce discussions in order to throw their points of view in parallel to demographers (on demographic principles), sociologists and economists, whose views and work are rated appropriate and syllogistic for application to society's development. Time demands that Social Geography and geographers may need to look beyond the study of numbers and distributional qualities of population for better professionalism.

Ecosystem analysis of tribal populations, in particular, generates valuable information for record (Mookherjee, 1997). Caste, tribe, or linguistic approach in measuring various social dimensions is quite old in academic research and mapping evaluation. The dominance of such research which evoked great strides came up from the social statistics created by the census, particularly India's census from 1901. It threw open the opportunity to individual scholars to bring out politico-economic consequences. As noted earlier, the ethnologies brought out were the instruments to create consensus on habitat and society. However, post-independent India saw it in transition due to their governance and policies. Tribes and regions bring typical identity which gave valuable insights to measure social mobility (Roy, 1983). Tribal regions are weakening now and becoming mobile due to economic aspirations and the spread of education. Though the aged tribals remain in their original habitats, the younger ones move from their cores, leaving their roots. This field awaits attention of the geographers in India for in-depth field-oriented studies.

Statistical testing and multivariate methods in development and diversification leading to scores are some of the specific and strong tools to measure social infrastructure. Not going into the history of such tools, it is felt that potential application in demographic and applied population investigations, much headway has been made on these themes. Macro interpretations are common to social scientists (Navaneethan and Saxena, 1999). Based on the methodologies of the Physical Quality of Life Index (PQLI of Morris, 1977), it has been found that literacy and basic resources are distinctly interrelated in the districts of India, indicating regional disparities that have social relevance. Districts are recreated and bifurcated constantly in India and so the studies on PQLI are to be built upon to provide impact of geographical inequalities in them in a regional perspective. And here lies an opportunity, which perhaps has not been availed enough by geographers, but is at least taken up by today's planners to accept everything possible of geographical, historical and economic interest of these areas.

Racial and linguistic composition are the strong social elements in a nation, region or area. About 2000 different peoples are known in the world of which small tribes numbering a few hundred and less, like the Andamanese-Minkopisians in India, and the largest such as the Indo-European in the world, are the constituents of the earth's population. Population is rising constantly and social problems have multiplied enormously (Brook, 1979). It is useful to relate language and space system in populations to learn lessons as to how such groups have adapted to modify the situation, adverse or favourable, for development in economic terms (Dutt, 1985b). Certain other models of assessment on language and economic space are also available to be generated by geographers in this raw but topical field of investigation, particularly given the diverse yet democratic set-up of India (Roy, 1986).

Another view point which underlies the realm of Social Geography is the subject matter of social and economic implications to human needs and dispersals on universal scale. This relates to needs of food, health services, education and migration to the masses. The occident and orient have seen great epidemics of cholera, smallpox, kala-azar fever, and plague. Britain lost over two million lives in the middle of the nineteenth century due to cholera alone. Europe's Black Death in 14th century was a horrible human catastrophe (Dutt et al. 2008). Deaths in India from plague, malaria and influenza were in millions during 1920s–30s numbered in the millions. Many masterpiece studies were conducted and models were designed for research purposes and to assess such investigations of population health conditions.

Scholars are quite aware of the contribution of Geddes (1941–42) who explained the socio-historical relevance to population, famine and disease interpretations. His mapping of the trend of population still provides a model for social welfare. Such exercises need to be taken up for studying the calamitous earthquake on 26 January, 2001 that occurred in Gujarat, where more than hundred thousand people (official estimates claim 30 thousand) succumbed to their death. The task of rebuilding socioeconomic values is a challenge to socio-political institutions. India faces almost regular droughts, floods and hazards in specific regions at various intervals. Constant geographic researches may provide a good ground to create awareness by geographical interpretations, and this may bring a social obligation to the geographers to deal with such issues.

Implications of Demographic Zones to Society

Demographic diversity poses a challenge to the social and economic development in its inter-relations, as far as the theoretical considerations are concerned. This is particularly important for India. Demographic zoning is quite important as a tool for categorizations like 'agricultural regions', 'geo-physical regions', 'planning regions', etc. Demographers in India have recognized the strategy of using demographic zones created by geographical concepts. The Indian scenario in establishing such zones is now about 40 years old. It commenced with the study of levels of development in India (in two volumes (Mitra, 1964), followed by Sengupta and Sadasyuk (1968) in one volume) on regionalization based on under-population vis-à-vis over-population in India. This was rounded out by Roy's (1988–1990) regional divisions of India (in 30 volumes) providing viable units of planning and population data gathering under the aegis of the Indian census. All these above works were compiled in an abridged form to avail the materials to general people by a demographer (Bose 1994). It is noteworthy that a general consensus is recognized and supported by demographers to achieve goals of population and development by this strategy, which in turn, may give a sound footing to social development in India.

Micro-Population Concerns

Ninety districts in India were chosen for vigorous family welfare programmes and evaluation of earlier efforts towards welfare. This has now been expanded in scope by the efforts of India's National Commission on Population (2001) by selecting 135 districts of India to fully adopt the registration of birth, death and marriages, ensure full education till 14 years of age and to ensure provision of basic needs like water, nutrition, immunization of children against preventive diseases, and development of roads. In addition, observation and investigation into the sex ratio of the general population, as well as sex ratios of the child population of seven years or older, and those up to six years of age are other concerns (Census, 2001). It is now evident that in addition to the population policy framework, social planning strategy may be of great importance the coming decades of the twenty-first century. It is high time for social geographers to take up their own proposals and evaluate studies of such districts in their research to provide the governments with the lapses and gains in social welfare. This will enhance the quality of geographic research as regards social commitment.

The Outlook and the Future

To sum up, the points put forth and described here are mere generalizations of the selected valuable studies and thoughts that have enriched social aspects of geography. Modernization is taking place very rapidly and is complex in its materialistic dimensions. Social values are breaking away rapidly as well. Now, Social Geography is not limited to a definite order, neither does a definition exist of it. It is true that it is not only a study of society, settlement, land use, urban landscape, or their integration as a whole but neither is it for social upliftment alone. It is competitive to treatment of the subject matter, area and the content. Social issues are complex in developed areas and more so in underdeveloped regions, irrespective of continents and nations. These complex issues require intensive focus to encompass various methodologies, perspectives, and an equation with other social scientists across the world.

There is no doubt that the new emerging technologies of GIS and remote sensing can assist the analysis considerably, but the philosophical bases in geography have to be given meaningful thought concerning the welfare of population, societies, and other areas. No Geography can aptly be regarded 'social' when the inferences are drawn from the intensive studies by primary collection and creation of databases on various regions, habitations and populations. Synoptic studies may not enrich the subject, rather they may require rewriting Geography in the present context; hence the burden and responsibilities of developing and furthering the scope of 'social geography lies on the new generations of younger geographers.

Editors' Note

The editor's have attempted to conform to standards of non-sexist language throughout this book. However, when terminologies predate the universal adoption of such standards, and have a tradition of usage during a certain era of geographic scholarship, then original usages have been retained.

References

Akhtar, R., A. K. Dutt, V. Wadhwa (eds.), *Malaria in South Asia: Eradication and Resurgence during the Second Half of the Twentieth Century*, Dordrecht: Springer, 2010.

Beteille, A., (with M. N. Srinivas), *Society and Politics in India, Essays in a Comparative Perspective*, Delhi: Oxford University Press, 1991, p. 317.

Bose, A., *Demographic Zones in India*, Delhi: B. R. Publishing Corporation, 1994.

Brook, S., 'Ethnic, Racial and Religious Structures of the World Population Data & Perspectives', *Population and Development Review*, 1979, pp. 505–534.

Brunhes, J., *Human Geography*, London, 1952.

Burgess, E. W., 'The Growth of the City', *Proceedings of the American Sociological Society*, Vol. 18, 1923, pp. 85–89.

Census of India 1978, Indian *Census and Anthropological Investigations*, New Delhi: Xth International Congress of Anthropological & Ethnological Sciences.

Census of India 2001, *Provisional Population Totals*, New Delhi.

Dickinson, R. E., *The West European City: A Geographical Interpretation*, London: Routledge & Kegan Paul Ltd., 1951.

Dube, S. C., *Indian Village*, London: Routledge & Kegan Paul, 1955.

Dube, S. C., *India's Changing Villages, Human Factors in Community Development*, London: Routledge & Kegan Paul, 1960.

Dutt, A. K., 'Cities of South Asia', in S. Brunn and J. Williams (eds.), *Cities of the World*, New York: Harper & Row Publishers, 1983, pp. 325–370.

Dutt, A. K., 'Cities of South Asia', in S. Brunn and J. Williams (eds.), *Cities of the World*, New York: Harper Collins, Second edition, 1993, pp. 351–387.

Dutt, A. K., Y. Xie, Frank J. Costa, and Zhengmao Yang, 'City Forms of China and India in Global Perspective', in A. K. Dutt, Frank J. Costa, S. Aggarwal and A. G. Noble (eds.), *The Asian City: Processes of Development, Characteristics and Planning*, Dordrecht: Kluwer Academic Publishers, 1994, pp. 25–52.

Dutt, A. K., *Global Urbanization Trends, Forms and Density Gradients*, Allahabad University, Professor R. N. Dubey Memorial Foundation, 2001.

Dutt, A. K. and George Pomeroy, 'Cities of South Asia', in S. D. Brunn, J. D. Williams and D. J. Zeigler (eds.), *Cities of the World*, New York: Rowan & Littlefield, Third edition, 2003, pp. 330–371.

Dutt, A. K., Allen G. Noble and G. D'Sa, 'An Historical View of Density Gradients of Calcutta: A Colonial City', *National Geographical Journal of India*, Vol. 31, No. 4, 1985, pp. 269–279.

Dutt, A. K., Chandra Khan and Chandra Sanguan, 'Spatial Pattern of Languages in India: A Cultural-Historical Analysis', *Geojournal*, Vol. 10, No. 1, 1985b, pp. 51–74.

Dutt, A.K., Hiran Dutta, Rais Akhtar and Malinda McVay, 'From Black Death to Surat Plague of 1994: A Quantum Leap in Medical Science Development', in A.K. Dutt, H.N. Mishra and Meera Chatterjee, (eds.), Explorations in Applied Geography, New Delhi: Prentice Hall, 2008, pp. 472–490.

Forde, C. Daryll, *Habitat, Economy and Society: A Geographical Introduction to Ethnology*, London: Methuen & Co. Ltd., 1938.

Geddes, A., 'Half-a-Century of Population Trends in India: A Regional Study of Net Change and Variability, 1881–1931', *Geographical Journal*, Vol. 98, 1941, pp. 228–253.

Geddes, A., 'The Population of India: Variability of Change as a Regional Demographic Index', *Geographical Journal*, Vol. 32, 1942, pp. 562–573.

Gottmann, J., *Megalopolis: The Urbanised North-eastern Seaboard of the United States*, New York: The Twentieth Century Fund, 1961.

Hartshorne, R., 'The Nature of Geography', *Annals of the Association of American Geographers*, New York: Geography in World Society, Lippincott Co., 1939, pp. 27–46. (Also see Meyer, A. H. and H. J. Strietelmeir, 1963).

Harris, C. D., 'A Functional Classification of Cities in the United States', *Geographical Review*, Vol. 33, 1943, pp. 86–99.

Hodson, T. C., *India: Census Ethnography 1901–1931*, Delhi: Manager of Publications, 1937.

Houston, J. M., *A Social Geography of Europe*, London: Gerald Duckworth & Co. Ltd., 1953.

Hutton, J. H., *Complete Survey of Tribal Life & Systems*, Census of India, Vol. I, No. 3, B: Ethnographical, Delhi: Manager of Publications, 1931.

Karan, P. P., 'Development of Geographic Thought in India', *National Geographic Journal of India*, Vol. 34, Nos. 1–4, 1992, pp. 179–193.

Kayastha, S. L., *The Himalayan Beas Basin: A Study in Habitat, Economy & Society*, Varanasi: National Geographical Society, 1964.

Mookherjee, S., 'Lineage & Non-Lineage Communities: Laupal , Purulia', *Annals of the National Association of Geographers, India*, Vol. 17, Nos. 1 and 2, 1997, pp. 80–85.

Morris, D. Morris, *Measuring the Condition of the World's Poor: the Physical Quality of Life Index Measure*, New York: Pergamon, 1977.

Navanethan, K. and P. C. Saxena, 'Multi-variate Graphical Methods for Development', *Demography India*, Vol. 28, No. 1, 1999, pp. 111–122.

Roy, B. K., 'Certain Issues of Language & Habitat: A Case Study of Tribal Areas of Chotanagpur Plateau', *Rural Systems*, Vol. 1, No. 2, 1983, pp. 135–140.

Roy, B. K., 'Languages and Economic Space in India', *Avadh Journal of Social Sciences*, Vol. 3: 1986, pp. 1–8.

Roy, B. K., 'Quality of Man in India', *GeoJournal*, Vol. 15, No. 4, 1987, pp. 335–346.

Sachchidananda, *Culture Change in Tribal Bihar: Munda and Oraon*, Calcutta: Bookland Pvt. Ltd., 1964.

Singh, K. S., *People of India*, Vols. 1–3, Calcutta: ASI, 1992–95.

Smithsonian Institution, Bureau of American Ethnology, Washington DC, 1946–1979.

Stamp, L. D., *Land of Britain: Its Use and Misuse*, London: Longman's Green & Co., 1948.

Stoddard, R. H., 'Trends in Published Research in India', *The Roots of Indian Geography*, Varanasi: National Geographical Society, 1992, pp. 159–166.

Taylor, G., *Geography in the Twentieth Century*, New York: Philosophical Library, 1957.

Trewartha, G. T., 'A Case of Population Geography', *Annals of the Association of American Geographers*, Vol. 43: 1953, pp. 71–93.

Vidal de la Blache, *Principles of Human Geography*, London: Constable, 1926.

Yates, E. M., 'Quality of Man', *GeoJournal*, Vol. 15, No. 4, 1987, pp. 327–333.

5

Methodological Developments in Social Geography

SUDHIR K. THAKUR

Taafe (1974) identified three major traditions in geography: 'spatial organization', 'man–land relations' and 'area study'. The first tradition, spatial organization, is defined as the arrangement of objects in geographical space. The second tradition, man–land relations, investigates the relationships between humankind and nature or biophysical environment. The third tradition refers to the study of places and regions and identifies the unique characteristics of those regions. These three views can be considered as separate but overlapping, leading to an integration of the three traditions. Geography as a discipline has two systematic components – human and physical. Physical geography studies the geographic aspects of the natural environment on the surface of the earth, and human geography studies the social, economic, urban and rural settlement systems of human populations. The focus of both these systematic components is: (i) to study the distribution and spatial structure of objects, (ii) to understand the processes explaining the spatial structure, and (iii) to use spatial policies to correct the maldistribution of these resources. Also important are the local and global forces influencing the spatial processes.

Geographers and non-geographers often ask whether there is unity in the approaches of the different components of geography. Imagine a volcanic eruption in Mount Etna and the 9/11 attack on the World Trade Centre – though one is a physical phenomenon and the other is a social geographic phenomenon, both were outcomes of a long-drawn process of disequilibrium and unrest. What methodologies can be used to understand these outcomes? Can similarities, parallels and differences be drawn between these two processes? Is there unity in these two processes? The physical geographic process will be understood by employing a scientific method, such as logical positivism. The social geographic process will be examined by using a quantitative, qualitative or humanistic approach, which might also include logical positivism. Further, Geographic Information Sciences that include Geographic Information Sciences that include Geographic Information Systems (GIS) and Remote Sensing techniques, can also be employed (GIS) for the spatial exploration and mapping of data. Social geography is a systematic sub-field of human geography:

> [It] studies spatial settings of social structures, mutual influences of social structures and geographical environment and searches for ways and methods of optimizing these relations from the viewpoint of rational satisfaction of human needs. Otok (1981) in Otok (1988, p. 11)

The focus in social geography has shifted from the study of 'social area analysis', 'poverty', and 'segregation' using a quantitative approach, to unravelling 'social inequalities' and the study of 'geography of differences' and 'social justice' using humanistic and Marxist approaches (Harvey, 1973). Further, social geography evolved to include the study of geographies of race, gender, sexuality, disability, crime, poverty, health, housing and social movements, among other topics as new areas of research. Jones (1984) posited that quantitative methodology in social geography cannot explain social processes since it does not take cultural values into consideration. He suggested that quantitative methods should be utilized at macro scales and qualitative at micro scales. The blending of the two methods provides an enhanced understanding of social processes. To study social issues a variety of approaches have been utilized: quantitative, qualitative, GIS, feminist and mixed method approaches. The purpose of this chapter is to investigate the methodological developments in social geography and examine the trends in the application of various methodologies in the past half century. The chapter is divided into four sections: this first section has provided a motivation for undertaking this research; the second section discusses the quantitative and qualitative methodologies in social geographic research; the third section reviews selected social geographic themes, and; the fourth section concludes the findings. The aim of this chapter is a broad review of the selected topics and not an exhaustive appraisal of all areas in social geographic research.

Methodological Developments

Quantitative Methods

Quantitative methods (QM) are research techniques that are used to gather measurable data on a given phenomenon. There are two main types of methods in quantification: mathematical and statistical. The former (mathematical methods) are used to explain the logical relationship between variables to prove a theory. They are used to derive formal models from a set of initial abstract assumptions. The latter (statistical methods) are used for hypothesis testing and verification using empirical data. The various statistical techniques used by geographers can be classified into four groups: descriptive statistics, inferential statistics, multivariate statistics and spatial statistical techniques. In the first group, geographers use simple concepts such as ratio, percentage, proportions, cumulative frequency, standard deviation and central tendency to study geographical phenomena. For example, Nelson (1955) used the standard deviation method to group American cities. Inferential statistics are those techniques which are used when data are not uniformly distributed and are obtained by sampling techniques. The various inferential techniques such as chi-square and Spearman-rank correlation became popular in geography after 1965. Although QM did not gain popularity in sub-fields of geography such as historical and cultural geographies, they were expected to become popular as behavioural variables to be utilized in statistical analysis. Multivariate regression analysis is a branch of statistics which deals with a large number of variables and consists of techniques such as factor analysis, principal component analysis, canonical analysis and multi-dimensional scaling. The last group, spatial statistics, included three sub-groups of techniques: pattern analysis, flow analysis and predictive analysis. Pattern analysis in geography has been a traditional method in which the distance, direction, pattern, shape, and dispersion of a phenomenon are analyzed. Flow analysis is used to analyze the interactions taking place amongst places and regions such as in the case of migration, trade and capital movement. Three techniques, i.e., gravity model, graph theoretic models and linear programming, borrowed and adapted from social physics, neoclassical economics, networks and graph theory, became popular in this category (see Berry, 1968; Fotheringham, 2009).

In the first phase of efforts in using QM, it was necessary to overcome the biased results that non-spatial statistics produced. Regression analysis assumes that data are normally, independently and identically distributed. But in reality spatial data are not independently and identically distributed since similar values for a variable tend to cluster together. This leads to a bias in parameter estimates due to spatial autocorrelation present in the data (Griffith, 1987). This bias can be detected and incorporated into the measurement process by running spatial regression models or geographically weighted regression models (Fotheringham et al., 2002; Anselin, 1988). Several geographers have argued that geographical phenomena cannot be measured and analyzed using the lens of QM. Harvey (1973, p. 128) posited that "the quantitative revolution has run its course, and diminishing marginal returns are setting in". Barnes (1998) argued that the use of correlation and regression was a social and cultural artifact for social surveillance and control. It ascended "as an eminently practical pursuit, reflecting the interests of those who pursued it" (Barnes, 1998, p. 212). Further Barnes (1994) presented a re-evaluation of the quantitative revolution in human geography. The very justification of QM which is based upon 'universality', 'logicalness', 'objectivity', 'simplicity' and 'precision' is beset with contradictions.

Qualitative Methods

Qualitative methods are research tools that investigate an in-depth understanding of human behaviour and the reasons that govern human behaviour. These research tools are concerned with how the world is viewed, experienced and shaped by social actors. These tools provide access to the motives, aspirations and power relationships that account for how places, people, and events are composed and represented (Esterberg, 2001). These methods became important in geography as the quantitative tradition declined and the humanistic tradition ascended. Crang (2002) posited that qualitative approaches have had a long association with cultural, social and feminist geographies as a reaction to quantitative geography. These methods have been developed through a variety of research inquiry traditions such as biographic study, phenomenological studies, grounded theory studies, ethnographic studies and case studies (Creswell, 1998). A biographic study accounts for the experiences as narrated to the investigator or found in documents or archival materials about a person. The second, phenomenological study examines the meaning of the lived experiences for an individual or for several individuals about the concept or the phenomenon. It is the study of the structures of consciousness as experienced from the first-person point of view. The third, grounded theory is a method that emphasizes generation of theory from data in the process of conducting research. In this method the researcher collates interview data, visiting the field multiple times, and develops and interrelates categories of information. Further, the analyst prepares a theoretical proposition or hypotheses. The fourth, ethnographic study, describes a social group or system based on the first-hand fieldwork. This methodology employs participant observation to provide a holistic understanding of a social group based on the premise that a system's components cannot be understood in isolation of the whole. The fifth and last tradition is the case study where an in-depth, longitudinal examination of a single event or case is conducted. A case study need not necessarily be a qualitative study. It can be a mix of quantitative and qualitative evidence to understand a situation or an event.

Hay's *Qualitative Research Methods in Human Geography* (2005) is an excellent addition to the corpus of growing literature and texts written with an audience of geographers in mind. This book deals with topics such as 'power, subjectivity and ethics', 'cross-cultural research', 'qualitative research design', 'interviewing', 'oral history', 'focus group', 'archival sources', 'questionnaires', 'discourse analysis', 'observational research', 'participatory action research', 'coding qualitative data', 'computers and qualitative data', 'writing qualitative geographies' and 'communicating qualitative geographies for public consumption'. An appraisal of selected publications in social geography reveals:

> [T]here is an apparent tension between the creativity of the qualitative research process–which implies contingent methods to capture the richness of context dependent sites and situations – and evaluation – which implies standardized procedures and modes of reporting. (Baxter and Eyles, p. 505)

Baxter and Eyles (1997) focus on the evaluation of established qualitative methodologies. They have developed a set of criteria for establishing rigour in qualitative geographic research. These four criteria are 'credibility', 'transferability', 'dependability' and 'conformability'. The first criterion, 'credibility' is defined as a description of a human experience which would be recognized by a person who has not experienced it, and understood clearly by a person who has experienced it. The second criterion, 'transferability', refers to the fitness of the findings from a study outside the sample, case study or real world experiences. The third and fourth criteria, 'dependability' and 'conformability' denote the degree to which it is possible to deal with instability, followed by the minimization of biases by the investigator and his/her interpretation (Baxter and Eyles, 1997). Further, Bailey, White and Pain (1999) argue that a standardized process of evaluation is difficult in qualitative research while maintaining creativity in the implementation of research design. Using 'grounded theory' they establish a framework for achieving the two – 'science and creativity'.

Review of Methods and Social Geographic Issues

Social Area Analysis

American sociologists Shevky and Bell (1955) proposed a link between urban social structure and residential patterns with economic development and urbanization of cities. This process of urban social change was called 'increasing scale of society' (Shevky and Bell, 1955). The early social geographers were interested in understanding the changing character of modern society in a spatial context. A central theme addressed was the measurement of social spatial differentiation. As the skill levels of workers increased they tended to move out of the central city area to the outskirts, thereby differentiating themselves from the rest of the population and identifying with more homogenous groups of population. Two statistical techniques, namely, factor analysis and principal component analysis, became important techniques to study urban socio-spatial differentiation. The factor analysis technique is a data reduction technique and allows the analyst to understand the relationships between social, economic, demographic and housing characteristics with the objective of identifying common patterns in the data. The goal is to produce a new set of hybrid variables called 'factors' or 'components' which account for the measurable amount of variance in the input data. The patterns of spatial variations that the factors describe are collectively called 'factorial ecology' (Knox and Pinch, 2000). It tests the general hypothesis that the pattern of residential differentiation can be reduced to a small number of general constructs (Davies, 1984).

The social area analysis was developed as a method to analyze census tracts. Most of the studies that have used factorial ecology models found that residential differentiation in most cities in the western, industrialized and developed world is dominated by three dimensions. The first is called 'socioeconomic dimension'. It takes into account the income, education, occupation and home values of individuals and families to determine their social status in society. The second dimension is called 'family status'. This construct shows that as the distance from the city centre increases, the average age of the adult resident declines and/or the size of the family increases. The third dimension is called 'ethnic status'. It captures the trend that for some families 'ethnicity' is a more important residential location determinant than is family or social status (Murdie, 1969; Rees, 1979).

Western Studies

Shevky and William (1949) studied the multidimensional character of Los Angeles and further used this approach to analyze the urban social structure of the San Francisco area (Shevky and Bell, 1955). Social geographers both within the United States and Europe applied this method to understand the evolution of societies in association with social trends such as urban social structure, crime, voting behaviour and demand for intra-urban transportation. The study of factorial ecology of cities has been an important research theme in social geography since the 1950s. Murdie's (1969) study of metropolitan Toronto was the first study of a major city in the developed world focusing on urban change during the period 1951–61. His study demonstrated that the three indices (socio-economic, social and ethnic status) were complementary and not competitive descriptions of urban social structure. His study also demonstrated that each index was linked to a particular urban form in metropolitan Toronto for 1961. The family status was linked with concentric zones, economic status with sector pattern, and ethnic clusters with multiple nuclei patterns of urban forms.

White (1987) did a comparative study of 24 cities in the US and found that with respect to the 'ethnicity' dimension there was pronounced variation across regions. The analysis established that the spatial clustering of African American population is most prominent where the African American population is the dominant minority population. Ray (1971) applied canonical analysis to explore the spatial relationships among socioeconomic variables for Canada, for city and county census data for 1961. His findings revealed that the urban growth and form in Canada are tied together by a set of centripetal and centrifugal forces. These forces operate at the inter-continental scale (linking Canadian hinterland with

European hinterland), continental scale (linking Prairie and Atlantic hinterlands with Ontario–Quebec hinterland) and regional scales (linking the metropolitan peripheries to their metropolitan centres). These forces are expressed via differences occurring at various scales in the relationship between immigration and cultural diversity expressed through education, occupation and income. Knox and Pinch's (2000) factorial ecology study of Baltimore for 1980 used 20 variables. These variables collapsed to four major dimensions explaining 72 per cent of the variation in the original data set. The first dimension called 'underclass' was strongly and positively associated with extreme poverty and disadvantage, rented accommodation and single-person households. The second dimension termed 'socioeconomic status' (combining income, education, occupation and material possessions) identified the high and low status areas explaining a little over 18 per cent of the total variance. The third dimension called 'young migrants' identified those census tracts which were inhabited by a high proportions of in-migrants, young people, Spanish speaking people and male population. This dimension explained a little over 14 per cent of the total variance. The fourth and last dimension termed 'black poverty' explained seven per cent of the total variation and was associated with families living in poverty and single parent families in Baltimore city. In terms of the social geography of the city, the inner city was associated with the 'underclass' and the northern and western parts of the city were associated with the 'socioeconomic status' dimension (Knox and Pinch, 2000).

Non-Western Studies

A pioneering study was done by Berry and Spodek (1971) comparing the ecologies of a sample of Indian cities. The study analyzed Indian cities for the year 1961 (Ahmedabad, Bombay, Kanpur, Madras, Poona and Sholapur) and made two observations on patterns. First, cities displayed 'dual city structure' with the 'British cantonments' in one area and prestigious residential areas in the other. The residential patterns followed the core – periphery distribution with high-status neighbourhoods in central areas and low-status neighbourhoods at the periphery. Also, there were newer institutional areas devoted to government and education. The second pattern was the distinction between familial areas and neighbourhoods housing new male migrants located around the commercial cores such as docks, mills, and new factory estates. Further, industry located at the periphery had promoted limited suburbanization and was a contributing factor for the development of specialized neighbourhoods in all cities. Berry and Rees (1969) study on Calcutta's ecology revealed a similarity with the American South in terms of the link between race and status in a system of castes. Dutt et al. (1989) used trend-surface and factor analysis focusing on 22 variables and a hundred wards to analyze the socio-economic structure of Calcutta for 1981. A comparison with the earlier study (Berry and Rees, 1969) showed that the economic basis of 1981 maintained the sector characteristics, while social status continued in a concentric pattern, though both have shown an outward shift away from Central Business District (CBD). New variables that were used in the study revealed that industrial land uses were peripherally located and had negative association with residential land uses. The finding that is new as compared to Berry's study is that in 1981, centrally located dense population areas are also heavily used for retail and office businesses (Dutt, D'Sa and Monroe, 1989; pp. 151–162).

Over the last several decades factorial ecology models have provided an improved understanding of residential differentiation as cities grew and the occupational structure changed with modernization. Factorial ecology is a sophisticated technique for describing the central elements of the urban socio-spatial structure. Its output depends upon a rich data set invariably derived from the censuses of various nations, regions and local area statistics. This kind of analysis has been constrained by several factors such as 'lack of data', 'spatial autocorrelation' and 'definition of urban areas' (Knox and Pinch, 2000). The social area analysis has been constrained by lack of data since the full range of socioeconomic characteristics of the population are not available. The census offices do not have adequate resources to compile detailed information on sensitive subjects such as religion, people's lifestyle and daily activity patterns. Another problem that arises in the factor ecology studies is the presence of spatial autocorrelation. Census areas are one way of arrangement of urban areas. Would a different factorial ecology have been produced if a different spatial arrangement of census sub-areas had been chosen? This leads to the larger question: Is the difference a product of scale-specific processes or an outcome of the data set arrangement? A further issue that needs to be resolved is the degree to which factorial ecologies cover functional as opposed to administrative urban areas. Most social area analyses studies have used the city as the unit of study. As urbanization takes place, cities grow and the ecological structures of the various parts of the cities get differentiated (Knox and Pinch, 2000).

Spatial Dimension of Poverty

Poverty is an economic and social condition whereby people in different geographical regions of the world are not able to meet the minimum requirements of food, shelter and employment for their sustenance. Social geographers have studied poverty by taking suitable measures of poverty (such as percentage of households below a certain income level) and mapping them across different spatial units to understand the spatial dimensions of poverty. The subsequent object has been to understand the causes of poverty and to determine whether spatial policies can be implemented for its mitigation. A seminal study was undertaken by Watson (1951) for Hamilton, Ontario, to demonstrate a remarkable concentration of unemployment, neglect, desertion and delinquency in the 'city's shatter zones'. Brunn and Wheeler (1971) used factor analysis to identify the determinants of poverty in low income counties in the US for 1960. The study identified six dimensions of poverty – socioeconomic status, agricultural productivity, demographic composition, agricultural holdings and investment, degree of urbanization and manufacturing. Cooke and Marchant (2006) investigated the spatial distribution of high poverty neighbourhoods both between and within Metropolitan Statistical Areas (MSA) using regression analysis. Their study made three observations – first, the number of poor census tracts declined during the decade of the 1990s in the southern and midwestern regions; second, there had been an increase in high poverty neighbourhoods in the inner ring suburbs of three areas (California's Central Valley, Los Angeles and Sunbelt cities), and third, in the declining inner core of stagnant cities in the northeast there had been an increase in poverty associated with rise in population. Further, Partridge and Rickman (2006) studied the spatial variations in poverty rates across the US in the 1990s at the state and county levels. The study identified high incidence of poverty in the inner cities and remote rural areas though anti-poverty gains were made nationally during the same period. Their study further examined the success and failure of anti-poverty policies in different locations. Using regression methodology they explored the spatial, demographic and economic determinants of poverty. More specifically, they argued that place-based policies must be locally contextualized since different locations might be experiencing poverty due to different reasons such as low job growth, tight labour market and lack of access to job locations.

Spatial poverty is an important dimension of poverty analysis and can be examined at the macro (state and regional) and micro (urban areas) scales. The spatial pattern of regional poverty and urban poor as well as its causes and characteristics have been of interest to social geographers in India. National governments are able to reduce poverty rates at the national level through anti-poverty policies but high incidence of poverty remains in various pockets in cities, hinterlands and remote areas. It is necessary to examine the regional pattern of poverty and its inter-regional variations within a nation to gain an enhanced understanding of deprivation and destitution. Dayal (1989) identified rural poverty patterns in India using consumer expenditure data and the notion of regional poverty lines (based on regional food habits and prices). The analysis revealed pockets of regional poverty in the northeast and central plateau regions; the most prosperous regions were located in the northwestern part of India. A correlation and regression analysis of rural poverty in India during 1971 suggested high income concentration in the western and northwestern regions and low income concentration in the eastern and southern regions of India. The statistical analysis revealed that agricultural development, size of holdings and family size have a positive influence on incomes, and landlessness has a negative impact on poverty. A negative correlation between low caste population density and household income suggests the persistence of unfair social structure as a cause of poverty in India (Dayal, 1985). The average nutritive values of food intake by individuals were utilized to examine the regional concentration of hunger in India between 1973 and 1983. Results showed concentration of food poverty in coastal states in India and its persistence over time. Food poverty has declined in half the states in India but has increased in the other half. Food poverty increased in those states which experienced an increase in food production and further the quality of food intake improved in those states where food poverty had declined (Dayal, 1993).

The northeastern region of India comprising the Indo-Gangetic plain and the eastern coastal plain is densely populated in rural areas and this generates push factors leading to migration and slum formation in cities (Mukhopadhyay and Dutt, 1997, pp. 325–362). In the case of Calcutta (Mukhopadhyay and Dutt, 1993, pp. 181–186) it was found that most slums formed at a medium distance from the city centre, as slums were neither concentrated near the core nor in the periphery of the city. A descriptive stage model accounted for the motivation factors for rural–urban migration. Also, apart from the spatial growth of slums, a cyclical growth of slums in Calcutta was identified where slum dwellers were enmeshed in a vicious cycle of poverty and different generations in the family were not able to free themselves from the web of perpetual poverty. This is shown in a model where a slum dweller comes from a village, gets a low paid job, has a large family, low income, low levels of education for children and the cycle is repeated through generations (Dutt, Mitra and Halder, 1997, pp. 413–425. In Delhi slums, male members travel more than female members in the conduct of their daily activity (Dutt, Tripathi and Mukhopadhyay, 1994, pp. 309–326).

The problem of urban poverty has been the subject of government policies for slum improvement in India. It started with the bulldozing activities of the 1950s through to the improvement and conservation attitudes of the 1960s with greater emphasis on improving hygiene and sanitation and on to further bulldozing and clearing of slums in the 70s. In Calcutta these public policy measures have been reflected in plans of the Calcutta Metropolitan Planning Organization (Dutt, Halder and Mitra, 1998). In another study on pavement dwellers it was observed that dwellers resided near the most congested parts of the CBD, such as transportation nodes and districts with intensive commercial activity. This can be explained by the availability of better opportunities for employment in a competitive environment. The major finding is that the shorter the distances from the CBD, the more densely populated are the sidewalks (Dutt, Mukhopadhyay and Halder, 1994, pp. 337–352).

Housing Geographies

Housing provides individuals and families with shelter, protection from the vagaries of nature, an investment opportunity, gateway to a job and services, and social support. Housing is the most important asset in which households make an investment. It is a dominant land use in every city, county and state in the nation. Housing is available to individuals and families based upon their need and ability to pay. It can be state-subsidized or constructed by land developers in the private sector. In either case housing is a resource which is unevenly distributed geographically with variable costs and quality.

The quality and quantity of housing is expressed through attributes such as condition and character of houses, maintenance, lot size, square foot, open space and location. Social geographers have explored various themes in the geography of housing consumption. First, housing outcomes may be viewed as a spatial reflection of social differentiation. Second, housing may be considered as a resource with desirable characteristics which households may wish to acquire (social status, wealth and living space). Third, housing policy, directly or indirectly, shapes the social structure of societies by positively impacting the supply of residential space.

Social geographers have utilized various methodologies ranging from qualitative, quantitative and GISciences to analyze housing problems in geographical space. Dutt et al. (1991) used a qualitative methodology (questionnaire survey) to analyze the housing preferences of residents in the centrally-planned city of Warsaw, Poland. Their study revealed three aspects of housing preferences in a centrally-planned city. First, the analysis revealed higher preference for single-family homes as compared to multi-family homes. Second, this preference was higher among white-collar workers as compared to blue-collar workers. Third, most city dwellers preferred a mix of single-family homes, noise free, and spacious housing with service facilities in their proximity. A quantitative methodology with spatial hedonic price models have been advocated in housing geography where a set of structural and location attributes are selected as independent variables and median sale prices as the dependent variable to analyze the cause and effect relationship between housing attributes and median price. Yu et al. (2007) studied the spatial dimensions of house prices in Milwaukee, Wisconsin, using GIS and geographically-weighted regression approaches. Their results demonstrated better model performance and predictive accuracy as compared to the ordinary least squares approach. The results show the implications of spatial constraints on housing prices.

Disease and Health Geographies

Geography of health and disease studies the spatial patterns of mortality, morbidity, wellbeing, and healthcare, and the relationship between environment and patterns of the above aspects in the population. Medical geographers have explored themes such as the study of the 'spatial ecology of disease', 'disease diffusion and spread patterns' and 'comparison of the patterns of diseases with the distribution of presumed environmental risks'. A quantitative spatial analysis approach has been utilized along with mapping and GIS for visualization of the analysis of such themes.

A vital contribution of medical geographers and epidemiologists has been the application of 'spatial point pattern analyses' in the understanding of geographical incidence of diseases. Spatial analytic methods (quadrat and nearest neighbour analyses) do not capture the spatial variation in population density, and if the aim is to identify spatial clustering around a source point, then kernel estimation is a more appropriate approach (Gatrell, Bailey, Diggle and Rowlingson, 1996). Recently many researchers have utilized a mixed-method approach combining quantitative and qualitative approaches to analyze geographic health problems. This mixing of methods is often referred to as 'triangulation' and may be either 'simultaneous' or 'sequential'. An analysis is simultaneous when quantitative and qualitative data analysis is implemented at the same time. It is sequential when the quantitative is followed by the qualitative approach or vice versa (Gatrell, 2002). Gatrell and Bailey (1996) have emphasized the use of software environments in the study of geographical epidemiology, healthcare planning and location of facilities. The importance of statistical methods in the identification of disease clusters and in disease mapping has been emphasized by Marshall (1991). He pointed to the significance of statistical methods in identifying the relationships between disease rates and social, demographic and environmental factors.

Another important area of geographic health research is healthcare delivery systems and spatial equity in the distribution of medical facilities, especially in developing nations (Rushton, 1988; Massam et al., 1986). 'Location-allocation modelling' (Ghosh and Rushton, 1987) has been extensively utilized to determine the optimum arrangement of services in relation to population distribution or demand points (Tewari, 1992). Kumar (2004) applied location-allocation and logistic regression approaches to evaluate the location efficiency and geographic accessibility of healthcare facilities in Rohtak and Bhiwani districts in northwest India. His analysis concluded the presence of spatial inequality and location inefficiency in the distribution of healthcare facilities both in the public and private sectors, but was accentuated in the private sector as compared to the public sector. Ayeni, Rushton and McNulty (1987) studied the geographic accessibility of dispensaries and child welfare centres in rural Nigeria. Their analysis revealed low relative efficiency in the location of these facilities although the number of facilities increased between 1979–82. An optimal allocation of the facilities would have improved the utilization of the facilities by 12 and 16 per cents for dispensaries and child welfare centres, respectively.

The cause of disease and resultant death could be due to illness, environmental factors such as pollution, lack of healthcare, non-availability of physicians, and socio-economic factors. A regression analysis for a small suburban area in Chicago for the 1960s showed a strong association of infant deaths and measles with income (Pyle and Rees, 1971). This speaks of the lacuna in the American health system and resultant inequity amongst various social groups. Pyle's (1973) cartographic and correlation analysis of measles in Akron, Ohio for 1970–71 suggested that a more equitable distribution of vaccine provision could have averted the spread of the disease.

The Acquired Immune Deficiency Syndrome (AIDS) problem in the US has a regional dimension of spread pattern. The paper by Dutt et al. (1987) on AIDS was the first of its kind in a geographical journal. The two regions where the disease first appeared were the northeastern region, centered in New York City, and the western region, centered in San Francisco and Los Angeles, from where it had spread to other MSAs, cities and towns (Dutt et al., 1987, 456–471). The killer disease, once confined to the periphery, had now spread to the heartland, which signalled the gravity of the AIDS problem in the US. Dutta and Dutt (1978), based on their global malaria occurrence study, posited that the problem of malaria is endemic and its periodic recurrence is inherently geographic based upon physical factors such as rainfall, altitude, humidity and temperature. The persistence of malaria is also exacerbated by economic and cultural factors. There is an endemic malaria zone around the equator. In the incidence of malaria, analysts have observed a geographic shift northwards with the movement of the sun and southwards during southern summer.

The regional need for physicians was explored in an analysis of the healthcare requirements in a two-county region of Ohio. While technological improvements could decrease the demand for physicians; population changes due to economic progress or decline could alter the need for medical care. Also, the changes in population cohorts like the geriatric population, females of childbearing age and the birth rate of the area could alter the demand for physicians. In addition, the occurrence of new or existing endemic health problems can alter the need for medical attention in the region (Munroe and Dutt, 1984, pp. 83–85). In the Summit and Portage counties in Ohio while there is no general shortage of primary healthcare physicians, specific areas showed lack of obstetricians and pediatricians as compared to the demand for such services (Dutt, Dutta, Jaiswal and Monroe, 1986, pp. 443–455).

An anthology on the medical geography of India discussed the spatial and ecological aspects of health and disease, problems of nutrition in relation to socio-cultural factors and the geography of the healthcare delivery system in India (Akhtar and Learmonth, 1985). The problem of malaria has plagued India since antiquity. Though the disease was thought to be controlled, a resurgence had taken place in several pockets by 1965. Two west-central states, Gujarat and Madhya Pradesh, had shown resurgence due to factors that show strong association with monsoon rains, higher humidity, vegetation, tribal habits and rice cultivation (Dutt, Akhtar and Dutta 1980, pp. 317–330). In a later paper, he (along with his colleagues) used the annual malaria parasite index for 1978 and 1993 to study the spatial incidence of malaria in Indian cities. The findings showed a regional shift in the higher incidence of malaria from the northwestern region surrounding Delhi and in the states of Punjab and Haryana in 1978 to the southeastern coast, northern and southern parts of Chennai. The disease is connected to *anopheles stefensi*, a malaria vector that is well suited for the environmental conditions in urban areas. This spatial shift in malarial intensity is the result of people losing resistance to the disease after about a decade. Therefore the disease shifts from one region to the next in a ten year cycle (Akhtar, Dutt and Wadhwa, 1998, pp. 151–168). South Asian malaria origin diffusion and myth eradication have been discussed in this recent book (Akhtar et al, 2010).

Ghosh (2006) studied the impact of mass media on mother's knowledge of prenatal care in selected regions in India. The multivariate logistic function analysis revealed a north–south divide among the selected Indian states (Himachal Pradesh, Uttar Pradesh, Karnataka and Andhra Pradesh). The effect of awareness and use of prenatal care services were stronger in the north as compared to the south. The reasons for greater awareness in the southern region are higher education and social status, as well as exposure to a wider variety of alternative services and information.

Social Geographies of Crime

Social geographies of crime focus upon the study and interrelationships between crime, space and society through the associations between social and spatial analyses of offenders, offences and the location of crime. Smith (1986) provided a broad examination of the national and local dynamics associated with the spatial distribution of crime in the United Kingdom (UK). She integrated a broad spectrum of criminological research with the sociological approaches of social organization and change. Pain (2000) discussed the notion of crime due to fear, social identity (gender, sexuality, age and race) and social exclusion. She argued that the importance of 'place' and 'community' has often been relegated and needs to be recognized in crime research. The overarching questions that most crime specialists ask is where criminals live, where crime occurs and whether there is a geographical link between the location of offenders and offences. Most of the early criminologists linked regional patterns of crime to the social and physical environment of offenders.

Broadly speaking, two explanations have been provided to understand crime patterns. The first is called 'social disorganization thesis'. This thesis postulates that poverty and social deprivation have strong positive correlation with crime (Shaw and Mackay, 1942). Further, high levels of population turnover and ethnic heterogeneity contributes to social disorganization. Recent research has established the interconnection of crime with five factors–'demographic', 'economic', 'social', 'family disruption' and 'urbanization' (Andresen, 2006). The second explanation is called the 'routine activities theory' or the 'lifestyle-exposure-to-risk' hypothesis (Cohen and Felson, 1979). This thesis argues that the convergence of offenders and offences depends upon the absence of capable guardians to protect the home environment. It is expected that households engaged in routine activities (work, school and entertainment) would lead to a higher degree of guardianship of the home, and hence a lower risk of crime. Two lifestyle variables which are important indicators of such victimization risks are 'size of the family' and 'spare time activities'. A large family would mean that there is continuous surveillance of the household and smaller size would mean lack of vigilance. Further, spare time activities are associated with behavioural patterns at times (such as evening, early mornings and weekends) and locations (such as pubs, theatres, streets) where high incidence of offences takes place. These two approaches were utilized to investigate the spatial dimension of automobile theft and violent crime in Vancouver, British Columbia for the year 1996. A spatial regression approach identified 'high unemployment' and 'young population' as the strongest predictors of criminal activities in the region (Andresen, 2006). The 'routine activity theory' and the 'rational choice hypothesis' explained the location site selection rationale of serial killers for disposing of bodies (Lundrigan and Canter, 2001). The study for 126 cases in the US and UK showed that crime domains would be in close proximity to the homes of the criminals. Also, the domain size (area) would vary by offender and would increase over time.

A quantitative methodology has been employed by most crime researchers including those within social geography. Large cities have pockets of crime activities in dilapidated areas such as found in the inner cities. A spatial analysis of Chicago's suburban areas showed two forms of spatial association with respect to crime rates. First, there is a distance–decay effect in violent crimes from the downtown area; and second, there is a positive spatial autocorrelation such that one suburb's violent crime rate is positively correlated with the neighbouring suburb's crime rates. Further, the distribution of property crime rates is associated with the location of retail and manufacturing activities. Thus, the distance for property crime extends several miles across the suburban boundaries (Brown, 1982). The spatial pattern of residential burglaries has been explored for the city of London, Ontario region (1998–2001). A geographically weighted regression approach showed significant local variations in the relationship between the risk of residential burglary and the 'average value of dwellings' and 'percentage of the population in multi-family housing'. The pattern of residential burglary was an outcome of three behavioural scenarios – 'target attractiveness scenario' in relatively wealthy communities in the outskirt neighbourhoods of the city, 'opportunistic activity scenario' in relatively deprived area in the inner city, and a combination of the two scenarios in the neighbourhoods adjacent to the University of Western Ontario area (Maczewski and Poetz, 2005).

The spatial pattern of crime in India has an explicit regional dimension which stands out distinctly. The cities located in the 'north-central subculture region' show a major concentration of violent, economic and group crimes (Dutt and Venugopal, 1983; Dutt, Noble and Singh, 1979). The regional crime pattern has spread southwards embracing parts of Rajasthan, Gujarat, Maharashtra and Madhya Pradesh. Over the last two decades the intensification of crime can be attributed to political factors like protection of criminal elements, use of criminals by politicians and, less importantly, crime due to caste and religious differences and terrorist activities (Pomeroy, Wadhwa and Dutt, 1999, pp. 292–302). A micro level study of Ajmer city found that crime varied spatially within the city (police jurisdiction areas). Within the old commercial area, property crime and pickpocketing were rampant. Theft of cycles and motor parts was common in central areas and affluent residential areas. Other kinds of criminal activities identified were burglary, theft and robbery. Death due to consumption of contaminated liquor had a high occurrence in the city. Their location reflected the place of manufacture or the site of consumption (Dutt, Noble and Sharma, 1985, pp. 57–72). A stepwise regression and canonical analysis of crime patterns in Delhi for the periods 1971, 1981 and 1991 revealed four spatial patterns. First, crime location has gradually shifted from the core to the periphery of Delhi. Second, urbanization, rapid growth of population, high migration, unemployment, industrialization and emergence of slums have shown a positive association with crime; while density of population, large number of people per household and Scheduled Castes do not show a positive correlation. Third, economic crime occurred where people were engaged in tertiary sector activities. Fourth, the study observed an inverse relation between literacy rate and crime, that is, when literacy rate is high, crime is low (Bhushan, 1997).

An area that has gained popularity in the study of crime patterns is the application of GIS, specialized computer software and prediction models to understand the local dynamics of crime. Murray et al. (2001) utilized spatial analysis techniques and GIS in the exploratory spatial analysis of crime in Brisbane, Australia. He and his colleagues argued that GIS is not only a mapping tool but could be used for internalizing information such as the relationship between the physical environment and the spatial patterns of criminal activity. The spatial clustering and spatial analysis techniques were utilized to identify outliers and significant groupings of similar suburbs. Modelling software such as Crimestat has been developed for crime mapping. This software by inputting data can give spatial description summaries of overall patterns, spatial autocorrelation (if the data shows randomness, concentration or dispersion), identify 'hotspots', performs interpolation, space–time analysis and journey-to-crime modelling (Levine, 2006). A new procedure for the identification of temporal-spatial pattern in crime has been developed using the 1996 arson data for Buffalo. The method combines nearest neighbour technique and cumulative sum methods to identify deviations from expected geographic patterns. This analysis can be implemented for smaller regional units (Rogerson and Sun, 2001).

Social Aspects of Regional Development and Planning

Broadly speaking, planning refers to the formulation and implementation of the economic, social, environmental, spatial and sectoral development strategies. The terms local and regional development and planning refer to those plans, strategies and policy interventions that address the problems of development at the local and regional levels such as city, county, state, inter-regional, river basin, watershed or other spatial units of development. Planners address problems that arise from uneven spatial development between and within regions. The social dimension of planning attempts to clarify the relationships between social factors and land use planning at the local and regional levels (So and Getzels, 1988). In particular, social planning addresses the variety of needs within a community and pays attention to the equity and distributional implications of planning. Further, the purpose of social planning is not simply to identify the distributional impact of planning but to mitigate such impact that places disadvantaged groups in an adverse situation as compared to the rest of the population (So and Getzels, 1988).

Urban social geographers have utilized the methodology of identifying a geographical problem, selecting a suitable spatial scale and testing of spatial hypotheses with respect to social phenomena. The results are mapped through space in order to identify spatial patterns and propose processes that explain cause and effect relationships in geographical space. This methodology utilizes spatial analysis techniques and GIS for visualization and interpretation of results. A geography and planning school, *Akron School of Planning Studies* has vigorously attempted this methodology over the last several decades to provide insights into the social and regional dimensions of planning. This school was led by a team of internationally reputed scholars (Professors Allen G. Noble, Ashok K. Dutt and Frank J. Costa) along with their colleagues and students from around the globe to study regional development in developed and developing nations.

Some of the major works in international regional development planning were conducted in the study of Belgian and Dutch planning problems (Dutt and Costa, 1985; Dutt and Costa, 1992). Both the volumes are the first comprehensive treatment of analyzing planning and development experience in these areas in the English language. The book on Belgian planning and urban development addresses the issue of planning impact for Belgium in the context of the European Economic Community (EEC), the impact of linguistic divisions on the content of planning legislation, the planning and development in the two largest cities of Brussels and Antwerp and smaller cities of Brugge, Liege and Louvain-la-Neuve (Dutt and Costa, 1992). The planning of Louvain-la-Neuve demonstrated a certain creativity in urban planning where a pedestrian town has been made operational in an age of high speed automobiles and the idea of 'super-sized new towns' has been discarded in favour of a manageable small town (Dutt and Costa, 1992, p. 207).

The Netherlands has practiced both planning and market mechanisms to solve its spatial development problems. Organizationally, planning in the Netherlands is divided into three tiers – national, provincial and municipal. There are also three levels of planning associated with the organizational distinction – macro, meso and the micro. While macro planning examines national aggregates (such as employment, gross national product (GNP) and production), meso planning deals with sectoral planning in the functional version and provincial planning in the geographical version. Micro planning relates to a single project in a given location. The Netherlands follows regional planning in industrialization which means balancing the development of provinces. While the provinces are responsible for meso and micro planning, the national government undertakes macro planning. Economic and physical planning is enunciated at the national level where the economic considerations are directive and physical matters suggestive. There is a lack of coordination between national and provincial planning. There does exist a comprehensive approach to planning at the provincial level (Dutt, 1968, pp. 670–685). Dutch planning has achieved more success with the problem of lagging area development and decongestion. While the concept of Garden Cities has been implemented in the form of New Towns in Britain, it has taken the form of 'Industrial Nuclei in the Stimulus Areas' in the Netherlands (Dutt, 1970, pp. 321–335). The Dutch experience in the implementation of project planning in protecting the people, land and property in the Delta region from high floods is a remarkable achievement in terms of reclaiming land from the sea (Dutt and Heal, 1979, pp. 131–141). The origination, exemplary effort, technological, economic, developmental and environmental benefits have been the strong points of planning. The Delta project demonstrated how regional planning approaches can be implemented to achieve regional environmental security, regional development, accentuation of tourism and recreation potential, and increasing the agricultural base (Dutt and Heal, 1985, pp. 184–202).

In the Asian urbanization development process theme, the Akron School of Planning has enhanced the understanding of the Asian urbanization process and its characteristics, development and planning. There are divergent paths and policy responses in Asian urbanization and planning which leads to the recognition of a varied range of institutional arrangements. These arrangements are the causal factor of the policy responses to planning (Costa, Dutt, Ma and Noble, 1988). A differential urban growth pattern has been found for regions in Asia. In the mid-twentieth century east and west Asia were more urbanized than Asia as a whole. By the year 2025 they will remain more urbanized. Southeast Asia was least urbanized in 1950 but had a high rate of urbanization in 1965. West Asia remains the most urbanized and will continue to remain so (Dutt et al., 1994, pp. 6–10). Also, an interesting comparison can be made between nineteenth century American and European urbanization with twentieth century Asian urbanization. While urban pull factors in migration was the main cause of European and American urbanization in the nineteenth century, the Asian urbanization is characterized by natural increase and rural push factors (Parai and Dutt, 1994, pp. 369–372). Urbanization in Asia is positively related to per capita growth in Gross National Product (GNP) and export value, but negatively related to fertility. Economic growth has not been uniform in terms of spatial development and each country depicts different characteristics. A descriptive model portrays the linear evolution of societies till the point where the proportion of population becomes urbanized (Dutt et al., 1996, pp. 1–14).

Urbanization and economic development have an intertwining relationship. As rural societies transform to urban societies, their urban forms and settlement patterns change dramatically. Moustapha, Costa and Noble (1985) note that Saudi Arabia's urbanization is taking place at a faster pace than the nation's capacity to manage it. Thus, a planned intervention in the process of urban development is the key to managing growth (Al-Oteibi et al., 1993). In response to this urban problem a *gemeinschaft-gesellschaft* model has been proposed for Arabic towns to unite the traditional and urban forms into a coherent physical settlement (Costa and Noble, 1986). This model reconciles western planning techniques and the Islamic culture of Arabic cities. This model focuses particularly on 'subdivision planning' and 'building codes'. The model of urban development includes four components: (i) each individual household should have privacy, (ii) a small, intimate neighbourhood space should be provided where the population could mingle without contravening family or religious rights, (iii) an area for the location of economic activities should be present, along with (iv) a compact, low-rise character of building development in relation to climate and family privacy (Costa and Noble, 1986, p. 169).

Conclusion

Social geography is a subfield of human geography that gained importance during the 1960s and 1970s. It studies social geographic problems in society and the associated spatial structure which underpins the social relations in geographic space. It aims to understand the distribution of spatial objects and identify its social spatial structure, to understand the processes explaining spatial structure, and to utilize spatial policies to correct geographic imbalances. Two methodologies were important in social geographic research – quantitative and qualitative. The quantitative methodology became popular in social geography particularly in the 1960s, since it was based on scientific principles and methods. This approach, identified with the scientific principles and methods of positivism (the philosophy of science), which had gained popularity at this time in the natural and engineering sciences. The methodology was subsequently applied to study social geographic problems such as urban social areas, poverty, crime, housing, food and nutrition, culture, health and diseases.

The second methodology adopted by social geographers was the qualitative approach. Analysts have argued that social geographic issues were not amenable to quantitative analysis. Qualitative methods investigate human behaviour and the reasons that govern human behaviour. These tools provide access to the motives, aspirations and relationships that account for how places, people and events are composed and represented. This methodology includes various techniques such as biographic study, phenomenological studies, grounded theory studies, ethnographic studies, and case studies.

A review of selected areas or themes in social geographic research demonstrates the shifts in the application of any one methodology towards a hybrid approach to understand social geographic phenomenon. To sum up, no single methodology is appropriate or sufficient to adequately analyze social geographic problems, and research indicates that there is a need for a hybrid approach to analyze social geographic issues.

References

Akhtar, Rais and A.T.A. Learmonth (eds.), *Geographical Aspects of Health and Disease in India*, New Delhi: Concept Publishing Company, 1985.

Akhtar, R., A. K. Dutt and V. Wadhwa, 'Health Planning and Resurgence of Malaria in Urban India', in A. G. Noble, F. J. Costa, A. K. Dutt and R. Kent (eds.), *Regional Development and Planning for the 21st Century*, Aldershot: Ashgate, 1998, pp. 151–168.

Akhtar, R., A. K. Dutt and V. Wadhwa, 'Malaria in South Asia: Eradication and Resurgence during the Second Half of the Twentieth Century', Dordrecht: Springer, 2010.

Al-Oteibi, S., A. G. Noble and F.J. Costa, 'The Impact of Planning on Growth and Development in Riyadh, Saudi Arabia, 1970–1990', *GeoJournal*, Vol. 29, No. 2, 1993, pp. 163–170.

Andresen, M. A., 'A Spatial Analysis of Crime in Vancouver, British Columbia: A Synthesis of Social Disorganization and Routine Activity Theory', *Canadian Geographer*, Vol. 50, No. 4, 2006, pp. 487–502.

Anselin, Luc, *Spatial Econometrics: Methods and Models*, Kluwer Academic Publishers, 1988.

Ayeni, B., G. Rushton and M. L. McNulty, 'Improving the Geographic Accessibility of Healthcare in Rural Areas: A Nigerian Case Study', *Social Science and Medicine*, Vol. 25, No. 10, 1987, pp.1083–1094.

Bailey, C., C. White and R. Pain, 'Evaluating Qualitative Research: Dealing with the Tension between Science and Creativity', *Area*, Vol. 31, No. 2, 1999, pp. 169–183.

Barnes, T. J., 'Probable writing: Derrida, Deconstruction, and the Quantitative Revolution in Human Geography', *Environment and Planning A*, Vol. 26, No. 7, 1994, pp. 1021–1040.

Barnes, T. J., 'A History of Regression: Actors, Networks, Machines, and Numbers', *Environment and Planning A*, Vol. 30, 1998, pp. 203–233.

Baxter, J. and J. Eyles, 'Evaluating Qualitative Research in Social Geography: Establishing "rigor" in Interview Analysis', *Transactions of the Institute of British Geographers*, Vol. 22, No. 4, 1997, pp. 505–525.

Berry, B. J. L., *Spatial Analysis: A Reader in Statistical Geography*, Englewood Cliffs, New Jersey: Prentice Hall, 1st ed., 1968.

Berry, B. J. L. and P. H. Rees, 'The Factorial Ecology of Calcutta', *The American Journal of Sociology*, Vol. 74, No. 5, 1969, pp. 445–491.

Berry, B. J. L. and H. Spodek, 'Comparative Ecologies of Large Indian Cities', *Economic Geography*, Vol. 47, 1971, pp. 266–285.

Bhushan, P. S., *Crime, Criminals, and Society*, Manisha Publications, New Delhi, 1997.

Brown, M. A., 'Modeling the Spatial Distribution of Suburban Crime', *Economic Geography*, Vol. 58, No. 3, 1982, pp. 247–261.

Brunn, S. D. and J.O. Wheeler, 'Spatial Dimensions of Poverty in the United States', *Geografiska Annaler: Series B, Human Geography*, Vol. 53, No. 1, 1971, pp. 6–15.

Cohen, L. E. and M. Felson, 'Social Change and Crime Rate Trends: A Routine Activity Approach', *American Sociological Review*, Vol. 44, 1979, pp. 588–608.

Cooke, T. and S. Marchant, 'The Changing Intrametropolitan Location of High Poverty Neighborhoods in the US, 1990–2000', *Urban Studies*, Vol. 43, No. 11, 1971–1989.

Costa, F. J. and A. G. Noble, 'Planning Arabic Towns', *Geographical Review*, Vol. 76, No. 2, 1986, pp.160–172.

Crang, M., 'Qualitative Methods: the New Orthodoxy', *Progress in Human Geography*, Vol. 26, No. 5, 2002, pp. 647–655.

Creswell, J. W., *Qualitative Inquiry and Research Design: Choosing Among Five Traditions*, New Delhi: Sage Publications, 1998.

Dayal, Edison, 'Wealth and Poverty in India', *GeoJournal*, Vol. 11, No. 4, 1985, pp. 369–382.

Dayal, Edison, 'Rural Poverty in India: A Regional Analysis', *Journal of Rural Studies*, Vol. 5, No. 1, 1989, pp. 87–98.

Dayal, Edison, 'Regional Changes in Food Poverty in India', *GeoJournal*, Vol. 30, No. 2, 1993, pp. 167–177.

Davies, W. K. D., *Factorial Ecology*, Aldershot: Gower, 1984.

Dutt, A. K., 'Levels of Planning in the Netherlands with Particular Reference to the Regional Planning', *Annals of the Association of American Geographers*, Vol. 58, No. 4, 1968, pp. 67–685.

Dutt, A. K., 'A Comparative Study of Regional Planning in Britain and the Netherlands', *The Ohio Journal of Science*, Vol. 70, No. 6, 1970, pp. 321–335.

Dutt, A. K. and F. J. Costa (eds.), *Public Planning in the Netherlands: Perspectives and Change Since the Second World War*, Oxford University Press, 1985.

Dutt, A. K. and F. J. Costa (eds.), *Perspectives on Planning in Belgium*, Dordrecht: Kluwer Academic Publishers, 1992.

Dutt, A. K. and S. Heal, 'Delta Project Planning and Implementation in the Netherlands', *Journal of Geography*, Vol. 78, 1979, pp. 131–141.

Dutt, A. K. and S. Heal, 'The Delta works: A Dutch Experience in Project Planning', in A. K. Dutt and F.J. Costa (eds.), *Public Planning in the Netherlands*, Oxford: Oxford University Press, 1985, pp. 184–202.

Dutt, A. K. and G. Venugopal, 'Spatial Patterns of Crime among Indian Cities', *Geoforum*, Vol. 14, No. 2, 1983, pp. 223–233.

Dutt, A. K., S. Jr. Achmatowicz-Otok and Anna Achmatowicz-Otok, 'Residential Preferences in the City of Warsaw', *GeoJournal*, Vol. 24, No. 3, 1991, pp. 285–292.

Dutt, A. K., R. Akhtar and H. M. Dutta, 'Malaria in India with Particular to two West-Central States', *Social, Science and Medicine*, Vol. 14, 1980, pp. 317–330.

Dutt, A. K., F. J. Costa, L. J. C. Ma and A. G. Noble (eds.), *Asian Urbanization: Problems and Processes*, Berlin and Stuttgart: Gebruder Borntraeger, 1988.

Dutt, A. K., A. Halder and C. Mitra, 'Shifts in Slum Upgrading Policy with Special Reference to Calcutta', in A. G. Noble, F. J. Costa and R. Kent (eds.), *Regional Development and Planning for the 21st Century*, Aldershot: Ashgate, 1998, pp. 151–168.

Dutt, A. K., Chandreyee Mitra and A. Halder, 'Slum Location and Cycle of Poverty: Calcutta Case', *Asian Profile*, Vol. 25, No. 50, 1997, pp. 413–425.

Dutt, A. K., A. Mukhopadhyay and A. Halder, 'Sidewalk Dwellers in Calcutta', in A. K. Dutt, F. J. Costa, S. K. Aggarwal and A. G. Noble (eds.), *The Asian City:*

Processes of Development, Characteristics, and Planning, Dodrecht: Kluwer Academic Publishers, 1994, pp. 337–349.

Dutt, A. K., A. G. Noble and K. Sharma, 'Variations of the Spatial Patterns of Crime in Ajmer City, India', *Indian Journal of Criminology*, Vol. 13, No. 1, 1985, pp. 57–72.

Dutt, A. K., A. G. Noble and S. Singh, 'Is there a North-central Subculture of Violence in India', *The National Geographical Journal of India*, Vol. 25, No. 2, 1979, pp. 101–111.

Dutt, A., Gerardine D'Sa and C. B. Munroe, 'Factorial Ecology of Calcutta Revisited', *GeoJournal*, Vol. 18, No. 2, 1981, pp. 151–162.

Dutt, A. K., S. Tripathi and A. Mukhopadhyay, 'Spatial Spread of Daily Activity Patterns of Slum Dwellers in Calcutta and Delhi', in A. K. Dutt, F. J. Costa, S. K. Aggarwal and A. G. Noble (eds.), *The Asian City: Processes of Development, Characteristics and Planning*, Dodrecht: Kluwer Academic Publishers, 1994, pp. 309–325.

Dutt, A. K., F. J. Costa, S. K. Aggarwal and A. G. Noble, 'An Introduction to the Asian City', in A. K. Dutt, F. J. Costa, S. K. Aggarwal and A. G. Noble (eds.), *The Asian City: Process of Development, Characteristics, and Planning*, Dordretch: Kluwer Academic Publishers, 1994, pp. 6–10.

Dutt, A. K., H. M. Dutta, J. Jaiswal and C. Munroe, 'Assessment of Service Adequacy of Primary Health Care Physicians in Two County Region of Ohio, USA', *GeoJournal*, Vol. 12, No. 4, 1986, pp. 443–55.

Dutt, A. K., C. Munroe, H. M. Dutta and B. Prince, 'Geographical Patterns of AIDS in the United States', *Geographical Review*, Vol. 77, No. 4, 1987, pp. 456–471.

Dutt, A. K., N. Chiang, A. G. Noble, J. F. Williams and Bednarek (eds.), *Urbanization Trends in Asia*, Fourth Asian Studies Center, Michigan State University, 1996, pp. 1–14.

Dutta, H. M. and A. K. Dutt, 'Malarial Ecology: A Global Perspective', *Social Science and Medicine*, Vol. 12, 1978, pp. 69–84.

Esterberg, K. G., *Qualitative Methods in Social Research*, Boston: McGraw Hill, 1st Edn., 2001.

Fotheringham, A. S., Chris Brundson and M. Charlton, *Geographically Weighted Regression: the Analysis of Spatially Varying Relationships*, John Wiley and Sons, Ltd., 2002.

Fotheringham, A. S., and P. A. Rogerson, *The Sage Handbook of Spatial Analysis*, New Delhi: Sage Publications, 2009.

Gatrell, A. C., 'Geographies of Health: An Introduction', *Methods and Techniques in the Geography of Health*, Oxford: Blackwell, 2002, pp. 50–88.

Gatrell, A. C. and T. C. Bailey, 'Interactive Spatial Data in Medical Geography', *Social Science Medicine*, Vol. 42, No. 6, 1996, pp. 843–855.

Gatrell, A. C., T. C. Bailey, P. J. Diggle and B. S. Rowlingson, 'Spatial Point Pattern Analysis and its Application in Geographical Epidemiology', *Transactions of the Institute of British Geographers*, New Series, Vol. 21, No. 1, 1996, pp. 256–274.

Ghosh, A. and G. Rushton (eds.), *Spatial Analysis and Location-Allocation Models*, New York: Van Nostrand Reinhold Company, 1987.

Ghosh, Debarchana, 'Effect of Mother's Exposure to Electronic Mass Media on Knowledge and Use of Prenatal Care Services: A Comparative Analysis of Indian States', *Professional Geographer*, Vol. 58, No. 3, 2006, pp. 278–293.

Griffith, Daniel, 'Spatial Autocorrelation: A Primer', *Association of American Geographers*, 1987.

Hay, Iain (ed.), *Qualitative Research Methods in Human Geography*, Melbourne: Oxford University Press, Second edition, 2005.

Harvey, D., *Social Justice and the City*, John Hopkins University Press, 1973.

Jones, E., 'Post-positivist Social Geography', *GeoJournal*, Vol. 9, No. 3, 1984, pp. 241–245.

Kumar, Naresh, 'Changing Geographic Access to and Locational Efficiency of Health Services in Two Indian Districts between 1981–1996', *Social, Science and Medicine*, Vol. 58, 2004, pp. 2045–2067.

Knox, P. and S. Pinch, *Urban Social Geography: An Introduction*, Essex: Prentice Hall, Fourth edition, 2000.

Levine, Ned, 'Crime Mapping and the Crimestat Program', *Geographical Analysis*, Vol. 38, 2006, pp. 41–56.

Lundrigan, S. and David Canter, 'Spatial Patterns of Serial Murder: Disposal Site Location Choice', *Behavioral Science and Law*, Vol. 19, 2001, pp. 595–610.

Maczewski, J. and A. Poetz, 'Residential Burglaries and Neighborhood Socioeconomic Context in London, Ontario: Global and local regression analysis', *Professional Geographer*, Vol. 57, No. 4, 2005, pp. 516–529.

Marshall, R. J., 'A Review of Methods for the Statistical Analysis of Spatial Patterns of Disease', *Journal of the Royal Statistical Society*, Series A, Vol. 154, No. 3, 1991, pp. 421–444.

Massam, B. H., R. Akhtar and I. D. Askew, 'Applying Operations Research to Health Planning: Locating Health Centers in Zambia', *Health Planning and Policy*, Vol. 1, No. 4, 1986, pp. 326–334.

Moustapha, A. F., F. J. Costa and A. G. Noble, 'Urban Development in Saudi Arabia Building and Subdivision Codes', *Cities*, Vol. 2, No. 20, 1985, pp. 140–148.

Mukhopadhahy, A. and A. K. Dutt, 'Slum Dwellers Daily Movement Patterns in Calcutta Slum', *GeoJournal*, Vol. 29, No. 2, 1993, pp. 181–186.

Mukhopadhahy, A. and A. K. Dutt, 'Geographic Patterns of Indian City Slums with Particular Reference to Calcutta', in Rais Akhtar (ed.), *Contemporary Approaches to Indian Geography: Essays in Honor of Professor Mohammed Shafi*, New Delhi: APH Publishing, 1997, pp. 325–362.

Munroe, C. and A. K. Dutt, 'Projecting Physician Requirements in a Two-county Region in Ohio', *Social Science and Medicine*, Vol. 18, No. 1, 1984, pp. 83–85.

Murdie, R. A., *Factorial Ecology of Metropolitan Toronto, 1951–1961*, University of Chicago, Department of Geography, Research Paper No. 116, 1969.

Murray, A. T., Ingrid McGuffog, J. S. Western and P. Mullins, 'Exploratory Spatial Data Analysis: Techniques for Examining Urban Crime', *British Journal of Criminology*, Vol. 41, 2001, pp. 309–329.

Nelson, H. J., 'A Service Classification of American Cities', *Economic Geography*, Vol. 31, No. 3, 1955, pp. 189–210.

Otok, Stanislaw, 'Research Problems in Social Geography', in S. Otok (ed.), *Research Approach to Social Geography* Warszawa, 1988, pp. 7–18.

Pain, Rachel, 'Place, Social Relations and the Fear of Crime: A Review', *Progress in Human Geography* Vol. 24, 2000, pp. 365–387.

Parai, A. and A. K. Dutt, 'Perspectives on Asian Urbanization: An East-west Comparison', in A. K. Dutt, F. J. Costa, S. K. Aggarwal and A. G. Noble (eds.), *The Asian City: Process of Development, Characteristics and Planning*, Dordrecht: Kluwer Academic Publishers, 1994, pp. 369–389.

Partridge, M. D. and D. S. Rickman, *The Geography of American Poverty: Is There a Need for Place-Based Policies?* W. E. Upjohn Institute for Employment Research, MI: Kalamazoo, 2006.

Pomeroy, G., V. Wadhwa and A. K. Dutt, 'Spatial Patterns of Crime in Indian Cities', in G. Chapman, A. K. Dutt and R. Bradnock (eds.), *Urban Growth and Development in Asia: Living In Cities*, Vol. 2, Aldershot: Ashgate, 1999, pp. 292–302.

Pyle, G. P., 'Measles as an Urban Health Problem: The Akron Experience', *Economic Geography*, Vol. 49, No. 40, 1973, pp. 344–356.

Pyle, G. F. and P. H. Rees, 'Modeling Patterns of Death and Disease in Chicago', *Economic Geography*, Vol. 47, No. 4, 1971, pp. 475–488.

Ray, Michael, 'From Factorial Ecology to Canonical Ecology: The Spatial Interrelationships of Economic and Cultural Differences in Canada', *Economic Geography*, Vol. 47, 1971, pp. 344–367.

Rees, Philip, *Residential Patterns in American Cities*, Department of Geography, University of Chicago, Research Paper No. 189, 1979.

Rogerson, P. and Y. Sun, 'Spatial Monitoring of Geographic Patterns: An Application to Crime Analysis', *Computers, Environment and Urban Systems*, Vol. 25, 2001, pp. 539–556.

Rushton, Gerard, 'The Roepke Lecture in Economic Geography Location Theory, Location-allocation Models, and Service Development Planning in the Third World', *Economic Geography*, Vol. 64, No. 2, 1988, pp. 97–120.

Shaw, C. R. and H. D. Mackay, *Juvenile Delinquency and the Urban Areas: A Study of Rates of Delinquency in Relation to Differential Characteristics of Local Communities in American Cities*, Chicago: University of Chicago Press, 1942.

Shevky, E. and M. Williams, *The Social Areas of Los Angeles*, University of California Press, 1949.

Shevky, E. and W. Bell, *Social Area Analysis: Theory, Illustrative Application and Computational Procedures*, Stanford, CA: Stanford University Press, 1955.

Smith, S. J., *Crime, Space and Society*, Cambridge: Cambridge University Press, 1986.

So, F. S. and Judith Getzels, *The Practice of Local Government Planning*, Municipal Management Series, International City/County Management Association, Second edition, 1988.

Taafe, E. J., 'The Spatial View in Context', *Annals of the Association of American Geographers*, Vol. 64, No. 1, 1974, pp. 1–16.

Tewari, V. K., 'Improving Access to Services and Facilities in Developing Countries', *International Regional Science Review*, Vol. 15, No. 1, 1992, pp. 25–37.

Watson, J. W., 'The Sociological Aspects of Geography', in G. Taylor (ed.), *Geography in the Twentieth Century: A Study of Growth, Fields, Techniques, Aims, and Trends*, London: Methuen, 1951.

White, M., *American Neighborhood and Residential Differentiation*, New York: Sage Foundation, 1987.

Yu, Danlin, Y. D. Wei and C. Wu, 'Modeling Spatial Dimensions of Housing Prices in Milwaukee, WI', *Environment and Planning B*, Vol. 34, No. 6, 2007, pp. 1085–1102.

6

Geographies of Disability: An Emergent Theme in Social Geography

VANDANA WADHWA

According to sociologist Len Barton (1996, p. 3), one charge of his field is to relate social structures to the 'lived reality of people in particular social settings'. If 'particular social settings' includes a person's spatial setting, then the same charge is true for social geography. These relationships between social structures and lived realities are particularly meaningful in disability geography – one of the more recent streams of social and human geography. This chapter seeks to introduce the reader to this field, giving a brief glimpse of the evolution and development of disability studies in the larger realm of the social sciences, particularly in geography.

As with any other introductory work, it runs the risk of giving the subject superficial treatment by trying to present too much in too short a space. However, since disability geography still does not find adequate representation in mainstream social geography books or curricula, it would be appropriate to provide an overview of the field to the reader. While breadth is prioritized over depth, the latter is not eschewed altogether. Using a phenomenological approach, I have tried to highlight the prominent role of social environments in the creation of disability through a comparative examination of shifting meanings of disability across space. Thus, the two-fold aim of this chapter is to highlight disability and persons with disabilities as important components of society and social geography studies, and to underline the importance of social contexts in the creation of disability.

Understanding 'Disability'

Western medical and social science have long regarded disabilities as explainable within a biomedical model that views disabilities as deviations from the 'normal' healthy body, promoting the worldview that disabled persons are somehow inferior or damaged. Additionally, the biological impairment itself is seen to be the cause and source of the disability (Barton, 1996; Gleeson, 1999; Oliver, 1996; Williams, 2001). The medical model has emphasized '…curing, concealing, or fixing bodies so that individuals could be made to "pass" as normal' (Snyder 2005, p. 481). Even the WHO's first (1980) version of the International Classification of Impairments, Disabilities and Handicaps (ICIDH) contained terminology and nomenclature that reflected a neglect of social contexts and barriers in the creation of disability (Altman, 2001).

However, the medical model was challenged by a developing body of thought, positing disabilities as social constructs produced by barriers presented by normative social and physical structures rather than deficiencies within a body itself. In 1976, the Union of Physically Impaired Against Segregation (UPIAS) articulated their understanding of disability as an isolating, oppressive and exclusionary experience imposed by society on those with organic impairments (Albrecht, 2005b; Oliver, 1990; Snyder and Mitchell, 2006). Further, work by Vic Finkelstein extending this line of thought led to the development of the 'social model of disability' by Michael Oliver in 1983 (see Oliver, 1996). He posited that disability is not necessarily rooted in the body but in the body's socio-physical environment that might present barriers to full participation in common activities of life. This model was instrumental in shaping new understandings of disability as a product of overarching socio political and economic structures rather than of biomedical causes alone (Dear et al., 1997; Oliver, 2004; Thomas, 2004).

Definitions, Concepts, Terms and Issues

The definition or description of disability is a difficult endeavour – it often includes physical and mental conditions and impairments, chronic illnesses, substance abuse, the perception of disability (as in towards persons living with HIV/AIDS), and even in some literature, such serious socioeconomic disadvantage as homelessness (Dear et al., 1997). There is no common understanding of what constitutes 'disability'. Where various impairments lie on the spectrum of 'disability' is often a matter of contention and varied interpretation. Such disabilities would include developmental disabilities, those acquired later in life rather than at birth, those that are neurological or psychological and might not seemingly hamper life functions, invisible disabilities, obesity, chronic conditions and syndromes and others that often lie on the threshold of 'disability' (Altman, 2001; Cooper, 1997; Cormode, 1997; Parr, 1997; Temkin, 1971; e-mail communication with Disability Geography scholar Michael Dorn on September 27, 2008; also see Chouinard et al. 2010 for a varied representation of identities that might be labelled as 'disabled').

The meaning of many related terms is also contested, as in the differentiations made between 'impairment' and 'disability' (Oliver, 1990; Parr and Butler, 1999; Thomas, 2004). In 1976, UPIAS put forward a definition of 'impairment' understood as loss or malfunction of limb, organ or mechanism, and of 'disability' as exclusionary experiences created by society as a result of the impairments; these definitions have been widely supported by disabled people themselves (Oliver, 1990, p. 11). But, some emphasize that impairment and disability are both cultural constructs as opposed to the former having a 'natural' or biological connotation. According to these arguments, the former varies culturally, not only because it can be the product of the socio-cultural environment where one lives, but also because of perception – it might or might not be classed as the cultural evaluation of a physical or mental condition as a deviation from the norm. Disability is understood as a negative social response to what has been culturally evaluated to be an impairment (Abberley, 1987; Oliver, 1990; Shuttleworth, 2003; Shuttleworth and Kasnitz, 2005).

Impairment, as understood under the UPIAS definition, might not necessarily be a disability if the socio-physical environment poses no barriers and if it is not evaluated to be negative. An apt and oft-cited example of how 'impairment' is culturally constructed and might not be a disability can be found in Nora Groce's 1985 study of seventeenth century Martha's Vineyard in the United States, where a large proportion of the population was deaf. However, this did not constitute a disability for them since most residents – deaf and hearing – had mastered a form of sign language, effectively rendering the 'impairment' a simple difference rather than a disability (Scheer and Groce, 1988).

One other area of contention within disability studies and advocacy is the issue of labels. For example, in the US, the favoured language in disability studies is to emphasize the personhood of the individual who has the disability, thus leading to descriptors such as 'persons with disabilities'. In the UK and Oceania, the term 'disabled persons' is preferred due to its greater politicisation power of highlighting a group of persons facing discrimination (Albrecht, 2005a; Gleeson, 1999; Priestly, 2001).

Leading disabilities scholar Irving Zola sought to prioritise personhood over disability due to his strong belief that the condition of disability was too universal to call for differentiation into a separate class of people. The foundation of this belief was that almost everyone at some stage of life faces or will face some disability due to factors such as ageing, chronic illnesses, the survival of premature infants, and survival through better technology and medical advances, though such factors might cause some impairments (Zola, 1989). Others believe that this leads to unreal assumptions about personhood since 'disability is an essential part of the self' in the disabled person's life and cannot be separated from their person or treated as secondary (Oliver, 1990, p. xiii).

Also of contention in debates on disability and identity is the issue of 'difference'. Reynolds (2007) exhaustively reviewed this debate through discourse analysis, pointing out that activists and advocates prefer to emphasize difference since it provides a platform for the creation of rights-oriented polemics, while academics seek to emphasize commonalities lest discourses of differences cause them to be reified, particularly in the form of discrimination.

On the note of discrimination, just as discussions on gender and race must include the examination of sexism and racism, disability brings to the fore questions about the process that makes it an oppressed category. 'Ableism' might be described as attitudes, actions and institutions, intended or unintended, which negate or ignore differing abilities and thus create socioeconomic, political and physical barriers for those who do not fit the 'norm' of able-bodiedness (Butler and Bowlby, 1997; Chouinard, 1997; Levi, 2005; Turner, 2001).

Evolution of Disability Studies and Disability Geography

The study of the disabled body and the experiences of persons with disabilities is not particularly new – such studies and accounts can be found in various disciplines dating back to ancient times (Albrecht, 2005b). What is new is the treatment of disability studies as a field of study in itself, carving its own distinctive theoretical underpinnings and changing its epistemological stance away from subject/object positivistic perspectives and 'colonized' interpretative exercises that have prioritized the researcher's voice over those of the participants (Oliver, 1996). There has been a greater engagement in the field by persons with disabilities, not as mere objects of study, but as active participants and researchers. In fact, disabled scholars have contributed greatly to the growth and development of disability studies (Gleeson, 1999). Barnes (2004) provides a full review of the evolution of disability studies in the social sciences.

Organized disability activism has been around for some decades, and many of the texts and theorizations in disability studies have flowed from it (Campbell and Oliver, 1996; Oliver, 1996; Shakespeare, 2000; Turner, 2001; Whyte and Ingstad, 2007). In fact, Snyder (2005) calls disability studies the 'theoretical arm' of the disability movement. Gleeson (1999) traces a 'coherent discourse' on the topic to the mid-twentieth century, gaining momentum with the US civil rights movement. Moreover, critical discourse from the fields of feminism and race studies in the 1970s and '80s was crucial to the theoretical development of the field, as were the contributions of disabled academics (Barton, 1996; Gleeson, 1999).

Some scholars were already fully engaged in disability studies by the 1980s, for example, with the establishment of the Society for the Study of Chronic Illness and Disease in the US, renamed the Society for Disability Studies in 1986, under whose aegis the hallmark journal *Disabilities Studies Quarterly* was published. A parallel development was the launch of the British journal *Disability, Handicap and Society*, later renamed *Disability and Society*. In fact, the pioneering efforts of the British in the realm of disability studies have preceded and influenced American conceptualizations of disability. Publications and conference sessions, as well as the establishment of programmes of disability studies also took place in these countries and across the rest of the western world in Canada and Australia through the 1980s. However, major theoretical developments came to the field only in the 1990s (Cormode, 1997; Gleeson, 1999; Shakespeare, 2000; Snyder, 2005; Whyte and Ingstad, 2007).

Disability studies within geography followed a similar trajectory of development as in other social science fields, that is, it was mostly absent from scholarly discourse until the 1990s (Gleeson, 2001; Park, Radford and Vickers, 1998; Parr and Butler, 1999). While some works on disability geography were published in earlier decades, particularly in the areas of mental health and social services including institutionalization (see reviews of this trajectory of development of Disability geography in Chouinard et al. 2010; Crooks, Dorn and Wilton, 2008; Gleeson, 1999; Park et al., 1998), much of the work on disabilities was within the rubric of medical geography (Johnston, 2000; Worth, 2008).

Encapsulating the very latest in disability geography debates, Crooks et al. (2008) condensed the contents of a Disability Symposium held at the 2007 Annual Meet of the Association of American Geographers, and found that many of the presentations were reflective of developments in disability geography literature, mainly along the themes of 'the changing parametres of disability; the complex relationships between disabled people and technologies; and the struggle for citizenship'. (Crooks et al., 2008, p. 884). Similar themes resound in an even more recent compilation of Disability Geography studies (Chouinard et al. 2010, preface), with the addition of Disability Geography's emphasis on 'the bodily experiences of people with impairments. . . .'

Theories and Models in Disability Geography

While a large number of theorizations and models of disability exist (Altman, 2001), we will look at the major ones that have permeated into disability geography. The 'medical model' and 'social model' have been the most influential (Johnston, 2000; Parr and Butler, 1999). Traditionally, disability was studied within medical geography, embedded in the 'medical model' based paradigm of the times (Chouinard 2010; Johnston, 2000), but since the 1990s, geography has mostly favoured the 'social model', (Gleeson, 1999), although it has been criticized on a number of grounds. This prompted the rise of other variations and refinements, such as the 'sociospatial model', and 'embodied disabilities' (Gleeson, 1999; Johnston, 2000; Park et al., 1998; Worth, 2008).

Critiques of the Social Model

Despite its success in highlighting the role of social barriers in creating disability, the social model has been perceived as assuming a simplistic causal relationship between disability and the external environment at the cost of ignoring the reality of the impairment (Oliver, 2004). However, as Oliver (2004) and Barton (1996) explain, social causality does not imply denying the actual corporeal situation, but rather one's identity is not solely described by what the medical establishment ascribes it (usually as deficient in one or more aspects).

The social model has also been deemed insufficient since it lacks the complexity required to explain the heterogeneous nature of disability arising from intersections of class, race and gender, among other factors, as also the multifaceted nature of disability that can include chronic illnesses, mental, physical and sensory impairments, and even socioeconomic condition. Thus, the social model is critiqued for viewing disability as a monolithic identity, wherein it runs the risk of being essentialist in nature (Butler and Bowlby, 1997; Dyck and O'Brien, 2003; Oliver, 2004). On the other hand, some scholars fear that emphasizing the heterogeneity of disabilities might result in a return to an individual-based medical model (Butler and Bowlby, 1997; Parr, 1997).

Embodied Disabilities

By the end of the twentieth century, another approach that gained ground in disability studies in general was that of embodied (lived) experiences, and this trend has been apparent in disability geography as well (Dorn and Laws, 1994). This approach attempts to do away with the artifice that is the divide between the medical and social models (Gleeson, 1999; Whyte and Ingstad, 2007; Williams, 2001), and is essentially an effort to examine the effects of the larger socioeconomic and political structures on the daily, lived experience of the disabled person, thereby providing an account of both the corporeal and social realities and barriers (Whyte and Ingstad, 1997).

In geography, too, it has been argued that the social model has effaced the experience of the body (Gleeson, 1999) and failed to recognize 'corporeality', prompting the development of 'embodied materialism' by Gleeson (1999), a fusion of historical–geographical materialist and embodied accounts of disability. For social geography, this change is important not only in that it is a new paradigm in disability geography, but also that this approach operates at the most elemental level of society – the human body. This paradigm does not recognize the divorce between bodily realities and environmental barriers, but seeks to employ the lens of the body as it negotiates the human or social and natural barriers of its surrounding space (Park et al., 1998; Worth, 2008).

Socio-Spatial Model

Dear et al. (1997, p. 471) provide an additional dimension to the social model by adding the construct of space.

> The confluence of a broad range of attitudinal determinants within specific locales produces a 'landscape of (in)tolerance'. Within each locale, various forms of disability may be interpreted and responded to differently. This is true at the national, regional and local level. We have emphasized that space does not merely reflect the social construction of disability; instead, space itself is integral to the production and perpetuation of disability.

The geographies of disability must take into account the fact that not only does space (as a social construct and product of social power relations) present a landscape of oppression, but also that everyday navigations of these power relations and the socio-spatial structures they create present barriers. Therefore, its effect is at once physical and psychological in nature (Gleeson, 1999). We will delve further into this aspect in the following sections.

Epistemology and Tools

'Nothing about us, without us' was the slogan disability activist Friday Mavuso gave to the disability movement, signalling the demand for the right to participate in research, activism and decision making. However, Vera Chouinard takes this even further and calls for developing an empowerment aspect in research (Chouinard, 1997).

Traditional positivist and interpretive epistemologies can be hegemonic since they tend to discount the experiences and voices of the 'subjects'. This prompted the development and promotion of alternative methodologies that transition from observation of the 'subject' and interpretations of their situations and actions to participatory and praxeological research, either incorporating such 'subjects' or undertaken by them (Chouinard and Crooks, 2003; Oliver, 1996; Snyder, 2005). In the case of disability studies, Oliver (1996) contends that even the latter methodologies do not always provide for a voice for disabled persons since the basic power structure of who is being studied and who translates it into academic or policy studies does not change. Oliver (1996) lobbies for an 'emancipatory' methodology that would empower persons with disabilities through control over how their situations, actions and needs are presented.

Various methods that have traditionally been used in disability studies have included those associated with positivistic and interpretive methodologies, but more engaged methods such as participatory action research, critical discourse analysis and ethnographic accounts, including those autobiographical in nature are gaining favour (Brown, 2001; Park et al., 1998; Snyder, 2005; Worth, 2008).

Disability and Postmodernity

The very complexity of disability and the inability to adequately theorize it within the medical or social model has led some scholars to turn towards post-modernist, post-structuralist, and feminist post-modern approaches (Corker and Shakespeare, 2002; Thomas, 2004; Williams, 2001). Post-modernism cannot yet fully grasp the topic of disability either, presenting many problems such as running the risk of imperialist hegemony by imposing western concepts of postmodernism onto non-western cultural sensibilities and realities (Ghai, 2002). Nevertheless, it presents a useful perspective for engaging disability studies into a broader theoretical framework, whilst informing these same frameworks through the realities of disability.

A Cross-Cultural Study of Disability

Historically, different societies and cultures have had varying responses to impairments, determining whether or not it is deemed or becomes a disability. Barnes (1996) and Scheer and Groce (1988) provide a review of this 'human constant' across times and cultures, showing how some societies have viewed impairments as blessings, others as a negative, and yet others simply as a difference with no connotation of either negativity or inferiority. However, Barnes (1996) concludes that Western cultures have mostly been marked by prejudice against persons with impairments, although, contrary to some other accounts, Gleeson (1999) finds that at least in feudal England, persons with impairments were largely able to participate in society. The view of disability as an individual concern has been more pronounced since the advent of industrialization and capitalism, leading to oppressive socioeconomic and political structures for those with impairments (Barnes, 1996; Gleeson, 1999; Oliver, 1990; Thomas, 2004). This last aspect of the effect of capitalist structures is particularly relevant in the present study.

Traditional and non-Western cultures have had varying responses to disability as well (Ingstad and Whyte, 1995, 2007; Priestly, 2001) but as things stand now, most accounts point towards the experiences of disabled persons in developing countries as marred by bias and ableist practices and behaviour, intended or otherwise (Bhambani, 2005; Devlieger, 2005; Ghai, 2001, 2002; Stone, 2005). While there is now a growing concern for the rights and life needs of persons with disabilities in many parts of the developing world (Albrecht, 2005a; Filmer, 2008), prevailing trends of social marginalization and stigmatization, along with the debilitation brought about by poverty, dearth of economic and educational opportunities, and lack of access to basic needs including healthcare presents a very mixed outlook for the disabled in this part of the world (Fuller, 2005; World Bank, 2007). However, Ingstad (2001) cautions against harbouring 'myths' regarding widespread abuse and neglect of the disabled and lack of activism in the developing countries.

Theoretical Framework

One of the dominant theoretical underpinnings of disability is that it is a social construct – it derives meaning from how societies with their socio-cultural institutions and practices render a body functional or disabled. Additionally, Massey (1994) states that not only is space a social construct but that society is spatially constructed as well.

> … And so, to the aphorism of the 1970s – that space is socially constructed – was added in the 1980s the other side of the coin: that the social is spatially constructed too, and that makes a difference. In other words, and in its broadest formulation, society is necessarily constructed spatially, and that fact – the spatial organization of society – makes a difference to how it works. (Massey, 1994, p. 254)

Imrie (2000) invoked this 'geography matters' mantra to make the case that where one lives makes a difference in terms of what one might expect to have access to. In the case of disabled persons, services and other goods are available to them only if they are within accessible mode and distance from them. Campbell (Campbell and Oliver, 1996, pp. 184–185) relates how, despite accomplishing all or more than an able-bodied person, attitudes of discrimination and bigotry often make it impossible to 'claim' space in society, where space refers to social space rather than physical.

It necessarily follows that if space is important to the construction of society and its material and cultural being, then where one lives will affect and indeed mould the understandings and perceptions of what it means to be disabled in that society. Therefore, disability takes on different meanings over different spatial contexts (Priestly, 2001; Whyte and Ingstad, 1995, 2007). Ingstad (1995) provides a good example of this by comparing the experience of blindness in Norway as compared to Botswana. She admits that while the biomedical situation might essentially be the same, it is the contexualized situation brought about by intersections of socio-cultural and economic conditions that make the lived experience of the same disability extremely dissimilar in two different places. In Norway, technological and socio-politically created support systems enable a great degree of mobility and independence in life, where such values are prioritized. On the other hand, in her study area of Botswana, such independence was not acceptable since the community would think of it as abandonment by the family. Moreover, the technological assistance of the 'white stick' was redundant due to culturally prevalent generational bonds that provided the person in Ingstad's (1995) study a ready guide in her grandchild, keeping both woman and child feeling functionally important.

Study Methodology

According to Albrecht, "Disability studies refutes the equation of disability with inferiority and instead aims its analytical lens at the social obstacles that produce disability as a devalued experience." (Albrecht, 2005a, p. xiv) This is precisely what this present account seeks to do. There are many accounts of cross-cultural differences in the perception of what might constitute a disability, or even how the same biomedical condition might be seen as different types of disabilities (Ingstad and Whyte, 1995, 2007; Priestly, 2001). What sets this account apart is the unique and additional benefit of a comparative study of the shifting meanings of disability across space, as based on the experiences of the same person. To the best of my knowledge, such a cross-cultural study has not been done so far.

According to Whyte (1995), studying questions of disability experience has usually involved one of the two methodologies – the evolution of the concept through history and over space, or the more specific study of a person's experiences of it. The former runs the risk of over-generalization, and the latter, while an in-depth approach, cannot provide a more general context or generate a larger theory. Whyte (1995) argues for a balance of the approaches. The present study falls in the latter category, but attempts to build a larger context through referencing pertinent literature.

Disability studies favours the use of methodologies that provide voice and agency, particularly in the case of reflexive work by a disabled scholar (Worth, 2008). Since experience is held to be the source of knowledge and phenomenology allows for tapping such knowledge, phenomenological methods such as experientialism can become powerful tools of description and analysis available to disability studies (Snyder and Mitchell, 2006). The methodological tool I have used here is 'self-experientialism', that is, the use of my own accounts of the experience of disability across two cultures. Such a tool is widely used in disability studies in general (Priestly, 2001; Williams, 2001) and also in disability geography, as can be seen in various autobiographical works including Chouinard (1996), Golledge (1997), Guelke (2003) and Moss (1999).

> Personal experiences ... help the reader 'see' society and our discipline through others' eyes. The intention in not to evoke sympathy or pity but to encourage the reader to understand more fully the environments [she] negotiates daily. (Chouinard and Grant, p. 139 in Worth, 2008, p. 309).

Therefore, in such studies it is important to remember that it is the account of the experience of disability that is of importance, not so much the illness or impairment (Williams, 2001).

The Study: Cultural Contexts and the Shifting Nature of Disability

I was diagnosed with a common neurological condition when I was 16 years old. Most often, it is easily controlled through appropriate medication and presents no problems to educational, social, or work-related aspects of a person's life. However, in case of particularly difficult and untreatable cases, or in the absence of appropriate care, the condition can take on a degree of severity that can cause grave harm and even death. My condition was a rather run-of-the-mill case, and as such should not have presented any major problems. However, attitudinal and physical barriers created a situation where a biological condition was negatively construed to be an 'impairment', and eventually presented an indisputable 'disability'.

My account will span the time I spent in India, where I was born and lived for 24 years, and move to my experiences in the US, where I have lived since then for well over a decade.

India: Role of Stigma in Turning 'Impairment' to 'Disability'

While there is an immense body of work on disabilities about and from the developing world, these have not received much attention until very recently, and even then are informed by the dominant Western paradigms and understandings of disability (Ghai, 2002; McEwan and Butler, 2007). The situation of most of the disabled in developing countries is well summed up in the unvarnished words of disability activist Joshua Malinga: 'While people in the rich world are talking about independent living and improved services, we are talking about survival' (Stone, 2001, p. 50).

In India, issues regarding rights and needs of persons with disabilities have long been considered of no consequence – these are matters to be dealt with by the individuals and their families, and the dominant discourse is embedded in the philosophy of *karma* (Bhambani, 2005; Ghai, 2002). The first census regarding disabilities was performed only in 1981, the first time since independence in 1947, and that too only because 1981 was declared the International Year of the Disabled. India's need to live up to its image as a ratified member of the United Nations (UN) Resolution of 1970 that reaffirmed obligations to the UN charter made this possible. Since then, full legal rights have been guaranteed to persons with disabilities only with the passage of the Persons with Disability Act of 1995, enacted after much pressure from disability advocates and the Disability Rights Group in particular. Despite this, the government only reluctantly included disabilities as a category in the 2001 census as a result of the pressure from these same activist groups that have grown considerably in the last few decades. This reluctance reflects the negative attitudes and lack of importance accorded to the issue, as obvious from its absence from the political agenda (Bhambani, 2005; Ghai, 2002).

Without considering multiple intersections of caste, class, gender, ethnicity and religion, a discussion of disabilities can, at best, be essentialist. But the risk needs to be taken to provide some sort of overview of the situation in India. Depending upon data sources, an estimated 70 to 110 million of the nation's billion-plus population can be characterized as disabled (Ghai, 2002; Murdick et al., 2004; World Bank, 2007). Disability is either pitied, as belied by the use of the term *bechara* (poor thing, or without recourse), or denigrated and stigmatized as deviance and abnormality. Usually, persons with disabilities are oppressed, marginalized and stigmatized into a general state of silence, both of the spirit and in terms of their own feelings about their situation and capabilities (Bhambhani, 2005; Ghai, 2001, 2002; Murdick et al., 2004).

A revealing study by Nag (2000) shows how certain neurological conditions are stigmatized in Indian society. In his sample of 100 married women, all kept their condition secret from their potential spouses at the insistence of their parents. Those taking treatment kept their pills in unmarked or mismarked bottles, which were usually given some innocuous label of a headache or backache medication. Thirteen women eventually revealed their medical histories to their husbands, and all thirteen were sent back to their natal homes. Overall, Nag (2000) found that women who have such conditions face a great degree of discrimination and stigma, their parents pay large dowries to get them married, and if they do get married, they often face cruelty, threats of divorce, separation or redundancy and other stresses in their marital homes.

Nag (2000) also studied the lives of 13 men with the same condition, and found them to face no such problems in potential or actual marital life, except that in most cases, demands for dowry were for lower sums of money. The men did, however, face greater economic barriers than those who did not have such a condition. Therefore, his study is a rich presentation of the gendered nature of disability in India, as caused by social prejudices and related stigma. Inhorn and Bharadwaj describe stigma as:

> "… an attribute of a person that is deeply discrediting to social identity. How soon a stigma discredits one's very personhood depends upon its visibility. (Inhorn and Bharadwaj, 2007, p. 85)"

Thus visible 'disfigurements' hold immediate stigma, but a neurological condition like mine that is not immediately discernable would only be stigmatized if known. Therefore, I was encouraged (read remonstrated) that I should keep it secret, lest it jeopardize my and my family's position in society at large, particularly the chances of finding a life partner. This is akin to Das and Addlakha's (2007) observations regarding how disabilities are regarded in Indian society, wherein these are seen to be part of and hold consequences within larger social networks rather than restricted to the body of the individual.

Their study also highlights the highly gendered nature of disability, where women with disabilities are regarded as doubly disadvantaged, in that being marked as disabled would 'imperil the[ir] "life projects"' (129). Likewise, Abu Habib (1995) finds that while there is no restriction on disabled men to marry, disabled women rarely find a life partner (my parents' fear), unless a heavy dowry has been paid.

Therefore, the disability I faced was not that I was unable to carry on usual life functions, but that I may potentially be regarded and stigmatized as 'damaged goods' by society as a whole, and thus even by my parents. The stereotypes, ignorance and stigma resulted in lack of appropriate and sustained medical care despite the fact that I came from a middle class, literate family like Nag's (2000) sample population. Over a short period, my neurological condition worsened, lost some of its invisibility and morphed into a disability – both in terms of the fact that I faced biased attitudes, eliciting a mixed response of curiosity and revulsion (although all talk or explanation of it was shunned), and that it affected several life functions such as learning and cognition.

However, the effects on other life functions such as mobility and access were limited, if any, and towards the end of my stay in India, I was treated by a very competent practitioner of *Unani* medicine (a form of Greek medicine adapted by traditional Islamic physicians), who was able to keep my impairment from presenting any difficulties or experience adverse pharmacological reactions. On both counts of stigma and effect on life functions, this was a very different experience from the one I would have in the US.

US: Landscapes of Exclusion

Disabled persons number almost 50 million in the US, about 20 per cent of the population (Siebers, 2006). Yet, persons with disabilities have consistently lower rates of educational attainment, earnings, home ownership and franchisement than their non-disabled counterparts. Poverty is higher in this demographic and only 27 per cent are employed, as opposed to 78 per cent of the non-disabled people (Chouinard, 1997; Schwartz et al., 2005). Nevertheless, there is a much greater awareness of the rights, issues and concerns of persons with disabilities in the US. The American Disability Act (ADA) of 1990, along with various other civil rights laws covering health, employment, work and housing protections provide many avenues of recourse to persons with disabilities (Bickenbach, 2001).

When I came to the US, I was able to access appropriate medical care for my neurological condition. However, I was cautioned that I would probably have to take medications all my life, which presented several problems such as severe drug toxicity during the initial stage and the phenomenon of iatrogenic (here, drug-induced) disabilities, or adverse drug effects (ADEs) over the long term. ADEs are negative health outcomes caused by side effects of medications and can be permanent in nature. As a result, I not only developed a number of endocrine and metabolic disorders, but also musculoskeletal and further neurological issues which, within the context of urban US life, became a disability.

> For disabled people, the physical construction of urban space often (re)produces distinctive spatialities of demarcation and exclusion, from the lack of access to public transport systems to the absence of visual clues or guides in towns to enable vision-impaired people to move with ease. Indeed, the sociospatial patterns of ableist values are etched across the city in numerous ways, forming a type of architectural apartheid. (Imrie, 2001, p. 232)

I became, and remain, physically isolated by the fact that I cannot independently use my own mode of transport – a situation many persons with disabilities contend with. Moreover, it is not so much my neurological condition that precludes driving, as do impairments caused by the ADEs, particularly when combined with American urban form and design. Living within city limits where transit networks are densest is not always an option due to cost and other circumstances. Someone like me would have to live very close to a public transit line in order to retain a modicum of mobility and independence. This brings us to the first problem presented by US culture – a spatial structure reflective of the capitalist political economy (Gleeson, 1999, 2001).

> The human landscape can be read as a landscape of exclusion. … Because power is expressed in the monopolization of space and the relegation of weaker groups in society to less desirable environments, any text on the social geography of advanced capitalism should be concerned with the question of exclusion. … The simple questions we should be asking are: who are places for, whom do they exclude and how are these prohibitions maintained in practice? … [we need] an account of barriers, prohibitions and constraints on activities from the point of view of the excluded (Sibley, 1995, pp. ix–x).

Zoning and other land use regulations, as well as market-influenced processes such as suburbanization and separation of functions have produced landscapes that reproduce injustices of segregation and isolation (Young, 1990; Gleeson, 1999; Wolch and Dear, 1993). This leaves many people marginalized, not just the disabled but also the low income, elderly and any others who might require public transit services. Despite smart growth efforts, most zoning practices have encouraged sprawl, and transit systems are not conducive to non-traditional patterns of mobility (see Gleeson 2001).

Almost all major needs are oriented around auto access (Zola, 1989). As a result, all aspects of life are affected – employment, recreation, access to medical, food and other retail needs (Gleeson, 2001). The meshing of multiple aspects of a person's life makes life in the city and the larger area that much more difficult – problems getting to place of work, to physicians, to events, effectively limiting such participation. For me, this ineffective planning of space and means of access have become greater barriers in light of the ADEs, where even walking a mile to a transit node or other facilities is a herculean task.

The last aspect based on cultural conceptualizations of a society steeped in ableist modes of thinking particular to the American culture's prevalent notions of efficiency and worth is the inability of most people to figure out–(i) Why I don't drive (despite my explanation, it is usually chalked down to fear or inability to adjust to the 'American' way of life); (ii) Why I don't have a permanent job (she's probably not good enough), or; (iii) Why I feel so strongly about public transit systems ('Boston's system is good, right? Why complain?' Certainly, it is good, but only if one lives in the Greater Boston area. The rest of the system is geared towards conventional ableist patterns of peak-time traffic and work-life assumptions, which do not apply to everyone).

This inability to understand my particular situation in the context of a culture that prizes independence is usually transmitted to me in subtle language or the brushing off of concerns as matters not to be aired in public (Zola, 2003), and not unlike the mechanisms of interaction described by Giddens (1984, in Young, 1990) where latent or other biases are operationalised at a subconscious level and often displayed by subtle actions, behaviour or words, sometimes absolutely well intentioned, but demeaning nevertheless.

Tying the Narrative

Stigma itself is a changeable construct of society – it varies over space and cultural context, as well as type of impairment (Shuttleworth, 2003). This was the major barrier I faced in India, which excluded me from claiming social space. However, the upside of the socioeconomic and political milieus was that physical access to space did not present a problem with the heavy investment in public infrastructure, as well as the existence of the informal economy where one could find rickshaws aplenty or tri-autos through the operation of the small-scale sector of the formal economy. The eventual access to non-allopathic treatment also resulted in a very functional and ADE-free situation.

Diametrically opposed to such an experience of disability, in the US, I did not have to face any stigma as a direct result of the impairment. However, the operation of dominant socioeconomic and political structures presented many barriers to physical access, and thus to full participation in society and to social space. At times, my inability to 'fit in' with the prevalent lifestyle of independent mobility and access due to such barriers resulted in negative social responses as well. Additionally, the healthcare system, also steeped in the capitalist mechanisms of 'bottom line' – what Gary Albrecht called the 'disability business' – does not adequately address well-being and preventive care (Albrecht and Bury, 2001; Donchin and Purdy, 1999; Mosher, Gosden and Beder, 2004), as a result of which I ended up with more problems than with which I had begun.

As it stands today, in India, the Persons with Disabilities Act of 1995 lays down reservation mandates for the disabled in many walks of life, but if the foremost rung of making a life in the modern world – education – is broken, stepping to others is almost out of the question. While there is no reservation or quota for disabled persons in education, free education to all those under 18 years of age is mandated (Government of India, 1996). However, there are too many barriers in the way of obtaining education and training for a disabled person, such as negative attitudes, lack of human and monetary resources, and political will, as well as gender bias that works against girls and their ability to get a fair chance at education (Kalyanpur, 2008; Thirumurthy and Jayaraman, 2007).

Similarly, in the US, the ADA provides the right to accommodations and other laws protect against discrimination. However, there is not much use in constantly fighting individual cases if society and its attendant aspects of work, recreation, transportation and architecture are all structured in a way that make it extremely difficult for some persons to participate – this includes single parents, part-time students, elderly and disabled, among others.

The shortage of flexible jobs and the rigidity of many of these social structures result in lack of job opportunity and loss of income (Schriner, 2001). Additionally, it is assumed that accommodations afforded by protective laws must result in an 'abled' life just as any able-bodied person – it does not account for alternative ways of everyday life apart from the conventions of work or functionality (Siebers, 2006). For example, flexible work schedules and job sharing would provide greater opportunities for persons with disabilities to make a living wage, while keeping employers adequately staffed at all times.

Thus, the barriers in the US are created by the overarching political economy where interests of marginalized groups have not yet been fully realized (Albrecht and Bury, 2001; Barnes, 1996; Gleeson, 1999). Even in the face of international efforts such as the revision and reclassification of the ICIDH 1980 to recognize the social nature of disability, it remains largely seen as a health parameter as opposed to a phenomenon embedded in a larger socio-political structure (Snyder and Mitchell, 2006).

Conclusion

Efforts at the international level to alleviate the situation of persons with disabilities were formally initiated by the UN in the early 1970s. Later, 1981 was declared the International Year of the Disabled, and 1983–92 the International Decade. Many other countries and regions followed suit, enacting a number of legislations and organizing around disability rights issues, keeping the disabilities agenda alive at least on paper (Whyte and Ingstad, 2007; Albrecht, 2005b; Priestly, 2001). While noticeable strides have been made towards this goal in many countries, so much needs to be done yet. It is hoped that the sum of all these efforts will bring disability rights and issues to the fore. It is at this point that Zola's (1989) emphasis on universalism is useful since the entire global population is likely to benefit from such awareness.

One of the surest ways of getting to that goal is active representation of disabled people's rights and experiences by disabled persons themselves – in decision-making processes, and on regulatory, advisory and decision-making bodies (disability activist Barbara Chandler, personal communication on October 11, 2007). Parr (1997) also rightly points out that ableism is promoted by the exclusion of the disabled from decision making processes, a fact that Gleeson (1999, p. 2) also mentions in the context of disabling environments of the West. He notes that oppressive spaces are largely created because of the exclusion of disabled persons from the 'discourses and practices that shape the physical layout of societies'.

At this point in time, it is telling that the words 'racism' and 'sexism' are a common part of our vocabulary, but ableism is a term recognized by very few (Siebers, 2006). As Gleeson (1999) and Chouinard (1997) so powerfully point out, disability geography needs to be more than the mapping of spatial patterns of persons with disabilities or a mere description of their experiences, but must be able to contribute towards their resistance movement.

I believe that the first place to begin would be to examine the history of such oppression and recount the development of resistance to it, particularly through the accounts of disabled persons and scholars. Such critical discourse and emancipatory approaches, including works by those mentioned in the study methodology section, have helped to make signal landmarks and seminal contributions. This chapter has been an effort in the same direction, presented in a mainstream work, in the hope of sparking the interest of fellow scholars and students of social geography.

Author's Note

This chapter is dedicated to the memory of disabilities scholar Dr Todd J Reynolds. He died in June 2008, but his work and dedication to disability scholarship lives on. Also, great thanks to Dr Michael Dorn for his insight and critique that helped refine this work.

References

Abberley, P., 'The Concept of Oppression and the Development of a Social Theory of Oppression', *Disability, Handicap & Society*, Vol. 2, No. 1, 1987, pp. 5–19.

Abu Habib, L., 'Women and Disability don't Mix! Double Discrimination and Disabled Women's Rights', *Gender and Development*, Vol. 3, No. 2, 1995, pp. 49–53.

Albrecht, G. L. and M. Bury, 'The Political Economy of the Disability Marketplace', in G. L. Albrecht, K. D. Seelman and M. Bury (eds.), *Handbook of Disability Studies*, Thousand Oaks, CA: Sage Publications, 2001, pp. 585–609.

Albrecht, G. L., 'Introduction', *Encyclopedia of Disability*, Thousand Oaks, CA, London and New Delhi: Sage Publications, Vol. 1, General edition, 2005a.

Albrecht, G. L., *Encyclopedia of Disability*, Thousand Oaks, CA, London and New Delhi: Sage Publications, Vols. 1–5, General edition, 2005b.

Altman, B. M., 'Disability Definitions, Models, Classification Schemes, and Application', in G. L. Albrecht, K. D. Seelman and M. Bury (ed.), *Handbook of Disability Studies*, Thousand Oaks, CA: Sage Publications, 2001, pp. 97–122.

Barnes, C., 'Theories of Disability and the Origins of the Oppression of Disabled People in Western Society', in L. Barton (ed.), *Sociology and Disability: Emerging Issues and Insights*, New York: Longman Publishing, 1996, pp. 43–60.

Barnes, C., 'Disability, Disability Studies and the Academy', in J. Swain, C. Barnes, S. French and C. Thomas (eds.), *Disabling Barriers–enabling Environments*, London: Sage Publications Inc., 2004, pp. 28–33.

Barton, L., 'Sociology and Disability: Some Emerging Issues', in L. Barton (ed.), *Sociology and Disability: Emerging Issues and Insights*, New York: Longman Publishing, 1996, pp. 3–17.

Bhambhani, M., 'Disability Policy: India' and 'Experience of Disability: India', in G. L. Albrecht (ed.), *Encyclopedia of Disability*, Thousand Oaks, CA, London and New Delhi: Sage Publications, Vols. 1 and 2, 2005.

Bickenbach, J. E., 'Disability Human Rights, Law, and Policy, in G. L. Albrecht, K. D. Seelman and M. Bury (eds.), *Handbook of Disability Studies*, Thousand Oaks, CA: Sage Publications, 2001, pp. 565–584.

Brown, S. C., 'Methodological Paradigms that Shape Disability Research' in G. L. Albrecht, K. D. Seelman and M. Bury (eds.), *Handbook of Disability Studies*, Thousand Oaks, CA: Sage Publications, 2001, pp. 145–170.

Butler, R. and S. Bowlby, 'Bodies and Spaces: An Explanation of Disabled People's Experiences of Public Space', *Environment and Planning D*, Vol. 15, No. 4, 1997, pp. 411–433.

Campbell, J. and M. Oliver, *Disability Politics: Understanding our Past, Changing our Future*, London and New York: Routledge, 1996.

Chouinard, V., 'Like Alice through the Looking Glass: Accommodation', *Academia Resources for Feminist Research*, Vol. 24, Nos. 3 and 4, 1996, pp. 3–11.

Chouinard, V., 'Making Space for Disabling Differences: Challenging Ableist Geographies', *Environment and Planning D*, Vol. 15, No. 4, 1997, pp. 373–81.

Chouinard, V. and V. Crooks, 'Challenging Geographies of Ableness: Celebrating How Far We've Come and What's Left to be Done', *The Canadian Geographer*, Vol. 47, No. 4, 2003, pp. 383–85.

Chouinard, V., E. Hall and R. Wilton (eds.), *Towards Enabling Geographies: 'Disabled' Bodies and Minds in Society and Space*, Surrey, England: Ashgate, 2010.

Cooper, C., 'Can a Fat Woman Call Herself Disabled?', *Disability & Society*, Vol. 12, No. 1, 1997, pp. 31–41.

Corker, M. and T. Shakespeare, 'Introduction: Mapping the Terrain', in M. Corker and T. Shakespeare (eds.), *Disability/Postmodernity: Embodying Disability Theory*, London and New York: Continuum, 2002, pp. 1–17.

Cormode, L., 'Emerging Geographies of Impairment and Disability: An Introduction', *Environment and Planning D*, Vol. 15, No. 4, 1997, pp. 381–390.

Crooks, V., M. L. Dorn and R. D. Wilton, 'Emerging Scholarship in the Geographies of Disability', *Health and Place*, Vol. 14, 2008, pp. 883–888.

Das, V., and R. Addlakha, 'Disability and Domestic Citizenship: Voice, Gender, and the Making of the Subject', in B. Ingstad and S. R. Whyte (eds.), *Disability in Local and Global Worlds*, Berkeley and LA, CA: University of California Press, 2007, pp. 128–148.

Dear, M., S. L. Gaber, L. Takahashi and R. Wilton, 'Seeing People Differently: the Socio-spatial Construction of Disability', *Environment and Planning D*, Vol. 15, No. 4, 1997, pp. 455–480.

Devlieger, P., 'Experience of Disability: South Saharan Africa', in G. L. Albrecht (ed.), *Encyclopedia of Disability*, Thousand Oaks, CA, London and New Delhi: Sage Publications, Vol. 2.

Donchin, A. and L. M. Purdy, 'Introduction', in A. Donchin and L. M. Purdy (eds.), *Embodying Bioethics: Recent Feminist Advances*, Lanham, MD: Rowman & Littlefield, 1999, pp. 1–15.

Dorn, M. and G. Laws, 'Social Theory, Body Politics, and Medical Geography: Extending Kearns's Invitation', *The Professional Geographer*, Vol. 46, No. 1, 1994, pp. 106–110.

Dyck, I. and P. O'Brien, 'Thinking about Environment: Incorporating Geographies of Disability into Rehabilitation Science', *The Canadian Geographer*, Vol. 47, No. 4, 2003, pp. 400–413.

Filmer, D., 'Disability, Poverty, and Schooling in Developing Countries: Results from 14 Household Surveys', *World Bank Economic Review*, Vol. 22, No. 1, 2008, pp. 141–163.

Fuller, B., 'Developing World', *Encyclopedia of Disability*, Thousand Oaks, CA, London and New Delhi: Sage Publications, Vol. 1, 2005.

Ghai, A., 'Marginalisation and Disability: Experiences from the Third World', in M. Priestley (ed.), *Disability and the Life Course: Global Perspectives*, Cambridge, UK: Cambridge University Press, 2001, pp. 26–37.

Ghai, A., 'Disability in the Indian Context: Post-colonial Perspectives', in M. Corker and T. Shakespeare (eds.), *Disability/Postmodernity: Embodying Disability Theory*, London and New York: Continuum, 2002, pp. 88–100.

Gleeson, B., *Geographies of Disability*, New York: Routledge, 1999.

Gleeson, B., 'Disability and the Open City', *Urban Studies*, Vol. 38, No. 2, 2001, pp. 251–265.

GOI, 'The Persons with Disabilities (equal opportunities, protection of rights and full participation) Act, 1995'. *Source*: http://ccdisabilities.nic.in/Act%201.htm, (last accessed 1 September 2008).

Golledge, R., 'On Reassembling One's Life: Overcoming Disability in the Academic Environment', *Environment and Planning D*, Vol. 15, No. 4, 1997, pp. 391–409.

Guelke, J. K., 'Roadkill on the Information Highway: Repetitive Strain Injury in the Academy', *The Canadian Geographer*, Vol. 47, No. 4, 2003, pp. 386–399.

Hahn, H., 'The Politics of Physical Differences: Disability and Discrimination', *Journal of Social Issues*, Vol. 44, No. 1, 1988, pp. 39–47.

Imrie, R., 'Disabling Environments and the Geography of Access Policies and Practices', *Disability & Society*, Vol. 15, No. 19, pp. 5–24.

Ingstad, B., 'Public Discourses on Rehabilitation: From Norway to Botswana', in B. Ingstad and S. R. Whyte, *Disability and Culture*, Berkeley and LA, CA: University of California Press, 1995, pp. 174–195.

Ingstad, B. and S. R. Whyte (eds.), *Disability and Culture*, Berkeley and LA, CA: University of California Press, 1995.

Ingstad, B., 'Disability in the Developing World', in G. L. Albrecht, K. D. Seelman and M. Bury (eds.), *Handbook of Disability Studies*, Thousand Oaks, CA: Sage Publications, 2001, pp. 772–792.

Ingstad, B. and S. R. Whyte (eds.), *Disability in Local and Global Worlds*, Berkeley and LA, CA: University of California Press, 2007.

Inhorn, M. C. and A. Bharadwaj, 'Reproductively Disabled Lives: Infertility, Stigma, and Suffering in Egypt and India', in B. Ingstad and S. R. Whyte, *Disability in Local and Global Worlds*, Berkeley and LA, CA: University of California Press, 2007, pp. 78–106.

Johnston, R. J., 'Disability, Geography and', in R. J. Johnston, *et al.* (eds.), *The Dictionary of Human Geography*, Oxford: Blackwell Publishing, 2000.

Kalyanpur, M., 'The Paradox of Majority Underrepresentation in Special Education in India: Constructions of Difference in a Developing Country', *Journal of Special Education*, Vol. 42, No. 1, 2008, pp. 55–64.

Levi, S. J., 'Ableism', *Encyclopedia of Disability*, Thousand Oaks, CA, London and New Delhi: Sage Publications, Vol. 1, 2005.

Massey, D., *Space, Place, and Gender*, St. Paul, MN: University of Minnesota Press, 1994.

McEwan, C. and R. Butler, 'Disability and Development: Different Models, Different Places', *Geography Compass*, Vol. 1, No. 3, 2007, pp. 448–466.

Mosher, L. R., R. Gosden and S. Beder, 'Drug Companies and Schizophrenia: Unbridled Capitalism Meets Madness', in J. Read, L. R. Mosher and R. Bentall (eds.), *Models of madness: Psychological, Social and Biological Approaches to Schizophrenia*, New York: Brunner-Routledge, 2004, pp. 115–130.

Moss, P., 'Autobiographical notes on chronic illness', in R. Butler and H. Parr (eds.), *Mind and Body Spaces: Geographies of Illness, impairment, and disability*, London: Routledge, 1999, pp. 151–162.

Murdick, N., P. Shore and M. M. Chittooran, 'Cross–cultural Comparison of the Concept of "Otherness" and its Impact on Persons with Disabilities', *Education and Training in Developmental Disabilities*, Vol. 39, No. 4, 2004, pp. 310–316.

Nag, D., 'Gender and Epilepsy: A Clinician's Experience', *Neurology India*, Vol. 48, No. 2, 2000, pp. 99–104.

Oliver, M., *The Politics of Disablement: A Sociological Approach*, New York: St. Martin's Press, 1990.

Oliver, M., 'A Sociology of Disability or a Disablist Sociology?' in L. Barton (ed.), *Sociology and Disability: Emerging Issues and Insights*, New York, Longman Publishing, 1996, pp. 18–42.

Oliver, M., 'If I had a Hammer: the Social Model in Action', in J. Swain, C. Barnes, S. French and C. Thomas (eds.), *Disabling Barrier–Enabling Environments*, London: Sage Publications, Inc., 2004, pp. 7–12.

Park, D. C., J. P. Radford and M. H. Vickers, 'Disability Studies in Human Geography', *Progress in Human Geography*, Vol. 22, No. 2, 1998, pp. 208–233.

Parr, H., 'Mental Health, Public Space, and the City: Questions of Individual and Collective Access', *Environment and Planning D*, Vol. 15, No. 4, 1997, pp. 435–454.

Parr, H. and R. Butler, 'New Geographies of Illness, Impairment and Disability' in R. Butler and H. Parr (eds.), *Mind and Body Spaces: Geographies of Illness, Impairment and Disability*, London: Routledge, 1999, pp. 1–24.

Priestley, M., 'Introduction: The Global Context of Disability', in M. Priestly (ed.), *Disability and the Life Course: Global Perspectives*, Cambridge, UK: Cambridge University Press, 2001, pp. 3–14.

Reynolds, T. J., 'A Dualism in Production of Difference', Annual Meet of the Association of American Geographers, Boston, MA, 2007.

Scheer, J., and N. Groce, 'Impairment as a Human Constant: Cross–cultural and Historical Perspectives on Variation', *Journal of Social Issues*, Vol. 44, No. 1, 1988, pp. 23–37.

Schriner, K., 'Disability Studies Perspective on Employment Issues and Policies for Disabled People: An International View', in G. L. Albrecht, K. D. Seelman and M. Bury, *Handbook of Disability Studies*, Thousand Oaks, CA: Sage Publications, 2001, pp. 642–662.

Schwartz, J.A., *et al.*, 'Disability Policy: United States', in G. L. Albrecht (ed.), *Encyclopedia of Disability*, Thousand Oaks, CA, London and New Delhi: Sage Publications, Vol. 1, 2005.

Shakespeare, T., 'Introduction and Part one: From Activism to Academia', in T. Shakespeare (ed.), *The Disability Reader: Social Science Perspectives*, London: Continuum, 2000, pp. 1–7.

Shuttleworth, R. P., 'Disability/Difference', in C. R. Ember, and M. Ember (eds.), *Encyclopedia of Medical Anthropology: Health and Illness in the World's Cultures*, New York: Springer, 2003, pp. 360–374.

Shuttleworth, R. P. and D. Kasnitz, 'Cultural Context of Disability', in G. L. Albrecht (ed.), *Encyclopedia of Disability*, Thousand Oaks, CA, London and New Delhi: Sage Publications, Vol. 1, 2005.

Sibley, D., *Geographies of Exclusion: Society and Difference in the West*, London and New York: Routledge, 1995.

Siebers, T., 'Disability Studies and the Future of Identity Politics', in L. M. Alcoff, *et al.* (eds.), *Identity Politics Reconsidered*, New York: Palgrave MacMillan, 2006, pp. 10–30.

Snyder, S. L., 'Disability Studies', in G. L. Albrecht (ed.), *Encyclopedia of Disability*, Thousand Oaks, CA, London and New Delhi: Sage Publications, Vol. 1, 2005.

Snyder, S. L. and D. T. Mitchell, *Cultural Locations of Disability*, Chicago: University of Chicago Press, 2006.

Stone, E., 'A Complicated Struggle: Disability, Survival and Social Change in the Majority World', in M. Priestley (ed.), *Disability and the Life Course: Global Perspectives*, Cambridge, UK: Cambridge University Press, 2001, pp. 50–65.

Stone, E., 'Experience of disability: China', in G. L. Albrecht (ed.), *Encyclopedia of Disability*, Thousand Oaks, CA, London and New Delhi: Sage Publications, Vol. 2, 2005.

Temkin, O., *The Falling Sickness: A History of Epilepsy from the Greeks to the Beginnings of Modern Neurology*, Baltimore/London: The John Hopkins Press, Second edition, 1971.

Thirumurthy, V. and B. Jayaraman, 'Special Education in India at the Crossroads', *Childhood Education*, Vol. 83, No. 6, 2007, pp. 380.

Thomas, C., 'Disability and Impairment', in J. Swain, C. Barnes, S. French and C. Thomas (eds.), *Disabling Barriers–Enabling Environments*, London: Sage Publications, Inc., 2004, pp. 21–27.

Turner, B. S., 'Disability and the Sociology of the Body', in G. L. Albrecht, K. D. Seelman and M. Bury (eds.), *Handbook of Disability Studies*, Thousand Oaks, CA: Sage Publications, 2001, pp. 252–266.

Whyte, S. R., 'Disability: Between Discourse and Experience', in B. Ingstad and S. R. Whyte (eds.), *Disability and Culture*, Berkeley and LA, CA: University of California Press, 1995, pp. 267–291.

Whyte, S. R. and B. Ingstad, 'Introduction: Disability Connections', in B. Ingstad and S. R. Whyte (eds.), *Disability in Local and Global Worlds*, Berkeley and LA, CA: University of California Press, 2007, pp. 1–32.

Williams, G., 'Theorizing Disability', in G. L. Albrecht, K. D. Seelman and M. Bury (eds.), *Handbook of Disability Studies*, Thousand Oaks, CA: Sage Publications, 2001, pp. 123–144.

Wolch, J. and M. Dear, *Malign Neglect: Homelessness in an American City*, San Francisco: Jossey-Bass, 1993.

World Bank, '*People with Disabilities in India: From Commitments to Outcomes*'. *Source*: http://siteresources.worldbank.org/DISABILITY/Resources/Regions/South%20Asia/PeoplewithDisinIndia.pdf (last accessed 18 August 2007).

Worth, N., 'The Significance of the Personal within Disability Geography', *Area*, Vol. 40, No. 3, 2008, pp. 306–314.

Young. I. M., *Justice and the Politics of Difference*, Princeton, NJ: Princeston University Press, 1990.

Zola, I. K., 'Toward the Necessary Universalizing of a Disability Policy', *The Milbank Quarterly*, Vol. 67, Suppl. 2.2, 1989, pp. 401–428.

Zola, I. K., *Missing Pieces: A Chronicle of Living with a Disability*, Philadelphia: Temple University Press, 2003.

7

Geography and Personality of Region: The Context of Culture

A. B. MUKERJI

As far back as the Stone Age, humankind has been inquisitive about its environment. Over a period people identified themselves with the land they occupied. With bounded lands they encountered elements created by nature and sooner or later, filled the area with elements they themselves created out of elements that existed independent of them. Geography as a formal discipline and an informal engagement, had, as its principal concern, the acquisition of knowledge and understanding of an identified and identifiable land area. Geography is always interested in evolving methods of exploring the land and creating an image of it.

These images, created through protracted encounters with the land and of real and perceived configurations, may be designated the personality of the region. Thus, the personality of a specific region can be conceptualized – firstly, through the perceptions of the inhabitants and their mode of living that has evolved to weave through the myriad moods of seasons and ecological subtleties such that the habitat can no longer be understood apart from the habits of the inhabitants, and secondly, through the interaction and synthesis in the minds of geographers, historians and archaeologists.

A Brief Overview of the Origins of Personality Studies of Regions

A survey of the extant literature on the theme clearly reveals two varieties of contributions. The first variety of research comprises a small section that is explicit in the use of the term 'personality' in their titles. In contrast, the second variety might be considered 'implicit personality' studies as these do not use the term personality in their titles or in their texts but are developed through the technique and are set in the mould of the explicit personality studies. The number of publications in the second category is very large and only a few examples could be given in this discussion for the purposes of illustration and understanding.

A literature search reveals only 11 contributions that belong to the first group (Fleure, 1921; Blache, 1928; Fox, 1938; Sauer, 1941; Subbarao, 1958; Summers, 1960; Daniel, 1964; Evans, 1973a, b, c; Dunbar, 1974), making Fleur and Blache the pioneers of such work. There could be some more of these contributions because scholars who developed their synthesis of a specific region might still be publishing in journals and books that belong to a variety of disciplines in addition to geography. The 11 papers mentioned here have been published in periodicals, serials and books, and are not easy to track down and the reason is cited below.

In India, certainly unaware of Sauer's ideas, Deshpande published 'Western India' (1948), hailed by many discerning critics as classic research that reminds one constantly of the spirit of 'personality' studies. Perhaps his sources of inspiration and influence were largely Vidal de la Blache and Jean Brunhes, even though he was quite familiar with the research and writings of the Poona group of archaeologists. Another Indian example is provided by Mukerji (1986), who described the 'region of seven sisters' (Assam, Meghalaya, Nagaland, Tripura, Mizoram, Manipur and Arunachal Pradesh) as bound together by the fact that their peripheral location in northeast India looks beyond the boundaries than towards the Indian core. Culturally, they belong to different groups but their location holds them together. Mukerji (1986) develops this view with Kniffen's ideas at the back of his mind, and considers the unity of at least six of the seven states as stemming from their opening onto the Brahmaputra Valley.

There are many papers that are inspired directly or indirectly by the concept 'identity' or 'personality', always implicit but not difficult to search out. In many papers on cultural ecology, cultural landscapes or cultural geography, one can discover the original concept of personality that is organized around the people, their traditions and their territorial organizations. Singh and Khan (1993) provide an appealing example from India. Several of the papers included in Fox (1977) can be considered as 'personality' studies. The Indian examples are far fewer than those from France, England, Ireland and the United States (US). Good regional interpretations that are not based on analysis but on synthesis would answer to the description of 'personality' studies. For example, Dhussa (1990) in which Awadh, the setting of Premchand's short stories and novels is described, or Delhi (Dhussa, 1988) or Mourne Country (Evans, 1967), where the descriptions basically hinge on landscapes and social life.

Kniffen in particular influenced Mukerji (1986) and Singh and Khan (1993), the latter two being fully aware of Sauerian ideas and the role of history, folk-culture, modes of living and traditional social–territorial patterns. Singh and Khan's work must be considered an excellent example of the personality concept of a rather inaccessible, special region in which the Meos have pursued a distinctive way of living for the last five centuries in such a way that Meos have become identified with the Mewat area and vice-versa. Few examples of such brilliant conceptualization exist in the corpus of the geographical literature of India. Undoubtedly, this is the only penetrating study of the cultural geography of a specific, well-known but not well-understood region of India that has been developed within the mould of 'personality' studies where the authors are unaware of the personality concept but are eminently successful in illustrating personality ideas.

Nature of Personality of Region

We can do well to give a quotation from Sauer's 1941 paper on the 'personality' of Mexico in order to initiate our discussion on what exactly is the nature of the personality of a region. Sauer wrote:

> The designation 'personality' applied to a particular part of the earth embraces the whole dynamic relation of life and land. It does not deal with land and life as separate things but with a given land that is lived in by a succession of peoples who have appraised its resources for their times in terms of their capacities and needs, who have spread themselves through it as best suited their ends and who have filled it with the works that expressed their particular way of life. (Sauer, 1941, pp. 353–354).

The necessity for discussing the nature of the concept of personality is simply that it has never been attempted before and also because it helps in understanding the elements that constitute the personality of a specific region and the methods to capture it. We also wish to suggest that there must be a general nature of the concept that appealed to historians, pre- and post-historians, archaeologists, historical–regional geographers, archaeologist–geographers and geographers of folklore, all of whom have contributed to the growth of this genre regardless of the discipline they belong to. All of them were tied together by the historical evolution of culture–habitat relationships in specific areas.

Sauer's statement throws light on the nature of personality that he conceived and used. Still, it is not easy to fully comprehend its nature. To add to our difficulty, it has been argued by Buttimer (1978) that personality and *pays* (fr.: region) became so deeply rooted in the minds of geographers and ordinary folk that the concepts eventually assumed the nature of charisma, as indeed was the case of *Le Geographie Humaine* in which the seeds of the concepts lay deeply embedded.

It can be suggested that the personality of a specific region may or may not be real. Whether it now appears elusive to the scholars having a mindset of positivism or seems difficult to comprehend to those who are absorbed in the imperatives of immediacy, the personality of *paysage* had exercised a powerful hold on the thinking of French geographers and populace for nearly a century. These inhabitants had an objective correlative for personality; it certainly was not a mental construct. Its reality was thinly veiled by historical evolution and this veil could be lifted by scholarly study.

Personality studies are, in essence, historical geography. Its reality has been demonstrated in one small evocative paper, 'To know the Land and Its People' (Kniffen, 1960, pp. 20–23). Kniffen's 1963 paper (pp. 291–299) further strengthens it. When it comes to word-painting of a real scene, there can be few parallels to the one provided by Demangeon (1927), whose haunting word-painting of a part of the British Isles described the brooding silence, the rustling and whispering of heath grass and the chirping of a bird or two breaking the prevailing loneliness. In a similar mode, perhaps one can convey the sense of the landscape of fear; that of Lahaul and Spiti, one of the best examples of the high cold deserts of the Himalayas. The sense of isolation, being pitched against howling winds, sliding mountains, the vastness of the space where the mountains pierce the skies is overwhelming – the land is dead, no flower blooms and no bird flies. This is a region that is numbing to the senses. One slowly freezes to death, mentally and physically. This is a region where one is faced with the relentless pounding of primordial energy. Word-painting was more than enough to bring out the reality of the personality.

It must now be clear that personality is not holistic in the usual Hartshornian sense that is produced by integration of the elements that constitute a region. One can emphasize that the process of integrating is incongruous with the idea of personality of a region. The process of synthesis in the 'personality' has underpinnings of Vidalian philosophy with regard to the relation between people and their milieu. No such philosophy is discernible in the case of regional integration. 'Personality' is different from 'character', which is the Hartshornian designation of a region, if not altogether a dogma. The difference is further accentuated by the fact that all 'personality' studies are based on the usage of the term 'personality' in the region or '*pays*' itself and is further demonstrated through substantive research. Finally, in all such studies the regions are identified and their contents are organized around a single historical-cultural element. Consider how Sauer weaves the personality of Mexico around silver mining or Stanislawski around viticulture in the widest sense.

It is clear from our discussion that there is no particular objective in identifying and portraying personality. The French geographers wrote on small regions more for scholarly delight than to solve any particular problem faced by the region at the time. Indeed there is delight in pure scholarship that is inspired and initiated by any theme that catches our eye and captures our imagination and not by the imperatives of exigency. Secondly, as Vidal suggested, all studies of 'personality *paysage*' were meant to, when claimed explicitly or implicitly, to illuminate the relationship of society and milieu. The readers of such texts were most often intelligent or aware groups, laypersons, curious individuals and scholars representing many disciplines and many branches of geography, including physical geography, who found in each such study a compact and succinct treatment of the physiography of the region. There was a wide readership of such writings, especially in France of Vidalian times and also in England and Ireland.

Personality Making Elements

There are a large number of elements that together constitute personality. These elements have been embedded in personality till the time a scholar arrives on the scene and starts the process of discovering personality. There are clearly two types of elements, those that are largely the endowments of nature, and others that are created on the landscape. Both the elements are perennially in a state of flux and can be observed and recorded. The endowments of nature mostly undergo changes very slowly and imperceptibly. When culture groups enter a specific region, they change both natural and human affects during their occupancy. Such changes would represent their technological capabilities and their needs mainly dictated by their traditions, traditional habits and value systems. Each successive historical succession has indeed left markers on the ground, the so-called relict features. Drained marshes (*Acacia arabica*) of Holland, woodlands in the former forestlands, sal (*Shorea robusta*) and sheesham (*Dalbergian sissoo*) in the Shiwalik hills tell us of the efforts of culture groups to modify or transform the natural endowments. In identifying and synthesizing the personality of a region, the geographer is continually encountering the relict features of natural endowments and human elements. Sauer's phrase 'cultural landscape' and 'natural landscape' easily answer these conditions of change and modification. Elements that were once part of a region's personality have now disappeared and new elements have appeared in their place. The vast unbroken narrow stretches of tall grasslands infested with tigers, and elements that characterized the *terai* of Uttar Pradesh and Bihar till the 1940s now no longer exist; instead we have large plantations of sal, sheesham and bans (*Dendro calamus strictus*). One can only succeed in reconstructing the past and discovering the personality of the *terai* that has at least partly disappeared from the land through archival records, the British Settlement report, forest reports, the relic forests in scattered patches, folk tales and memories in the minds of Tharus and Bhokshas (the indigenous inhabitants of the *terai*). One must remember that there are many elements of personality formation that are fixed natural endowments, such as terrain, climate and natural boundaries, whose significance depends on their assessment by different culture groups in their times, and their meanings change as a response to historical processes and events.

Location and Extent

Of the two kinds of locations, mathematical and relative, it is only the latter that plays a role in personality formation. Examples can be drawn from around the world of how relative location has gone into the making of personality. In India we have the examples of Sunderbans and Meghalaya. Sunderbans is located between the rivers and distributaries of Bangladesh and West Bengal. It projects as a vast cone upwards to the north, piercing the northern Gangetic Plain of West Bengal and is fronted by the treacherous canyons and shoals of Bay of Bengal to the south. There has been no east–west movement through the Sunderbans; the relative location has enabled the preservation of the life that originated in an uncharted past. Its relative location is the basis of its isolation and for its development into a cultural–ecological region. Meghalaya, a big chunk of peninsular mass breaking away from its parental body in the geological past, has a unique relative location. The southern Brahmaputra plain, a narrow strip with turbulent streams like Kopili penetrating into the body of the plateau through narrow fingers of alluvium, forms the state's northern margins; while the vast Brahmaputra and its ever-changing channels run along the western scarp of the plateau, terrifying humans and nature in equal measure. Silchar Valley separates it from Nagaland in the south and Manipur in the east. Its relative location has bred and sustained the quality of isolation for a long time in a larger spatial context where influential changes through the centuries have been characteristic. The continuing quality of separateness has allowed the Garo, Khasi and Jaintia tribes to develop and continue to speak Garo (Assamese–Burman language family), Khasi (Austric language family), and Monkhmer language family that originated in the Thailand plateau. Meghalaya's personality is tribal in nature. Brittany in France could be another good example. Here the relative location of the region in the central part of hills and valleys is joined by the Breton Massif in the east of France and the sea that invades through the indented coast into the land where for long the people have continued to speak Breton, a language that belongs to the Celtic language family. Here again, the isolation caused by topographic inaccessibility has led to the formation of a unique personality, much as the personality of Wales. In the case of Chile, the country is fronted all along its length by the Pacific Ocean to the west and shielded by the backdrop of the mighty, inhospitable and inaccessible Andes to the east that shut it off from the enormous hunks of land of Brazil and Argentina. Its strip-like attenuated shape, and its frontage and backdrop have shaped its personality.

An important feature of relative location is that at some places, at certain stages of development, it might determine whether the area plays the role of culture hearth and centre of diffusion. Mexico's relative location facilitated its playing the role of culture hearth in the cultivation of cereals and vegetables, maize, tomato and as a centre of diffusion, beyond the Pacific to Mexico and beyond the Atlantic to India and Africa. In a brief but succinct manner, Kniffen (1951, p. 585) relates the relative location of Chile, without ever referring to its personality, to the southward movement of the Spaniards in the fourteenth century (Santiago was founded in

1542). The Spanish imprint on the landscape still persists; most of the monumental buildings are of Spanish design and Spanish is the common language throughout the country.

In India, one can think of two contrasting examples. The mountainous region of Ladakh, one of the earliest and most powerful culture hearths of Buddhism and preserver of the Lamaist traditions, has a unique personality which has been formed by, *inter alia*, its enormous extent. Goa, in sharp contrast, is a tiny region that has long played the significant role of the culture hearth of Portuguese culture, and an important centre of diffusion for the cultivation of maize, potato, tobacco and a whole series of crops first grown in Latin America. Due to its small size the region displays a remarkably uniform Portuguese cultural landscape that has shaped its personality.

What about physiography? Certainly it also plays a part in personality formation. Kniffen (1951, p. 585), in portraying the personality of Chile provides a compact treatment of its physiography that almost prompts one to discover its personality. Again, in his paper on the lower Mississippi Valley, Kniffen (1980) provides a comprehensive discussion of the natural landscape that includes physiography, climate, vegetation, wildlife and the river systems. Even this kind of pointed description of the natural landscape, including some historical reconstruction, has helped shape the personality of a region. In his classic essay on Mexico, Sauer (1941, p. 35) does not provide a treatment of physiography separately but weaves in its lineaments and mineral-related colonial activities in an inimitable manner that characterizes his writings, reflective and laced with historical features of the areas. Sopher's paper (1977) on Rohilkhand and Awadh describes in detail the features of the region's earlier physiography including the marshlands that in historical times prevented the flow of people between the two states and allowed them to develop independent of each other. Rohilkhand and Awadh, on the basis of historical evolution, social structure, modes of production and occupancy patterns, stood as different entities even though they are separated by social gradients. Awadh, a largely Hindu area that was the hearth of Bhars and Chandravanshi Rajputs, developed in innumerable alluvial basins separated by tracts of flood-free interfluves, while Rohilkhand, much of it a vast, inhospitable and uninhabited *terai*, was the heartland of Rohilla Afghans who spent most of their time fighting battles. Physiography provided the setting in which culture groups worked out their destinies and established their distinctive occupancy patterns. Physiography of a region provides a basis for setting of cultural areas and their evolution; some of these areas grow into culture hearths and others have helped their spread during the historic times: such a spread also sets the direction and speed. In the description of personality the cultural processes during historical times are found to be inextricably related to physiographic features.

The paper by Singh and Khan (1993, pp. 151–155) does not include the word 'personality' in its title but suggests that both the authors are aware of Sauer's Mexico and Fox's Britain. The paper provides a brilliant discussion of the ecological niches and physiography whose lineaments, when necessary, are interwoven with culture and historical processes. Physiography, in their portrayal, emerges as one of the basic elements that shapes the personality and constructs the cultural geography of Mewat, an extremely well defined culture-ecological area. The Aravallis receive pointed attention from them as do the valleys and ridges of the topography, the valleys functioning as the interaction corridors and the ridges as the interaction barriers. They highlight the correspondence in the landscape of *pals* and *gotra* (clan sub-structures) and individual valleys. Physiography in their discussion is related to historical processes of peopling and culture growth. Beyond doubt, it is not environmental determinism but the physiography that is an integral part of Mewat's personality. With the physiography is also interwoven the climatic details, the native vegetation, the quality of soil and land for agriculture, and the availability of water. When reading this paper, one is distinctly reminded of Sauer's treatment of Mexico.

Primeval and Original Vegetation Cover

It is now well known that nowhere on the earth does one find primeval vegetation except for some remote and inaccessible places. Humans have modified and altered the original vegetation cover by one technique or another to the extent that today much of the original cover has been replaced by one that is very largely cultural. It is still natural vegetation but so many events of invasion, replacement and succession have taken place that the species diversity might have either been increased or decreased and new species have colonized the changed vegetation cover. This natural vegetation cover in many cases has contributed to the personality of a region. How does it contribute to personality? Firstly, it is an element of the natural landscape that in itself is a personality-forming element. Secondly, the cover directs the process of clearing and occupancy in a particular pattern. Thirdly, the natural vegetation cover determines the limits of cultivation and forestry in the largest sense. Utilization or non-utilization of the natural vegetation cover is, by itself, an interesting question that is relevant to personality formation. As in the discussion of the other three elements we shall now provide examples to demonstrate how natural vegetation cover enters the process of personality formation. The best examples, of course, come from India. We have already mentioned the Sunderbans delta, an amphibious landscape of land and water which is inextricably laced with distributaries that are in different stages of decay and death. It is given a unique personality by vast forests of mangrove which are almost completely inhabited by *sundari* (*Haritiera fomes*) species. It is, essentially, a one-species forest. The forest is sufficiently dense and being the natural habitat of the Royal Bengal tigers, thwarted all early occupancy attempts. Similarly, the tall elephant grass that so characterizes the *terai* of Uttar Pradesh and Uttaranchal and Bihar becomes a basis of the personality of the *terai*. Like the Sunderbans region, the *Terai* is haunted by man-eating tigers, and dare-devil elephants (that defy both grass and tigers); such defiance is also demonstrated by two original tribal groups of *Terai*, Tharus and Bhokshas. The *terai* still retains, at least in large parts, its original character that adds to the portrayal of its personality. Outside of India, one encounters the vast loess plains of Great Alfold, the most extensive steppes in the Danube basin, well known as *puszta*. At present, the *puszta* is covered by unbroken stretches of wheatlands, dotted with agglomerate rural settlements scattered through the area. The personality of the Hungarian plains is well underscored by the *puszta*.

The Lineaments of History in the Personality of a Region

Many regions have their personality rooted, *inter alia*, in the lineaments of their history. Without this historical basis it is extremely difficult to fully understand the significance of vicinal location, the processes of the occupation of the land, gaining control over indigenous resources and modification of the original natural and cultural landscapes of the region. Historical lineaments must lead to an understanding of the movement and diffusion through region-specific culture processes. The lineaments are not concerned with the succession of dynasties but with the succession of cultural groups. Rajputs, Muslims, Moghuls and Marathas and later the English were not just ruling political groups, they represented cultural groups, they generated cultural processes in their own times that changed the region of Malwa and its personality. Each succeeding group left its mark on the region, giving it a striking personality. While the process of capturing the control of a region is an important theme, clearly the more substantial feature of the historical configuration is the creation of imprints of the cultural artifacts on the landscapes of a region at specific periods. There are regions that are, relatively speaking, bereft of history; others are intertwined with their historical processes to such a degree that they can easily be described as historical regions. In India, there are many examples – Malwa, Awadh, Rohilkhand, Bundelkhand, Mithila, the Assam Valley, the Kashmir Valley, Rayalaseema and the Thar Desert (also known as Marusthali). Each of these regions has a strong personality that can be discovered or captured, and each region has marked historical lineaments and have been the context of the interplay of historical processes.

The Structure of Rural Society

The structure of rural society would basically refer to the pattern of land ownership or the ownership, control and even use of the means of production, that is, who owns the means of production and who gets to use these means by whatever patterns of relations of production. Secondly, it refers to the social classes that may be traditionally based or to a system in which wealth is acquired by any means that differentiate the classes. Thirdly, it would refer to groups of people inhabiting a region whose personality we are attempting to discover, who can be classified on some identifiable basis.

Singh and Khan (1993, pp. 158 and 161) point out the case of villages in the Mewat region, a culture-area that has a distinctive personality with as many as 13 dominant clans; these do not form classes in the Marxian sense but constitute social groups within the Meo tribe. There is an array of farming, artisan and service castes, all adding to a complex social structure of its rural society. The really striking and noteworthy feature of this social structure is the presence of a large number of clans within one single tribe, the Meo. In the Sunderbans, several castes and the indigenous people and Bangladeshi refugees would be characteristic. Meghalaya, although a totally tribal area by definition, has a structure of rural society that is comprised only of tribes: Khasis in the Khasi district, the Garos in the Garo district, and the Jaintias in the Jaintia district. Within the Khasi tribal society one finds the Siyem (King), the chieftains, the underlords and the Khasi farmers. This is a tribal system to concentrate power in the hands of tribal chieftains and is equally integrated into the system of production. In some regions of India, the structure of rural society is comprised of a vast array of castes, which as a group, can be classified in accordance with the Marxian production organization system into the landowning caste group, artisan caste group, service caste group and labouring caste group. In many areas, even in areas where urbanization and industrialization have made inroads and have seriously impacted the village way of life, one can still observe the continuation and flourishing of the *jajmani* system, essentially a production organization system in which all the caste groups are interlinked and interdependent. On the other hand, in some regions, as in the Gujrot culture region of Haryana, there are very few caste groups; indeed, in innumerable Gujjar villages, there is no other caste than the Gujjars. Within such villages the only perceptible structure is comprised of clans (*gotras*) and lineages. The only difference in status that can be observed here is between clans that came and founded the village and acquired the ownership of the land and water resources, and those who came later and were given land by the founders, who were designated as the dominant clan by Mukerji (1976, pp. 95–115). Some regions are characterized by dominant clans such as the Ahirwal (Ahirwati) or Jatot or Gujrot; others are characterized by the presence of a dominant caste, if the caste dominance is conceived both in terms of the amount of landownership and numerical preponderance, in addition to the social status in the regional caste hierarchy which is integral to the Sanskritic social structure. The personality of a region that is related to a specific social system can be observed in many parts of the country, but caste-structure related regions are specially prominent in northwestern India which includes Haryana, western Uttar Pradesh, parts of Punjab, Jammu, the outer section of Himachal Pradesh and practically the whole of Rajasthan. In most of Rajasthan, there is a repetitive combination of rajputs, brahmins, and businessmen (*jains* and *banias*), but there are regions which are the heartland or the hearth of specific tribes as Meenawati and Mewat. It is surprising that one does not find any discussion on social structure as an element of personality in western writing. On the other hand, in a Muslim-dominated region, such as Rohilkhand, contrary to widespread belief, there is an entire range of professional groups – *dhobi, mochi, bhishti, teli, rangrej, saees* (one who tends horses) and *julaha* among several others. All Muslims are neatly arranged into two groups – *ashraf* (Sheikh, Syed, Moghul and Pathan) and *ajlaf* which is comprised of all the artisan, service, and labour professional groups that correspond to the Hindu caste structure of higher castes and lower castes. The word *jati* is anathema to Muslims but the individual groups have practically all the attributes of Hindu *jatis* and conform to the same. In any discussion of the personality of Rohilkhand one will have to consider the dominance of the Muslims, both in number and power, and their unique social structure. However, in no other large part of India do regions tend to get identified with a specific dominant caste, clan, tribe or tribal-caste as in northwestern India (including Rajasthan), where Nesfield (1931) had classified the dominance of Jats, Gujjars and Ahirs.

Regional Cultural Fabric

The term 'fabric' here would include elements that are part of the personality of a region – linguistic wealth, origin and evolution of culture regions, cultural landscape, deities and festivals, religion including folk religion, and traditional technology. One would like to consider all the material and non-material traits of the regional cultural fabric but such a comprehensive list would be interminably long. The difficulty of selecting a particular element in preference to others is further compounded by the fact that no one element can be used as a surrogate for another element. There would be general agreement that some elements are very specific to a particular region and therefore more important than others in conveying some idea of the personality of a region.

Linguistic Wealth

Language and religion can be considered as the two most important elements that shape both regional culture and the personality of a region. It is through language, the most immediate and universal means of expression, that culture spreads through a region and among the members of a specific culture group so that eventually the language becomes identified with a region and vice versa. Spoken language is the first means of communication. Its basic cultural function, however, is to diffuse a culture and sustain it. In the absence of a comprehensive inventory and distribution pattern of all the material and non-material traits of culture the first solid basis of identifying or constructing them should be considered as the most satisfying, reasonable and rational basis for the culture regions of a large country like India. Even the successively lower-order regions, at least up to the third level, can be identified on the basis of language sub-groups and dialects. The Aryan culture region extending mainly to the north of the Vindhyachal ranges should be considered as the first order, the Hindi culture region is the second order and this is followed in the third level by Bhojpuri, Mithila, Braja and Awadh culture region based as they are on the dialects that are the components of the Hindi language. Such culture regions as those based on language family, language members and the constituent dialects have evolved through history gradually getting interwoven with the regional cults and regional literature and even visual expressions such as cinema. The culture region based on language is always deeply rooted in the historical beginnings of a region and, hence, also has territorial stability and historical continuity. Awadhi, a dialect in which Tulsidas wrote *Ramcharitamanas*, and Braja, the dialect in which Surdas wrote his Krishna poetry (both are poet-saints of the medieval periods of Indian history), are enough evidence of the historical depth of the beginning and evolution of the Awadhi and Brajabhasa dialects of the Hindi language. A similar age can be ascribed to Maithili language in which another great poet-saint of the medieval period, Vidyapati, wrote his cult Krishna poetry. It is Brajabhasa, Awadhi and Maithili that have so greatly contributed to the personality of Braja, Awadh and Mithila. Outside of the Hindi or Aryan culture region, we have a widespread but scattered coverage of the Austric language culture region that is definitely older than all other culture regions of India. Within this larger region we have second-order regions such as the Santhal and Ho regions. Of the two, the Santhal is a very well-defined region with a territory of its own and, more importantly, a very developed culture described as the Santhali culture. Thus, we observe that both the classical (Sanskritic) and the traditional culture regions are found in India, both having deep historical roots.

Dutt et al.'s (1985) work on linguistic pattern of India made an outstanding contribution to the field. A portion of their work has been reproduced in Chapter 16 of this book. Khubchandani (1993, pp. 101–115) in a paper on 'India as a Socio-Linguistic Area', which might as well read 'India as a Cultural-Linguistic Area', argues for the plurality of cultures and hence of languages. It can be asserted that the plurality or a wide spectrum of languages has provided the basis for the emergence of culture regions. We suggest that such culture regions, founded on a single dominant language and a large number of the constituent dialects, be termed as *kshetra*. Historically, such regions appeared on the scene centuries ago when dialects were the main means of communication within their respective group of speakers. Awadhi, Brajbhasha, and Maithili are older than Hindi, that is, the classical higher form of Hindi. As the linguistic-cultural region has many dialects prevailing even up to the present, it represents diversity and not homogeneity. As mentioned earlier, in the culture region based on language the first-order culture region is founded on the dominant language and the second-order regions are founded on the constituent dialects. There is an overarching unity in such linguistic-cultural regions that encompass a variety of dialects, folk religions, cults, and even climate and physiography in such a manner that an inhabitant, for example, of Brajabhoomi will be able to completely understand what is being communicated to him by an inhabitant of Awadh or Mithila, simply because all these dialects share the common linguistic character of Hindi and the concepts of life and land in the largest sense. Nor is a linguistic-cultural region an insular region, as is demonstrated with empirical evidence by Khubchandani (1993); it interacts with other cultural regions, occasionally absorbing through the processes of contact, diffusion and movement, the languages and other cultural traits and in the process introducing a little heterogeneity along the borders of the language-based culture region, but the core remains stable and displays continuity. Khubchandani illustrates this generalisation on the basis of the Konkani culture region. Indirectly, he illuminates one of the basic features of a culture region. Although Khubchandani does not say so explicitly, it is amply clear in his arguments that the dominant language used completely at least in the core area of linguistic-culture region is not the only basis or even the most significant basis for its identification as such. One would have great difficulty in accepting it. Any one who is engaged in identifying or constructing the cultural-geographical regions of India would have no option but to use the dominant regional language in achieving this task. Easily, the most important justification for doing this in India is the known fact that distributions of all the basic material and non-material cultural traits that should go into the making of a culture region and, thereby, of its personality and the distribution and areal coverage for dialects is more or less known with a certain degree of assurance. Also, as is well documented and discussed by Bose (1961), they can easily function as surrogates for the characteristic culture traits or elements that go into the evolution of a culture region and its personality. Bose would rather like to emphasise certain selected material culture traits for the identification of culture regions or areas. What we are arguing for here is a broad congruence or correspondence in cores of linguistic-culture regions and the culture regions founded on the regional distribution of material culture traits. As Bose himself displays, the *chauchala* (four-gabled) pyramidal roof form (four convex gables made of straw and branches, having a low, pointed junction at the intersection of the four walls) practically disappears when one moves from the Bangla culture region of which it is so highly characteristic, and crosses to the Bangla– Bihar culture region border. It is extremely difficult to prove, today, whether the distribution of material culture traits is older or younger to the distribution and evolution of a language that contributes so significantly to the identification of the personality of a region.

Religion in the Making of Personality of Region

Religion is another important element that contributes to the conceptualization of personality of a region, although perhaps a little less so than language. While in each major religion one can find the concurrent existence of several sects and adherents of several reformist religious groups, religion as a whole can still help in discovering the personality of a region, in particular, in two situations. Firstly, in the domain of a major religion there are smaller areas or regions mainly inhabited by people who belong to a branch of this major religion and, secondly, in a country which is overwhelmingly the domain of a major religion there could be or are indeed several other religions, the number of whose adherents is considerable. In both situations, a major religion or a large division of a major religion or a major sect or group of followers could contribute significantly to the evolution of the personality of a specific region. Both language and religion are important elements but their distributional patterns are very complex, hence, generalizations have to be made with great caution. Further, it is very rarely that one strikes upon a region, large or small, which at one particular time has all its population adhering to one and only one religion and that too a major, world-scale religion. Despite all the complexities, examples are available in some part of the world or other which reveal directly or indirectly the dominance of religion, and which show the personality to be woven into the region's dominant religion or its components.

India is overwhelmingly dominated by a single ancient religion both in ethos and number of followers. In a scenario of religious multiplicity on the national scale and diversity of religions at the level of the constituent regions and states, we can easily identify states and regions whose personality is strongly supported by one or the other religion. Let us first consider the Valley of Kashmir, which in more senses than one is an Islamic region, very well defined and delimited by physiography, and with Islam and its behavioural aspects inseparably interwoven into the fabric of the society and all aspects of life. The regional personality is further heightened by the unique Dardic language they speak. In contrast one finds Orissa, preponderantly Hindu in population and entirely Hindu in ethos. It has remained deeply rooted in the Hindu religious and social system since the times of Emperor Ashoka, and even under the rule of the Mughals it remained entrenched in its Hindu character. Islam, then a powerful proselytizing religion, could not make any inroads into the region. Today's Orissa was called the Kalinga Janapada during the Ashokan era and later Vedic and Puranic periods. Orissa and the Valley of Kashmir provide undoubtedly the best examples of the regions whose personality is deeply and extensively permeated by religion. In the Valley of Kashmir, it is the mosques and tombs, the *maqbaras* (tombs), and the typically Islamic terraced gardens (Nishat and Chashmashahi) which organize the space and life of the society. In Orissa the same function is performed by the great temples, small religious places and sites, religious fairs and festivals, and temple-sited periodic markets. In both the regions life revolves around religion. Perhaps no other region in India can claim the same kind of religion-based personality as these two.

Dutt has made a remarkable contribution in identifying religious regions of India. His work in collaboration with Satish Davgun has studied origin, diffusion and spread of religion in India (1979, 1982 and 1985; also see chapter 16). Extending along the northwestern borders and located throughout its length north of the main Himalayan ranges (the Zanskars) lies the trans-Himalayan belt comprising Ladakh, Lahaul and Spiti, a solidly Buddhist region where Mahayana Buddhism or Lamaistic Buddhism has been in continuous practice since ninth century AD. The main Himalayan ranges are pierced by innumerable high passes that remain snowbound for almost eight to ten months a year. The Buddhist region and its description is justified on more than one base. It remains an introverted spatial entity. More than any element that goes into the making of its personality, Mahayana Buddhism acts as the genius loci. Life and land are organized around the monastery. The diurnal cycle and the cycle of the seasons follow the precepts and directions of the Buddhist religion. The region is obviously a westward and southward extension of western Tibet, in physiography, race, religion, language and practically all elements of the mode of living. Traders, transportation and tourists indeed introduced changes but the essentials of life and land remain the same, and the traditional way of living continues. Lamaism, by expressing itself in a myriad of ways and activities, plays a major role in the formation of the personality of the trans-Himalayan region. It promotes a sedentary mode of living where ecologically-sustained crops, including those used in the performance of religious rituals, are preferred in cultivation to any other crops. Simplicity in life is prominently observable. Cattle husbandry based on yak and zebu and related species including hybrids and crossbreeds are widespread; butter is used in the lamps of the monasteries. Pastoralism that originated in Tibet along with all other culture elements and settled agriculture, all having religious roots, have made the region sufficiently distinctive so as to be marked out as a Tibetan culture region (Karan and Mather, 1976, p. 490). In few regions in India does one find such a clear evidence of the relocation of an entire culture-complex that is essentially religious in origin and nature as in the trans-Himalayan belt where its language, religion, and the entire mode of living that originated in Tibet diffused through the high passes into Ladakh, Lahaul and Spiti, and also to a great extent to Sikkim and Arunachal Pradesh. In this region, practically everyone practices Buddhism and speaks and writes the Tibetan language. The *gompa* is the symbol of the continuity of a tradition. In its territorial domain it is the seat of both spiritual and temporal power, giving directions to the laymen and the lamas alike in their daily work pattern. The *gompa* is the immediate seat of learning of religion and the Tibetan language. Already sitting on the highest of the hills and with its vertical development touching the sky, the *gompa* has provided the universally followed model for folk dwellings, all of them being vertical or mountain type of dwellings. Cattle and humans live in the same building. The *gompas* function as institutional nodes (Karan and Mather, 1976, p. 491). Art was developed here, and painting, dance and music had their beginnings and development in its extensive premises. Its own solitude and aloofness from the outer world provided an inspiring ambience for learning. Lamaist Buddhism has generated a characteristic school of painting of *thangka*, displaying glorified and deified lamas, grotesque and bizarre imagery that could frighten, and also of *mandalas* and a large range of paintings on cotton scroll, walls, ceilings and even wood. There is nothing secular in the paintings, they are Lamaist Buddhist in essential character and their purpose is religious. Lamaist Buddhism has another expression, a particular form of music that is very different from any other school of music prevailing in India. Lamaist music reveals the concepts of Lamaism and the legends of the Buddhist epic (Karan and Mather, 1976, pp. 504–505). It is *gompa* music and is played in the monasteries accompanied by the blowing of horns, the beating the drums and cymbals, and a range of other musical instruments. Finally, one is struck by the organized vertical and territorial structure of the *tantricised* Lamaist-Buddhist trans-Himalayan people (Sopher, 1967, p. 63). A paper by Singh (1976, pp. 351–369) illustrates in a most convincing manner the generalization put forth by Sopher. In the paper, Singh analyses the components of the territorial organization of *gompas* in Ladakh, which is equally applicable to the *gompas* in Lahaul and Spiti. This paper illustrates the vertical structure of Ladakhi (Buddhist) society with laymen at the base and the Head Lama or *Kushak* at the top. The middle level is occupied by a group of lamas and *chomos* (nuns) each of them having a clearly assigned function to perform. There is no other area in India that has its personality so deeply founded and rooted in such an ecclesiastical–spatial system as Ladakh, Lahaul and Spiti; the system is at once spiritual and temporal and aims at self-preservation and self-sustenance.

In some areas of the world where the dominant religion has existed for long historical periods, one observes a distinctive landscape that is essentially created by the specific religious faith of most of its inhabitants. Examples can be found in many parts of India and other countries. The Ladakh landscape created by Lamaist Buddhism is dominated by the *gompas*, *chortens*, vertical houses and terraced fields that surround the *gompa*. The Orissa Hindu landscape is dominated by thousands of large and small temples with their *shikharas* (tops) reaching out to the skies, the divine realm.

An emphatic expression of religion in the creation of a culture region and its personality is through a series of pilgrimage centres and the associated landscape features. Pilgrimage, the act of travelling to a pilgrimage centre and worshipping the deity in a house of god located in a sacred space or within a sanctified site is an integral part of many religions–Hinduism, Islam, Christianity, Sikhism, Buddhism and Jainism. In each case there are areas which can be described as holy, sacred or pure regions, a region of pilgrimage in which one finds a heavy concentration of pilgrimage centres, pilgrimage routes, houses of worship, and buildings where the pilgrims stay. The entire culture-complex of pilgrimage spreads over this sacred region. Here one finds sacred woods, gardens (Buddhist *viharas*), rivers, mountains, peaks and even caves. Both Onkareshoara and Kamakhya Hindu deities are established (*staphita*) in caves or in pits, the former in the Ujjaini and the latter in the Gauhati pilgrimage regions; one walks down, and not up, to touch the deities and offer prayers. Innumerable shrines and small temples are scattered through such areas, all connected by ancient pilgrimage routes and pedestrian paths and lined by groves, gardens and pilgrim rest houses (*dharmshalas*), each with a well or by the side of a spring or a stream and a large central open space, the site of meditation. A classic area that answers to this description is Uttarakhand (mainly Garhwal, but also part of Kumaon). The entire area is a Hindu religious region whose personality is almost entirely based on its Hindu character. It is mountainous and the pilgrimage centres are located virtually in every altitudinal belt. It is rightly referred to as *devabhumi* or *tapobhumi* (the land of gods and of meditation). Uttarakhand's religion-based personality is made prominent by the presence of the *tirthas* (pilgrimage centres) dedicated to all the major Hindu deities – Siva, Vishnu and Brahma, the destroyer, the preserver and the creator, respectively (Bhardwaj, 1973, pp. 88–89). Every aspect of land and life in Uttarakhand is rooted in Hindu religion. The landscape bears this out more than any other component. From Haridwar, where Ganga, the holiest of all Hindu rivers, descends onto the plains, via Kedarnath to Rishikesh and Badrinath, everything one observes on land, in people, their activities, their economy, the structures, the roads and the forests proclaim the great sacredness of the region and reflects the ultimate Hindu Khand (realm). Here, every place has a Hindu name, every word is derived from the Sanskrit language, the language of the Hindu scriptures. The rivers and the confluences (*sangamas*) are worshipped at specific *tirthas*. The confluences, termed *prayagas*, are situated on the holy rivers Ganga and Yamuna and their tributaries, such as Devaprayag located at the confluence of Bhagirathi and Alakananda. Similarly, there are five *kedaras* (related to Siva) and five *badris* (related to Vishnu), the most famous of them being Kedarnath and Badrinath. These 15 holy places are all joined to each other by ancient pilgrimage routes, and the entire system accompanied by pilgrimage rest houses and pilgrimage-related structures form the sacred religious region. There is no other example of such a region in India and, perhaps, none in the world. Except for the Mormon culture region which is large and extensive, what we have in most parts of

Europe and India is really the sacred space, a landscape feature that has characteristics which conform to the conception proposed by Yi-fu Tuan (Tuan, 1978, pp. 84–99). Apart from the great differences in dimensions, the religious culture region such as Uttarakhand (now Uttaranchal) has become holy because of its *tirthas* while the much smaller sacred space has to be endowed or sanctified by a religious faith. In the Hindu religion, a mountain peak or a confluence or the point where a holy river descends onto the plains or a forest (*tapovan*) will not, by itself, become a sacred space unless there is a *tirtha* located on it and there are large numbers of interlinked *tirthas* and associated religious landscape features.

Finally, let us briefly consider the role of one special aspect of Hinduism that helps evolve the personality of a specific region. The special theme is that of sacred cows and their *goshalas* and *pinjrapoles* (both homes of the cattle). This absolutely brilliant and original theme has been investigated by Deryck Lodrick (Lodrick, 1981). Lodrick, in discussing the distribution of the *goshalas* and *pinjrapoles* in India very clearly highlights the state of Gujarat as having the maximum concentration of this landscape element (Lodrick, 1981, pp. 31–34). He also points out the convincing correlation between the concentration of the members of the Jain community, all of them rich businessmen and all of them practicing *ahimsa* which in its simplest sense would refer to non-violence. The behavioural expression of *ahimsa* in relation to the phenomenon of *goshalas* is the total avoidance of any food item of animal origin. It would be natural, obvious and logical for the Jains to nourish an attitude of protection towards cows, bovines and even birds, and to contribute generously for the construction of buildings that will be home to these animals when they are old and uncared for. The cow, to the Jain, is the ultimate symbol of sacredness, and protecting them and caring for them when they are old or abandoned is considered to be an act of piety and virtue (*punya*). *Goshala* is a religious institution for the Hindus, Jains and Sikhs alike but the Jains make the largest donations for their maintenance and operation. Also, one cannot forget that the cow is an integral element in the Krishna cult that includes in its distribution practically the whole of Gujarat. Some of the oldest *goshalas* and also Jain settlements can be found in the Kathiawar region of Gujarat, which in turn is linked to ancient ports and convergence of trade routes in the hinterland of the Gulf of Cambay. In addition to the Jains, the business community has played an important role in the dispersal of cow cult and Krishna cult, and the survival and continuity of the *goshalas*. It is logical and not incidental to find the heaviest concentration of the *goshalas* and much later of the Gandhi *Gosadan* (another name of *goshalas*, obviously named after Gandhi, himself a member of the Modh banias and unquestionably the greatest of the believers, practitioners, protagonists and propagators of *ahimsa* in Indian history, and a protector of the cow). Although *goshalas* are found in large numbers in Rajasthan and in small, scattered bunches in the metropolis of Kolkata, they contribute very markedly to the making of the personality of Kathiawar and Gujarat.

A discussion of the role of language and religion in the making of a region's personality strongly affirms that they are the most powerful personality elements, language more so than religion since the followers of the same religion living in different regions speak different languages. The Muslims of the Kashmir Valley speak Kashmiri, a part of the Dardic language family; those of Kerala speak Malayalam, a member of the Dravidian language family; and the Muslims of Bengal speak Bengali, which is part of the Aryan language family. However, in regions differentiated on several other element complexes, religion plays a very significant role. All other elements, such as those encapsulated by the mode of living, crops, fruits, type of agriculture, land tenure, agricultural or occupational implements, handicrafts, house types, rural settlement types, modes and vehicles of transportation can go together or separately in the making of the personality of a specific region, but the difficulty in using them has reduced their value in the understanding of a region's personality. Their repetitive occurrence or distribution, for one thing, limits their use for this specific purpose. Apart from these elements, there is landscape, which can be put to greater effect in the portrayal of personality.

Landscape

Since 1928, when Carl O. Sauer published his seminal paper 'The Morphology of Landscape' (Sauer, 1928, pp. 19–54), the phenomenon or element of landscape in the portrayal of areas or regions had been gaining increasing importance. When we consider landscape we are really referring to this humanised landscape, although the existence of a natural landscape, partly on land and entirely in the premises of landscape morphology, cannot be denied.

Within India, practically no geographer has cared to portray the landscape in a research paper except the solitary paper that deals with the Telengana rural landscape (Mukerji, 1964, pp. 100–126). This landscape, developed over the last thousand years with the settling of the farmers from coastal Andhra Pradesh who were practicing paddy cultivation on incipient terraces and along the valley bottom of the streams that were dammed in a particular physiographic context, displays a high degree of stability and continuity and occurs repetitively over the entire Telengana region. Three basic components have been discussed here – field landscape, settlement landscape and house types. At a later time, serious research was attempted on the Shiwalik hills rural landscape (Mukerji, 1976, pp. 95–115). In yet another paper, the same author applied the methodology and basic concept of cultural ecology to the study of rural settlements of the Chandigarh Dun (Mukerji, 1982, pp. 337–354). Much of the uniqueness of the cultural landscape is established by a careful study of the field pattern, settlement types and settlement pattern and also by a clear evidence of their repetitive character over a considerable part of the Dun, sufficiently enough to enable us to suggest that its personality is to some extent formed by the cultural ecology and landscape of the region. Indian geographers and social scientists have not only ignored the study of personality of India's immensely varied spectrum of regions but also of a more richly rewarding array of landscapes, both cultural and natural, and have, on the other hand, invested so much of their time, energy and intellectual effort on the transient and temporary questions of regional identity, which are in their very premise political in nature.

That India has a vast wealth of unique regional landscapes is a fact far too obvious to be stressed. But the fact that hidden within these regional landscapes are much of its history, culture, mode of living, and indeed all other personality forming elements is not readily understood. Anyone who has travelled widely from Srinagar (Kashmir) to southern-most Kanyakumari, and from Dwarka on the western coast to Kamakhya (Gawahati, Assam in the extreme northeast), would be struck by the immense variety of landscapes. All four of the five basic theme clusters can be applied to the study of these landscapes (culture, culture history, culture area, culture ecology and culture landscape). The Kerala landscape that provides the basis for its unique personality is related to the plantations on the hills and paddy and coconut groves on the coastal plain, with settlements without an apparent boundary merging one into the other as a continuous line of homes, each of them sitting in their own green garden. Unending miles of parallel linearity, the coast line, the coast plain, the settlements, the roads, the houses, and the plantation-covered hill slopes – the landscape is compelling. Contrast this with the stark barrenness and overwhelming solitude and silence of the Marwar desert plains. After plains, few and small settlements situated near the holes or pits of water sitting on the clay pans underlining the sand exist; with a small number of unbounded fields and almost no cultural landscape features. There are few features in the cultural landscape, the list of which might not even be one-fourth of what we observe in Kerala. Quite clearly, the immediate reason for the difference in the personality of the two regions is the unforgettable difference in their landscapes.

Capturing the Personality of Region

After a lengthy but not surely a complete discussion of the elements that form the personality of a region, it would be but logical to attempt an understanding of the ways of capturing the personality of a region. Essentially, these ways would be historical and cultural that would involve the prominent lineaments of ecology in an equal measure. One could suggest, a priori, the following ways of reaching the goal – (i) lineaments (ii) painting (iii) folklore (iv) regional religious cults, deities and festivals (v) folk life (vi) sculpture and handicrafts (vii) dance (viii) regional languages and dialects. Of the eight ways we here propose the fourth and the eighth have already been discussed in some measure to be accepted as surrogates of these ways. The third and fifth can be merged into a more meaningful category of folk life. The seventh way, dance cannot have an application outside of India. Even within India we have regional forms or schools of dance but the regions are highly restricted. We do not have a distinctive form of music that characterizes a particular region only, neither do we have distinctive schools or forms of dance for each and every region or culture area of the country. Kathakali is typical of Kerala as Kuchipudi is of Orissa or Bharatanatyam is of Tamil Nadu and Andhra Pradesh. But artists belonging to different language (linguistic) states can practise and become the exponents of one or the other forms of classical dance and music. Not all the cultural regions or areas of India have a unique form of dance or music. On the other hand, there are forms of regional folk dances and music (Bihu of Assam, Garba and Dandiya of Gujarat and Bhangra of Punjab) that correspond to the pan-Indian system of festivals and cycle of seasons. These forms do not fit into the major forms of classical dances that might even point to unity in India (Chaki-Sircar et al.,

1982, pp. 147–165, also see Chapter 19 of this book). In classical music of India one can recognize two semi pan-Indian schools, the Karnataka and Hindustani, but within each there are innumerable *gharanas* (families) that have distributions that completely disregard regional boundaries. Most curiously the principal exponents of a *gharana* that belongs to Hindustani music might have spent his entire life in the region of the Karnataka school of music. The great schools of music (Karnataka and Hindustani) have their major exponents from among all kinds of religions and all kinds of language groups. This is significant. The domain of Hindustani music spreads across linguistic boundaries. Some of the greatest exponents of Hindustani music are Muslims. The greatest of them all, Ustad Alauddin Khan (of Maihar), was a Bengali Muslim and Bhathande and Paluskar were Marathi Brahmins. The Karnataka school is certainly more rigid and orthodox, its major exponents are mostly Hindus and a majority of them are upper-class Brahmins. These details illustrate that music and dance are of little help in capturing the personality of a specific region. Of all the folk culture elements, perhaps only folk art has received high scholarly attention of two geographers, E. C. Mather and P. P. Karan (Mather and Karan, 1982, pp. 165–195), reproduced in Chapter 18 of this book.

In complete contrast to Constable and Turner, we have the schools or *gharanas* (families) of paintings that have been discussed with great affection and empathy by Sopher (Sopher, 1986, pp. 3–9). Sopher's immediate aim was to use these paintings for a deeper understanding of the nature of place in India. Indirectly, however, the paintings that he used and the analysis he attempted contributed to capturing the personality of the Rajasthan culture area. Some of the paintings used by Sopher belong to and intend to portray specific regions of Rajasthan such as Mewar, Marwar, Haraoti specifically represented by Bikaner, Udaipur, Bundi, and Deccani paintings. The paintings reveal the royal or noble domestic architecture, the animals (horse and cow), the Rajput fabric with regional prints, Rajput dress, banana plants, curvilinear gable roof forms, and lastly, human figures arranged in sequence of distances and with objects in their hands that unmistakably convey the hierarchical social structure, along with a very clear separation of a rural–urban landscape in the background, full of houses, buildings and a watchtower very clearly separated from the former by a belt of large trees with dense foliage. The larger number of female characters in all the paintings would suggest a yearning of the Rajput society to have a large number of women around, even though the actual practice among them is to have their number reduced by one means or other.

There should be no doubt that the principal and the most effective way of capturing the personality of a region is through the humanistic understanding, perception and interpretation of creative literature. Regional literature, novels, short stories, poetry and essays serve our purpose best. In order to answer the question as to how literary geography or simply regional literature helps us in capturing the personality of a region, we may refer to the earlier discussions in this paper on the nature of personality and the nature of region in personality studies. Briefly, in both, the paramount emphasis is on individual perception and subjective evaluation of a region in its totality, helping in the understanding of the personality of a specific region. Creative literature involves both the processes and thus leads us to our purpose of capturing the personality of a region.

It is not our purpose to discuss such themes as landscapes in literature (Salter and Lloyd, 1989, pp. 1–32), and image and substance (Noble and Dhussa, 1990, pp. 49–65), since our purpose is to evaluate the capacity and the extent to which literature helps us in capturing the personality of a region, mainly the regions drawn from India and some from other parts of the world. The roots of this kind of study are found in 'the best geographer has never disregarded the aesthetic qualities of landscape to which we know no other approach than that of the subjective' (Sauer, 1925, p. 48). He further argues that 'the task of geography is conceived as the establishment of a critical system which embraces the phenomenology of landscape, in order to group in all its meaning and colour the varied terrestrial scene' (Sauer, 1925, p. 25).

Types of scenarios (landscapes and region's visible manifestations) have great influence on literature (Geike, 1970, pp. 58–59). A whole genre of studies sprung up to illustrate the generalizations proposed by Wright on the place of imagination in geography (Wright, 1947, pp. 1–15; Baker, 1931, pp. 257–269; Darby, 1948, pp. 426–443; Paterson, 1965, pp. 146–152; Spolton, 1970, pp. 88–96; Pocock, 1978; Alexander, 1986, pp. 38–49; Tuan, 1985, pp. 56–60; Salter, 1981, pp. 142–155; Aiken, 1979, pp. 331–348; Dhussa and Bhardwaj, 1988, pp. 33–40; Dhussa, 1990, pp. 95–108; Salter, 1978, pp. 69–83; Tuan, 1978, pp. 194–206; and Singh, 1985, pp. 291–318; Dutt, Ashok K. and Ramesh Dhussa, 1981; Dutt, Ashok K. and Ramesh Dhussa, 1983).

Several points may be noted from the very thin bibliographic reference corpus presented here. Since our concern here is with region and its personality, we have not included any reference on studies on urban images and geographical interpretations of novels dealing with urban life and landscapes. We have not been able to include references in non-English research publications. All the research articles included in the references have been published by geographers who are broadly familiar with the general concepts of cultural geography and humanistic geography. They have interpreted the novels and poetry and their perception of regions with depth and convincing familiarity. Many questions will remain – the absence of a paper on the Lake District of Wordsworth's poetry, a specific region on the land is ignored; why could the Indian geographers not research on Brindabanlal Verma's Bundelkhand novels (*Jhansi Ki Rani, Garh Kundar, Virata Ki Padmini* and *Mrignayani*), or Mohar Singh Yadav's *Panjar Dharti* that deals with a specific region, Rahr of Alwar (Rajasthan)?

Conclusion

In delineating the background of the concept of personality a path of historical analysis was taken. Three sub-concepts, origin, diffusion and the use of the concept of personality were discussed in detail. Originating in the early twentieth century in France with Vidal de la Blache, his philosophical and regional formulations of *pays*, genre de vie, habitat and the inhabitants, and the concept of personality of region were soon implanted in England. The concept was proposed and applied first in geography and then had an independent origin in archaeology and claimed as its practitioners both archaeologists and geographers. In addition, it was reinterpreted so as to include folk life. Thus, it has had three beginnings – geography, archaeology and folk culture. The network of diffusion from the source of geography has been both wide in space and deep in time; Vidal's influence of '*personalite*' can be seen in a writing from more recent times. Diffusion from archaeology and folk studies has spread through geographers more than through archaeologists. The most striking feature of the history of the concept of 'personality' is the persistence of its original meaning as endowed by Vidal and his contemporary, Fleure in England. It was '*totalite*' undoubtedly but it was comprehended by perception, reflection and synthesis of the objective reality. Personality studies acquire excellence only by dealing with a cultural region in its most comprehensive meaning.

Throughout the entire discussion, at one point or the other, we have emphasized the stability of the personality of a particular region. Indeed, this is its most significant quality and is almost entirely based on the stability of patterns of elements that constitute personality over long historical periods ranging from eight to ten centuries. The character of the region largely explains it, which as we have emphasized is a culture region that shares a regional culture. Internal developments and adoption and assimilation of externally originated elements characterize this. Physical-geographical elements do not change, or change very slowly; the elements of cultural origin, on the other hand, might change perceptibly over shorter periods of time but the patterns, relative to each other, persist. This is more true of religion, language and art. Hence, the personality of a region displays a striking continuity.

Since the studies by geographers engaged in 'personality studies' are hinged on a culture region, it is but logical that they would attempt to capture the personality not through the analysis of data in a mechanical way that is supported by techniques and methodologies of positivistic approach. Culture elements, traits and trait complexes cannot be clubbed together mathematically since their interrelationships are not functional or empirical but genetic. One of the alternative ways of regional analysis is to reflect on the perception of the painters and novelists. Literature, of the two, is more important. Within the field of creative writing that comprises the core of the corpus of literature, novels can help us best in capturing the personality of a region. This genre of writing expresses the novelists' deep perceptions of the natural and cultural landscapes of a culture region.

The detailed discussions on the nature of personality, the history of the use of the concept of personality, the elements that constitute personality and the methods of capturing the personality of a region have been able to establish that the personality of a region is ingrained in it and is not contingent upon the immediacy of externalities and therefore scholarship related to the theme is relevant to itself. Unlike the current concern for the 'identity of a region' that is a response to the recent polemics of identity, the theme of personality, by itself, does not contribute to the solving of a problem of a region. Its ultimate relevance is to a better understanding of a region and, thus, to a high order of scholarship as was attained by Blache, Fleure, Fox, Demangeon, Evans, Sauer, Stanislawski and Subbarao, the most prominent geographers to have written on the personality of a region.

References

Aiken, C. S., 'Faulkner's Yoknapatawapha County, Geographical Fact into Fiction', *Geographical Review*, Vol. 67, 1977, pp. 1–29.

Aiken, Charles S., 'Faulkner's Yoknapatawpha County: A Place in the South', *Geographical Review*, Vol. 69, 1979, pp. 331–348.

Aiken, Charles, S., 'A Geographical Approach to Faulkner's "The Bear"', *Geographical Review*, Vol. 71, 1981, pp. 446–459.

Alexander, David, 'Dante and the Form of the Land', *Annals, Association of American Geographers*, Vol. 76, 1986, pp. 38–49.

Baker, J. N. L., 'The Geography of Daniel Defoe', *Scottish Geographical Magazine*, Vol. 47, 1931, pp. 257–269.

Berdoulay, V., 'The Vidal-Durkheim Debate', in Richard Peet and Marwyn Samuels (eds.), *Humanistic Geography*, Chicago: Maroufa Press, 1978, pp. 77–91.

Bhardwaj, Surender M., *Hindu Places of Pilgrimage in India*, Berkeley: University of California Press, 1973.

Blache, Vidal de la, *Tableau de language Geographie de language France*, Paris: Librairie Hachette, Vol. 1, No. 1, 1903.

Blache, Vidal de la, *The Personality of France*, London: Alfred Knopf, 1928.

Bose, N. K., *Peasant Life in India: A Study in Indian Unity and Diversity*, Calcutta: Anthropological Survey of India, 1961.

Bowen, E. G., 'Le Pays De Galles', *Trans. Inst. of British Geographers*, Vol. 26, 1959, pp. 1–25.

Brunhes, Jean, *Geographie Humaine de language France*, Paris: Librairie Plon, 1920.

Buttimer, Anne, 'Charisma and Context: The Challenge of Le Geographie Humaine', in Richard Peet and Marwyn Samuels (eds.), *Humanistic Geography*, Chicago: Maroufa Press, 1978, pp. 58–76.

Cohn, Bernard S., 'Regions Subjective and Objective: Their Relation to the Study of Modern Indian History and Society', in Bernard S. Cohn (ed.), *An Anthropologist Amongst the Historians and Other Essays*, New Delhi: Oxford University Press, 1987, pp. 100–136.

Daniel, G., 'The Personality of Wales', in I. I. Foster and L. Pocock (eds.), *Culture and Environment*, London: Routledge and Kegan Paul, 1964, pp. 7–25.

Darby, H. G., 'The Problems of Geographical Description', *Trans. Inst. Of British Geographers*, Vol. 30, 1962, pp. 1–14.

Darby, H. G., 'The Regional Geography of Thomas Hardy's Wesse', *Geographical Review*, 1964, pp. 426–444.

Demangeon, A., *Iles Brittanniques*, Paris: Librairie Armand Colin, 1927.

Deshpande, C. D., *Western India*, Dharwar: Students' Own Book Depot, 1948.

Dhussa, R. C. and Surender Bhardwaj, 'Delhi as Viewed by Expatriate Writers', *The National Geographical Journal of India*, Vol. 34, No. I, 1988, pp. 33–40.

Dhussa, Ramesh, 'Premchand's Writings: A Gold Mine of Geographic Images', *The National Geographical Journal of India*, Vol. 36: 1990, pp. 95–108.

Dostal, Walter, 'The Shhuh of Northern Oman, A Contribution to Cultural Ecology', *Geographical Journal*, Vol. 138, No. I, 1972, pp. 1–8.

Dunbar, Gary S., 'Geographical Personality', in H. J. Walker and W. G. Haag (eds.), *Man and Cultural Heritage*, Baton Rouge: Louisiana State University Press, 1974, pp. 25–35.

Dutt, Ashok K., and Ramesh Dhussa, 'Novelist Sarat Chandra's Perception of his Bengali Home Region,' *GeoJournal*, 5:1, 1981 pp. 41–53.

Dutt, Ashok K., and Ramesh Dhussa, 'Novelist Sarat Chandra's Perception of Bengalis in Probash (Foreign Lands). A Literary Geographic Analysis,' *The National Geographical Journal of India*, Vol. 29, Parts 3 and 4, 1983, pp. 188–206.

Dutt, A. K., Chandra Khan and Chandra Sanguan, 'Spatial Pattern of Languages in India: A Cultural-Historic Analysis', *Geojournal*, Vol. 10, No. 1, 1985, pp. 51–74.

Dutt, Ashok K., and Allen Noble, 'Religious Diversity Patterns of Rajasthan within an Indian Framework,' *Asian Geographer*, Vol. 4, No. 2, 1985, pp. 137–144.

Dutt, Ashok K., and Satish Davgun 'Patterns of Religious Diversity in Allen G. Noble and Ashok K. Dutt (eds) *India: Cultural Patterns and Processes*, Boulder, Colorado: Westview Press, 1982, pp. 221–246.

Dutt, Ashok K., and Satish Davgun 'Religious Patterns of India with a Factoral Regionalization,' *GeoJournal*, 3:2, 1979, pp. 201–214.

Evans, E. E., *Mourne Country, Landscape and Life in South Down*, Dundalk, 1967.

Evans, E. E., *The Personality of Ireland, Habitat, Heritage, and History*, Cambridge: University Press, 1973.

Evans, E., 'The Personality of Ulster', *Trans. Inst. Of British Geographers*, Vol. 51, 1973, pp. 1–19.

Evans, E. E., 'The Personality of Wales', B.B.C. Radio Lecture, Cardiff, 1973.

Fleure, Herbert, 'Regions Humaines', *Annales de Geographie*, Vol. 26, 1917, pp. 161–174.

Fleure, H. J., 'Countries as Personalities', *The Nature*, Vol. 5, 1921, pp. 573–575.

Fox, Cyril, *The Personality of Britain, Its Influence on Inhabitant and Invaders in Prehistoric and Historic Times*, Cardiff: University of Wales Press, 1938.

Fox, Richard G., *Realm and Region in Traditional India*, New Delhi: Vikas Publishing House Pvt. Ltd., 1977.

Francaviglia, R. V., 'The Mormon Landscape: Definitions of an Image in the West', *Proceedings, Association of American Geographers*, Vol. 2, 1970, pp. 59–61.

Geike, Archibald, *Types of Scenery and their Influence on Literature*, Washington: Kennikat Press, 1970, pp. 58–59.

Hart, J. F., *The Look of the Land*, Englewood Cliffs: Prentice-Hall, 1975.

Hudson, Brian J., 'The Geographical Imagination in Arnold Bennett', *Trans. Inst. of British Geographers*, Vol. 7, No. 3, 1982, pp. 365–380.

Issac, Eric, 'The Act and the Covenant: The Impact of Religion on the Landscape', *Landscape*, Vol. 11, 1962, pp. 12–17.

Jackson, B. K., 'Religion and Landscape in the Mormon Culture Area', in Karl Putzer (ed.), *Dimensions of Human Geography*, Chicago: Chicago University Press, 1977, pp. 100–128.

Jha, Makhan, *Dimensions of Pilgrimage*, New Delhi: Inter-India Publications, 1985.

Johnson, K. B., *Order Upon the Land*, New York: Oxford University Press, 1976.

Jordan, Terry G., *The European Culture Area*, New York: Harper & Row Publications, 1973.

Jordan, Terry G. and Lester Rountree, *The Human Mosaic*, New York: Harper and Row Publishers, 1979.

Karan, P. P. and Cotton Mather, 'Art and Geography: Patterns in the Himalaya', *Annals, Association of American Geographers*, Vol. 66, No. 4, 1976, pp. 487–515.

Khubchandani, L. B., 'India as a Socio-Linguistic Area', in Aijazuddin Ahmad (ed.), *Social Structure and Regional Development*, Jaipur: Rawat Publications, 1993, pp. 101–115.

Kirk, William, 'The Role of India in the Diffusion of Early Cultures', *Geographical Journal*, Vol. 141, No. I, 1975, pp. 19–35.

Kniffen, F. B., *The Primitive Cultural Landscape of the Colorado Delta*, Berkeley: University of California Press, 1931, pp. 43–66.

Kniffen, F. B., *The Natural Landscape of the Colorado Delta*, Berkeley: University of California Press, 1932, pp. 149–244.

Kniffen, F. B., *The Indian Mounds of Iberville Parish*, New Orleans: Geological Bulletin, 1938.

Kniffen, F. B., *Pomo Geography*, Berkeley: University of California Press, 1939, pp. 353–400.

Kniffen, F. B. and Richard Russell, *Culture Worlds*, New York: Macmillan Company, 1951, p. 585.

Kniffen, F. B., 'To Know the land and its People', *Landscape*, Vol. 9, 1960, pp. 20–23.

Kniffen, F. B., 'The Physiognomy of Rural Louisiana', *Louisiana History*, Vol. 4, 1963, pp. 291–299.

Kniffen, F. B., *Louisiana, Its Land and People*, Baton Rouge: Louisiana State University Press, 1968.

Kniffen, F. B., 'Material Culture in the Geographic Interpretation of the Landscape', in Miles Richardson (ed.), *The Human Mirror: Material and Spatial Images of Man* (ed.), Baton Rouge, Louisiana State University Press, 1974, pp. 252–267.

Kniffen, F. B., 'The Lower Mississipi Valley: European Settlement, Utilization and Modification', in H. J. Walker and R. A. Detro (eds.), *Cultural Diffusions and Landscapes*, Baton Rouge: Louisiana State University Press, 1990, pp. 3–34.

Kosambi, D. D., *The Culture and Civilisation of Ancient India in Historical Outline*, New Delhi: Vikas Publishing House, 1977.

Lodrick, Deryck O., *Sacred Cows, Sacred Places*, Berkeley: University of California, 1981.

Mather, E. M. and P. P. Karan, 'The Geography of Folk Art in India', *India: Cultural Patterns and Processes*, Colorado: Westview Press, 1982, pp. 165–195.

McIntire, William, *Prehistoric Indian Settlements of the Changing Mississippi River Delta*, Baton Rouge: Louisiana State University, 1958.

Meinig, D. W., 'Introduction', *The Interpretation of Ordinary Landscapes*, New York: Oxford University Press, 1979, pp. 1–7.

Meinig, D. W., 'Geography as an Art', *Trans. Inst. of British Geographers*, Vol. 8, No. 3, 1983, pp. 314–329.

Morgan, F.W., 'Three Aspects of Regional Consciousness', *Sociological Review*, Vol. 32, 1938, pp. 68–88.

Mukerji, A. B., 'Cultural Landscape of a Telengana Village: A Morphogenetic Study', *Geografia*, Vol. 3, No. 1, 1964, pp. 11–42.

Mukerji, A. B., 'Rural Settlements of the Chandigarh Siwalik Hills: A Morphogenetic Study', *Geografiska Annaler*, Vol. 58B, No. 2, 1976, pp. 95–115.

Mukerji, A. B., 'Cultural Ecology of Rural Settlements in the Chandigarh Dun Region', in Allen G. Noble and Ashok K. Dutt (eds.), *India: Cultural Patterns and Processes*, Boulder: Westview Press, 1982, pp. 337–354.

Mukerji, A. B., 'The Region of the Seven Sisters: A Distant View', *Indian Geographical Journal*, Vol. 61, No. 1, 1986, pp. 1–12.

Neruda, Pablo, *Selected Poems*, New York: Grove Press, 1961, pp. 12–13.

Nesfield, J., *Brief View of the Caste System of the Northwestern Province*, Allahabad: Government Press, 1931.

Noble, Allen G. and Ramesh Dhussa, 'Image and Substance', *Journal of Cultural Geography*, Vol. 10, No. 2 1990, pp. 49–65.

Onaki-Sircar, Manjushree and Parbati K. Sircar, 'Indian Dance: Classical Unity and Regional Variations', in Allen G. Noble and Ashok K. Dutt (eds.), *India: Cultural Patterns and Processes*, Colorado: Westview Press, 1982, pp. 147–165.

Paterson, J. H., 'The Novelist and his Region: Scotland through the Eyes of Sir Walter Scott', *Scottish Geographical Magazine*, Vol. 81, 1965, pp. 146–152.

Planhol, Xavier de, 'L'Islam dans la physiognomie geographique de la Peninsule Iberique', *Revue Geographique des Pyrennes et du Sud-Ouest*, Vol. 63 : 1962, pp. 274–281.

Pocock, D. C. D., *The Novelist and the North*, Durham: University of Durham, 1978.

Pockock, D., 'The Novelists' Image of the North', *Trans. Inst. of British Geographers*, Vol. 4, No. 1, 1979, pp. 62–77.

Price, Edward T., 'Viterbo: Landscape of an Italian City', *Annals, Association of American Geographers*, Vol. 54, 1964, pp. 242–275.

Raza, Moonis, 'Extent and Boundaries of Sube Awadh: 1560–1605, A Study in Historical Geography', *The Geographer*, Vol. 12: 1965, pp. 21–28.

Rees, Ronald, 'Constable, Turner, and Views of Nature in the Nineteenth Century', *Geographical Review*, Vol. 73, No. 3, 1982, pp. 253–269.

Salter, C. and W. J. Lloyd, *Landscape in Literature*, Washington: Association of American Geographers, 1969.

Salter, Christopher, 'Signatures and Settings: One Approach to Landscape in Literature', in Karl W. Butzer (ed.), *Dimensions of Human Geography*, Chicago: Chicago University Press, 1978, pp. 69–83.

Saltar, Christopher, 'John Steinbeck's The Grapes of Wrath', in D. C. D. Pocock (ed.), *Humanistic Geography and Literature*, London: Croom Held, 1981, pp. 142–155.

Sankalia, H. D., *Studies in Historical and Cultural Geography and Ethnography of Gujarat*, Pune: Deccan College, 1949.

Sauer, C. O., 'Conditions of Pioneer life in the Upper Illinois Valley', *Illinois State Geological Survey,* Bulletin 27, 1916, pp. 153–163.

Sauer, C.O., 'The Morphology of Landscape', *University of California Publications in Geography*, Vol. 2, No. 2, 1925, pp. 19–54.

Sauer, C. O., 'The Barrens of Kentucky', *Kentucky Geological Survey*, Vol. 6, No. 25, 1927, pp. 123–130.

Sauer, C.O., *Prehistoric Settlements of Sonora*, Berkeley: University of California Publications in Geography, 1931.

Sauer, C. O., *The Road to Cibola*, Berkeley: University of California Publications in Ibero-Americana, No. 3, 1932, pp. 1–38.

Sauer, C. O., 'The Personality of Mexico', *Geographical Review*, Vol. 31, 1941, pp. 353–354.

Sauer, C. O., 'Foreword to Historical Geography', *Annals, Association of American Geographers*, Vol. 31, 1941, pp. 1–24.

Sauer, C. O., Homestead and Community on the Middle Border', *Landscape*, Vol. 12, No. 1, 1962, pp. 3–7.

Sauer, C. O., 'Status and Change in the Rural Midwest – A Retrospect', *Austrian Geographical Society*, Vol. 105, 1963, pp. 357–365.

Singh, Harjit, 'Territorial Organisation of Gompas in Ladakh', *Himalaya, Centre National de la Recherche Scientifique,* Paris, 1976, pp. 351–369.

Singh, Jaipal and Mumtaz Khan, 'The Cultural Landscape of Mewat', in Aijazuddin Ahmad (ed.), *Social Structure and Regional Development*, Jaipur: Rawat Publications, 1993, pp. 151–181.

Singh, Rana P. B., 'The Personality and Lifeworld of Varanasi as Revealed in Shiv Prasad Singh's Novel, A Study in Literary Geography', *National Geographical Journal of India*, Vol. 1, 1985, pp. 291–318.

Spolton, L., 'The Spirit of Place: D. H. Lawrence and the East Midlands', *East Midlands Geographer*, Vol. 5, 1970, pp. 88–96.

Sopher, David E., *Geography of Religions*, Englewood Cliff: Prentice-Hall, 1967.

Sopher, David E., 'Rohilkhand and Oudh, An Exploration of Social Gradients Across a Political Frontier', in Richard G. Fox (ed.), *Realm and Region in Traditional India*, New Delhi: Vikas Publishing House, 1977, pp. 281–307.

Sopher, David E., 'Place and Landscape in Indian Tradition', *Landscape*, Vol. 29, No. 2, 1986, pp. 3–9.

Stanislawski, Dan, *The Individuality of Portugal*, Austin: University of Texas Press, 1959.

Stanislawski, Dan, *Portugal's Other Kingdom, The Algarve*, Austin: University of Texas Press, 1963.

Stanislawski Dan, 'Dionysus Westward: Early Religion and the Economic Geography of Wine', *Geographical Review*, Vol. 65, 1975, pp. 427–444.

Subbarao, B., *The Personality of India*, Baroda: Baroda University Press, 1958.

Summers, R., 'Environment and Culture in Southern Rhodesia: A Study of the Personality of a Land-locked Country', *Proc. Amer. Phil. Society*, Vol. 104, 1960, pp. 266–292.

Tuan, Yi-Fu, *Space and Place*, London: Edwin Arnold, 1977, p. 86.

Tuan, Yi-Fu, 'Sacred Space: Explorations of An Idea', in Karl Butzer (ed.), *Dimensions of Human Geography*, Chicago: Chicago University Press, 1978, pp. 84–99.

Tuan, Yi-Fu, 'Literature and Geography: Implications for Geographical Research' in David Ley, et. al., (eds.), *Humanistic Geography*, Chicago: Naroufa Press, 1978, pp. 194–206.

Tuan, Yi-Fu, 'The Landscapes of Sherlock Holmes', *Journal of Geography*, Vol. 84, 1985, 56–60.

Tuan, Yi-Fu, *Topophilia*, New York: Columbia University Press, 1990.

Tuan, Yi-Fu, 'Realism and Fantacy in Art, History, and Geography', *Annals, Association of American Geographers*, Vol. 80, No. 3, 1990, pp. 435–447.

Watson, J. W., 'The Soul of Geography', *Trans. Institute of British Geographers*, N. S. 8, 1983, pp. 385–399.

West, Robert C., *Cultural Geography of the Modern Tarascan Area*, Washington: US Printing Office, 1948.

West, Robert and John P. Augelli, *Middle American, Its Lands and Peoples*, New Jersey: Prentice Hall, 1968.

West, R. C., *The Mining Community in Northern New Spain, The Parral Mining District*, Berkeley: University of California Press, 1949.

West, R. C., *Colonial Placer Mining in Colombia*, Baton Rouge: Louisiana State University Press, 1952.

Wright, J. I., '"Terrae Incognitae", The Place of the Imagination in Geography', *Geographical Review*, Vol. 37, 1947, pp. 1–16.

Zelinsky, Wilbur, 'Generic Terms in the Place Names of the Northeastern United States', *Annals, Association of American Geographers*, Vol. 45, 1955, pp. 319–349.

Zelinsky Wilbur, 'An Approach to the Religious Geography of the United States, Patterns of Church Membership in 1952', *Annals, Association of American Geographers*, Vol. 51, No. 2, 1961, pp. 141–147.

Zelinsky, Wilbur, *The Cultural Geography of the United States*, Englewood Cliff: Prentice Hall, Inc., 1973, p. 21.

8

Social Planning: A Spatial Perspective

FRANK J. COSTA

The boundaries of social planning are very elastic. In its broadest sense, social planning is concerned with collective action taken to create better living conditions and a brighter future for individuals and groups viewed from this perspective. It encompasses a vast range of activities that are difficult to examine in their totality. Thus, it becomes useful to adopt a specific focus to examine social planning and social planning issues. The focus adopted in this review is spatial or geographic. The intent is to analyze the spatial dimension of selected social planning initiatives within a specific social context – urban society.

Social Planning Issues

As stated earlier, the range of social planning concerns is vast and contains a multitude of sub-areas and issues. These include – (i) racism and sexism, (ii) ageing, (iii) child care and education, (iv) housing, economic opportunity and social justice, (v) public health, (vi) public safety and crime, and (vii) quality of life issues including access to cultural and leisure benefits.

Each of these sub-areas or issues has a spatial component. For example, racism and ethnicity are often reflected in segregation patterns. Economic opportunity may be limited in certain geographic areas. Public health indicators may vary by geographic regions and crime patterns frequently exhibit a particular spatial pattern.

Architectural or Physical Determinism

Addressing social planning concerns from a spatial perspective frequently involves the adoption of an architectural or physical determinism argument. This is the 'built form' version of environmental determinism. In its main outline this argument posits the thesis that specific types of built form configurations or designs (which can be either spontaneous or planned) of neighborhoods and cities can result in improved behavior patterns of their populations.

This argument has provided the intellectual basis for a large number of planning theories and policies including Howard's Garden City, the Pullman experiment in Chicago, post World War II British New Towns and most famously, large-scale high-rise public housing developments of the 1950s and the 1960s both in America and Europe. A parallel and related argument holds that spontaneously created urban forms can also have a beneficial impact on people. New urbanism idealizes the European village and the small nineteenth century American towns as models for new development. Jacobs (1961) attributed the safe conditions of early twentieth century ethnic neighborhoods in large American cities to their village-like character in which most residents were involved in neighbourhood social life. She developed her famous 'eyes on the street' argument to account for the healthy social life and safety of these areas.

The scale of environmental intervention depends to a great extent upon the prevailing political philosophy of a specific place or period. Socialist or welfare-state governments proposed and carried out plans for massive changes in the physical form and, consequently, the social make-up of their societies. The transformation of the urban and regional geographies of the United Kingdom (UK), Sweden and the Netherlands during the 1950s and 1960s is testimony to the political strength of the architectural or physical determinists. In the United States, on the other hand, powerful conservative forces prevented the realization of large-scale public intervention in the urban and regional fabric. Change did occur but it was dictated primarily by private forces. Urban renewal and suburbanization resulted in the reorganization of the physical space of cities and regions but these were largely directed by private rather than public initiative.

The Re-Emergence of Spatial Concerns in Social Policy: An Analysis

In the 1950s and 1960s many scholars predicted the eventual demise of 'place' communities because of the improvements underway in communication and transportation. People would find the need for geographic propinquity to services and social activities superfluous because those improvements in communication and transportation would overcome the impediments imposed by space and distance. The Webbers in their important essay on 'Culture, Territoriality and the Elastic Mile' saw perceptions of space as related to social class. They hypothesized a continuum of need for geographic propinquity, which was bounded on one end by intellectual elites whose primary group affiliations were not based on kinship, ethnicity, nationality or place of residence and at the opposite end working class groups, whose primary group affiliations were based upon these very factors. Society was evolving in a way favouring the growth of non-place communities at the expense of place communities. The Webbers voiced a concern that public policy as articulated by intellectuals would ignore the needs of increasingly marginal communities (Melvin and Webber, 1967).

In recent years, a different perspective on the importance of place or physical space has taken hold. There has been a resurgence of concern for 'roots' and 'place', especially among the intellectual and economic elite who were supposed to be in the forefront of the creation of 'non-place' communities. 'Gentrification' of architecturally and historically significant older neighbourhoods and the growth of exclusionary zoning practices in many suburban communities bent upon preserving their 'special' character are evidence of this new concern for space (Appleyard, 1981).

Geographers and land use planners continued to attach great importance to space in the creation of social communities even when it was out of style with many sociologists and psychologists. Berry's (1973) concept of a 'mosaic culture' at the base of urban and regional spatial organization and Chapin's (1956) theory of land use are extremely important aids in understanding the social forces underlying spatial form. Berry describes the emergence in the US, of 'a society with a number of parallel and distinctively different lifestyles'. These divergent groups occupy different parts of the urban or regional setting thus creating a 'mosaic' of internally homogeneous communities (Berry, 1973). For Chapin (1956) the observable urban land use pattern results from certain kinds of actions, which, in turn, are derived from particular sets of values as shown in Fig. 8.1.

Implicit in both the Chapin and Berry perspectives is the importance of social groups in the creation of visible urban form. We can 'read' a

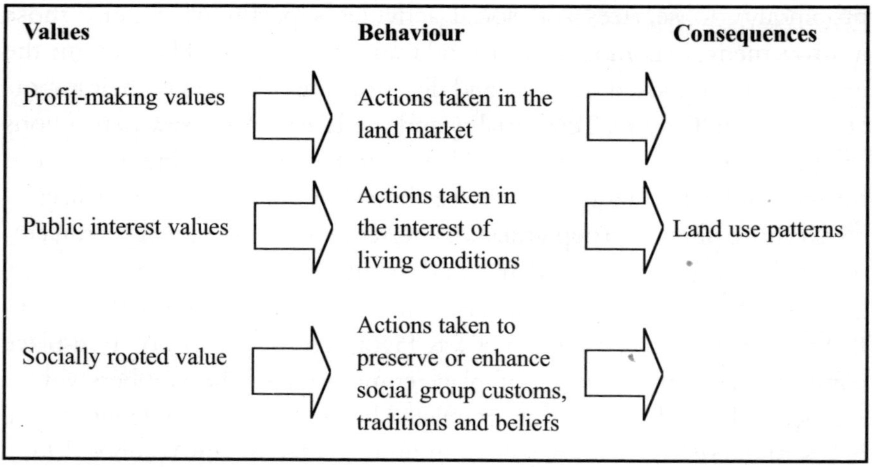

Fig. 8.1 Value/Behaviour/Consequence.

city's social characteristics through careful interpretation of its physical condition. This is essentially the domain of social geography.

Origins of Modern Social Planning

The emergence of the uniquely different industrial town during the eighteenth and nineteenth centuries marked a watershed in the history of human settlements. Nothing before resembled the physically vast, densely populated and terribly polluted environments of these towns. Earlier theories and concepts about cities were of no help in understanding these new conditions.

Eventually, a new body of social theory was created to explain the impact of these new settlements and to predict how they would change human society. In general, these theories described a bleak future of increasing size for cities and decreasing strength of rural or small-town based traditional ties and allegiances. People within cities would become cut off from their traditional social group moorings. Eventually, this social isolation would produce negative psychological consequences. Durkheim even foresaw an increase in the suicide rates for those living in cities. Most social theorists predicted increasing levels of crime and other forms of social deviance. Social planning as a professional movement in modern society owes its origins to the environmental conditions and related social theory of this time.

Emergence and Development of American Social Planning

The growth in the size of both rural and urban populations in the early nineteenth century set into motion some of the first social assistance programmes. Among the most important of these was poor relief, which attempted to provide public subsidy for the poor and the destitute. Most of these early relief programmes assumed a distinction between the 'deserving' and 'undeserving' poor. Deserving poor were in poverty through no direct personal fault. They included the handicapped, the blind, the mentally ill, and in some cases the aged. Poor relief programmes of the period sought to remove, or at least alleviate, their condition of poverty through a variety of mechanisms, most notably through the asylum or poorhouse.

Another means by which public expenditure and public action in the realm of social policy got underway in the pre-Civil War period was through the creation and development of the public school system. Later in the century, and especially after the Civil War, when America's industrial expansion caused great growth in cities, a number of new social programmes were initiated. Among these was the settlement house movement, which sought to work with immigrant families and poor rural migrants to teach them American values on one hand and to adapt to life in crowded cities on the other hand. The settlement house movement had a direct impact on the introduction of organized recreational programmes in urban areas. Public and privately sponsored playgrounds were established in crowded city neighborhoods to provide a wholesome outlet for the physical energies of urban youth.

An important mid-nineteenth century development prefigured on an even larger physical scale, the later playgrounds and settlement house movement. This was the successful policy of creating large urban parks, a policy typified by Central Park in New York City. Here, as with playgrounds, the rationale was based on providing space for wholesome and socially permissible forms of recreation. The arguments used in support of Central Park's creation were especially interesting. The urban poor if denied the amenity of public open space would direct their hostile energies towards the urban middle class and the wealthy. Central Park could act as a social pressure valve, permitting the release of the pent-up frustrations of the underclass. Housing reform was another mid-to-late nineteenth century social programme aimed at improving the quality of life for the poor and the working class. Here, efforts were made to reduce speculative pressures in land development by forcing landowners to construct apartment tenements in such a way as to increase the amount of sunlight penetrating into a building and to improve the circulation of air through and around tenement buildings. First in New York City, and later in other cities, new building codes were proposed and adopted which restricted 100 per cent lot coverage by requiring open courts within buildings and walls between them.

Settlement House Movement

The early twentieth century saw the proliferation of private, non-profit social service agencies. Many of them were attached to religious organizations and were engaged primarily in poor relief or charity and family services. Very little development in the social services realm occurred until after the Great Depression and most specifically with the New Deal legislation of the 1930s. New Deal legislation is significant for a number of reasons. For the first time in the history of America, the federal government assumed a major role in development and implementation of social policy. Also, the foundations of all subsequent social policy initiatives were laid down at this time. Most significant among these was the Social Security Act of 1935 and the federally-financed public housing programme.

The New Deal era was full of promise in the realm of social planning. Rexford Tugwell's plan for federally-financed new towns was a bold policy calling for the creation of socially and physically balanced communities. The neighborhood unit concept, although developed in the late 1920s, was put into practice during the 1930s. Important examples of incorporating a social dimension into neighborhood planning include Radburn in New Jersey, Sunnyside Gardens in New York City and Chatham Village in Pittsburgh.

With the coming of World War II, public initiatives in social policy development faded. Very little change occurred in social policy immediately after the war except for the much-heralded, but largely flawed, urban renewal programme of the 1950s and 1960s. Most social policy analysts now believe that urban renewal exacerbated social problems by destroying 'place' communities and replacing them with impersonal residential high-rise apartment towers.

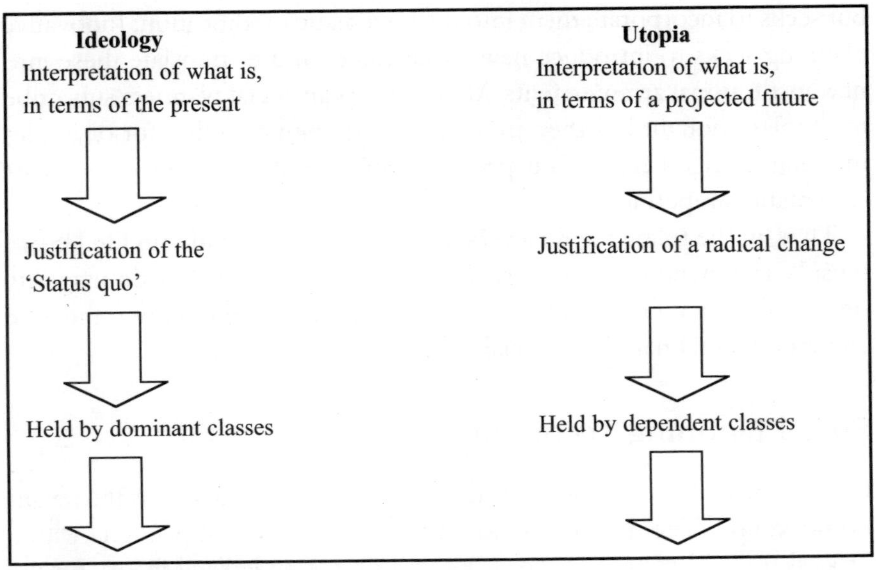

Fig. 8.2 Contrast between Ideology and Utopia.

The most recent set of nationally directed and financed social programmes was the Great Society programme of the mid-to-late 1960s. These programs owe their formation largely to the urban riots of the era which greatly disturbed both national and local leadership of the cities throughout the country. As the violence subsided and middle-class counter pressure increased, even these programmes began to be cut back or eliminated. At the present time, we are faced with a situation in the US in which we continue to find ourselves without a comprehensive social planning policy. Most of the socially-based planning initiatives described earlier owe their creation to the existing political and economic establishment's need to preserve their positions in society. American society, based on the principles of private enterprise and personal initiative, has resisted public sector dominance except in times of emergency, such as during the Depression years of the 1930s.

In his book, *Ideology and Utopia* (1936), Manheim contrasts ideological and utopian thought displayed in Fig. 8.2. Manheim identifies specific planning approaches which derive from each school of thought. Planning allocation is based upon ideological thought while innovative planning is utopian. Ideological thought assumes the continuing validity of traditional social values and norms. It seeks to preserve these through a process of system-wide balancing which takes into account special social concerns but seeks to incorporate them into the systematic modification. Innovative planning seeks to introduce new social values and to translate these into new institutional arrangements. Many American social planners subscribe to utopian thought but they are constrained from planning for or implementing change because our private enterprise ideology prevents major systematic tampering.

Thus, in the following review of social planning activities in the US, we must bear in mind the ideological limitations imposed by American society on social policy development and the consequent non-comprehensive and incremental nature of social planning efforts in the US.

Social Planning Techniques

One of the earliest and most influential social planning device is the neighborhood unit. The neighborhood unit combines physical planning with a process for achieving social goals. Essentially, the underlying theory for the neighbourhood unit is the creation of small-scale social communities in which personal ties among the residents would be strengthened by geographic propinquity and shared use of social and community institutions. A central role is given to the elementary school because the greatest proportion of neighborhood social interaction should occur here.

The theoretical rationale for the neighborhood unit is largely derived from the nineteenth century urban social theory which viewed cities as essentially destructive of social values associated with the idealized small town or rural community. Social theorists realized that the growth of large-scale urban settlements could not be reversed. What they sought to create was a network of small-scale neighborhoods in which social life would approximate the character of the idealized small town. Concurrently, the economic advantages of demographic concentration could also be achieved. In a way, the neighborhood unit concept reflects the 'mosaic culture' concept described earlier. What the proponents of the neighbourhood did not realize was that forces associated with the preservation of social group identity were actually creating a series of small-scale communities or neighborhoods without any planning intervention.

A more recent adaptation of the neighborhood unit concept is found in the work of Costa and Noble (1986) on Saudi Arabian cities. They propose an approach to urban design and planning which combines the conscious creation of small-scale communities within the framework of the modern town. The small-scale communities can be viewed as cells within a network of modern transportation and communication linkages. Thus, a resident can reside in the relative social security of his 'place' community, yet still take advantage of the economic life of the larger town. Although proposed by Costa and Noble for Arab towns where traditional family-centered social values are of great importance, the concept can be adapted to urban communities in other cultures as well.

One of the most interesting experiments in social planning in the US was the 'equity' planning programme developed in Cleveland by Norman Krumholtz in the early 1970s. Krumholtz and his planning staff saw the residents of the city as victims of an 'exploitative planning process' in which the local interests of an increasingly impoverished and non-white central city lay within an affluent and largely white urban region. He was opposed to the construction of the urban freeway, which in his view destroyed city neighborhoods for the sake of increasing vehicular mobility of suburban commuters. He opposed the City of Cleveland's financial support and tax abatements for a major new office complex in the Central Business Distinct (CBD) because its benefits would accrue primarily to its developers and its costs would be borne by city residents. These two examples demonstrate that its costs would be borne by city residents and also demonstrates the 'equity' or 'advocacy' positions taken by the planning staff (Krumholtz, 1982).

In retrospect, the Cleveland equity planning program did not succeed, primarily because Krumholtz failed to establish political coalitions of sufficient strength to guarantee its success. The Cleveland equity planning approach is permeated with the values and goals of social planning and for this reason it is an effort of historic significance. For the first time a major city sought to improve the physical and economic conditions of its citizens through planning by extracting financial concessions from more affluent suburban constituencies and wealthy public utilities.

Defensible Space

An important spatial adaptation intended to avoid problems of social pathology and to provide for a safe living environment is often referred to as 'defensible space'. Proponents of this spatial planning technique argue that urban crime is a social problem amenable to reduction or in some cases, eradication through space manipulation and design. Their premise is that the gradual de-personalization and de-collectivization of urban space result in unsafe or crime-prone areas or districts within cities. Traditional urban space or neighborhoods, such as those described by Jacobs in the *Death and Life of Great American Cities* and Gans in *The Urban Villagers* have largely vanished from most cities. Within these enclaves a sense of common origins and common economic conditions worked to create a sense of community. Most people tended to know one another and 'looked out' for each other. These spatial communities were, in essence, *gemeinschaft* cells within a larger *gesellschaft* setting of the city. The economic and social mobility associated with advanced societies has largely destroyed these vestiges of 'small town' or *gemeinscahft* life.

However, the need for physical security associated with place remains and a new branch of social planning has evolved to meet this need. This is 'defensible space'. Essentially, 'defensible space' involves the physical reorganization of existing space or the creation of new space to reduce or eliminate the incidence of anti-social or criminal behaviour.

Oscar Newman, a pioneer in the development of the concept, compares two geographically adjacent public housing projects in St Louis, the Pruitt-Igoe homes made up of high-rise apartment buildings in a park-like setting and the smaller Carr Square village composed of two-storey row houses in a conventional city block setting (Newman, 1995). While Pruitt-Igoe, soon after its construction, began to fall into physical disrepair and social chaos, the Carr Square village survived as a safe and healthy enclave in an otherwise decaying district. Newman attributes this disparity in outcome to the physical design and organization of each development. Pruitt-Igoe lacked a clear demarcation between public and private space. People living there had no sense of identity with or control over their space. Residents of the Carr Square village, on the other hand, had a greater sense of control over their space. Reasons for this include minimizing the amount of public space in favour of a carefully delineated set of private spaces. Each household had control over its own back and front yard areas. People felt a sense of ownership over these private spaces as opposed to the lack of 'propriety feelings' among residents of Pruitt-Igoe.

Defensible space advocates argue that design solutions which give residents a sense of ownership and control over their own space as well as the common spaces of their neighborhoods will, in the long run, make for safer conditions. Thus, space manipulation is at the base of the 'defensible space' movement. In a way this can be described as the reintroduction of *gemeinsehaft* social values in an otherwise spatially ill-defined and physically dangerous urban environment.

New Urbanism

The rapid growth of the new urbanism movement is testimony to the dissatisfaction of segments of the building industry and the design community with the persistent pattern of sprawl and unplanned decentralization occurring in most American metropolitan areas. As noted earlier, private sector forces have worked to create a transformation in the American landscape. Vast, dispersed tracts of development serviced, almost exclusively, by private automobiles have become the American development paradigm. Critics lament the monotonous 'sameness' that characterizes most of this development. Regional distinctiveness and local uniqueness have been lost, which, they assert, has destroyed a 'sense of place'. As Stein once said about Oakland when visiting from San Francisco – "There is no there there".

New urbanists propose an alternative to sprawl which emphasizes the creation of physically contained neighborhoods of housing, parks and schools placed within walking distance of shops, civic or local service and mass transit. Mass transit networks are the framework for the region and tie together its various parts with an efficient system of buses and trains. If we examine the theoretical roots of new urbanism we quickly discover that most derive from repackaged old ideas. Paramount among this is garden city theory and neighborhood planning, especially Clarence Perry's neighbourhood unit concept which treated the urban neighborhood as the building block for the city and region. Kunstler identifies eight specific factors that under gird *New Urbanism* (Kunstler, 1996). These are: (i) The neighborhood is the primary unit for planning, (ii) Each neighbourhood should be limited in size and should have well defined boundaries, (iii) Secondary units for planning are urban corridors which function as both lines of communications and boundaries and districts or special use areas, such as CBDs or industrial zones, (iv) The neighborhood should contain a mixture of land uses, not just different residential types but also compatible services and commercial uses, (v) Buildings should be aesthetically designed and should help to define public space, (vi) Streets should be designed to facilitate movement within neighborhoods and, of equal importance, to deter movement through neighborhoods, (vii) Urban design principles including the use of terminating vistas and the incorporation of pockets of green space within neighborhoods should be encouraged, and (viii) The application of architectural design standards to the entire neighborhood should be encouraged to facilitate an aesthetically harmonious development.

Conclusion

New urbanism is the most recent and most discussed new development in the spatial approach to social planning. Many of its basic tenets are borrowed from earlier ideas and techniques. Aspects of the garden city theory and the neighborhood unit concept and Lynch's theory of city image can be found in the eight factors listed above. Additionally, a certain disdain for the city and an appreciation for the small town or village traceable to nineteenth century social theory permeates new urbanism.

Throughout all of these various approaches a common thread of thought is evident and that is spatial manipulation impacts the psyche of people. The approaches discussed here are intended to have a 'beneficial' impact. They are all exercises in social engineering and reflect the underlying ideology of environmental determinism.

References

Appleyard, D., 'Place and Non place, the New Search for Roots', in J. de Neufville (ed.), *The Land Use Debate in the United States*, New York: Plenum Press, 1981.

Berry, B. J. L., *The Human Consequences of Urbanization*, New York: St. Martin's Press, 1973, pp. 64–66.

Cafferty, P. J., 'Planning for Diverse Human Needs', in F. S. So and I. Stollman (eds.), *The Practice of Local Government Planning*, Washington, DC: International City Management Association, 1979, pp. 507 and 509.

Chapin, F. S., *Urban Land Use Planning*, Urbana: University of Illinois Press, 1965.

Costa, F. J., and A. G. Noble, 'Planning Arabic Towns', *Geographical Review*, Vol. 76, No. 2, 1986, pp. 160–172.

Jacobs, Jane, *The Death and Life of Great American Cities*, New York: Vintage Books, 1961.

Krumholtz, N., 'A Retrospective View of Equity Planning', *Journal of the American Planning Association*, 1982, pp. 163–183.

Kuntsler, James Howard, 'Home From Nowhere', *The Atlantic Monthly*, 1991, pp. 43–66.

Mannheim, K., *Ideology and Utopia, Chicago: International Library of Psychology*, Philosophy and Scientific Method, 1936.

Melvin, M. and C. C. Webber, 'Culture Territoriality, and the Elastic Mile', in W. Eldredge (ed.), *Taming Metropolis*, New York: F. Praeger, 1967, pp. 35–53.

Neufville de, J. I., 'Land use a tool for social policy', in J. I. de Neufville (ed.), *The Land Use Debate in the United States*, New York: Plenum Press, 1981, p. 3.

Newman, Oscar, 'Defensible Space: A New Physical Planning Tool for Urban Revitalization', *Journal of the American Planning Association*, 1995, pp. 149–155.

Perry, C. A., 'The Neighborhood Unit, A Scheme of Arrangement for the Family Life Community', *Monograph 1, Neighbourhood and Community Planning, Regional Survey of the New York and its Environs*, New York, Vol. 7, 1929.

Timmermans, J. M. and J. W. Becker, 'Social Planning in the Netherlands: Organization and Practice', in A. K. Dutt and F. J. Costa (eds.), *Public Planning in the Netherlands*, Oxford: Oxford University Press, 1985, pp. 87–106.

III
Social Geography from a Global Perspective

9

Regional Patterns of Spanish-Language Newspaper Publication in the United States, 1848–1992

MAURA E. HUNTZ AND ROBERT B. KENT

Population data from the decennial census of the United States (US) can provide a reasonable picture of the changing distribution of people of various Hispanic origins in the country during the last 150 years. Beyond simply enumerating population distributions, some census data, like home ownership and language spoken at home, do provide a sense of the degree to which Hispanics have settled permanently in particular regions and the extent to which they have maintained important cultural traditions such as language use. Thus, census data can provide an index to the permanence of Hispanic populations and to their degree of assimilation in the US. However, these data cannot illuminate the degree to which Hispanics have established institutions to maintain and to recreate Hispanic culture in the alien cultural context of the US. To gauge the extent to which Hispanics, or for that matter other immigrant groups, attempt to maintain and recreate their culture in the new cultural milieu, one must examine the extent to which they establish institutions to do so. Typically, social institutions like churches, schools and ethnic clubs fulfil this function, while ethnic-based businesses and the mass media like newspapers, radio and television often play a supplemental role in preserving and strengthening ethnic identity.

More than 50 years ago, in his book, *Spanish-Speaking Groups in the United States*, John Burma (1954, p. 38) predicted that the Spanish-language press in the US would disappear within 15 years. Nothing, it turned out, could have been further from the truth. Burma could not have anticipated the historical forces that encouraged the migration of Spanish-speaking immigrants from many Latin American countries to the US – revolutions and civil wars, economic dislocation and distress, growing awareness of employment opportunities in the US and the decreasing friction of distance. In 1950 Hispanics accounted for about three per cent of the population of the US. In barely 40 years this statistic tripled, reaching almost 10 per cent in 1990. Population projections suggest that by 2050, Hispanics will account for over 20 per cent of the nation's population (US Department of Commerce, 1993, Vol. 2). Rather than disappearing (as Burma had so forcefully suggested), the Spanish-language press in the US has prospered and grown during the latter half of the twentieth century, largely driven by the continuing immigration of Spanish-language speakers from Mexico and other parts of Latin America.

A variety of scholars and writers, ranging from those interested in the history of journalism to those concerned with the Hispanic experience in the US, have examined the Spanish-language press in the country. Studies have examined historical, sociological, demographic, linguistic and business dimensions of Spanish-language newspaper publication in the US (Gutiérrez, 1980; Shoemaker et al., 1985; Guernica, 1982; Veciana-Suarez, 1987). Indeed, as the financial significance of the Spanish-language press has increased in the last decades of the twentieth century, trade journals like *Editor & Publisher, Quill* and *Advertising Age* provide increasingly frequent coverage of the Spanish-language print media.

The geographical dimension of Spanish-language newspaper publication has received little attention in literature. Important among these, however, have been regional studies focussing on specific areas in the US. These include studies focussing on the southwest (Gonzales, 1977), the US–Mexico borderlands (Griswald de Castillo, 1977), states and cities with large Spanish-speaking populations (Chacón, 1977; Oczon, 1979; Trevino, 1991), and the diffusion of the Spanish-language beyond the borderlands into interior states (Smith, 1990). Most recently, a paper has examined the historical geography of the establishment of Spanish-language newspapers throughout the US (Kent and Huntz, 1996).

This research paper examines the regional geography of Spanish-language newspaper publication in the US over nearly a century and a half, from 1848 until 1992. It documents a portion of ongoing research into the geographical manifestations of Hispanic media growth and diffusion currently underway in the US. Specifically, it expands on the earlier research of Kent and Huntz (1996) which focussed narrowly on an examination of the principal historical periods when Spanish-language newspapers were established in the US. In this report, a more regionally-focussed analysis identifies the principal geographical concentrations of Spanish-language newspaper publication during the last 150 years and the historical evolution of newspaper publication within each region. The report also provides an overview of the characteristics of Spanish-language newspapers by region – specifically the publication frequency of these newspapers and their longevity. The study is limited to a consideration of those Spanish-language newspapers published in the coterminous states and territories of the US, and does not include Spanish-language newspapers published in Puerto Rico or other offshore areas once occupied or controlled by the US.

Methodology

The geographical and historical evolution of Spanish-language newspaper publication in the US is established using a combination of source materials. These include several bibliographic publications by scholars of the ethnic and Spanish-language press, notably Rios and Castillo (1970 and 1972) and Wynar and Wynar (1976) as well as trade publications and guides (Ayer and Sons, 1933–1992; Editor & Publisher, 1959–1990; National Research Bureau, 1986; Standard Rate and Data Service, 1988–1992). The time period examined runs from 1848–1992, and data on all Spanish-language newspapers published during this period was tabulated. The search of these materials attempted to establish the years during which each newspaper was published, the specific geographical location of the newspaper and the publication periodicity of each paper – daily, weekly, monthly or other.

The available data are often far from ideal and information on many papers is incomplete. For example, while nearly 600 Spanish-language newspapers were published during the period, information clearly identifying the beginning and ending dates of publication is only available for about a quarter of the total. Similarly, nearly a quarter of the newspapers published are classified as not being published on a daily, weekly or monthly schedule. Many papers may have ended up in this category because it was simply impossible to classify them more accurately based on the information available.

Regional Patterns

Nearly 600 daily, weekly, monthly and irregularly issued Spanish-language newspapers have been published between 1848 and 1992. Using the data provided on the city of origin of each newspaper, seven principal regions can be identified. Four of these regions lie in the southwest – California, Arizona, Upper Rio Grande Valley and Texas, while the rest are found east of the Mississippi – Greater New York City, Florida, and Chicago (Fig. 9.1).

Spanish-language newspaper publication has been most intense in the southwest. In terms of the absolute number of newspapers published, the Upper Rio Grande Valley, running northward from El Paso in Texas to the upper reaches of the river's course in northern New Mexico and southern Colorado, is the most significant. One hundred and eighty newspapers have been published here, and most have been published in or around El Paso, Albuquerque and Santa Fe (Table 9.1 and Fig. 9.1).

Fig. 9.1 Spanish-language newspaper regions of USA.

This area has been one which has been characterized by long standing Hispanic settlements dating from 1600 AD in the north and by the continuing immigration of Mexican nationals, particularly in the south in and around Las Cruces, Mesilla and El Paso.

Table 9.1 Data for publication frequency and years in print of Spanish-language newspapers in the USA by region, 1848–1992.

	Daily			*Weekly*			*Monthly*			*Irregular/Other*			*Total*		
Region	*Mean years*	*No.*	*%*	*Mean years*	*No.*	*%*	*Mean years*	*No.*	*%*	*Mean years*	*No.*	*%*	*Mean years*	*No.*	*%*
California	22	6	4	12	93	62	10	11	7	9	39	26	13	149	100
Arizona	–	1	4	24	20	71	–	1	4	5	6	21	21	28	100
Upper Rio Grande Valley	19	14	8	19	112	62	1	2	1	18	52	29	19	180	100
Texas	29	13	9	12	86	59	3	5	3	13	43	29	13	147	100
Chicago	34	3	16	8	14	74	7	1	5	6	1	5	11	19	100
Florida	28	2	8	17	21	81	5	1	4	10	2	8	17	26	101
Greater New York	45	2	6	11	17	52	16	6	18	8	8	24	13	33	100
TOTAL	25	41	7	15	363	62	9	27	5	13	151	26	15	582	100

Sources: Rios and Castillo, 1970 and 1972; N.W. Ayer and Sons *Directory of Newspapers and Periodicals*, 1933–1992; *Editor and Publisher International Yearbook*, 1959–1992; *Standard Rate and Date – Hispanic Media and Markets*, 1988–1992; *The Encyclopedia Directory of Ethnic Newspapers and Periodicals in the United States*, 1976.

If we consider the number of newspaper foundings in strictly numerical terms, California and Texas are virtually tied in terms of their significance – with 149 and 147 newspapers founded in each area respectively (see Table 9.1 above). San Francisco and Los Angeles in California have been the undisputed leaders, with Spanish-language newspaper publication beginning earlier and lasting longer in these three cities than in any others. Lesser and more recent concentrations have developed in San Jose, San Diego and Calexico. In the last 50 years Central Valley towns, especially Sacramento, Fresno and Bakersfield, have been home to a modest number of Spanish-language papers. In Texas, Spanish-language newspaper publication has been concentrated in the southern portion of the state, notably along the US–Mexico border. In contrast to California, publication in Texas has been focused in a more limited number of centres – major border towns, namely, Brownsville and Loredo and larger interior cities like San Antonio, Corpus Christi, Houston and Dallas/Fort Worth.

Arizona, the fourth area of concentrated Spanish-language newspaper publication in the southwest, stands as an area of limited consequence in contrast to the three other regions. Only 28 newspapers have been founded here, with most having been published in Tucson, a historic centre of Mexican settlement. Phoenix represents a secondary centre, with most other towns boasting Spanish-language newspaper publication being located along the US–Mexico border.

East of the Mississippi River, three smaller concentrations of Spanish-language newspaper publication stand out – New York, South Florida and Chicago. New York City and its environs have the longest history and not unexpectedly, the largest number of papers, a total of 33. The publication of these papers has clearly centered on New York City, although Spanish-language newspapers have been published in northern New Jersey, southern Connecticut, Philadelphia, Boston and even Washington, DC. South Florida has published a total of 26 papers, focussed on two principal nodes – Tampa and Miami. Finally, Chicago represents a third area of significance. The city and its surrounding region, including southwestern Michigan, have been home to 19 newspapers published in Spanish – most established since 1950.

A handful of Spanish-language newspapers, less than one per cent of the total, have been published in cities and states far removed from these regional concentrations. Six papers could not be readily assigned to any of the seven principal regions because of their disparate locations – Washington, Utah, Oklahoma, Missouri and Georgia.

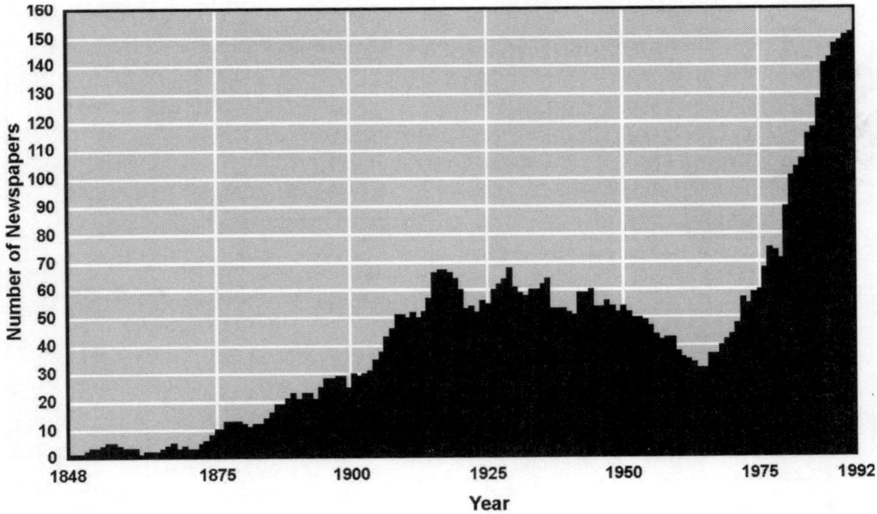

Fig. 9.2 Cumulative growth of Spanish-language newspapers in USA in 1848–1992.

Newspapers in Print

While Spanish-language newspapers were published as early as 1808 in the US, it was not until the end of the Mexican–American War in 1848 that Spanish-language newspaper publication developed serious momentum (Fig. 9.2). Early on, the numbers were few, never exceeding more than ten newspapers in publication in any one year until 1876. In the years that followed, the publication of Spanish-language newspapers increased well into the early decades of the twentieth century, peaking at 68 in 1929. Between 1930 and 1945, the number of Spanish-language newspapers in publication remained fairly constant, hovering around 60 per year. But beginning in 1945, a period of relative decline began. Each year for nearly 20 years the number of newspapers in print decreased, reaching a nadir of 33 in 1965. Since the late 1960s, however, the growth of the Spanish-language press has been dramatic, with the number of published newspapers increasing in nearly every year and standing at 152 in 1992.

Geographically, the pattern of Spanish-language newspaper publication has varied (Fig. 9.3). In the southwest, the publication of Spanish-language newspapers began in the middle of the 1800s, while east of the Mississippi Spanish-language newspapers did not appear until around the turn of that century. Furthermore, the absolute number of newspapers published in Spanish has also been much larger in the southwest than in

Fig. 9.3 Spanish-language newspapers, 1848–1992.

the eastern states. In addition, most of the regions west of the Mississippi have experienced periods of growth as well as decline during the century and a half covered in this study. In eastern US by contrast, Spanish-language newspaper publication remained comparatively insignificant in all areas until the mid-1960s, but has grown steadily in the ensuing three decades (Fig. 9.3).

In the southwest, the profiles of the number of newspapers in print in any one year among the four regions are distinct, indicating the different populations and social histories which have typified in each region (Fig. 9.3). In the Upper Rio Grande Valley, Spanish-language newspaper publication grew steadily throughout the second half of the nineteenth century, reaching a peak between 1910 and 1915 when over 30 newspapers were published yearly. This period happens to coincide with the time New Mexico was admitted as a state into the US in 1912. In subsequent decades, the number declined steadily, dropping into single digits in 1960. By 1975, however, the number had grown to about 10 and has remained relatively constant in the 1990s. In California, continuous, although sometimes limited, growth in Spanish-language newspaper publication has been the rule. Throughout most of the nineteenth century, the number in print in any one year rarely exceeded five, and was often less than five. At the turn of the 19th century, the number jumped to 10 per year and then grew slowly to between 20 to 25 by 1930. For nearly 50 years the number of Spanish-language newspapers in the state remained constant at this level, but tremendous growth occurred from the early 1980s onwards. By the early 1990s over 65 newspapers were published in Spanish in California. In Texas, the newspaper publication pattern represents something of a contrast between the Upper Rio Grande Valley and California. Few Spanish-language newspapers were published between 1848 and 1880, but a slow, steady growth began since 1880. The number of papers in print reached 10 by 1890 and reached a peak of between 25 and 30 between 1915 and 1920. These numbers declined subsequently, but a comparative stability reigned between 1920 and 1960, with the number of newspapers in print in any one year standing between 15 and 20. The 1960s and 1970s represented something of a nadir for Spanish-language newspaper publication in Texas with fewer than 10 papers in print annually. By 1980, this pattern of decline was reversed and the number of papers grew steadily, exceeding 20 in print each year by the early 1990s. In Arizona, Spanish-language newspaper publication has never been very significant, at least in numerical terms. Spanish-language newspapers began to be published in Arizona in 1875, but the number in print only exceeded five in the years between 1920 and 1925 when six were published. In the ensuing decades their numbers slowly declined, and by 1975 no Spanish-language papers were published in the state. By the early 1990s, one newspaper had again begun publishing in Spanish.

East of the Mississippi, all three regions are characterized by a similar temporal pattern of Spanish-language newspaper publication – slow, steady growth throughout the twentieth century (Fig. 9.3). Newspapers published in Spanish appeared first in New York in the late 1890s and the early 1900s in Florida. Chicago lagged behind, with the first Spanish-language paper appearing in 1930. In New York and Florida, no more than one newspaper was published regularly during any one year until well into the 1930s and in Chicago this pattern continued into the early 1970s.

In the late 1960s and the early 1970s newspaper publication in Spanish boomed in all three regions, with between five and ten newspapers in print each year. Growth has continued steadily since the 1970s in all three regions, and by the early 1990s between 15 and 20 Spanish-language newspapers were in print each year in metropolitan regions of Chicago, New York and South Florida (Fig. 9.3).

Publication Frequency and Longevity

A key trend in the publication frequency of Spanish-language newspapers has been the dominance of weekly newspapers (Table 9.1). Weekly newspapers have dominated the Spanish-language press since the 1850s. Over 60 per cent of all Spanish-language newspapers published have been weeklies. Weeklies have also dominated regionally, with every region recording at least half of all papers being published as weeklies. In the New York metropolitan region, weeklies have been the least significant, where they have represented just over 52 per cent of all newspapers in print. Florida stands at the opposite extreme, where over 80 per cent of the newspapers published have been weeklies.

In absolute terms, the number of weeklies published has been greatest in the traditional core regions of the southwest. The Upper Rio Grande Valley has dominated weekly newspaper publication, where 112 have been published. California and Texas follow with 93 and 86 weeklies, respectively. In the remaining four regions, the number of weeklies range between 14 and 21.

The popularity of weekly newspapers may be attributed to the narrowly focussed mission of these publications and the fact that they can be produced inexpensively. Generally, weekly publications focus on community news, public service information and local advertising. Publication costs are often borne by local business advertising which caters to the Spanish-speaking population and the weeklies can often be distributed free of charge at key points throughout the community or city. The weekly format also provides considerable flexibility to the publisher, permitting the paper to vary its length and hence its costs, allowing many weeklies to remain in print for many years.

On an average the publication longevity of Spanish-language weeklies nationally stands at about 15 years, although there are notable regional differences (Table 9.1). The average publication longevity of weeklies in

Arizona and the Upper Rio Grande Valley have been the highest, 23.5 years and 19.1 years, respectively. The average number of years in print has been the shortest in the Chicago metropolitan region, 7.7 years.

Weeklies have continued to represent a significant component in Spanish-language newspaper publication in the US in the 1990s. In 1992, over 90 weeklies were in print across the country and these represented about three-quarters of all Spanish-language newspapers circulating nationally (Table 9.2). The greatest number of weeklies is published in California, where 44 were in print in 1992. Texas followed with 18, while the remaining regions each accounted for ten or less.

Daily newspapers have comprised a small proportion of all Spanish-language newspapers published in the US over the last century and a half, only 7 per cent. Nevertheless, the comparatively small percentage belies their importance. The simple fact of daily publication underscores their visibility and importance in local and regional Spanish-speaking communities as vehicles for both news and commerce. In addition, on an average individual daily newspapers remain in print for much longer than weeklies, monthlies or irregularly published papers. Forty-one daily newspapers were published; on an average they were published for about 25 years, much longer than the mean publication years for the next closest category of newspapers, about 15 years for weeklies (Table 9.1).

The geographical distribution of daily Spanish-language newspaper publication in the US shows considerable variation (Table 9.1). About two-thirds of all daily papers have been published in just two of the newspaper regions identified in this study, the Upper Rio Grande Valley and Texas, 14 and 13, respectively. California, where just six daily papers have been published, stands as a somewhat distant third in terms of the total number of dailies published. Each of the remaining regions has produced less than a handful of daily papers, between one and three. Nevertheless, these small numbers may be somewhat deceptive. While only two dailies have been printed in Florida, the mean number of years in print is 28. For the three dailies which have been published in Chicago the average number of years in print is 34, and in New York the average number of years in print is 45 years.

In the early 1990s, over ten daily Spanish-language newspapers were in print in the US. With the exception of Arizona, all regions boasted at least one daily newspaper printed in Spanish. Texas led with three, followed by Chicago, New York and Florida with two each. Surprisingly, despite its

Table 9.2 Data for publication frequency and years in print of Spanish-language newspapers in the USA by region, 1992.

	Publication Frequency														
	Daily			*Weekly*			*Monthly*			*Irregular/Other*			*Total*		
Region	*Mean years*	*No.*	*%*	*Mean years*	*No.*	*%*	*Mean years*	*No.*	*%*	*Mean years*	*No.*	*%*	*Mean years*	*No.*	*%*
California	12	1	2	15	44	81	11	3	6	22	6	11	15	54	100
Arizona	–	–	–	5	1	100	–	–	–	–	–	–	5	1	100
Upper Rio Grande Valley	63	1	10	10	8	80	–	–	–	60	1	10	39	10	100
Texas	45	3	13	12	18	78	1	1	4	11	1	4	16	23	99
Chicago	21	2	18	10	8	73	7	1	9	–	–	–	11	11	100
Florida	28	2	14	21	10	71	5	1	7	18	1	7	22	14	99
Greater New York	45	2	15	16	6	46	28	3	23	23	2	15	25	13	99
TOTAL	36	11	9	14	95	75	14	9	7	24	11	9	19	126	100

Sources: N.W. Ayer and Sons *Directory of Newspapers and Periodicals, 1933–1992; Editor and Publisher International Yearbook, 1959–1992; Standard Rate and Data – Hispanic Media and Markets, 1998–1992.*

large Hispanic population and constant influx of immigrant Spanish-speakers, California only published one Spanish-language daily. Most of these papers had long publication histories. The mean years in print exceeded 35, with one paper in the Upper Rio Grande Valley being published continuously for over 60 years (Table 9.2).

Spanish-language newspapers with monthly publication schedules have been few. Since 1848, only 27 have been published, representing less than five per cent of all Spanish-language newspapers in the US (Table 9.1). Only one or two have ever been published in Arizona, the Upper Rio Grande Valley, Chicago or Florida. The largest number of monthlies has been published in California, yet this represents only 11 newspapers. The publication runs of these monthlies have been comparatively short. The average number of years in print is slightly less than 9. In California and New York, where the most monthlies have been printed, the mean number of years in publication is the longest, 10 and 15 respectively. In the early 1990s, a total of just nine Spanish-language monthly newspapers were in print and these were found in just five of the regions (Table 9.2). Only one monthly was published in Chicago, Texas and Florida, while California and New York accounted for three each. The publication longevity of the monthlies in New York is notable, an average of nearly 30 years (Table 9.2).

Spanish-language newspapers with irregular publication schedules have accounted for fully one-quarter of all papers published in the United States (Table 9.1). Their publication has been concentrated almost exclusively in three regions in the southwest – the Upper Rio Grande Valley, Texas and California. In each of these regions these newspapers have represented between 25 and 30 per cent of all papers ever published. East of the Mississippi, papers published on irregular publication schedules have not been common. Only one has been published in Chicago, two in Florida and eight in New York. Newspapers on irregular publication schedules have become less significant in recent decades. In the early 1990s, only 11 such papers were in print in the US, representing just less than nine per cent of all Spanish-language newspapers. Over half of these were published in California, with the remaining regions accounting for two or less each (Table 9.2).

By the 1990s two regions, California and Texas, dominated the geographic pattern of Spanish-language newspaper publication (Fig. 9.4). The publication of over 60 per cent of all Spanish-language newspapers in the US occurs in these two areas (Table 9.2). California accounts for the most, 43 per cent of the total, while Texas accounts for just 18 per cent. With the exception of Arizona, where only one Spanish-language paper was in print in the early 1990s, the remaining Spanish-language newspapers are evenly distributed between the other four regions. Among this group that includes Florida, New York, Chicago and the Upper Rio Grande Valley, the percentage of the total number of Spanish-language newspapers published nationally ranges between 11 per cent and eight per cent, respectively.

Conclusion

This research note outlines the evolving regional geography of Spanish-language newspaper publication in the US over the last 150 years. Spanish-language newspapers have constituted a constant presence in coterminous US since the close of the Mexican–American War in 1848, but their publication has been concentrated in a few geographically discrete regions. Historically, the three most important regions have been the Upper Rio Grande Valley, Texas and California, each accounting for at least one-quarter of all Spanish-language newspapers published. Each area corresponds to a region of historic Mexican and Spanish settlement, as well as continuing immigration from Latin America throughout much of the period under study. Newspapers have been published in Spanish in each of these regions since the mid-1800s. East of the Mississippi, Spanish language newspapers have a more recent history, their publication dating largely from the years since 1950. Publication in the east has focused on three metropolitan regions – New York, Chicago and South Florida. In these regions, the presence of a large number of Spanish speakers from a range of Latin American countries has fuelled newspaper growth in recent decades.

By the early 1990s, the historical patterns of the regional dominance of Spanish-language newspapers in the southwest had given way to a more geographically disbursed pattern. California and Texas continue to represent the principal regions of Spanish-language newspaper publication, but the significance of both the Upper Rio Grande Valley and Arizona has declined. However, all three eastern regions, New York, Chicago and South Florida, have strong Spanish-language presses which are likely to continue to grow. Two dailies are published in each of the regions. By comparison, Texas boasts just three dailies and California only one.

Despite the success of the Spanish-language newspapers in the later decades of the twentieth century, diverse pressures threaten the future of this ethnic press. Newspaper readership is declining among most groups in the US, and the Spanish-language press is not immune to this process. In addition, other media are exerting strong pressure on Spanish-language newspapers. The number of Spanish-language radio and television stations has grown impressively in the last two decades, especially in large metropolitan markets, precisely where recent growth has also occurred in the Spanish-language press. The number of listeners and viewers has also increased dramatically. Furthermore, as access to the World Wide Web becomes more generalized, many Spanish-speaking immigrants may increasingly utilize the Web to access national and regional newspapers in their country of origin rather than depending on Spanish-language newspapers published in the US for news from 'home'.

Since the late 1980s much more exacting data on the nature of publishing in Spanish-language newspapers and periodicals has become available than that which provided the basis for the data used in this research note. As the Hispanic market has become larger and more attractive for advertising campaigns, marketers and advertisers have demanded more precise data. Future research utilizing these data, especially circulation numbers and the geographical extent of the paper's distribution at the level of counties and Areas of Dominant Influence (ADIs) will likely provide a distinctly different vision of the significance of Spanish-language newspaper publication in different regional contexts in the US.

References

Burma, John H., *Spanish-Speaking Groups in the United States*. Durham, NC: Duke University Press, 1954.

Chacón, Ramon, 'The Chicano Immigrant Press in Los Angeles: The Case of 'El Heraldo de Mexico', *Journalism History*, Vol. 4, No. 2, 1977, pp. 34–41.

Editor and Publisher Co., *Editor and Publisher International Yearbook*, New York: E&P Publications, 1959–1990.

Gonzales, Juan, 'Forgotten Pages: Spanish-language Newspapers in the Southwest', *Journalism History*, Vol. 4, No. 2, 1977, pp. 50–55.

Griswald de Castillo, Richard, 'The Mexican Revolution and the Spanish-language Press in the Borderlands', *Journalism History*, Vol. 4, No. 2, 1977, pp. 42–47.

Gutiérrez, Felix, 'Latino Media: An Historical Overview', *Nuestro*, October 1980, pp. 25–28.

Guernica, Antonio, *Reaching the Hispanic Market Effectively: The Media, the Market, the Methods*, New York: McGraw Hill, 1982.

Kent, Robert B., and Maura E. Huntz, 'Spanish-language Newspapers in the United States', *Geographical Review*, Vol. 86, No. 3, 1996, pp. 446–456.

N. W. Ayer and Sons, *N. W. Ayer and Sons Directory of Newspapers and Periodicals*, Philadelphia: N. W. Ayer and Sons, 1933–1992.

National Research Bureau, *The 1987 Media Encyclopedia Working Press of the Nation–Newspaper Directory 1*, Chicago: Automated Marketing Systems, Inc., 1986.

Oczon, Annabelle, 'Bilingual and Spanish-language Newspapers in Territorial New Mexico', *New Mexico Historical Review*, Vol. 54, No. 1, 1979, pp. 45–52.

Shoemaker, Pamela J., *et al.*, 'Spanish-language Print Media Use as an Indicator of Acculturation', *Journalism Quarterly*, Vol. 62, No. 4, 1985, pp. 734–741.

Smith, M. M., 'The Mexican Immigrant Press Beyond the Borderlands', *Great Plains Quarterly*, Vol. 10, No. 2, 1990, pp. 71–85.

Standard Rate and Data Service, *Hispanic Media and Markets*, Skokie, IL: Standard Rate and Data Inc., 1988–1992.

Trevino, Roberto R., 'Prensa y Patria: The Spanish-language Press and the Biculturation of the Tejano Middle Class, 1920–1940', *Western Historical Quarterly*, Vol. 22, No. 4, 1991, pp. 451–472.

U. S. Department of Commerce, Bureau of the Census, *Hispanics Americans Today*, Current Population Reports, Population Characteristics, Washington DC: GPO, 1993.

Veciana-Suarez, Ana, *Hispanic Media USA: A Narrative Guide to Print and Electronic Hispanic News Media in the U.S.*, Washington DC: The Media Institute, 1987.

Wynar, Lubomyr R., and Anna T. Wynar, *Encyclopedia Directory of Ethnic Newspapers and Periods in the United States*, Littleton, CO: Libraries Unlimited, Inc., Second edition, 1976.

10

Enterprise Zones in a Global Perspective: Socioeconomic Consequences

SAMUEL THOMPSON AND ASHOK K. DUTT

Scholars of economic development contend that socioeconomic conditions in economically-depressed urban areas can be improved if those urban areas utilize economic development projects as a means to attract private investment in the form of new businesses. An increase in the number of businesses, representing new economic development projects in the urban areas, would increase job opportunities and enhance the quality of life of the residents. From the perspective of government officials, the enterprise zone programme can be a means by which private investment capital could be attracted into local areas which, in turn, would revitalize the local economy. In order to understand the intricacies of the enterprise zone concept, there is a need to refer to the British and Dutch experiences of two decades following the Second World War. Hong Kong's economic experience in recent times has also influenced the United Kingdom (UK) and the United States (US) as they attempt to address blighted conditions.

In order to address rapid loss of jobs in central cities, the enterprise zone concept was developed as a way to aid or reduce economic depression in many communities. The zone concept is recognized as a means to create jobs and to ease pressure on local governments to provide social services with a diminishing tax base. In light of these economic difficulties, state and local governments have attempted to try to reverse the slide of their respective economies caused by a combination of declining tax revenues and rising demands for services (Spindler and Forrester, 1993, p. 28). In essence, governments have to finance services out of diminishing revenues.

The enterprise zone is unique because it concentrates on providing development incentives, such as tax breaks and fewer local and state regulations in selected geographical areas experiencing severe economic difficulties. In essence, an enterprise zone is a targeted approach for enticing new businesses while at the same time retaining old ones, enhancing job creation and improving the overall welfare of the local community. The targeted nature of an enterprise zone makes it possible to devote resources to a particular area in order to accelerate community and business participation in bringing about better economic conditions.

> ... targeted economic development represents a break from traditional economic development, as practiced by state and local governments, and an expansion of community economic development, as practiced by community development corporations ... it is concerned with where the good jobs are, how to gain access to them, how to create jobs, and how to support businesses likely to hire poor people, how to make bad jobs into good jobs, and how to support disadvantaged people as they enter the labour market. Hence, it must creatively join economic development, employment training and human services if real and sustainable pathways to employment are created. (Giloth, 1995, p. 280).

Historical Development of Enterprise Zones

The emergence of enterprise zone proposals for economic development can be traced to several areas including Hong Kong, the UK, the Netherlands, India, China and the US. As most of these countries, the UK also faced economic difficulties in its declining urban areas. After significant job losses in the manufacturing sector, the UK faced an increase in unemployment in the 1970s. With rising unemployment, the British Government initiated a nationwide forum in the mid-1970s in an attempt to formulate new urban policies to revitalize declining urban areas. Among those who proposed solutions to urban unemployment was Peter Hall, a British urban geographer and planner. Hall conceptualized his ideas after observing the magnitude and success of free economic enterprise being conducted without the influence of the government in Hong Kong.

Hong Kong

Hong Kong has developed into one of the major ports and commercial centres linking various parts of the world. It is the financial capital of Asia and the world's third most important banking and financial centre, trailing only to London and New York (Lo, 1992, p. 2). Hong Kong has prospered as a freeport based on a *laissez-faire* policy which allowed private enterprise to develop with minimum interference from the government (Lo, 1992, p. 12). Accordingly, Lo (1992) suggests that history, geography and political factors have made it possible for Hong Kong to blend the best of Western and eastern cultural elements (Lo, 1992, p. 3).

Hong Kong's high level of development did not occur in a vacuum. Early development strategies focussed on small-scale industries using less sophisticated technology, cheap labour and an orientation towards exports (Lo, 1992, p. 13). Over the years Hong Kong has been transformed into an industrial giant, heavily dependant on export-oriented manufacturing industries and specializing in light consumer goods such as textiles, clothing, electronics and plastics. This skillful crafting of Hong Kong's economy was made possible because of the minimal role of government. The role of the Hong Kong Government was restricted to providing a secure and stable environment; it was for the people to fully engage their energies in economically productive pursuits to improve their standards of living (Lo, 1992, p. 14). In fact, the Hong Kong Government encourages investment by pursuing a liberal policy of free enterprise with no discrimination against overseas investors (Humann, 1992, p. 38). One of the most free and open marketplaces anywhere on the globe, it has found its way in the modern world through the ingenuity and drive of its people, low taxes, rule of law, respect for business and property rights, tremendous physical infrastructure and unbridled capitalism (Perkin, 1999, p. 272).

As a relatively small economic entity, Hong Kong nevertheless plays a far larger role in global business and finance than its size suggests (Perkin, 1999, p. 272). The successes of Hong Kong are evident in the form of high economic growth rates and the high standard of living. Its success is often linked to Asian values and culture, leading to an emphasis on the work ethic, thrift, family loyalty, personal discipline and self-reliance (Rowley and Fitzgerald, 2000, p. 2). These attributes have seemingly been supported and encouraged by a regime of unfettered market forces and freewheeling capitalism (Rowley and Fitzgerald, 2000, p. 2). Thus, it is not surprising that in an attempt to revitalize central cities, western countries began to emulate the strategies that made Hong Kong an economic power in East Asia.

United Kingdom

The UK is the first market economy based country to recognize that even in an advanced economy like its own, there are depressed areas with stagnant or declining economies. This led to increased hardship for the people of the area and deterioration in the socioeconomic conditions. There was high unemployment in the areas of industrial decline resulting in immigration of the local population to areas where industry was still thriving. Such labour force movement was heightened during the Depression of the early 1930s. The result was that the British Parliament passed the following acts: (i) The Special Areas (Development & Improvement) Act of 1934; (ii) The Special Areas Reconstruction (Agreement) Act of 1936; and (iii) The Special Areas (Amendment) Act of 1937 (Dutt, 1969). In the 1930s, Britain thus initiated a national industrial policy encouraging industrial relocation to the special areas in order to combat economic hardship and social deprivation. Though this effort was designed as a short-term measure, the policy continued after the Second World War with modifications. The old term 'Special Area' was replaced with 'Development Area', following the enactment of the Development Areas Act. The Act led to the designation of eight development areas. Of the number of designations, six were in England – Southwest, Westham, Merseyside, South Lancashire, West Cumberland and Northeastern England; and the remaining two were in Scotland – mid-Scottish and Scottish highlands.

In 1940, the Barlow Commission report suggested a four-point remedy with alternative industrial distribution and location. The remedies were: (i) Decentralization of industries and industrial population from congested urban areas; (ii) Balancing of industrial development among the various natural regions; (iii) Diversification of industries in each such region; and (iv) Limiting continued immigration of industrial labor to London and the surrounding areas (Royal Commission Report, 1940, p. viii).

Several years after the Second World War, Britain experienced political changes as the Labor Government was replaced by the Conservatives towards the end of the 1950s. Conservatives placed minimal emphasis upon the Development Areas strategy. The Labour Government further modified the Development Area concept in 1965 after they replaced the Conservatives. They eliminated smaller Development Districts based on growth criteria and substituted them with vastly enlarged Development Areas. These changes not only focussed on the elimination of unemployment in much larger areas but were also linked to the general strategy of development of a region. The newly defined Development Areas (Fig. 10.1) made the boundaries much broader than those of the growth centres (Rodwin, 1970, p. 140).

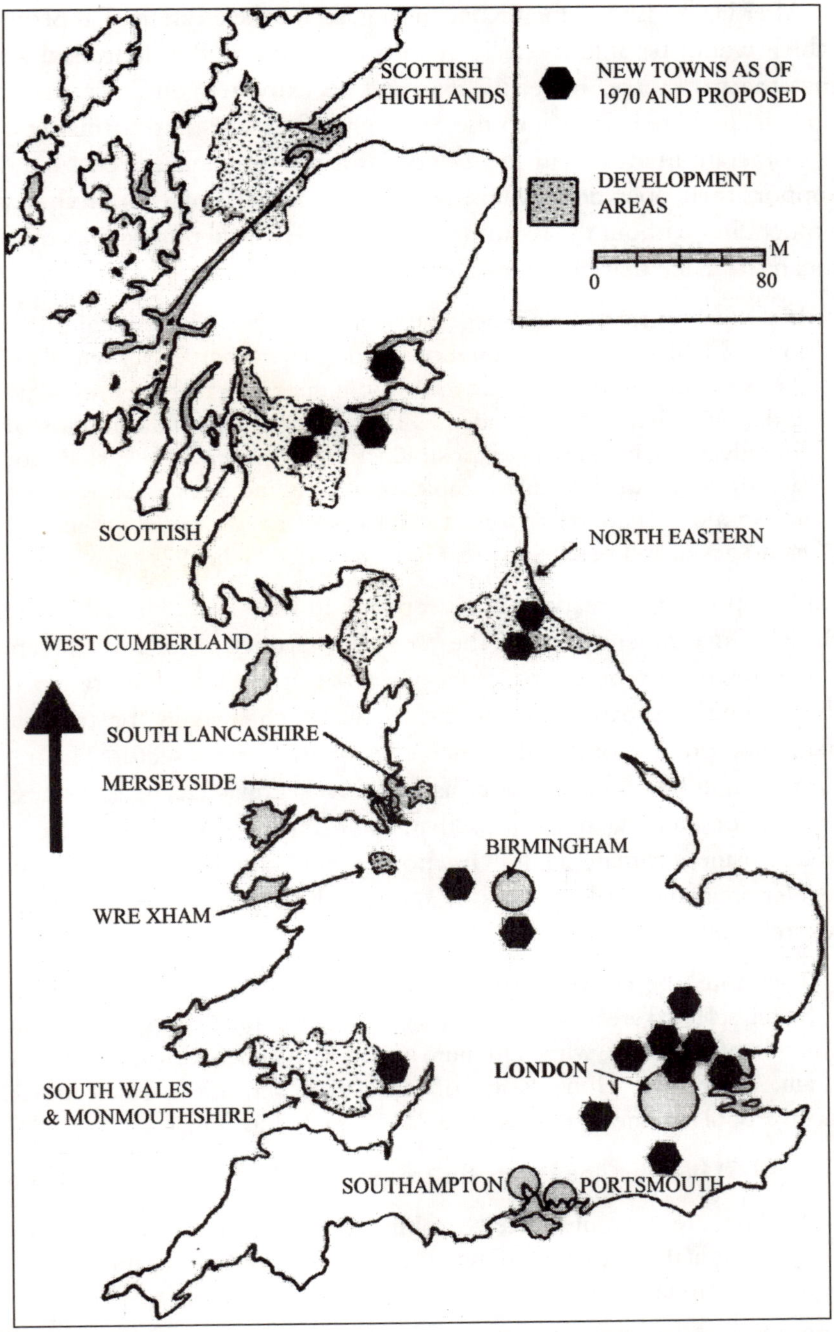

Fig 10.1 Location of development areas and new towns in 1970 (included are proposed ones).
Source: Modified from Dutt (1970, p. 326).

After Hall's visit to Hong Kong, he argued for the creation of businesses which would be able to easily absorb residents of the depressed areas into the workforce. In reality, it would be extremely difficult to attract knowledge-based firms into the inner cities because these firms tend to agglomerate in areas with necessary infrastructure and skilled labour to support their operations. Thus, urban areas in need of economic development but without the requisite infrastructure could pursue unorthodox means to make that possible.

> If we really want to help inner cities and cities generally, we might have to use highly unorthodox methods. One major source of their ills is that so many of their people ... so the inner city studies tell us again and again ... have been stranded high and dry by the rapid evolution of the advanced industrial (or postindustrial) economy. Their skills (or lack of skills) were readily useable in an early industrial economy, but are no more. If we try to force them to catch up, we may do them and us no good, and perhaps a great deal of harm (Hall, 1977).

Hall proposed the creation of "Freeports" in June 1977. He called on the British Government to make the "freeport" attractive for foreign capital and foreign entrepreneurs, especially from East Asia. He argued that the decline in urban areas was the result of changes in the traditional manufacturing sector and the emergence of the service sector. The transformation in traditional industry had negatively impacted small businesses, known for creating more jobs than large businesses. To resurrect the small business climate, Hall's "freeport" would eliminate or reduce taxes, regulation and social services and would be tried on a small-scale in severely depressed areas.

> Therefore, the answer might be to accept … the Freeport solution. Small, selected areas of inner cities would be simply thrown open to all kinds of initiative, with minimum control. In other words, we would aim to recreate Hong Kong of the 1950s and 1960s inside inner Liverpool or inner Glasgow (Hall, 1977 quoted in Butler, 1981, p. 96).

Hall (1977) built his arguments for freeports in the following statements:

A. The areas would receive minimal government regulation to encourage the creation of small businesses and the attraction of foreign capital.

B. Goods and services produced or sold in the zone would be free of taxes based on what he called "shameless free enterprise".

C. There would be no need for wage and price controls in the freeports. The only departure from the national norm is that no social services (education, health and welfare) would be provided because of the reduction in taxes, coupled with the fact that the whole process at this stage is experimental.

D. There would be no restrictions on the manner of participation in the freeports (Hall, 1977).

The rationale behind the freeport is that innovations would lead to the development of high-skill jobs and new companies. The success of high-skill companies would accelerate the development of supporting service sector establishments where low-skilled individuals could participate in the economy. According to Hall's argument, the participation by both skilled and unskilled labor in the labour force would systematically turn around the depressed areas. Hall, however, cautioned that the freeport is not a panacea for all urban areas because some areas have unique problems or have deteriorated to a point beyond revitalization.

Conservative Party leaders identified with Hall's radical proposal for economic development. Prominent among the Conservatives was Sir Geoffrey Howe (former member of the House of Commons, Chancellor of the Exchequer and Foreign Secretary in the Thatcher Government) who coined the term 'enterprise zone' to describe Hall's proposal. In a 1978 speech, Howe suggested that the poor economic conditions associated with declining urban areas were the result of strict national government regulation, tax burdens and other obstacles that tend to impede efforts by the same government to revive an area (Butler, 1991, p. 28).

Howe's solution was a revision of Hall's freeport concept. In the enterprise zone, government should encourage economic freedom and innovation and reduce taxes and regulation. This would stimulate business risk-taking and the creation of jobs. Moreover, the enterprise zone would lead to a type of economic and social experimentation that would return depressed urban areas to the period when they used to be centres of creativity, opportunity and job creation (Butler, 1991, p. 29). The enterprise zone would cover an area not more than two square miles with no restriction on land use, and within which the suspension of price and wage controls would hold. Local and national governments would relinquish any land they may own in the freeport area which would be auctioned to the highest bidder. Howe's enterprise zone concept seemed very radical, especially the proposal to eliminate planning controls in the freeports. Given the UK's strong town planning tradition, planning controls in the freeports were modified, but not eliminated. Howe's ideas were finally implemented when the Conservative Party under Margaret Thatcher took power with the general election of 1979. The new government created 12 enterprise zones through legislation towards the end of 1980 (Butler, 1991, p. 29).

The legislation centred on the Local Government Planning and Land Act 1980 and the Financial Act 1980, which made it possible for local authorities, new towns or urban development corporations to begin the process of designating enterprise zones on an experimental basis (Morrison, 1987, p. 85). Each of the zones would benefit from fewer land use regulations, property and corporate tax exceptions, and incentives to train potential workers or employees (Morrison, 1987, p. 85).

Between 1980 and 1981, the British Government created the first group of enterprise zones, namely Clydebank, Belfast, Swansea, Corby, Dudley, Speke, Salford, Trafford, Wakefield, Hartlepool, Tyneside and the Isle of Dogs (Morrison, 1987, p. 85). Similarly, between 1983 and 1984, another group of zones was created, namely Allendale, Glanford, Middlesbrough, Northeast Lancashire, North West Kent, Rotherham, Scunthorpe, Telford, Wellingbrough, Delyn, Milford Haven, Invergorden and Tayside (Great Britain Department of the Environment (GBDE), 1987, p. 13). All the cities in the programme had acute economic problems.

Once all the enterprise zones became operational, an attempt was made to monitor economic activities in each of the zones. A consulting firm, Roger Tym and Partners, analysed economic data based on the first two years of the programme (Morrison, 1987, p. 90). Roger Tym and Partners concluded that within the first two years, the first group of zones attracted cumulatively 725 businesses that created 8,065 jobs (Tym, 1984, p. 144). In 1987, the Department of the Environment requested another study of the enterprise zones. This study was conducted by PA Cambridge Economic Consultants, with a focus on the number of businesses and jobs created in the zones and the contributions of the zones in revitalizing the local areas (GBDE, 1987, p. 1). This study found the zones to be useful as a means to central city revitalization.

The Dutch Stimulus Areas and Associated Social Planning

In the Netherlands, a new regional industrialization policy was introduced in 1951 to encourage industrial growth in the less developed northwest and southwest regions. The objectives of the policy were: (i) Mitigation of out-migration from less developed areas; (ii) Reduction of unemployment; and (iii) Balancing the development between high and less developed regions.

In 1952, the Dutch Parliament enacted the regional industrialization policy in order to correct the imbalance in development through: (i) Recognition of the problem area; (ii) Selection of 42 nuclei of industrialization within the area; (iii) Provision of state subsidy to industrial establishments in the selected nuclei (new ones or the expansion of old ones); (iv) Improvement of 'residential climate' in the industrial nuclei; (v) Development of the infrastructure of communications in the less developed provinces as a whole; and (vi) Temporary relief from the unemployment situation by subsidizing out-migration (Dutt, 1968, p. 677).

The strategy of development followed encouragement of industrial development at a number of nuclei of the problem areas rather than that throughout its total area (Fig. 10.2). It was thought that these nuclei would act as growth centres and spread the development in the surrounding area. The problem areas, also designated as stimulus areas, were in the northern, southeastern and southwestern parts of the country. There were 47 such nuclei at the end of the 1960s. Industrial development was subsidized in these areas and infrastructural development was accentuated. All these also led to a new generation of socio-planning as planned development of community centres, resettlement houses, youth clubs, health centres and libraries was subsidized with capital investment and operating cost. These stimulus areas also received subsidies for sport fields, swimming pools and workshops for handicapped people. The agricultural areas after stimulus areas received improvement subsidy as well as subsidies for resettlements (ibid). It was also proposed that government should create a climate more conducive to private enterprise by cutting public expenditure, lowering taxes and deregulating business activities. 'Public investment, government participation in important private projects and the maintenance of demand for goods and services are elements of such an economic policy' (Van Delft and Kwaak, 1985, p. 121).

China's Economic Zones

Until 1978 China pursued a policy of self-reliance. After 1978 China followed the open door policy and joined the globalization process by embracing free market-based capitalism. There were four Special Economic

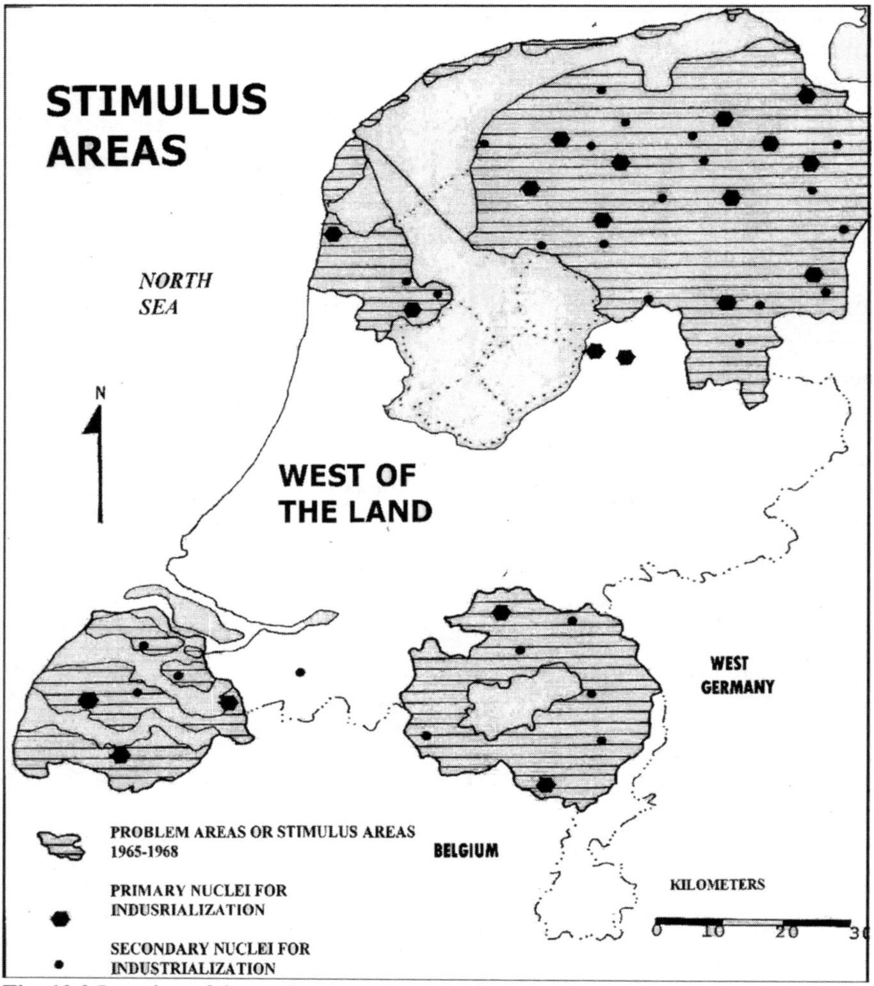

Fig. 10.2 Location of three stimulus areas and primary and secondary nuclei for industrialization: 1965–1968.

Source: Modified from Dutt, 1968, p. 68, and Dutt, 1970, p. 328.

Zones (SEZs) mostly opened in southern China. The economic growth was prompted by foreign investment and exports. In the eastern coastal regions, more opened zones and cities were recognized. In the 1990s, Podong district was opened by the Chinese Government outside Shanghai as an economic zone. The Government also announced stimulation of high-tech industries. With the Government's support the high-tech industry situated specially in the opened zone multiplied. The Yangtze region became a leader of technological development.

> The region has undertaken tremendous efforts to globalize its economy and enhance its education and high-tech industries. In 2001, the region attained US$ 73.9 billion foreign investment, accounting for 32.3 per cent of the national total (Zhang, 2003).
>
> It is led by cities of Shanghai, Hangzhou, Suzhou and Nanjing, as well as Wuxi and Ningbo, and many other cities. The Yangtze delta has established hundreds of varied development zones, and it is reported that Shanghai alone has established more than 200 development zones, many with a focus on foreign investment and high-tech industry (Wei, 2007, p. 35).

In general, the size of SEZs in China is large, having multi-product industrial townships with huge cost benefits, including those of input taxes. In comparison, SEZs in India are small.

India's Special Economic Zones

The SEZs in India were started in 1965. By the year 2000 their total number was eight. They were all located near an airport or harbour as they were known as Export Processing Zones, with their products earmarked for export. Though there were residential parts in some of these zones the emphasis was heavily on production. In the year 2000, there was a policy change by the Government of India in which these zones were converted to SEZs. The Central Government planned their locations near the large cities. The SEZs provided an infusion of industries, offices and other employment (Dutt and Noble, 2008, p. 296).

The number of SEZs started to proliferate when the impact of globalization was witnessed. The demand for export production attracted both indigenous and foreign capital which required a spatial stimulus and facilities for export-oriented areas free from restrictions prevalent in other locations. By 2006, over 400 applications were filed for setting up more SEZs. By then over half of them were approved by the Government. In the SEZ areas the entrepreneurs are given tax breaks and ready infrastructure to lure investors in export-oriented industries. In 2006 and 2007, as much as US$5 billion worth of foreign direct investment was expected by the SEZs. By December 2008, about 530 SEZs were formally approved by the Government. A majority of them were IT SEZs, with a minimum area of only 10 hectares.

> Developers, helped by the government, acquire cheap land. Incentives to investors include a five-year holiday on profit tax, and exemptions

from import and exercise duties and from some licensing requirements. Moreover, to qualify for the benefits, a manufacturer in a SEZs needs only be a net earner of foreign exchange over a five year period rather not just an exporter. Reliance Industries, India's biggest private sector company, is planning enormous, town-sized SEZs near Mumbai and in Haryana, near Delhi, most of the others are tiny. The minimum area for a 'multi-product' SEZs is 1,000 hectares (3.9 miles), for a 'product-specific' zone, it is 100 hectares, and for information technology, biotechnology and jewelry, just ten hectares. (*The Economist*, October 2006, pp. 45–46)

Mahindra World City

The first SEZ in India is situated 25 miles south of the Chennai airport. The strategy of the SEZs is the same as that of SEZs in China. They are government-planned projects with better infrastructure. They provide new employment and attract foreign investment. Efforts are made not to build such a city on productive agricultural land. In the case of Mahindra World City this strategy was followed satisfactorily, but in the state of West Bengal a new SEZ was planned on the fertile agricultural land adjacent to the northern fringe of Calcutta Metropolitan District.

> Apart from the Mahindra and Reliance, which are Indian investors, Dell, Accenture and Timken are interested in building their own SEZs. The Mahindra World City, spread in areas of 1,300 acres, has wide roads, street lighting, sewer and water facilities, private security, cable provision and power station. Thirty-two international and domestic companies have already bought space in this zone. Tax breaks and start-up monies are provided by the government. In the SEZs, land acquisition is facilitated by the government. Will such SEZs be as successful as in China? (Rai, 2006, p. 5)

In the SEZs land acquisition is facilitated by the government, making it easier to start enterprises for the investors as the latter do not have to go through the hard and difficult process of land acquisition.

Singur: A Failed Effort

The town of Singur, 25 miles to the north of the city of Kolkata and at the fringe of the Calcutta Metropolitan District, was chosen to be a site for an enterprise zone for making the world's cheapest car, Nano by Tata

Motors, which had earlier acquired Jaguar and Land Rover luxury car brands from the Ford Motor Company. The Tatas are well known Indian entrepreneurs. Their company is headquartered in Mumbai and they are known as one of the most powerful business magnates of India. They have also earned a reputation of being a socially responsible employer.

> Encouraged by the Communist Party of India [Marxist], the party that runs the state and has been seeking to attract investment, Tata has invested about US$345 million in the plant and attracted about 60 suppliers to set up shop nearby to ensure that the car would start rolling off production lines in the last three months of this year. The plant and its suppliers are located on almost 1,000 acres of land that had been purchased from farmers. Construction on the plant began in January 2007, employing about 4,000 people at it peak. (Bellman and Beckett, 2008, A8)

Though the Government acquired the land for Tata, many farmers complained that it was done without their consent and with insufficient compensation. As a result, thousands of farmers protested.

> Behind the protest is Mamata Banejee, a firebrand politician who has used the demonstrations and the massive publicity they have garnered to portray the Communists as insensitive to the interest of small farmers and local constituents. The leader of the Trinamool Congress, a rival state party, Ms Banerjee has held nightly rallies at the manufacturing site. She is demanding the return of about 400 acres of the site, saying the land she wants returned was taken from farmers against their will. Tata denies that it grabbed land from farmers. (Bellman and Beckett, 2008, A8)

By September 2008, Tata had already invested US$350 million and they were faced with the possibility of relocation of their Nano factory to another part of India. By October 2008, the Tatas decided to relocate their Nano plant to the state of Gujarat which had a more favourable investment climate. This resulted in a great financial loss to the company. The state of Bengal, which has already turned into an unattractive place for new industrial plants due to political problems and labor unrest, will not reap the benefits of the Nano.

> Nano plant was projected to create close to 20,000 jobs: about 1,000 at Tata itself, about 7,000 at parts makers and about 12,000 businesses expected to sprout up around the site and its employees (Bellman and Beckett, 2008, A8).

Kolkata has already fallen behind in industrial development compared to other Indian cities, namely, Bengaluru, Hyderabad and Mumbai.

SEZ and Impact of Economic Slowdown

The economic slowdown that started at the end of 2008 has forced several SEZ entrepreneurs to repeal the government 'approval' or limit the size of their land holdings.

> Obviously, near standstill in the credit market and the pervasive demand crunch (the latter causes the former to persist even as partly resulting from it), has forced the developers to plead inability to get enough firms to buy SEZ slots. The viability of many SEZs, which are being developed or about to be developed is in doubt. But that should not convince one to mindlessly buy the argument that these SEZs are in trouble purely due to the economic slowdown, which the developers claim they did not anticipate to be one of such gravity (Narendranath, 2008).

Since the SEZs are not allowed to sell their acquired land, they are afraid to be stuck with their bought property. They are therefore trying to find ways to get out of their land investments. At the same time many SEZ developers are left high and dry as they are sitting on land banks without the needed funds to either develop them or attract investors. Thus, the moral and economic stability of SEZ model of India is in question (ibid.).

United States and Enterprise Zones

The *laissez-faire* approach to economic development was introduced into the US by conservatives who expressed their dissatisfaction with government policies. In 1979, the Heritage Foundation, based in Washington, DC, proposed the use of enterprise zones and urged policy-makers to pursue the concept in the US (Butler, 1991, p. 27). Stuart Butler, an analyst with the foundation, played a significant role in developing the concept in the US. Similar to the Conservatives in Britain, Butler believes that government programmes have in part failed to ameliorate the plight of depressed cities. Butler sees the enterprise zone as an attempt to revive failing small businesses. He further argues that the enterprise zone would be an ideal place for economic experimentation with its suspension of rent control and minimum wage requirements (Butler, 1981 and 1991).

Butler also revised the original 'freeport' and enterprise zone proposals by Hall and Howe. Hall had argued for the creation of freeports only in sparsely populated derelict areas in England, devoid of government regulations and taxes. Howe proposed and revised the enterprise zone as a way to promote industrial parks where manufacturing would flourish and jobs would be created by business firms in the zone. The idea of free enterprise without government intervention was promoted. On the other side of the Atlantic, the approach to the enterprise zone concept was more comprehensive than what the British had in mind. Butler (1981) saw enterprise zones as a tool to initiate overall community development. Butler believes in a planned unit development form of enterprise zone where there is diversity or a mixture of commercial, industrial and residential use in the same area.

Based on the brief history and continued revision in the original enterprise zone concept, a possible conceptual model for the US (Fig. 10.3) can be proposed consisting of six elements – job creation in depressed neighbourhoods; expanding the economy; encouraging local enterprise; social improvement; innovation and experimentation; and globalization (Butler, 1981, p. 139).

Proponents of enterprise zones believe that creating jobs in the depressed areas of a city is one of the main objectives of the concept. For job

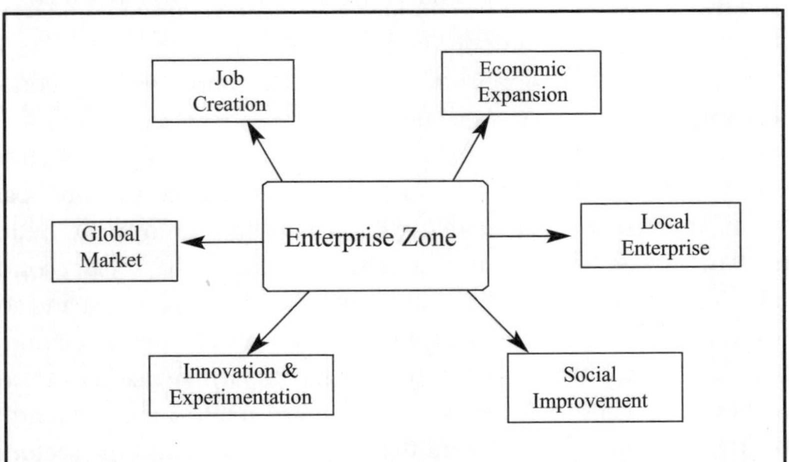

Fig. 10.3 Enterprise zone in the US.

Source: Thompson, Samuel, K., Enterprize Zones: Current Planning Efforts by State and Local Governments in New Jersey, unpublished dissertation, University of Akron, Ohio, 2001.

creation to come to fruition, small businesses must be encouraged because they create the bulk of employment in cities for semi-skilled and unskilled individuals. Governments should eliminate barriers that tend to hinder small businesses and provide a conducive atmosphere for those interested in investing in the depressed areas. Large firms also should be encouraged to participate in the zone because they can provide valuable technical assistance to small firms, which may lead to the creation of additional small businesses.

Butler comments that while the principal goal of enterprise zone programmes is the creation of jobs, the effort to create jobs in the central cities should not be carried out to the detriment of the whole regional economy. The purpose of the enterprise zone is not to orchestrate the redistribution of economic activities in favour of residents in a particular area or city (Butler, 1981, p. 40). Support for enterprise zones will diminish if the intent is to redistribute economic activities. What the enterprise zone does best is to highlight the resourcefulness of an area in embracing the available resources to improve the locality socially, economically and politically. The enterprise zone provides an area with opportunities to revive its economy by renovating abandoned and dilapidated buildings and assisting welfare recipients, unemployed individuals and small-scale investors.

Enterprise zones should be conducive to the development and nurturing of small businesses among the local residents, who can be made to recognize that there are opportunities available to improve their economic conditions. The enterprise zone concept gives residents an optimistic view of the future and the desire to rebuild the local economy through local initiative (Butler, 1981, p. 140). Furthermore, economic stability is likely to be maintained if local residents participate in employment creation, instead of depending on non-residents to direct the local economy. Residents, rather than outsiders, are likely to show high interest and social value in their communities or central cities. Also, the enterprise zone will provide legitimacy to small businesses and informal market activities, which, in turn, will provide jobs and necessary skills to the residents.

Blair and Endres (1994) found that the informal economic sector had been largely ignored in the literature by economic development researchers. They argued for the inclusion of benign informal sector activities in any planning strategy geared towards central cities. These informal activities have great potential for inner-city residents; accordingly, they should be integrated into the mainstream.

> The opportunity cost of participating in informal activities is lower for individuals without mainstream employment opportunities ... a dense net of social and institutional relationships characteristic of some urban neighbourhoods has been shown to be useful in supporting the informal economy. Many productive informal activities operate with one foot in the informal economy and one foot in the mainstream economy. Mainstream activities sometimes shelter the informal economy. Many inner-city commercial operations are small proprietors in which tax avoidance is relatively easy and work rules and other regulations can be skirted (Blair and Endres, 1994, p. 287).

Overall, development in the informal sector and other areas in the formal sector will add to the expansion in the regional and national economy.

Although job creation is the goal of the enterprise zone, it cannot be successful without parallel improvements in the social realm of the depressed areas (Butler, 1981, p. 141). The social aspect must be taken into consideration because if the residents are unwilling to help themselves, incentives alone cannot bring about improvements in the locality. Community organizations should be active in developing tailor-made community-wide programmes, self-help projects and neighbourhood watch programmes to make the community safe from crime and drugs. These programmes would bolster the social fabric of an area, and the presence of new and old businesses would add to the improvement of the area. Finally, a partnership between local residents and the business sector would go a long way towards revitalizing the area socially and economically.

The enterprise zone, in theory, will accelerate a process where innovation and experimentation are encouraged through individual and group efforts. These processes may lead to a breakthrough in business ventures that could help the local area immensely. It takes time for a breakthrough to emerge because few ideas reach the stage of full production. For every single idea that turns into successful production, there are hundreds of failures that are finally abandoned (Hisrich, 1986, p. 78). The zone should create an environment which will be attractive to risk-takers. There should be no obstacles which would inhibit free creativity and risk-taking. Without this opportunity for innovation and experimentation, it is likely that not many will succeed in the zone. With several risk-takers, it is likely that one or more innovations will have an impact beyond the local area. Certainly, most small businesses have experienced at least one or more failures before succeeding in a venture.

With the emerging global market, local communities will derive substantial economic benefit from export-oriented businesses. These firms normally export to regional, national and global markets. With technological advancement, local firms can efficiently market their products over a wide area because of the elimination of trade barriers through associations such as the North American Free Trade Association (NAFTA). Moreover, firms with tremendous innovative capabilities can take advantage of emerging markets for their products. The reciprocal effect for local residents will be further job creation as firms expand globally.

The American approach seeks to improve the lives of zone residents in many ways. This approach involves residents and businesses in shaping policies that govern the implementation of zone programmes and neighborhood activities. In the end, this coalition between residents and businesses strengthens local support for the enterprise zone programme.

Case Studies: Enterprise Zones at the State Level

The literature on the subject is filled with studies on employment and fiscal impact of enterprise zone programmes and reviews of state enterprise zone programmes (Rubin and Wilder, 1989; Erickson and Friedman, 1991; Wilder and Rubin, 1996). Other studies have focussed on national enterprise zone programmes across several states. Most of these studies encompass a variety of research techniques, including case studies, statistical analyses and surveys of zone businesses and administrators.

This case study addresses the cost–benefit issue by focussing on New Jersey's Urban Enterprise Zone programme (UEZ). Rubin (1990) was interested in determining the impact of the UEZ programme on New Jersey when benefits accruing from UEZ-induced economic growth are compared with costs associated with the program. The study used the Input/Output (I/O) Model to estimate the full effect of economic change in a specific geographic area. The I/O Model is a method which represents an economy in a system of linear equations; the economy is disaggregated into individual industries which are grouped into Standard Industrial Classifications (Rubin, 1990, p. 113).

The I/O Model made it possible to differentiate economic growth resulting from enterprise zone activities from the growth which would have occurred without an enterprise zone programme. This study finds that the UEZ programme is a cost-effective tool in the state's economic development arsenal, yielding US$1.90 in state and local taxes for every dollar in tax revenues forgone by the state as a result of tax exemptions to UEZ businesses (Rubin, 1990, p. 106). What is extraordinary about this study is that it measures the full impact of UEZ incentives, such as direct increase in economic activity associated with UEZ firms, plus the additional or multiplier effects resulting from this economic activity rippling through the New Jersey economy (Rubin, 1990, p. 113).

Grasso and Crosse (1991) contributed to the evaluation of enterprise zones by summarizing specific findings by the US General Accounting Office (GAO) regarding the enterprise zone in Maryland. The GAO found that employment among participating firms in zones studied did increase by 76 per cent during the four years following the implementation of the enterprise zone programmes (Grasso and Crosse, 1991, p. 127). Upon further analysis, however, the GAO found that the growth could not be exclusively attributed to the zone programme.

Grasso and Crosse's study provides no evidence that the Maryland Enterprise Zone Programme increased employment in the areas the GAO studied. Possibly, the problem with the Maryland programme was that the administrators had not done enough to promote the zones. Marketing is an essential part of economic development; therefore, concerted effort has to be made to sell locations in blighted areas to potential employers. Maryland officials disagreed with the GAO's conclusion because the enterprise zone programme was never intended as the last option for revitalizing poor areas. Instead, officials used the program to augment other economic development programmes within the state.

Enterprise zone policies and strategies at the state level vary in terms of incentives and implementation. Some states employ the use of such classic enterprise zone elements as tax breaks and regulatory relief. Other states engage in an active or interventionist role such as assisting in the securing of loans, raising venture capital and infrastructure improvement.

Elling and Sheldon (1991) explore the significance of differing programme components for the success of 47 enterprise zones in the states of Illinois, Indiana, Kentucky and Ohio. They used coefficient of variation, controlling for years of zone operation, to determine the extent of variation in economic activity among the four states. The authors noticed variations in zone economic activity existed across the four states. The mean number of firms investing annually in Indiana's zones was ten times greater than the number investing in Ohio zones (Elling and Sheldon, 1991, p. 141). Conversely, the median investment per zone per year in

Ohio was more than double that occurring in Illinois' zone. These interstate differences suggest that variation in state level provisions affects the success of enterprise zones. State differences may also reflect other economic advantages of a state or its general economic climate.

Another enterprise zone study involves shift-share technique to uncover any evidence demonstrating the effectiveness of the enterprise zone as an economic development tool. Rubin and Wilder (1989) used the shift-share technique to analyse the impact on employment in the enterprise zone in Evansville, Indiana. They measured changes in zone employment based on regional growth effect, proportional shift and differential shift. The regional growth effect determines whether changes in certain economic sectors in the zones are influenced by the larger metropolitan area. The suggestion was that growth in the zone occurred because it was integrated into the larger region and shared in the growth of the area, and not because the zone had an edge over other areas (Rubin and Wilder, 1989, p. 421). The authors found that employment growth in the zone was part of the overall general growth in the Evansville Metropolitan Area.

Impact of Stimulus Development Programme on Socioeconomic Conditions

Whether in North America, Europe or Asia, economic conditions do fluctuate from time to time, affecting a spectrum of people, businesses and cities. It is not uncommon to observe high unemployment rates, migration of business and people, low revenue collection and dilapidated structures in once prosperous cities. The proliferation of SEZs, social plans, export promotion zones or enterprise zones, while designed to generate jobs, also lead to an improvement in the human condition such as strengthening peoples' skills and abilities to capitalize on available jobs in the zones. In areas with depressed economic conditions, human capital investment uplifts individuals and educates them, to participate in this venture. Education of citizens has the tendency to remove uncertainties among existing or new businesses about labour availability and their skill levels. Globally, non-profit organizations, civic leaders, churches and city officials come together and set up centres to assist residents looking to learn new skills or in search of jobs in a depressed area. The ultimate goal of training or retraining is to make local residents employable and reduce unemployment.

A focus on social conditions has become the norm as cities implement development programmes, particularly to aid people who are unable to help themselves socially and economically. To that end, community organizations and city officials are active in developing tailor-made community-wide programmes, self-help projects and neighborhood programmes designed to help people in need. These programmes bolster the social fabric of an area and build a sense of community among residents in an area. In a sense, partnerships among organizations, public officials, local residents and the business sector would go a long way in revitalizing the cities both socially and economically. Many Community Development Corporations (CDCs) and community support groups are working to enhance the employability of local residents. They build contact networks and link prospective employers with potential employees. The role of CDCs has expanded beyond the traditional focus on housing and business development to include human services, community empowerment and building social capital (Cowan et al., 1999, p. 325). The profile of non-profit organizations, coupled with their experience, makes them highly appropriate to participate in enterprise zone projects to help local residents. When areas or communities have a long history of decline, extreme poverty and minimal development opportunities, often organizations, government officials and individuals join efforts to create an environment where labour needs of employers can be addressed. With the community organizations playing an important role, local residents may find it easier to build trust, share information and create lasting bonds, translating into a stronger pool of labour. As people gain new skills or improve their existing skills, the ultimate result would be people gaining employment and paying taxes, thus reducing the burden on communities with high unemployment rates such as in the UK, the Netherlands, India, China and the US.

Conclusion

The concept of enterprise zone, export promotion zone, problem areas and many others with such designations are intended to stimulate the economy of a particular area, city or region in different parts of the world in order to bring about socioeconomic advancement. Many governments have supported economic development programmes with investment capital and other measures to spur investment. Thus, the enterprise zone programme, industrial growth programme, open door policy or SEZs is a testament to how governments continue to offer incentives, regulatory relief and tax abatement schemes to encourage the private sector to contribute to job growth and socioeconomic betterment. In essence, there is a strong public–private partnership to advance conditions favourable to economic development. Instead of an adversarial relationship, governments and businesses seek a common goal of improved economic conditions by working to create economic growth in an area, region or country. The role of government and private sector partnership emanates from experiences, especially after the Second World War as evidenced in the UK, followed by the Netherlands in the 1950s, India in the 1960s, China in the 1980s and the US in the 1990s. Even though economic zone policies were meant to provide economic stimulus, the benefits were intended to bring about societal benefit and advancement of general social well-being.

The concept of economic zones, stimulus zones and development areas underwent radical change during the last 60 years. The earlier emphasis was on government stimulus and government-set guidelines. This is changing in favour of free and open market economy where private investors have a greater role and governments act as facilitators. All enterprise zone activities do not end in success. Some end up in dire failure as in Nandigram and Singur in West Bengal, India. In a free market economy where democracy prevails, such as in India, one has to take into consideration the will of the people. Acquiring productive farmland from farmers without their full satisfaction can create such a negative atmosphere that new investors will hesitate to allocate their investment and the existing investors may have to withdraw from their projects after making commitments.

References

Bellman, Eric, and Paul Beckett, 'Modernization Foes in Rural India Send Message to Investors: Protest Drive Tata to Stop Building Mini Car Plant', *The Wall Street Journal*, Wednesday, 3 September 2008, A8.

Blair, John P. and Carole R. Endres, 'Hidden Economic Development Assets', *Economic Development Quarterly*, Vol. 8, 1994, pp. 286–291.

Butler, Stuart M., 'The Conceptual Evolution of Enterprise Zones', in Roy E. Green (ed.), *Enterprise Zones: New Directions in Economic Development*, Newbury Park, CA: Sage Publications, 1991, pp. 27–40.

Butler, Stuart M., *Enterprise Zones: Greening the Inner Cities*, New York, NY: Universe Books, 1981.

Cowan, Spencer M., *et al.*, 'Factors Influencing the Performance of Community Development Corporations', *Journal of Urban Affairs*, Vol. 21, 1999, pp. 325–340.

Dutt, Ashok K., 'Levels of Planning in the Netherlands, with Particular Reference to Regional Planning', *Annals of the Association of American Geographers*, Vol. 58, No. 4, 1968, pp. 670–685.

Dutt, Ashok K., 'Regional Planning in England and Wales: A Critical Evaluation. Part II: The London and Birmingham Areas as Case Studies', *Plan*, Vol. 10, No. 3, 1970.

Dutt, Ashok K., 'A Comparactive Study of Regional Planning in Britain and The Netherlands', The Ohio Journal of Science, Vol. 17, No. 6, 1970, pp. 321–335.

Dutt, Ashok K. and Allen G. Noble, 'Growing and Changing of Cities and the Spread of Urbanization in South Asia', in Ashok K. Dutt, H. N. Misra and Meera Chatterjee (eds.), *Explorations in Applied Geography*, New Delhi: Prentice-Hall of India Ltd., 2008, pp. 275–307.

Elling, Richard C., and Ann Workman Sheldon, 'Determinants of Enterprise Zone Success: A Four State Perspective', in Roy E. Green (ed.), *Enterprise Zones: New Directions in Economic Development*, Newbury Park, CA: Sage Publications, 1991, pp. 136–154.

Erickson, R. A., and S. W. Friedman, 'Comparative Dimensions of State Enterprise Zone Policies', in Roy E. Green (ed.), *Enterprise Zones: New Directions in Economic Development*, Newbury Park, CA: Sage Publications, 1991, pp. 155–176.

Giloth, Robert, 'Social Investment in Jobs: Foundation Perspectives on Targeted Economic Development during the 1990s', *Economic Development Quarterly* 9: 1995, pp. 279–289.

Grasso, Patrick G. and Scott B. Crosse, 'Enterprise Zones: Maryland Case Study', in Roy E. Green (ed.), *Enterprise Zones: New Directions in Economic Development*, Newbury Park, CA: Sage Publications, 1991, pp. 122–135.

Great Britain Department of the Environment (GBDE), *An Evaluation of Enterprise Zone Experiment*, Prepared by PA Cambridge Economic Consultants, London: Her Majesty's Stationery Office, 1987.

Hall, Peter., *Green Fields and Gray Areas, Papers of the RTPI Annual Conference*, Chester, London: Royal Town Planning Institute, 1977 (address to RTPI).

Hisrich, Robert D., *Entrepreneurship, Intrapreneurship, and Venture Capital*, Lexington, MA: D. C. Heath and Company, 1986.

Humann, David., *Doing Business in Hong Kong*, Hong Kong: Price Waterhouse Press, 1992.

Lo, C. P., *Hong Kong*, London: Belhaven Press, 1992.

Morison, H., *The Regeneration of Local Economies*, Oxford: Oxford University Press, 1987.

Narendranath, K. G., 'SEZs left high and dry, need succour', *The Economic Times*, Times of India, 16 December 2008.

Perkin, Ian K., 'Barren Rock to World Entrepot: Recent Economic Developments and Issues', in Albert H. Yee (ed.), *Whither Hong Kong: China's Shadow or Visionary Gleam*?, New York: University Press of America, 1999.

Rai, Saritha, 'Oases of Modernity Amid India's Desert of Public Services', *New York Times*, 3 October 2006, Section C, p. 5.

Rodwin, Lloyd, *Nation and Cities; A Comparison of Strategies for Urban Growth*, Boston, New York, Atlanta, Geneva, Illinois, Dallas, Palo Alto: Houghton Mifflin Company, 1970.

Rowley, Chris and Robert Fitzgerald, 'Managed in Hong Kong: Economic Development, Competitiveness and Deindustrialization', in Chris Rowley and Robert Fitzgerald (eds.), *Managed in Hong Kong: Adaptive Systems, Entrepreneurship and Human Resources*, Portland, OR: Frank Cass, 2000, pp. 1–12.

Royal Commission on the Distribution of Industrial Population, *Report HMSO*, Cmd. 6153, London, 1940, p. viiii.

Rubin, B. M. and M. G. Wilder, 'Urban Enterprise Zones: Employment Impacts and Fiscal Incentives', *Journal of the American Planning Association*, Vol. 10, 1989, pp. 3–17.

Rubin, Marilyn Marks, 'Urban Enterprise Zones, Do they Work? Evidence from New Jersey', *Public Budgeting and Finance*, Vol. 10, 1990, pp. 3–17.

Spindler, Charles J. and John P. Forrester, 'Economic Development Policy: Explaining Policy Preferences Among Competing Models', *Urban Affairs Quarterly*, Vol. 29, 1993, pp. 28–53.

Tym, R. and Partners, *Monitoring Enterprise Zones: Year Three Report*, London: Roger Tym Associates, 1984.

The Economist, 'India's Special Economic Zones: Cash Cows', 14 October 2006, pp. 45–46.

Van Delft, A. and A. Kwaak, 'National Development and Economic Policy in the Netherlands since 1945 with Special Reference to Regional Economic Policy', in Ashok K. Dutt and Frank J. Costa (eds.), *Public Planning in the Netherlands*, Oxford: Oxford University Press, 1985, pp. 107–121.

Wei, Yehua Dennis, 'Process of Globalization, Social Milieu and Multiple Trajectories in the creation of Technopoles', in Baleshwar Thakur, George Pomeroy, Chris Cusack and Sudhir K. Thakur (eds.), *City, Society and Planning*, Essays in Honour of Professor A. K. Dutt, New Delhi: Concept Publishing Company, Vol. 2, 2007, pp. 23–41.

Wilder, Margaret G. and Barry M. Rubin, 'Rhetoric Versus Reality: A Review of Studies on State Enterprise Zone Programs', *Journal of the American Planning Association*, Vol. 62, 1996, pp. 473–491.

Zhang, G. L., 'A Comparative Analysis of Urban Economic Development in the Yangtze Delta' (in Chinese), *Urban Forum*, Vol. 4, 2003, pp. 40–43.

11

Multi-faceted Regional Inequality in China

YEHUA DENNIS WEI AND CHI KIN LEUNG

Regional inequality is an important area of academic inquiry and government policy. Scholars, however, disagree over the trend of regional inequality and the forces underlying it. Neoclassical doctrines suggest that regional differentials will eventually be equalized under efficient markets and factor mobility conditions, while divergence perspectives, especially dependency and structural schools, contend that spatial disparities are inevitable and self-reinforcing (Borts and Stein, 1964; Soja, 1980). Empirical evidence in developed and developing countries is mixed. This is especially so in transitional economies where the pace, scope and consequences of reforms are uneven.

Foreign Direct Investment (FDI) has had a far-reaching impact on host economies, such as capital formation, employment, technology, trade, economic growth and core-periphery relations (Taylor and Thrift, 1982; Dicken, 1998). On the one hand, FDI is regarded as a dynamic force in economic development providing capital, creating jobs, spreading new technology, promoting trade and improving economic well-being. On the other hand, FDI is considered to be responsible for economic dependence, cultural imperialism and the intensification of core-periphery relationships in developing countries. The recent rapid globalization of economic activities and changing roles of government institutions further compound the patterns and processes of regional inequality. Globalization is increasingly recognized in the development literature as a factor that further marginalizes the periphery and generates new forms of poverty and inequality (Hirst and Thompson, 1996; Sassen, 1991). However, there is a lack of theoretically-informed empirical work on the impact of FDI on regional inequality in developing transitional economies.

Given the concern for national stability, studies of regional inequality in China, especially since the economic reforms, are numerous (Fan, 1995;

Wei, 2000a; Wei and Fan, 2000). These studies generally show that the disparities between the coastal and inland provinces have been increasing since China's economic reforms. The increasing disparities have been attributed to several factors including fiscal policies, investment allocation and internal migration. However, the impact of globalization and FDI on regional inequality has not been adequately investigated, even though several publications have analysed the geographical distribution and network relations of foreign investment in China (Gong, 1995; Leung, 1993; Leung, 1996; Hsing, 1998). Since China is the world's second largest recipient of international capital flows and because FDI generally prefers coastal areas, the impact of globalization and FDI on regional inequality in China can be substantial. This chapter, therefore, aims to assess the impact of globalization and FDI on regional inequality in post-Mao China.

In the following sections we will examine the development of foreign economic policy and FDI in post-Mao China in the context of globalization. The impact of FDI on regional inequality in China will then be assessed. Through a case study of Jiangsu Province the chapter will further assess the impact of globalization and FDI at the sub-provincial level. This chapter defines FDI strictly in an economic sense. Investments from the Greater China areas (Hong Kong, Macau, Taiwan) are considered part of FDI. As China has absorbed most of its FDI since the early 1990s, this chapter focuses its analyses on the 1994–1999 period when the impacts of FDI during the first twenty years of reforms were most pronounced.

Reform, Location, and Spatial Distribution of Foreign Investment in China

Since the implementation of economic reforms in 1978 China has gradually restructured its state-controlled economy. A part of the reform measures was to open up the economy, encouraging foreign investment and trade with the objectives of promoting advanced technology and export growth. China's adoption of the open-door policy came in a period during which the volume of international investment and trade was rapidly expanding, a situation due in part to the increasing wage levels of advanced economies, spatial separability of production functions and capability of large firms to articulate their networks over distance. The entry of newly industrialized Asian economies, including the Greater Chinese economies of Hong Kong and Taiwan, into various post-industrial stages of development further contributed to the expansion of international investment and trade flows.

However, China's process of opening up to the outside world has been gradual and spatially uneven. Following the introduction of the Joint Venture Law that permitted foreign investment in 1979, China established four Special Economic Zones (SEZs) in 1980 as experimental sites for the open-door policy. All four SEZs were located in South China – Shenzhen, Zhuhai, Shantou in Guangdong, and Xiamen in Fujian (Fig.11.1). A major goal of selecting these four zones was to attract investment from Hong Kong and overseas Chinese, a strategy that was deemed necessary at that time given the lack of an attractive investment environment for non-Chinese firms. Nevertheless, despite the provision of certain investment incentives, such as income tax reduction and duty exemptions, the

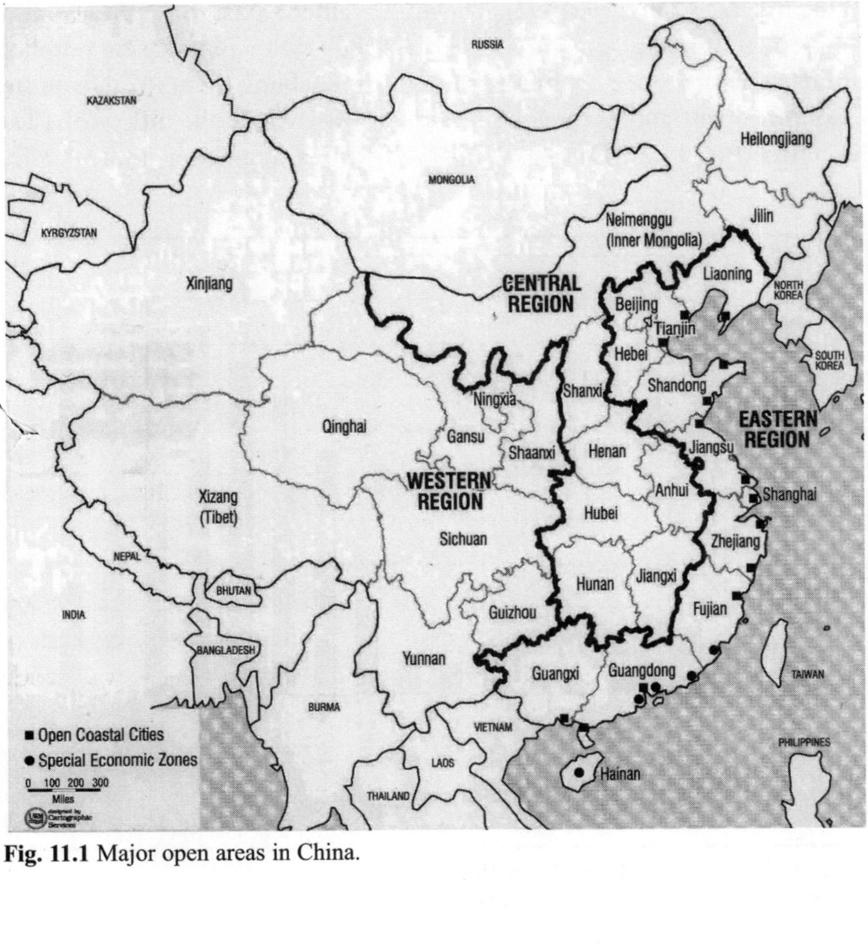

Fig. 11.1 Major open areas in China.

inflow of foreign investment to China at that time remained insignificant because of the infancy of the open-door policy. During 1979–83, China only received US$ 1.8 billion in FDI (State Statistical Bureau (SSB), 2000). FDI in that period came primarily from Hong Kong and was concentrated in hotel construction activities.

As economic reforms progressed from 1984–1986, China extended the provision of investment incentives for foreign firms to 14 other coastal cities (from Beihai in Guangxi to Dalian in Liaoning) and three open areas (Zhujiang, Minnan and Changjiang) (Fig. 11.1). This extension broadened the bases for foreign investment and created a more balanced spatial structure of foreign investment along the coast. To further attract foreign investment, the State Council approved 'Twenty-Two Articles for Foreign Investment' in 1986, offering additional incentives to foreign firms including greater access to the domestic market and autonomy in hiring practices (Howell, 1993). The improvement in the investment environment continued throughout the late 1980s with an increasing number of areas granted open economic status, thus enabling them to enjoy more autonomy in attracting foreign investment. As a result, the inflow of FDI hastened (Fig. 11.2). During 1984–1989, China attained a total of US$

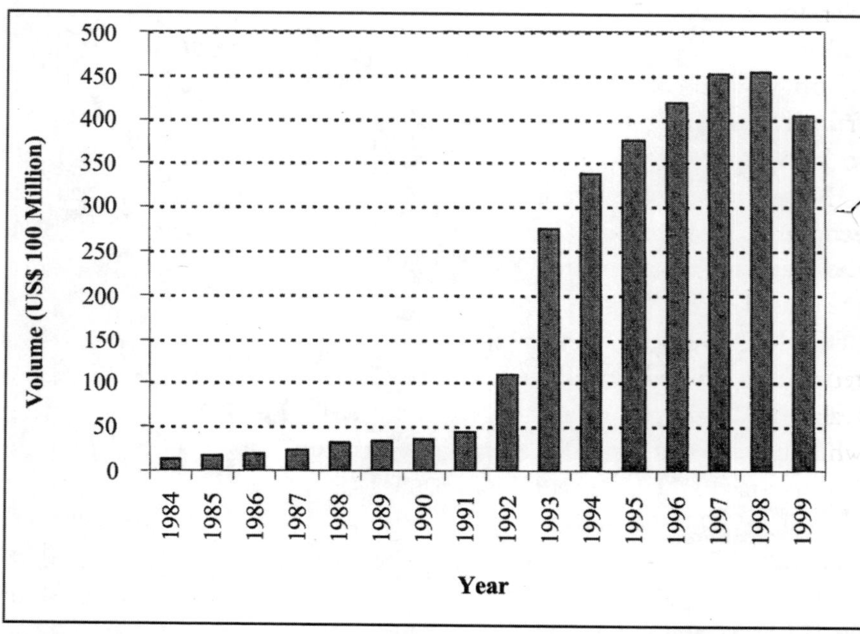

Fig 11.2 The growth of FDI in China, 1984–1999.

13.7 billion in FDI (SSB, 2000). Compared to the previous period, FDI in this period continued to come primarily from Hong Kong, but it comprised a higher level of manufacturing investment as Hong Kong in the mid-1980s began to decentralize its production activities, particularly to Guangdong.

Despite the disruption caused by the Tiananmen incident in 1989, China continued to deepen its economic reforms and open-door policy throughout the 1990s. Since 1993, foreign firms were able to enjoy preferential treatment in most of China, with more areas opened up for FDI. Foreign firms were also able to enjoy a broader range of investment incentives and simpler procedures for investments (Fu, 2000). The increasing sophistication of the investment environment and the greater autonomy of local governments in attracting foreign investment augmented the open-door policy.

As a result, foreign firms, especially global corporations, began to establish their operations in China in a significant manner. In addition, China eliminated most of the restrictions on capital inflows from Taiwan and South Korea. These two economies quickly emerged as two of the primary source economies of China. During 1990–1999 China realized a total of US$ 290.4 billion FDI, an amount that was nearly 19 times more than that of the 1979–1989 period (SSB, 2000). The upsurge in investment inflows from other countries brought about a significant diversification of origins and sectoral composition of inflows. The proportion of FDI from Hong Kong declined from 54.9 per cent in 1990 to 40.6 percent in 1999.

Nevertheless, the substantial inflow of FDI has produced a highly uneven economic landscape in China. Due to better international accessibility, the majority (approximately 87.7 per cent) of realized FDI is located in the coastal region (Figs. 11.3 and 11.4). Although there was gradual diffusion of FDI into the central region, the western region remained an insignificant recipient of foreign investment. From 1983 to 1999, the share of China's realized FDI in the central region increased from 1.1 to 9.4 per cent, while the amount of FDI in the western region declined. In 1999 these two regions together accounted for only 12.2 percent of the total amount of realized FDI in China.

Of all the coastal provinces, Guangdong has attracted the largest amount of FDI (Table 11.1). But as other coastal provinces gradually opened up for foreign investment, the dominance of Guangdong in the national structure of FDI declined. Guangdong's share of realized FDI in China

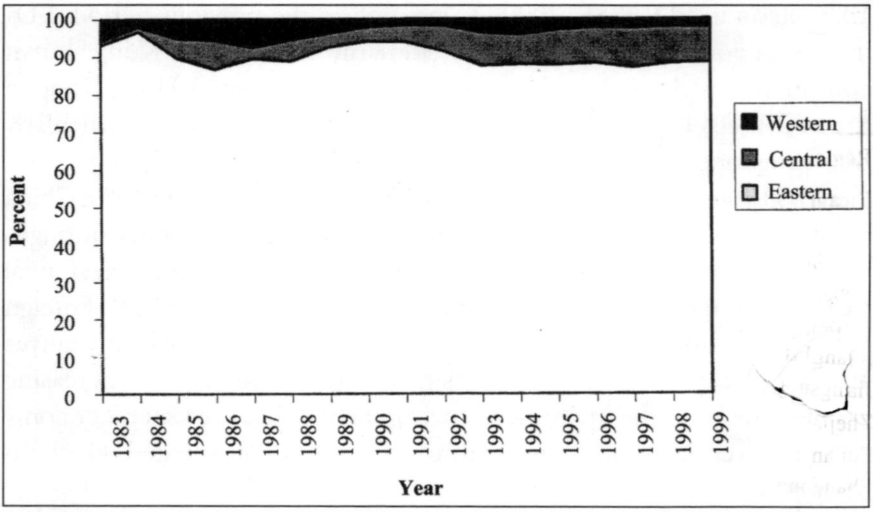

Fig. 11.3 Regional distribution of FDI in China, 1983–1999.

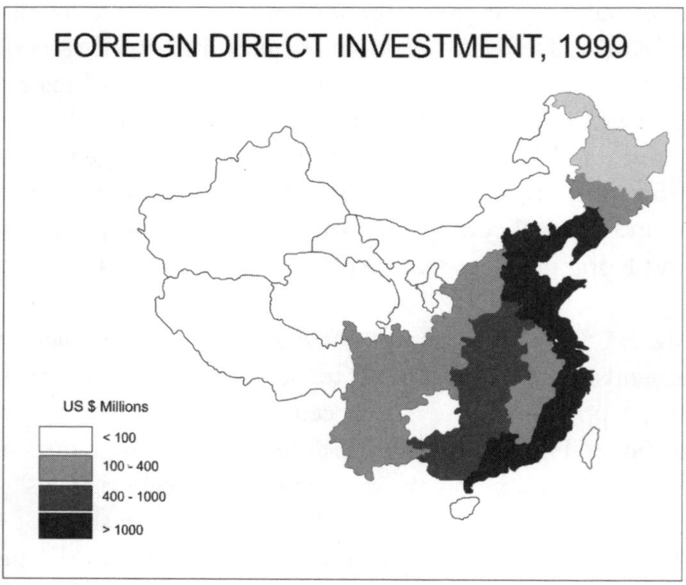

Fig 11.4 Provincial distribution of FDI in China in 1999.

declined from 69.4 per cent in 1983 to 29.2 per cent in 1999. Meanwhile, the amount of FDI attracted by Jiangsu, Fujian, Shanghai and Shandong increased (Table 11.1). This regional shift of FDI from Guangdong to other coastal provinces reflects the increasing openness of China's economy and sophistication of the investment environment. Foreign firms

Table 11.1 Provincial Distribution of FDI in China (US$ Millions), 1983–1999.

	1983		*1990*		*1999*	
	Total	*Per cent*	*Total*	*Per cent*	*Total*	*Per cent*
Region	577	100.0	3,242	100.0	39,935	100.0
Eastern Region	536	92.9	3,045	93.9	35,050	87.8
Beijing	76	13.1	277	8.5	1,975	4.9
Tianjin	5	0.8	83	2.6	1,764	4.4
Hebei	1	0.2	39	1.2	1,042	2.6
Liaoning	7	1.2	248	7.6	1,062	2.7
Shanghai	11	1.9	177	5.5	2,837	7.1
Jiangsu	9	1.5	141	4.3	6,078	15.2
Zhejiang	3	0.4	48	1.5	1,233	3.1
Fujian	16	2.8	290	8.9	4,024	10.1
Shandong	3	0.5	151	4.7	2,259	5.7
Guangdong	400	69.4	1,460	45.0	11,658	29.2
Guangxi	6	1.1	30	0.9	635	1.6
Hainan	0	0	101	3.1	484	1.2
Central Region	6	1.1	122	3.8	3,747	9.4
Shanxi	0	0	3	0.1	391	1.0
Nei Monggol	3	0.6	11	0.3	65	0.2
Jilin	0	0	17	0.5	301	0.8
Heilongjiang	1	0.2	25	0.8	318	0.8
Anhui	0	0	10	0.3	261	0.7
Jiangxi	0	0	6	0.2	321	0.8
Henan	0	0	10	0.3	521	1.3
Hubei	0	0	29	0.9	915	2.3
Hunan	2	0.4	11	0.3	654	1.6
Western Region	34	5.9	75	2.3	899	2.3
Sichuan	19	3.3	16	0.5	341	0.9
Guizhou	0	0	5	0.2	41	0.1
Yunnan	0	0	3	0.1	154	0.4
Xizang	0	0	–	–	–	0.0
Shaanxi	3	0.4	42	1.3	242	0.6
Gansu	13	2.2	1	0.0	41	0.1
Qinghai	0	0	–	–	5	0.0
Ningxia	0	0	1	0.0	51	0.1
Xinjiang	0	0	7	0.2	24	0.1

Source: State Statistical Bureau, 1992, 2000.

were able to better exploit factor advantages in other Chinese coastal provinces, especially those in the Changjiang Delta region. The competition among provinces for FDI intensified as provinces and localities were allowed to either utilize their resources to establish development zones, provide additional incentives for foreign firms, or both.

It can be seen that the concentration of FDI in China and the subsequent diffusion of it within the coastal region are attributable in part to the various stages of the open-door policy by the Central Government. Places that were first opened up for foreign firms are the primary centres of FDI, while those opened up later are secondary foci. As ties with Greater China economies, especially Hong Kong, was a primary determinant of the establishment of the SEZs at the beginning, Guangdong naturally accrued most of the FDI in the 1980s. The subsequent opening up of the coastal region promoted the gradual diffusion of FDI in that region. The presence of established industrial bases, international port facilities and large domestic markets facilitated the diffusion. This was especially true for the coastal provinces in the East China region with Shanghai, the largest industrial and economic centre in China, as another major centre of foreign investment. Although most of the central and western regions are now able to compete with the coastal region for foreign investment under similar terms as prescribed by the Central Government, the lower levels of industrial capabilities and international accessibility there remain the primary determents of FDI inflows.

In addition to the policy of the Central Government and geographical factors, the actions of local governments are also instrumental in producing this uneven FDI landscape (Wei, 2000b). Localities in the coastal region vary significantly with respect to the ingenuity and flexibility of government administration, with some being more active in promoting FDI inflows than others. Within the authority prescribed by the Central State, local governments can provide additional incentives to foreign firms including lower land use fee, income tax refunds, subsidies, and cost-free services. Some localities even use their personal relationships with Central Government officials so as to attract some large foreign ventures of repute to their territories. Localities with greater financial capabilities or better relations with the Central Government are likely to secure more FDI inflows. This is especially true for the more developed areas of the coastal region. The less developed areas of the coastal region, along with most of the central and western regions, are unlikely to have such competitive advantages.

Foreign Investment and Regional Inequality in China

While the actions of central and local states have produced a spatially uneven investment landscape, the forces of globalization can accentuate or moderate such regional differences. To minimize risks, foreign investors generally prefer the following areas of host economies for their investments – coastal locales, economic centres and special districts. Coastal locales offer foreign investors better accessibility to required inputs and the world market. These locations are especially important for outward-oriented ventures engaging in time-sensitive activities. Economic centres, on the other hand, provide foreign ventures greater local connections and market potential. These locations are especially important for inward-oriented ventures that focus on host markets. For both outward and inward-oriented ventures, special districts furnish lower investment overheads and simpler operational environment for specific types of investments. Free-trade areas, for example, provide import or export ventures, or certain types of import tariff exemptions, while high-technology areas offer technology-complex ventures, lower income tax or longer tax holidays. FDI tends to accentuate regional differences in host economies that have disparate spatial economic structures. The reverse is true when host economies have more balanced structures.

Aside from the level of investment, the regional consequences of FDI vary with the properties of global capital and of the local economy. At a macro-structural level, other things being equal, FDI accentuates regional differences if it significantly varies in space with respect to capital formation, employment generation and income growth. In China, during 1994–1999 FDI was a major source of capital formation in all core coastal areas – Guangdong-Fujian, Shanghai-Jiangsu, and Beijing-Tianjin (Table 11.2). In all core areas, FDI accounted for at least 15 per cent of total fixed asset investments in the period. The contribution to capital formation from various sources differed among the three areas. Investments from Greater China, as a group, were a more important contributor to capital formation than other sources in the Guangdong-Fujian area.

The Greater China economies, however, were not a significant source of capital formation in areas such as Shanghai, Jiangsu and Tianjin. Of the other coastal provinces, Hebei and Zhejiang had low levels of capital formation accounted for by FDI, as they are in the shadow areas of Beijing-Tianjin and Shanghai, respectively (Table 11.2). The higher degrees of

Table 11.2 Capital Formulation, Employment Generation and Wage Level of FDI by Province.

	Percent FDI Contribution to Total Fixed Asset Investment (cumulative, 1994–1999)		*Change in Urban Employment 1994–1999 (million persons)*			*Wage Level by Ownership Sector, 1999 (Yuan)*	
	Foreign	*Greater China*	*Total*	*Local*	*Foreign*	*State*	*Others inc. Foreign*
Beijing	12.5	9.5	–0.26	–0.43	0.17	9645	12575
Tianjin	14.3	3.4	–0.51	–0.75	0.24	8072	10522
Hebei	4.4	1.2	0.17	0.10	0.07	5653	5625
Shanxi	4.7	0.8	–0.28	–0.27	–0.01	5596	5810
Inner Mongolia	1.2	0.2	–0.29	–0.31	0.02	4996	4283
Liaoning	8.5	3.3	–2.40	–2.58	0.18	5894	6648
Jilin	8.3	1.5	–1.17	–1.21	0.04	5765	5820
Heilongjiang	1.8	1.4	–1.43	–1.48	0.05	4985	6309
Shanghai	12.9	4.2	–0.85	–1.24	0.39	11015	13186
Jiangsu	11.7	3.4	–0.68	–0.96	0.28	7186	7740
Zhejiang	4.9	2.0	0.17	0.07	0.10	7734	8672
Anhui	4.4	1.0	0.41	0.37	0.04	5600	7680
Fujian	11.0	12.1	0.28	–0.19	0.47	6609	8076
Jiangxi	2.5	1.5	–0.39	–0.41	0.02	5050	7275
Shandong	5.4	1.8	1.75	1.42	0.33	6356	5850
Henan	2.6	2.7	0.71	0.61	0.10	5265	5197
Hubei	6.0	4.1	0.19	0.17	0.02	5411	5754
Hunan	2.6	1.4	0.37	0.35	0.02	5412	5897
Guangdong	10.4	11.1	0.76	0.17	0.59	9494	10569
Guangxi	6.0	2.1	0.16	0.14	0.02	5525	6480
Hainan	14.4	5.7	–0.11	–0.12	0.01	5365	8579
Sichuan	2.9	2.1	–0.67	–0.74	0.07	5476	6338
Guizhou	2.2	0.8	0.03	0.02	0.01	5125	5613
Yunnan	2.2	1.5	0.32	0.30	0.02	6419	6863
Tibet	0.1	0.0	–0.01	–0.01	–	11519	12411
Shaanxi	1.8	0.8	0.33	0.32	0.01	5142	6054
Gansu	3.2	1.4	–0.08	–0.08	0.00	6131	6734
Qinghai	0.7	1.0	–0.03	–0.03	–	6946	6176
Ningxia	1.7	0.6	0.03	0.02	–	5819	5888
Xinjiang	0.8	0.8	–0.16	–0.16	0.00	6067	6626
CHINA	7.1	3.9	–3.64	–6.91	3.27	6280	8261

Source: State Statistical Bureau 1995, 2000.

private entrepreneurship in Zhejiang further attributed to the low levels of capital formation by FDI. The significance of FDI to capital formation declined with increased distance from the coast. With the exception of Sichuan (including Chongqing which became a municipality in 1997) none of the inland provinces had more than 5 per cent of their total fixed asset investments from FDI. The remote western region of China in particular had very limited foreign investment, and much of that was for resource and infrastructure development.

The same three areas – Guangdong-Fujian, Shanghai-Jiangsu and Beijing-Tianjin – similarly shared strong employment generation through FDI (Table 11.2). By 1999, these three areas accounted for 65.7 per cent (4.03 million) of all urban employment generated by FDI in China. Guangdong in particular had 1.43 million jobs created by FDI. The number multiplies when it includes the employment generated by industrial processing activities. The majority of the provinces in the three areas had at least 10 per cent of the employment accounted for by FDI. In other coastal provinces, including Hebei and Zhejiang, FDI was not a significant source of urban employment. As with capital formation, the effect of FDI on employment generation declined with distance. In the central and inland regions FDI was not a significant source of urban employment. It accounted for less than two per cent of urban employment in all non-coastal provinces.

It should be indicated that FDI not only generates direct employment but it can also induce indirect employment growth by developing supplier relationships or other linkages with local firms. However, FDI, may hamper employment growth if it displaces local firms. This situation arises when FDI competes with indigenous firms in similar product or market areas. Of the six provinces in the three core areas, only Guangdong experienced employment growth in both the foreign and local sectors because of the high degrees of outward-oriented FDI. The other five provinces suffered from a decline in employment in the local sector. Foreign ventures were a significant displacement force as they were primarily market entry investments. That Guangdong had parallel employment growth in the local sector indicates the competitiveness of local firms. The longer history of open-door policy, and the better access to latest world market trends because of its proximity to Hong Kong incubated a significant number of local firms that are capable of competing with foreign ventures. In all non-coastal provinces FDI was not a significant source of employment growth. It only generated 0.92 million urban employment by 1999.

With respect to income growth, FDI created a larger multiplier effect in Beijing-Tianjin, where firms had a wage level 30 per cent higher than state enterprises in the same area (Table 11.2). The income multiplier effect was somewhat moderate in the two other core regions. FDI in Shanghai-Jiangsu and Guangdong-Fujian had a wage level approximately seven to 22 per cent higher than their equivalent state enterprises. The difference in wage levels reflects the greater number of high-level positions in the Beijing-Tianjin area, as a higher proportion of foreign firms locate their China headquarters or liaison offices in Beijing in particular. The greater proportions of manufacturing activities, especially in Guangdong and Jiangsu, accounted for the smaller wage differentials between the foreign and state sectors. It is interesting to note that in these areas FDI does not necessarily have higher wage levels than state sectors. This was the case for two coastal provinces (Shandong and Hebei) and three non-coastal provinces (Inner Mongolia, Henan and Qinghai). Higher degrees of production specialization in the local sectors, such as energy production in Inner Mongolia and Henan, was one of the factors for this difference.

The higher wage levels that accompanied FDI, along with the corresponding increase in wage levels among local firms, inevitably increased the income gap between the coastal and the non-coastal region. In 1994, the difference in average worker wage between the highest (Shanghai in the coastal region) and the lowest ranking provinces (Heilongjiang in the non-coastal region) in the nation was 4,030 yuan (SSB, 1995). In 1999, that difference (between Shanghai in the coastal region and Shanxi in the noncoastal region) increased to 10,576 yuan (SSB, 2000). With the exception of Tibet, because of heavy state subsidies, four of the six provinces in the three core areas (Shanghai, Beijing, Tianjin and Guangdong) had an average annual worker wage of at least 10,000 yuan in 1999. In addition to Shanxi, other provinces that had one of the lowest levels of average worker wage in 1999 included Henan and Inner Mongolia. The dominance of coal extraction and processing activities, and the corresponding absence of higher value-added industries, are the factors underlying the lower wage levels in these three provinces.

The same increase in regional disparities can also be observed along the lines of Gross Domestic Product (GDP) and government revenue. In 1994, the three core areas shared 30.6 per cent of China's GDP and approximately 35.8 per cent of government revenue. In 1999, the percentages increased to 33.4 and 38.1, respectively. A significant portion of the increase in GDP and government revenue (+0.91 and +0.84 estimated percentage points respectively) came from Guangdong where FDI had greater contribution to capital formation or employment generation or both (SSB, 1996 and 2000). The increases in GDP, and especially government revenue, are important as the provinces have more power to secure greater autonomy for dealing with foreign firms from the Central Government. The provinces also have more resources for improving their investment environment and for providing additional incentives to foreign investors. As a result other provinces, especially those in the non-coastal region, are less capable of competing for foreign investment. This causes the disparities between the coastal and the non-coastal regions to persist.

Perhaps one of the most important impacts of FDI on the disparities between the coastal and the non-coastal regions is the uneven distribution of technological and managerial capabilities that foreign investment produces. Given the higher level of technology and managerial sophistication of foreign ventures and the corresponding higher wage levels, the coastal locales where FDI is concentrated become the primary destinations of first-rate professionals and workers from other provinces, especially for those from the non-coastal region. The outward migration of these workers not only discourages foreign investment inflows but also hinders the long-term development of the non-coastal provinces. Firms in major non-coastal provinces such as Shanxi and Hubei have to offer higher wages than their coastal counterparts in order to retain some of the first-rate professionals and workers. In 1994, the three core areas accounted for 34.6 per cent of scientific researchers and polytechnical services workers in China. In 1999, the percentage increased to 35 per cent. The proportional increase is much larger when only top ranked engineers, scientists and managerial personnel are considered, as reflected by the larger proportional increase in the number of patents granted to the three core areas in the coastal region, from 32.1 per cent in 1994 to 37.4 per cent in 1999.

Foreign Investment and Regional Inequality in the Jiangsu Province

Besides disparities in FDI distribution within China as a whole, FDI is also unevenly distributed within the individual provinces of China. Through a case study of Jiangsu we will further reveal the uneven distribution of

FDI within provinces and the impact of globalization and FDI at the sub-provincial level. Representing the dynamic coastal provinces, Jiangsu is a major recipient of FDI in China. Historically, Jiangsu had closer ties with the international economy than many other provinces of China since the 1840s, when Shanghai and Nanjing were opened up for foreign investment and trade. Southern Jiangsu (Sunan) in particular has been better integrated into the international market than other areas of China.

As analyzed previously, China's open-door policy is spatially uneven and foreign investment is concentrated in China's coastal provinces. Jiangsu is one of the coastal provinces of China that have enjoyed preferential open-door policies. Favourable state policy and local initiatives have stimulated the increase of foreign investment in Jiangsu. From 1985 to 1999, FDI in Jiangsu increased from US$ 11.9 million to US$ 6.4 billion (Jiangsu Statistical Bureau (JSB), 2000).

While lagging behind Guangdong and Fujian in the early post-Mao stage of opening up to the outside world, Jiangsu has made considerable efforts to attract FDI. In 1984, Nantong and Lianyungang were among China's 14 open coastal cities designated to attract foreign investment and promote foreign trade. In 1985, all cities and counties in Sunan, including Suzhou, Wuxi, Changzhou and 12 counties under its jurisdiction, became open areas. These local governments obtained preferential policies in the approval of investment projects, tax relief for using foreign capital, tariff reduction on import and the retension of exchange earnings. Therefore, in the mid-1980s most of the open areas in Jiangsu were located in Sunan and enjoyed the advantage of early action, while in the rest of Jiangsu, only two cities – Lianyungang in northern Jiangsu (Subei) and Nantong in central Jiangsu (Suzhong) – were opened for foreign investment. Gradually, the open-door policy was extended to the rest of Jiangsu. In 1988, more areas in central Jiangsu were opened to foreign investment. Overall, 9 cities and 40 counties in Jiangsu were opened up for foreign investment and trade. However, Xuzhou and Huaiyin, two municipalities in Subei, were still not opened to foreign investment and trade. This year the first wholly foreign-owned enterprise was established in Changzhou, a city located in Sunan. In the following years more cities and counties in northern Jiangsu became open areas. To compete for foreign investment, numerous open districts have been established in Jiangsu, often with subsidies from local budgets. Even townships and villages in Sunan have attracted some foreign investment.

Foreign investors are interested in locations with favourable policies provided by the Central Government, a more developed infrastructure, strong support of local governments and close ties with international markets. Favorable state policy and local conditions have steered the bulk of foreign investment to Sunan. In 1995, 72.1 per cent of FDI in Jiangsu was concentrated in Sunan, with Suzhou alone attracting 48.7 per cent of FDI. FDI in northern Jiangsu was considerably less than Sunan, largely due to less favourable state policies and local conditions. Figure 11.5 illustrates the concentration of FDI in Sunan in 1995. Large gaps exist among cities in attracting foreign investment. For example, FDI in Suzhou (US$ 559 million) was much larger than that in Huaiyin (US$ 16 million). Among counties, Zhangjiagang attracted the most investment with US$ 600 million in FDI, followed by Kunshan (US$ 505 million), Jiangyin (US$ 252 million) and Wuxian (US$ 251 million), all located in Sunan. Several counties in northern Jiangsu, including Fengxian, Lianshui and Sihong, had FDI amounting to less than half a million dollars.

Patterns of FDI can be further understood by an analysis of the uneven distribution of open districts in Jiangsu. In 1995, Jiangsu had 12 national-level open districts. Except for Nantong in Suzhong and Lianyungang in Subei, ten of them were located in Sunan. Suzhou municipality alone had five national-level development districts, while none of the counties in northern and central Jiangsu had national-level open districts. In Sunan, Kunshan's open district is one of the largest county-level open districts of China. In 1999, Kunshan attracted US$ 5[illegible]0 million FDI and ranked the first among the counties in Jiangsu (JSB, 2000).

Such patterns of FDI have had tremendous impact on regional inequality in Jiangsu. During the post-Mao period, rural inter-county inequality and inter-regional inequality across southern, central and northern Jiangsu increased dramatically. Inter-regional inequality across Sunan, Suzhong and Subei, based on coefficient of variation (CV) of per capita gross value of industrial and agricultural output, almost doubled from 0.33 in 1978 to 0.64 in 1995. Correspondingly, CV for rural inter-county inequality increased from 0.45 in 1978 to 1.04 in 1995, an increase of 131 per cent. The counties with the fastest economic growth are all located in Sunan, including Kunshan, Zhanjiagang, Wuxi, Wuxian, Wujiang, Taicang, Wujin and Jiangyin. The rapid growth of these counties in Sunan has contributed greatly to the rise of the north–south gap and rural inter-

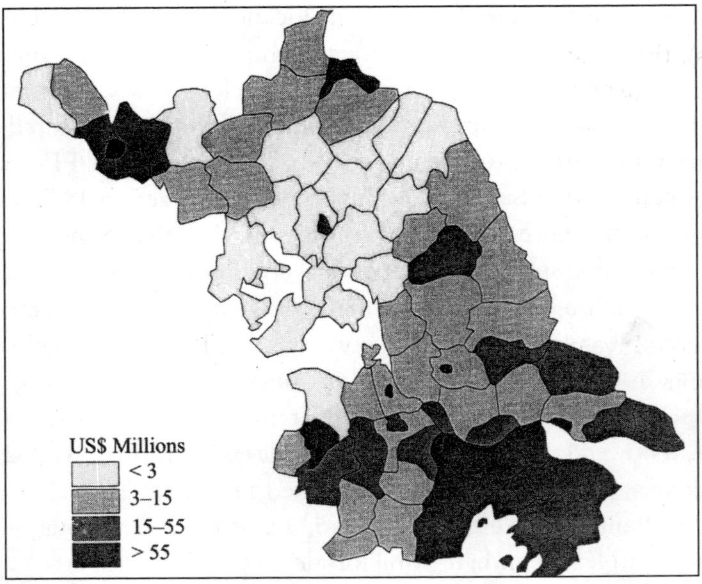

Fig. 11.5 The distribution of FDI in Jiangsu Province, 1995.

county inequality. The growth of Sunan's counties is due largely to local efforts and factor endowments and also due to the infusion of foreign investment.

The uneven geographical distribution of FDI is one of the major factors leading to the rise of the Sunan–Subei gap in Jiangsu. In 1998, foreign investment accounted for 16.3 per cent of total fixed assets investment in Jiangsu (JSB, 2000). Subei, with a poorer, more rigid economy, tends to rely more heavily on the state budget. With declining state budget support for local spending, Subei has been struggling to find alternative sources of financing for economic development. The concentration of FDI in Sunan has provided substantial capital for its economic growth and further increased the gap between Sunan and Subei in investment.

Since FDI brings modern technologies and management techniques (United Nations Conference on Trade and Development, 1999), regions with more FDI, Sunan in this case, tend to enjoy a higher level of technology and management skills. Such a gap in technology has been extended by the technology policy of China which provides preferential policies to localities with such advantages, such as Suzhou and Nanjing, while localities in Subei have been de-emphasized by China's technology policy. Moreover, since much of export in China is from Foreign Invested Enterprises (FIEs), the concentration of FDI in Sunan has led to the increasing gap between Sunan and Subei in foreign trade, another factor leading to the rise of inter-regional inequality in Jiangsu.

State-Owned Enterprises (SOEs) in China have been undergoing tremendous restructuring and have been laying off workers. With the dramatic increase of FDI, FIEs have become a major source of job growth in Jiangsu. In 1999, Suzhou municipality had 383,259 people employed in FIEs, and FIEs employed more workers than any other sector (that is, the state, collective or private sector) in Kunshan, Changshu and Zhangjiagang (Suzhou, 2000). FIEs also tend to provide higher wages for their workers, which increases the wage gap between Sunan and Subei. FDI's multiple effects have also provided job and income opportunities for the local enterprises which have developed production relations with FIEs. In summary, FDI has become an important factor in the increase in the Sunan–Subei gap and the emergence of a group of counties in Sunan.

While FDI in Subei has increased in recent years, the gap between Sunan and Subei in FDI remains large. The favourable investment conditions and preferential policies have sustained Sunan's attractiveness to foreign investment and maintained the inflow of FDI into Jiangsu. Meanwhile migrants have provided an abundant labour force for the FIEs in Sunan. The locational concentration of FDI makes the task of reducing poverty and regional inequality difficult.

Conclusion

This paper has examined the development of foreign economic policy and the rise in FDI in post-Mao China in the context of globalization. The adoption of an open-door policy, coinciding with a period during which the volume of international investment and trade was rapidly expanding, led to significant inflows of FDI into China. The inflows of FDI concentrated first in Guangdong and were later diffused to other coastal provinces especially those on the Yangzi delta. However, after 20 years of the open-door policy the inflows of FDI to non-coastal regions remains limited.

In addition to the coastal/non-coastal divide, FDI further gave rise to a differentiated landscape within the coastal region, with Guangdong–Fujian,

Shanghai–Jiangsu and Beijing–Tianjin as the core areas. In these core areas FDI was a significant source of capital formation, employment generation and income growth. These core areas gradually expanded their share of China's GDP, government revenue, and technological and managerial capabilities. Due to this they are more capable than other areas in attracting foreign investment and in long-term economic development.

The forces of globalization operate similarly at a sub-provincial level. FDI concentrated in the more developed parts of Jiangsu created a development divide between the southern and northern parts of the province. The case of Jiangsu further illustrates the importance of local ingenuity and government policy in attracting FDI to sub-provincial localities.

With the gradual opening up of interior China, the Central Government has indicated a gradual elimination of location-based open-door policies. However, the declining control of the Central Government has made localities major players in attracting foreign investment. The importance of FDI in job generation and economic growth has stimulated competition among local governments in China to provide preferential policies in land, infrastructure, tax and finance to attract foreign investment. Consequently, numerous local-level open districts have been established and huge agricultural lands have been converted to industrial use, leading to the rapid decline of cultivable land in China. Problems such as corruption, unfair competition and labour malpractice have also emerged in many cities. More efforts are needed to address the social and environmental impact of FDI in China.

*This research was supported by grants from the Geography and Regional Science, and China, Taiwan, Mongolia and Southeast Asia Programs, National Science Foundation of US (Grant BCS-0004357 and BCS-0004281), and the Natural Science Foundation of China (41028001).

References

Borts, G. H. and J. L. Stein, *Economic Growth in a Free Market*, New York: Columbia University Press, 1964.

Dicken, P., *Global Shift*, London: Paul Chapman, 1998.

Fan, C. C., 'Of Belts and Ladders: State Policy and Uneven Regional Development in post-Mao China', *Annals of the Association of American Geographers*, Vol. 85, No. 3, 1995, pp. 421–449.

Fu, J., *Institutions and Investments: Foreign Direct Investment in China during an Era of Reforms*, Ann Arbor: University of Michigan Press, 2000.

Gong, H., 'Spatial Patterns of Foreign Investment in China's Cities, 1980–1989', *Urban Geography*, Vol. 16, No. 3, 1995, pp. 198–209.

Hirst, P. and G. Thompson, *Globalization in Question*, Cambridge, MA: Blackwell, 1996.

Howell, J., *China Opens its Doors*, Colorado: Lynne Rienner Publishers, 1993.

Hsing, Y., *Making Capitalism in China*, New York: Oxford University Press, 1998.

Jiangsu Statistical Bureau (JSB), *Jiangsu Tongji Nianjian (Jiangsu Statistics Yearbook)*, Beijing: Chinese Statistics Press, 1996–2000.

Leung, C. K., 'Personal Contacts, Subcontracting Linkages, and Development in the Hong Kong-Zhujiang Delta Region', *Annals of the Association of American Geographers* Vol. 83, No. 2, 1993, pp. 272–302.

Leung, C. K., 'Foreign Manufacturing Investment and Regional Industrial Growth in Guangdong Province, China', *Environment and Planning A*, 1996, pp. 513–536.

Sassen, S., *The Global City*, Princeton, NJ: Princeton University Press, 1991.

Soja, E., 'The Socio-spatial Dialectic', *Annals of the Association of American Geographers*, Vol. 70, No. 2, 1980, pp. 207–225.

State Statistical Bureau (SSB), *Zongguo Tongji Nianjian (China Statistical Yearbook)*, Beijing: China Statistical Press, 1992–2000.

Suzhou Statistical Bureau, *Suzhou Tongji Nianjian (Suzhou Statistical Yearbook)*, Beijing: Chinese Statistical Press, 2000.

Taylor, M. and N. Thrift, *The Geography of Multinationals*, London: Croom Helm, 1982.

United Nations Conference on Trade and Development (UNCTD), *World Investment Report 1999: Foreign Direct Investment and the Challenge of Development*, New York: United Nations, 1999.

Wei, Y. H. D., *Regional Development in China: States*, Globalization, and Inequality, London: Routledge, 2000a.

Wei, Y. H. D., 'Locational Patterns of Foreign Investment in China', in A. G. Noble, B. Thakur, A. B. Mukherji, and F. J. Costa (eds.), *Geographic and Planning Research Themes for the New Millennium*, New Delhi: Vikas Publishing House, 2000b, pp. 163–183.

Wei, Y. H. D. and C. C. Fan, 'Regional Inequality in China: A Case Study of Jiangsu Province', *The Professional Geographer*, Vol. 52, No. 3, 2000, pp. 455–469.

12

Social Geography of the Minorities in Israel

ELISHA EFRAT

The State of Israel made great efforts to absorb hundreds of thousands of Jewish immigrants during the 1950s and 1990s. It has prepared for them a physical, economic and social infrastructure in the country and has integrated them into a community that is prospering by the day. Unfortunately, Israel has not done enough for the Arab minorities. The Arabs who live in the sovereign territory of Israel form a large share of the country's population, own much land in regions where they reside and are very much involved in Israel's politics. The Arab minorities who live in 'a State within a State', deserve a more serious treatment from the governmental bodies of Israel because of their demographic weight in the total population and their occupancy of large areas along the Israeli border with Judea and Samaria. The scope of the chapter is up to the September 2000 conflict, as it conspicuously marks some of the ramifications of these social geographic elements mentioned above.

Demographic Background

At the end of 1991, the minorities in Israel totalled 1,200,000 – about 17 per cent of the population in Israel. Their share in the total population is similar to that of the Jewish populations that reside in the new development towns. Most of the minorities are concentrated in the Northern District, including Upper and Lower Galilee. In 1991, this district comprised about 48 per cent minorities, a fact which demonstrates that both, minorities and the Jewish peoples in Galilee were demographically almost in complete balance. In the central mountainous part of Galilee, excluding the valleys of Hula and Lake Kinneret in the east, the valley of Visreel in the south and the coastal plain of Acre, which since the late 1880s has been the cradle of Jewish settlement in the northern part of the Land of Israel, the minorities comprised about 75 per cent of the total population. The percentage of the minorities in the Northern District is 2.7 times higher than in the total population of Israel, which just reaches 17 per cent. The number of minorities' settlements in the Northern District was 90 in 1999 and they comprised a quarter of all the settlements in this region. The number of their settlements with more than 5,000 inhabitants was 51, among them the town of Nazareth with 57,200 inhabitants, and Shefaram with 26,800 inhabitants. In Galilee, there are Arab villages with more that 10,000 inhabitants each, as Tamra with 21,300, Merar with 16,400, Sakhnin with 20,400 and Arabe with 14,800. Tamra and Sakhanin, for instance, had a population size similar to the Jewish town of Zefat which had 24,000 inhabitants. Nazareth, in fact, is bigger than any other Jewish town in central Galilee. The minorities of Israel are concentrated mainly in two regions, in the Eron valley, and along the eastern part of the coastal plain. In each of these areas thousands of minorities live in small towns and villages. The biggest Arab town in the Eron valley is Um el-Fahem and some other big villages such as Kara and Kafr Kara have about 11,000 inhabitants each. In the eastern coastal plain, there are large Arab settlements at Baqa el Garbiye with 17,400 inhabitants, Tira with 17,500 inhabitants and Taybe with 27,000 inhabitants. The latter two have gained the status of municipalities. These regional concentrations of minorities in Israel create two conspicuous phenomena – a definite regional majority of Arabs in central Galilee and a dense Arab populated strip along the eastern coastal plain, parallel to the 'Green Line'. The minorities in Israel, numbering 1,200,000 people have ownership, right of possession and direct influence over the cultivation and exploitation of about 250,000 acres of land, or about 10 per cent of Israel's territory north of the valley of Beer Sheba. Their villages are dispersed mainly between the Nazareth mountains in the south and the Lebanon border in the north (Fig. 12.1). The minorities comprise, as mentioned earlier, 17 per cent of the total population of the country and reside in 130 settlements. A quarter of them live in mixed Jewish–Arab towns like Jerusalem, Yafo, Lod, Ramla and Acre, a third in the rural settlements in Galilee and the rest in the Eron valley and the eastern coastal plain. Additionally, there are about 100,000 Bedouins who live in the Negev and Judean deserts. The Arab population which resides along the eastern

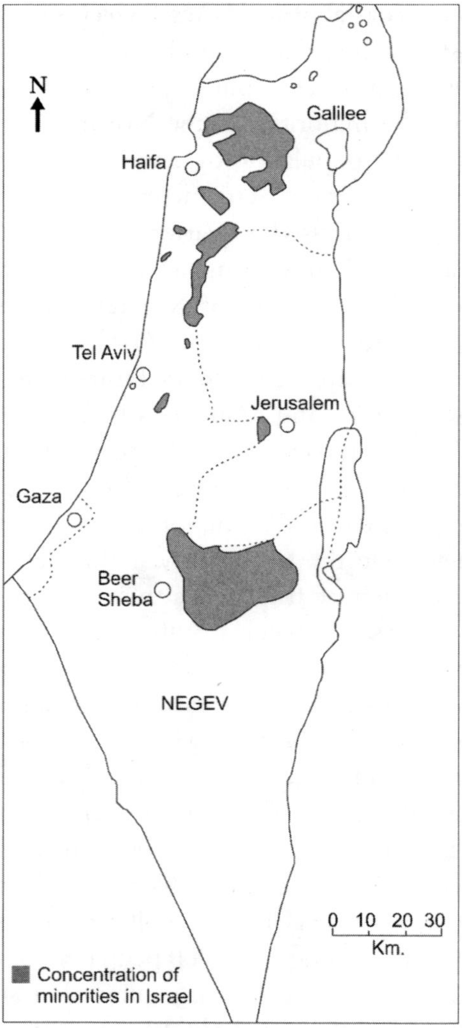

Fig. 12.1 Concentration of minorities in Israel.

coastal plain, from Eron valley in the north to the Modiin region in the south, once belonged to a wider Arab region, to a great triangle of space whose angular points were the towns of Nablus, Tulkarm and Jenin. A remainder of it belongs now to Israel's sovereign territory where about 100,000 Arabs are resident. In this area, as in other Arab villages of Galilee, a regional homogenous system of services is developing along main communications axes and around large villages with 5,000 inhabitants and more. About two-thirds of the rural Arab population is integrated in these regional systems, but are gradually taking the form of isolated areas within the State of Israel. The minority population has increased much since the establishment of the State of Israel. In 1948, they totalled not more than 156,000 people. The increase in their numbers in the 1970s and 1980s was about 3.5–4 per cent per annum, one of the highest in the world. The birth rates among the Arabs decreased, but so did the death rates, which kept the total increase high. More than 75 per cent of the Arabs in Israel were born after 1948. The Arab population does not have any need to emigrate, they live in big families and are bound to their lands. The official governmental plan for population distribution towards the year 2020 envisages more than 1.5 million minority inhabitants in the country with a large section of them in settlements with more than 10,000 inhabitants each. The minorities are at present on a trend of economic and social change. While before 1948 their economy was based mainly on autarchic farms on small plots of land, after the establishment of the State, their economic basis has changed considerably. Their agricultural activity became integrated into the modern economy of Israel which increased their production and resulted in a higher standard of living. Because of their commercial connections with the urban markets in Israel and their economic and social interrelations with the Israeli population, their traditional barriers of rural life were broken. More of them worked outside their villages, their occupation in agriculture declined and more than half of their workforce in the rural settlements is now engaged in non-agricultural activity. This change increased their income, but at the same time, also split their paternal homes into smaller families. The national aspirations of minorities increased the demands for new building sites, public institutions and conversion of agricultural land in use for housing. Lately, more industry has been initiated and developed in the Arab villages, which is the first sign of semi-urbanization. The Israeli Government encouraged local government in the Arab sector to a certain degree, and in the last years of the twentieth century, some large villages received the status of towns.

Arabs and Jews: A Spatio-Social Sketch

The difference in the geographic and demographic patterns of Arab and Jewish populations is one of the major political, economic and social issues in Israel. In Israel, the Jewish population receives greater economic priority, and their advantages are higher in the densely populated Jewish areas of the central parts of the country. Their disadvantages lie mainly in the Arab-populated areas of Galilee and the eastern coastal plain. The Government tries to decrease these disadvantages with a policy of encouraging Jewish population distribution into these peripheral regions. The Arabs, on the other hand, find advantage in being concentrated in certain regions of the country where they are able to encourage the sprawl of their settlements and to seize open land for expansion, but suffer disadvantages of life in the periphery, which decreases their opportunities for occupation, level of services and standard of living (Fig. 12.1).

Not much had been done by the Israeli authorities to advance the minorities' standard of living in the periphery. Regional and local planning efforts have not been developed equally in the Jewish and Arab sectors resulting in differences in construction, housing infrastructure, roads, public institutions and industrial zones. Compared to the urban and rural planning that exists in the Jewish sector, the planning of the Arab villages is still backward. No clear conceptions regarding the image and character of a rural Arab village exist; nor are there any notions about its special architectural features or the new ways of construction that should be adopted. Not many planners and architects are engaged in the field of Arab village planning in cooperation with their inhabitants. Many villages lack approved outline schemes and modernization has still not reached all of them. Although rural planning is at a very advanced stage in many countries of the world, with interesting solutions to different kinds of rural problems, in the Arab sector of Israel not much has been implemented. The Israeli Government directs national and local development in the Arab sector at a slow pace. At the local level it aspires to improve housing, basic rural infrastructure and to diversify occupations, while at the national level it acts to prevent Arabs from building on government-owned land and to keep a demographic balance between Jews and Arabs through strong policies. The first level seems to be constructive, but it is connected with town planning restrictions in the villages and with strict steps taken against deviations from the rules, despite the fact that population density in the Arab villages is very high and the economic and demographic pressure under which the population lives often compels them to infringe the law and to change arable land into land for other uses. The Government's approach to the minorities' situation does not provide enough solutions to the real problems they face. Although the

Government made efforts to improve development in the Arab sector, what remains very conspicuous is the Arab population's continuous struggle against confiscation of their land in Galilee for Jewish settlement, and also the Bedouins' struggle against their displacement from the pasture lands that they owned in the past. The Bedouins of the Negev were driven out from the lands on which they lived for generations and were relocated to some unsuccessful settlements, east of Beer Sheba, where the government wanted to settle them despite the fact that these settlements did not fit their way of life. One of the well-known expressions of the Arab population against the discrimination faced by their sector is the 'Land Day' celebrated every 31 March. This celebration highlights several facts – the minorities' identification with the Palestinians in the administrative territories under Israeli occupation; the deepening of national identity between the Arabs on both sides of the 'Green Line'; and the support they give to their local leaders who struggle to achieve civil rights. 'Land Day' has a political and social meaning for the minorities, especially because of the 'Intifada', an uprising in the territories in 1987 and again in 2000, which has influenced their nationalistic emotions. It reveals the root of the problems which the Arab face – land for them is a symbol and an essence. They relate to their land as the origin of their existence and the territory which gives them a real stake in this country. They believe that they have always lived on this land. But now they suffer discrimination, living without full civil rights and as low-ranking citizens. Their nationalistic aspirations are similar to those of the Palestinians in the occupied territories. The 'Green Line' which separated them in the past did not make them better Israelis. Since Israel does not demonstrate a clear minority policy, their future in the framework of the Jewish State remains uncertain. The minorities in Israel represent some irreversible basic facts which may not please many Israeli politicians. Seventeen per cent of Israel's population which owns hundreds of thousands of acres of land are to some extent discriminated against in planning and development. This population is urbanizing very rapidly. It does not emigrate and needs adequate physical infrastructure for modern living. It has advanced in education, economy and social needs. It constitutes a nationalistic population which conflicts with Israel's political aims. It is located adjacent to Israel's borders with the territories along the 'Green Line', with all the security problems that lie beyond it. In order to improve the situation of the minorities, it is necessary to prepare for them a timely social, economic and settlement plan on a national scale according to their social characteristics: to develop a hierarchy of regional settlements with service centres of different sizes, to develop models of modern rural building, to release to a certain degree agricultural land for housing, commerce and industry, and to foster the construction of public institutions, roads, industrial zones and parks in the larger villages and semi-urban settlements.

Conclusion

After the gradual absorption of the Jewish mass-immigration in the 1950s and 1990s and all the new towns that had been constructed for that purpose, the time has come to devote financial sources to the Arab sector. Such a step may prevent further political tension in the area. There is still a danger that the minorities in Israel, influenced by the Palestinians in the occupied territories, may rise up again as in October 2000 and demand autonomy for themselves within the sovereign State of Israel if further feelings of being discriminated against do not come to an end. The identification of the Arab minorities with the Palestinians' outburst of anger after the tragic massacre at the Cave of Machpela at Hebron in 1994 revealed the hidden wrath they harbour against the Government. One dramatic painful occurrence brought about an Arab revolt against the army and the Government, expressed by pelting stones on vehicles, mass public demonstrations with burning of tyres on highways and other symptoms of anger which were not seen earlier. Their feelings of discrimination, which lie under a thin cover of tolerance, suddenly burst out after the first spark that was light at the Temple Mount in Jerusalem. The formation of a policy in regard to the Arabs of Israel is not so difficult, since an agreed policy exists. It is not a matter involving the solutions of a nationalist conflict, but one of granting equality to citizens of the country. An examination of all party platforms shows that there is no disagreement among them on this point. The problem is only one of integrating minorities into a national and regional system. The time has come to direct more resources towards the minorities. Such a step is likely to avert possible political tensions in the future, such as 'Land Days' and memorial days which reflect the frustration of the minorities who wish to live in a democratic country.

References

Efrat, E., *Israel – A Contemporary Political Geography*, Bochum: Universitätsverlag Dr N. Brochmeyer, Vol. 17, 1996, pp. 126–130.

Grossman, D., 'Arab Settlement Activity in the Sharon and its Margins', in R. L. Singh (ed.), *Geographic Dimensions of Rural Settlements*, Varanasi: NGSI, 1976.

Khamaisi, R. and A. Gonen, *The Arabs in Israel on the Wake of Peace*, Jerusalem: Floersheimer Institute for Policy Studies, 1993.

Khamaisi, R., *Issues in Planning and Development of Localities in the Palestinians Entity*, Jerusalem: Floersheimer Institute for Policy Studies, 1994.

Khamaisi, R., 'Land Ownership as a Determinate in the Formation of Residential Areas in Arab Localities in Israel', *Geoforum*, Vol. 26, No. 2, 1995, pp. 211–224.

Kipnis, B. and I. Schnell, 'Challenges in the Distribution of Arabs in Mixed Jewish-Arab Cities in Israel', *Economic Geography*, Vol. 52, No. 2, 1978, pp. 168–180.

Portugali, J. and M. Sonis, 'Palestinian National Identity and the Israeli Labour Market', *The Professional Geographer*, Vol. 43, No. 3, 1991, pp. 265–279.

Portugali, J., *Implicate Relations: Society and Space in the Israeli–Palestinian Conflict*, Dordrecht: Kluwer Academic Publishers, 1993.

Schnell, I., 'The Israeli Arabs: The Dilemma of Social Integration in Development', *Geographische Zeitschrift*, Vol. 78, No. 2, 1990, pp. 78–92.

Schnell, I., 'Perceiving Ethnic Space: Israel–Arab Cognition of the Central Galilee', *Geography Research Forum*, Vol. 12, 1992, pp. 62–80.

Schnell, I., 'Urban Restructuring in Israeli Arab Settlements', *Middle Eastern Studies*, Vol. 30, No. 2, 1994, pp. 330–350.

Soffer, A., 'Geographical Aspects of Changes within the Arab Community of Northern Israel', *Middle Eastern Studies*, Vol. 19, No. 2, 1983, pp. 213–243.

Viftachel, O., 'Geopolitical Aspects of Stability in a Biethnic State: The Case of the Arabs in Israel', *Politics*, Vol. 23, No. 2, 1988, pp. 448–456.

Viftachel, O., *Planning a Mixed Region in Israel: The Political Geography of Arab-Jewish Relations in the Galilee*, Avebury: Gower Publishing, 1992.

Viftachel, O., 'The Political Geography of Ethnic Protest: Nationalism, Deprivation and Regionalism among Arabs in Israel', *Transactions: Institute of British Geographers*, Vol. 23, No. 1, 1997, pp. 91–110.

13

Urban Sprawl and Socioeconomic Change in the Kathmandu Valley, Nepal

KRISHNA PRASAD POUDEL

Nepal is the most densely populated country in the Himalayas, where the population has grown from 5.5 million in 1930 (Zurink and Karan 1999) to 23 million in 2001 (Central Bureau of Statistics (CBS), 2002). Kathmandu Valley is located in a tectonic depression in the central Himalayas over flat lacustrine soils deposition. Geographically situated in the central part of Nepal, Kathmandu is the capital of the country. The Valley has a centripetal flow of rivers and streams originating in the surrounding hills and flowing out to the south from a narrow gorge. Kathmandu is located within the valley of the Bagmati river system, eight tributaries of which drain the city. The river system has always been the city's main source of water for drinking and irrigation and it holds religious, cultural and social value for the Nepalese (Asian Development Bank/International Centre for Integrated Mountain Development, (ICIMOD), 2006). Three local administrative districts – Kathmandu, Lalitpur and Bhaktapur lie in the Katmandu Valley. According to the Local Self-Governance Act 1999 of the Government of Nepal, these districts are further divided into smaller local administrative and development units – one metropolitan city, one municipality and 57 Village Development Committees (VDCs) in Kathmandu district, one sub-metropolitan city and 41 VDCs in Lalitpur district, and, two municipalities and 16 VDCs in Bhaktapur district. The district boundary in most cases follows the water divide except for a small southern part of Lalitpur district (Fig. 13.1). The urban inhabitants are confined to the central part of the Valley whereas the rural settlements are distributed across the outer fringes up to the foothills.

The three districts in the Valley cover 899 square kilometres or approximately 347 square miles, which is six per cent of the total area of the

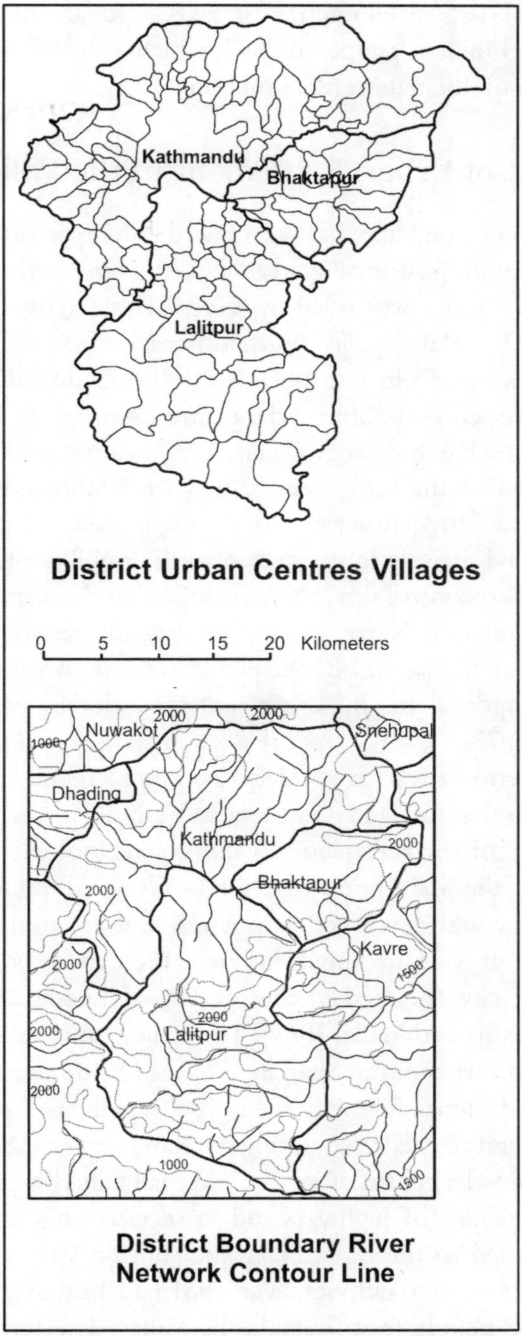

Fig. 13.1 Kathmandu Valley, a bowl-shaped depression with a narrow outlet to the south; urban area is located in the central part and interconnected across all three districts.

country (147,181 square kilometres or 56,827 square miles) and were inhabited by 1.63 million people in 2001, which is seven per cent of the total population of the nation (23.2 million).

Development of Urban Settlement in the Valley

Human habitation in the Valley has been traced to long before the Christian era. The '*Vanshavalis*' (historical genealogical documents) record that initially Kathmandu Valley was ruled by 'Gopal Bansi' (cow herders) from 900 to 700 BCE; by 'Mahisapalas' (buffalo herders) from 700 to 625 BCE; and by 'Kirat' Kings from 625 BCE to CE 100 (ICIMOD, 2007). The Valley was developed as a commercial centre even before 600 BCE, during the time of the Kirati dynasty (Malla, 1978). Zurink and Karan (1999) have mentioned that the settlement history of Kathmandu Valley goes back to as early as fifth century CE. In 494 CE, a group of powerful families, the Licchhavi dynasty in connected to the nobility of India, joined in a power block to control the mountain area that corresponds to much of present day central Nepal. After the eleventh century, Kathmandu (*Kantipur*), Lalitpur (*Patan*) and Bhaktapur (*Bhadgaoun*) became the capitals of small local kingdoms and the urban settlement developed around these capitals (Malla, 1978).

For a long period these urban centres remained the entrepot trade centres of goods that originated in India and Tibet. However, the growth and development of the Kathmandu Valley towns took place only during the latter part of the Malla period (AD 1476–1768). All these three towns in the valley grew and developed as political and economic centres and became capitals of various kingdoms over the centuries. The security afforded by the city encouraged the growth of handicrafts, trade and commerce (Shrestha and Malla, 1969). The Valley came under the rule of Gorkha King Prithwi Narayan Shah in 1769 and Kathmandu became the capital of unified Nepal. The city then grew rapidly as a political, commercial and cultural centre. Even during the Rana regime (1846–1950), the capital city remained a centre of power and maintained its importance of centrality. The opening of highways and air services and the provision of urban amenities led to the rapid expansion of the Valley. The political change from monarchy to democracy in 1951 had a significant impact on the migration of people from outside the Valley. The fertile valley was gradually peopled by migrants from the surrounding hills and outside

(Shrestha and Malla, 1978). The Valley has two principal landforms – alluvial and flood plains along the rivers and somewhat more elevated river terraces, locally called '*tars*'. The urban centres are mostly located in flat areas, with a slope of less than one degree and with soils of a predominantly loamy texture characterized by boulders (Haack and Khatiwada, 2007). Dutt and Geib (1998) stated that though Kathmandu Valley comprises a small area of the country, it is:

> ... economically the most prosperous region and socially prestigious ... The per capita income is the highest in the Valley which also has the higher literacy rate, better communications as well as sanitation facilities. The existence of a political capital in Kathmandu and productive agricultural land around it in the Valley has turned it into an attractive region. (Dutt and Geib, 1998, p. 281)

Population Growth and Demography

Kathmandu was first connected to India by air in 1953 and by motor road in 1956, and to Tibet (China) in 1965. The construction of highways and introduction of air services, along with increasing developmental activities with India and Tibet, led to the rapid development of the Valley. Three centres, one each from Kathmandu, Lalitpur and Bhaktapur, developed as urban centres. According to the 1961 Census, the three centres of the Valley had a total population of 204,097. Kathmandu alone accounted for over half with 122,507 inhabitants. In 1971, the Valley's population was 244,583, reaching 363,507 in 1981. After the political changes in the country in 1990, two large settlements of the Valley (Madhyapur Thimi and Kirtipur) were incorporated as a municipality. The total urban population of the Valley reached 995,966 in 2001. This amounts to a 60 per cent share of the total population of the three districts of Kathmandu Valley (CBS, 2002). In the last 50 years the urban population of Kathmandu Valley has increased nearly five-fold (Fig. 13.2). It is projected that the population of the Valley will reach 2.5 million in 2020 compared to 1.6 million in 2001 (Kathmandu Valley Town Development Committee, 2002). Three major reasons have been cited for increase in the urban population of Nepal – natural increase of population in the designated urban locations, in-migration from rural areas and abroad to urban areas, and reclassification of urban areas, which includes both boundary expansion of existing urban locations and declaration in gazette of new

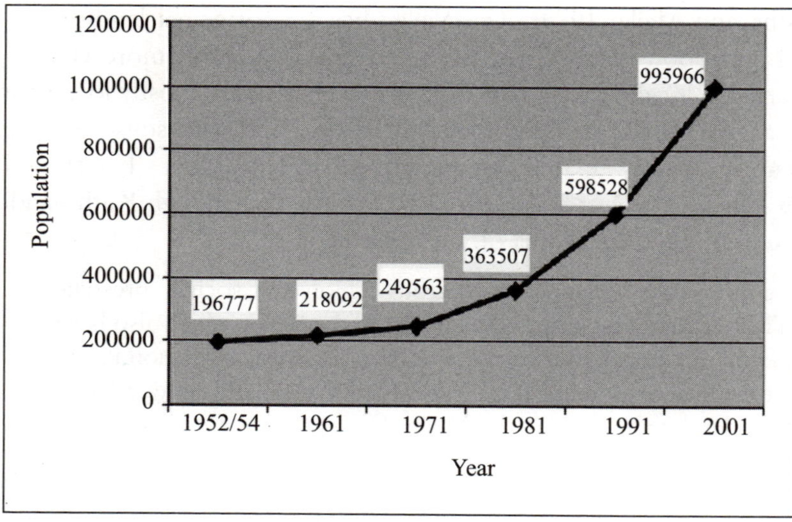

Fig. 13.2 Urban population of the Kathmandu Valley, 1961–2001 (Compiled from CBS 1961, 1971, 1981, 1991 and 2001).

localities as urban municipalities (Gurung, 1998). These reasons also apply to the Kathmandu Valley.

The population growth rate in urban areas is higher than that in the rural part of the Valley. Over the last two decades, the growth rate of the urban areas has remained over five per cent. The rate of urban growth has constantly increased from census years 1961 to 2001, whereas the rural area had an abrupt high rate of increase in 1971 and thereafter, the rate of increase slowed to slightly over two per cent (Fig. 13.3).

Along with the growth of population, the demographic composition has also changed in both rural and urban areas. According to the 2001 Census, the urban area of the Valley had a population of 996,000 with a male/female ratio of 112.7, whereas the rural area had a population of 629,000 with a male/female ratio of 102.6. The urban area showed a slightly decreasing trend in the 0–14 years age group. The 20–24 age group has the highest representation in the urban area. The rural area has not shown a clear decreasing trend in that age group (Fig. 13.4).

The age–sex composition of the population reveals that the urban population has a trend towards a concentration of youth. In-migration and transient populations seem to be the reasons behind this development.

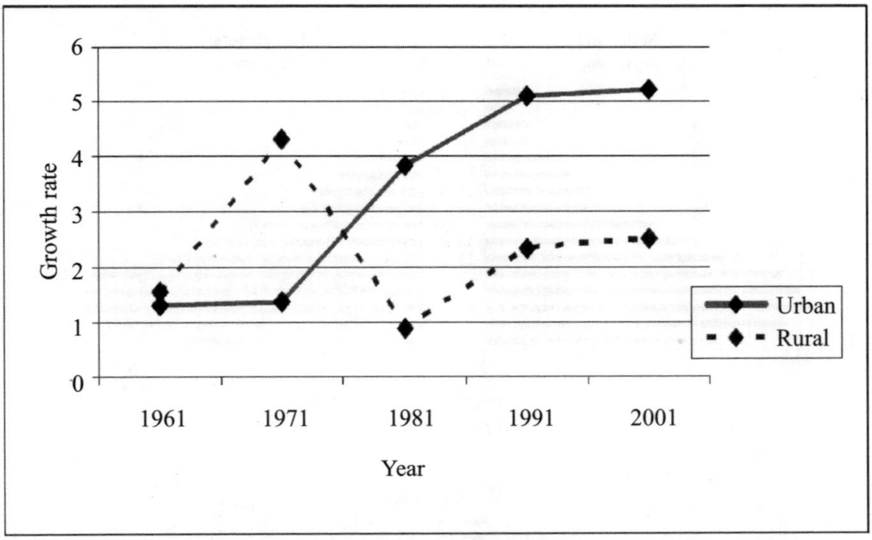

Fig. 13.3 Population growth in the Kathmandu Valley, 1961–2001 (CBS, 2003).

Urban Space Management

Both vertical and horizontal space of the Valley has been expanding tremendously with the increasing population (Fig. 13.5). Urban centres are confined to the central part of the Valley, where the population is densely concentrated. Even in 1961 it was reported that the Kathmandu Valley was one of the most densely populated areas in Nepal. The concentration of population was over 1000 persons per square kilometre in the Valley, whereas the urban part of the Valley had over 30,000 people in a square kilometre (Malla, 1969). According to the 2001 Census, the concentration was extremely high in the central part of the Valley (Fig. 14.6). Kathmandu Metropolitan City (KMC), Laitpur Sub-Metropolitan City (LSMC), Bhaktapur, Madhyapur, Thimi and Kirtipur municipalities are five designated urban areas. They are also confined to the central part of the Valley. Therefore, the outskirts of the valley has a smaller population.

KMC covers a 52 square kilometre area (20 square miles) and it had a population of over 672,000 in 2001. Crude density of the KMC is around 13,000 persons per square kilometre. The city core has an extremely high number of people living in a congested area. The city core also has a large number of temporary migrants who live in compact commercial-cum-residential and functional units. Because of the high concentration of

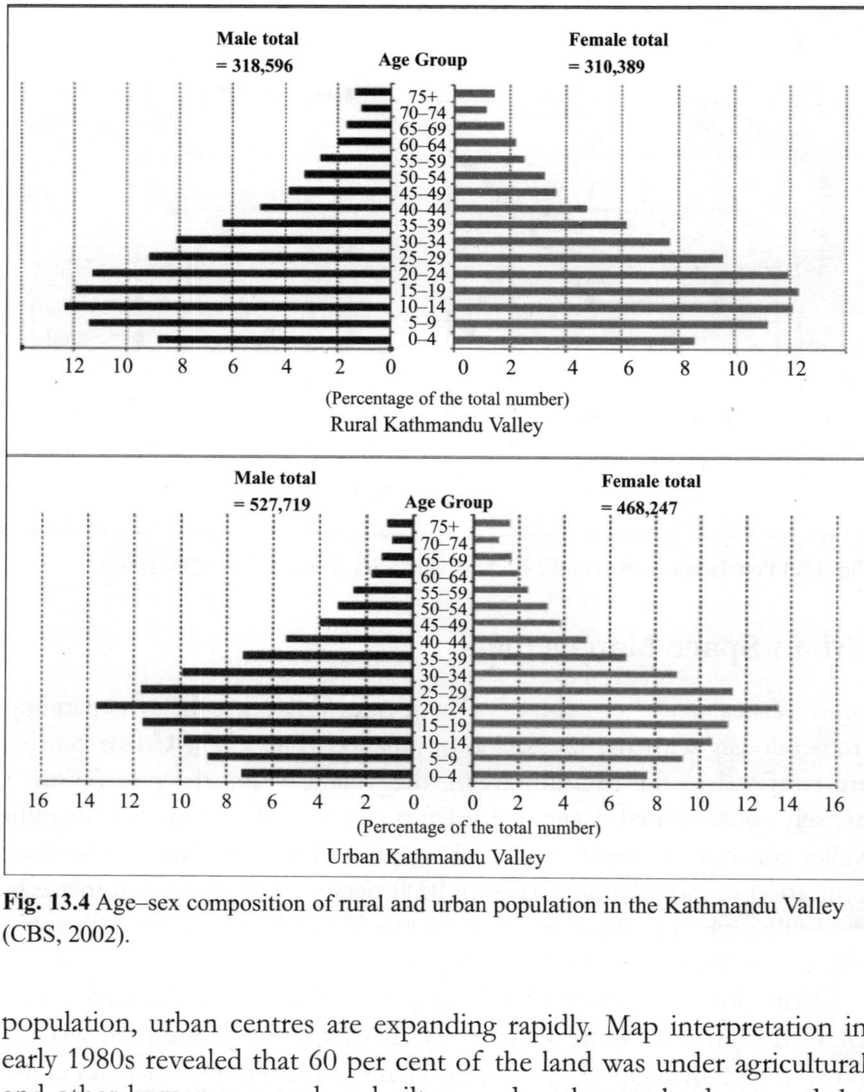

Fig. 13.4 Age–sex composition of rural and urban population in the Kathmandu Valley (CBS, 2002).

population, urban centres are expanding rapidly. Map interpretation in early 1980s revealed that 60 per cent of the land was under agricultural and other human use, such as built-up and settlement land use, and the remaining 40 per cent was under forest, fallow grazing, water bodies and wasteland categories (Poudel, 1983–84). The share of built-up areas in the Valley was 4.8 per cent in 1984 but has increased to 11 per cent in 1991 and 17.62 per cent in 1998, whereas agricultural land was 64 per cent in 1984, 56 per cent in 1991 and 43.72 per cent in 1998 (Koirala, 1998). There is a clear declining trend in available agricultural land and an increase in built-up area (Fig. 13.7).

Fig. 13.5 Urban space expansion in Kathmandu Valley.
A. Photograph of first high rise residential complex in the Valley, then under construction in Dhobighat, Lalitpur–an example of vertical expansion of urban space (photograph taken from the Tribhuvan University side by author on 4 May, 2008).
B. Expansion of urban structures towards the agricultural fields (photograph taken from the Chobhar Hill of the Nakhu area of Lalitpur by author on 01 May, 2008).

Concrete structures have been erected on a large part of the Valley floor. Thapa *et al.* (2008) have compared satellite imagery data of Bouddha area of Kathmandu for 1967 with the same for the years 1991 and 2007. They concluded that the predominantly rural agricultural landscape had gradually changed to a peri-urban landscape with increasing human settlement in 1991, and almost all such space had been transformed into built-up

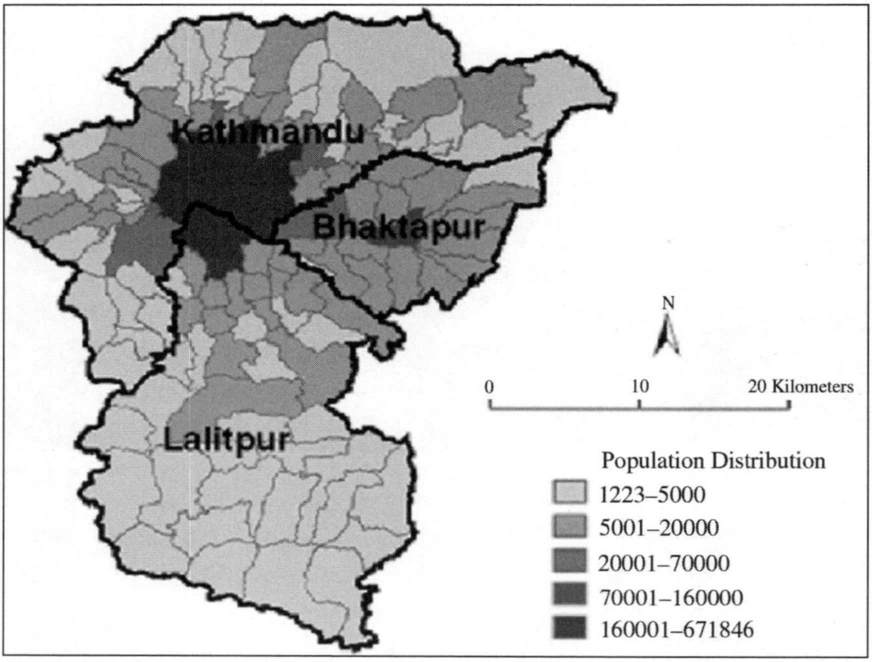

Fig. 13.6 Population distribution in the Kathmandu Valley, 2001 (CBS, 2002).

area by 2007. It is evident that the urbanization process in the Valley is taking place too rapidly, which has great impact on its urban management, environmental condition and emergency coping strategies. The old core of the city was well developed during the medieval period (fourteenth to seventeenth century) and the city had been gradually expanding to the periphery. In the past, houses were closely concentrated because of socio-cultural, religious, ethnic, political and economic factors. The traditional localities have been transformed into a continuous array of residential and commercial blocks (Fig. 13.8).

Thus, the present urban core has remnants of old structures with very few modern amenities and safety measures. Growing expectations of the new generation for more open space, wider roads and modern amenities forced the traditional core-area dwellers to shift to the urban fringe. In the meantime, abrupt lifestyle changes of the countryside elite, power seekers, upper-middle class workers, businessmen, government employees and students caused a sudden influx of population into the Valley. This, in turn, resulted in an abrupt increase in urban land value. It is estimated

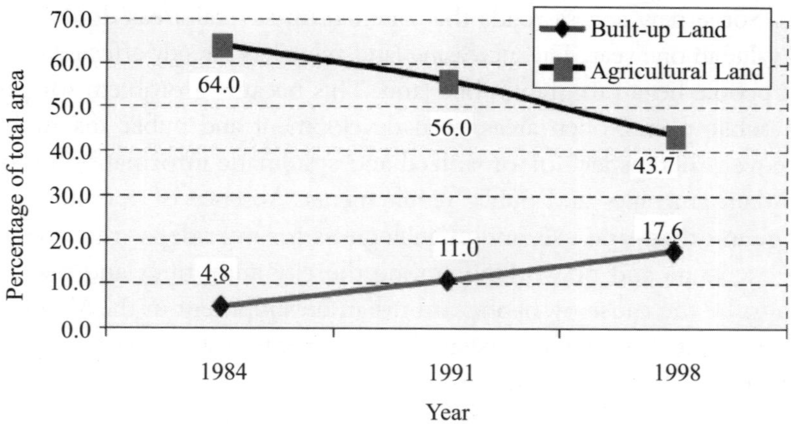

Fig. 13.7 Land use change in the Kathmandu Valley (Poudel, 1983–84; Koirala, 1998).

Fig. 13.8 IKONOS satellite image of core city of Kathmandu, i.e. Rani Pokhari, Asan and Indrachowk area, 1999.
Source: Kathmandu Metropolitan City, Kathmandu, Nepal.

that urban land value has increased by 40 to 50 per cent annually in recent years. Some new access roads that opened up several areas doubled the land value in one year. The increasing land value has directly affected public land; people began to grab public land. This became a problem for planning public places, open areas, road development and public institutions. Moreover, there is lack of organized and systematic information regarding urban amenities and public requirements. Absence of monitoring of change in urban land use, and unwillingness for inter-departmental database exchange and networking among the city authorities and planners seem to be the cause of haphazard urban development in the Valley. All these present a barrier to sustainable urbanization and development in the Valley.

Urban In-Migration Management Issues

Being a historical market centre, political capital and cultural centre, the Valley gained popularity among the people as their desired destination since its early days (Malla, 1978; Zurink and Karan, 1999). After being conquered by the Gorkha King, the Valley witnessed a further strengthening of its political power and strategic importance. Gradually, people from other parts of the country and even foreign nations migrated to the Valley in large numbers. Between 1984 and 1998, approximately 6,300 hectares (24 square miles) of fertile and productive agricultural land was lost to urbanization, industrialization, and quarrying of sand, soil and stone. Between 1984 and 1994, the Valley's urban area increased from 3,096 to 8,378 hectares (12 to 32 square miles) and 5,282 hectares (20 square miles) of fertile agricultural land was lost to urbanization (Ministry of Population and Environment (MoPE), 1999). It is estimated that more than half of the Valley's high grade land, that is, 43 percent of the existing agricultural land, will be lost to urban sprawl by 2010 (Halcrow Fox and Associates 1991, MoPE, 1999). The migrant population accounted for 11.1 per cent of the total urban population in 1981. This proportion has increased in the past decade because of political conflict. A study carried out by ICIMOD in 1993 (MoPE, 1999) revealed that migration contributed to less than 10 per cent of the urban population of Kathmandu between 1952–1961, about 6 per cent between 1961–1971, jumping to about 42 per cent between 1971–1981, and over 64 per cent between 1981–1991. The percentage of migrant population is comparatively less in Lalitpur

Table 13.1 Population of Kathmandu Valley and place of birth, 2001.

Kathmandu Valley	*Total population*	*Total native born (%)*	*Born in same district (%)*	*Born in other district*		*Foreign born (%)*
				VDC (%)	*Municipality (%)*	
Urban	995,966	96.97	61.52	30.66	4.77	3.03
Rural	628,985	99.39	79.05	18.93	1.38	0.62

Source: Central Bureau of Statistics, 2002.

and Bhaktapur districts, which increased 47 per cent and 12 per cent respectively between 1981 and 1991. According to the 2001 Census, nearly 40 per cent of the urban population was born elsewhere but lived in the Valley (Table 13.1). The proportion of the population born in the same location was higher in the rural part of the Valley. This reveals that the in-migration rate is higher in the urban part of the Valley in comparison to its rural counterpart.

A large part of the country is poor and has very low per capita income. According to the National Living Standard Survey (2004) the national average annual per capita income was Rs. 15,162 (US$ 236.35 given the foreign exchange rate on 4 May, 2008[1]) (CBS, 2004). The urban centres are considered better off in terms of income opportunities compared to the rural areas. In urban Kathmandu, average annual per capita income was US$ 715 as compared to US$ 396 in other urban areas of the country. This has clear influence in pulling rural and small urban area populations to Kathmandu city. The so-called Maoist insurgency and political insecurity in the countryside over the last several years also caused a sudden flux of in-migration into the capital (Thapa and Sijapati, 2003). From the field study undertaken, it was observed that the majority of middle to lower-middle class people, who were often categorized as "better off" classes in the rural areas, came to seek a better and safer livelihood in the Valley. Due to the amount of money needed to invest in land to build even a small house, the migrants have preferred to live in fragmented land plots of 100 to 200 square metres. These groups have basically concentrated in areas of poor road accessibility and fewest urban amenities. On the other hand, property dealers and brokers also took advantage of dealing in small plots because they had a large number of buyers. This process caused more congested and haphazard urban settlements. Squatter settlements are another aspect of urban settlement. In 1985, there were 17 squatter settlements in the Valley with a total population of 3,000 (MoPE, 1999). In 1994, there were 33 squatter settlements with a

Fig. 13.9 Photograph of squatter settlements along the bank of Bagmati River at Thapathali (taken by author, 17 April 2008).

total population of 15,000 (Thapa, 1994). Sixty per cent of these squatter settlements were on public land (MoPE, 1999). The number of squatter settlements increased rapidly, and in 2003 this number was reported to be 64 (ICIMOD, 2007). The rate of addition of new huts is also high. New huts have appeared spontaneously in several locations. Recently-constructed squatter huts can be seen along the banks of Bagmati River that are within the monsoon flood zone of the river (Fig. 13.9). Most squatter huts found along the river are traditionally left uninhabited due to their location in a highly vulnerable monsoon flood zone. The inhabitants who do stay here have no drinking water, sanitation or electricity.

Rapid urbanization is a sign of economic prosperity for a city, but it also brings biophysical changes that have a great and often problematic impact upon the living environment. The metropolitan region of Kathmandu Valley is surrounded by hilly terrain and now has limited land resources for new developments. Burgeoning population, unguided urban development and daunting urban environmental problems are serious concerns in the Kathmandu Valley. Haphazard and unguided processes of change in land use invite such diverse consequences as inadequate housing and urban services; added by air pollution in the city (Pradhan, 2004; Thapa *et al.*, 2008). The haphazard construction and unplanned development that took place after the Kathmandu Valley Physical Plan of 1967 was documented by the Department of Housing and Physical Planning. However, the authorities have not undertaken any real planning even after the documentation of the issues and guidelines. This is a clear example of poor regulatory mechanism and a lack of sensitivity on the part of the authorities.

Conclusion

Kathmandu Valley, a bowl-shaped geographical area located in the central part of Nepal, is the capital city of the country. A large number of historical temples and beautifully carved wooden and stone materials in the house and public dwelling units in urban Kathmandu Valley signify the prosperous historical past of the Valley. Nearly a million people were recorded in the defined urban area in 2001. With approximately an equal-sized transient and permanent population, the Valley comprises nearly two million inhabitants altogether, which reflects an annual growth rate of over five per cent. In the past few decades, Kathmandu Valley's city centre has turned into an ill-planned area. Physical infrastructure lacks adequate planning and is becoming chaotic. Unplanned settlement units are mushrooming over the fertile agricultural lowland. Poor road access, haphazard construction and large influx of population have brought about negative environmental consequences. All the holy rivers and streams have been reduced to sewage canals. Polluted and odorous air rising from the rivers adds to the air pollution in the Valley, which already faces considerable vehicular emission. Open and green areas are also being consumed by concrete structures or vehicle parking areas. Kathmandu Valley needs substantial planning and management to improve its urban, social and environmental sectors.

Editor's Note

All dollar figures are for this approximate time-frame in 2008, when the author undertook a field study of the Kathmandu Valley area. Dollar conversions not standardized by purchasing power parity.

References

Asian Development Bank (ADB) / International Centre for Integrated Mountain Development (ICIMOD), *Environment Assessment of Nepal: Emerging Issues and Challenges*, Kathmandu: ADB/ICIMOD, 2006.

Central Bureau of Statistics (CBS), *Population Census 2001*, Kathmandu: His Majesty's Government of Nepal (HMG–Nepal), 2002.

CBS, *Population Monograph of Nepal*, Kathmandu: CBS, HMG–Nepal, *Vols. I and II*, 2003.

CBS, *Nepal Living Standards Survey 2003/04*, Kathmandu: CBS, HMG–Nepal, *Vols. I and II*, 2004.

Dutt, Ashok K. and M. Margaret Geib, *Atlas of South Asia, A Geographic Analysis by Countries*, New Delhi: Oxford & IBH Publishing Co. Pvt. Ltd., 1998.

Haack, B. N. and A. Rafter, 'Urban growth analysis and modeling in the Kathmandu Valley, Nepal', *Habitat International*, Vol. 30, 2006, pp. 1056–1065.

Halcrow Fox and Associates (HFA), *Kathmandu Valley Urban Development Plans and Programs*, Kathmandu: Government of Nepal, Department of Housing and Urban Development / HFA.

HMG–Nepal, *The Physical Development Plan for the Kathmandu Valley*, Kathmandu: HMG–Nepal, Department of Housing and Physical Planning, 1969.

ICIMOD, *Kathmandu Valley Environment Outlook*, Kathmandu: ICIMOD, 2007.

International Union for Conservation of Nature (IUCN), *Regulating Growth: Kathmandu Valley, Draft Report*, Kathmandu: IUCN, 1995.

Koirala, Hridaya Lal, 'Issues of Urban Environment in Kathmandu Valley: A case study of Kathmandu Metropolitan City', *The Himalayan Review (Nepal Geographical Society)*, Vol. 30, 1998, pp. 1–18.

Kathmandu Valley Town Development Committee (KVTDC), *Long Term Development Concept of Kathmandu Valley*, Kathmandu: Ministry of Physical Planning and Works, KVTDC, 2002.

Malla, Upendra Man, 'Presidential Address Delivered at the Inauguration of International Geographical Field Meeting in Nepal on December 8, 1968', *The Himalayan Review (Nepal Geographical Society)*, Vols. 2 and 3, 1969–70, pp. 62–74.

Malla, Upendra Man, 'Settlement Geography of Kathmandu Valley from 600 BC to 1000 AD', *Geographical Journal of Nepal*, Vol. 1, No. 1, 1978, pp. 28–36.

Ministry of Population and Environment (MoPE), *Environmental Planning and Management of the Kathmandu Valley*, Kathmandu: Government of Nepal, MoPE, and IUCN, 1999.

Poudel, Krishna Prasad, 'Quantitative Analysis of Drainage System of the Kathmandu Valley', *The Himalayan Review (Nepal Geographical Society)*, Vol. 15, 1983–84, pp. 21–38.

Poudel, K., Poudel, Krishna Prasad, 'Kathmandu Valley Citizens in the Bowl at Risk', Presentation at a Seminar on Vulnerable Cities; Hazards, Risks and Preparedness, Department of Geography, Delhi School of Economics, University of Delhi, Delhi, 18–19 March 2005.

Pradhan, Pushkar K., 'Population Growth, Migration and Urbanization: Environmental consequences in Kathmandu Valley, Nepal', *in Jon D. Unruh, Maarten S. Krol and Nurit Kliot (eds.), Advances in Global Change Research*, Netherlands: Springer, Vol. 20, 2004, pp. 177–199.

Shrestha, Chandra Bahadur and Upendra Man Malla, 'Urban Centers of the Kathmandu Valley', *The Himalayan Review (Nepal Geographical Society)*, Vols. 2 and 3, 1969–1970, pp. 33–38.

Thapa, D. and B. Sinjapati, *A Kingdom under Siege: Nepal's Maoist Insurgency, 1996 to 2003*, Kathmandu: The Printhouse, 2003.

Thapa, K., *Up-gradation of Squatter Settlements in Kathmandu: Public Intervention and People's Participation*. New Delhi: School of Planning and Architecture, 1994.

Thapa, Rajesh Bahadur, Yuji Murayama and Shailja Ale, 'City profile: Kathmandu', *Cities*, Vol. 25, 2008, pp. 45–57.

Zurink, David and P. P. Karan, *Life on the Edge of the World Himalaya*, Baltimore and London: Johns Hopkins University Press, 1999.

14

Ave Maria: A Planned Town in Collier County, Florida

JOHN E. BENHART AND HARRY 'BUD' PILARSKI

Located in southwest Florida, Collier County is one of the largest and wealthiest counties in the state. Larger than the state of Delaware, Collier County was created in 1923 and was named after Barron Gift Collier, a businessman born in Memphis who promoted the region's development and the completion of the Tamiami Trail in 1928 using his personal fortune from streetcar advertising. The County includes important environmental preserves such as the Everglades National Park, Big Cypress Wildlife Preserve and Ten Thousand Islands as well as urban settlements such as Naples, Marco Island, Everglades City and Immokalee (Fig. 14.1). The population of Collier County has increased from 6,500 in 1950 to over 325,000 in 2008. Development has been concentrated along the Atlantic Gulf Coast from Marco Island to Naples and northward to Vanderbilt Beach near Pelican Bay.

A centre for vegetable farming and cattle raising, Immokalee is an unincorporated community in the northeast portion of Collier County. A significant seasonal influx of migrant workers to Immokalee serves the vegetable farms and orange groves in the surrounding areas. The Immokalee region has the lowest per capita income in Collier County and over 80 per cent of its population is Hispanic. Immokalee was near the early route of soldiers from the Seminole War who pursued the Seminole tribe into the Big Cypress Forest Reserve. Settlers began occupying Immokalee in the 1870s. In the vicinity of Immokalee is the planned town of Ave Maria which was established in 2006.

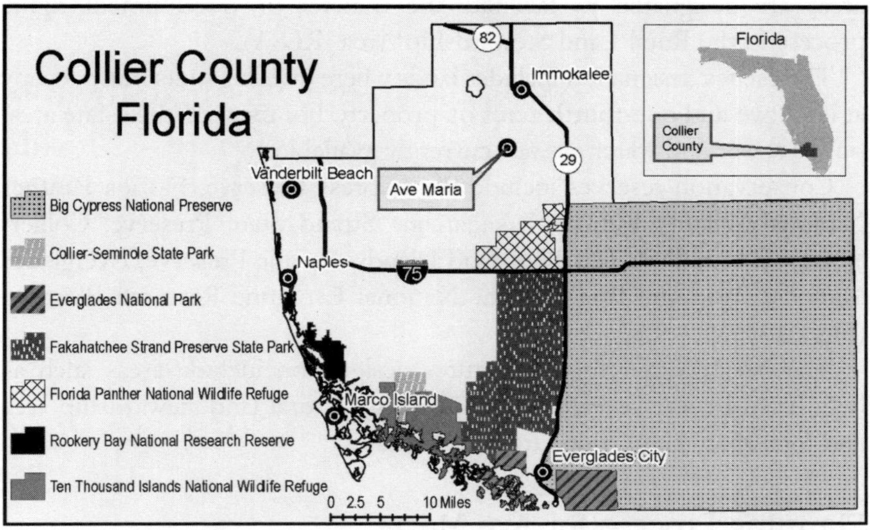

Fig. 14.1 Location of Collier County; West side is the Gulf of Mexico and in most of the east and south is the Everglades swamp. The location of Ave Maria is in the north, less than 10 miles from state route 29.

Planning Concepts

Collier County has a strong and comprehensive management plan for development, land use, economic growth, environmental protection and preservation of quality of life (Collier County Growth Management Plan, 2005). To protect the environment, the County has emphasized the need to conserve important natural, scenic, agricultural, historic and environmentally-sensitive areas (Haner, 2007). Stewardship areas have been incorporated in the regional planning process to preserve flowways, rural lands, water retention zones and habitat regions (Weeks, 2006).

Zoning for Collier County has been based on the growth management plan that designates zoning districts for urban areas, agricultural and rural areas, large estates, conservation reserves and for other special uses (Future Land Use Map, 2004). Urban designations include a mixed-use district, a commercial district and an industrial district. The regional infrastructure includes central water and sewer facilities, with police and fire protection for densely populated areas. Intensive residential developments are concentrated along the Gulf of Mexico.

The agricultural or rural designation includes a mixed-use district located in an extensive rural land stewardship overlay. Sending and receiving areas are designated to facilitate the transfer of development rights process in the Rural Land Stewardship Area (RLSA).

The estates designation includes lands where dwelling units must occupy at least two and one-fourth acres of property. For most of the estate area, public sewer and water are not currently available.

Conservation reserves include Big Cypress Preserve, Florida Panther National Wildlife Refuge, Fakahatchee Strand State Preserve, Collier-Seminole State Park Ten Thousand Islands Aquatic Preserve, Everglades National Park, and Rookery Bay National Estuarine Research Preserve (Fig. 14.1).

The overlays and special features designation include areas such as high hazard coastal areas, airport noise area, rural land stewardship area and the urban–rural fringe transition zone.

Planning Process for Ave Maria

Ave Maria is the first development within the recently established 195,000 acre RLSA of eastern Collier County (Nath, 2005). The RLSA provides incentives for environmentally-sensitive Stewardship Sending Areas (SSAs) which enable the development of less sensitive Stewardship Receiving Areas (SRAs) within the RLSA. Under the RLSA overlay, stewardship credits are generated from the designation of SSAs, which ensure protection of natural resources and agriculture. Accrual of these credits entitles development in SRAs where new communities are permitted and natural resource values are low (Marsh, 2005). The town of Ave Maria is the first SRA to be designated under the RLSA programme.

The initiative for the creation of the town came from a unique opportunity to locate a new private university in Collier County, Ave Maria University (AMU). The Barron Collier Company, a long-time property owner, donated the campus site. The company formed a partnership with AMU named New Town Development, LLLP, to jointly develop the new town of Ave Maria (Ave Maria University and Ave Maria Town, 2006). AMU is expected to serve emerging demand for higher education in southwest Florida.

The entire site of the town of Ave Maria falls within an open or undesignated area of the RLSA, which implies that it has minimal natural resource value and is suitable for designation as a SRA. Under the RLSA natural resource scoring system, no part of the town approaches the threshold of significant natural resource value.

However, the town of Ave Maria will enhance protection of natural resources. As provided by the Collier County RLSA policies, natural resources will be protected and agricultural activities will be retained through the establishment of SSAs that generated the stewardship credits needed to entitle the town. Including the acreage of the SSAs utilized to entitle the preliminary development agreement, approximately 17,000 acres have been dedicated as SSAs to entitle the town (Development of Regional Impact, 2004). The 17,000 acres of SSAs are subject to a stewardship easement, which preserves the natural resources and protects existing agricultural activities within these areas by prohibiting future development. The SSAs thus fulfill the intent of the RLSA program to entitle development through assured protection of areas with high natural resource values (Field Visits, 2007).

Town of Ave Maria

The town of Ave Maria helps to advance southwest Florida's economic goals. Construction for the planned town of Ave Maria began in 2006, launching a new regional economic centre that will provide 1,200,000 square feet of retail and office space and will generate a significant number of new jobs in the rural portion of Collier County (Carpenter, 2006). The town and University will cover 5,000 acres occupied by 20,000 people in the mixed-use compact development area. Barron Collier Corporation and Tom Monagham, Domino Pizza founder and Ave Maria University Chancellor, have worked closely in planning and development of the town and University. The Oratory, rising over 100 feet and with a seating capacity of 1,100, is the focal point of the University and surrounding town. It is located in the centre of a European style plaza, surrounded on the north, south and east sides by the town's commercial core and open to the University's central linear green to the west. The town centre, occupying over 330,000 square feet, will house retail space on the ground floor, with condominiums on the floors above. Its Prairie school architectural design includes green copper roofs.

The master plan includes residential neighbourhoods connected by a network of low-speed streets and sidewalks; a mixed-use town centre that will provide residents and students with essential goods and services; and civic gathering places for entertainment and dining. The development is planned in two five-year phases that began in 2006 and will continue through 2016.

Ave Maria is planned as a walkable community that facilitates efficient pedestrian and bicycle movement, including monitoring the number of motorized vehicles in the outside lane, vehicle speed, lane condition and availability of sidewalks and greenways. Major downtown planning options for the European town centre include (i) Commercial core with residential upper floors, (ii) Energy efficient structures, (iii) Total pedestrian and bicycle accessibility, (iv) Linear green throughout town and to the University, (v) Prohibition of incompatible development, and (vi) Residential neighbourhoods connected by a network of low-speed streets, sidewalks and bicycle paths connected to a compact mixed-use town centre.

In the two years since the Ave Maria development began in 2006, four new major developments have begun, which are (i) A new beltline I-75 to Highway 82 east to Route 29 south to I-75 east (Alligator Alley) – the new beltline will open rural eastern Collier County to increased traffic and development (Fig. 14.1), (ii) The new town of Big Cypress, a 3,700 acre development adjacent to Ave Maria, (iii) Tradepost Industrial Commercial Park in Immokalee as part of the Federal Empowerment Zone to provide employment in the nation's most impoverished urban and rural areas, and (iv) Expansion of Immokalee Airport.

These new developments affirm the power of change and reveal how these land use changes help to establish the planned town Ave Maria. The town of Ave Maria will occupy over 4,000 acres, with the University occupying an additional 1,000 acres. Residential development will include custom homes, town homes, condominiums and apartments connected in an energy-efficient manner to the town centre. The town plan includes 1,000 moderate-income owner-occupied housing units, 700 low-income housing units and 200 very-low-income housing units.

A public elementary and middle school and a private Catholic K-12 school will be located on site. A new high school a few miles from Ave Maria will serve the community. Police, fire and emergency medical services will be located in Ave Maria. The Collier County Sheriff's Department will serve the town of Ave Maria. Sixty acres of both active and passive recreational parks, wetland conservation districts and a championship golf course are included in the master plan. The town developers have committed to donate a 28-acre site within 10 miles of Ave Maria to the Habitat for Humanity of Collier County for the construction of 150 affordable housing units.

Ave Maria will broadly include five land uses (i) 11,000 residential dwelling units, (ii) 690,000 square feet of retail or service space, (iii)

510,000 square feet of office space, (iv) 400 hotel rooms, and (v) 6,000 student housing units. The planning for Ave Maria has considered its proximity to coastal urban areas and the anticipated demand for housing to support faculty, staff and administrative employees of Ave Maria University.

Ave Maria University

AMU is the first Catholic University built in the United States in over 40 years. The University's location at the centre of Ave Maria makes it an integral part of town planning. The new campus officially opened in August 2007. Six campus buildings were completed for the 2007 fall semester, including the library, the dining hall, the first classroom building and three residence halls (Carpenter, 2006). Approximately 600 students were expected at AMU for the 2008 fall semester. Eventually, AMU will serve 6,000 students.

The Phase I five-year AMU plan, beginning in 2006, includes the Oratory, Library, Student Activities Centre, Science and Technology Building, University Pool and three residence halls. The Phase II plan, ending in 2016, includes a sports and recreation centre, four undergraduate residence halls, a grotto and a graduate academic building. The Ann Arbor, Michigan, Ave Maria School of Law has moved to the new campus in Collier County; future development includes a law school building.

The town square – the heart of Greek, Roman and medieval towns – has often survived as an important open space (McCarthy, 2008). The newly planned town of Ave Maria has developed features of medieval town squares in Europe and integrates university greenways into a town vista from the Oratory. Close access to the compact mixed-use town centre provides the University with convenience, accessibility, energy conservation and a social gathering place (Benhart, 2007). In addition to providing greenways and vistas, the University offers the town of Ave Maria a gathering space for meetings, educational opportunities, technology and library resources. The multiple-use joint planning applied for the town of Ave Maria and the University serves as a model for future town planning.

Cultural Geography and Planning

The multiple-use planning addressed specific urban principles of ethnic, cultural and generational diversity (i) People should accept the society, not seek to destroy it, (ii) The common bond of economic welfare creates some social integration, (iii) Destabilizing tendencies of non-acculturated newcomers are limited, and (iv) Living wage levels are maintained (Wadley, 2008).

The above principles of urbanism generate some interesting questions for the planned town of Ave Maria in its close proximity to the community of Immokalee – How will a more up-scale, highly educated population of Ave Maria impact a region dominated by a lower income, less educated Hispanic population? Will Ave Maria have a positive or negative impact on the Immokalee region? Will the location of Ave Maria help improve educational opportunities and per capita income for Immokalee residents? Will the location of Ave Maria increase property values and commodity prices and thus displace residents of Immokalee? How will the new cultural diversity impact social integration? Will a process of social change occur because of the interaction of significantly diverse cultures in Ave Maria and Immokalee? How will living wages and quality of life improve or decline in the Immokalee region? How will the recent severe local economic downturn during 2007–2009 in Collier County impact the future of Ave Maria? How will Ave Maria benefit from the population of Immokalee? How will the location of affordable housing surrounding Immokalee improve living conditions for local residents? Many of these questions will be answered as the communities of Ave Maria and Immokalee interface. This new development assuredly offers an opportunity for economic, ethnic, cultural and generational diversity in the planned town of Ave Maria and the Immokalee community, to cooperate in developing a vibrant geographic region in eastern Collier County.

Summary

The planned town Ave Maria is the first development within the recently established 195,000 acre RLSA of eastern Collier County. Construction for the town of Ave Maria began in 2006 to develop a new regional economic centre that will provide 1,200,000 square feet of retail and office space and generate a significant number of new jobs. Ave Maria will occupy 5,000 acres with over 20,000 people in a mixed-use compact development.

Barron Collier Corporation and Tom Monaghan, Domino Pizza founder and AMU Chancellor, have worked closely in developing the town and university plan. The University's location at the centre of Ave Maria makes it an integral part of town planning. This major development will enhance economic, ethnic, cultural and generational diversity in the planned town of Ave Maria and the Immokalee community, offering a dramatic opportunity to cooperate in developing a vibrant geographic region in eastern Collier County. The multiple-use planning for the town of Ave Maria and the University serves as a model for future town planning.

Note

1. Field visits and interviews at Ave Maria groundbreaking and during town and university construction and development 2006, 2007, and 2008 by Dr. John E. Benhart, Sr.

References

Ave Maria Development Company, *Development of Regional Impact*, Barron Collier, Inc., 2004.

Ave Maria University, *Ave Maria University and Ave Maria Town, Florida*, www.naples.avemaria.edu, 2006.

Benhart, John E. Sr. and H. Stephens, 'Land Use Planning Initiatives in Pennsylvania', in B. Thakur et al. (eds.), *City Society and Planning*, (In honour of Professor A. K. Dutt), New Dehli: Concept Publishing Company, Vol. 3, 2007, pp. 208–223).

Collier County Planning Department, *Collier County Growth Management Plan*, 2005.

Community Development and Environmental Services Division, Graphics and Technical Support Section, Future Land Use Map, Collier County Florida, 2004.

Marsh, William, *Landscape Planning: Environmental Applications*, Hoboken: John Wiley and Sons, Inc., 2005.

McCarthy, Linda and Boian Koulov, 'Cities of Europe', in Stanley Brunn (ed.), *Cities of the World*, New York: Rowman and Littlefield Publishers, Inc., 2008, pp. 201–254.

Interview with Dr. Carole Carpenter, Vice President for University Relations, Ave Maria University, 2006.

Interviews with Ananta Nath, P. E. Chief Consulting Engineer, Big Cypress Basin, South Florida Water Management District, 2005, 2006, 2007 and 2008.

Interview with Judy Haner, Intergovernmental and Community Outreach Specialist, Big Cypress Basin, South Florida Water Management District, 2007.

Interviews with David Weeks, Chief of Comprehensive Planning, Collier County Florida, 2005 and 2006.

Wadley, David, 'The Garden of Peace', *Annals of the Association of American Geographers*, Vol. 93, No. 3, 2008, pp. 652–685.

IV
Social Geography in the Indian Context

15

Socio-cultural Regions in Prehistoric and Historic India

SURYA KANT

Geographical factors provide the stage for cultural groups to work out their destinies and establish distinctive occupancy patterns. The evolution of cultural regions, emergence of cultural cores, and the direction and speed of cultural diffusion are greatly controlled by the prevailing geographical conditions of a region. Thus, the historical experiences of the people living in different geographical regions have been strikingly different. Such a situation is more marked in countries like India where the large areal extent, vast physical diversity and unique geographical location have made it a known case of unity in diversity in terms of the cultural pattern.

The physical framework of the Indian subcontinent determined the initial migration routes as well as the choice of the settlement area (river valleys or interfluvial tracts) by the incoming cultural streams originating from different parts of Asia. The scarcity of food and the presence of natural barriers, such as rivers, hill ranges, or desert expanses curbed their freedom of movement. Over the wide open valleys and the undulating plains on the plateau, they could also perceive social barriers erected along the contact lines between different ethnic groups and enforced by social customs. It may be assumed that the primeval culture domains were ethnically homogeneous and socially defined as their violation invited conflict, followed by internecine wars. Initially, there was a remote possibility of cultural overlap. Subbarao (1958, pp. 8–35) used detailed archaeological data to demonstrate the preservation of mutual exclusiveness in the remote hill tracts. In contrast, the cultural groups occupying the river valleys of the Indo-Gangetic plains were always under constant pressure from fresh invasions and were pushed into the bordering marginal lands, such as hills, deserts or densely forested areas. Those who were pushed or drifted to such marginal lands or so-called refuge zones were able to preserve their original ethnic traits. Hence, they remained unaffected by fresh waves of incursions – a regular feature of the zone in and along the main corridor of movement connecting the Kabul Valley with the North Indian plains. The prevailing physical features, thus, finely supported the scope for the plurality of cultural forms and their survival over time – the newer elements getting assimilated by the groups living all along the main route of migration, and the old, the primitive and the archaic elements remaining a distinctive feature of isolated regions at the margins of the former type of areas. Perhaps, it is because of the dominant role of physical factors that until very recently, several studies used to describe the historical geography of India as the persistent interaction of three types of zones – perennial or nuclear zones, route zones, and zones of relative isolation.

This raises the questions – how were the socio-cultural regions formed, and how did they evolve through different phases of Indian history and prehistory? Several attempts have been made in archaeology (Allchin, 1963; Fairservis, 1971; Richards, 1933; Sankalia, 1963; Subbarao, 1958; Wheeler, 1959), history (Kosambi, 1972; Pannikar, 1955; Toynbee, 1961) and geography (Schwartzberg, 1977; Singh and Khan, 1993; Sopher, 1977; Spate, 1957) to understand the nature of the association between the geographical factors and cultural elements in Indian history. Most of these works draw inspiration from Richards' pioneering work.

In case of India, one has to face several challenges to comprehend any such study. Some of the difficulties are mentioned below:

(i) Due to limited archaeological evidence, the prehistoric scene in India is quite hazy. The few inadequate investigations on this period leave vast gaps in information to be filled with conjecture. Many sites were accidentally discovered. The selection of sites for digging was subjective. Borrowed concepts were used for archaeological excavations. Greater focus was placed on some sites over others. The Archaeological Survey of India faced several administrative and financial difficulties. All such problems pose serious limitations on the authenticity and wider application of the available evidence.

(ii) Despite the widespread occurrence of tools used by early humans in India, no definite geographical picture of the development of Paleolithic cultures can be reconstructed. Each site was an isolated discovery and represented a type in itself.

(iii) Archaeological sites reveal the evidence of cultural overlaps rather than cultural successions, making the task of cultural regionalisation all the more challenging. There exist wide gaps in information, and cartographic tradition is practically missing in a large part of Indian history. In fact, it is extremely difficult to demarcate the boundaries of socio-cultural regions before the British period beginning in the nineteenth century.

(iv) Archaeological work at several Harappan sites has shown the presence of lower layers yielding evidence of pre-Harappan (Neolithic) cultures. Ironically, these lower levels at many of the Harappan sites have not yet been dug out because of physical difficulties (for example, high water table), leaving the question of Harappan–pre-Harappan connections unsolved and speculative.

(v) While the regions of attraction possess evidence of a complete cultural succession reflecting a remarkable continuity, the regions of isolation present a different picture. Their archaeological record is discontinuous. Whatever cultural influences managed to reach there were virtually impounded as no new influences could percolate.

(vi) Lack of a history-writing tradition with exact chronology and established accuracy through documentary evidence for the available ancient Indian literature introduces complexities. It results in a large body of uncorroborated data and ill-recorded traditions to make a historical and chronological treatment difficult. Hence, well-corroborated Indian history begins around 600 BCE in the North, and slightly later in the South. Moreover, in complete contrast to ancient Egyptian and Babylonian civilizations, where the script of writings of the people who had lived there could be deciphered, the script of writings of a type preserved on the seals of the Indus Valley people has still not been deciphered satisfactorily. Consequently, we cannot apply the concept of prehistory (preliterate societies) and history (literate societies) at least in the case of the Indus Valley civilization. The Indus Valley civilization cannot be placed under either of the two categories, history or prehistory. Indian history prior to 600 BCE, especially the period of the Indus Valley civilization, is generally termed as proto-history (Subbarao, 1958; Sankalia, 1963). The same terminology has been accepted here by organizing discussions under prehistory, proto-history and history.

Broadly, prehistory in India extends from about 400,000 to 2500 BCE, proto-history from 2500 BCE to 600 BCE, and history begins thereafter.

To examine the formation and evolution of socio-cultural regions in different periods, varied sources have been used. The discovered tools, skeletons, paintings, sculptures and art pieces have been used for the prehistoric period, architectural design of buildings, pottery, jewellery, religious symbols, arts and seals for the proto-historic period, and contemporary literature, inscriptions and coins for the historic period.

However, it is advisable to keep all such above-mentioned constraints in mind while looking into the following discussion on the evolving process and pattern of socio-cultural characteristics of society in India.

Prehistoric Period (400,000–2500 BCE)

Despite the earliest traces of human activity in India going back to the second inter-glacial period between 400,000 and 200,000 BCE, no direct evidence is yet available to throw light on the nature of this population and their physical characteristics. Tools left by these people are the only evidence to reconstruct the story of the early human cultures present from the Palaeolithic (Old Stone Age) to the Neolithic (New Stone Age) and the Chalcolithic (metal-using cultures) periods.[1] It is almost impossible to identify socio-cultural regions on the basis of existing information, yet the geographical interpretation of artefacts belonging to different prehistoric phases helps us to understand the process of human adaptation to existing ecological conditions and pattern of their movements pertaining to this adaptation. Also, it will help in discovering the emergence of certain localities repeatedly visited by the early humans in the course of spatial diffusion of such cultures.

The cultural geography of India customarily recognizes three types of regions in India – regions of attraction, isolation, and relative isolation. The archaeological records of the regions of isolation and relative isolation, being of a discontinuous nature, are generally filled with conjecture. The Potwar region (now in Pakistan) and the region around Madras (now Chennai), which have been systematically studied, belong to significantly different physical conditions and typology, suggesting a sequence. de Terra and Menghin have termed these as 'Sohan' industry and 'Madras' industry (or 'Peninsular' facies) of the Early Stone Age in India (Subbarao, 1958, p. 50). We will next discuss these regions using the same terminology.

The traces of human cultures discovered in the Sohan (Soan in early writings) river valley, a tributary of the Indus in the northwest of Rawalpindi

(Pakistan), reveal that people living in this part were hunters who used crude stone tools. Such tools, found buried in the glacial as well as the fluvial terraces of the river, belong to the Old Stone Age. The tools collected from the fluvial terraces present a complete stratigraphic record of the series of climatic changes that occurred during the Pleistocene times. It is with this stratigraphic record of the tools that the Sohan valley sprang into prominence as one of the most celebrated sites of the lower Palaeolithic period.[2] The evolution of tool-making techniques took place in three distinctive stages – pre-Sohan, Sohan, and late-Sohan (de Terra and Paterson, 1939). Each successive phase revealed a technological advancement over the previous one. Thus, while the pre-Sohan tools were based on flakes, the Sohan and the late-Sohan varieties consisted of core tools. In fact, the early Sohan group, which belonged to the second inter-glacial period, consisted mostly of choppers and other scraping tools made on flat, truncated pebbles (Subbarao, 1958, p. 53). Typologically, they were subdivided into several groups ranging from Clactonian to Levalloisian (prepared platform techniques named after Levallois, a site near Paris).

Placing the evidence in its proper environmental context, de Terra and Paterson noted a direct relationship between the climatic changes and the rise of early human cultures. It may be postulated that the tools unearthed from the terraces must have been left behind by the early humans over the surface of the Sohan river valley. The downward movement of the glaciers and the fluvial drift that followed the melting of the snow might have displaced the tools from their original sites. Perhaps the Potwar plateau located between River Indus and River Jhelum became one of the earliest sites of the diffusion of early human cultures in the Indian subcontinent (Fig. 15.1). The advances and retreats of glaciers implied vast fluctuations in the global temperature regimes. This must have resulted in far-reaching changes in the earth's environment, particularly in its climate and vegetation cover. The ancient hunters and food-gatherers must have remained on the move in the wake of these changes (Ahmad, 1999, p. 87).

Sohan-type tools have also been found in other parts of North India. Lal (1956, pp. 58–92) found such tools in the terraces of the sub-Himalayan river valleys of Satluj, Beas and its tributary, Banganga (Himachal Pradesh). Similar tools have also been found scattered on the banks of the river Yamuna (in Bundelkhand), the Chambal, and the Banas (in eastern Rajasthan). The pebble-based core tools (choppers and scrapers) appear to have a southern limit along the 22°N latitude, with Mayurbhanj

POTWAR REGION

A. Physical Setting

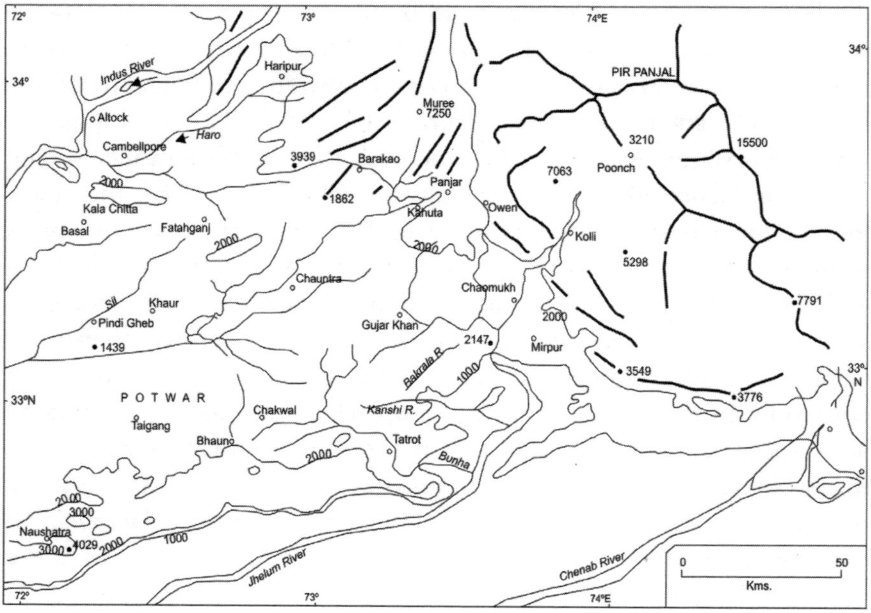

Fig. 15.1.A Physical setting of Potwar region of Punjab plain.
Source: After de Terra and Paterson, 1939.

B. Distribution of Prehistory Sites

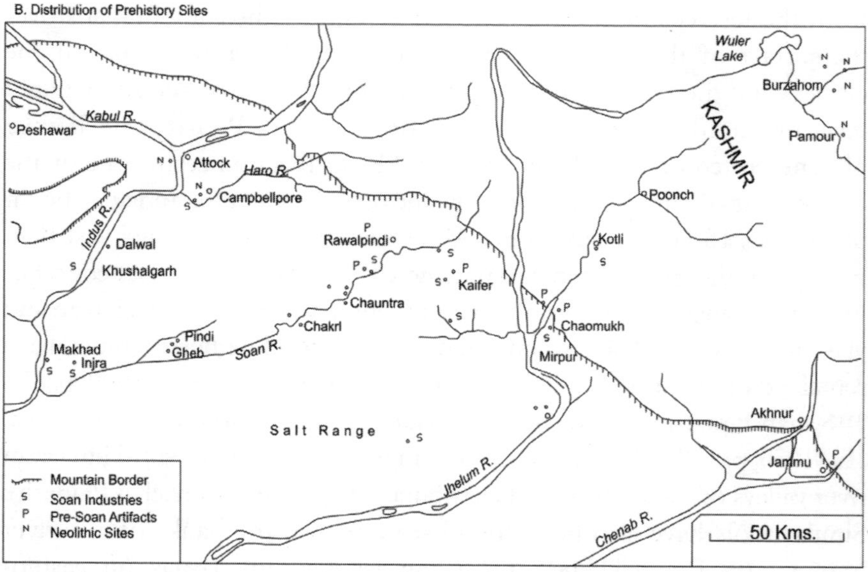

Fig. 15.1.B Location of prehistoric sites in Potwar region of Punjab plain.
Source: After de Terra and Paterson, 1939.

(Orissa) as the southern limit. Despite the widespread occurrence of these tools, no definite geographical picture of the development of Palaeolithic cultures can be reconstructed. As is generally known, the river valleys of the North Indian Plain have not yielded any tools. If the ancient hunters left behind any tools, they might be buried under the thick mantle of alluvium deposited during the successive phases of fluvial activity.

The tools discovered in and around Madras (now Chennai) and other parts of peninsular India belong to a different tool-making tradition. Instead of pebble chopping tools, the tools found here mostly consist of hand axes and cleavers made on cores and flakes. These tools, representing the 'peninsular facies' of the Early Stone Age in India, are Acheulean[3] in topology and suggest an independent development in the region lying to the south of the Narmada. Some observers have noted similarities between the Madras hand axes and the tools found on the East African plateau, suggesting a possible connection. Such tools have been found in a vast area encompassing the peninsular region. Chennai is recognized as an area where the earliest tools were unearthed at the site of Vadamadurai.

Evidently, overwhelming archaeological evidence scattered over the peri-glacial areas in the northwestern Himalayas as well as the peninsular plateau support the appearance of Palaeolithic hunters on the Indian scene. However, incomplete knowledge makes systematic geographical interpretation of the Old Stone Age sites almost impossible. Evidence also suggests that there was a transitional phase between the Upper Palaeolithic and the Neolithic period, called the Mesolithic period. During the Mesolithic period, one comes across overwhelming evidence of tiny flint tools known as microliths. A multitude of these tools, including blades, scrapers, burins, triangles, crescents and lunates have been collected from sites scattered all over the country. The Mesolithic period marks a change from flakes to the microlithic tradition (Allchin and Allchin, 1968, p. 78). The tools are generally made of finer varieties of rocket, such as jasper, chert, agate and quartzite. Also included in the findings are composite tools made of stones fixed to bones or wood, as well as remains of pottery. These new varieties of tools indicate sophistication in the techniques of tool-making, an imperative of the multiplying human needs. Insofar as the geography of the Mesolithic sites is concerned, nothing can be said with certainty.

Although these tools are widely distributed in India, no evidence has yet been found from either the Ganga valley or the Himalayas. Sites have been extensively studied in western, central and southern India. In western India, tools have been found in the states of Gujarat and Rajasthan and in the Malwa region in the valleys of River Mahi and River Banas. A layer at Langhnaj (Mahesana district) has yielded black, red and red-and-black potsherds. Copper and iron tools have also been found at higher levels. Sites are also situated in Maharashtra, particularly in the upper Godavari valley (for example, Nevasa), Salsette Island and Ellora. Other important Mesolithic sites fall in Singrauli basin (for example, Lekhania rock shelters in Mirzapur district), in the Damodar valley (for example, Birbhanpur) and in Chaibasa, Chakradharpur, Santal Parganas, Durgapur, Bankura, Singhbhum, Keonjhar, Mayurbhanj and Sambhalpur. Other rock shelters, such as the one at Adamgarh Hill in the Narmada valley, are rich in the cultural remains of the Mesolithic period. Several sites have been excavated in parts of southern India, particularly in Chitradurga, Kurnool and Bellary districts (for example, in Brahmagiri). Not all the sites reveal a cultural continuity.[4]

The evidence of the microliths indicates a gradual transition of the Palaeolithic hunters and food-gatherers to an agriculture-based production economy. Such a transition was, however, a slow process spanning millennia. Interestingly, some of the ancient hunters continued to remain with the Palaeolithic mode till very late in history. For them, agriculture remained a peripheral activity, if they engaged with it at all.

Proto-Historic Period (2500–600 BCE)

With the transition to settled life, agricultural communities domesticated a number of plants and animals, learnt to kindle fire, increased production to support large-scale agricultural communities, developed pottery, settled villages and towns in large numbers and began to use metals. Thus, the society in India entered a new phase of socio-cultural life. Humanity, adopting 'an aggressive attitude to [its] environment' (Childe, 1952), learned to grow food crops, tamed wild animals, made pots and wove garments.

Proto-historic cultures, found in different parts of the subcontinent, are characterized by wide variations in aesthetic and technological traditions, but at the same time present certain mutual influences and contacts. In some parts of the country, highly developed urban-based civilizations have been found, comparable to those of West Asia in time and stature. In contrast, there were highly primitive Stone Age cultures surviving in certain areas. The ecology and geography of these cultural regions can explain this differential development. Three sub-cultural phases – pre-Harappan, Harappan, and post-Harappan – are identified in the proto-historic period (Subbarao, 1958, pp. 85–88).

The earliest village sites of the Neolithic cultures in the Indian subcontinent were dug out from the relatively smaller river valleys of Baluchistan. Emergence of the first Neolithic communities on the Indo-Iranian borderlands suggests the possibility of an eastward shift of the agricultural mode of production from West Asia to the Indian subcontinent. The oldest village sites in West Asia located in Turkey, Palestine and Iraq probably belong to the seventh or the eighth millennium BCE. The cultures found at dig-sites in Baluchistan are, however, much younger and are dated around the middle of the fifth millennium BCE. Their rise in Baluchistan and in other parts of the Indus Valley, however, represents a remarkable development. In fact, traces of Neolithic cultures have been found over a vast geographical area encompassing the Baluchistan uplands, the Indus basin and the adjoining areas in northern Rajasthan.

The small rivers in the Baluchistan Hills – Zhob, Beji, Pishin Lora, Dasht, Kel, Hingoli and Hub, to name only a few – in their neatly carved-out valleys, offered ideal conditions for the rise of primeval village settlements dependent on some form of agriculture, coupled with the rearing of animals. Water supply in these rivers was seasonal, permitting crop sowing at different levels along the riverbanks. There are many sites in the Indus basin, Ganga Valley, Malwa plateau, Gujarat, Rajaputana, Maharashtra, Andhra Pradesh, Karnataka (Krishna basin), Tamil Nadu and Orissa from where evidence of this cultural phase was collected (Subbarao, 1958, pp. 85–87). Archaeological evidence throws light on the nature of the artefacts as well as houses and pottery traditions. Some of the important sites are Kili Gul Mohammed, near Quetta, Rana Ghundai in the Lora Lai valley, Periano Ghundai in the Zhob valley, Kots Diji, east of the Indus, and Mundigak in the south-eastern region of Afghanistan. The evidence collected from these sites shows how the food-producing mode sustained these communities. This mode of production eventually spread to other areas in the Indus Valley and set the stage for the rise of a civilization, the first of its kind in Indian history.

These people belonged to several cultures, differentiated primarily by different types of painted pottery. Each culture had distinctive features of its own, but all were of the same generic pattern as those of the Middle East. Though their settlements were small, rarely more than a few acres in extent, their material standards were comparatively high. They knew the use of metal.

These pre-Harappans, who laid the foundation of the Indian cultural tradition were the typical representatives of an agrarian society. Figurines of mother goddesses (for example, Zhob goddesses) and *pipal* leaf motifs on pottery leave much to be inferred about the origins of Indian civilization. In many ancient cultures the worship of the Mother Goddess was associated with that of the bull, and the pre-Harappans were no exception. Bull figurines have, in fact, been discovered. The bull forms a favourite motif for the decoration of the pottery of Kulli and Rana Ghundai, one of the most important of the Zhob sites (Basham, 1967, p. 14).

In the early part of the third millennium, well-organized civilizations developed in northwestern India in the Indus Valley region, contemporary to the well-known Egyptian and Mesopotamian cultures. The sites of the Indus Valley Civilization, known as Harappan Culture (c. 3000 BCE to c. 1500 BCE), are widely distributed from Rupar in the Punjab foothills to Lothal and Rangpur on the Gulf of Cambay and from the Makran coast to Kalibangan on the dry bed of the Ghaggar in northern Rajasthan. Alamgirpur, east of Yamuna, appears to be the eastern-most outpost.

The transformation of a Neolithic culture with its modest beginnings in Kili Gul Mohammad, Rana Ghundai, Kot Diji and Kalibangan into a civilization with a substantial food-producing economy to support an urban society, predominantly engaged in the artisan goods industry and in a widespread exchange of these goods on a commercial scale, must have been a time-consuming process. Evidence suggests that the civilization had already set in by the beginning of the third millennium BCE. The fact that it could sustain itself for one full millennium and a half testifies to its ecological viability. The food-producing economy in a dry region with scanty rainfall could have been possible only in the event of rivers carrying a sufficient supply of water to the agricultural fields. The Indus and its tributaries allowed the people to grow a variety of crops in the dry regions of Sind, Punjab and northern Rajasthan, as these rivers carried with them a large volume of snowmelt in the peak summer season. The main crops were wheat, barley and sesamum. There is no clear-cut evidence of the cultivation of rice, but it has been established that Harappans grew and used cotton. Perhaps the surplus from agriculture was transferred to the numerous towns, such as Mohenjo Daro on the Indus, Harappa on the Ravi, and Kalibangan on the Saraswati, to allow people necessary freedom to engage in the manufacture of artisan goods. The raw materials for these industries came from far and near. A variety of minerals were used – zinc, copper and precious stones from the Aravallis, cotton and other agricultural raw materials from Sind and the Punjab plains, wood and ivory from the surrounding forests, and pearls from the sea. Trade in these goods, domestic as well as external, became a characteristic feature of the Indus Valley people (Ratnagar, 1981). Probably every merchant or mercantile family had a seal bearing an emblem, often of a religious character, and a name or brief inscription in the tantalizingly indecipherable script. It was this commerce that sustained the civilization for so long. However, no significant change came with the passage of time indicating that a certain equilibrium had already been reached. The basic economic activity continued for centuries without any modification. This unparalleled continuity suggests 'the unchanging traditions of temple' rather than 'the secular instability of the court' (Piggott, 1950). It is believed that a priestly class under the theocratic state managed to extract social surplus in order to maintain a semblance of law and order.

This glorious civilization suffered a sudden decline around 1500 BCE. The precise reasons are yet unknown, but destruction due to a natural catastrophe such as floods could have been one of the reasons. Attacks by the Aryans could be another plausible reason. However, recent research also suggests that climate change and human adaptation took place, as also the possibility that the Aryan tribes were migrants into the already declining area, rather than invaders bringing about a sudden change; past colonialist agendas and recent nationalist polemics have further muddied an already complex matter (Lawler, 2008). Regardless, what is known is that evidence ends abruptly as the Harappan mounds show a sudden break in the layers containing cultural remains. In fact, both the beginning and the end of this civilization is obscure as the currently available archaeological data throw little light on such issues.

The Neolithic cultures outside the Indus basin made a late appearance, not earlier than the first half of the first millennium BCE. However, in recent years, more and more evidence has been put forward to suggest that the Neolithic cultural tradition started in pre-Harappan times in at least some regions of India. For example, in the case of Burzahom in the valley of Kashmir, chronologically the evidence goes back to the second half of the third millennium BCE. The tools dug out from the Karewa beds at Burzahom include remains of grey and black burnished pottery, stone axes and a variety of stone and bone tools. The evidence also suggests that the Burzahom culture possibly had an affinity with the Neolithic cultures of East Asia, particularly Manchuria. The practice of burying dogs with their masters was a peculiar trait common to the two regions.

The archaeological evidence collected from sites in Southern Deccan (Karnataka), such as Brahmagiri, Sanganakallu, Piklihal, Maski, Tekkalakota, Hallur as well as from the ash mounds of Utnur and Kupgal, along the banks of River Krishna and River Godavari, reveals a widespread use of ground stone axes. Domestication of animals such as goats, sheep and cattle was common. The Neolithic settlements were nestled on the granite hill slopes which were mostly terraced. Chronologically, these cultural phases have been placed c. 2500–1800 BCE. The cultural succession suggests a second phase (c. 1800–1500 BCE.) in which these earlier cultural traits continued along with the use of copper and bronze. A third phase has also been identified, dating back to c. 1400–1050 BCE, in which the use of metals increased considerably. These Neolithic communities were mainly dependent on cattle raising, although cultivation of gram and millet was adopted as a means of supplementary subsistence in the third phase of cultural development (Allchin, 1963). In the first phase, Hissar and certain sites in Baluchistan and Iran influenced the Deccan Neolithic cultures, particularly in the pottery tradition. During the second phase, the cultural influences seem to have emanated from Malwa, and in the third phase, from Maharashtra (for example, Jorwe type of pottery).

Evidence of other Neolithic cultures comes from eastern Rajasthan and the Malwa plateau. The remains collected from Ahar and Gilund in the Banas basin in eastern Rajasthan suggest a peculiar Banas Neolithic culture with unique characteristics–an absence of stone tools but numerous copper axes and a variety of black-and-red ware (Sankalia, 1964, p. 194). In addition, Nagda and Navdatoli, two sites in the Malwa region, yielded a variety of artefacts (stone blades, copper tools and painted black-and-red ware), indicating the emergence of the Neolithic culture. These were mainly cattle-raising communities that also domesticated sheep and goats. Chronologically, these cultural phases belong to three different periods, assigned dates from c. 2015 to 1380 BCE.

From the geographical spread of Neolithic cultures in the Indian subcontinent, Allchin and Raymond (1968) concluded that Saurashtra, eastern Rajasthan and Malwa appeared to have acted as centres of diffusion of post-Harappan culture through the rest of India. Locationally, these regions were situated at the junctions of routes and it is likely that they became scenes of intermingling of different cultural traits, Harappan as well as West Asian. A synthesis of these traditions took place in these nodal regions from where they spread to other parts of India. This diffusion of cultural traits possibly took three routes – a southern route passing through Maharashtra and the Deccan, an eastern route passing through the Narmada and Betwa Valleys, and a northern route leading to the Ganga Valley.

Information about the post-Harappan period is generally available from the literary works of the Aryans, such as *Rig Veda* (the oldest of the Vedic texts), *Brahmanas* (prose commentaries related to Vedas, particularly regarding sacrifices), *Puranas* (Sanskrit encyclopaedic literature related to Hindu scripture and lore) and the epics (the *Ramayana* and the *Mahabharata*). It is assumed that the late Harappan sites of Rupar (Punjab) and Alamgirpur (Ganga–Yamuna doab) played a significant role in the diffusion of Harappan (and post-Harappan) influences in the Ganga Valley. Sites in Maharashtra and in the Deccan where extensive archaeological work has been done bear testimony to this diffusion theory. Sites in the Tapi Valley, viz., Prakash and Bahal, as well as those in the Godavari and Krishna Valleys, viz., Jorwe, Nevasa, Daimabad, Chandoli, Sonegaon and Bahurupa, have yielded evidence of a stone industry associated with copper and bronze tools and pottery (Sankalia, 1963, p. 203). These cultural phases have been dated as c. 1700–1050 BCE. The evidence collected from Eran on River Betwa, and Tripuri on River Narmada, indicates the possible routes through which the Malwa influences were diffused through the central and eastern regions of India. Archaeological remains also show a transition towards the Iron Age around 1040 BCE.

The gradual expansion of the post-Harappan influences over the Ganga Valley occurred along the routes connecting Alamgirpur with the rest of the region, sites that faded away soon after the end of the Harappan phase. This is evident from a sudden break in cultural continuity from the late Harappan phase to the Iron Age. The ochre-coloured pottery generally associated with copper hoards is thought to belong to the late Harappan and the post-Harappan phases. Later excavations at Atranjikhera in the Etah district confirmed these connections. A comparative study of the archaeological remains collected from Harappa, Rupar, Autha (Punjab),

Alamgirpur, Hastinapura, Atranjikhera, Ahichchhatra (the Doab and the upper Ganga Valley), Noh (Indo-Gangetic divide region), Sarawasti, Kosambi, Rajghat, Prahladpur, Chirand and Sonpur (middle Ganga Valley) corroborate these conclusions (Thapar, 1990, pp. 71–72). The different pottery types discovered at these sites help in the reconstruction of the sequence in cultural succession from ochre-coloured ware (c. 1200 BCE), painted greyware (c. 800–600 BCE) to the northern black polished ware (c. 200 BCE). At many of these sites, iron tools have been found in intermediary beds around 1000–800 BCE.

In the geography of *Rig Veda*, Yamuna appears to be the eastern limit. Subsequent streams of the Aryan tribes who moved eastwards are believed to have composed *Yajur Veda* and *Atharva Veda* as well as the later texts in regions lying to the east of the Yamuna, from Hastinapura to Magadha. The middle Ganga valley was populated after the forests were cleared. A story in the *Satapatha Brahmana* reveals that the land across the River Gandak was uncultivated and marshy because 'it had not been tasted by *Agni Vaisvanara*'. It became fit for settlement after *Agni* (fire) had crossed the river. The migrants moved and settled in the valley through two routes, northern and southern.[5]

Historic Period (600 BCE Onwards: Socio-cultural Regions in the Ancient Period

The eastward dispersion of Aryan settlements in the later Vedic period (800 to 322 BCE) led to the emergence of small states in the western Gangetic plains. States (*janapadas*) emerged as monarchies as well as republics, the latter representing a model of tribal democracy.

Tracing the transition from lineage to state, Thapar (1990, pp. 70–115) argued that monarchies were a peculiarity of the fertile Ganges valley. On the other hand, the states that emerged on the northern and the southern periphery of the valley were mostly republics. This distinction owed its origin to the ecological differences as expressed in the surplus generating potential of the two types of ecological zones. Understandably, the republics must have been the first states to emerge. Gradually, they were transformed into monarchies. Those ousted from the monarchies continued to establish new republics on the periphery of the Ganga Valley. Thus, monarchies and republics had an interesting geographic pattern of distribution. The transformation of republics into monarchies also marked a transition from

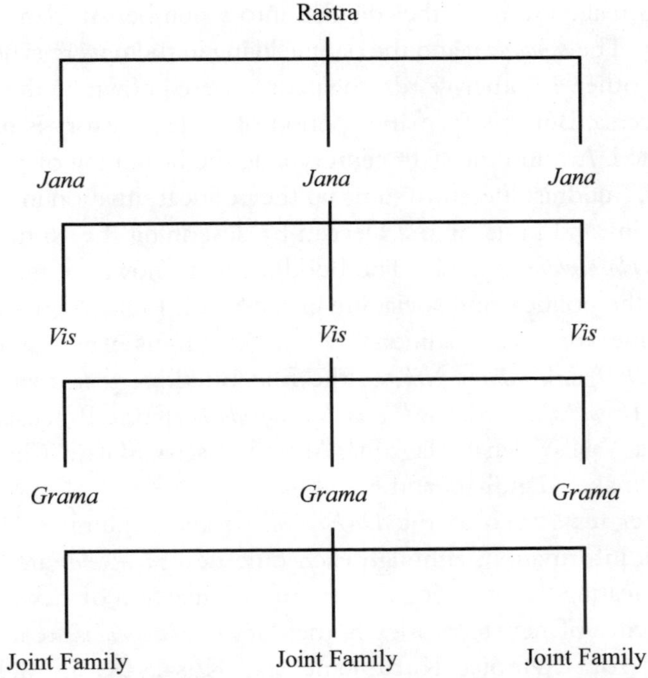

Fig. 15.2 Hierarchical structure of socio-cultural regions evolved in Vedic India (based on joint family system and clan solidarity).

the egalitarian tribal social order to a caste-based hierarchical structure. Gradually, different caste groups got associated with different occupations, leading to a further augmentation of the caste-based society. Over time, caste-specific occupational specialization also contributed to the diversification of the economy on a progressive basis, with the cities developing at nodal points as centres of trade and industry.

In the initial stage, the territorial system which the Aryans evolved was founded on the ethos of the joint family system, clan integrity and tribal identity. The smaller units were successively integrated with higher order spatial units right up to the level of the tribal state, known as rashtra (Fig. 15.2). The village (*grama*), canton (*vis*) and people (*jana*) formed the successive units in sequential order, the physical features usually indicating their loosely defined boundaries. In the post-Vedic period, the country was deemed to be composed of five broad socio-cultural realms – *Udicya* (North India), *Pracya* (East India), *Praticya* (West India), *Madhyadesa* (Central India) and *Daksinapatha* (South India). Around 500 BCE, these five broad realms were further divided into a number of clan territories (*janapadas*). The *janapadas* and the people living in them were synonymous with each other. In other words, the people were known by the *janapadas* and vice versa. But this formative period of Indian history is not firmly documented. Around the sixth century BCE, the beginning of the historical period, Buddhist literature sums up the political situation in the North Indian plains and parts of the Deccan by describing the 16 major kingdoms or *sodasa mahajanapadas*. The Buddhist texts, however, make no reference to the political and social life in the South India. Nonetheless, we may assume that the traditional Tamil kingdoms were in existence (Davies, 1959). *Anguttara Nikaya*, the first Buddhist text, mentions the following 16 *mahajanapadas (sodasa mahajanapadas)* – Kuru, Panchala, Kosala, Kasi, Malla, Vajji (Videha), Magadha, Anga, Surasena, Matsya, Chedi, Vatsa, Avanti, Asmaka, Gandhara and Kamboja.

The later texts such as the *Digha Nikaya* and a number of *Puranas* repeat this information, although each time new *janapadas* are added to the list indicating the on-going process of colonization of new tracts and the emergence of new territories. Sometimes the *janapadas* are mentioned as twins (for example, Kuru–Panchala, Kosala–Kasi, Malla–Vajji, Surasena–Matsaya and Chedi–Vatsa). This process of coming together of two neighbouring *janapadas* may be a political response to the overarching authority of certain nodes of power emerging as empires. By the time of Buddha, *Madhyadesa* of *Bharatavarsa* ('India' of that time) had already emerged as the major ecumene of Aryan settlement outside the Indus basin. In fact, the Sapta-Sindhava region appears to have faded away as the Ganga Valley came into prominence. *Madhyadesa* was protected by natural boundaries which made it the most secure region, just as its rich resources of land, water and congenial climate added immensely to its agricultural potential. The mid-Indian uplands, the Chhotanagpur plateau and the Rajmahal hills defined its southern and southeastern boundary. The deltaic tract of Bengal, emerging as the core of the Vanga *janapada*, was a much later development. In such a fertile plain, early Aryan settlements must have emerged on the banks of the rivers and on the land reclaimed from the surrounding forest. The pioneer villages that emerged on the cultivated tracts eventually came to be organized into territorial units, that is, clan territories, republics and kingdoms. Hierarchically organized politico-territorial arrangement of settlements was based on clan segmentation and consolidation, which gradually developed at every level of Hindu states irrespective of size or ruling dynasty (Mukherjee

1923, p. 238). Elemental to such a system were the notions of family property, clan solidarity and tribal affinity. Territorial organization for micro-level administration, as mentioned in the *Mahabharata* and the *Manusmriti*, was based on the decimal system. Villages were grouped into units of ten, twenty, hundred and thousand for administrative purposes and their chiefs were designated as *dasgrami, vimsapatipa, satgrami* and *adhipati* respectively (Hopkins, 1888, p. 84). Tribal states had duly recognized core territories but their peripheries were loosely defined. Physical features such as rivers, mountains and forests covering vast stretches of land usually formed their boundaries.

Cities emerged on the banks of rivers and became the foci of political authority. Hastinapura, Ahichchhatra, Kausambi, Ayodhya, Saket, Kasi (Varanasi), Shravasti, Vaishali, Rajagriha, Ujjaini and Taxila emerged as nodes of power attracting a large population of landed elite, artisans, warriors and administrators. With the growth of trade, some of these political centres acquired commercial importance as well and in some cases the latter became the chief focus of activity. Thus, Taxila in Gandhara retained its commercial importance since it had access to West Asia, particularly after sixth century BCE when it lay on the eastern margin of the Achaemenid empire. The importance of control over river traffic, which gradually grew in importance, was demonstrated in the rise of Pataliputra, the capital of the Mauryan Empire, due to its location near the confluence of the major rivers of the Ganga Valley. Thus, the site and situation of these capital towns played a significant role in determining their importance as a core of economic and political power. Fortification in the form of a wall and look-out towers enclosed the urban settlements and separated them from the surrounding areas, thus demarcating the urban area from the rural. But this separation was by no means absolute since the links between the two remained strong (Thapar, 1990, pp. 91–92).

Madhyadesa became the heartland of the Ganga Valley civilization. Gradually, local dialects developed with a literary tradition, in certain cases became the repository of folk culture, art, religion and philosophy. This resulted in the process of cultural diversification between the *janapadas*. Each *janapada* evolved its own dialect or language and produced its own *Puranas*. These were the beginnings of cultural regionalism that distinguishes India so characteristically.

The clearing of the forests in the Ganga Valley and the establishment of an agrarian system had led to the creation of powerful kingdoms in this area. These were to dominate the history of northern India for many centuries. Further, it was the continuous but veiled conflict between pre-Aryan and Aryan culture that modified and changed the pattern of Aryan culture. The development of India as we know it, stems from the arrival of the Aryans and the socio-cultural life they brought along with them. No doubt, there were several other, often oppositional forces that also played a significant role in affecting the pattern of socio-cultural life in India.

The Sudra cultivators, who cleared the forests, were mainly responsible for agricultural development. Many of them were landless labourers, which weakened their status. Untouchables, a category lower than Sudras, came to be recognized during this period. They are described as having a language different from that of the Aryans. Their occupations such as rush-weaving and hunting came to be looked upon as extremely low.

This period made the most significant contribution to the evolution of social institutions and religion in India. The origin of Hinduism in India can be traced to the arrival of the Aryans in the subcontinent. The Aryans not only contributed to the Sanskrit language, the idea of caste-based society and religious sacrifice, and the philosophy of the *Upanishads* (speculative philosophical appendices to the *Puranas*), but were also instrumental in the clearing of land for large-scale agriculture. Still more important was the generation of new ideas and institutions, either through acceptance or opposition to such contributions. Sanskrit had developed as the language of the educated upper castes and remained a unifying factor among the upper castes throughout the subcontinent for many centuries. The caste system, evolved during this period and having a considerable role in determining political institutions, has survived in India for more than two thousand years despite efforts to break its grip. At a different level, the opposition to caste and Vedic sacrifices was the prominent feature of later social movements. From the metaphysical subtleties of the *Upanishads* sprang many of the later systems of thought.

The social and political life under the monarchical system was dominated by the Brahmin political theories. Social and political power lay with the *rajas* and the representatives at the assembly who were generally of Kshatriya origin. The divine nature of kingship was also established. For being the transmitters of divinity, the priests too were not considered as ordinary mortals. The throne and priesthood worked hand in hand. Cattle rearing was no longer the primary occupation; agriculture had taken root in many areas. Land was either owned collectively by the villagers or by a tribal chief who hired labourers to work on it. Undoubtedly, land was the most important source, but not the only source of income for the chiefs. Trade in agricultural commodities had taken root in the social and economic life of North India. Towns had come into existence as centres of industry and trade. Towns such as Shravasti, Champa, Rajagriha, Ayodhya, Kaushambi, and Kashi were of substantial importance to the economy of the Ganga plain. Urban centres were important not only in trade but also in administrative control. A desire to have control over trade routes among the important principalities in the Ganga Valley gave impetus to empire building. Those having strategic and economic advantage won in the power game. Magadha, under King Bimbisara emerged victorious and established itself as the centre of political activity in northern India, a position which it maintained for centuries. The victory of Magadha was a victory for the monarchical system, now firmly established in the Ganga Valley.

The changing features of social and economic life, such as the growth of towns, expansion of the artisan class, and the rapid development of trade and commerce, were closely linked with another sphere – that of religion and philosophical speculation. The conflict between the established orthodoxy and the aspirations of newly rising groups in the urban centres must have intensified the process, resulting in a remarkable richness and vigour in thought rarely surpassed in the centuries to come. The ascetics and the wandering sophists of the earlier age maintained a tradition of unorthodox thinking. In general, philosophical speculation ranged from determinism to materialism. Thinkers such as the *Ajivikas* were followers of a philosophy of complete predetermination – destiny which controlled even the most insignificant action of every human being. These sects were regarded with scorn and were accused of immoral practices by the orthodox. The Brahmins were particularly harsh, since the materialists objected to the senseless rituals and ceremonies on which the priests insisted, and which were their livelihood. Two of these puritanical sects, Jainism and Buddhism, finally evolved into independent religions. Jainism remained mainly confined to the Ganga Valley, though later on it moved to western, northern and southern parts of the country. Jainism spread rapidly among the trading community, its emphasis on non-violence (*ahimsa*) prevented agriculturists from joining it since cultivation involved killing of insects and pests. Jains specialized in conducting the exchange of manufactured goods and acting as middlemen, confining themselves to financial transactions. Thus Jainism came to be associated with the spread of urban culture. Buddhism as a religion was more popular than Jainism.

In Buddhism, salvation lay in achieving *nirvana* or freedom from the cycle of rebirth. The doctrine of *karma* was essential to the Buddhist system of salvation. The introduction of monastic orders accelerated education since the monasteries became a source of learning in addition to that offered by the Brahmins. More importantly, men and women of all strata of society were accepted as monks and nuns. Education was therefore not restricted only to the elite few. The acceptance of nuns was a revolutionary step considering that Brahmin orthodoxy was gradually trying to place limitations on women's priestly activities.

Both Buddhism and Jainism were opposed to brahminical orthodoxy, denied the authority of the *Vedas* and were antagonistic to the practice of animal sacrifice, by then a keystone of brahminical power. Both appealed to the downtrodden castes (the *Vaishyas* who were economically powerful but not granted corresponding social status, and the oppressed Sudras). Though Buddhism and Jainism did not directly attack the caste system, they were nevertheless opposed to it and can, to that extent, be described as non-caste movements (Thapar, 1990, p. 68). This provided an opportunity for those of low caste to opt out of their caste by joining a non-caste sect. The lack of expenses involved in worship, as contrasted with Brahminical worship, also attracted the same stratum in society.

The Buddha, who intended his message to reach the lower strata of society, used to deliver his teachings in the popular language, Magadhi, in preference to Sanskrit. The followers of Buddhism were mainly traders, artisans and farmers. Brahmin Buddhists were looked upon as renegades by their caste fellows. Kshatriya adherents of Buddhism and Jainism were theoretically something of an anomaly since warriors can hardly be supporters of non-violence; but the Kshatriya tribes in the republics supporting Buddhism were also professional warriors. Buddhism and Jainism were, thus, closely linked with urban centres and largely associated with the lower castes. The same pattern was repeated in later centuries with the various phases of the *Bhakti* movement, the social content being an essential part of their religious doctrine. People became prosperous, particularly with the expansion of trade. Political control was still largely with the Kshatriyas and Brahmins, but the mercantile classes were economically ascendant. Buddhism and Jainism were their answers to Brahminism (Thapar, 1990, p. 69).

The beginning of the eighth century CE set the process of decline in classical Hindu culture and degeneration in the political system. This facilitated the conquest of the subcontinent by foreign powers. For this reason, the period from the eighth to the thirteenth century is sometimes referred to as 'the dark age' of Indian history. However, many institutions of present-day India began to take shape during this period. Feudalism evolved during this period as the basis for the political economic structure, survived in a broad sense until recent times and influenced the development of society accordingly. Many of the sub-castes that evolved during this period continue to function in the social hierarchy. The languages spoken in the various states of India today are derived from the regional languages spoken in thirteenth century India. Religious cults, as distinct from established religion, also emerged at this time, and still dominate the lives of the rural population today.

It was around the beginning of this period that the secondary *prakrits* (Middle Indo-Aryan languages related to, yet different from Sanskrit), namely *Sauraseni, Ardha magadhi, Magadhi* and *Maharashtri*, became the literary *apabhramshas* (literally 'falling down'), corrupt forms of *Prakrit.* The modern vernacular came through them as the tertiary *prakrits. Apabhramsha*, after its origin in the northwest, travelled with migration streams, scattering and settling in central and western India after the Hun invasions. *Apabhramsha* heavily influenced the *Prakrit* of the Jains and it is here that the link between the older and the newer languages is evident.

Regional interest and variation was beginning to express itself in many forms, including architecture and sculpture where the breaking away from classical models is evident in the temples of this period. There are three regions in the north – Rajasthan and Gujarat in western India, Bundelkhand in central India, and Orissa in eastern India – where large, elegant temples have survived. The overall architectural style is similar, conforming to the *nagara* or north Indian style, but this does not exclude local variation.[6]

The reluctance of the upper classes of the North to admit popular deities into their religious system led to the creation of a clear-cut distinction between the religion of the elite and the religion of the masses in this period. More sophisticated forms of Hinduism held sway in the upper echelons of society. The use of the term Hinduism to cover both the *Vaishnava* and *Shaiva* following that comprise the two major sects of the Brahmanical religion, came into popular use only after the arrival of the

Arabs and Turks, who used the word Hindu primarily to refer to the inhabitants of the Indian subcontinent and to distinguish themselves from the native inhabitants. The term persisted and is now associated only with the Brahminical religion of the subcontinent, although the Arabs and the Turks only vaguely differentiated between the Hindus and the Buddhists, Jains, and other religions. With the gradual decline of the latter, the term was applied only to *Vaishnavas* and *Shaivas*.

Many of the changes introduced into Hinduism at this time were the result of a compromise between orthodox belief and popular demand for a more personal religion.[7] Image worship increased substantially and a multitude of new deities were introduced, necessitating the building of shrines and temples to house them. The incarnations of Vishnu became more popular and interest in the *Puranas* and epic literature, particularly through their versions in regional languages, provided a tradition in which to incorporate the legends of the incarnations, the most popular being Krishna tradition, after the philosopher of the Bhagavad Gita. The cult became popular in the Mathura region, from where it rapidly spread to other parts of northern India. At the popular level, Krishna and his favourite, the milkmaid Radha, were worshipped as part of a fertility cult.

Buddhism and Islam, both being institutionalized proselytizing religions, came into conflict as both attracted the same potential following. This led to a strong antagonism between the two. Attacks on Buddhist monasteries resulted in an exodus of Buddhists from eastern India to Southeast Asia. Islam found its largest following in previously Buddhist areas of India: the northwest and the east.

Socio-cultural Regions in the Medieval Period

Following the successful campaigns of the Afghans and the Turks, a new political order had emerged on Indian soil. With the establishment of Muslim rule in India in the thirteenth century, the Muslims became the ruling minority and the Hindus the ruled majority. The incoming Turks and Afghans tended to settle in the towns, giving rise to a vigorous urban culture. Initially, this did not greatly change either the pattern of Indian culture or the political and administrative institutions and practices. In many cases local rulers and chiefs continued to rule as before.

However, as evident from the development of the *Bhakti* movement, the challenge to the social pattern was intensified. Since caste loyalty was stronger than political loyalty, the significant impact of Islam was upon the social structure as new sub-castes and sects within these castes began to emerge and were permeated with Islamic ideas. To this extent, the earlier pattern of assimilation of foreigners was repeated. In spite of its egalitarian philosophy, the influence of Islam did not lead to the disappearance of caste. In fact the social dynamism of Islam was somewhat reduced in India as Islam succumbed to and accepted caste in society, where the *Shaikhs* and the *Sayyids* (members of the high *Ashraf* caste) had a caste status analogous to that of Hindu *dvijas* (twice born); thus, the threat to the caste system was slight. Authority and social prestige remained with the castes traditionally associated with power. The lack of vertical mobility through the caste hierarchy in society isolated the castes from each other. By the same token, it isolated new thought within the castes. This made the *Bhakti* movement politically ineffective during this period. However, in subsequent centuries the followers of Nanak (recognized as the first Sikh guru), for instance, developed into an effective political community. But the traditional pattern of opposition to orthodoxy was to continue until the late nineteenth century, when the emergence of the Indian middle class caused a new social and political pattern to evolve.

The Mughals, who stepped into the shoes of the Sultans in 1526, made wide-ranging changes in administrative organization. The facts of geography along with those of history and political reality were kept in mind while rationalizing the existing division of space for administrative purposes. That is why one sees a discernible continuity from the *janapadas* to the Mughal *subahs* (provinces). While the political structure underwent many changes in the intervening period of two millennia, the political divisions were more or less built on the legacy of socio-cultural regions. Ahmad (1999, p. 106) attempted a comparison between the Mughal provinces and the 16 *mahajanapadas* to find a broad correspondence between the two. The Mughals built their provincial structure on this very edifice. One of the best examples of geographical factors being duly recognized in the rationalization of provincial boundaries is revealed from the administrative boundaries of Punjab. Known as *subah* of Lahore, Punjab was bounded by the River Indus in the West and by the River Satluj in the East. Notably, the term Punjab, denoting the land of five rivers, came into wider currency during the reign of Akbar. This shows that there were attempts to keep the physical and administrative boundaries of historically evolved primary divisions coterminous (Kant, 1988, p. 39).

According to *Ain-e-Akbari* (a chronicle on political institutions during the times of Emperor Akbar), the Mughal empire was divided into 16 primary divisions or provinces in 1601. Later on, as a result of consistent Mughal effort to extend the imperial frontiers towards the South, four more provinces (Aurangabad, Bidar, Bijapur and Haidarabad) were added to raise the number of provinces to 20 in 1707 (Habib, 1982, pp. vii–viii). Each province (*subah*) was further subdivided into *sarkars* and each *sarkar* into *mahals* or *paraganas*. The *sarkars* of the Mughal period, as secondary divisions at the provincial level, corresponded to *aharas* of the Maurya period and *Vaishyas* of the Gupta period (Kant, 1988, p. 40). While the *mahals* or *paraganas* were revenue subdivisions created for the collection of tax on land, a single *mahal* or a cluster of *mahals* having homogeneous soil and climatic conditions were designated as a *dastur*. A separate revenue code (*dastur-al-amal*) applied to each *dastur*. Irr a way, the *dasturs* may be seen as analogous to agricultural regions (Ahmad, 1999, p. 101). According to *Ain-e-Akbari*, the *subah* of Lahore was divided into five *sarkars* and further into 232 *paraganas*. Such a system of territorial organization of administration at the sub-regional level was a continuation of the traditional system of clan territories evolved during the ancient period within the framework of micro-level ecological units.

It may be interesting to examine the nature of correspondence between the *janapadas* and the Mughal provinces of the sixteenth century. Notably, the Mughal *subah* of Delhi extended over the Kuru *janapada*. Agra occupied the *janapadas* of Surasena and Panchala. Allahabad focussed on Vatsa and Awadh on Kosala. The *subah* of Bihar was an amalgam of Malla, Vajji, Magadha and Anga *janapadas*. The *subah* of Bengal represented a later extension of territory and occupied the Vanga *janapada*. However, Vanga was not mentioned in the *Anguttra Nikaya*. The *subah* of Malwa occupied the Avanti *janapada*. In the northwest, the *subah* of Kabul had grown out of the core *janapadas* of Gandhara and Kamboja. The Mughal *subah* of Kabul was much larger and marked an outgrowth of the core region of Gandhara. In the process of expansion it embraced the territories of Jammu and Kashmir. Evidently, there had been a broad correspondence between the *janapadas* and the Mughal provinces. At the sub-provincial level, the territorial arrangement of administration had remained the same, as evolved during the ancient period on the basis of ecological parameters. Nevertheless, the *janapadas* were expected to grow from their core areas during a span of 200 years with the peopling process and occupation of new lands in the peripheral areas.

Persian was the official language during this period. Persian influence penetrated deep into the world of ideas and left a permanent imprint on Indian socio-cultural life, architectural design, art and administrative practice. The mystical and freethinking ideas of the *sufis* were carried out in India in accordance to the great tradition of Persian poets. The Persian love of poetry and song found a ready resonance in Indian hearts. Even today, *mushaira*, public assembly of poets to recite poems to a critical audience, is an important event in North India. Through the Mughals, Persia became the school of manners for *Hindustan* (Spear, 1990, p. 50).

Persian tastes, ideas and attitudes are so embedded in North India that they are often thought to be local products. Persian influenced Urdu and also Hindi to some extent. But perhaps the most lasting of Persian influences was administrative. Persian nomenclature and administrative concepts were so pervasive that they were found among the fighting Marathas when they were struggling to be free of the Mughals (Spear, 1990, p. 51). Even today, almost all of the terminology used in revenue administration in India is derived from the Persian language – *khasra, khatauni, zamabandi, intakal* and *mukhtiarnama.*

Summary

The evolution of socio-cultural regions in India, spanning a period of about 6000 years, was initially dominated by geographical factors. A combination of physical characteristics, such as form and slope of land, drainage, soil cover, natural vegetation and climate provided diversity in production potential. Consequently, the alluvial plains attracted numerous cultural streams. On the periphery of these plains, the rim of hills and uplands permitted the continuance of primitive economic modes unaffected by change over time. Broader environmental setting and diversified ecological niches, thus, provided the basis for different kinds of socio-cultural regions. Nevertheless, the diverse socio-cultural traditions that the incoming human groups brought in from the areas of their origin, coupled with their capability to transform the natural environment, played a significant role in the evolution and emergence of regional differentials in socio-cultural patterns of the subcontinent.

In spite of archaeological evidence supporting the presence of early humans in India in the second inter-glacial period, no direct evidence is yet available to throw light on the nature of social institutions, cultural traditions and other characteristics of such people. The two tool-making industries discovered in India are characterized by different tool-making traditions. While the pebble chopping tools dominate in the Sohan type of tool-making industry, the tools discovered from the sites of the Madras type mostly consist of hand axes and cleavers made of cores and flakes. Madras-type tools, Acheulean in topology, suggest an independent development of culture across the region lying to the south of the Narmada.

With the emergence of settled life and the gradual spread of agricultural communities in the Later Stone Age, societies on the subcontinent entered into a new phase of socio-cultural development. These communities differed widely in aesthetic and technological traditions. The ecology and geography of these cultural regions largely explained these differences. Such differences, coupled with consequent socio-economic variations among these communities, became the basis for the language cultures on the subcontinent at a later stage. In the perennial nuclear regions, highly-developed urban-based civilizations coexisted with highly primitive Stone Age cultures in the areas of isolation. Depending upon ecological setting, there existed socio-cultural variations within the broad cultural regions. The territorial rooting of different culture groups took place during this period.

The diffusion of Aryan settlements from the Indus Valley to the Ganges Valley in the later Vedic period led to the emergence of monarchies and republican states on the soils of the Ganga Valley, ushering a new era in socio-cultural and political developments on the subcontinent. During this period, cultural traits diffused through several routes.

In the initial stage, the territorial system which the Aryans evolved was founded on the ethos of the joint family system, clan integrity and tribal identity. The smaller units were successively integrated with higher order spatial units right up to the level of the tribal state, known as *rashtra.* The village (*grama*), canton (*vis*) and people (*jana*) formed the successive units in sequential order, the physical features usually indicating their loosely defined boundaries. In the post-Vedic period, the country was deemed to be composed of five broad socio-cultural realms – *Udicya* (North India), *Pracya* (East India), *Praticya* (West India), *Madhyadesa* (Central India) and *Daksinapatha* (South India). These broad realms were further divided into a number of clan territories (*janapadas*) in the North Indian plains, 16 of them being territorially large and politically strong (*sodasa mahajanapadas*). These *janapadas* were synonymous with the people and vice versa. The origin of Hinduism in India can be traced back to the coming of the Aryans to the subcontinent. The Aryans not only contributed to the Sanskrit language, the idea of caste-based society and religious sacrifice, and the philosophy of the *Upanishads*, but also played a key role in the clearing of land for large-scale agriculture. Sanskrit had developed as the language of the educated upper castes in this period and continued to be a unifying factor among the upper castes throughout the subcontinent for many centuries. The caste system, evolved during this period and having a considerable role in determining the nature of political institutions, has survived in India for more than 2000 years despite efforts to break its grip. However, the opposition to caste and Vedic sacrifices became a prominent feature of later social movements.

The period from the eighth to the thirteenth century saw the degeneration of classical Hindu culture and political institutions, yet it also witnessed the shaping of many institutions of present-day India. Feudalism as the basis of the political-economic structure took root during this period, survived in a broad sense until recent times, and influenced the development of society accordingly. Many of the sub-castes and religious cults that evolved during this period continue to exist in the current social hierarchy and milieu. Most of the modern regional languages spoken in India are today derived from the languages spoken in thirteenth century India.

The establishment of the new political order in the thirteenth century made the Muslims the ruling minority and the Hindus the ruled majority. Under the influence of Islam several new sub-castes and sects within castes emerged in Indian society. This repeated the earlier pattern of assimilation of foreigners. The lack of vertical mobility in the caste-based society isolated the castes and the thinking within the castes, rendering new socio-political movements ineffective during this period. In subsequent centuries, however, some movements gained traction, such as that by the followers of Nanak.

Though the socio-cultural pattern and the political regions remained almost unaltered during the early Muslim rule in India, the Mughals made wide-ranging changes in administrative organization in the sixteenth century. The facts of geography along with those of history and political reality were kept in mind while rationalizing the existing division of space for administrative purposes. The creation of the Mughal *subahs* (provinces) reflected a discernible continuity from the *janapadas*. While the political structure underwent significant change in the intervening period of two millennia, the political divisions with some modifications were built on the legacy of traditional socio-cultural regions that had evolved as clan territories based on the ecological framework during the ancient period.

Persian, which was the official language during this period, penetrated deep into the world of ideas and left a permanent imprint on Indian socio-cultural life, architectural design, art and administrative practice. Though Persian is no longer spoken in India today, its influence is seen on Urdu and Hindi, both being widely spoken in India, the former being an official language in Pakistan. *Hindustani*, the everyday language of the North, is deeply indebted to it. Perhaps the most lasting of Persian influences was administrative; Persian terminology is still very popular in India, especially in revenue administration.

Evolved through a long period of prehistory and history, the socio-cultural regions displayed their broad monolithic nature in terms of the Aryan–Dravidian origins in two quintessential geographic divisions, northern and southern India. Clearly demarcated by the Vindhyachal–Satpura ranges, peninsular India is insular in character and the Great Plains of northern India along with the Himalayan region present a picture of cultural synthesis. These two basic characteristics, insularity and synthesis, have continued to be reflected in those socio-cultural regions which have evolved through time.

Acknowledgement

The discussion with Dr. A. B. Mukerji, Professor (Retd.) of Geography, Punjab University, Chandigarh, has been extremely helpful in the preparation of this article. His help is gratefully acknowledged.

Notes

1. There is no consensus on the naming of different phases of Pleistocene culture in India. B. Subbarao (1958) and Bridge Allchin (1959) attempted to solve this problem by naming them Early Stone Age (Earlier Pleistocene), Middle Stone Age (Later Pleistocene) and Late Stone Age (Microlithic), but not to the satisfaction of all.
2. The Sohan valley technique of tool-making became a reference point in comparative archaeology for checking the antecedents of similar tools discovered in other parts of India. It was due to the pioneering work of de Terra and Paterson (1939) that it became possible to place the whole set of evidence collected from the Sohan river terraces in its proper perspective. By correlating human cultures with the sequence of climatic changes during Pleistocene times, de Terra and Paterson set

the stage for a meaningful study of the Palaeolithic cultures in India. Here, tools were found in four of the five terraces of the Sohan river. The lithic evidence was collected from the terraces of the second glacial, second inter-glacial and the third glacial phases.

3. The term, Acheulean, takes its origin from St Acheul, a suburb of Amiens in France, where rice industries of the culture have been excavated recurring from the terrace grovels of the Somme.
4. For example, sites from where the hand axes were collected do not reveal a cultural succession to the Mesolithic phase. However, the *teri* (sand dunes of wind deposits in coastal areas) sites in southern Tamil Nadu have yielded evidence of transition from the Palaeolithic to the Neolithic cultures.
5. The former followed the foothills of the Himalayas, probably taken by Videgha Mathava and the latter followed the south bank of the Yamuna and the Ganga at the base of Vindhyan outcrops. The northern route turned south following the rivers, particularly the Gandak which joined the Ganga at a point not too far from Pataliputra, where it also met the southern route (Thapar, 1990, p. 70).
6. The *nagara* temple was square in plan but gave the impression of having a cruciform shape owing to graduated projections in the middle of each of the four sides. The central tower was tall, inclining gradually inwards in a convex curve.
7. By the end of the twelfth century, two sects, Buddhism and Jainism, were dominant in northern India. Jainism was restricted mainly to the Jain community in western India. Buddhism, mainly in eastern India, was fast losing support. Buddha had been incorporated into the Hindu pantheon as an incarnation of Vishnu. But the popular mind never quite accepted this – the worship of Buddha by non-Buddhists remained a formal and deferential relationship with the god. The militaristic values of the feudal system no doubt found the Buddhist and Jaina emphasis on *ahimsa* (non-violence) unpalatable. Where the idea of non-violence survived was amongst the leaders of the devotional cults, opposing violence for the same reasons as did the Buddha.

References

Ahmed, A., *Social Geography of India*, Jaipur: Rawat Publication, 1999.

Allchin, B., 'The Indian Stone Age Sequence', *Journal of the Royal Anthropological Institute of Great Britain and Ireland*, Vol. 93, No. 2, 1963, pp. 210–234.

Allchin, B. and Raymond Allchin, *The Birth of Indian Civilization*, Hammondsworth: Penguin Books, 1968.

Allchin, B., 'The Indian Middle Stone Age: Some New Sites in Central and Southern India, and their Implications', *Bulletin of the Institute of Archaeology*, Vol. 2, 1959, pp. 1–35.

Allchin, F. R., *Neolithic Cattle-Keepers of South India – A Study of the Deccan Ashmounds*, Cambridge: Cambridge University Press, 1963.

Basham, A. L., *The Wonder That was India*, New Delhi: Rupa & Co., Third edition, 1967.

Childe, Gordon V., *New Light on the most Ancient East*, New York: Grove Press, Inc., Fourth edition, 1952.

Davies, C. C., *An Historical Atlas of the Indian Peninsula*, Oxford: Oxford University Press, 1959.

de Terra, H., 'The Quaternary Terrace System of Southern Asia', *Geographic Review*, January 1939.

de Terra, H. and T. T. Paterson, *Studies on the Ice Age of India and Associated Human Cultures*, Washington: Carnegie Institution of Washington, Publication No. 493, 1939.

Fairservis, Walter A. Jr., *The Roots of Ancient India: The Archaeology of Early Indian Civilization*, London: George Allen & Unwin, 1971.

Habib, Irfan, *An Atlas of the Mughal Empire*, Delhi: Oxford University Press, 1982.

Hopkins, E. W., 'Position of the Ruling Caste in Anceint India', *Journal of American Oriental Society*, p. 13.

Kant, Surya, *Administrative Geography of India*, Jaipur: Rawat Publications, 1988.

Kirk, William, 'The Role of India in the Diffusion of Early Cultures', *Geographical Journal*, Vol. 141, No. I, March 1975, pp. 19–35.

Kosambi, D. D., *The Culture and Civilization of India in Historical Outline*, New Delhi: Vikas Publishing House, 1972.

Krishnaswami, V. D., 'Stone Age India', *Ancient India*, Vol. 3, 1947, pp. 11–57.

Krishnaswami, V. D., 'Progress in Prehistory', *Ancient India*, Vol. 9, 1953, pp. 53–79.

Lal, B. B., 'Palaeoliths from the Beas and Banganga Valleys, Punjab', *Ancient India*, Vol. 7, 1956, pp. 58–92.

Lawler, Andrew, 'Indus Collapse: The End or the Beginning of an Asian Culture?', *Science*, Vol. 320, no. 5881, 2008, pp. 1281–1283.

Mukherjee, R. K., *Democracies of the East: A Study in Comparative Politics*, London: P. S. King, 1923.

Pannikkar, K. M., Geographical Factors in Indian History, Bombay, 1955.

Piggott, S., *Prehistory of India*, London: Harmondsworth, 1950.

Ratnagar, Shereen, *Encounters: The Westerly Trade of the Harappan Civilization*, Delhi: Oxford University Press, 1981.

Richards, F. J., 'Geographic Factors in Indian Archaeology', *Indian Antiquary*, Vol. 62, 1933, pp. 231–243.

Sankalia, H. D., *Prehistory and Protohistory in India and Pakistan*, Bombay: University of Bombay, 1963.

Sankalia, H. D., 'Middle Stone Age Culture in India and Pakistan', *Science*, Vol. 146, 1964, pp. 365–374.

Schwartzberg, J. E., 'The Evolution of Regional Power Configurations in Indian Subcontinent, in Richard G. Fox (ed.), *Realm and Region in Traditional India*. New Delhi: Vikas, 1977, pp. 197–233.

Sellman, R. R., *An Outline Atlas of Eastern History*, London: Edward Arnold, 1954.

Singh, Jaipal and Mumtaz Khan, 'The Cultural Landscape of Mewat', in A. Ahmad (ed.), *Social Structure and Regional Development: A Social Geographical Perspective*, Jaipur: Rawat, 1993, pp. 151–181.

Sopher, David E., 'Rohilkhand and Oudh: An Exploration of Social Gradients Across Political Frontier', in Richard G. Fox (ed.), *Realm and Region in Traditional India*, New Delhi: Vikas, 1977, pp. 281–307.

Spate, O. H. K., *India and Pakistan*, London: Methuen & Co., 1957.

Spear, Percival, *A History of India*, New Delhi: Penguin Books, Vol. 2, 1990.

Subbarao, B., *The Personality of India*, Poona: University of Baroda, Archaeological Series No. 3, 1958.

Thapar, Romila, *A History of India*, New Delhi: Penguin Books, Vol. 1, 1990.

Thapar, Romilla, *From Lineage to State*, Delhi: Oxford University Press, 1990.

Toynbee, Arnold J., *Between Oxus and Jumna*, London: Oxford University Press, 1961.

Wheeler, Sir M., *Early India and Pakistan*, New York: Frederick A. Praeger, 1959.

16

Distinct Regional Cultural Identities of India Based on Religion and Language

ASHOK K. DUTT

In collaboration with S. DAVGUN (Religion Section),
CHANDRAKANTA C. KHAN and CHANDRALEKHA SANGWAN
(Language Section)

Diverse cultures of India give rise to regional variations in both material cultures (settlement patterns, temple designs, house types, bullock carts, plow construction and way of dressing) and non-material cultures (language, criminal behavior, religion, dance forms, castes, music, god forms and perception of Indian heritage). These characteristics are so vividly pronounced regionally that one sometimes wonders if the country really possesses any harmony. There is, nonetheless, an inherent unity that has been created amidst the rich cultural heritage nurtured over 5000 years (Dutt and Noble 1982). The following aspects of culture in relation to religion and language have been examined to identify spatial implications in the country.

There exists a deep nexus between religion and culture. Since the impact of religion on culture varies spatially in accordance with its area of dominance, the phenomenon of religion as a geographic aspect is of great importance to the cultural and political geography of India. Indians take their religion seriously. For an average Indian his or her belief in religion is very deep. When the British Raj was divided into India (a secular state) and Pakistan (an Islamic nation) in 1947, there was a deep Hindu-Muslim divide, which often erupted into riots. As time passed most of the Hindus who wanted to migrate from West and East Pakistan (now Bangladesh) to India completed their migration journey and, similar was the case with the Muslims who wanted to migrate from India to Pakistan.

There were only a few Hindus left in Pakistan (former West Pakistan), while about 11 per cent of the population of Bangladesh continues to be Hindus. In India about 13.4 per cent of the population are Muslims, who appear destined to live in India for good. Compared to the end of the 1940s, there appears a generational gap at the beginning of the new millennium with a new generation of Muslims bought up in India who have never ever visited Pakistan and with very few near relatives or friends migrating to or visiting from Pakistan. Moreover, the news of discriminatory treatment meted out to the *Mujahirs* (Indian Muslim migrants to Pakistan) in Karachi and *Biharis* (Muslim migrants from Bihar) in Bangladesh come as signals to the Indian Muslims that they are not welcome migrants either in Pakistan or Bangladesh. Thus, the Indian Muslims have become a part of national political system.

Both Muslim and Hindu leaders have started to use religion as an instrument for vote gathering. Muslims vote for candidates who protect them, while Hindu fundamentalists thought that by playing the 'Hindu Card' they could obtain a majority support in the elections because India has an overwhelming majority (80.5 percent) of Hindus. The Hindu fundamentalists had been in the political field since even before the country's independence. Their political support among the masses was weak until the end of the 1980s. Their major political party initially was named Hindu Mahashaba; the name changed into Jana Sangh and now, they are called the Bharatiya Janata Party (BJP). BJP altered the political arena in the May 1996 national elections by winning 30 percent of the parliamentary seats (or members) and 24 percent of popular vote. In the election of 1999, the BJP obtained only a little over one-third of the parliamentary seats, its 24-party alliance, mostly with non-fundamentalists, had a 55 percent majority in the Indian parliament. BJP support waned in Uttar Pradesh state that lies at the center of India's Hindi heartland which often holds the key to who rules India. As a result, the parliamentary elections of 2004 and 2009 brought back the Indian National Congress Party (with its allies) to power. Up until the present time, the norm had been that whichever political party wins a majority of parliamentary seats from the heartland, rules India.

Spatial Implications of Religion: Hinduism

India has many religions, some of which originated in India, and some which were grafted onto her religious milieu. Hinduism, Buddhism,

Table 16.1 Changing religious composition of India, 1881–2001

Census		*Hindus*	*Muslims*	*Christians*	*Sikhs*	*Buddhists*	*Jains*
1881	i	75.1	19.97	0.71	0.74	0.07	0.49
1891	i	74.2	20.41	0.77	0.68	0.09	0.51
1901	i	72.9	21.88	0.98	0.77	0.1	0.47
1911	i	71.7	22.39	1.21	1	0.11	0.41
1921	i	70.7	23.23	1.47	1.06	0.12	0.39
1931	i	70.7	23.49	1.77	1.28	0.23	0.37
1941	i	69.5	24.28	1.91	1.4	0.12	0.37
1951	ii	84.99	9.93	2.3	1.74	0.45	0.36
1961	iii	83.5	10.69	2.44	1.79		
1971	iii	82.7	11.21	2.6	1.89	0.7	0.47
1981	iv	80.4	11	2.4	1.9	0.7	0.5
1991	iv	81.3	12.1	2.3	1.9	0.8	0.4
2001	v	80.5	13.4	2.3	1.9	0.8	0.4

Sources: i Davis, K. 1968. *The Population of India and Pakistan*, New York: Russell and Russell, p. 179.

ii *India 1960*, Delhi: Publication Division, Government of India, 1960, p. 43

* excludes states of Jammu and Kashmir and Part B Tribal Areas of Assam

iii *Census of India*, 1971, Religion Series I – India Paper 2 of 1972, (Delhi Manager of Publications), p. 11

iv *Statistical Outline of India 2005–06*, Mumbai: Tata Services Ltd., 2006

v Census of India, 2001, www.censusindia.net

Jainism, and Sikhism all originated in the country, but Islam and Christianity were brought into the land from West Asia. According to the 2001 census, shown in Table 16.1, Hinduism continues to be the major religion in India; a little over 80 percent of the total population is Hindu.

Though the basic contents of Hinduism (as contained in the *Rig Veda*) were brought to India by the Aryans about 1,500 BC, the religion is still considered to be indigenous to the country because all later developments of this religion, in theoretical as well as practical terms, occurred on the Indian subcontinent. This religion consists of numerous beliefs and practices, and has given rise to different socio-religious institutions. Hindus were the original settlers of the land of the Indus River. Modern Hinduism has gradually evolved from an early Vedic Brahmanism, the religion of the Aryans, who were an ancient Indo-European people. At present, Hinduism is a diverse conglomeration of doctrines, cults, and ways of life.

As a Hindu dominated country, Hindus have had a great impact on the cultural geography of India. Table 16.1 displays the slight decline in the proportion of the Hindu population in India during the 1881–1941 and 1951–2001 periods. During the former period, this decline was due more to the conversion of low caste Hindus to other religions.

> Up until recent times the Hindus did not, and in many areas still do not, regard the untouchables as properly among the faithful and did not admit them to Hindu temples (Davis 1968, p.179).

Thus, many of the low caste Hindus were attracted to other religions such as Islam, Christianity, Sikhism, and Buddhism. In Table 16-1, the proportion of Hindus in the total population shows an abrupt increase from 1941 to 1951, which was due to the partition of British India in 1947 into India and Pakistan. Many Muslims left India and moved to Pakistan; in return many Hindus from (West) Pakistan and East Pakistan (now Bangladesh) migrated to India. Consequently, this caused an increase in the number and percentage share of the Hindus in the total population. After 1951, again there is a slight decline in the proportion of the Hindus in the total population, which is a continuation of the 1881–1941 trend. Though conversion to other religions is one of the important reasons, there are other demographic reasons, such as low fertility, which explain the gradual decline in the share of Hindus in the total population. Hindus have a low fertility compared to Sikhs, Muslims and Christians (Pethe 1973).

Hinduism has only been slightly affected by the other religions that originated in India or came since, but at the same time has had a strong impact upon them. For example, Christianity, Sikhism and Islam have inherited the Hindu caste system in some form.

Distributional Pattern of Hindus

Generally, Hindus are spread all over India with lesser concentration in the periphery. They exceeded 80 percent of the total population in 256 districts out of the 356 (Census of India 1971). There are a few areas where the Hindus make up more than 95 percent of the population, such as in most of Orissa state and the adjoining districts of Madhya Pradesh. In seven districts of the country, they are more than 99 percent. Figure 16.1 provides the relative importance of Hindus in the spatial perspective. The only areas which do not have a Hindu predominance are the Punjab plains, Kashmir, the western part of Uttar Pradesh, the north-eastern part of India, central Maharashtra and the Malabar Coast. The spatial distributional pattern of the Hindus has not undergone any major change since at least 1881, when the first census was taken, till 1947.

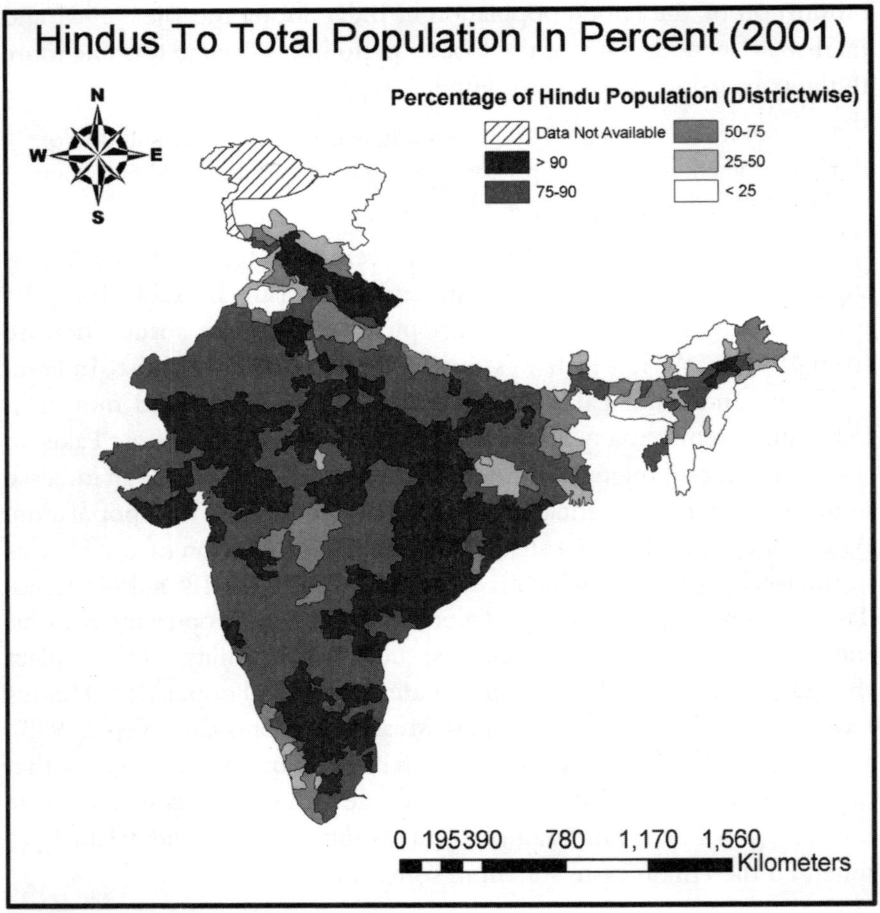

Fig. 16.1 Distribution of Hindus in India.
Source: Census of India, 2001; (Modified from Nag, 2007).

The comparison of the present distribution map with that of the other census years, such as 1941 (Brush 1949) and 1961 (Gosal and Mukerji 1970), does not reveal any major changes in distributional patterns, except for the mass Hindu exodus from Pakistan in 1947. Despite a few local changes at the time of the partition, Hindus have retained their overall majority in most districts (Gosal and Mukerji 1970).

One isolated region of a high concentration of Hindu population covers the mountainous northern districts of Uttar Pradesh and Uttarakhand. This area, due to its hilly and inaccessible topography, remained undisturbed, and Islam and Christianity did not make any gains there.

Most of the central and southern India is dominated by Hindus, although there are a few pockets where their share decreases to some extent. Again, the vast area of Hindu predominance in central India remained beyond the influence of Islam and Christianity. As compared to the Indo-Gangetic plains, this region was a forested area with rugged topography and low soil fertility, which did not attract the Muslim invaders and kings. In the south another zone of high concentration of Hindus includes the northern districts of Tamil Nadu and the adjoining districts of Karnataka, where Hindus are a little more than 90 percent of the total population. This region also was not disturbed by the intrusion of foreign religions because it was not only far away from the Muslim core areas of Delhi-Agra, but being on the eastern coast, was on the leeward side of the main Christian and Islamic trade routes. Both of these regions, central India and the southern zone, have been relatively undisturbed centers of Indian (Hindu) civilization (Moreland and Chatterjee 1945).

The eastern half of the Gangetic Plain, western Rajasthan, Gujarat, most of Maharashtra, Karnataka Pradesh and the southern part of Tamilnadu, in contrast, are less dominated by Hindus.

A few districts, particularly in the state of Jammu and Kashmir, and in the north-eastern states of India, have a much lesser predominance of Hindus, who constitute less than 30 percent of the population of these areas. It remains a fact that the areas of low Hindu concentration are found on the periphery (Brush 1949).

In Jammu and Kashmir and Punjab, Hindus form only a small percentage of the total population. Jammu and Kashmir state is overwhelmingly Islamic, while Punjab is the Sikh state. Another region lacking a Hindu predominance is western Uttar Pradesh, where Muslims are found in sizeable numbers.

This region formed the Core Area (Delhi-Agra) of Muslim rulers for a long time period (1194–1857). The north-eastern part of India, except for the Brahmaputra Valley, has a low concentration of Hindus. This region includes the northern districts of West Bengal, and districts along the international border in Assam, Meghalaya and Nagaland. In these hilly, tribal areas, large scale conversion of the tribals to Christianity is one of the chief reasons for the low percentage of Hindus besides there is the prevalence of animism as well. "The Hindu influence never extended to these isolated tribal regions" (Gosal and Mukerji 1970, p. 93). The tribal area of the Chota Nagpur region around Ranchi, now in the newly formed state of Jharkhand, also has a low concentration of Hindus. In southern India, the Malabar coastal plain also has a low proportion of Hindus in the total population. Since early historical times this coast had trade links with both the Islamic and Christian worlds, and thus has been influenced by these religions. Overall, the non-Hindu religions have made their impact either by immigration or by conversion, and have lessened the Hindu predominance in a few areas of the country.

Islam[1]

Islam came to India along with invaders from Persia, Afghanistan and Western Asia, during the 8th to 11th century AD. Later on, Muslims ruled over the major part of India. Many people were forced to be converted into Islam, while many low caste Hindus embraced Islam voluntarily as a reaction to Hindu high caste tyranny. An overwhelming majority of the Muslims in India are the descendents of converts from Hinduism (Lamb, 1968). Sunnis outnumbered Shias 3 to 1, in 2001 (Statesman's Yearbook 2006, p. 825).

In present day India, Islam is the largest "minority" religion. Over 13 percent of the total population of India is Muslim. India ranks third in the world in Muslim population, next only to Indonesia and Bangladesh. This large number exists despite a huge exodus at the time of the partition in 1947; during the 1961–71 decade, Muslims in India experienced an increase of 30.85 percent, which is comparatively higher than the growth rate of the total population (24.80 percent). According to Table16.1, their share in the total population has generally been gaining. Although during the early period Muslims increased their proportion by conversion, later on the source of gain apparently lay in the greater fertility (Pethe 1971). One of the reasons of higher fertility among Muslims is that there is no restriction on widow remarriage (Davis 1968). Also, family planning programs are not very popular among them. *Mullahs* enforce religious taboos against family planning. During the 1975–77 emergency, the government's family planning program enforcement received the greatest resistance from the Muslims. Immediately following the emergency, Mrs Indira Gandhi faced a resounding defeat partly because of Muslim apathy to her Congress Party. In the Hindi Belt where Muslims are in sizable numbers, they disowned the party in the 1977 national elections.

The abrupt reduction in the share of the Muslims in the total population in the 1951 census was the result of the partition. In British India,

Muslims formed about one quarter of the population. At the time of partition in 1947, many Muslim-majority areas were incorporated into Pakistan and many Muslims from Indian territory migrated to Pakistan. Consequently, the proportion of Muslims in India decreased substantially. But the Muslim population has experienced a steady increase since 1951 census.

The increase in the Muslim population is not spatially uniform. Few areas have experienced tremendous growth, and that is mainly due to illegal immigration of Muslims from Bangladesh. In 2001, the proportion of Muslims to total population of Assam and West Bengal had increased to 30.9 percent and 25.2 percent respectively. Tripura is the only state in India which, during 1961–71, experienced a decline in the Muslim population. This state had very few Muslims, but in 2001, 8 percent of the state population were identified as Muslim. The states surrounding Bangladesh have experienced a higher population increase, due both to the migration of Hindu refugees and illegal Muslim immigration from Bangladesh (erstwhile East Pakistan).

Distributional Pattern of Muslims

Muslims are concentrated in a few local areas only, whereas in the rest of the country they are sparsely distributed. Muslims are mostly concentrated in those areas which were under Muslim rule for a long period.

Muslim areas are concentration and spread all over north India. Except for Jammu and Kashmir, there is no other state where Muslims have an absolute majority. This state is quite near to the migration routes of the Muslim invaders from the north-west and the majority of the inhabitants were forced to adopt Islam. The absolute majority of Muslims in Kashmir was never challenged by immigration of a large number of Hindus in Jammu in particular since India's Independence in 1947 or an out-migration of some Muslims from the Srinagar Valley to Azad Kashmir in Pakistan. As this area remained isolated and economically underdeveloped, out-migration occurred to other states of India.

Another region of a high concentration of Muslim population covers the western part of Uttar Pradesh, a region under Muslim political control for most of the 12th–18th centuries. Uttar Pradesh was 18.5 percent Muslim in 2001. In addition, the Delhi-Agra core area and Lucknow, great seats of Muslim culture since the 13th and the 18th centuries respectively, attracted a large Muslim population both of foreign and indigenous origins (Mukerji 1972). Muslim concentration is also found around the international border with Bangladesh. The northern districts of West Bengal and the Assam Valley have comparatively a large number of Muslims. These districts and Bangladesh form the region where a large number of low caste Hindus embraced Islam during the Muslim period of Indian history (1206–1757). Also, these Indian border districts experienced an infiltration of Muslim refugees from Bangladesh prior to and during the liberation war of 1971.

In the districts of Jaisalmer and Bikaner in Rajasthan state, about 24 percent and 12 percent, respectively, of the population were Muslims. These districts are contiguous to Muslim dominated Pakistan and represent an extension of Pakistan's Muslim concentration region. One of the important features of the Muslim population in these districts is that over 90 percent are rural (Gosal and Mukerji 1970).

Muslims form about 20 percent of the total population in the areas where Islam penetrated and converted many local people, particularly in north India. The regional variations of the Muslim distribution are the results of many factors, such as: (i) forced conversion in north-west India, (ii) voluntary conversion of low caste Hindus in north-east India, (iii) conversion of people in the Malabar area through seaborne contact with Islamic traders from the Middle East, (iv) the impact of the Delhi-Agra Muslim core area on the Ganga-Jamuna plains, and (v) the effects of regional Muslim kings in south India (Dutt, Chatterjee and Geib 1976). As most converted Muslims came from low caste poor Hindus, even today Muslims in India remain in more poverty compared to other religious groups. One indicator of the poverty rate is the literacy rate. Only 48 percent of Muslims in 2001 were literates compared to 55 percent Hindu, 69 percent Christians, 61 percent Sikhs, 62 percent Buddhists, and 84 percent Jains.

Muslims are in majority only in a few districts, mostly in the State of Jammu and Kashmir, which, in 2001, consisted of 67 percent Muslims. An interesting feature of the distribution of Islam in the country is its urban bias; i.e. percentage of Muslims in India living in urban areas. This is mainly the result of the fact that the early Muslims settled in the urban centers where trade and craft flourished, and this trend continued due to their specialized skills, which found a greater market in the urban areas. Moreover, they also came as administrators, support staff and soldiers, who always resided in urban centers. As much as 36 percent of the Muslim population lives in urban areas. Such urban bias of Muslims is surpassed only by the Jains in India.

Sikhism

Sikhism was founded in Punjab during the late 15th century AD by Guru Nanak Dev. It was only after the early 18th century, however, that this sect began to become distinctly separated from the Hindus. Owing to its geographic location between the Muslim and Hindu dominated areas at that time, Sikhism had long shown a militant tendency. This religion had diffused mainly within the Punjab area.

Sikhs constitute less than 2 percent of India's population. Although there is hardly any part of India where they are not found, their overwhelming concentration is in present Punjab. Since the Independence of India in 1947, Sikhs have been struggling for a state with a Sikh majority; and due to their majority in Punjab, they were successful in getting the former Punjab divided into Punjab (a Sikh majority state) and Haryana (a Hindu majority state). This bifurcation took place in 1966. The Sikh community in Punjab accounts for about 80 percent of the total Sikh population of India (Gosal and Mukerji 1970).

The Sikhs form the fourth largest religious community in India, and their total is 19.2 million (2001 Census). During 1961–71, the growth rate of the Sikh population was 32.28 percent, only next to that of the Christians. Such a high growth rate was due to the conversion of Hindus to Sikhism. In contrast to Hinduism, Sikhism in principle does not have a rigid caste system. Moreover, Sikhism's willingness to accept converts explains why the Sikh community grew more rapidly than the rest of the Indian population. Among Sikhs, widow remarriage is allowed and is widely practiced. This also results in higher fertility.

> Not only do the Sikhs apparently have a high fertility rate, but also, on the basis of slender evidence, they have a low mortality (Davis 1968, p. 183).

The Sikhs recorded a tremendous growth from 1881 to 1921, an increase of about 75 percent, which is shown in Table 16.1 (Krishan 1971). This rapid increase in the Sikh population was mainly due to the conversion of the Hindus, particularly in the then Punjab province and other princely states in the Punjab plains. During 1921–41, the Sikhs maintained their previous increase rate, again due to voluntary conversion and increasing natural growth resulting from decline in mortality. During the 1941–51 decade, the Sikh population increased only 9.3 percent, probably owing mainly to a higher rate of mortality and instability caused by riots at the time of the partition in 1947. The partition was preceded by savage Sikh–Muslim riots; about 2.5 million Sikhs were forced to leave Pakistan (Singh 1953), and most of them settled in Indian Punjab.

Distributional Pattern of Sikhs

The distributional pattern of the Sikh population in Fig. 16.2 indicates that they are mainly confined to the Punjab and the surrounding districts of Jammu and Kashmir, Himachal Pradesh, Haryana and Rajasthan. It was during the British rule over India that Sikhs started migrating to other parts of India, settling in various urban centers (Dutt and Davgun 1979).

Hoshiarpur and Jullundur are the districts from where out-migration of Sikh farmers occurred to other areas in India (Krishan 1971). During the 20th century, many Sikh cultivators from these districts also moved to the newly established Canal Colonies towards the north and west of Lahore. Many Sikhs from the central districts of Punjab emigrated to foreign countries, such as Malaysia, Hong Kong, the Fiji Islands, the East African countries, the United Kingdom, the United States of America and Canada, This out-migration was especially pronounced from the rural areas (Gosal and Mukerji 1970), and was stimulated because of the small size of landholdings, water logging of the soils, and population pressure.

Outside Punjab, two adjacent areas, Chandigarh (16.1 percent) and Haryana (5.5 percent) have the greatest concentrations of Sikhs in India. Ambala, Karnal and Hisar districts in Haryana received many Sikh farmers from the central part of Punjab; also at the time of the partition of India, some Sikhs from Pakistan were rehabilitated in these districts, as well as in the canal irrigated areas of the Ganganagar district of Rajasthan. The land reclamation in the *terai* districts of Nainital in Uttar Pradesh during the early 1950s attracted many Sikh cultivators. In the state of Jammu and Kashmir, Jammu district has a large number of Sikhs. At the time of the partition many Sikhs from the Sialkot region in north east Pakistan moved into this area, mainly due to its close proximity. Delhi is four percent Sikh. These Sikhs are mostly refugees from Pakistan, engaged in trade, commerce, transport and administrative services.

Sikhism was confined spatially in the Punjab region, mainly because the regional language of Punjabi and the newly evolved *Gurmukhi* (from the mouth of the *Guru*) script were used to propagate it in written and

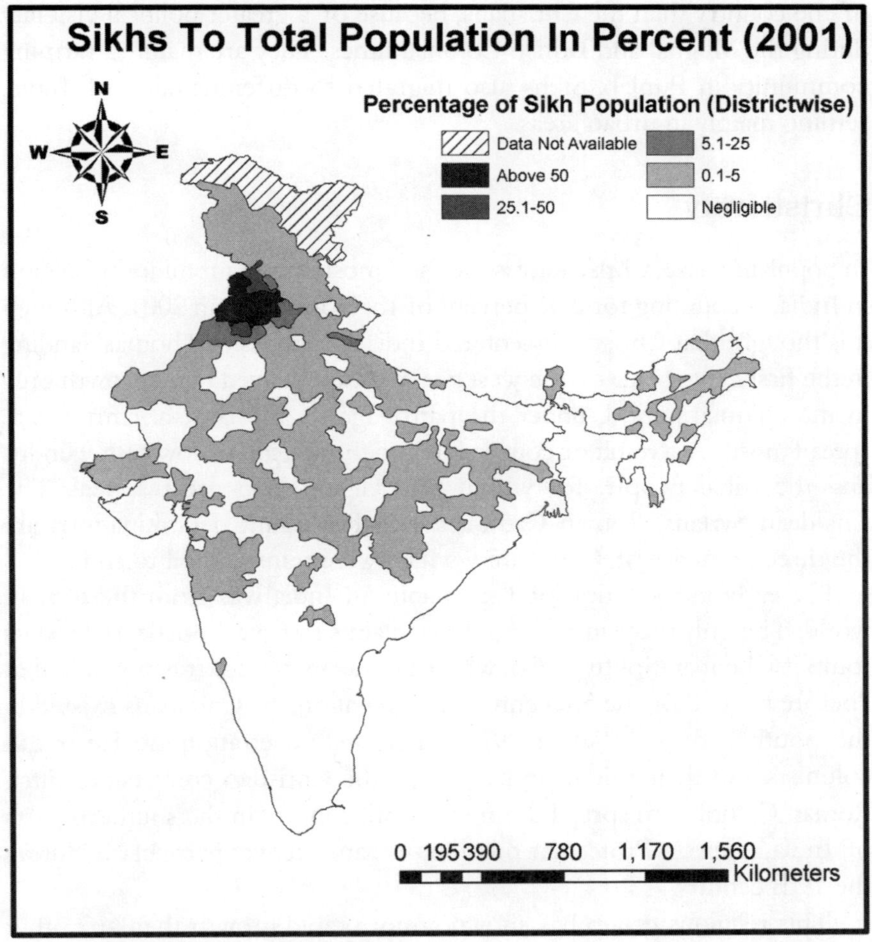

Fig. 16.2 Distribution of Sikhs in India.
Source: Census of India, 2001; (Modified from Nag, 2007).

spoken forms. Also, the Sikh *Gurus* only operated from the Punjab plains and the surrounding areas, and were busier trying to survive the persecution of the Muslim rulers, than to strive for areal expansion (Dutt and Davgun, 1977).

Presently, Sikhs, due to their enterprising nature, are found all over India. Their concentration in Punjab increased since the Partition due to the immigration of the Sikhs from the Pakistan side of the border to the Indian side. They are the fourth most significant religious group in India, but have had a greater impact on the socio-cultural and economic milieu of the country than the Christians, because of a greater political visibility during the Mughal and British Colonial times. They are mainly a farming community in Punjab. Sikhs also migrated to different parts of India, settling mainly in urban areas.

Christianity

In population size, Christianity is the third most important minority religion in India, accounting for 2.31 percent of the population in 2001. Although it is thought that Christianity entered India as early as St Thomas' landing in the first century AD on the west coast, it experienced rapid growth only in the colonial period, under the patronage of the British. Christianity spread mostly as a result of conversion into the religion of low caste Hindus and the tribal people, for whom the religion held great appeal. The Chaldean Syrians, Roman Catholics, and Protestant denominations are the three branches of Christianity which were transplanted to India.

The early introduction of Christianity in India was from the Roman world. The only place in the world that claims to have Apostle *St Thomas's* tomb is Chennai (South India), where he was martyred. It is possible that "before the end of the 5th century congregations of Christians existed in the South" (Brush 1949, p. 91). Later on, penetration by European colonists and their rule in India revived the Christian conversion. First, Roman Catholicism spread during the 15th century in the southern parts of India; later on Protestant missions became active, particularly during the 19th century.

This religious group has shown a more rapid growth than any other religious community in India. Between 1881 and 1971, Christians almost quadrupled their proportion although in terms of the country's total it still remains quite low. The percentage share of the Christians in the total population of India has shown a regular increase. During 1961–1971, the growth rate among the Christians was 32.6 percent, which was the highest among all other religious groups in India. After the independence of India in 1947, the new government discouraged Christian missionaries to convert. Mizoram experienced an 86.09 percent increase; Nagaland, 66.76 percent; Meghalaya, 46.98 percent; Manipur, 26.03 percent. These increases are the result of the conversion of the tribal population to Christianity as well as migration of Christians from Islamic East Pakistan, now Bangladesh (Brush 1949). In contrast, the tribal district of Ranchi

(Bihar; now Jharkhand) had only 17.70 percent increase in the Christian population.

Distributional Pattern of Christians

The distribution of Christians in India is quite uneven and spotty. Christianity is most widespread in the north-eastern and southern parts of India (Fig. 16.3). There were nine districts in 1971 where Christians had a majority. Most of these areas are in north eastern India.

In south India, Kerala has a large Christian population. In northwest India, Gurdaspur district is the only district in Punjab where 6.5 percent of the population is Christian. The tribal area in Chota Nagpur plateau,

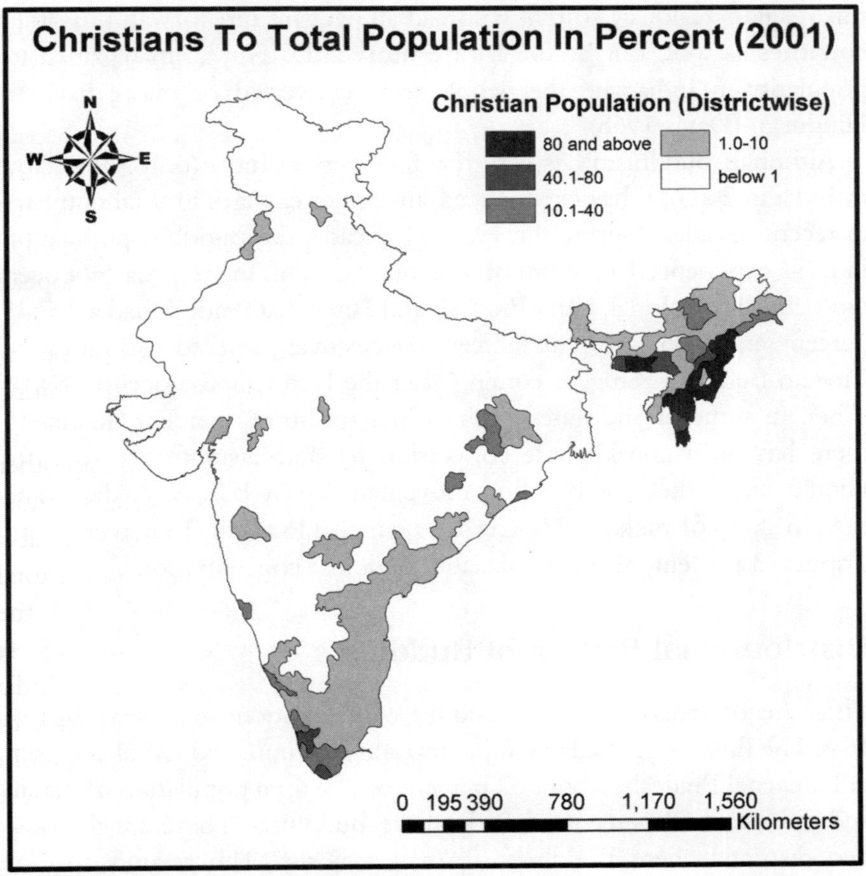

Fig. 16.3 Distribution of Christians in India.
Source: Census of India, 2001; (Modified from Nag, 2007).

now the newly created state of Jharkhand was 4.1 percent Christian in 2001. Christian missionary work has been very active there since the early decades of the last century.

Buddhism

Buddhism originated in India. It is ironic that it has very few followers left in its country of origin. Buddhists comprised only 0.8 percent of India's population in 2001. Buddhism originated in the north-eastern part of India, during the 6th century BC, as a movement to reform the malpractices of Hinduism. Soon it became a popular religion all over India, and a few kings adopted it as their state religion. The Maurya King Asoka (269 to 232 BC), whose kingdom pervaded the sub-continent, encouraged this religion zealously so that it spread all over his territory and to other countries as well. But by the 10th century A.D., Hinduism regained its popularity in India and the people were converted en masse back to Hinduism (Davis 1968).

Although Buddhism has very few followers in India (only 7.9 million in India in 2003), it has experienced important changes in total numbers in recent decades. During the 1961–71 decade, the Buddhist population in India experienced a growth of 17.2 percent. This increase has not been uniform all over India. Uttar Pradesh and Himachal Pradesh had a 207.45 percent and 98.67 percent increase, respectively, due to the influx of Tibetan Buddhist refugees coming after the Han Chinese occupation of Tibet. In some of the states, such as Maharashtra (6 percent Buddhist), there has been considerable conversion to Buddhism from low caste Hindus under the Neo-Buddhist movement led by B.R. Ambedkar. The eastern states of Sikkim (28 percent), Arunchal Pradesh (13 percent), and Tripura (3 percent) also have sizeable Buddhist concentrations.

Distributional Pattern of Buddhists

Three major areas that mark Buddhist concentrations are shown in Fig. 16.4. The first covers Ladakh in Jammu and Kashmir, and Lahul and Spiti in Himachal Pradesh. About 62 percent of the total population of Lahul and Spiti, and 52 percent of Ladakh are Buddhists. These are the only two districts where Buddhists form a majority. The second area of Buddhist concentration is the Kameng district of Arunachal Pradesh,

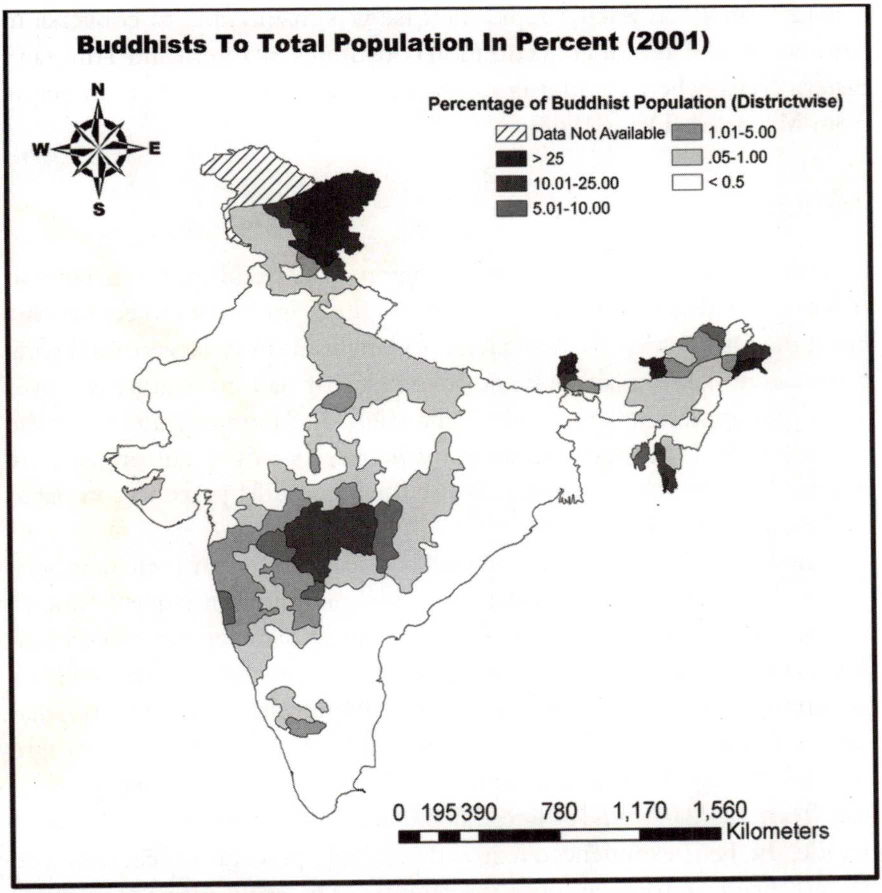

Fig. 16.4 Buddhist Percentage total population by districts.
Source: Census of India, 2001; (Modified from Nag, 2007).

two-fifths of the population are Buddhist. These pockets of Buddhism in the Himalayan region have persisted for a long time. Hinduism, and later on Islam, did not invade these areas because of their remoteness and isolation. Also these areas, being close to Tibet, received continuous immigration of Tibetan Buddhists (Gosal and Mukerji 1970). The third area of Buddhist concentration covers most of Maharashtra where many low caste Hindus were encouraged to embrace Buddhism in the 1950s as a result of Ambedkar's Buddhist movement in which low caste Hindus were encouraged to become Buddhists in order not to face social discrimination; resulting in Maharashtra experiencing a spectacular increase in the Buddhist population, from 2,487 in 1951 to 2,789,501 in 1961 and

3,264,233 in 1971. Such a rapid increase was mainly due to conversion. Another area of minor concentration constitutes Mizoram and Tripura in eastern India, where Buddhists are the descendents of ancient immigrants from Myanmar (Davis 1968).

Jainism

Jainism is both a philosophy and a religion. Like Buddhism, this religion also originated as a movement to reform Hinduism in the 6th century BC. From the 5th century AD, many regional kingdoms in India accorded royal patronage to Jainism, although no ruling king of national stature was ever a Jain. Jains represent 0.4 percent of the total population of India as per the census of 2001, but they are the most literate as 84 percent of Jains are literate. Their female literacy rate is also the highest (81 percent) compared to the other religious groups.

Jains have not experienced any substantial increase in their numbers; rather, they seem to be slow-growing. Such a condition is partly due to almost a total restriction of widow remarriage. Conversion to this religion is not encouraged and furthermore, some Jains have converted back to Hinduism. In 1881, Jains constituted 0.49 percent of the total population of India, whereas in 1971, they formed 0.47 percent; this is a slight decrease though in absolute numbers, they have doubled their population from 1,222,000 in 1881 to 2,605,000 in 1971. During the 1961–71 decade, the Jains experienced a growth of 28.48 percent, which, however, has not been uniform all over the country. The rapid increase in many areas is mainly due to migration of Jains from north-west India.

Distributional Pattern of Jains

The Jains are spread largely in the western part of the country. If we draw lines joining Bikaner with Jabalpur and Jabalpur with Shimoga, we find that the area toward the west of these lines are thickly inhabited by Jains. Fig.16.5 shows this distribution. Jains do not form more than 7 percent of the total population of any district. The largest number of Jains is found in Maharashtra, which accounts for 27 percent of all the Jains in India; Greater Mumbai has a high concentration.

Though Maharashtra has the largest number of the Jains; Rajasthan, Gujarat, Madhya Pradesh and Karnataka have large areas with concentrations of Jains. However, even in these states, Jains constitute a very

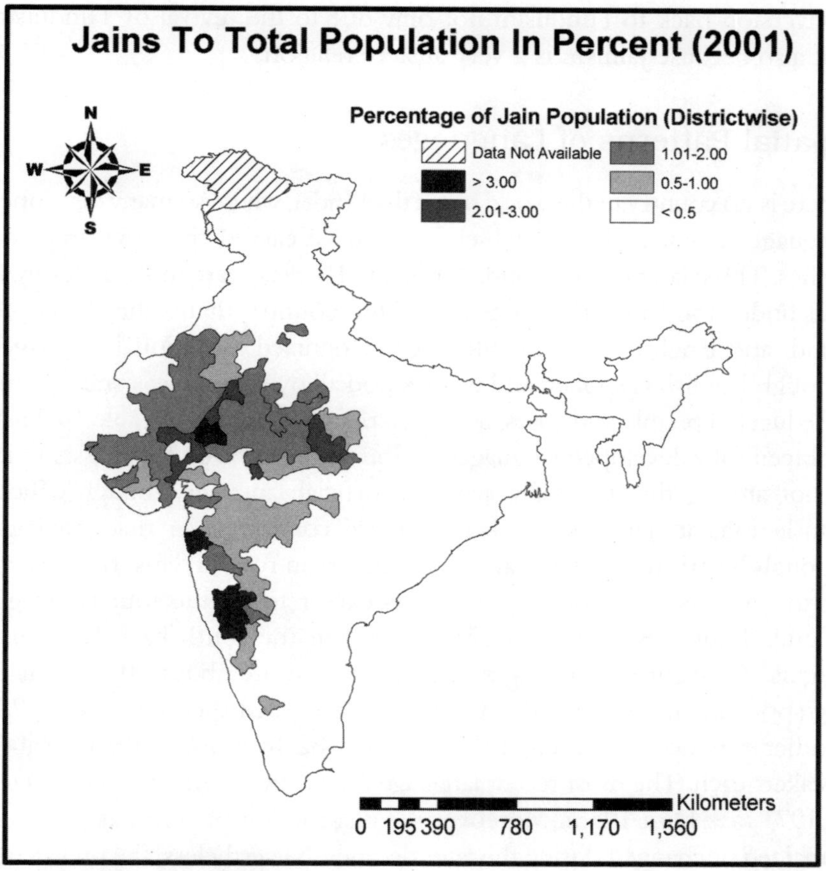

Fig. 16.5 Distribution of Jains in India.
Source: Census of India, 2001; (Modified from Nag, 2007).

small percentage of the total population. There are only eight districts in the country which have more than 4 percent of their population as Jains.

The Jains are essentially urban dwellers. Their urban percentage (59 percent of the total Jains) exceeds that of rural (41 percent). Jains are mostly engaged in commerce and industry, both urban occupations. But in two states, Karnataka and Rajasthan, a majority of the Jains are rural inhabitants. Probably most Jains have migrated to other parts of India from these two states during the last few centuries. Jains have been an important influence in the Indian economy, primarily because of their association with significant business activity in the country. Several prominent business families in India are Jains. There has been some conversion back to Hindusim not only due to the revival of Hinduism, but also because Jainism is a very austere religion.

Spatial Patterns of Languages

There is no country in the world other than India, where so many developed languages occur and so in which many have carved their own regional niches. Three languages – Hindi, Urdu and English – are more widespread and understood in different parts of the country than other language. Hindi and English are consitutionally recognized as national languages. Though English is spoken and understood all over India by a small group of educated people and elites, it is not a people's language. Table 16.2 lists eighteen fully developed languages of India. Only one of them, Kashmiri, is not among the nationally accepted official language, though official transactions in Jammu and Kashmir are conducted in that language. Though North Indian languages have an Aryan root in Sanskrit, brought by the Aryans in about 1500 BC in its earlier form, the four languages (Tamil, Telugu, Kannada and Malayalam) in the south have Dravidian origins. All eighteen languages together constitute about 90 percent of the spoken language in India. Census has recorded the existence of 281 mother tongues in the country, of which 82 have more than 100,000 speakers each. The most recent language census by districts was conducted in 1971 (see Dutt 1985). Moreover the distribution pattern has generally remained unchanged during the later decades. Nevertheless, the prevalence of so many mother tongues and languages creates an extreme heterogeneity. Though each state has a state language, there may be one or more subregions in that state where some other language is dominant. In some cases, the official state language is, in fact, a minority language (Dutt and Geib, 1998, p. 114).

Hindi Belt: India's Power House

Hindi is the state language of nine states (Bihar, Jharkhand, Uttar Pradesh, Uttarakhand, Madhya Pradesh, Himachal Pradesh, Chhattisgarh, Rajasthan, and Haryana) and one Union Territory, Delhi. Most other native languages are official state languages of single states. Bengali is the state language of both West Bengal and Tripura while Marathi is an official language of both Maharashtra and Goa. Urdu, the mother tongue of only about 5.18

Table 16.2: (Source:http://www.censusindia.gov.in/Census_Data_2001/Census_Data_Online/Language/Statement1.htm)

Rank	*Language*	*Speakers*	*Percentage*
1	Hindi dialects	422,048,642	41.03%
2	Bengali	83,369,769	8.11%
3	Telugu	74,002,856	7.19%
4	Marathi	71,936,894	6.99%
5	Tamil	60,793,814	5.91%
6	Urdu	51,536,111	5.01%
7	Gujarati	46,091,617	4.48%
8	Kannada	37,924,011	4.69%
9	Malayalam	33,066,392	3.21%
10	Oriya	33,017,446	3.21%
11	Punjabi	29,102,477	2.83%
12	Assamese	13,168,484	1.28%
13	Maithili	12,179,122	1.18%
15	Bhili/Bhilodi	9,582,957	0.95%
14	Santali	6,469,600	0.63%
15	Kashmiri	5,527,698	0.54%
16	Nepali	2,871,749	0.28%
17	Gondi	2,713,790	0.27%
18	Sindhi	2,535,485	0.25%
19	Konkani	2,489,015	0.24%
20	Dogri	2,282,589	0.22%
21	Khandeshi	2,075,258	0.21%
22	Kurukh	1,751,489	0.17%
23	Tulu	1,722,768	0.17%
24	Meitei (Manipuri)	1,466,705	0.14%
25	Bodo	1,350,478	0.13%
26	Khasi	1,128,575	0.112%
27	Mundari	1,061,352	0.105%
28	Ho	1,042,724	0.103%
29	Sanskrit	14,135	0.001%

percent of the Indians and state language of only one state – Jammu and Kashmir, has a greater areal spread than Hindi, which is a mother tongue for about 41.03 percent of the population. Moreover, the north-central India, designated as the *Hindi Belt*, has the main concentration of Hindi speaking people.

The Hindi Belt has determined the outcome of all national elections of the country since 1952. The Indian National Congress (INC), which held power from the time of India's independence until 1975, had been voted into power by securing a majority in the Belt. In the 1977 election, immediately after the imposition of the much hated "emergency measures" gagging democracy, Indira Gandhi's Congress Party was voted out of power with solid disapproval of the Belt. The comeback of Indira Gandhi-led CP in 1980 could not have happened without the regained support of the Belt. Similarly, in the second half of the 1990s the BJP and its Alliance succeeded in holding on to the power only by a majority support of the Belt. In 2010, the ruling Congress Party at the center holds its majority with the support of regional parties mostly from Bihar and Uttar Pradesh. Thus, the heartland of India (Hindi Belt), has mostly played a dominant role in deciding India's political hegemony, while the south and most other peripheral areas have played a subsidiary role.

Hindi

Hindi is the official language of the Union Government. It is numerically the most predominant mother tongue. However, its area is very sharply demarcated. It is popularly spoken only in the north-central part of the country. The Hindi language can be divided into three strata: a) the local or village level dialects; b) 16 sub-regional dialects (*Khari Boli, Hariani, Braj Bhasha, Kanauji, Bundeli, Awadhi, Bagheli, Chhattisgarhi, Maithili, Bhojpuri, Magahi, Jaipuri, Mewati, Malwi, Marwari, and Pahari*), and c) standard Hindi, written in the *Devnagri* script which has roots in *Nagri* and *Brahmi* (Saxena and Sahai 1971).

Hindi, in its earlier form, established itself like other New Indo-Aryan languages around 1000 AD though the actual spoken form of Hindi was in use by 1300 AD (Nigam 1972). It emerged from *Saurasene Apabhramsa*, which was spoken in the region surrounding Delhi and was influenced by dialects from Punjab, Haryana and Western Uttar Pradesh (Nayar 1969).

The *Bhakti* (devotional) movement, starting in the 11th century during the early Muslim rule in India, followed by the secular poetry movement of the 15–17th centuries AD contributed immensely to the development of the language. The *Bhakti* movement was a manifestation of Hindu preservation to withstand the religious pressures given forth by the Islamic rulers. The popular regional dialects, as they were used to reach the masses, eventually resulted in the enrichment of poetic lyricism not only in Hindi, but in all other "New" Indo-Aryan languages. As a result of the movement, a number of very significant literary contributions were made in various sub-regional dialects of Hindi: the lyrics of Vidyapati in *Maithili*, *Ramcharitmanas* of Tulsidas, poems of Kabir in Awadhi, and the poetry of Surdas in *Braj Bhasha*.

The beginning of the 19th century marks the inception of modern Hindi. The second half of the 20th century witnessed its increasing momentum culminating in its designation as the official language of the Union Government. The most well known Hindi literati of the 20th century include Prem Chandra (novelist), Jai Shankar Prasad (dramatist) and Yaspal (fiction writer). Spatially, there exists a sharp dichotomy between the Hindi speaking and non-speaking regions. Hindi speakers are concentrated in north-central and west-central parts of the country.

This sharp dichotomy between the Hindi speaking and non-Hindi speaking areas does not only coincide with the broad division of the "New" Indo-Aryan family of languages in the North and Dravidian family of languages in the south, but with other new non-Hindi New Indo-Aryan language areas, such as Gujarat, Maharashtra, Orissa, West Bengal, Assam and Punjab which have relatively much less of a proportion of their population that have Hindi mother tongue speakers. It is, nonetheless, a fact that the southern third of the peninsula, the coasts of Orissa, Andhra Pradesh, Maharashtra, Gujarat and northern two-thirds of Jammu and Kashmir have less than 1 percent mother tongue Hindi speakers by districts, partly because they are distantly located and separated by physical barriers from the historic Hindi core of western Uttar Pradesh and Delhi region. People with Hindi as mother tongue adhere to a kind of distance-decay characteristics from the core, surrounded by an intermediate area with a lesser number of Hindi speakers and an outer area with a negligible number.

Since the mid-19th century, Hindi established itself as a language with core areas in Varanasi, Allahabad and Lucknow. All three have great universities that have nurtured the Hindi language. After the Independence of 1947 and Hindi's status as the official national language, the country's capital of Delhi became the main focus of literary and publishing activities of this language. Over three-fourths of the population in the National Capital Region speak Hindi as its mother tongue.

Urdu

Urdu is considered a "homeless" language by many because it has not been officially adopted as a state language in the states where it has the maximum concentration. The Muslim majority state of Jammu and Kashmir has adopted it as an official language despite the fact that the overwhelming majority of people in that state speak Kashmiri as a mother tongue. Unlike other mother tongues, Urdu does not have a regional core area where a majority of people in any single state or district speak the language. It is spoken as a mother tongue by over 5 percent of the total population of the country. At the national level it is the mother tongue of the majority of Muslim population in north central and western India.

The word "Urdu" is of Turkish origin and means "the army". It originated as an army language of the 13th and 14th centuries when the Delhi-based sultans hired Turkish and Afghan generals and militia; the sultans themselves were of the same origin. Thus, it was the language of the army which, from its pidgin origin, gradually found its way into the royal courts of the sultans and Moghuls and mingled with local dialects, derived from Hindi of the Delhi region, and came to be known as "*urdu-e-Mualla*" or "the high Urdu" (Amani 1974). This mixture gradually developed into a fully grown Urdu language by the 16th and 17th centuries and in the process the rich Persian language influenced it greatly. The north Indian Muslims thought Urdu to be a "new discovery", but in actuality this was no more than a Muslim version of Hindi or Hindustani. When the north Indian Muslims established their regional kingdoms or administrative headquarters in the south, they carried with them this language. Hyderabad City, the former capital of the Nizam, thus became a strong bastion of Urdu. Urdu, while adopting Perso-Arabic script, was based on the same idioms as Hindi (Saxena and Sahai 1971).

Urdu became not only the court and official language of the Muslims but also the popular spoken language of many people. To north Indian Muslims, Urdu obtained a sort of Islamic approval because their language is written in the same script as the holy *Koran*. While developing a large body of literature, it acquired regional identities in Delhi, Lucknow,

Lahore, Hyderabad, Patna and Murshidabad. With the coming of the British and the consequent spread of English, Urdu lost its position as a royal language.

Urdu has a limited concentration in two sub-regions, one along the Gangetic Plains of Uttar Pradesh and Bihar and the other in the south, in the erstwhile Muslim strongholds of Nizam in Hyderabad, and the sultanates of Mysore, and Bijapur. The uniqueness of Urdu lies in its widespread dispersion. Its absence in the states of Assam, Jammu and Kashmir (in spite of official status) and Kerala which support a substantial proportion of Muslim population is to be noted because Muslims in India in most instances associate themselves with Urdu. The Muslims in these states, situated far away from the Delhi–Uttar Pradesh Urdu core, seem to have adopted their own regional languages. Located in the periphery of the country, they remained least affected by the Urdu language of the rulers housed in the same Delhi–Western Uttar Pradesh core areas in which Hindi was also lodged for centuries.

Marathi

Marathi is a regional language of the new Indo-Aryan group. Marathi is the official language of Maharashtra. Konkani, spoken in the southern Konkan coast, is considered to be its only real dialect. Konkani is now the official language of Goa with 51.5 percent of the state population speaking the language.

No reference to Marathi language has been found earlier than the 8th century AD (Tulpule and Kulkarni 1971). During the earlier stages, and at the time of *Bhakti* movement, a great bulk of religious literature grew in Marathi. However, through the efforts of Shivaji, the founder of the Maratha kingdom in the 17th century, the language was 'purified' to the original Sanskrit base and the Persian influences of the Muslim period were eliminated as a reaction against Aurangzeb's (1659–1707) Islamic bigotry. When the Maratha kingdom expanded to adjacent Gujarat, Madhaya Pradesh and Orissa, the language was spread to these areas.

Karnataka in the 18th century had a confederal association with Baroda in Gujarat and Gwalior and Indore in Madhya Pradesh. As a result a large number of Marathi speakers migrated to these places causing a spread farther away from its core area.

Moreover, when the British divided India into three super-regional Presidencies (Bengal, Madras and Bombay) and introduced an English system of education in the Presidency town headquarters of Calcutta (Kolkata), Madras (Chennai) and Bombay (Mumbai), a large number of the newly-educated elites migrated from these three towns to different parts of the Presidency carrying with them their speech; Bengali speakers migrating to non-Bengali parts of the Bengal Presidency; Tamil to non-Tamil Madras Presidency; and Marathi spreading into non-Marathi areas of the Bombay Presidency. Marathi speakers thus spread into Gujarati, Hindi, Telugu and Kannada areas.

However, over 90 percent of India's Marathi speakers remain concentrated in the state of Maharashtra. Greater Mumbai capital of Maharashtra has a relatively low proportion (42% according to 1971 census) because of a large number of Gujarati, Hindi, Sindhi, Tamil, and Kannada migrants.

Bengali

Bengali and Assamese are the eastern most branches of the new Indo-Aryan languages and are linguistically associated with, *Gauda* and *Magadhi Apabhransas*. *Gauda*, an eastern manifestation of *Magadhi*, evolved in north Bengal in the then capital region of Gour before the first millennium AD and eventually branched into *Dhakki* which gave rise to Eastern Bengali, spoken in Bangladesh, and to Bengali and Assamese by about 1200 AD.

Bengali emerged as a distinct language not later than *circa* 1000 AD. Its thousand years of history presents three stages of development. The early stage (*circa* AD 1000–1200), Old Bengali is represented by mystic songs (*Carya-padas*). The second stage (*circa* AD 1300–1750), or Middle Bengali, is represented by a copious literature beginning from the latter half of the 15th century. At this stage the language received a large number of Persian (and Arabic) as well as a few Turkish and Portuguese vocables. The third stage (since 1750), Modern Bengali, has a very rich literature in poetry and prose. It has received vitality from contact with the English language (Sen 1971, p. 21).

As a part of the general *Bhakti* movement of the country (*circa* AD 1300–1750), *Viasnavism* (a form of religious belief) swept the countryside of Bengal during the Middle Bengali period. During the same period *Ramayana* and *Mahabharata* were translated into Bengali by Krittivasa and Kashirama, respectively. Bengali was the first language to experience a modern renaissance; other Indian literature followed Bengali. Bengali poets, authors and novelists inspired others in India to begin the process of modernization in their own languages.

Although the initial impetus was given to Bengali in its earliest core of north Bengal, the subsequent cores moved to Nadia (Nabadwip in particular), Murshidabad and Kolkata as a result of historic necessities. During the last 500 years a strong connectivity developed among these cores because each is tied to the Baghirathi-Hooghly distributory of the Ganges River. Like Marathi to Mumbai and Tamil to Chennai, the center of Bengali currently remains very strongly tied to the location of its former Presidency town Kolkata, which is home to the bulk of Bengali cultural and literary activities.

Bengali mother tongue speakers have diffused farther away from their original core in West Bengal and Bangladesh because of several factors. First, Kolkata was not only the headquarters of Bengal Presidency, which had jurisdictions over West Bengal, Bangladesh, Assam, Meghalaya, Mizoram, Orissa and Bihar, but was also the capital of British India from 1772 through 1911. Such a situation caused migration of educated Bengalis to non-Bengali areas as an aid to the administration because the British recruited them as they needed educated Indian administrators, postal and railway workers and clerks to man the lower-level positions. Second, starting from the middle of the 19th century, Kolkata became the pioneer and the main seat of the English language-based Western education system in north India. For several decades, the Calcutta University, established in 1857, not only served north India, but Myanmar as well. This resulted into a large-scale migration not only to the Presidency, but all over north India. Though these migrants spoke Bengali as their mother tongue, their male bread-earners could speak English as a second language. Third, starting from 1946 when Hindu–Muslim conflicts reached a peak in Bengal, a large number of Bengali speaking Hindu refugees from Bangladesh migrated not only to West Bengal, but to Tripura, Meghalaya, Assam, Bihar and Andhra Pradesh for resettlement either on their own or sponsored by the Indian Government.

Tamil

Tamil is the main language of the Dravidian family. It reached maturity earlier than others in the family. Due to its vocabulary and grammar

Tamil was able to influence the development of the other Dravidian languages. It is also the oldest living Indian language. The origin of the word, Tamil, comes from the Sanskrit word "*Dravida*" which was corrupted to 'Danrila' and ultimately 'Tamil' (Iyengar 1965). Other than the Tamil speaking core of Tamil Nadu and Pondicherry, the adjacent states of Karnataka, Andhra Pradesh, Kerala and parts of Maharashtra have sizable numbers of Tamil speakers. Tamils also sailed to Malaysia, Sri Lanka, Myanmar, Singapore, South and East Africa (Nigam 1972). In Sri Lanka, Liberation Tigers of Tamil Eelam have been demanding a separate state for the north and eastern parts of the country. Over 7 percent of Singapore's population speaks Tamil, which is also one of its official languages.

Malayalam

Malayalam is the official language of Kerala where its core is also lodged. Tamil and Malayalam were the same before the 15th century when the latter separated as a distinct language of the Kerala region.

The highest proportion of Malayalam speaking population in Kerala is in the district of Malappuram (99.83 percent), followed by Alleppey (98.75 percent). Mahe, an administrative district of Pondicherry, but physically an enclave of Kerala, has 99.57 percent of its population speaking Malayalam. Lakshadweep, a group of islands in the Arabian Sea, with Muslim majority, is overwhelmingly Malayalam speaking. A large number of people in Andaman and Nicobar Islands speak Malayalam. They are partly the second and third generation of Moppilla rebels, expelled to Andamans as a punishment meted out to them by the British for their "criminal" conduct. Economic opportunities have promoted Malayalam speaking people to migrate not only to nearby but also to distant places like Chennai, Greater Mumbai region, and Sundargarh in Orissa. The Persian Gulf states, during the last several decades, received a large number of Muslim and Christian migrants from Kerala to work as labourers and domestics.

Malayalam originated in Kerala in the 14th century. Up to that time, Sentamil or Tamil was spoken in the region (Iyengar 1965). The earliest work in Malayalam is *Si Ramas Ramacharitam* (Iyengar 1960), published in the 14th century. During this period the language developed considerably, mainly through a grammatical and rhetoric work of the 15th century known as *Lilatilakam* (Nigam, 1972).

In the 16th century, Malayalam underwent a metamorphosis that resulted in what is today called 'Modern Malayalam'. The credit for this goes to Ezhuthachan, who is known as the father of modern Malayalam (Nayar 1965). His works combine Sanskrit with Tamil dominated Malayalam, and come under the category of 'Manipravalam'. By the beginning of the 18th century Malayalam literature was fully developed, and was freed from Tamil influence and developed a bias for Sanskrit. It was in this period that the missionaries and evangelists from the West made their contributions to Malayalam by compiling dictionaries in the language, translating the Bible into simple prose, and writing original works in prose and verse on Biblical themes. Books on astronomy, astrology, mathematics, and medicine were also written during this period by scholars in Sanskrit (Nayar 1965). Great emphasis was given to western education which emphasized the use of Malayalam (Nair 1977). This greatly enriched the language in prose and verse.

Kannada

Kannada is the official language of Karnataka where most people speak this language. Outside the state of Karnataka, adjoining Tamil Nadu, Maharashtra and Andhra Pradesh attracted working Kannada speaking migrants in plantations, cotton textile mills and other non-farming activities. The spread of Kannada-speaking people in non-Kannada areas of Greater Mumbai, Thana and Pune in Maharashtra, Chennai City and Ramanathapuram in Tamil Nadu and Sikkim is primarily the result of employment opportunities offered in those areas.

Kannada has a rich literature, second only to Tamil among the Dravidian languages. The earliest remnants of Kannada are some inscriptions from 5th century AD. The period from AD 925 to 1150 was dominated by Jain writings in praise of the *Tirthankaras*. In the 12th century, Maga Chandera wrote the *Pamachandia Charita Purana* a Jain version of the Ramayana. With the establishment of the Vijaynagaram Empire in the 14th century, patronage was given to the language by the kings, who were themselves scholars, and wrote in Kannada and Sanskrit. Vijaynagaram, the capital city, became the center of Kannada literary activities. By the early 17th century, a full grammar of Kannada was prepared in Sanskrit. During the 17th century, the Christian missionaries in Goa published a number of works in Kannada. Leonardo Cinnonma wrote a grammar and language dictionary in Kannada, which was published in 1776 (Nigam 1972). The main centers of the present-day Kannada literary activities are Bengaluru, the capital of Karnataka and Mysore, former capital of the regional sultans before the British took over the area in the late 18th century.

Telugu

Telugu, like Kannada and Tamil, attained a separate individuality among Dravidian languages and its own unique history. Its core area encompasses all of Andhra Pradesh and the Yanam district of Pondicherry. Telugu is a well developed language. The oldest specimens of Telugu, so far available, go back to the 7th century. The Telugu script, which is almost identical to the Kannada script, is known to have taken shape by 1000 AD, from the Pahlava script of the 7th century AD, which in turn, like all other Dravidian and most New Indo-Aryan language scripts, was derived from *Brahmi* (Nigam 1972).

With the establishment of the British rule in India, Chennai became the center of studies in Tamil and Telugu, and the first Telugu book was printed in 1796. Contact with Western literature and science brought a new period of development.

Under the influence of the nationalistic movement of 1905 and of Bengali literature of Bankim Chandra Chatterji and Rabindranath Tagore, a new literary group to represent all that was progressive and nationalistic under the name of '*Sahiti Samiti*' was formed; this society was oriented towards European literature (Nigam 1972). Vishwanatha Satyanarayana was the greatest poet of this period (Nigam 1972). Before Andhra Pradesh was given the status of a new state based on language in 1953, the city of Chennai continued to be the major center of Telugu literary activities, but afterwards, the center gravitated to the Andhra state capital of Hyderabad, which for the last 300–400 years had also remained a secondary core of Urdu language (Nigam 1972).

In comparison to other Dravidian languages, Telugu is spoken most widely outside its linguistic core. Its transitional linguistic frontiers extend considerably into the adjacent Kannada (Karnataka) and Tamil (Tamil Nadu) speaking areas. The Telugu migrants have also moved to more distant places, such as Greater Mumbai and Jalgaon in Maharashtra, the steel city of Rourkela in Orissa, the railway town of Kharagpur in West Bengal, and Lakhimpur district of Assam; all in search of employment.

Gujarati

Gujarati became the official state language of Gujarat when it attained statehood in 1960. The Gujarati core lies in Gujarat where 90% of the speakers reside. Gujarati speakers are also found in the adjoining state of Maharashtra, particularly in Greater Mumbai.

The Gujarati language is connected with the Marwari dialect of adjacent Rajasthan and until about 1000 AD both were similar. In turn, Marwari had close affinity with *Braj Bhasha*, a form of Hindi spoken in Western Uttar Pradesh. Gujarati literature, the genesis of which dates back to about 1000 AD, is divided into Old (up to 1450), Middle (1450–1800) and New (1800 to the present) periods. The Old Period is characterized by Hindu and Jain religious contributions, particularly resulting from the *Bhakti* Movement which took shape in the 11th century when Muslim invaders started to plunder Gujarat and finally when the Delhi-based sultans occupied it two centuries later. The Parsis, who migrated from Persia to southern Gujarat coasts during the 10th century, also contributed to the Gujarati literature, particularly after they adopted this language to be their own starting from the 14th century (Chatterji 1963). During the Middle Period, Gujarati separated from Marwari, but continued its *Bhakti* tradition. It also added patriotic flavor in its literary compositions inspired by Shivaji's liberation struggle.

The Western influence permeated into the New Period with changing literary forms and content. Nature related and real life portraits became more prominent. Mahatma Gandhi (1869–1948) wrote extensively in Gujarati in addition to his contributions in English and Hindi. According to Chatterji (1963):

> His style had been conspicuous for its simplicity and directness, terse and to the point, and a model of clarity, and fully expressive of his great ideals of love, charity and adherence to Truth without fear for favor (p. 245).

The Gujarati speaking region is physiographically isolated with the sea coast to the southwest, the Thar Desert to the west, the Aravali hills to the north and northeast and the hilly and forested tracts to the south. Ahmadabad, the major city of Gujarat, has 80 percent of its population speaking Gujarati. The westernmost district of Kutch bordering Pakistan's Sindhi-speaking province of Sind, poses a different aspect as it forms the transition between Sindhi and Gujarati populations. Only 56 percent of

Kutch population speaks Gujarati as their mother tongue, while 42 percent speak *Kachhi*, a dialect of Sindhi.

Outside the Gujarati core of Gujarat, Greater Mumbai has about 18 percent of its population speaking Gujarati. There the Gujarati businessmen are a prominent segment of the society. Sizable numbers of Gujaratis have migrated eastward all the way to Kolkata and, similarly, southwards to the cities of Chennai, Hyderabad and Madurai. Over 50 percent of Indian migrants to the United States is Gujarati. Certain sections of business in India, particularly the wholesale and large-scale commodity sales, are a Gujarati specialty though many Gujaratis have entered the manufacturing sector in more recent times. Ambani brothers, India's richest with strong ties to manufacturing and service sectors are Gujaratis. They operate from Mumbai.

Oriya

Oriya is the official language of the state of Orissa. About 93 percent of the country's total Oriya mother tongue speakers reside in Orissa. Oriya has branched out from the eastern *Magadhi Apabhramsha* and is classified under the Eastern group of the New Indo-Aryan like Maithili, Assamese and Bengali; all four are considered sister languages. The *Munda* group of languages continues to influence this language (Nigam 1972). Old Oriya (10–13th centuries) is enriched by religious literature. The Middle Oriya Period (1300–1850) was initially influenced by saint *Chaitanya Maha Prahbu* of Nabadwip (Bengal), who spent considerable time in the sacred city of Puri. During the 16th and 17th centuries, Oriya was influenced by Sanskrit. Modern Oriya started in about 1850 and was influenced by western literature. *Probashi* Bengalis, who migrated to Orissa from the middle of the 19th century, contributed their share in modernizing Oriya. Oriya which has virtually the same script as Bengali, Assamese and Maithili, has changed considerably in recent times and has acquired a special form of its own.

People with Oriya as its mother tongue, show a high concentration in the coastal and plain areas of Orissa. Outside the Oriya core, the Oriyans have been attracted by the non-agricultural employment opportunities, such as in the Singhbhum district of Jharkand, Ujjain, Indore and Kolkata. Such migrations have also taken place to the metropolis of Kolkata and the tea gardens of Assam.

Punjabi

Punjabi is the official language of Punjab, and its core lies in the Punjab State of India and Punjab province of Pakistan. West Punjabi (*Lahnda* or *Hindki*), like the East Punjabi, evolved from the West and Northwest *Apabhramsha*, and was considered to be one of the bases on which the modern Punjabi language evolved. Western Punjabi or *Lahnda* is not spoken in India and is essentially a language of the Punjab province of Pakistan.

Punjabi literature started to take form when Guru Nanak founded the Sikh religion in the 15th and 16th centuries. He wrote mainly in Urdu mixed with Hindi and Punjabi. In 1588, the fifth Sikh Guru, Arjan Dev, compiled the *Adi Granth*, the sacred Sikh scripture, but written in old Hindi. A new Punjabi script called *Gurmukhi* was introduced in the 16th century, which was based on *Sharda* script of Kashmiri and *Nagri* Hindi.

The Punjabi language during the 17th century was written in three scripts: Perso-Arabic, *Nagri* and *Gurmukhi* (Bhal 1971). Today, Gurmukhi, which means 'proceeding from the mouth of the Guru', is the official script of the language. Punjabi literature is famous for its romances written mainly in the 18th century. Though Punjab is the place where the great Sanskrit language evolved about 2500 years ago, the development of a new Indo-Aryan language in the region in the form of Punjabi was greatly impeded because: i) during the Muslim invasions and occupation from the 11th through 18th centuries, this region was mainly influenced by Persian and Urdu; ii) the powerful Hindi language, which was never much different from Punjabi, always influenced and often overwhelmed Punjab from its eastern Haryana side; and iii) the use of three different scripts until recent times added confusion to literary activities at various levels. Therefore, Punjabi never had enough momentum to amass richness like most other new Indo-Aryan languages.

Punjab came under the British rule in 1848. The Muslim revival encouraged Urdu, while the Hindu revival encouraged *Sanatan Dharma* and strengthened Hindi. The Punjabi language was again neglected. After Independence in 1947, West Punjab in Pakistan came to be heavily influenced by Urdu, and East Punjab by Hindi. In 1961, when the Punjab state included Hindi speaking Haryana and parts of Himachal Pradesh, only 41% of its population had Punjabi as their mother tongue. In 1966, however, the Punjab state was reorganized based on language and thus Haryana and Himachal Pradesh were separated from it, raising Punjabi speakers in the new state to 62 percent.

Assamese

Assamese is the official and state language of Assam. It belongs to the Eastern group of the new Indo-Aryan family of languages, having been developed from the Magadhan *Apabhramsa*. Assamese as an independent language and literature appears to have begun in the 14th century AD. Prior to this time it was similar to Old Bengali (Chatterji 1960).

Assamese diverged from Old Bengali, which was centered in the Gour region of North Bengal. It entered the Brahmaputra Valley of Assam through the west. It was, therefore, not unexpected that Kamrup in the West Assam became the main seat of Assamese literature from its inception through the 16th and 17th centuries. It was the Kamrup-based western dialect of Assamese that influenced the language of all Assam during this period and even today it is claimed to be the mother of Assamese. The Ahom kings of Burman origin in East Assam (13th through 19th century), who brought Tibeto-Burman influences into Assamese language, caused the ascendancy of the eastern dialect over the west, and by the 17th century, Assamese spoken around Sibsagar district became the standard form. After Assam was annexed by the British in 1826 and made a part of Bengal Presidency, two significant things happened: 1) Western forms entered into Assamese literature through Kolkata-based elites and the local missionaries, and 2) Gauhati in central Assam turned into the major center of political and cultural activities causing an ascendancy of central Assamese dialect in the language. Bengali has also influenced Assamese considerably from its inception to this day and both languages share the same script. According to the 1971 census, 99.39 percent of native Assamese speakers lived in Assam.

Spatially, Assamese is confined to its core Brahmaputra Valley with very little expansion beyond its immediate vicinity. Only a few Assamese have migrated beyond their own core. Located at the extreme eastern end of the Indo-Aryan language area and surrounded by physical barriers on all sides, the west Assamese people were not only relatively isolated, but historically, they thrived in the Brahmaputra Valley in virtual linguistic isolation.

Kashmiri

Kashmiri is spoken in the western half of Jammu and Kashmir and is spoken by about 54 percent of the total state population. It is mainly concentrated in the Srinagar Valley and the adjacent mountains. In Srinagar district about 93 percent are Kashmiri speaking. There is some dispute about the linguistic classification of Kashmiri, although Grearson places it into the *Dardic* group of the sub-Iranian branch and did not include it in the Indo-Aryan family of languages (Sarkar, 1964). Chatterji points out the possibility that the Aryans, who came to India around 1500 BC, also went to Srinagar Valley before 1000 BC and took with them an Aryan dialect which eventually gave rise to the base of Kashmiri (Chatterji 1963). North Indian Brahmins later introduced Sanskrit into Kashmiri resulting into overlaying of Indo-Aryan elements over *Dardic* base (Chatterji 1963).

Thus, from early times, Kashmiri has been profoundly influenced by Sanskrit and *Prakrit* languages but after 13th century AD the influence of Persian language occurred because Persian was the court-language and the medium of elite literature in Kashmir. The language benefited from the incorporation of idioms and words of Persian, but it also suffered through borrowing of poetic epithets, phrases, hackneyed imagery and figures of speech (Bamzai, 1973).

With Urdu as the official language of Kashmir State, the Perso-Arabic script has been commonly used for the Kashmiri language.

Sindhi

Sindhi is classified under the NW group of the Indo-Aryan sub-family. Sindhi has preserved some of the archaic linguistic features of the *Apabhramsa* of the earlier times and is related to West Punjabi. Among its different dialects *Vicholi* of Hyderabad in Sind is considered to be the standard. The Sindhi linguistic frontier crosses the international boundary and one of its dialects, *Kachhi* in India, extends into Kutch of Gujarat.

After Independence and partition in 1947, when most Sindhi speaking Hindus were forced out of Sind in Pakistan, they migrated en masse as refugees and settled in the cities of west-central India, not far from their place of origin. Mumbai, with well over two percent of its people speaking Sindhi, has become the main center of Sindhi culture and literature in India. 90 percent of people speaking Sindhi in India are spread over in four west-central states: Gujarat (36.26 percent), Maharashtra (25.22 percent), Madhya Pradesh (14.44 percent), and Rajasthan (14.33 percent).

Chatterji's comment that "Sindhi does not have an extensive literature" (1963, p. 36), has its roots in the historical evolution and geographical setting of Sind, which is situated at the mouth of the Indus and buffered from the rest of India by the inhospitable Rajasthan (Thar) desert and swamplands of the Rann of Kutch. Sind was influenced first by Dravidian and, then, by Aryan civilizations for about 4500–5000 years and developed a form of Sanskrit based *Apabhramsa*, which came southwards from Punjab along the Indus Valley, during the first millennium AD. It was during that formative stage of Sindhi language that an Arabic invasion took place in the 8th century AD. The invaders came both by the coastal lands and by Arabian Sea from the west. This invasion placed Hindu culture and language under seige and their existence was threatened by Islamic rulers.

When, however, Sindhi as a new Indo-Aryan language evolved from its *Sanskrit-Prakrit-Apabhramsa* roots around 1000 AD, it never gathered enough literary momentum. Being physically removed from India's mainstream culture, literary inspiration from the *Bhakti* movement was not received, and other literary contacts with India were also broken. It may be noted that *Bhakti* movement had inspired all new Indo-Aryan languages and is partly responsible for the accentuated development of north Indian regional languages. Sindhi, during the last 1200 years, has been greatly influenced by Persian and Arabic languages. Even their traditional script based on Kashmiri *Sharda* and similar to Punjabi *Gurmukhi* was relinquished in favor of an extended Perso-Arabic script, which was formally adopted as a script for Sindhi by the British during the 19th century. As the recent Sindhi migrants to India prefer *Nagri* for their writing (Chatterji 1963), the language in India has also adopted the same script officially.

Comparative Historical-Geographical Setting of Four Peripheral Languages

Retardation of Sindhi literary endeavors poses a certain unique relationship with the spatial setting that needs to be discussed in a comparative framework of three other peripheral languages of the Indian sub-continent: Punjabi, Kashmiri and Assamese. The Punjabi language also underwent a retarded development, but not to the extent of Sindhi, and reasons lie not in its physical isolation like Sind, but in other factors. First, the Punjab plains were situated on a 'march zone' of all northwestern invaders and conquerors. It was here that an initial trial of strength between the invaders and the invaded occurred for the occupation of the 2500-km-wide Indo-Gangetic plains. These factors created countervailing forces to healthy literary activities. Second, the Islamic invasion and occupation which continued through the 18th century, came about at a time when the Western dialect and *Apabhramsa* was evolving into a new Indo-Aryan Punjabi language. Third, the richer Persian, Urdu and Hindi literary influences dwarfed Punjabi ever since its embryonic stage. Thus, the poverty of both Sindhi and Punjabi languages were caused by severe constraints imposed by physical and historical factors during most of their developmental stages.

Kashmiri, on the other hand, in its isolated mountain habitat, had already developed into a new Indo-Aryan language before the Islamic occupation. The strong Sanskrit influence during its formative stage was also a great help in fostering its individuality. The Muslim rulers were generally benevolent and encouraged the local Kashmiri language which resulted in enrichment of Kashmiri with Persian.

Assamese evolved at the northeastern periphery of India in the relative physical isolation provided by Brahmaputra Valley. It was neither retarded by Islamic invasion nor did any other sub-family of language ever threatened its structure like Sindhi. Though Burman Ahom rulers (13th through 19th century), who ruled from eastern centers of the valley, brought with them a Tibeto-Burman language, it was never forced upon the Assamese. Assamese derived inspiration from strong *Bhakti* movement-based literary centers of Nadia in West Bengal (Nawadip in particular), in addition to the strong influence of modern Bengali literature since the 19th century. All these resulted into a rich heritage of Assamese literature.

Linguistic Diversity

Language diversity results when people in sizable numbers speak more than one language within a specified area or district. If sizable groups of people speak each of the different languages in the same area, the diversity is magnified. Therefore, the question arises as to which geographic area we should refer to. If we consider the country as a whole and limit our data base to 18 languages and other languages, it may be concluded that India is extremely diversified. However, if we consider the states and union territories of the Indian Union, we will find that the diversity levels will vary from very high in Punjab and Jammu and Kashmir to low in Andhra Pradesh and Kerala. Similarly, if the diversity is assessed at the district level, only a few districts will be found to have high linguistic diversity. It is, therefore, apt to state that India's linguistic diversity is very pronounced at the national level and it is generally low at a local or district level.

Dutt et al. 1985 study, based on district level data, reveals that the district units are generally linguistically homogeneous. There are only a few large areas, mostly away from the Indus-Ganges Valley and the coastal plains where greater diversity can be identified. More accessible plain lands, where population densities are high, are, thus, less diversified.

Several high diversity pockets are associated with the metropolitan cities such as, Kolkata (Calcutta), Chennai (Madras), Mumbai (Bombay), Bengaluru (Bangalore), and Hyderabad because the general pull factor attracts in-migrants to those cities from different linguistic areas. Similarly, the steel towns of Jamshedpur (Jharkhand) and Rourkela (Orissa) have higher diversity. Greater Mumbai is the most diverse among Indian cities. It attracts Gujarati (18 percent), Urdu (11 percent), Hindi (10 percent), Tamil (2.62 percent), Sindhi (2.6 percent), Telugu (2.16 percent), Malayalam (2.12 percent), Kannada (2.10 percent), Punjabi (1.49 percent), and Bengali (0.38 percent) native speakers, other than the regional Marathi, which constitutes 42 percent of the city (note: all percentage figures are based on 1971 census data since no such district or city-wise information were published afterwards). Mumbai is the only South Asian megacity where the mother tongue of the surrounding region is spoken by less than 50 percent of the populace.

Linguistic diversity is associated with large tracts of Deccan Plateau; also true of Assam Hills which historically have remained less accessible to the new Indo-Aryan and Dravidian languages giving rise i) to the development of local languages that remained confined to micro pockets, and/or ii) to retention of pre-existing Austric and Tibeto-Burman languages.

In the linguistic frontier areas such as Kutch (Gujarat) and Jammu (Jammu and Kashmir), where more than one language converges with sizable numbers of other/others, diversity increases. Indian linguistic pattern is largely characterized by dominance of a single language in a district. Most districts have over 80 percent of their people speaking a single language. A few districts that do not conform to a single language dominance show a strong correlation with decreasing diversity index (Dutt et al. 1985). The scatter diagram confirms that the district level linguistic diversity in India is, thus, generally a phenomenon related to a single language dominance. The Indian linguistic pattern may, thus, be characterized as "deconcentrated concentration".

Concluding Remarks

Both religion and language have made deep imprints in setting India's cultural patterns. Though the Hindu religion, the oldest of India's major religions, came to the country along with the migration of the Aryans around 1500 BC, the languages evolved much later. The mother language of the Aryans were Sanskrit and from that root evolved most North Indian languages. The Dravidian languages in the south possibly had its roots before the Aryans, but they flourished much later. In this way, Hindu, Buddhist and Jain religions are older than existing languages in India, but later religions, such as Islam, Christianity and Sikhism evolved when other languages were already formed. There are, of course, some relationship between religion and language because Hindus are associated with Hindi and other north Indian Sanskrit-based languages, while Urdu is primarily a Muslim language. Sikhs are associated with *Gurmukhi* script of the Punjabi language. Kashmiri, the language of Kashmir, has a majority of Muslim speakers. Even though this language had a Sanskrit root, conversion from Kashmir into Islam turned most Kashmiri speakers to the Islamic religion. Christians speak regional languages, but the missionaries have established educational systems with English as the medium of instruction. As a result, a large number of Christians are bilingual. They speak their regional language and are also fluent in English.

In spatial spread, Hinduism virtually spreads all over India, whereas the Hindi speakers are only found in northern India. Therefore, the spread of the single major religion is much wider than that of any single language.

Acknowledgements

This chapter is largely based on three publications. They are 1) Dutt, A.K. and Davgun, S. "Religious Patterns of India with a Factoral Regionalization," *GeoJournal* 3.2 (1979): 201–214, (2) Dutt, A.K., Khan, C. and Sangwan, C. "Spatial Pattern of Languages in India: A Cultural Historical Analysis," *GeoJournal* 10.1 (1985): 51–74, (3) Dutt, A.K. and Geib, M. 1987. *Atlas of South Asia*. Boulder, Co. and London: Westview Press, pp. 26–29, 110–119. Chapters reproduced with permission from copyright holders.

Note

1. Map of Muslim population distribution was not included in Census of India 2001 (Nag 2007), and thus cannot be reproduced here.

References

Amani, K.Z. 1974. 'The Status of Urdu Language in India: A Geo-Political View,' *Geographer*, 212, pp. 15–36.

Bamzai, P.M.K. 1973. *A History of Kashmir*. Delhi: Metropolitan Book Co.

Bhal, Kali Charan. 1971. 'A Grammatical Sketch of Punjabi'. in Nigam, R.C. (ed.), *Grammatical Sketch of Indian Languages with Comparative Vocabulary and Text*, Census of India 1971, Part I, Series I, Language Monographs 2, 1961 Series.

Brush, J.E. 1949. 'The Distribution of Religious Communities India,' *Annals, Association of American Geographers*, 39, pp. 81–98.

Census of India. 1972. *Religion*, Series I India, Paper 2 of 1972, p. 11.

Chatterji, S.K. 1960. 'Assamese,' in Majumdar, R.C. (ed.), *The History and Culture of the Indian People*. Bombay: Bharatiya Vidya Bhavan.

Chatterji, S.K. 1963. *Languages and Literatures of Modern India*. Calcutta: Prakesh Bhawan.

Chatterji, S.K. and Katre, S.M. 1973. 'Languages,' in *The Gazetteer of India, Country and People*, Vol. I. Publications Division, Government of India.

Chatterji, S.K. and Majumdar, R.C. 1969. 'Telugu,' in Majumdar, R.C. (ed.) *The History and Culture of the Indian People*. Bombay: Bharatiya Vidya Bhavan.

Das Gupta, Jyotirindra. 1970. *Language Conflict and National Development*. Berkeley

Davis, K. 1968. *The Population of India and Pakistan*. New York: Russell and Russell.

Dutt, A.K., Chatterjee, S.P. and Geib, MM. 1976. *India in Maps*. Dubuque Iowa: Kendall/Hunt Publishing Co. 1976.

Dutt, A.K. and Davgun, S. 1977. 'Diffusion of Sikhism and Migration Pattern of Sikhs in India,' *GeoJournal*, 1.5, pp. 81–90.

Dutt, A.K. and Davgun, S. 1979. 'Religions and Patterns of India with Factoral Regionalization', *GeoJournal*, Vol. 3.2, pp. 201–244

Dutt, A.K. and Geib, M. Margaret. 1998. *Atlas of South Asia*. India: Oxford & IBH Publishers.

Dutt, A.K., Khan, Chandrakanta, and Sangwan, Chandralekha. 1985. 'Spatial Pattern of Languages in India: A Culture-Historical Analysis.' *GeoJournal* 10.1, pp. 51–74.

Dutt, A.K. and Noble, G. 1982. *India: Cultural Patterns and Processes*. "Patterns of Religious Diversity" in Boulder, Colorado: Westview Press Inc., pp. 221–246

Gosal, G.S. and Mukerji, A.B. 1970. 'The Religious Composition of Indian Population: A Spatial Analysis,' *Tijdschrift voor Econ. en Sociale Geografie*, 61, pp. 91–100.

Harshe, R.G. 1966. 'Marathi,' in Majumdar, R.C. (ed.) *The History and Culture of the Indian People*, 5. Bombay: Bharatiya Vidya Bhavan.

Iyengar, K.R. Srinivasa. 1960. 'Malayalam,' in Majumdar, R.C. (ed.) *The History and Culture of the Indian People*. Bombay: Bharatiya Vidya Bhavan.

Iyengar, K.R. Srinivasa. 1965. 'Tamil and Tamilakum,' in Majumdar, R.C. (ed.) *The History and Culture of the Indian People*. Bombay: Bharatiya Vidya Bhavan.

Iyengar, K.R. Srinivasa. 1966. 'Telugu,' in Majumdar, R.C. (ed.) *The History and Culture of the Indian People*. Bombay: Bharatiya Vidya Bhavan.

Krishan, G. 1971. 'Distribution of Sikhs outside the Punjab, India,' *The Indian Geographical Journal*, 46, pp. 35–41.

Lamb, B.P. 1968. *India: A World in Transition*. New York: Praeger Publishers.

Nag, P. 2007. *Cultural Heritage Atlas of India*. Kolkata: National Atlas and Thematic Mapping or Origin Station of India.

McDonald, J.R. 1972. *A Geography of Regions*. Dubuque, Iowa: W. M. C. Brown Co. Publishers.

Moreland, W.H. and Chatterjee, A.C. 1945. *A Short Cultural History of India*. New York: Longmans, Green and Co.

Mukerji, A.B. 1972. 'Distributional Aspects of Muslim Population in UP., 1961,' *The Geographer*, 9, pp. 16–29.

Nair, S.K. 1977. 'Malayalam,' in Majumdar, R.C. (ed.) *The History and Culture of the Indian People*. Bombay: Bharatiya Vidya Bhavan.

Nayar, S.K. 1965. 'Malayalam,' in Majumdar, R.C. (ed.) *The History and Culture of the Indian People*. Bombay: Bharatiya Vidya Bhavan.

Nayar, Baldev Raj. 1969. *National Communication and Language Policy in India*. New York: F.A. Praeger Publishers.

Nigam, R.C. 1972. *Language Handbook on Mother Tongues in Census*. New Delhi: Census Centenary Monograph, N. 10, Office of Registrar General.

Pandit, P.B. 1971. 'A Grammatical Sketch of Gujarati,' in Nigam, R.C. (ed.), *Grammatical Sketch of Indian Languages with Comparative Vocabulary and Text*, Census of India 1971, Part I, Series I, Language Monographs 2, 1961 Series.

Pethe, V.P. 1973. Hindus, Muslims and the Demographic Balance in India, *Economic and Political Weekly*, 8:2, pp. 75–78.

Sarkar, Amal. 1964. Handbook of Languages and Dialects in India. Calcutta: Firma K.L. Mukhopadyay.

Saxena, Babu Ram and Ramnath Sahai. 1971. 'A Grammatical Sketch of Hindi,' in Nigam, R.C. (ed.), *Grammatical Sketch of Indian Languages with Comparative Vocabulary and Text*, Census of India 1971, Part I, Series I, Language Monographs 2, 1961 Series.

Sen, Sukumar. 1971. 'A Grammatical Sketch of Bengali,' in Nigam, R.C. (ed.), *Grammatical Sketch of Indian Languages with Comparative Vocabulary and Text*, Census of India 1971, Part I, Series I, Language Monographs 2, 1961 Series.

Singh, K. 1953. *The Sikhs*. London: George Allen and Unwin Ltd.

Statesman's Yearbook, The, Barry Turner, (ed.), New York: Palgrave Macmillan, 2006.

Tulpule, S.G. and Kulkarni, S.B. 1971. 'A Grammatical Sketch of Marathi,' in Nigam, R.C. (ed.), *Grammatical Sketch of Indian Languages with Comparative Vocabulary and Text*, Census of India 1971, Part I, Series I, Language Monographs 2, 1961 Series.

17

Linguistic Diversity Changes in India: A Regional Analysis, 1971–2001

RAJRANI KALRA

India is a land characterized by 'unity in diversity' amidst a multicultural society. This is symbolized by variety in culture such as different languages, religions, castes, house types, dance forms and dietary patterns (Noble and Dutt, 1982). Of these cultural traits, language is an important instrument of cultural identity since it is through this medium that different groups of people communicate with the world and express a sense of identity to a place. Often, social tensions emerge when a certain segment of society feels ostracized from social and economic processes of development due to lack of knowledge of the dominant and prevalent language. This often leads to granting linguistic minorities special privileges to accommodate them in the process of mainstream national social and economic development.

India is considered to be the world's most linguistically diverse nation. The Eighth Schedule of the Constitution specified 14 major languages and a concerted effort has been made to fully develop all these languages in the interest of national integration and development. Subsequently, eight more languages were included in the schedule and these were: Sindhi (1969), Konkani, Manipuri and Nepali (1993), Bodo, Dogri, Maithili and Santhali (2003) (Sengupta, 2009). According to the 2001 Indian Census approximately 96.6 percent of the Indian population spoke these 22 scheduled languages with another 100 non-scheduled languages spoken by a minimum of 10,000 people in different regions (Census of India, 2001). The 2001 Census of India has declared 22 schedule languages (Table 17-1).

India is characterized by an astounding degree of linguistic diversity since each state has adopted one or two of the 22 official languages for

Table 17.1 Twenty-two scheduled languages of India (2001).

Assamese	*Kannada*	*Oriya*	*Telugu*	Sindhi*	Maithili***
Bengali	*Kashmiri*	*Punjabi*	*Urdu*	Konkani**	Bodo***
Gujarati	*Malayalam*	*Sanskrit*		Manipuri**	Dogri***
Hindi	*Marathi*	*Tamil*		Nepali**	Santali***

Languages in italics: Original 14 scheduled languages
* An addition by the Constitution Twenty-first Amendment Act, 1967
** An addition of languages by the Constitution Seventy-first Amendment Act, 1992
*** An addition of four languages by the Constitution Hundredth Amendment Act, 2003
Source: Census of India, 2001; Kalra, 2007

conducting business and governance, and yet a few of the other major or minor languages could still be spoken by various population cohorts in different states. The diversity in Indian languages could be explained historically by the presence of numerous ancient kingdoms, each with its own language. Although the states were disintegrated and merged with other states due to territorial expansions and wars, the language spoken by the people remained intact. Later, during colonial rule new state lines were drawn which did not follow the former political or linguistic boundaries.

Given this background the purpose of this study is to explore the relationship between language and geography and the intertwining relationships among them. This research explores the impact of relative distance and location on the spread and development of Indian languages across geographical space. The overarching theme addressed in this chapter is if diversity in Indian languages can be identified at various geographical scales. Linguistic diversity can be ascertained at the national level (macro level) or the state and district levels (micro levels) by examining the spread of languages at the national level relative to the spread or concentration of various languages across geographical units. This study specifically formulates and comprehends the linguistic diversity in India for the years 1971 and 2001 at the sub-national or state levels.

Research Methodology

In this research, the census data for scheduled and non-scheduled languages have been used for the years 1971 and 2001. To conduct a detailed analysis the researcher has selected the mother tongue data related to languages as they cover the entire population. A mother tongue is defined as the language first spoken in childhood by a person. The Census of India provides linguistic records for scheduled and non-scheduled language data. This research has utilized all the fifteen scheduled languages and combined all the non-scheduled languages as 'other languages' and has aggregated them into one group. So, a total of sixteen mother tongues have been considered for analysis during the year 1971 and twenty-two mother tongues for the year 2001. There have been many changes during the period 1971 and 2001 in terms of administrative divisions of states, and inclusion of languages in the Constitution of India.

The study area consists of 28 states and 7 union territories for the year 2001, and 24 states and 6 union territories for the year 1971 for implementing the data analysis. This research has delineated the linguistic diversity of India by calculating the index of diversity modified by Dutt and Davgun (1985) for all the scheduled and non-scheduled languages of all states and union territories in India for the year 1971 and 2001. The index of diversity is used to explain the linguistic diversity pattern of India. An evaluation is also made of the changes that have been observed in the last three decades during the period 1971–2001. The diversity index can be measured statistically by calculating an index of concentration or diversification. A diverse society with various religions, languages and customs has a better prospect of national integration and social stability. Diversification has been studied by economic and urban geographers to explore the scale of concentration or spread in cities with respect to any economic or social characteristic such as religion, language, music, food consumption, industry, services, and high-technology.

Studies by Tress (1938), Rodgers (1957) and Conkling (1963) have analyzed patterns of diversification in cities according to the labor force absorbed within the industries in those cities. Shortridge (1976) refined the 'Lorenz Curve' method and calculated the religious diversity of the population in the United States. Warf and Winsberg (2008) have utilized four quantitative measures (simple counts, relative dominance, Shannon's and Simpson's entropy and probability based estimates) to measure religious diversity in the US. A modified index of diversity (Dutt and Davgun, 1982) was used to measure and interpret religious diversity patterns in Rajasthan (India).

This study has used the above revised index of diversity by Dutt and Davgun (1982) for calculating the linguistic diversity index for India. The values closer to +1.0 indicate less diversity, whereas values closer to −1.0

indicate high diversity. This study utilizes the index of diversity measure to generate maps showing the linguistic diversity ranging from very high to very low, and calculates the diversity index for all the Indian states and union territories as well. The index of linguistic diversity measures the degree of social and linguistic interaction among various linguistic groups of the society.

The index of diversity of all states and union territories for 1971 and 2001 have been calculated utilizing spreadsheets (excel). ARC-GIS 9.3.1 has been used to create maps that aid in interpreting spatial patterns of linguistic diversity in India. This research does not compare the selected time periods due to two types of data limitations. Firstly, there has been a change in the number of languages from16 [15 scheduled and 1 (all) non-scheduled] in 1971 to 23 [22 scheduled and 1(all) non- scheduled] in 2001; and secondly, the number of states and union territories have changed during the intervening period. The results for index of diversity were derived utilizing the following four steps: a) by computing state and union territory based proportion of population allocation for all the languages, b) ranking these values (language percentages) according to their magnitude, and c) calculating a diversity index for each state and union territory.

The diversity index is written as:

I= (D-E)/(M-E), where

I = Index of concentration (or diversity if lower values are considered as more diversified)

D=Cumulative percentage total according to the rank of each language in a state

E= Cumulative percentage total assuming even percentage distribution of each language

M=Maximum cumulative percentage total assuming 100 of the frequencies in Rank 1.

The 'D' is the cumulative percentage total, according to the rank of each language in a state. The term 'E' in the formula is calculated as the cumulative percentage total assuming an even percentage distribution of each language. For the year 1971 the 'E' was derived for 16 (15 scheduled +1 non-scheduled) languages assuming an even percentage, i.e., 100/16

=6.25 for each language. The final term 'E' was calculated as 850 for 1971. Further, for the year 2001, 23 languages were utilized in the study [22 scheduled +1 (non-scheduled)], and assuming an even percentage, i.e., 100/23=4.34, the final E was calculated to be equivalent to 1198.19. The term 'M' in the formula is the maximum cumulative percentage total assuming 100 of the frequencies in Rank 1 and was calculated as 1600 (16*100 =1600, where 16 was the total number of languages in the data set for the year 1971). Similarly, the term M for 2001 was equivalent to 2300 assuming 100 of the frequencies in Rank 1 (23 total languages were taken for the year 2001). Finally, the last step involves mapping the values for each state and union territory by using ARC-GIS 9.3.1, and classifying the values by using the quintile method and grouping them into five categories of 'very high', 'high', 'moderate', 'low', and 'very low' diversity. The values closer to 1 show the least diversity and values closer to zero show highest diversity. So, the diversity maps have been prepared for the time period 1971 and 2001. These maps illustrate the concentration and the spread in the geographical pattern of the languages of all the states and union territories of India.

Linguistic Diversity in India

The major linguistic regions of India have played a vital role in maintaining India's political, social and cultural identities. These states are not just administrative units but they symbolize the deep historical and cultural histories from which they have evolved to their present day landscapes (Adhikari and Kumar, 2007). There are regional linguistic issues in India due to which segments of the population demand for political division and fragmentation of states. All aspects of linguistic diversity cannot be addressed in this paper and hence the focus of this paper is limited to examining the spatial linguistic diversity of India. For instance imagine the core regions where people use the language as mother tongue; then around the core exist the linguistic frontiers where the predominant presence of the language begins to decline. Also, languages like Marathi, Bengali and Tamil retain the core region effect in the cities like Mumbai, Kolkata and Chennai, and spread to other places via migration of people and relocation diffusion. Likewise, Punjabi and Sindhi spread via migration of people and relocation diffusion as well (Kalra, 2007).

India's linguistic regions include languages belonging to more than one family and sharing traits which do not belong to the original families (Emeneau, 1956). Khubchandani (1993) argues that India is an example of contrived homogeneity since small speech groups consisting of several thousand or more people are able to survive in the midst of large linguistic communities. A recent study by the United Nations Educational, Scientific and Cultural Organization (UNESCO) has examined that several languages in the world are at the verge of extinction. It has identified 196 languages in India belonging to the 'scheduled', 'non-scheduled', and 'others' categories which have been classified as 'endangered'. Of these languages threatened by possible extinction, two (Manipuri and Bodo) belong to the Eighth Schedule categorization and have been classified as being 'endangered' and 'unsafe' (UNESCO, 2010).

Diversity Analysis of Indian Languages: 1971–2001

Linguistic diversity is a direct and an indirect gauge for social, political and economic expansion and it exists where substantial number of people speak more than one language within a particular region. Therefore, a higher number of spoken languages results in high linguistic diversity and a lower number of languages spoken in a region results in a lower diversity (Kalra, 2003).

The diversity index helps to depict the concentration and the spatial pattern of languages in all the states and union territories of India. In India the distribution pattern of languages has changed during the period 1971 and 2001. This is tied to the various economic, demographic, social and political factors that have brought transformation in India over the past three decades. Many new states have been carved out and new languages have been added to the scheduled category since 1971. Some states have developed economically and also had social and political upheavals. These factors have also played a vital role in changing the linguistic diversity in India.

The linguistic diversity in the year 1971 was high in the states and union territories of Jammu and Kashmir, Delhi, Chandigarh, Karnataka, Manipur and Tripura, whereas moderate to low diversity is observed in the states of Assam, Maharashtra, Gujarat, Orissa and Maharashtra. Low diversity was prevalent in Hindi-speaking states of Rajasthan, Bihar, Uttar Pradesh and Haryana (Figs. 17.1 and 17.2).

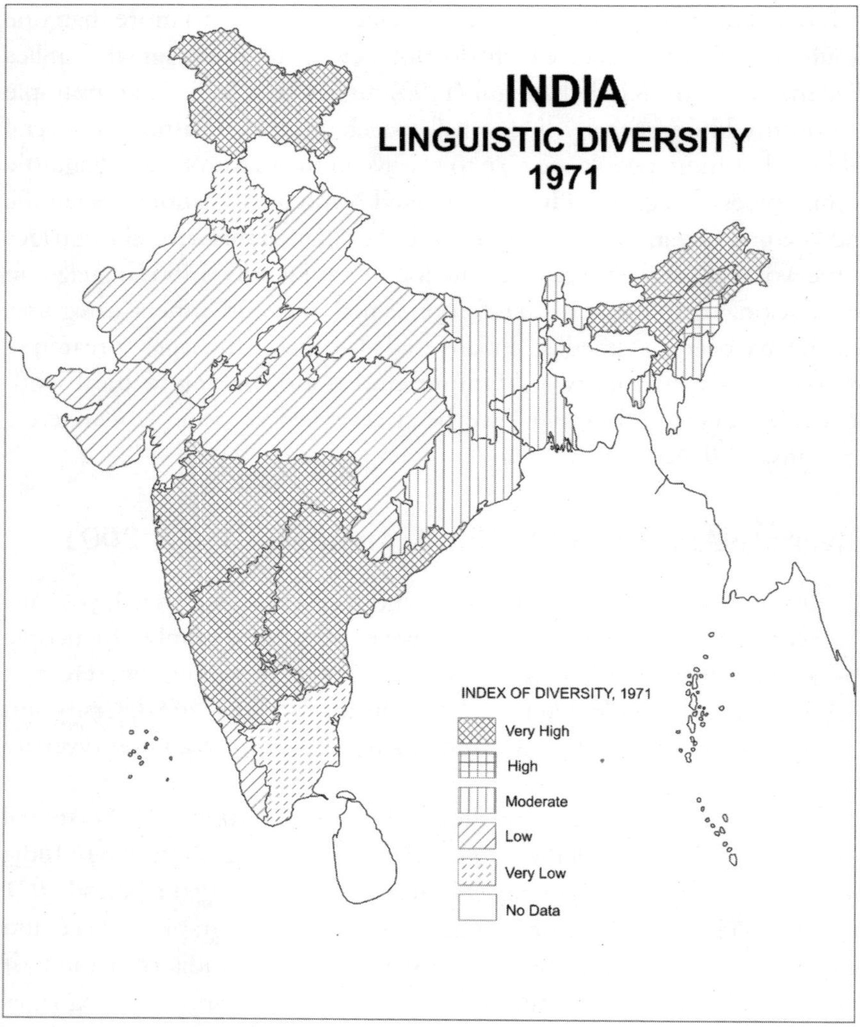

Fig. 17.1 Linguistic Diversity of India: 1971.
Data Source: Sekhar, 1971(Census of India, 1971),
Source: Kalra, 2007
Three newly formed states i.e. Jharkhand, Uttaranchal and Chhattisgarh were non-existent in 1971.

Jammu and Kashmir had high linguistic diversity in 1971 and was a very sought after destination due to its geographical landscape, natural beauty and wilderness (the mighty Himalayas); but in 2001 it changed to very low diversity because of increased political instability and the continued Kashmir dispute between India and Pakistan (Fig.17.3)

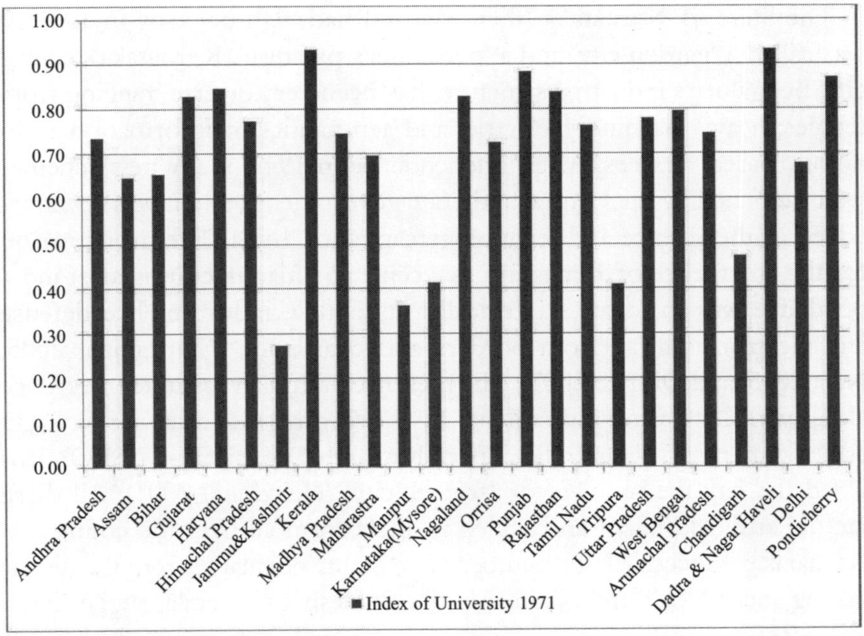

Fig. 17.2 Linguistic Diversity of Indian Languages-1971.
Data Source: Sekhar, 1971 (Census of India, 1971).

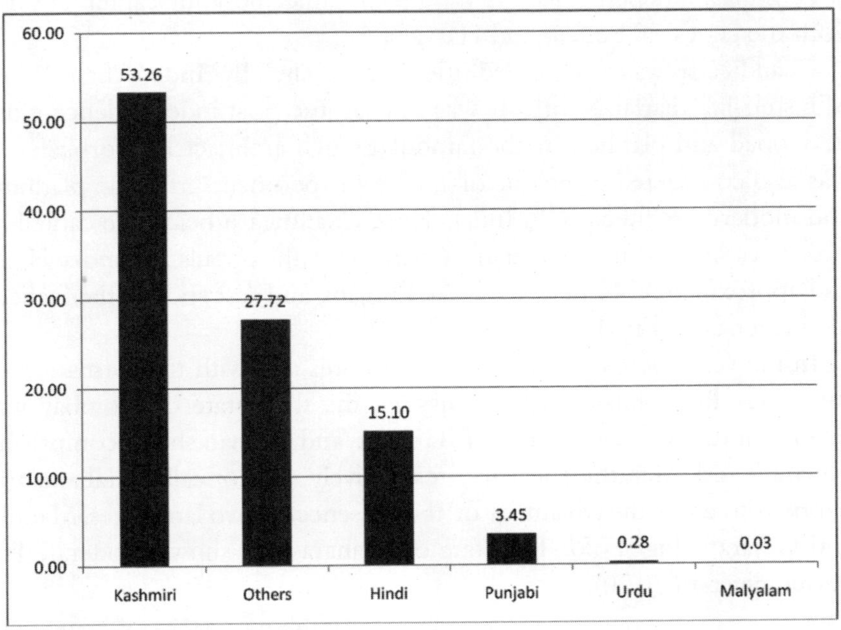

Fig. 17.3 Distribution of Languages in Jammu and Kashmir.
Source: Sekhar, 1971 (Census of India, 1971).

The State of Karnataka (then Mysore) had high diversity in 1971. It was called a 'garden city' and a 'pensioner's paradise'. Karnataka's capital city, Bengaluru's industrial structure, has been very diverse, ranging from textiles, heavy machinery, electric, and aeronautics to information technology based services. After independence in 1947, many new schemes were launched by the Central and State governments, and it was acknowledged as the science and technology capital of India. The major reason for the emergence of Bengaluru as a center of manufacturing after independence was to locate strategically susceptible industries like defense and electronics away from borders and coastlands (Chittranjan, 2005; Nair, 2005; and Dittrich 2007). The presence of Indian Institute of Science along with increasing investments by the Central Government in R&D establishments, such as Indian Space Research Organization (ISRO) provided the city the moniker of 'science city' (Heitzman, 2001). All these factors attracted talent and skilled workers from all over the country to Karnataka. Especially large number of migrants originated from the neighboring states like Tamil Nadu, Andhra Pradesh and Kerala, suggesting a 'distance-decay effect' (more migrants originated from states which are in close proximity relative to states that were further away). Chandigarh also had high linguistic diversity (0.47) in 1971 as it was a newly formed city after India's independence (1947) and became the joint capital city for both the states of Punjab and Haryana.

Chandigarh was also called the 'dream city' by India's first Prime Minister, Jawaharlal Nehru. It was one of the post-independence cities developed and planned by the famous French architect Le Corbusier. It was also considered to be one of the best experiments in urban planning and modern architecture in India. Thus, Chandigarh being the capital of two states (Punjab and Haryana), 56 percent of the population spoke Hindi and approximately 40 percent spoke Punjabi, and rest spoke other scheduled languages (Fig. 17.4).

In the year 1960, due to linguistic disputes and with the formation of the States Reorganization Commission, the then state of Bombay was divided into two new states of Gujarat and Maharashtra, comprising Gujarati and Marathi speakers, respectively. Historically, Maharashtra happens to enjoy the advantage of the presence of two languages, Marathi and Gujarati (Fig. 17.5). The state of Maharashtra shows moderate linguistic diversity (0.70).

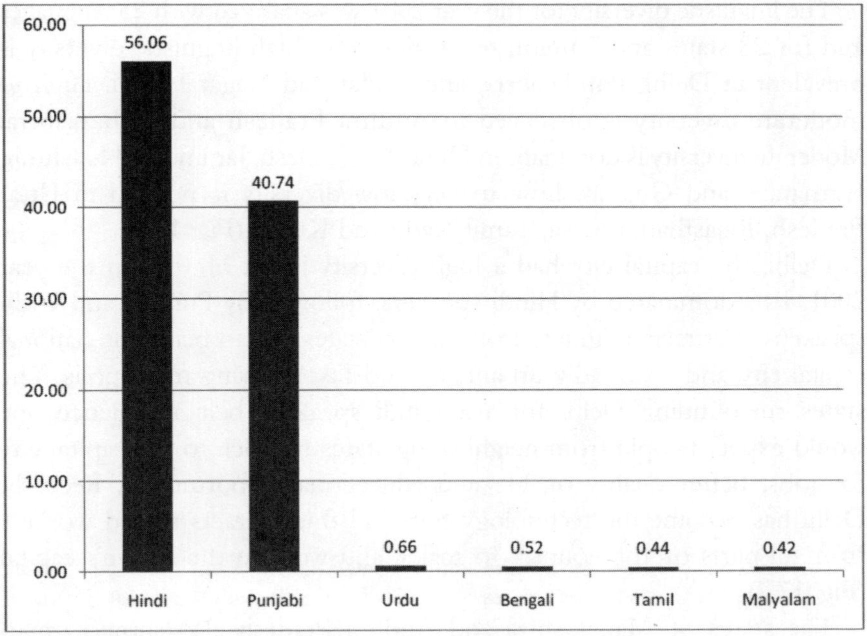

Fig. 17.4 Distribution of Languages in Chandigarh-1971.

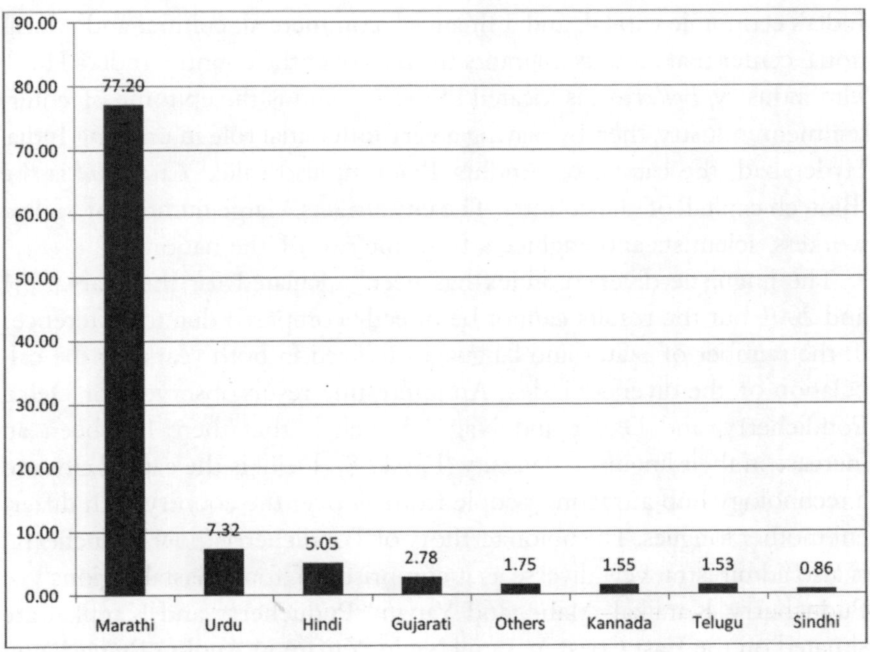

Fig. 17.5 Distribution of Languages in Maharashtra.

The linguistic diversity for the year 2001 was analyzed with 23 languages and for 28 states and 7 union territories. Very high linguistic diversity is prevalent in Delhi, Pondicherry, and Dadar and Nagar Haveli. High to moderate diversity is observed in Andhra Pradesh and Maharashtra. Moderate diversity is dominant in Himachal Pradesh, Jammu and Kashmir, Karnataka and Gujarat. Low to very low diversity is noticed in Uttar Pradesh, Rajasthan, Orissa, Tamil Nadu and Kerala (Fig. 17.6).

Delhi, the capital city had a high diversity index of 0.50 in the year 2001. It is dominated by Hindi speakers, followed by Punjabi and Urdu speakers. It attracts migrants from nearby states due to being the national capital city and an rapidly urbanizing and fast growing metropolis. The states surrounding Delhi form a Hindi speaking belt and hence one would expect people from neighboring states to flock to the capital city for jobs, better quality of life and educational opportunities. Recently, Delhi has become the technology hub and thus attracts skilled workers from all parts of the country to reside and work in the nation's capital (Fig. 17.7).

The states of Maharashtra and Andhra Pradesh also show high to moderate diversity. Mumbai (formerly the city of Bombay) is both the capital of Maharashtra and the largest metropolis of India. It is considered India's economic capital, and a financial, commercial, cultural and educational center that attracts migrants from all over the country. India's Hindi film industry, *Bollywood*, is located in the city and is the epitome of entertainment industry, thereby playing a very influential role in unifying India. Hyderabad, the capital of Andhra Pradesh, also called *Cyberabad* is the 'Biotech capital' of the country. The city attracts a large number of skilled workers, scientists and engineers from the rest of the nation.

The linguistic diversity index has been calculated for the years 1971 and 2001 but the results cannot be directly compared due to differences in the number of states and languages utilized in both years for the calculation of the diversity index. An interesting result observed for Delhi, Pondicherry, and Dadar and Nagar Haveli is that there has been an increase in their linguistic diversity (Fig. 17.8). Delhi is the capital city and a technology hub attracting people from all over the country with different mother tongues. The union territory of Pondicherry (now Puducherry) is also administratively diverse as it comprises of four coastal regions viz. Puducherry, Karaikal, Mahe, and Yanam. Puducherry and Karaikal are situated on the East Coast in Tamil Nadu, Yanam in Andhra Pradesh and

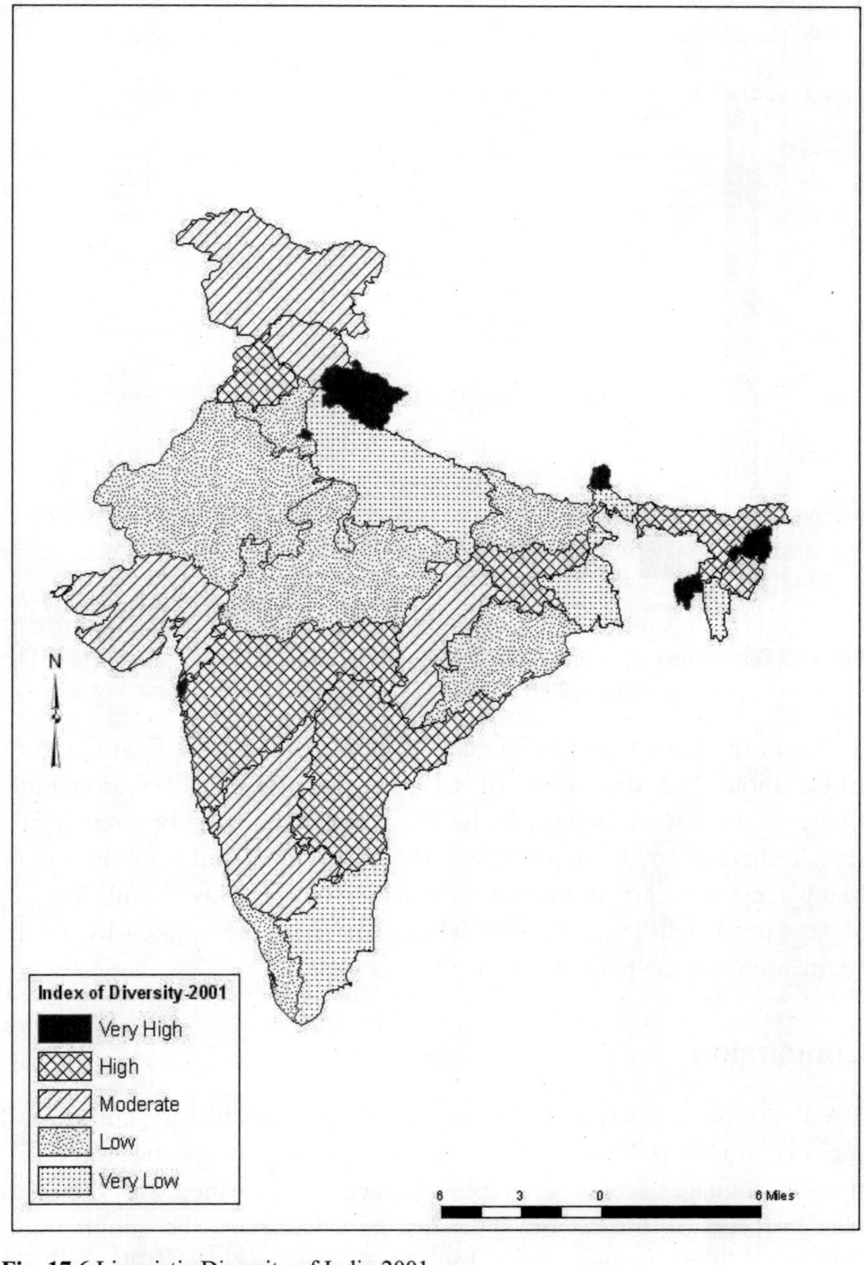

Fig. 17.6 Linguistic Diversity of India-2001.
Data Source: Census of India, 2001.

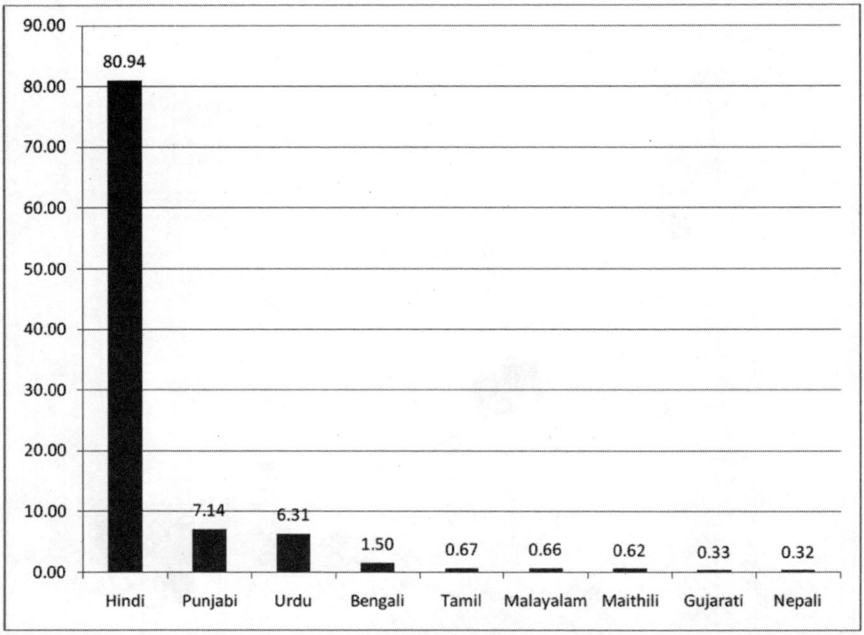

Fig. 17.7 Distribution of Languages in Delhi-2001
Data source: Census of India, 2001.

Mahe on the West Coast in Kerala. Pondicherry is on the East Coast of India, about 162 kms south of Chennai, located on the Coromandel Coast of the Bay of Bengal. It also has a rich history, as the French first set base here in 1670, followed by Portuguese, Dutch and English settlers. Many languages are dominant in this region such as Tamil, Telugu, Malayalam, English and French. These languages are spoken by a substantial number of people residing in this region.

Conclusion

The linguistic diversity in India portrays the region's history, culture and socio-economic processes of transformation. It portrays that the diffusion of languages across geographical space is intertwined with the complex histories of the region. This research delineates the geographical pattern of linguistic diversity in India during the periods 1971 and 2001 utilizing index of diversity approach at the state level. It sheds some light on the observation that India is linguistically diverse at the national level (macro scale) but homogeneous at the state level (micro level). Almost all

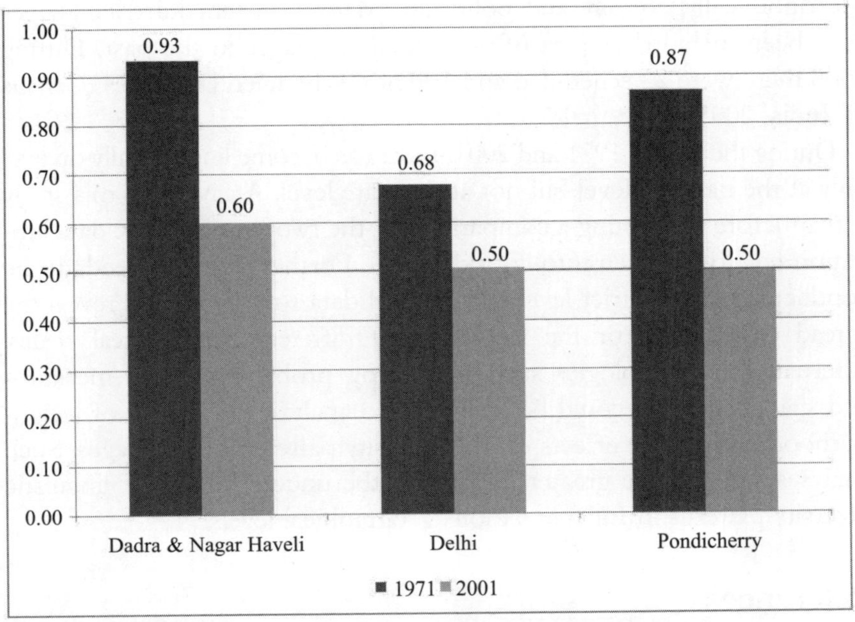

Fig. 17.8 Major Linguistic Diversity Index Change 1971–2001(Increase).

the states are dominant in one major language with few secondary languages spoken by some segments of the population. The results show remarkable change in few states and lesser changes in other states. The transition during the period 1971 and 2001 increased the linguistic diversity in few states, decreased in some and in some states there was no change at all.

The analysis has demonstrated that highly economically developed states and union territories such as Maharashtra, Delhi, and Tamil Nadu tend to have high linguistic diversity, and impoverished states tend to have lesser linguistic diversity. It reveals that dominant languages of bordering states have an impact upon the states which are economically developed and highly urbanized; if the neighboring state uses similar or same language, the probability of linguistic diversity will be quite low and vice-versa. An important observation is that apart from proximity and distance, the homogeneity of the languages depends on a region's social and political stability. Stability in a region plays a significant role in attracting people of diverse languages as in the case of major metropolises such as Delhi, Mumbai and Bengaluru.

Several non-scheduled languages are struggling to be included among scheduled languages to alleviate their importance in the linguistic hierarchy

– economically, socially and politically. Many non-scheduled languages have been included as part of scheduled languages in the past. During 2008 there were 22 scheduled and 100 non-scheduled languages (Census of India, 2001).

During the period 1971 and 2001, India has become linguistically diverse only at the national level but not at the state level. A caveat of this study is that before attempting a comparison of the two time periods, data limitation has to be taken into consideration. Further research needs to be conducted using district level or city level data to explore and reveal the spread of diversity or the lack of it at different geographical scales. Alternative methodologies such as entropy, probability based measures and spatial statistics could be employed to analyze the impact of neighborhood and cluster effects on the diversity patterns of languages. Such analyses will provide greater insights to the understanding of linguistic diversity patterns in India at various geographical levels.

References

Adhikari, S. and Kumar, R. 2007. 'Linguistic Regionalism and the Social construction of India's political space'. in B. Thakur, G. Pomeroy, C.Cusak and S.K. Thakur (eds.) *City Society and Planning: Essays in Honor of Professor A.K. Dutt*, Volume: Two: Society, pp. 374–392. New Delhi: Concept Publishing Company.

Conkling, E.C. 1963. 'South Wales: A case study in industrial diversification'. *Economic Geography*. 39 (3):258–272.

Census of India 2001. http://www.censusindia.gov.in

Census of India 2001. Data on Language. Statement 7. http://www.censusindia.gov.in/Census_Data_2001/Census_Data_Online/Language/Statement7.htm.

Dutt, A.K. 2003. 'India: A Geographic Preface'. In S. Ganguly and N. DeVotta (eds.), *Understanding Contemporary India* pp. 7–15. USA: Lynne Rienner Publishers, Inc.

Dutt, A. Khan, C. and Sangwan, C. 1985. 'Spatial Pattern of Languages in India: A Culture-Historical Analysis'. *GeoJournal* 10(1), pp. 51–74.

Dutt, A.K. and Devgun, S., 1982. 'Patterns of Religious Diversity'. In A. G. Noble and A. K. Dutt (eds.), *India: Cultural Patterns and Processes*, Boulder, Colorado: West View Press.

Dutt, A.K. and Davgun, S. 1979. 'Religions and Patterns of India with Factoral Regionalization'. *GeoJournal*, Vol. 3(2), pp. 201–244.

Emeneau, M.B. 1956. *India as a linguistic area. Language* 321, pp. 3–16.

Fishman, J. 1992. *Reversing Language Shift*. Clevedon: Multilingual matters.

Kalra, R. 2007. Indian languages and their dissemination: 1971–1991, In B.Thakur, G. Pomeroy, C. Cusack and S.K. Thakur (eds), *City Society and Planning*, *Volume 2: Society*, pp. 447–477. New Delhi: Concept Publishing Company.

Kalra, R. 2006. High-Technology and Urban development in Bengaluru, India. In J. Gatrell and N. Reid (eds.), *Enterprising Worlds: A Geographic Perspective on Economics, Environment and Ethics*, pp. 71–81.Netherlands: Springer.

Kalra, R. 2003. *Linguistic Diversity Changes in India: 1971–1991*, M.A Thesis, Department of Geography and Planning, University of Akron, Akron, USA.

Khubchandani, L.M. 1993. India as a Socio-linguistic Area. In A. Ahmad (ed.), *Social Structure and Regional Development: A Social Geography Perspective*, Jaipur: Rawat Publications.

Noble, A.G. and Dutt, A.K. (eds.) 1982. *India: Cultural Patterns and Processes*, Boulder, Colorado: Westview Press

Rodgers, A. 1957. 'Some aspects of industrial diversification in the United States'. *Economic Geography* 33 (Jan.), pp. 16–30.

Sekhar, C.A. 1971. *Social and Cultural Tables*, Census of India 1971, Series 1, India Part II-C i.

Sengupta, P. 2009. 'Endangered Languages: Some Concerns', *Economic and Political Weekly*, 44(32), pp. 17–19.

Tress, R.C. 1938. 'Unemployment and the Diversification of Industry'. *The Manchester School* 9, pp. 140–152.

United Nations Educational Scientific and Cultural Organization (UNESCO), 2010. *Atlas of the World's Languages in Danger*, United Nations Educational, Scientific & Cultural Organization, 3 Revised edition.

Warf, B. and Winsberg, M. 2008. 'The Geography of Religious Diversity in the United States', *The Professional Geographer*, 60(3), pp. 413–424.

18

The Geography of Folk Art in India

E. COTTON MATHER AND P. P. KARAN

With a few notable exceptions, cultural geographers have neglected the study of one of the most comprehensive spheres of human activity – vernacular or folk art, which embodies a complete record of man's life, work and experience. For both its materials and techniques, folk art depends on the character of a place as it expresses the physical and cultural environment as well as the distinctive mental perceptions of the people. As manifestation of human experience and aspirations, folk art is woven from the values and general patterns of life and culture of the people and as such, forms an aesthetic canvas that portrays the interactive elements of regional character.

The geography of art attempts to study various art forms as: (a) an expression of a region's physical, socioeconomic and cultural setting, and the people's distinctive values that orient, articulate or explain the culture, and (b) a record of a regional culture, an unerring clue to the life, experience and aspirations of a people. It is not concerned with dates, titles, names and biographies or with the sensuous value of works of art as individual independent objects. Rather it addresses itself to the physical and social conditions of origin and operation of a work of art, to the background of regional economic and cultural factors and forces that condition the forms of art and affect its motifs and themes, and also to its meaning in a given cultural region with all its aspirations, experiences and fulfillments. Art is viewed as the autobiography of a culture, expressing fully and profoundly the ideas, sentiments and faith of a region.

Folk art emphasizes not an individual's expression, but the expression of a cultural group rooted in its pattern of living and conditioned by its experiential interpretation of the character of the place. It represents a fusion of the environmental and metaphysical realms. Thus, it portrays the regional personality and serves as a beacon to its culture. While the political and economic framework of an area may change, the attitudes and values that vernacular art of a region records, and by which its cultural geography can be understood, remain vivid and eloquent. Folk art thus epitomizes and symbolizes the regional culture. It records the cultural heritage, transcendence, vitality, values and attitudes of the area within the context of its social milieu. The folk arts portray the visions and values of each major cultural region, and unfold the interaction between art and the physical, social and intellectual conditions in each region (Chattopadhyay, 1977). Each cultural region has evolved its own motifs and symbols of art depending upon the social, philosophical and religious thought of the area. Folk art may be viewed as a vivid areal tapestry which expresses the personality of a place and depicts the complex social values of its culture, as well as man's relationship to the world around him. Indeed, vernacular or folk art is the most effective and intimate source available to the cultural geographer to provide insight to the attitudes, values and experiences of a people.

From the vast triangle of land thrust out into the Arabian Sea and the Indian Ocean to the mighty bulk of the Himalayas are many modes of folk art expression, as distinctive as the contributions of the various nations of Europe to the culture of the West. The geography of India which helped to preserve her identity was also responsible for the partial isolation in which each major cultural region pursued its own ideals. Though frequently divided among several kingdoms during different historic periods, each region retained its general identity of style and development. This is not to say that there was no exchange between the regions. Each region transmitted ideas and received some influences, but each maintained its distinctive folk art. The art forms of India are vast and varied and differ from region to region as they take on elements from the local setting. In this chapter, one art from – folk painting – is used to illustrate regional patterns of folk art. No attempt is made to discuss all forms and styles of folk paintings in various areas of India; only a few selected examples from each region are used to show the relationship between art and geography. The regional pattern of folk painting in India is represented in Fig. 18.1.

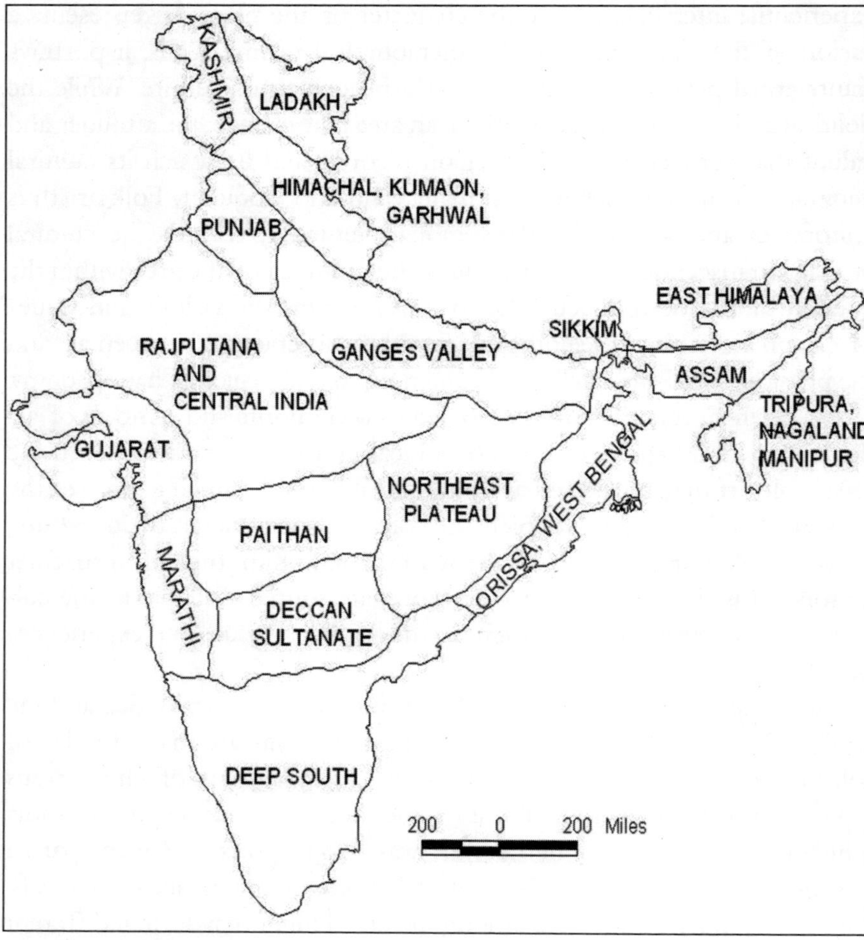

Fig. 18.1 India: Regional patterns of folk painting.

Regional Patterns of Folk Painting

Kashmir

The neat, park-like landscape of the Kashmir Valley and the trimmed gardens of the palaces, associated with the joys of outdoor life celebrated in Kashmiri songs and lyrics form the background of the design of visual arts in Kashmir. The Islamic prohibition of paintings, and especially of plastic representations of natural form, led to the development of geometrical and decorative pattern. The tendency towards conciseness of design and vigorous and subtle formalization became central to the style of Kashmir, as in Southwest Asia (Bamzai 1960; Dhar 1978). Flowers and plants are distilled into their pure geometrical forms and are repeated in elegant, eye-catching traceries on brocades and carpets, on manuscripts and pottery, on screens and friezes and on the columns, gates and architraves of mosques. The unrivalled elegance of form and colour that characterizes Kashmir folk art is the outcome of the search for the delights of the open-air life in the well-trimmed, elegant and bright gardens of the Valley, where people take refuge from the bare walls and crowded streets of the city. The brilliance and solidity of colours reflect not only the ever recurrent sharp, seasonal alterations of the landscape, but also the contrast between the blankness and dull monotony of the barren mountains and the luxuriant verdure of the Vale.

While the Muslim artists of Kashmir express their talents in designs and pictures of the flora and fauna of the area and in the portraits of famous personalities, the Hindu artists have concentrated on religious themes such as portraiture of the ten incarnations of Vishnu, the paintings of the Goddess Durga and the depiction of Shiva. However, the influence of Kashmiri landscape, dress and form dominate these paintings.

Ladakh, Sikkim and Darjeeling

The unique imagery of Lamaist Buddhism characterizes painting in the Tibetan culture and area of Ladakh, Sikkim and Darjeeling Himalayas. Two types of Lamaist imagery which express Tibetan culture are those of apotheosized Lamas and saints and of terrifying deities (Karan and Mather, 1976). Each Himalayan Buddhist monastery has its pantheon of Lamas. Most are idealized as divine figures, rather than reasonable likenesses of the persons portrayed. The grotesque and bizarre forms of terrifying deities painted by the artists on the *thangka*, or scroll paintings on cotton cloths, are a peculiar feature of Lamaist art. These images which have been interpreted as a release from psychic and culture tensions, illustrate the fears of people who reside in an inhospitable physical environment. The consistent order and harmony in the design of the *mandala* structure is the most complete and complex expression of the Tibetan's perception of cosmic reality (Karan and Mather, 1976). The *mandala's* design is geometrically precise, and its colours are always strong and luminous. To the Tibetan Buddhist, the phenomenal world is one of chaos and tension. The *mandala* is an attempt to project order and harmony into that world. It is an effective and graphic visualization of a world that exists in the mind of the people of the Ladakh and Sikkim Himalayas.

Eastern Himalayas, Manipur, Tripura and Nagaland

The folk painting of the tribal region of the eastern Himalayas displays less sophisticated aesthetic sense and a less complex medium of expression. The most common form of art is drawing on wood (Elwin, 1948). The entrance to the houses have some crude and simple drawings on the wooden frame, with some dots and lengthwise lines displayed in an unstructured way. Figures and lines are drawn with pine resin, the essence of which gives black dye.

The elaborate and elegant folk design called *Akoybi* in Manipur tells the story of a legendry snake, *Pakhamba*. *Akoybi* means circular and in the painting one circle joins the other, each being further broken into patterns with a significant motif. The colours used in *Akoybi* are two shades of red, as though one were the reflection of the other, with a little black and just a touch of white. Animal motifs dominate the art. A whole array of wild animals is represented against a black background divided into horizontal panels.

The sieves and winnowing fans of the people of this region are exquisitely decorated with folk art (Chattopadhyaya, 1959). The colourful bamboo and leaf headgear, made all over the area, illustrates another attractive folk art. Umbrella handles made of bamboo are also used for folk painting. A number of designs are etched on the handle in swift and deft strokes, bringing out leaves, creepers and plant motifs. In Tripura, painting is also done on screens made of finely split bamboo. The usual motifs are trees, creepers, animals, birds, stylized human forms and geometrical designs.

Himachal Pradesh, Kumaon and Garhwal

The hill states of the Punjab Himalayas, now merged in Himachal Pradesh, Kumaon and the Garhwal Himalayas contained a number of principalities founded by Rajput princes. Located in fertile valleys, these principalities were flanked by high ranges, thick forests and placid mountain lakes within which developed distinctive art forms. In folk painting the colouring is simple and soft and the overall effect is very pleasing. The painter draws inspiration from the Hindu epics, religious legends as well as popular folk stories. The paintings are characterized by a sensitive appreciation of the Himalayan landscape and the flowering countryside. They reveal the lyrical grace and the delicate sentiments of the artist. Painted scrolls depict epics, wars and exploits of hill chieftains.

The folk artists revel in the delineation of the penances of Shiva and the devotions and activities of Shakti in her varied manifestations in the austere and rugged background of the Himalayas. A fusion of spiritual and humanistic values and outlook gives rise to a supreme manifestation of creative art and experience in this region. Kailash, the Himalayan home of Shiva and Parvati, looms large in the folk paintings. The Himalayan landscape with jagged cliffs, deodar trees, snow-covered ranges and torrential streams are portrayed with great vividness. The folk art embodies a profound and delicate assimilation of transcendental and human values.

The symbolism of the love of Radha and Krishna finds wide expression in the wall paintings of Himachal Pradesh. The scenes are tense and aglow. Radha waits expectantly for Krishna, clothes in disarray through restless movements of impatience and eyes distended with pensive apprehension. The scene is heightened by lotus flowers languishing in a pool. Sometimes besides Radha there is a *gopi*, competing for Krishna's favours with a coy look and a pout on her lips. The earth is shown red with mature trees in full bloom and inviting fresh grass.

In Kumaon, the usual wall pictures are known as *bar boond* (dash and dot). The pattern is made by putting down a number of dots to make the outline of the design, then joining them together by lines in different colors (Upreti, 1957). It calls for intense concentration and immense patience, for an error in a single dot or dash can upset the entire composition. A simple, but very moving, picture is made every spring called *Nata Gandhana*, 'tying the knot of kinship'. Row upon row of grains are shown standing up side by side, symbolizing prosperity. The ears of the grain are joined to show intimacy and concord. The overall effect is of an imposing structure, executed in perfect symmetry.

Kumaon is also noted for its *pattas*, special pictures made on festival days depicting different deities, as also the deity's various aspects that are worshipped on this occasion. Large in size and running from one end of the wall to the other, they are divided into sections as they narrate long and involved stories. The wall paintings made in Kumaon to mark family rituals, like naming a child, the sacred thread ceremony, marriage and the like, have their basic designs around *Jiva Matrikas*, which means mother of living beings. The goddesses Kali, Lakshmi and Saraswati are painted as embodiments of the three powers, while Ganesh is there as the remover of obstacles, as also the Sun, giver of light. Two extreme borders at the top and bottom represent the Himalayas.

Assam

In Assam and North Bengal where rainfall is copious and natural and drainage defective, reeds grow in abundance in many swamps. The local people carve out the solid reed or join the different pieces together to make images, masks, toys, birds and interesting animal forms. They also scoop out the pith to paint on it images of gods and goddesses from the Hindu pantheon and characters from religious as well as profane legends. The lines on these folk paintings are bold and the colours soak into the surface to give it an overall soft tone which is the special charm of paintings on pith.

West Bengal and Orissa

In Bengal, painting, as a medium of cultural expression, developed in complete independence from the conventions of temple art and free from the influences of a royal court (Dey and Irwin, 1946–47; Dev, 1959). The painted scrolls and *pat* of rural Bengal represent one of the ancient folk arts surviving down to the present century (Ganguly, 1956). In the villages of 24-Parganas, Bankura, Midnapore, Birbhum and Burdwan, one still meets the *patuas* selling their *pats* – small, square illustrations – at village fairs. Painted usually on paper of the cheapest variety, sometimes even old newspapers, the *pats* represent themes from mythological stories, especially the dance of Krishan with the milkmaids and Ramachandra's fight with Ravana (Ghosh, 1945).

Pats from Orissa portray Jagannath, the Lord of the Universe, worshipped in the famous temple at Puri (Srinivasarao, 1960). The pilgrims who have flocked to Puri for centuries from every corner of India take back home a suitable memento, a Jagannath *pat*, to remind them of the Lord. The *pat* artists of Orissa also tackle secular subjects and manage to preserve the innocence of their inspiration, the vivacity of the colours and the peculiarly Orissan exuberance of the ornamentation. The painting is done on cloth which the artists prepare by coating the cloth with a mixture of chalk and gum made from tamarind seeds to give the surface a kind of leathery finish on which they paint with earth and stone colours.

Aesthetically, folk painting on pottery rates high in Bengal and Orissa. An interesting earthenware known as *Sakera hari*, is decorated with a variety of colours after baking. In another variety the painting is done on the raw pot with different kinds of clay, and colours then burned in.

The womenfolk of Bengal and Orissa design and stitch tattered rags into large and small-sized cloths and quilts (*kanthas*) and the visual symbols show lotus buds, trees, flowers, leaves, the sun, and animal and human figures, as well as scenes from Bengali *Mangala Kavyas* (Ganguly, 1956). The inner field has exquisite shades and the cloth is framed by a sari-border weaving pattern. The *kanthas* made in Bengal are characterized by great elaboration and flexibility of designs exhibiting clear and vigorous rhythms.

Northeast Plateau

The Santhals and other tribal people of the Northeast Plateau, who are widely scattered among the forests of Bihar, Orissa and Madhya Pradesh, build their houses with thick mud walls which provide canvas for some remarkable wall paintings. The Santhal paintings done by women, are geometrical, and their design makes them unusually fascinating (Bose, 1925). Their purpose is essentially aesthetic; to make the Santhal cottage a more cheerful place in which to live or to give it a new look before a wedding or a festival. The special charm of Santhal painting lies in the total absence of self-consciousness, in the simplicity of its vision. The resultant product is art in its most vernacular form, replete with vitality.

While the Santhals paint on white background, other tribes such as the Saoras, who live in the beautiful hills of Koraput and Ganjam, work on walls washed with a red clay, in paints made of white rice powder or black ash (Elwin, 1951). The pictures are painted in honour of the dead, to avert disease and to celebrate certain festivals. They are especially interesting as they are inspired by dreams and portray what the artist has visualized about the afterlife.

Ganges Valley

In the ancient cities of the Ganges Valley, and beyond them on the roads that link the still unsophisticated townships together, a distinctive style of folk painting persists (Bonnerjea, 1930; Bose, 1951). On the outskirts of cities such as Varanasi, Gaya, Allahabad, Ayodhya, Mathura and Hardwar, the walls of numerous temples, *dharamshalas* (free guesthouses for pilgrims) *akharas* (wrestling arenas) and *manyu* humble homes are gaily painted with what look like huge prints, composed in bold lines and filled with vivid colours. Paintings are executed on house walls to mark a marriage, an important social celebration or just to welcome an honoured guest. The painters prefer bright colours which are rarely mixed and there is very little shading. A preliminary sketch in bare outlines is sometimes drawn with a chalk, but artists with years of experience paint images straightaway with the brush, their sense of colour and proportion rarely failing them. Characters from religious legends predominate, but there are also floral patterns, birds and animals, and soldiers riding out to battle or on guard duty. Minor variations in style exist according to the social status of the patron and the locality.

In front of village homes the women draw circular patterns with a white liquid paste of ground rice (*alipana*) representing the pedestal of Lakshmi, the Goddess of Wealth. The footsteps of the Goddess are always painted and paths leading from the footsteps to the granaries. In various *alipana* designs, the sun, moon, stars, Shiva and Parvati on Mount Kailash, and Vishnu and Lakshmi on lotus leaves, as well as various heroes of the epics, are reproduced with great originality and imagination in white, red, green, yellow and black colours.

Another set of wall paintings are made by Muslim women of the Upper Ganges Valley who eschew figurative work, even animals, confining themselves to abstract designs and geometrical patterns that have no ritualistic connotations. An air of exuberant creativity pervades them, a desire to bring beauty into dull and drab mud habitations. These creations shows an innate sense of rhythm and design, sensitivity to the gambols of light and shade. Above all, they are subtly integrated into the entire structure, as though it were an original part of the house. The houses of the Meos on the outskirts of Delhi have typical wall paintings of this nature (Mago, 1963).

A unique form of decoration, a by-product of Indo–Islamic art, is ornamental writing in the Arabic script or Tughra calligraphy. These varied forms, including animals and birds, are made up by the use of letters. They may seem fanciful but are most effective. Sometimes a camel or a horse composed of these letters may contain a whole holy address or the sayings of some great sage. Often used as wall decorations, they are embellished by flora and fauna and make a most attractive wall painting.

Folk painting is also done on pottery in many areas of the Ganges Valley. For instance, near Varanasi decorated pots are made in flashy colours for marriages and festivals. The designs are mainly of animals, the tiger being prominent, together with leaves and flowers.

In the Middle Ganges Valley, the districts of Darbhanga, Muzaffarpur, parts of Monghyr, Bhagalpur and Saharsa, and the southern districts of the Nepal Terai form a distinct culture area called Mithila. Maithili is the literary language of the area and Mithila has an artistic tradition of its own as represented by the paintings done on mud walls by women of brahmin and *kayastha* families (Archer, 1949; Mishra, 1960; Mathur, 1966). These wall paintings are done in homemade colours from cinnabar, orpiment and vegetable matter, mixed with oil, water and milk, and applied with a brush made out of a the rag or with grass. Lampblack is used for dark shading. Favourite subjects include various gods and goddesses, floral and ornamental patterns, and animal forms, executed at the entrance, on the walls of a corridor, or in the room where the family deity is worshipped. There is hardly anything to surpass the intricacy and the exuberance of the designs done inside the bridal chamber at the bride's home, where a newly-married couple resides for at least one week. Over the centuries, Mithila wall paintings have retained their vitality and creativity which continues to be expressed in vivid forms with an uplifting quality.

Punjab

Wall paintings of deities, flowers and birds are usually made at festivals and special occasions such as weddings. *Devi* (Goddess) figures of Goddess Durga, locally called *Sanjhi*, are made during the Dusserah festival in October. After a wall has been neatly plastered with a kind of clay applique technique, the Sanjhi image is created by fixing star-shaped pieces of clay, which are first painted white, then given touches of orange, blue and yellow to make the *devi* a rich ensemble. The entire picture is a highly colourful mosaic. This process is largely a community activity and several women jointly produce the image. The body itself is abstract, yet the face is most expressive. The image is richly decorated with ornaments deftly made out of limestone and clay, topped by feathers, mirrors, stars and spangles or any shiny object for embellishment. Most interesting is the close identification between the *devi* and the women of this area, from the headgear down to the feet. Even a support for holding the pot on the head, commonly used by women, is placed on this figure. The entire composition is done with a free hand without drawing lines or measuring; nevertheless, its relationship to the size of the wall is remarkably balanced and the colours are harmoniously blended (Mago, 1978).

Rajputana and the Central Indian Upland

Feudal chiefs fought numerous wars in ancient Rajasthan and Central India, often amongst themselves to establish their kingdoms; later, to hold their own against external aggressors. Two essentially feudal qualities emerged from this constant participation in warfare – (a) chivalry, and (b) a deep regard for the honour of the clan. These, coupled with the tender feelings of the soldier for the sweetheart he had left behind at home, were the favourite themes of the bards of Rajasthan and Malwa, and the perennial sources of inspiration to the folk painters.

At another level, yet no less important, was the great Vaishnava revival of the fifteenth century which appealed to prince and peasant alike and proclaimed that the path to salvation lay in the worship of Krishna. Episodes from the life of Lord Krishna provide powerful inspiration for a great deal of artistic activity. The environment helped to nurture the traditional spirit of mystical pantheism, symbolism and detachment in painting, a vernacular folk art inspired by the renaissance of popular Hinduism in which the old metaphysical conceptions of the oneness of life and the immanence of the Divine are brought home to the rural masses by Hindi poetry, music and painting in terms of the popular Radha–Krishna motifs (Maduro *et al.*, 1976). Folk painting has been brought into close association with the daily routine and toil of life, the ordinary happiness and sorrow of man and woman. Regional landscapes with flowering mango, *champka* and *kadamba* trees, lakes with rose lotuses, green meadows with deer, cranes and peacocks, sunshine, heavy clouds and thunderstorms characterize the paintings of Rajputana and Malwa. Here the integration of the values of nature, metaphysics and concrete daily experience is more profound. The nuances of human love, the modes of melody and the elements of landscape all become perfectly fused in the folk painting. Rajasthan landscape art reveals the infinite in human loves, delights and sorrows. Thus, the region, metaphysics and collective feeling and vision of the people blend in the creation of art.

Gujarat

The Jain community played a very important role in the development of art in Gujarat (Fischer and Jain, 1977). According to tradition, the nobility and the moneyed classes in Gujarat established libraries, Jain *gyana bhandars* (literally storehouses of knowledge). They also commissioned artists to produce illuminated versions of the Jain sacred texts for these libraries, on palm leaf, paper or cloth and bound with wooden covers. The idiom of manuscript illustration served Jain and Hindu religious texts equally well and even extended to secular compositions. A cultured and affluent middle class, which flourished on commerce, gradually took over the patronage of art from the nobility. Folk paintings were produced for a popular market. Some of these reflected the life of the ordinary people who crowded to the many centres of pilgrimage in Gujarat, and offered glimpses into domestic interiors and interesting commentaries on dress and living habits. The 'market scene' in its iconography and atmosphere truly represents contemporary Gujarat as seen by an ordinary artist, who retained the old penchant for decorative borders and brilliant colour schemes.

In Gujarat, folk painting is also done on pottery. The pumpkin-shaped kitchen vessel is covered with floral designs in a naturalistic, stylized way, while on the neck of the vessel a plant is made to rest with leaves on either side of the central stem. It is presumed that here the painter's intention is to create an illusion that this plant is growing amidst wide shrubbery. Another popular design is a row of deer or swans or elephants or even tiny clusters of seeds around the concave of any bowl.

Local artists of Saurashtra execute frescos with vigour, covering large areas in vivid water colours, painting the rulers, soldiers and politicians with a keen eye for detail and for varying moods and tempos. Known as *Shilawat*, this style of painting is found today in Jamnagar, Dwarka, Junagardh and Bhavnagar on the walls of old residential buildings and even on mud walls, which portray huge paintings on mythological subjects, particularly the Krishna legends. Huge rocks in the hillocks also provide rural artists with a free canvas to paint on mythological themes and to record their impressions of village life.

Marathi

Written and illustrated on handmade paper, an astrological chart or horoscope has always been considered an important document. It is not only an elaborate forecast outlining the subject's career with biographical fidelity, but also a work of art in Maharashtra. The sun, moon, major planets and signs of the zodiac are depicted on the chart strictly as described in authoritative astrological texts. The paintings indicate a highly developed rural culture and a typically Marathi way of handling the brush. The human types in the art are so representative that a fully laid out astrological chart may be considered an interesting social document.

Contrasted with the astrological charts are the scenes of rural life depicted on village house walls, which exhibit man's delight in the pleasure of the senses and enjoyment of beauty on the one hand, and the impermanence of life and the injustice, cruelty and disaster that may come out of earthly desires and passions on the other.

Paithan

The Deccan Plateau is the home of a peculiar folk style of painting, remarkable for its originality and boldness of brushwork. The style is a fusion of the art of the miniaturist with that of the temple muralist, and the angularities of the drawings indicate a kinship with the not too distant Ellora (Chinmulgund, 1962). The subjects treated are from Hindu religious legends and the epics, village belles attending to their daily chores and other scenes from village life.

Folk art in this region is more intuitive and mystical, saturated with a sense of the infinitude of nature and of human destiny. One senses the poise and tranquility of the universe in which man is treated as an inseparable part. The rigidity of lines and crystallization of forms, as well as the stylization, translates man's inner poise and harmonious adjustment with the universe. Feudal styles and temple traditions, variously blended, have sunk into the fabric of the local practice of art. The brightly coloured, stylistic flowers, swans, parrots, and peacocks on the handloomed fabrics of this area also reflected a distinctive folk art.

Deccan Sultanate

A distinct influence of Islam pervades the folk painting in the Deccan, a product of luxury and ease developed under the Deccan Sultanates. By the end of the seventeenth century the Rajput forces sojourning in the Deccan with the army of Aurangzeb created a fusion of Rajasthan, Mughal and Deccani traditions. Folk paintings reflect this 'southern synthesis' and the simplicity of idiom and narrative skill.

Amongst certain groups in Andhra Pradesh, the practice of carrying a wooden box with the idol of the village deity on it persists. It is finely decorated with paintings in folk style using mainly red, blue and yellow colours. The common theme is built around *Yamaloka*, the world of the dead, and stories from ancient books. Folk paintings on cloth took very definite form in the Deccan, where the hand painted, dyed cloth known as *chintz* was originally made in Golconda, near Hyderabad City (Beer, 1970). This art spread along the eastern coast of India up to Tamil Nadu, with a major concentration at Masulipatnam. Paintings on cotton comprised a dazzling array of exotic flowers and foliage mostly in red, blue, purple, yellow and black.

This region is also noted for its *kalamkari* (picturization on cloth). They are exclusively hand-painted fabrics, used as tapestries and hangings in temples. Here vegetable dyes of deep rich shades are used with strong outlines in brown and black, all of which produce a bold and striking effect. The outlines of the drawing are traced out by freehand from memory. The final lines of the picture are drawn with a sharply pointed bamboo stick. The artist first fills in the background colours, then the various figures. Female figures are usually in yellow, gods in blue, demons in red and green, and some are left unpainted. The paintings are made up in panels, each depicting a story from the epic. The large ones narrate an entire story, the smaller ones important events such as Sita's marriage. The figures have a unique quality as forms take shape under the simple, free movement of the artist's hand.

The Deep South

In the deep South, the paintings of gods and goddesses on the small shrines in Tamil Nadu and on temple floors in Kerala, done with coloured powders, have all the vitality of folk paintings. The flat leather cutouts used for shadow plays in Karnataka are gorgeously painted articles of exquisite folk craftsmanship. Throughout the South, there is a shrine of Lord Ayanar in almost every Tamil village. Pottery horses, dogs and elephants are offered by the villagers as steeds for the god, who rides round the fields to drive out agricultural pests, blights, diseases and evil spirits. Potters show their skill and artistry in making these animal images. Village gates, guesthouses and temples, as well as places of family worship, show a rich variety of artistic decoration. On the walls the scenes of the epics, as well as the varied assortment of popular folklore and tradition, are treated as themes for painting. In the peasant's home, doorways and windows are carved and the clean earthen walls show paintings of animals, trees, swastika, trident and other symbols. In style they follow the patterns set by Chola images.

Ritualistic decorative designs called *kolam* are executed in the courtyard or the floor of the house in southern India. In south Kanara even the kitchens are decorated with *kolam* designs. The Chola rulers in the South made use of *kolam* floor designs extensively. These decorations, done mainly by women, are among the most expressive of folk arts.

The Tanjore area has developed a tradition of its own in folk painting on wood. The themes, which are from the epics, are naturalistic in outline, with perfect harmony and rhythm in the composition and colour blending. Though normally bright shades are used, Krishna is sometimes shown partly in white with little patches of colour. The speciality of these paintings lies in their ornamentation. With the use of gold leaves, gilt metal pieces and coloured stones, traditional jewellery pieces are reproduced on the bodies of these paintings until they are completely covered with adornment. While the faces are pleasing and expressive, they all conform to a standard pattern. The skill lies in composing and working out the ornamentation, especially with the balancing of the gold leaf and the coloured stones.

Fine specimens of folk painting on wood can be seen in some of Kerala's churches, whose rich wood carvings are embellished by appropriate colours. The foliage, floral designs, raiments of the personages depicted, wooden structures, borders of balconies, pedestals, all stand out festively, each harmoniously blending into the other like tones in an orchestra.

In the districts of Ramnathapuram, Tirunelveli and Kanyakumari, palm leaf products such as fans, mats and baskets are used for delicate artistic folk painting with abstract animal, bird and geometrical designs.

Conclusion

The regional patterns of Indian folk art coincide broadly with Spate's map of India's major cultural zones and 'perennially important historical structure-lines' (Spate, 1961). Vernacular art of India holds up a mirror to the distinctive geographical, behavioural and social environment of the area in which it exists. Spatial, ecological and cultural aspects of vernacular art should provide a major focus in Indian cultural geography. The study of folk art in India can give the necessary key for opening the door to new conceptions in cultural geography. As one of the most telling vehicles for the propagation and implementation of culture, which is the key to understanding behaviour, folk art is among the most interesting of man's creations.

Acknowledgements

The authors wish to acknowledge their sincere appreciation to M. Ali (Udhampur, Kashmir), N. P. Apte (Satara, Maharashtra), K. C. Barua (Guwahati, Assam), P. C. Dillon (Hissar, Haryana), R. N. Dixit (Bara Banki, Uttar Pradesh), K. M. George (Trivandrum, Kerala), D. P. Joshi (Akola, Maharashtra), K. L. Mehta (Baroda, Gujarat), R. N. Mehrotra (Hardwar, Uttar Pradesh), M. Mohanty (Puri, Orissa), B. N. Mukharji (Krishnanagar, West Bengal), S. Raghavan (Madurai, Tamil Nadu), C. Reddy (Masulipatnam, Andhra Pradesh), L. C. Sharma (Chamba, Himachal Pradesh), J. Singh (Bhatinda, Punjab), J. N. Singh (Jaipur, Rajasthan), R. N. Sukla (Dwarka, Gujarat), V. T. Tiwari (Raigarh, Madhya Pradesh), P. Verma (Guna, Madhya Pradesh) and L. N. Yadav (Darbhanga, Bihar) for facilitating field work in different areas of India and assistance in taking photographs of works of folk art.

Note

This chapter has been reproduced from Noble, A. G. and Dutt, A. K., *India: Cultural Patterns and Processes*, Boulder, CO: Westview, 1982, pp. 165–94, with permission from the copyright owners.

References

Archer, W. G., 'Maithil Painting', *Marg*, Vol. 3, No. 3, 1949, pp. 24–33.

Aryan, K. C., *Punjab Murals*, New Delhi: Rekha Prakashan, 1978.

Bamzai, P. N. K., 'Kashmir Valley Paintings', *March of India*, Vol. 12, July 1960, pp. 23–24.

Beer, Alice Baldwin, *Trade Goods: A Study of Indian Chintz*, Washington, DC: Smithsonian Institution Press, 1970.

Bonnerjea, B., 'Notes on Geometrical Ritual Designs in India', *Man*, Vol. 33, 1930, pp. 163–164.

Bose, P. N., 'Three Specimens of Santal Drawings', *Man in India*, Vol. 5, 1925, pp. 235–236.

Bose, S. K., 'Fold Art of Uttar Pradesh', *March of India*, Vol. 3, No. 10, October, 1951, pp. 27–28.

Chattopadhyaya, K. P., 'Art of Tribal Folk', *Journal of the Assam Research Society*, Vol. 13, 1959, pp. 34–36.

Chinmulgund, P. J., 'Paithan Painting', *Times of India Annual*, 1962, pp. 67–72.

Chattopadhyay, K., 'The Ecology of Folk Art', *Indian Horizons*, Vol. 26, No. 2, 1977, pp. 5–7.

Dev, C., 'An Outline of the Folk Art of Bengal', *Indian Folklore*, July–September 1959, pp. 196–205.

Dey, B. and John Irwin, 'The Folk Art of Bengal', *Marg*, Vol. 1, No. 4, 1946–47, pp. 45–54.

Dhar, Somnath, 'Folk Arts of Kashmir and Central Asia', *Indian and Foreign Review*, 1 July 1978), pp. 21–22.
Elwin, V., 'Saora Pictographs', *Marg*, Vol. 2, No. 3, 1948, pp. 35–44.
Elwin, V., *Tribal Art of Middle India*, Bombay: Oxford University Press, 1951.
Elwin, V., *The Art of the North-East Frontier of India*, Shillong: Director of Information, NEFA, 1959, p. 52.
Fischer, Eberhard and Jyotindra Jain, *Art and Rituals: 2500 Years of Jainism in India*, New Delhi: Sterling Publishers Pvt. Ltd., 1977.
Ganguli, K. K., 'Kantha, The Enchanted Wrap', *Indian Folklore*, April–June, 1958, pp. 3–10.
Ganguly, R. N., 'Patas and Patuas of Bengal', *Indian Folklore*, April–August, 1956, p. 60.
Ghosh, D. P., 'An Illustrated Ramayana Manuscript and Patas from Bengal', *Journal of the Indian Society of Oriental Art*, Vol. 13, 1945, pp. 130–138.
Ghosh, D. P., 'Folk Art of Orissa', *Indian Folklore*, April–August 1956, pp. 73–77.
Karan, P.P. and Cotton Mather, 'Art and Geography: Patterns in the Himalaya', *Annals of the Association of American Geographers*, Vol. 66, 1976, pp. 487–515.
Maduro, R., *Artistic Creativity in a Brahmin Painter Community*, Research Monograph Series, Berkeley, California: University of California, Center for South and Southeast Asian Studies, 1976.
Maduro, R., 'The Brahmin Painters of Nathdwara, Rajasthan', in Nelson H. H. Graburn (ed.), *Ethnic and Tourist Arts: Cultural Expressions from the Fourth World*, Berkeley: University of California Press, 1976, pp. 226–244.
Mago, Pran Nath, 'Murals and Mosaics from Villages Around Delhi', *Design*, pp. 22–25, 1978.
Mago, Pran Nath, 'Wall Paintings by Punjabi Peasants', *Design*, October 1963, pp. 33–36.
Mathur, J.C., 'Domestic Arts of Mithila', *Marg*, Vol. 20, No. 1, 1966, pp. 43–46.
Mishra, S., 'The Folk Art of Mithila', *Folklore*, September–October 1960, pp. 319–324.
Spate, O. H. K., in W. G. East and O. H. K. Spate (eds.), *The Changing Map of Asia*, New York: E. P. Dutton, 1961, pp. 127–130.
Srinivasarao, N., 'Folk Art of Orissa', *Folklore*, No. 3, May–June 1960, pp. 114–147.
Upreti, N. R., *Folk Art of Kumaon*, Amsterdam: Department of Anthropology, Royal Tropical Institute, 1957, pp. 7–9.

19

Indian Dance: Classical Unity and Regional Variation

MANJUSRI CHAKI-SIRCAR AND PARBATI K. SIRCAR

In the social environment of rigid hierarchy, the performing arts of India served to bridge the gap between the intellectual Sanskritic tradition and the popular folk tradition. Ancient Brahminic tradition forbade Sanskrit learning to the non-initiates, that is all those who were not 'twice-born'.[1] This restriction applied to all women generally, including those from the brahmin caste. Although the so-called 'high tradition' kept its doors closed against intellectual pursuits by common people, the latter enjoyed some measure of spiritual experience through theatre, dance, folklore, oral literature and other aesthetic media.

The most respected scripture of dance and drama, the *Natyasastra*, written by the Sanskritic scholar, Bharata, is so fundamental that it has become known as the fifth Veda.[2] Dancing, like other arts, became recognized as a spiritual experience. In fact, the performing arts provide a source of religious education to the common people, as well as serve as channels for mass communication of moral and ethical values, gained through commonly shared aesthetic experience.

The dance theatre of India represents a blending of 'high' and 'folk' traditions. All classical schools of Indian dance rely on the textual foundation of the scriptures, either of Bharata or of Sanskritic scholars. Dance *gurus* often refer to these texts in order to defend and protect their art. In fact, the very word 'classical' has some prestige attached to it, inasmuch as it signifies closeness to the 'high' tradition. However, each of the classical styles has evolved so as to have distinctiveness with regard to technique, form, musical expression and costume and, above all, the presentation of the Sanskritic themes.

On a regional level we recognize dance as an expression of the moral and aesthetic spirit of local culture. To analyse the uniqueness of each style, we need to study the physical and cultural environment of the people, their historical experience and their geographical relationship to external influences. These studies can illuminate a vital element of regional culture and their power to assimilate the 'high' tradition and to modify the latter into something of their own.

Such an examination of the regional dance culture bears witness to a very vital force operative in Indian society, one that has enabled India not merely to adapt to external influences, but to modify these to suit her own genius. The Sanskritic influence was thus not able to submerge the distinctiveness of regional dance styles, rather it interacted with the latter to flourish in diverse ways.

Regionalization of the Krishna Theme in Dance

From the vast repertoire of Sanskritic themes the most popular one – the Radha–Krishna theme – may be selected to illustrate the striking variation on the original love episode that developed in regional dancing. In Kathak, the classical style of dancing of northern India, Krishna appears as a Mughal prince, a sophisticated and sensuous lover. In Manipuri style, in northeastern India, Krishna is presented as a seven to eight year old cowherd in innocent love-play. In Kathakali of southwestern India, Krishna is shown as a powerful, strong and heroic personality. In Bharatanatyam, the female dance style of southwestern India, the dancer assumes the role of Krishna without taking his physical form. She can transform herself with facial expressions, characteristic postures and symbolic gestures. This interesting and significant variation in Krishna's form and role is recognizable not only in costume, make-up and dance technique, but also in the interpretation of the philosophy behind the legend.

Four Major Classical Schools of Indian Dance

This chapter focusses on the four major classical schools of Indian dance[3] and attempts to analyse their regional distinctiveness against the context of pan-Indian unity. Although these are regional schools, nowadays in large cities such as Mumbai (Bombay), Kolkata (Calcutta) and Delhi, one can experience them all through professional performers and teachers. These days Indian dancers often cross regional boundaries to study dances of other regions.

Kathak

In northern India the dominant classical dance style is Kathak. The word 'Kathak' means a storyteller, entertaining people with sacred mythologies, epical stories and folklore. In North India, the Ganges plain has experienced many foreign invasions usually coming through the northwestern mountain passes and fanning out across the riverine plains. Through the ages, the culture of northern India thus always had to adjust to newly introduced foreign elements. These experiences brought new dimensions to ancient artistic life.

Kathak dancing flourished most vigorously in Lucknow and Jaipur. The Lucknow school shows a more secular and entertaining quality, since it was greatly influenced by Muslim court patronage. This style flourished in North Indian royal courts from the fifteenth through eighteenth centuries. The Jaipur style, which developed away from such direct Islamic patronage, evinces a more religious flavour. Nevertheless, the influence of Islamic culture is still to be found in it.

The romantic love of Radha and Krishna is a favourite theme in Kathak. In the latter period of Islamic rule, the idea of Sufism spread over India. Sufism, the mystic philosophy of Islam, had come to India from Persia in the tenth century. At first the Sufis lived in Sind and Punjab, but later they migrated to Gujarat, the Deccan and Bengal and gradually became greatly influenced by Hinduism, especially Vaishnava philosophy. Individual personal devotion tended to become the basis for worship. Many devout Muslims, influenced by Sufism, became more tolerant of the Hindu way of worship, the devotion to Krishna and Radha. During the fifteenth and sixteenth centuries, along with the Bhakti movement, Radha–Krishna stories became popular and the Kathak groups took a fancy to these themes.

Although some of the Hindu performers were well known as great religious devotees, their dancing gave in to the secular approach of the Islamic rulers and patrons who, although serious patrons of this art, did not share the religious ideology behind the dance, nor did they look upon the Radha–Krishna model as an expression of divine love. During the Muslim period many dancers were imported into India from Persia and Central Asia for court entertainment. They had their own style which influenced the local dance and music. The reign of Emperor Akbar (AD 1556–1605) is marked by its enlightened approach to culture, when Kathak took a strong hold in the Mughal court. Very tolerant of other religions and cultures, Akbar married, among others, a Hindu princess and encouraged Hindu music, dancers and other arts. Kathak dancers achieved a high status under his patronage.

The present form of Kathak was established about a century and half ago in Lucknow by distinguished dancers from Rajasthan. The court of the last Nawab of Ayodhya became famous throughout India for the spectacular staging of opera-like dance stories in his luxurious palace, with court dancers, musicians and poets.

In such a luxurious, courtly atmosphere, Krishna was depicted as a mortal man and sensuous lover. The costume was greatly influenced by the Mughal style. Krishna appears in *churidar* (tight pants), embroidered cap and a long *kameez* (shirt), like a fashionable Mughal prince. His consort, Radha, dresses as a Mughal princess.

Bharata's *Natyasastra*, mentioned earlier in this chapter, notes three basic components in dance technique–mood, melody and rhythm–and two forms of dancing–*nrtta* (pure dance) and *nrtya* (acting dance). Kathak incorporates all these components. The presentation usually begins with an invocation. As it proceeds it becomes geared to the audience's verbal appreciation and exclamation. The dancer and the tabla player often go into a mock contest in speed and in complexities of rhythm. The performer is very conscious of the immediate response of the audience. The dance movement is characterized by a sensuous grace with subtle erotic gestures. The acting is refined and sophisticated. The music is especially composed for the dancing. It stays in the background and keeps in tune with the basic timing. The dancer and the tabla player interplay joint or separate exposition of rhythmic complexities over the basic timing.

During the Muslim period the practice of dancing in northern India, although a popular art, was not regarded as proper for women of good virtue. Dancing girls were professional women and regarded as a special class of entertainers mostly catering to a male audience, while the female population was segregated and kept behind curtains. Islamic influence tended to virtually exclude women from the public sphere. The unequal treatment of the female sex, entrenched in the Hindu social structure, was further accentuated during this period with the segregation of the sexes. The stigma on dancing as a profession has, however, been removed during the twentieth century to a certain extent. This stigma has been further eroded by popular cinema in India, where dance sequences are de rigueur.

In sum, we can say that Kathak, originally a Hindu art, found its present form after having been filtered through the powerful influence of Islamization which swept through northern India. The secularization of this art separated it from the mainstream of religious experience.

Manipuri

Manipuri dancing comes from the Manipur Valley in the state of Manipur, nestled in the northeastern corner of India. Within the Assam–Burma ranges lies the intermontane basin of Manipur, remote from the mainstream of historical and cultural development in India until the fifteenth century, when the Bengali Vaishnava preachers entered the secluded valley. Beginning in the eighteenth century, Manipur has gone through a long process of Hinduization. But despite the resulting transformation of the religious ritual, the indigenous culture has retained its vigour and vitality. Hence, pan-Indian Vaishnavism has found a very different expression in Manipur's socio-cultural environment.

Dance is an integral part of Manipuri religious life. The traditional rituals of the Meiteis, the people of the valley, especially the most important one, *lai harouba* (pleasure of the spirit), are dominated by dancing.[4] Dancing is a spontaneous expression of devotion among the Meiteis. In public rituals, such as the *lai harouba*, all members of the community may join. In the past, while women took a central role, men joined by forming an outer circle. Nowadays this is a rare practice. *Lai harouba* is conducted by a ritual trio consisting of *maiba* (male priest), *pena khongba* (player of a bowed instrument) and *maibee* (priestess), with the maibee taking the most important role. The dancing and chanting of these women priests ranges from an abundant vigour to a tender gentleness.

Female participation is also marked in Vaishnavite festivals. The women are ardent devotees of Krishna and celebrate each full moon by dancing, enacting Krishna's life and his traditional romantic love-play with the milkmaid. A young boy, who has not as yet acquired sexual knowledge, assumes the role of Krishna. The diminutive boy dances and is surrounded by grown women dancing as milkmaids in a spectacular, dazzling costume. Men play *poongs* (drums) and cymbals, sing outside the ritual centre and often, in devotional ecstasy, dance vigorously in *kirtana* (a communal form of worship through song, dance and music introduced from Bengali Vaishnavism).

Women's *kirtana*, known as *nyupi pala*, is quite common[5], in which the oldest living female member of the royal family takes the leading role. The entire *kirtana* is imbued with gentle and noble feminine ecstasy. During the festival of *Jhulanjatra* (July–August), the *nyupi pala* is celebrated all over the valley.

In all of this, the most striking fact is the prominent role assumed by women in public ceremonies, a very unusual feature in South Asian culture. Despite the royal effort toward Brahminization of Manipuri culture, Vaishnavism here had to accommodate within itself an older, traditional role of women as central figures in religious ceremonies. Meitei women have a prominent role in the economic and social life of Manipur, especially in the multi-village network of trade. Women are well known as skilled weavers. As a vast number of women also participate substantially in agriculture, vegetable gardening and fishing, women enjoy a great deal of independence and equality in marriage, divorce and other socio-legal spheres. The role of the woman priest is unique in the classic pattern of any patrilineal society. Men are allowed to officiate as women priests, but they are required to dress up as women! In dancing, there is no bar for the women to take the central role, nor is any stigma attached to this practice.

In Vaishnavite ritual, lyrics were borrowed from the Bengali language, with the Meitei script replaced by that of Bengali. Several brahmins were imported to officiate as Vaishnava priests. But all this had very little influence on Manipuri dance style. The ancient *lai harouba* movements were incorporated in Vaishnava rituals, and under royal patronage the style became more elaborate and refined. The religious movement brought a new vitality to dancing and several dance-plays were composed under the patronage of successive kings.

Manipuri dance technique stands alone among all the classical styles. The concept of *mudra* (symbolic gesture), sculpture-like angular position, stamping footwork, dramatic facial expression, characteristic of all other classical dances of India, are not so important in Manipuri. Originally based on a Meitei text, the style was influenced later by several Sanskirt treatises from Bengal. The classical *nrtra* (pure dance) and *nrtya* (amalgam of both dancing and acting) are combined. There was a conscious effort toward the transformation of a regional style into pan-Indian aesthetics, but the Sanskrit influence has only enhanced the existing style, without transforming it. The use of space in rich choreography, the continuous flow of the unbroken body line, the spring-like motion of the knees, especially the lightness of the footwork, and a special rendering of rhythmic variation are not to be found in any other style. The devotees surrender themselves to their eternal lord in their dancing, which is introvertive, with only the least notion of entertainment. A profound religiosity prohibits having an adult man assuming Krishna's role. In Manipuri, Krishna is a symbolic representation of the divine. A little boy's (or occasionally a woman's) presence as a romantic lover transcends the physical boundaries of earthy emotion.

To the *kirtana*, introduced from Bengal, the Meitei men added an extremely powerful and vigorous ecstatic dancing, which is far more complex and is apparently borrowed from their traditional war dance. Historically, the Meitei were known for their martial skill, having to defend themselves from successive invasions from Burma. Such vigorous dancing, an expression of their physical prowess, is sublimated in the ecstatic *kirtana*.

The traditional costume of *lai harouba* is typically Meitei. Women wear a hand-woven, sarong-like *fanek* and blouse. Men wear the *dhoti*[6] and turban. For the Vaishnava dances a new costume was designed which has no parallel elsewhere. The Vaishnava forehead mark of sandalwood paste and wood beads are worn by all the performers. Manipuri music is greatly inspired by the Hindustani or North Indian school. Nevertheless, it has retained its traditional quality based on its code of tonal composition.

Geographic isolation provided by the Assam–Burmese border ranges helped the Manipuri to preserve much of indigenous quality which later became embellished with the accoutrement of Vaishnava culture imported from Bengal.

Kathakali

Kathakali dance-drama comes from the Malabar coast of southwestern India. Part of India's southern-most state of Kerala, it was an area remote from Islamic imperial influence, but open to foreign influences via the sea. In Kerala there were several traditions of dance-plays performed by men and women of the performer castes, of which *Kuttiyattam* and *Krishnattan* were the two most well known. *Krishnattan*, depicting the legend of Krishna in performances lasting for eight nights, flourished under the royal patronage of the Zamorins of Calicut in the mid-seventeenth century. To rival the Zamorins, the Raja of Kottarakkara had another set of eight plays staged depicting the legend of Rama, which came to be known as *Ramanattam.*

Kathakali was born out of the joint tradition of these plays. But, instead of the members of the performer caste, this new dance was performed only by the *Nayar* warrior caste under the supervision of the *Nambudiri* brahmin caste. By the end of the seventeenth century, Kathakali attained its full flowering. The original Sanskritic text of the traditional plays yielded to the regional language, Malayalam. The costume had a profound change as well. One legend has it that the Raja of north Kottayam had a dream of each class of dramatic characters, in which he could only see their upper bodies. Thus, there is ample variation in the costume for the upper body, but the lower body costumes are designed in a way that they look as if they came out of the sea.

Instead of having the performance in the royal court, Kathakali came to be performed in public before the whole community. In the traditional dance, masks were worn by the performers, who sang and chanted dialogues. In Kathakali, the dancers remain silent, use a complex pattern of numerous hand gestures and wear highly elaborate facial make-up. It is known that the Raja of Kottarakkara once performed in the play without being recognized, such is the transformation through make-up and costume! The musical accompaniment, although persistent, never dominates. The performance is staged during the *Navaratri* festival in honour of the goddess Durga.

Kathakali dance-drama is staged as a ritual. The drama opens with the loud beating of the *kali-kottu* drum. Then follows the chanting of sacred verses in prayer, offering an invocation to the gods for the success of the performance. The initial dance is *todyam*, a devotional dance behind the curtain, after which comes *purappadu*, the starting point of the drama. When these preliminaries are over, the actual dance-drama begins with the enactment of mythical or epical stories through a vast range of symbolic gestures. In Kathakali there are 24 basic *mudras* which can be elaborated to create literally hundreds of *mudras* to develop a simulated speech pattern.[7] Hand gestures are combined with minute variations of facial expression. Drops are placed in the dancers' eyes to redden them in order to emphasize the expression of their eyes. Every mood and every scene is acted in minute detail. Kathakali is solely performed by men; women's roles are played by men wearing appropriate costume and make-up. The prevailing mood in Kathakali is heroic. Battle scenes are staged with shrieking noise and war cries along with loud drumming and singing. The stage is lighted only by one or two large oil lamps. The style of dancing is vigorous and masculine.

We may wonder why at this time in history the heroic *Nayar* created such powerful and spectacular drama. Was it the result of a reaction to some special social situation when the royal *Nayar* found themselves losing their grip on power in the face of foreign aggression? Was the spectacular grandeur of Kathakali a reaffirmation of the *Nayar–Nambudiri* social status? An examination of the tradional social status of the *Nayar* and their history of martial pride may throw some light on these questions.

The *Nayars* are a significant community in south Malabar. Historically, the royal families of Kerala lacked political centralization. The *Nayars* were the warriors on call in a matrilineal and matrilocal society. *Nayar* boys were trained at the military training ground, the *Kalari*, from the age of seven and eight so that they could achieve excellent martial skill. Their bodies were regularly massaged with sesame oil to make them nimble and flexible. Colonial writers often refer to the extraordinary courage of the *Nayar*. Willian Logan examined the family records of Zamorin and writes:

> . . . of an extraordinary ceremony in 1683, at which many *Nayars* dedicated themselves to death, and, after a last supper and solemn leave-taking of their families, flung themselves upon the Zamorion's guards, in an attempt to fight their way through to the Zamorin himself fifty-five perishing … in five days. (Logan, 1887, p. 93)

A British Governor of Bombay described the *Nayars* as warriors carrying naked swords like canes or walking sticks. As a matter of fact, the *Nayars* once had the power of life and death over all the so-called 'lower caste' people in the community.

The arrival of Vasco da Gama in 1498 on the Malabar coast began the sea-borne, foreign intrusion. The *Nayars* resisted such foreign incursion into their territory, but ultimately colonial domination was extended over the *Nayars*, and the *Kalari* became a dance training centre for *Nayar* boys and from here, gradually, Kathakali took its present shape. Thus, the birth of Kathakali may be considered very significant in relation to the prevailing social exigency. The *Nayars* were losing their glorious status in the community and the dance theatre was one way to channelize the ethos of their masculine pride. In a matrilineal society, in the absence of a male physiological priority in the lineage system, masculine pride, perhaps, needed to be reaffirmed.

The selection of heroic themes for Kathakali dance-dramas probably reflects the *Nayars*' need for the performance to reaffirm their male ethos. Kathakali is violent, acrobatic and athletic. The *Nayars* chose the themes from the mythical past, not the historic past, to create a supernatural aura of ritual dancing. The stories present the courage and nobility of the heroes and the subjugation of evil in violent, rather blood-chilling, and realistic battles. In contrast to the male character, the female character (played by young males) is presented in an exceedingly simple way, without any elaborate costume or make-up.

Yet there is another element in Kathakali. The entire drama is interlaced with religious belief, prayer and invocation, which uplifts the aesthetic pleasure to a spiritual level. The Kathakali costume resembles contemporary Portuguese dress of the period. The martial background of the *Nayars* helps to explain the rendering of heroic plays of the mythical past. The epical stories were already woven into the lives of the people through their enactment for centuries in Malabari theatres. The *Nayars* revitalized these stories by introducing the new form, Kathakali, rendered with royal grandeur and intricate technique. Traditionally, the *Nambudiris* were the social allies of the *Nayars*. This alliance was rejuvenated and maintained through Kathakali.

Clifford Geertz analyses sacred religious ritual as a community's attempt to deal with pain, bafflement and moral paradox (Geetz, 1972, p. 167). Religious ritual is a powerful means for the denial of chaos, since the ritual world lies beyond the realities of profane life. It helps the group ethos to survive in the paradox. Ritual dance supported and uplifted the *Nayar* morale in a powerful and satisfying way. The shifting orientation of the royal plays from the court towards the community and the use of the regional language indicates a conscious attempt at popular appeal.

However, the vibrant spirit of Kathakali gradually weakened under Christian missionary influence. Kathakali was almost dying when the Malayalee poet, Vallathol, established the Kerala Kalamandalam, a centre for Kathakali, at Shoranur in the 1930s. He opened its doors to all castes, although it is still an all-male school. Today, female dancers are able to study Kathakali at other places.

Bharatnatyam

Literally, Bharatanatyam means the dramatic art of Bharata, the author of *Natyasastra*, but it is an adopted name for an ancient dance form, *Dasiattam*, which gained currency only in the 1930s. *Dasiattam* means the dance of the *devadasis*, the maidens of the gods. The change of name, which was an attempt to remove its association with the *devadasis*, is very significant as a measure of the modern social value of dancing. In British times, Bharatanatyam ceased to be performed in the temple, the result of an anti-*devadasi* movement which was directed against corruption in the temples. Previously such dancing was confined to, and zealously guarded by, the *devadasis* and other women were barred from learning this art. *Devadasis* were also known to be well-versed in literature, mythology and music. At present, women from all castes may study this dance form.

The *devadasi* system was established between the ninth and eleventh centuries at the time of the temple-building period of the Chola dynasty. During the reign of Rajaraja in the eleventh century about 400 *devadasis* were attached to the temple of Tanjore alone. They received allowances from the temple, tax-free land and old-age pensions for their service to the temple. In the seventeenth century Tanjore became the capital of the Nayak successors of the Vijaynagar kings and Bharatanatyam dance has long been associated with the temple in this city. The Dravidian South was able to maintain a cultural identity in the face of political pressure from northern India. *Devadasis* were thus able to preserve the ancient dance tradition in its pristine form. The institution of *devadasi* remained quite strong until the eighteenth century. The temple of Kancheepuram, for example, had one hundred *devadasis*.

Abbe DuBois, the French missionary, offers an interesting account of their elegant lifestyle and social position in the late eighteenth century (Dubois, 1906, p. 586). Although *devadasis* were ceremoniously married to the temple deity, they eventually became temple prostitutes and thus their social position was ambivalent. These women were highly sophisticated and often quite learned in the arts, and their ritual status gave them a special prestige. They were visited by high-class and high-caste men. But their social function was obviously not that of women with normal upbringing. A daughter of a *devadasi* became a *devadasi* unless she was very unattractive. It was often presitigious to dedicate a daughter to the service of the temple. For example, in Coimbatore a class of musicians always dedicated at least one daughter as a *devadasi* (Zoete, 1953, p. 63). She would start her dance lessons early in childhood and continue for seven or eight years. Dedicated to the temple deity, she would perform dances regularly in the adjacent temple theater. In time some of the *devadasis* became entertainers in the king's court and would become known as *rajadasis* (maids of the king).

Devadasi dancing was based on stories from mythology and had religious lyrics and themes. The technique included highly sophisticated and complex patterns of music, rhythmic variation, systematic body positions and movements, facial expressions and hand gestures, all with a perfect sense of balance.

The Kancheepuram temple sculpture shows 108 *karanas* (dance positions and poses) from *Natyasastra*, which are actually used in dancing. The prescribed tradition of *ntra* and *nrtya* is maintained as is the presentation of the various moods defined in the dance scripture. The music is Karnataka, the extremely rich South Indian classical style, with lyrics in Tamil and Telugu. When the Tamil kingdom fell, the cultural focus shifted to the Telegu kingdom of Vijaynagar in the sixteenth century and the Telugu language achieved a position equivalent to that of Tamil.

The present form of Bharatanatyam was developed about a century ago by four brothers, all distinguished dance teachers and musicians. Traditionally, such teachers and musicians came from the male descendants of the *devadasis*. Not being literate, they had to depend on memory and on oral and aural modes of learning. This is perhaps one important reason for the adoption and modification of the techniques of the ancient dance treatise into the regional idiom.

One can assume that the richness and vitality of Bharatanatyam is an expression of a vital culture which grew out of the intellectual and aesthetic milieu of the Chola dynasty. The relative closeness of the style to the classical treatise is understandable from its unalloyed association with an intellectual brahminic tradition for several centuries. South Indian temple sculpture was greatly inspired by the dance of the *devadasis*. In a well-known treatise on Indian painting, King Vajrasena is advised by a sage to learn the art of dancing before that of icon-making (Vatsyayan, 1968, p. 380). This advice underlines the interrelationships of different arts and their fundamental unity. One can well imagine the intellectual and aesthetic world of South India which made possible the nurturing of the vital art of dancing. As a major source of inspiration to the musicians, poets, painters, singers and sculptors, Bharatanatyam is the quintessence of South India's artistic excellence.

Bharatanatyam was exclusively a solo dance style to be performed only by women. The dance style projects a powerful individuality and sensuous femininity. While in Manipuri dance the dancer's personality is diffused in communal devotion, in Bharatnyam the devotion of the *devadasi* is expressed on a personal level to her beloved god. The dance style in Bharatanatyam has a theatrical quality, the dancer being conscious of an audience. The profound individuality of the dancer can be appreciated in the context of the social position of the women who performed in this style. The high royal status gave them a special social position. They lived in the public eye, surrounded by critics, and with competition for success. They enjoyed equal status within their families. Their dance showed the distinctive stamp of a professional woman. That lifestyle and social position are now a thing of the past.

Indian Dance in Perspective

Each classical school of dance is in a way unique, standing on its own merits. This uniqueness is the product of distinctive physical and cultural environments in the four regions in which the different styles developed and the very different historical experiences through which each went.

Returning to the *Natyasastra* of sage Bharata, one can trace his concept of dance in each style. All four schools demonstrate the basic concepts of *nrtta* (pure dance) and *nritya* (acting dance) as indicated by Bharata, but significant differences in detail exist in the use of *mudra* (symbolic hand gesture) and *abhinaya* (theatrical acting). Bharatanatyam shows the greatest closeness to the ancient tradition, whereas Kathakali has developed a far more elaborate repertoire of hand-speech. In Kathak the classical technique of *mudra* is much less important and a spontaneous style of acting has evolved. Both in the use of *mudra* and *abhinaya* Manipuri is least influenced by the Sanskritic tradition. Thus, although the same Sanskrit verses of the Bengali poet Jayadeva's *Gitagovinda* are used in Manipuri in the far northeast, in Bharatanatyam in distant Tanjore and in Kathakali in Malabar, they find very different expressions in the respective dance styles. We are not aware of any Kathak performance to *Gitagovinda*, but since the romantic love-play of Radha and Krishna is the main theme in this dance as in *Gitagovinda*, it is quite possible that the same verses could be used. However, each of the styles generally uses the regional language for the theme songs, except for Manipuri, where both Bengali and Meitei languages are equally prominent.

The two schools of South India present a contrast to each other. Kathakali is essentially a male group dance-drama, while Bharatanatyam is a female solo dance. The group spectacle of Kathakali was not meant for the small temple theatre for which Bharatanatyam was devised, rather the former needs to be presented in a courtyard with a large space. Manipuri Vaishnava rituals are performed is a *mandapa* (large temple hall) or in the open temple courtyard, which helps the gliding movement and fluid motion to flow in space. Kathak, like Bharatanatyam, is performed within a restricted space.

When the verse 'Ashtapadee' of *Gitagovinda* is sung, drums of different timbre and resonance accompany the singing to create the mood and melody for each dance style. *Cenda* and *mandala* drums are used in Kathakali, *mridangam* in Bharatanatyam and *poong* in Manipuri. If one ventured to perform 'Ashtapadee' in Kathak, then the *tabla* and *pakwaj* drums would be used. Likewise the style of the music varies. Moreover, there are considerable differences in the way dance is appreciated by the audience in accordance with the social role of dance in the regional societies.

In the North the female dancers of the Kathak school had to survive in a male-oriented society, and they were excluded from the mainstream of life, having been classed as entertainers upon the secularization of their art. In the South the *devadasis* were entertainers, too, but their ritual status gave them a special privilege in the society. Although they were temple entertainers, *devadasis* were in demand during weddings and other auspicious occasions, and thus were not completely excluded from society. The *Devadasi* family system was mother-centred and the equal rights of sons and daughters indicate the social privilege of a *devadasi* in a male-oriented society. In contrast, Kathakali is a male dance style, from which females were excluded until recently. Our analysis suggests a significant correlation between the brilliant and vivacious femininity of Bharatanatyam and the institutional lifestyle of the *devadasis*, and between the heroic style of Kathakali and the violent power and masculine force of the *Nayar* ethos of the eighteenth century.

Of all the styles discussed, Manipuri appears to be the most purely devotional and communal in spirit. This quality may be traced to the historical and religious background of the Manipuri Valley and its relative isolation from the stress and strain of external forces in the rest of India.

Acknowledgements

This chapter has been reproduced from Allen G. Noble and Ashok K. Dutt (eds.), *India: Cultural Patterns and Processes*, 1982. Westview Press, pp. 147–164, with permission of the copyright holder of the book.

Notes

1. The 'twice-born', which include Brahmin, Kshatriya, and Vaishya, "are so-called on account of the initiation ceremony at which they are ceremonially reborn and assume the sacred thread, a ceremony not permitted to the Sudras," J. H. Hutton, *Caste in India*, 4th ed., Bombay, Oxford University Press, 1973, p. 64.
2. The *Natyasastra*, a treatise on Hindu dramaturgy and histrionics, is ascribed to Bharata-Muni, and is generally believed to have been composed between 100 BC and 200 AD. M. Gosh, *The Natyasatra*, ascribed to Bharata-Muni, Calcutta, Asiatic Society of Bengal, 1951, p. 3.
3. In India there are now six recognized classical schools of dancing. The two additional ones are *Odisi* and *Kuchipudi*. There are also different dance-drama traditions, such as *Bhagavatamela Natakam*, *Yakshagana*, and *Chhau*. Often it is hard to categorize them, since all have a classical basis with a strong folk influence.
4. *Lai Harouba* is led by women priests, the *Maibees*, assisted by women and female children.
5. *Rasheshori Kirtana* (introduced by Raja Jai Singh of Rajasthan in 1750) and *Jalakeli* (introduced by Raja Nar Singh) are the most important versions of this dance.
6. A five yard, thin, white cotton cloth closely wrapped around the waist and the legs to look somewhat like trousers.
7. One of the authors of this paper (MCS) recalls her 'conversation' with the poet, Vallathol, at the Kerala Kalamandalam, who used no spoken language, but only *mudras*.

References

DuBois, J. A., *Hindu Manners, Customs, and Ceremonies*, H. K. Beauchamp (trans. and ed.), Oxford: Clarendon Press, Third edition, 1906.

Geetz, C., 'Religion as a Cultural System', in W. A. Lessa and E. Z. Vogt (eds.), *Reader in Comparative Religion*, New York: Harper and Row, Second edition, 1972.

Logan, W., *Malabar*, 2 Vols., 1887. Quote in B. de Zoete, *The Other Mind*, London, Gollancz, 1953.

Vatsyayan, K., *Classical Indian Dance in Literature and Arts*, New Delhi: Sangeet Natak Academy, 1968.

Zoete, B., *The Other Mind*, London: Victor Gollancz, 1953.

20

Space, Gender and Social Value: Analyzing Gender Inequalities in Relation to Space

ANINDITA DATTA

The role of space in creating and sustaining gender roles and gender inequalities is a subject that needs further interrogation, particularly within the richly diverse Indian context. Drawn from the author's doctoral work, this paper is an attempt to examine the question of gender inequality in terms of gender disparities in social well-being. The role of space and region in creating and sustaining these inequalities is interrogated through fieldwork in two physically and socio-culturally dissimilar regions. The paper is divided into four sections. Section 1 briefly describes the framework of the analysis. Section 2 describes the social and physical spaces within which this analysis is located. The results of the study are presented in Section 3. Section 4 is the concluding section where an attempt at theorization is made.

Analysing Gender Inequalities in Relation to Space

While it has become fashionable and politically correct to address the question of gender inequality (however fleetingly) in academic discourse as well as in grassroots activism, there is an urgent need to locate it firmly within a valid framework of analysis. To begin with, it is erroneous to address the question of gender inequality in isolation from the social–spatial context that it appears in. Academic discourse cannot produce meaningful explanations if such issues are taken out of the total societal context and addressed in isolation. Secondly, reality differs over space and time. Situations are comparable only where geographical and economic realities are similar. If spatial comparisons are essential, efforts must be made to understand the different geographical and social realities that generate such contrasts. It is in this that the role of space is imputed. The particular set of spatial parameters that define a place also locate it within a particular social space. These social spaces vary according to the manner in which customs, rituals, kinship structures and gender roles are constructed. The characteristics of the social space within which a place is located would have a greater bearing on the question of gender inequality than the characteristics of the physical location. Even though the latter influences the former, the social space is not determined purely from the physical aspects of location such as terrain, climate, etc. Instead, state intervention, social movements, historical and economic realities leave a greater imprint on social spaces than the physical environment in which they are cradled. Yet these are often overlooked and explanations for questions of gender inequality are sought in purely physical aspects of the space. According to this author such a theorization is naive and essentially erroneous.

In this chapter, an attempt is made to analyse the question of gender inequality in terms of gender disparities in social well-being. The question of gender inequality is first located within a valid framework of analysis and then examined with due reference to the role of space in influencing the same. The paper is divided into five sections. Section 1 briefly describes the framework of analysis. Section 2 describes the social and physical spaces within which this analysis is located. The results of the study are presented in Section 3. Section 4 is the concluding section where an attempt at theorisation is made.

Framework for Analysis

There is a need to locate the question of gender inequality firmly within a valid framework of analysis. Such a framework needs to incorporate the role of space in creating and, more importantly, sustaining such inequalities. This is best solved by broadly locating the question of gender inequality within the ambit of the welfare geography and more specifically within the framework of the geography of social well-being. The state of social well-being connotes a state of happiness (or well-being) resulting from the fulfilment of basic and higher-order needs and leading to the ultimate goal of self actualization. The geography of well-being is defined best by Smith (1977) as who gets what, where and how. Where basic human needs are fulfilled, such well-being is influenced by the gratification of higher-order needs. However, in situations where even basic needs like nutrition and healthcare are often unmet, gender disparities in basic areas of social well-being assume added importance in understanding the problem of gender inequality. Gender disparities in the basic areas of social well-being, therefore, underlie the gender disparities in every other sphere of life at every other scale of investigation, from the local to the national and international.

Having located the problem of women's marginalization in the framework of gender disparities in social well-being, the question of scale remains to be tackled. Any enquiry in this realm must address the problem at the level of the household as the household is the primary unit where the gender disparities in the basic aspects of well-being are produced, reproduced and reinforced. Again, the location of the household within a particular social space and regional ethos would determine, to a great degree, the nature of inequality being produced and reinforced.

Investigation of gender disparities within a framework of 'who gets what, where and how' demands a few considerations. On the question of 'who', the population under investigation is not homogeneous and certain diverse elements are inherent within the social fibre. The first difference is along gender lines, dividing the population into the male and female components. This lends itself to further subdivisions on the basis of age, caste or class. Thus, gender itself is not a homogeneous category. Intra-gender disparities may well exist within the broad category of gender itself.

As mentioned earlier, gender disparities in the basic areas of social well-being, like health, nutrition and education, are both the cause as well as the effect of the marginalization of women from all spheres of life. Therefore, these need to be studied together in response to the 'who gets what, where and how' model. This assumes added importance as each of these aspects may influence the others.

The question of 'where' in the Smithian model implicates the role of space in creating and sustaining gender inequality. Regional cultures are formed through a long and complex process of interaction between people and the environment in which the human saga unfolds. The roles, status and positions accorded to women differ across regions and are greatly influenced by the economy and culture suggested by the environment. Therefore, it is obvious that diverse physical environments would lend themselves to specific constructs of gender roles. The extent of restrictiveness of feminine gender roles influences the degree to which women participate in the social and economic life of the community. Lower participation invariably translates into restricted mobility, lower visibility and less power attached to such roles both within the household and in the community. These in turn would determine the degree of son preference depending upon the relative value attached to feminine gender roles vis-a-vis the masculine. The higher the degree of son preference, the higher is the likelihood of greater gender inequality being reflected in the basic areas of well-being.

Finally, an understanding of the dynamics of such discrimination and its basis within distinct regional cultures addresses the 'how' in the 'who gets what, where and how' framework suggested here.

Relevance of the Study

Analysing any gender issue in the framework suggested here would draw its relevance from the following. Firstly, and most importantly, gender would not be erroneously studied in isolation. Rather, the problem of gender-based marginalization would be analysed in the context of gender disparities in the levels of social well-being. Secondly, the intra-gender dimension would also be highlighted by not treating gender itself as a homogenous category. This provides for a systematic framework for analysis. Further, by addressing the key areas of social well-being, such studies would not overlook important linkages. This would ensure that a more complete picture of reality is obtained. Moreover, this framework would ensure that the problem is addressed at its root by making the household the unit of analysis. Finally, by comparing gender disparities across environmental regions, the regional dimension would be brought out fully. In particular the specific characteristics of social space would be examined as they influence the construction of gender roles and have a bearing on the problem of gender inequality. As argued elsewhere in this paper, this dimension of space has hardly been addressed in unravelling the problem of gender inequality thus far. On all these counts, studies in the framework outlined here would make due contributions to the existing body of knowledge on the geography of gender in India. An earlier version of the framework suggested here has been discussed more fully in Datta and Sinha (1997).

Space, Gender and Social Value

The role of space and gender in the creation of social value is argued in this section. While the relationship between space and gender is by now well known, that between space, gender and social value needs to be reasoned out more elaborately. Unarguably, specific places lend themselves to particular constructs of gender in response to the demands of the physical and social environment. The manner in which these gender roles are constructed influence the nature of work carried out by women and men within a particular spatial context. The argument presented in this paper is that the level of well-being enjoyed by an individual is largely the outcome of the social value ascribed to the individual within the household. Such values are ascribed largely on the basis of the nature of work carried out (or expected to be carried out) by an individual. Thus, disparities in the nature of the work done by men and women are immediately translated into differential social values within the household and, as a corollary, into gender disparities in the core areas of social well-being.

Fieldwork in two contrasting regions shows that the nature of women's work may be influenced by environment, level of development and the prevalent regional ethos, all of which act in tandem to produce specific gender roles. Due to these differences, the nature of women's work varies from place to place and leads to differential social values being ascribed to the same. The outcome is a difference in the level of social well-being of women vis-a-vis men in both regions. As argued earlier, marginalization and deprivation in the important aspects of social well-being are largely a result of lower social and economic value placed on a subject. The social values ascribed to an individual is determined at two levels – the society and the household. Thus, women's marginalization and oppression is a two-tiered process.

Social value in the societal context is contingent on position in the social hierarchy which is based on social power derived through caste, land ownership or household income. In this context, therefore, the problem of women's oppression and marginalization could be seen as rooted in the intertwining of three exploitative systems that sustain and reinforce each other. These are the systems of patriarchy where men as a class are better placed than women; the system of caste where the higher castes appropriate for themselves a higher level of well-being than the lower castes; and the system of feudalism where ownership and control over the most important means of production (land) ensures a higher level of social well-being. Interestingly, in the Indian scenario each of these systems supports and reinforces the other two. A change in the structure of any one of these systems leads to a change in the prescribed social value and, therefore, in the levels of well-being.

Within the household, however, the nature of work carried out (or expected to be carried out in future) by each member of the household determines their social value. An analysis of men and women's work shows that, by and large, women tend to be engaged in unpaid work while men tend towards paid work. Also, while the purpose of men's work is ostensibly the sustenance of the household, field observation shows that a large component of women's unpaid work is extra-household work consisting of social networking, and creating and maintaining mutually-beneficial ties between households. Similarly, the small component of paid work undertaken by women may often be strongly guided by the motive of self actualization rather than sustenance. Further, women's participation in domestic work is trivialized and seen largely as an extension of or preparation for the woman's biological role in child bearing.

The immediate fallout of this gender disparity in the nature of work is that the economic value of women is lower than that of men within the household. Since the economic value of an individual is an important determinant of their social value, the social value of women remains intrinsically lower than that of the men in the household. This lays the foundation for a bias against women and girls in education, health and nutrition within the household.

Selection of Regions

In order to examine the role of space in creating and reinforcing gender inequality, the sample design called for study villages drawn from contrasting social and physical environments. To appreciate the role of development as well, the sample design demanded that these be situated at different levels of development. Accordingly, based on an intuitive understanding of the social geography of India, the regions chosen for study were the Awadh plains and the Uttarakhand region. Both can be sufficiently distinguished from each other not only in terms of the physical aspects of place such as terrain, climate and agro-climatic conditions but also in terms of economy, culture and society.

This difference in the characteristics of social space that these regions inhabit accrues from their location in the perennially nuclear region and region of relative isolation within the northern part of the country. The perennially nuclear regions along the Gangetic plain with their suitability for plough agriculture have strong patriarchal traditions reflected in poor position of women especially among the twice-born castes, whereas the surrounding hill and forests have somewhat fewer and weaker traditions of male dominance due to the greater participation of women in the economic activities of the community. This may be deduced by applying the core-periphery or distance decay model to the social sphere. History shows that the incursions into the Indian subcontinent occurred from the northwest and each successive wave of people moved eastwards along the Gangetic plain. It ought to be recalled that the earlier inhabitants who were displaced from the plains to the hilly and forested regions were agriculturists worshipping the Mother Goddess. The latter was probably the remnant of the established fact that mother–children groups were the first social units. They were not only units of consumption but also units of production. Mothers and children worked together as gatherers during the period of early hoe cultivation and adult men were only temporarily and peripherally integrated into these early matricentric or matristic units. These people who migrated into the hills are likely to have retained their belief in the Mother Goddess and more egalitarian construction of gender roles which were reinforced by the demands for women's labour due to the harsher terrain. Meanwhile the fresh migrants along the plain regions were pastoralists. Their preoccupation with gathering cattle wealth and inter-tribal skirmishes pushed women into the background of their social and economic lives. Later on the heavy plough agriculture where the main crops were wheat and millet, offered minimal roles to women, rendering their economic values low. In this strongly patriarchal set-up the mores of male dominance were high and consequently feminine gender roles were more restrictive. At a later stage in history, when new equations of power were being drawn along the Gangetic plains, the population from this region once again moved into the nearby hills. Though the harsher terrain of the new environment demanded a greater participation from the women, yet culturally ingrained ideologies of male dominance remained in the social psyche of the plains people to a degree and the subjugation of women by the men continued even in the mountains, though to a lesser degree than in the plains. This would effectively explain the constitution of a less potent version of patriarchy in the northern hills and mountains of the subcontinent.

Thus, as part of the perennially nuclear regions of the Gangetic plains, the Awadh plain, situated in the heart of the Indian 'cowbelt', is a fertile plain which has witnessed the human saga unfolding over its breadth since time immemorial. With its suitability for heavy plough agriculture the region offered minimal roles to women in agricultural production, thus effectively marginalizing them from the process of economic production and rendering their economic value lower than that of males (Miller, 1981). This marginalization, coupled with strong patriarchal traditions (which are both the cause and effect of each other), is reflected in a wide inter-gender disparity among the different parameters of social well-being in this region.

The Awadh plain or the Upper Ganga–Ghaghra Doab includes the districts of Barabanki, Hardoi, Kheri, Lucknow, Rae Bareilly, Sitapur and Unnao of Uttar Pradesh. (See Fig. 24.1). Drained by the Ganga and its tributaries, the region is a flat and featureless plain. In the south it is demarcated from the neighbouring regions by the Ganga, while its northern extent is demarcated by the Ghaghra. Various other tributaries of the Ganga like the Choti Saryu, the Gomti and the Sai irrigate this plain. Agriculture forms the most important economic activity in this area. Rice, wheat, sugarcane and mustard are the most important crops. Lucknow and Kanpur are the most important urban centres of this region and typically attract migrant labour (often seasonal) from the rural hinterland. Often the workers reside in their own villages and commute to these urban centres by public transport. Household and small-scale industries form an important segment of the rural economy. Of these, the crafts of *chikankari* and *zardozi* are perhaps the best known. Others include carpet-weaving, basket-making and brick-making.

In the present-day scenario, the region assumes socio-political importance in that it is an area where various political groups vie with each other to woo the large and socially diverse electorate. Much akin to the Heartland Theory of Mackinder (1919), political control over the Hindi heartland is seen as an important stepping stone to forming the government at the Centre. (Mackinder identified Eurasia as the Heartland and argued that political control over this region ensured worldwide supremacy.) Also, as an area where various social groups coexist in a fragile and carefully maintained harmony, the area has witnessed numerous instances of caste violence in recent years. Other than its location in the nation's political heartland, the region could also be said to be part of the patriarchal heartland of India where the structures supporting the institution of patriarchy are at their most potent. Crimes against women are among the highest in this region, coupled with low rates of female literacy and high rates of mortality – indicating the lower position and social worth of women vis-a-vis men in the region.

From the foothills in the south, the Uttarakhand region extends up to the snow-clad peaks of the Himadri in the north, marking the Indo–Tibetan boundary. The River Tons separates the region from Himachal Pradesh in the west, while the eastern boundaries are demarcated by the River Kali (Singh, 1989, p. 443). The Uttarakhand region includes the Almora, Chamoli, Dehradun, Garhwal, Nainital, Pithoragarh, Tehri Garhwal and Uttarkashi districts of Uttaranchal (Fig. 26.1).

In this region, the mountainous terrain and forest cover combine to form a region of out-migration (especially male selective out-migration). Women-headed households are quite common and women play an important role in agriculture. The harsher terrain, coupled with the male selective out-migration which typifies the region, demands a greater role from women in the productive economy and so renders their social and economic value higher. This combination of ancient historical legacy and contemporary economic roles leads to a far less restrictive construction of feminine gender roles in the region. The Uttarakhand region assumes a contemporary socio-political relevance in that it is a region of growing regional aspirations. The centrifugal forces arising out of an artificially created and superimposed regional structure are at play, giving rise to a significant regional movement in this area. This movement has since culminated in the formation of a new state of Uttaranchal. Importantly the region is located on the fringes of the patriarchal heartland where due to a feminization of the rural milieu the structure of patriarchy has been modified to lose much of its potency. It has witnessed several social movements where women have been initiators and active participants. The *Chipko* and *Beej Bachao* movements are cases in point (see Chapter 26 for the Chipko social movement analysis).

The Sample Design

The sample design called for the selection of two villages from each region. In each region, the two villages selected would be drawn from the best and least developed districts of the region in order to represent these levels of development. Accordingly, the best and least developed districts of each region were identified using the Centre for Monitoring the Indian Economy's (CMIE) Relative Development Index (RDI) for districts for the year 1993 (CMIE, 1993). Lucknow emerged as the most developed district of the Awadh plains. Unnao and Rae Barreilly both shared the lowest RDI scores and were the least developed districts of this region. For the purpose of the study Unnao was chosen to represent the least developed district. Similarly, in the Uttarakhand region, Dehradun with the highest RDI score emerged as the most developed district. Chamoli with the least RDI score was identified as the least developed district.

From the best and least developed districts of each region, two *tehsils* each were identified, again the most and least developed. This was done on the basis of a simple composite index based on various indicators of development. Then from each of the *tehsils*, a representative village was selected for conducting the field study (Datta, 1999). Thus, villages from the better developed districts and *tehsils* were closer to an urban centre, while those located at a greater distance from an urban centre were chosen to represent the less developed areas. Table 20.1 summarizes the sample design and shows the villages selected for the study.

Characteristics of the Study Villages

The four villages selected for the study were Amethi Salempur and Sohra Mau in the Awadh region and Karbari Grant and Saliyana in the

Table 20.1 Villages selected in study area.

The Awadh Plains (Region I)		*The Uttarakhand Region (Region II)*	
Most Developed District	Least Developed District	Most Developed District	Least Developed District
Lucknow	*Unnao*	*Dehradun*	*Chamoli*
Most Developed Tehsil	Least Developed Tehsil	Most Developed Tehsil	Least Developed Tehsil
Lucknow	*Hasanganj*	*Dehradun*	*Karanprayag*
Village Selected	Village Selected	Village Selected	Village Selected
Amethia Salempur	*Sohra Mau*	*Karbari Grant*	*Saliyana*
Number of Households	Number of Households	Number of Households	Number of Households
517	119	185	77
Percentage of Households Surveyed	Percentage of Households Surveyed	Percentage of Households Surveyed	Percentage of Households Surveyed
19. 5%	85. 4%	53. 5%	100 %

[1]Notional. At the time the field study was conducted, 1991 census data was unavailable.

Uttarakhand region. Amethia Salempur is located 18 km northwest of Lucknow on State Highway number 25. The village comprises five hamlets – Amethia, Naubasta, Baznagar, Samratnagar and Maulvi Khera. The approach to the village is by a *pucca* road. The settlement structure is dense and clustered with a marked segregation of dwelling units along caste lines. Such caste-based niches are named after the castes that occupy them such as Dhobiana, Pasiana, Chamrahi, etc. Hindus comprise 79 per cent of the sample while Muslims constitute 21 per cent of the sample. The sample comprises people belonging to 12 caste groups. The village is primarily a Scheduled Caste village. Within the sample, over 40 per cent of the population is aged below 15 years. Only 12 per cent of the population is over 45 years of age. As is well known, this type of age structure of the population with the largest proportion belonging to the youngest and the lowest proportion placed in the oldest age categories is typical of less developed regions with high rates of infant mortality and lower life expectancy in general.

Located on the Lucknow – Unnao–Kanpur National Highway, Sohra Mau is almost equidistant from both Lucknow and Unnao. While Lucknow is approximately 29 km away from the village, Unnao is situated at a distance of about 30 km. The approach to the village is by a *pucca* (paved) road. The National Highway traverses the edge of the village. The settlement structure is typically dense and clustered. The fact that an important road passes through the village has also influenced the settlement structure. On both sides of the road, houses have given way to shops and eateries to cater to the people that may choose to halt at the village. Dwelling units are clustered on caste lines. The clusters of each caste are separated from the others by a footpath or drain. The houses of the upper castes are mostly double-storied *pucca* (permanent) structures equipped with all necessary amenities like electricity, water, bathrooms, toilets and kitchens and are built around a courtyard. Lower caste houses are mostly *kutcha* (degradable) or semi-*pucca* (depending on the economic condition). In contrast to Amethia Salempur, Sohra Mau is a high caste village. This trend is reflected in the sample where the higher castes comprise nearly half of the sample households. Agewise, nearly 50 per cent of the sample population is below 20. Another 46 per cent is between 20 to 59 years. Only five per cent are over 60 years. The sex ratio of the sample is typically masculine, with only 790 females to a thousand males. The sex ratio is lowest in the below-five age group (559 females to 1000 males) indicating probable neonatal neglect of female infants.

Located in the Dehradun *tehsil* of Dehradun district, Karbari Grant is situated about 15 km south of Dehradun city. The village is situated on the Simla road which is used by the Army in shifting men and materials to and from Dehradun. Karbari is divisible into three distinct portions – Gorkha Karbari, Garhwali Karbari and Ganeshpur. Gorkha Karbari houses the Gorkha population of the village. Garhwali Karbari and Ganeshpur are home to the Garhwalis and Gadarias respectively. Settlements in Gorkha Karbari are dispersed. Small groups of houses are surrounded by fields. Garhwali Karbari has a more dense settlement pattern due to greater population pressure. In Ganeshpur the settlement structure is extremely dense and clustered. The houses are separated from others by narrow tracks or drains. In Gorkha and Garhwali Karbari, most houses are single, storied *pucca* or semi-*pucca* structures built of wood, bricks or cement. Ganeshpur has more *kutcha* houses. In these, the walls are built of mud and topped by tin or stone roofs. Most of the houses in Gorkha and Garhwali Karbari have separate toilets, bathing areas and kitchens but this is not so in Ganeshpur. The houses of the Gadarias in Ganeshpur have large cattle sheds and fodder storage areas. Nearly 44 per cent of the population is aged below 20. About 48 per cent is between 20 to 59. Only six per cent is aged over 60. This pyramid-shaped age distribution pattern reflects a high birth rate and low life expectancy. The sample has a positive sex ratio of 1095 females to 1000 males. This is in keeping with the character of the region in general and the village in particular. Apart from being located in a generalised area of male selective out-migration, the village population consists largely of Gorkhas and Garhwalis. Both communities have a glorious tradition of serving in the armed forces – resulting in a sizeable number of males being away from the village.

Saliyana is located in the Karanprayag *tehsil* of district Chamoli. The nearest town, Gairsen, is about 2.5 km away from village. Situated on a steep slope, the village is easily divisible into two quarters. The lower slopes house the higher castes while the higher slopes hold the lower caste dwellings. The village is approachable by a *kutcha* (unpaved) foot track leading off the main road that connects Adi Badri to Gairsen. The 2.5 km long trail ascends the slope housing the village and on reaching the settlements, bifurcates into smaller trails leading to individual houses. Along the higher slopes, housing the lower castes, the dwelling units are arranged along the terraces of the slope in a linear fashion. On the lower slopes, too, the houses of the higher castes are arranged along the slope terraces in small groups of two or three houses. However, here the arrangement is not strictly linear. These slopes contain more settlements and they are dispersed with hutments interspersed with agricultural holdings. The higher slopes, on the other hand, contain a cluster of linearly arranged houses surrounded by agricultural land. The houses are mostly *pucca* or semi-*pucca*. They are built using locally available materials like wood, slate, etc. Quite a number of houses are double-storied with the lower portion being used to house livestock and fodder. Very few houses have separate toilets. None have running water and only one or two units have electricity. Over 50 per cent of the sample is aged below 20. A little over 37 per cent is between 20 and 59 years of age, while only 7.5 per cent is aged over 60. This pyramid-like age distribution is further accentuated by the fact that, being an area of male selective out-migration, most of the males between the ages of 20 to 55 have emigrated from the village in search of employment. Some have taken their spouses and children along, leaving behind only the elders of the household. The sex ratio of the village is positive with 1088 females to 1000 males. This is in keeping with its character of being a region of male selective out-migration. The fact that the sex ratio is highest in the 20 to 44 age group (1530 females to 1000 males) bears this out.

Typically, the sample consists of only the higher castes and the lower service castes. This is the result of a combination of two factors–on the one hand, the emigration of the high castes into this region from the surrounding plains and on the other, the absence of fresh migrations into the village due to its being an area of out-migration.

Both the villages in the Uttarakhand region have a substantially larger proportion of their sample belonging to the higher castes, whereas both villages in the Awadh plains have a larger proportion of their sample belonging to the lower castes (see Table 20.2).

The proportion of female-headed households is the largest in both villages of the Uttarakhand region. This is typical of the region, since it is one of male selective out-migration. Conversely, in both the villages of the Awadh plains, the proportion of female-headed households is extremely low (Table 20.3).

A far higher proportion of the sample is literate in the Uttarakhand region as compared to the Awadh plains. Consequently, both women and men's literacy rates are significantly higher in the Uttarakhand region as compared to the Awadh plains. Perhaps a higher value placed on education

Table 20.2 Regionwise caste composition of sample.

	Number of Households in Sample			
	Region I		*Region II*	
Caste Categories	*Amethia Salempur*	*Sohra Mau*	*Karbari Grant*	*Saliyana*
High	1	45	53	53
Intermediate	49	9	19	0
Low	16	13	22	0
Lowest	34	33	6	24
Total	100	100	100	77

Table 20.3 Female-headed households.

Region / Village		*Share of Female-Headed Households*
The Awadh Region	Amethia Salempur	9%
	Sohra Mau	2%
The Uttarakhand Region	Karbari Grant	16%
	Saliyana	11.68%

Table 20.4 Literacy rate.

		Literacy rates	
Region	*Village*	*Women*	*Men*
The Awadh Plains	Amethia Salempur	53.1%	68.1%
	Sohra Mau	53.7	77.7%
The Uttarakhand Region	Karbari Grant	81.2	88.7%
	Saliyana	78.2	86.4%

as a means of social and economic mobility in this area of out-migration is responsible for this trend. In all villages, except Karbari Grant of the Uttarakhand region, men's literacy rates are higher than women's. In Karbari Grant, women's literacy is only marginally higher than men's (Table 20.4).

With the exception of Sohra Mau of the Awadh plains, all other villages report a positive sex ratio. Sohra Mau, in keeping with its character of a high caste village with strong patriarchal traditions and situated in a region where such ethos are reinforced, reports a negative sex ratio. Within the same region, however, Amethia Salempur reports a positive sex ratio (Table 20.5). A predominantly lower caste population where brahminical patriarchal values are low and its location at a higher level of development may be two factors responsible for this scenario. In the Uttarakhand

Table 20.5 Sex ratio: Awadh plains and Uttarakhand region.

The Awadh plains		*The Uttarakhand region*	
Village	*Sex Ratio*	*Village*	*Sex Ratio*
Amethia Salempur	1,029	Karbari Grant	1,095
Sohra Mau	790	Saliyana	1,088

Table 20.6 Work participation rates: Awadh plains and Uttarakhand regions.

Region	*Village*	*Men*	*Women*
The Awadh Plains	Amethia Salempur	53.6%	46.7%
	Sohra Mau	50.5%	52.6%
The Uttarakhand Region	Karbari Grant	53.3%	47.6%
	Saliyana	34.8%	44.6%

region, male selective out-migration along with the higher social value of females combine to create conditions favouring a positive sex ratio.

In both regions, men's work participation rates tend to be higher than those of women in the villages located closer to urban centres (Amethia Salempur and Karbari Grant), while the converse is true for the villages located at a greater distance from urban centres. Villages located closer to urban centres offer greater employment opportunities for men while in the others, women's work participation may be higher in the wake of male out-migration (Table 20.6).

Results of the Study

This study examined the gender disparities in the basic areas of well-being, that is education and health. Both outcomes in education and health sectors are theorized as being directly contingent on social value, which itself is ascribed within the household on the basis of the perceived and real value of the work carried out by an individual. Such work is in keeping with the manner in which feminine and masculine gender roles are constructed and the demands of the local and regional economy.

In both regions an examination of the components of women and men's work reveals that women's participation in paid work is abysmally low as compared to men's participation in the same. Domestic work is the main component of women's work. This category of work attracts a low social value, primarily on two counts–firstly, because it is unpaid and;

secondly, because it is seen as an extension of women's child bearing role and not as productive work requiring concerted bodily and mental efforts. Thus, women expend a better part of their time and energy in work that is unpaid (and therefore unrecognized), whereas men devote most of their time to work that is monetarily remunerated. Further, men are more often engaged in paid non-farm work rather than agricultural and allied work. Such work consists mostly of specialized jobs like masons, carpenters, tailors, electricians, painters, *zardozi* apprentices, porters, drivers, factory workers and clerical and defence jobs that require at least rudimentary training or apprenticeship. The small proportions of women who are engaged in paid work tend to be concentrated in agriculture and are paid less than their male counterparts. All these factors ensure that the social value placed on women on the basis of their work is intrinsically lower than that placed on men and men's work. This directly impacts the gender disparity in educational and health status.

Educational deprivation is an important tool in maintaining unequal gender, caste and class relations and thus perpetuating and sustaining the system and sub-systems of gender inequality. The analysis of educational inequalities as part of a larger scheme of inequalities perpetuated against women leads to the conclusion that in every social category, women form a sub-category that faces greater deprivation than men of the same group. This is because of their lower social value within the household.

Comparison of pooled and regional aggregates of enrolment and dropout rates, together with the levels of adult illiteracy, suggests educational deprivation among women and lower castes is stronger in the Awadh plains than in the Uttarakhand region. In the latter, strategies to restrict knowledge and perpetuate unequal power relations based on caste, class and gender lose their potency due to a modification in the structure of patriarchy itself. Thus, in both regions access to knowledge is directly proportional to the degree of power wielded through gender, caste and class.

Health is a function of the nutritional status and the management of morbidity in the household. The former is largely influenced by intra-household distribution of food. The latter consists of immunisations and medical care in the event of illness. Both distribution of food and management of morbidity at household level tend to favour the more valued members and therefore, are most strongly influenced by social worth. Thus, those most marginalized in terms of health status are those with lower social value and power.

Data on the current nutritional status, intra-household food allocation and the management of morbidity suggest that the same are also influenced by gender, caste and class. This trend is distorted in the Uttarakhand region and may be attributed to the success of intervention strategies on the one hand and a higher social value placed on women in the wake of male out-migration and subsequent change in the structure of patriarchy on the other.

Conclusion

In conclusion, a theoretical model based on the premises and findings of this study is attempted. As shown, both health status and access to knowledge (education) are influenced by social value. Social value is determined by the nature of work as well as ascribed by the systems of patriarchy, caste and feudalism. Social value ascribed by patriarchy is determined at birth by gender and is more or less a life long constant. Those assigned by caste and feudalism are contingent on caste of birth or marriage and land ownership. The social values assigned to an individual within each of these systems together with their social value within the household (determined by the nature of work) act and react to influence the determinants of health status and education. The dynamics of such an interaction effectively determines the level of social well-being of an individual. A change in any one of the systems (that is, that of patriarchy, caste or feudalism results in a consequent modification of the social value and, therefore, also in the levels of social well-being). Similarly, a higher value on the nature of work undertaken by a subject would positively influence her social value within the household and result in an enhanced level of well-being. This said, it must be added that all three systems cannot be over generalized but acquire specific regional nuances as they adapt and modify themselves to the particular local regional contexts they operate in.

The policy implications of this functional model are two-fold. While short-term measures may be more direct and aimed at correcting the imbalances in health and educational status, such measures must be backed by a sustained long-term policy to enhance the social value of females and oppressed groups. The media (especially audio–visual media) emerges as an important vehicle for such policy measures. Gender sensitization schemes aimed at recognizing the value of domestic work and thus increasing the social value of women are among some of the more workable solutions to gender disparity.

References

Datta, A., and S. Sinha, 'Gender Disparities in Social Well Being: An Overview', *Indian Journal of Gender Studies*, Vol. 4, No. 1, 1997.

Datta, A. 'Inter Regional Gender Disparities in the Levels of Social Well Being: A Comparative Study of Uttarakhand Region and Awadh Plains,' unpublished doctoral dissertation submitted to the Centre for the Study of Regional Development, Jawaharlal Nehru University, New Delhi (1999).

Mackinder, H. J., *Democratic Ideals and Reality*, London: Constable and Co., 1919.

Mies, M., *et al.*, *Women: The last Colony*, New Delhi: Kali for Women, 1988.

Miller, B., *The Endangered Sex: Neglect of Female Children in Rural North India*, Ithaca: Cornell University Press, 1981.

Singh, R. L. (ed.), *India – A Regional Geography*, Varanasi: National Geographical Society of India, 1989.

Smith, D. M., *Human Geography: A Welfare Approach*, London: Edward Arnold Publishers, 1977.

Subbarao, B., *The Personality of India*, M S University, Baroda, 1958.

21

Encountering Reservation and the Reimagining of Caste

APARAJITA DE

On an early August morning in 2006 while I was rushing from the Metro Station to the Department for the weekly discussion with my tutorial group, I caught a fleeting glimpse of a few students in front of the Faculty of Arts on a 72-hour hunger strike protesting against Mandal II.[1] On entering the D-School[2] campus I noticed that, despite being 8:30 in the morning, groups of students had gathered around J. P.'s tea stall and Ambarda's canteen and were engaged in heated discussions. By this time I should have expected a few surprises at the Department because waiting for me were my students, all of whom had turned up and that too much before the scheduled time of 9 a.m. One of them asked:

> 'Since the tutorial is for the course on Urban Social Problems may we discuss some of the social problems that we are facing today?' And well what is that problem? 'Of course, the future of India! With this reservation thing will India have any future? Will any of us have any future for that matter? What is the use of studying? It is all meaningless. Even if I do well there is no guarantee that I might get through the M.Phil [Master of Philosophy] course or any other. Come to think of it, it hardly matters how you fare in the exams. I guess at least some lucky ones are free of it. But supposing I do get through these courses, what then? Will I get a job? I have no future. I wish I was born anything but a *Kayastha*[3] ... I mean where are we heading?'

Promptly another student replied:

> In the right direction. I am a *Bharadwaj Brahmin* and we are considered to be at the top of the caste hierarchy in Rajasthan but I have no objection to this caste-based reservation policy. I think it is the right thing to do. We

> cannot allow this rotten tradition of caste system and the inequalities that it breeds to go on forever. For heaven's sake we are in the twenty-first century and it's high time that we leave our traditions in the past where they rightly belong. Don't you think that the higher castes have done enough damage to the lower castes? I'm sorry, I don't think of it as a problem but a solution to the problem that we, the upper castes, have created.

Nodding in agreement, and rather diffidently, one of them responded:

> I am a scheduled caste and I agree that the upper castes have dominated other castes but in my hometown it is the OBC (Other Backward Classes) who are the most powerful. They own land and all the bureaucrats and politicians are of their caste or are in their pockets. The OBCs dominate even the upper castes. Do they really deserve reservation? Would it not make them more powerful and dominate us even more?

In the light of the ongoing public debate and controversy surrounding the recent reservation policy, these are some valid questions to which there are no easy or obvious answers. On the surface, it appears to have opened up a new arena of conflict between the beneficiaries, the 'officially' disadvantaged backward classes and castes, and the non-beneficiaries, the forward classes and castes. But what is even more interesting is not how the public opinion is divided – the pro-reservationists vis-à-vis the anti-reservationists – but how caste and caste consciousness have survived. Each one of my students, irrespective of the positions they took regarding the reservation policy, were very well aware of the caste group that they belonged to. At this point I must admit that Srinivas almost sounds prophetic that:

> Caste is an institution of prodigious strength and it will take a lot of beating before it will die (Srinivas, 1962, p. 72).

My attempt in this paper is to understand how caste survives in the popular imagination and in the public discourse. In other words, by taking a close look at the ongoing public debate on reservation and the process of identifying backward classes and castes, I will try to understand how caste is popularly viewed and constructed.

Reservation and the Remaking of Caste

The public debate on reservation has essentially centred on the nature of development and the future that each one of us, whether upper caste, backward or lower caste, envisages for ourselves and the nation. Predictably, many think that reservation would thwart development by compromising on quality. Thus, the question of merit has emerged as one of the most contentious issues in the debate. Mohammed Rela, an internationally renowned liver transplant expert, who has been a beneficiary of the quota system thinks:

> … [t]oday, Indians are competing with the best in the world. India is being regarded as the world's intellectual capital. Increasing reservations will not only hamper merit, it will make other countries suspect Indian talent. The entire quota system should be abolished. India should make examinations an open, level playing field for only the meritorious to succeed. This will improve quality (Sinha, 2006, p. 10).

Likewise, Ballal, the Vice-Chancellor of Manipal Academy of Higher Education, admits that though he is not against reservations, he fears for India's future:

> [t]he fact remains that in the era of globalization, we cannot afford to compromise with quality. If we do we will get wiped out (Pandit, 2006, p. 14).

Not surprisingly, most believe that quotas favouring backward classes and castes 'is a phenomenon of allowing, protecting and promoting under-performance'[4], that puts India's future at stake, including theirs. On the other hand, pro-reservationists think that the idea of 'merit' and the 'meritorious' has been equated with skills, particularly one's command over the English language (Deshpande, 2006). Questioning the so-called standards of merit an anonymous blogger comments:

> What 'merit' are we talking of anyway? Scores in entrance exams at age of 17? Take the claim of 'merit based' entrance to all IIMs [Indian Institutes of Management] and dozens of other institutes. Approximately 25% of the CAT [Common Aptitude Test] is about English! Another 25% is about English Comprehension!!!! There you are!!!! About 50% so-called aptitude test is a hoax for someone who is from a non-English speaking background … Dhirubhai Ambani had a poor command over English. He would not have made it through CAT. So, what 'merit' are we talking of?[5]

Thus, many think that those who are trained in English language schools, primarily the upper castes, are inadvertently favoured in such entrance examinations rendering them meaningless. Hence, these entrance examinations should be done away with, especially in state-funded institutes as the state is accountable for ensuring equality through affirmative action.[6] Though the construct of merit has been questioned, pro-reservationists consider that a dilution of merit is a small price to pay for the upliftment of the less privileged as it would result in the dispersion of merit, educational expansion and end the monopoly of the so-called premier institutes and that of the upper castes (Raibagkar and Pisharody, 2006; Omvedt, 2006).

Here I would like to highlight how the popular construct of the caste system and that of caste runs through the entire discourse on merit, albeit implicitly. Irrespective of one's position of a pro-reservationist or an anti-reservationist or even that of one's caste, the popular construct of the caste system seems to follow a three-line theory, that of the upper, middle and lower castes (Madan, 1989). For anti-reservationists the three-line theory translates into markers of quality, with the higher castes being more advanced 'qualitatively' than the others. This belief is rationalized by their access to better schools and education. Thus, they fear the inclusion of backward classes and castes would affect quality and thereby the development and future of India. Interestingly, many pro-reservationists who speak of dilution of merit hold a similar belief. To many pro-reservationists the three-line theory also reflects the inequalities embedded within the caste system and how it further perpetuates inequalities between the upper castes and the middle and lower castes.

Let us now turn to what is perhaps the central theme of the public debate on reservation – that of achieving social equality and justice and creating equal access to opportunity. On 22 May 2006 as I attended the *Mahapanchayat*, a pro-reservation rally at New Delhi's Talkatora Indoor Stadium, I saw and heard activists chanting slogans and carrying placards that said, 'Opportunity Breeds Equality'. At an opportune moment I cornered one of the student activists from Jawaharlal Nehru University carrying the placard and asked her what her opinion was and why she personally made of the slogan. She responded with alacrity and rather aggressively:

> To me those who have doubts about reservations are the ones who clearly want development for themselves. They want to grab all the opportunities and advance at our cost. They are the ones who are discriminating against us on the basis of caste. Why should we be sacrificed for their development? This is oppression and it is nothing new. It is an age old tradition, almost a normal habit in our social history. Why should we allow them to call the shots, oppress us and label us as

> backward and for god knows how long? Is this country a democracy or what? We are here to demand our rights. And let me ask who do you think is responsible for our backwardness? Don't you think that it is time that they own up to it and pay for it instead of giving us lip service?

The anger and the frustration of being perpetually backward, primarily due to state inaction and denial of access to education as a result of the monopoly and control over education by the upper castes, is self evident and runs through the discourse of most pro-reservationists. According to Sharad Yadav:

> [t]he manner in which reservations to OBCs in higher educational institutions of Central Government is being opposed proves that even after 150 years [from the time the upper castes protested against the attempts of the colonial British Government to introduce educational programmes for the *Shudras* and *Atishudras*, the mindset of the Indian elite has not changed. They are not ready to accept any logic or see any reason for reservations. Simply put, they are suffering – whether they know it or not–from the mindset that *Shudras* are not fit for higher education and that they should not be given opportunities (Yadav, 2006, p. 11).

Bidwai too underlines the differences that are created from being "born in a highly educated *savarna* family [who] will have a totally different universe of knowledge, social contacts and elite acceptability – and wholly different access to information about the availability of study courses, colleges and private tutorial institutions, career options, professional advice, etc. S/he can always call 'Uncle' so-and-so in the civil service, judiciary or the medical profession to get useful tips" as compared to those born in backward families (Bidwai, 2006). Thus, to many it is only fair that OBCs be given reservation to recompense past oppressions and injustices and these reservations should not be confused with the issue of quality or merit (Hasan, 2006, p. 13). Understandably, reservation is also about acknowledging past oppressions that continue to this day. Even after years of independence most of the people from the oppressed castes have remained backward and live in appalling conditions in rural areas with no access to primary, let alone secondary education. An anonymous blogger writes:

> Just to put things in perspective. A student who is classified as belonging to OBC would have had to finish Class XII or graduation as the case may be so as to apply for IIT (Indian Institute of Technology) or

> IIM. The school or college he or she would hail from may or may not be noteworthy but the fact is that there has to be one. So, we are not talking about people who've been denied primary or basic education. That's a different lot altogether.[7]

The picture that emerges is that of a group of people who are eternally banished to the land of darkness and underdevelopment. The arguments clearly imply that reservation is not just an issue revolving around the idea of equality and social justice but is a moral question, of owning up to past wrongs, atoning for them and setting things right. The pro-reservationist reimagines a world that is just and equal and made possible through reservations for the backward and often suppressed lower castes. The underlying assumption here, though clichéd, is that caste is the social evil that is solely responsible for the backwardness and social misery of the lower castes. Implicit in the assumption is also the understanding that the caste system follows a rigid hierarchy, which has remained unchanged through much of India's social history.

On the other hand, anti-reservationists believe that reservation negates the very essence of democracy, equality and social justice. Likewise, Kejal[8] and an anonymous blogger opines:

> I consider reservation – be it based on caste, sex, religion or any other parameter – as a clear breach of democracy. Democracy essentially means all people of a nation are equal no matter what their origin, sex, caste, religion is.
>
> The year I got through JEE[Joint Entrance Examination], the 9th ranker in reserved category was 1900th rank in general category. That was when I felt that reservation was 'justice denied' to hundreds of deserving candidates.[9]

Many think that reservation of such proportions, nearly 50 per cent, destroys rather than restores the rule of equality to opportunity (Hamine, 2006, p. 14). Most interpret equality as sameness and homogeneity or to be treated on the same basis. Any reservation would then mean contravening this idea of equality as 'concessions' of this kind are based on the recognition of social difference and thereby treating different people differently. Anti-reservationists also dispute such one-to-one correlation between lower castes and backwardness as being over-simplistic. They often cite the existence of the creamy layer within OBCs as an outright contradiction of this rule:

> Sir, please check your OBC list again. The other day, a gentleman on TV said that there are more than 3500 castes in the list. Even affluent communities like the *Lingayats* of Karnataka and the *Nairs* of Kerala are included in it.[10]

They claim that that the concessions granted by the reservation policy will only be grabbed by the creamy layer within the OBCs and not reach the truly weaker sections of the society. P. Radhakrishnan insists that:

> If you look at the data of the last five years [in Tamil Nadu], you will see that it is only the creamy layer of the Other Backward Classes that gets all the benefits. If you look at the employment data, the MBCs[Most Backward Castes], the SCs[Scheduled Castes] and the STs[Scheduled Tribes] have not benefited. The real needy will benefit only when we remove the creamy layer. For the last 56 years, reservation has not reached the needy and there is data to show that.[11]

Moreover, such policies fail to incorporate the changing dimensions of caste and class in contemporary Indian society, particularly the upward mobility among the OBCs (Karanth, 2006, p. 12). Many anti-reservationists firmly believe that modern India has opened up newer horizons for those who may have been marginalized in the traditional social hierarchy. Bansal, thus clarifies:

> What I'm saying is, in a single generation you can flip from flop or flop from flip. My father studied under kerosene lamps, on a meagre scholarship. Effort combined with luck and ability, led to social mobility. A government job which took him to the four corners of the world. And to a universe of x-rays and gamma rays beyond that . . . . But, I believe class is not necessarily linked to caste. Now you may disagree with my view of the world and say no, caste is still a major impediment in social progress for a large number of Indians. And therefore, we need reservations. And I am ready to accept that argument–but on the basis of facts and statistics! . . . . NCBC [National Commission on Backward Classes] could have taken the initiative to define backward classes in a new way (e.g. people living in *kachcha* houses, not owning land, no access to drinking water = 1 disadvantaged class, across caste lines). But no, it insists on naming specific castes as backward class. (Bansal, 2006)

Others question the need for reservation after 60 years of independence, paving the way for demands to review the success of reservation policies.

> After spending almost five years and having used the same hostel, same books, same faculty, same campus and same infrastructure, why do you still need reservation? (Pandey, 2006, p. 12)

Many argue that if reservations have failed to remove disparities then there is no justification in increasing reservation quotas. Anti-reservationists have also alleged that reservation is a political gimmick based on votebank politics and has nothing to do with the upliftment of the backward sections. Its only goal is to divide people, tear apart the fabric of society and destroy social cohesion–a definite hangover of the colonial political culture of divide and rule that still dominates mainstream politics.

The path to social justice, pro-reservationists argue, can only be realized when people, no matter who or what they may be, come under the same set of rules and are not given concessions because they are from certain caste groups. Such concessions are in fact discriminatory as they give advantages to some at the cost of others. One of my students in mock fury claimed:

> Compensatory discrimination! They tell us it is discrimination in order to end discrimination. Anything can go in the name of justice isn't it? Hasn't it occurred to anyone that this cannot be justice? Justice is for all. It cannot be for some and injustice to others. We are being told that we must compensate for the injustices that we may have committed in our long gone pasts. Okay we may have done so but does it justify the present injustices that are being meted out to us? Is this justice or some kind of settling of scores? As per their logic, 50 or 100 years down the line we can also claim reservations. So we still have some hope. And then of course we can't raise the question of creamy layer within the OBCs. They can enjoy all the benefits and some more but we can't utter a single word of criticism because that would not only be a politically incorrect thing to do but we will most definitely be accused of being narrow-minded casteists.

Turning to the question of popular imagination of caste system and that of caste, anti-reservationist acknowledge the existence of a hierarchical caste system but are opposed to it being rigid and static over time. A non-rigid understanding of the caste system implies a more contextual and dynamic interpretation of the caste structure, on the one hand. On the other, many anti-reservationists have challenged the materialistic interpretation of the caste system where backwardness simply cannot be equated with lower castes, at least in some contexts. We must also notice the veiled references to caste and electoral politics that suggest that caste consciousness and the act of relating it to the discourse of development is not a simple social issue but is a much more complex issue of identity politics. As a blogger admits:

All I can say is that, if this has anything to do with the so-called social upliftment, the step that is being taken is only going to ruin the nation even more! Because, when a schoolboy gets newly admitted, before his classmates can know his name or where he lives, they will spread this news – Hey, this new Brahmin has joined our class or Oh! That girl, she is new and I am quite sure that she is a Dalit.[12]

Visions of Modernity and the Insistent Politics of Caste

'Nobody has ever lived in a Utopia. But most of us live by our utopias, explicit or implicit.'

(Nandy, 1987, p. 17)

Let me now turn to another contentious aspect of the debate – that of defining backwardness and the official or state identification of backward classes and castes. At the very outset, the reservation policy and the official process of identifying backward classes and castes has already been accused of having a caste bias. Bansal notes:

I feel, caste had become irrelevant to a significant number of young people. But now it may once again become top of the mind . . . And that, I think will ultimately damage the idea of India. Things are far from perfect today but we should be working towards making caste a non-issue. Not the issue. (Bansal, 2006)

But many differ, like Omvedt, who argues that paying attention to caste is not casteist as the social evil of casteism still persists in contemporary India. Here, caste is viewed as a privilege or disadvantage that facilitates or impedes development of particular caste groups with the obvious conclusion being that upper castes would always be more advanced and part of the upper echelons of society and the lower castes would form the lower classes (Omvedt, 2006, p. 20). Dirks observes that throughout the history of modern India, popular imagination of caste is dominated by the perceived illegitimacy of traditional caste hierarchy and by the need to overcome its ill effects, namely caste inequalities (Dirks, 1997). Caste is commonly viewed as an aberration, a relic of the past that still continues to have a disrupting influence on India's progress and development. Such non-modern and often backward and oppressive constructions of caste have no space in the popular discourse of a modern, progressive and developed India. Contrary to this popular construct of caste, caste too has undergone transformations over time and has reinvented itself to assume new forms, functions and goals, mainly a shift from sacred to secular goals.[13] The present public debate on reservation itself is clearly indicative of this shift. Understandably, caste in the present-day has emerged as an ideology used to contest and protect political and socioeconomic interests (Nandy, 1990).[14]

In this context, the state's attempt to create standardized categories, that fail to take into account the complex social processes of contexually varying reasons for deprivation, leads to static or frozen categories. This is considered by many as the primary problem in the official identification process of backward classes and castes (Jenkins, 2003). Moreover, caste divisions and boundaries are ambiguous and have over the years blurred,[15] further complicating the problem of identification.[16] Srinivas points out that historically caste has been more flexible than is generally recognized (Srinivas, 1960). In pre-British India families, larger groups and dominant caste groups acquired power by resorting to warfare or by serving rulers (Srinivas, 1968; Kolenda, 1978). During the British Raj such traditional avenues closed down, opening newer ones. One of them being the decennial Census introduced by the British that provided an opportunity for lower castes to claim a higher status (Rowe, 1968; Kothari, 1970; Appadurai, 1993; Bandyopadhyay, 1994). Clearly, the relationship between caste, class and backwardness is complex and multifaceted and must be treated contextually. Understandably, there have been demands for more sophisticated identification criteria.

> We should see other forms of deprivation and find ways to address them. There can be an index of grading people on the basis of their caste, parent's education and economic conditions.[17]

> It would be ideal in the long term if different institutions and governments could devise varying affirmative action formulae based upon a number of different criteria besides caste–including gender, economic status of family, quality of schooling received by parents, backwardness of region of origin, etc. Delhi's JNU [Jawaharlal Nehru University] has a decade-old admissions policy which gives extra points to OBCs, women and regional backwardness over and above a candidate's entrance examination score. This has significantly raised JNU's OBC intake (Bidwai, 2006).

The flip side to an identification criterion that bears a close link with backward classes and castes, more often than not, labels and stigmatizes those caste groups which it aims to emancipate. A blogger recounts:

> It was during this time [of Mandal Commission], I remember reading a letter in one of the newspapers where a girl had recounted how her friends started treating her differently when they found out that she was from the SC/ST quota. A meritorious student, the girl had written it had offended her no end to be looked down upon because her friends wrongly assumed that she got a seat in the college because of her caste.[18]

Though detractors suggest and have given instances of caste groups claiming lower status to get benefits from reservation policies some from backward caste groups have challenged such classifications and have categorically denied being backward. Rela, who belongs to a backward Muslim community, questions:

> Who is backward? Presently, it is based on caste. But it actually should be based on socioeconomic standard of a community. I applied through backward quota for my MBBS [Bachelor of Medicine and Bachelor of Surgery] entrance exam in Madras Medical College. State level exams had quotas in Tamil Nadu then. But I wasn't backward in any way, besides coming from a backward Muslim caste. I came from a business family, had the best of education, got dropped to school in a car. (Sinha, 2006, p. 10)

It led me to think that there may be a larger, less visible and subtle politics hidden within the issue of reservation–perhaps the 'politics of condescension' (Mehta, 2006). We are, in most likelihood, entrenching social distinctions between the so-called forward, elite castes and the backward castes. The identification of backward classes and castes with backwardness in a way is a social ordering of difference that is reminiscent of our colonial legacy. In our eagerness to achieve our vision of equality, the term backwardness has perhaps acquired an unchanging and rigid meaning. Put simply, it means that the so-called forward castes would perhaps remain forward forever, consolidating their hegemonic position over the 'other', backward castes. Sadly, there has been widespread acceptance by the backward castes of their own backwardness. A blogger writes:

> They come out proudly in the pro-quota rallies and announce … we are not capable people, we survive on the mercy of others. Why on earth they don't believe they are the same human species with similar brains, have they all fallen prey to the inferiority complex and are happy about that!!!?[19]

In other words, the backward is defining itself in terms of the definitions borrowed from the forward castes, further hardening the boundaries between the two. Implicit in this politics of condescension is the politics of catching up. Being backward, the OBCs must catch up with the forward castes and it is the moral duty of the historically forward caste to give them a chance to catch up. Raibagkar and Pisharody, perhaps unknowingly, express similar sentiments.

> When globalization became a reality, the government responded favourably to the demands made by industry captains for a 'level playing field'. Do you then expect someone to run a race with legs chopped off? (Raibagkar and Pisharody, 2006, p. 10)

Thus, the backward became an object of charity and experimentation whose pace of development, progress and emancipation are set by the forward and developed castes. The backward would eventually develop like the forward castes through education or through the generosity and aid of the latter (Nandy, 2004).[20] Equality and development for the backward castes is assumed to happen only when they follow a similar trajectory of development and progress like that of the forward castes.

Postcript

> My brother and I were incessantly drilled on the 'value of education'. It was held up as our only passport for the future. So we grew up striving for it, yearning for it. And that, I think, is the crucial X factor due to which certain kinds of young people make it through competitive exams. And others don't. . . .

The story of reservation is the story of development. As the story unfolds, so do our utopias – our dreams and our nightmares, the winners and the losers, the forward and the backward, the developed and the underdeveloped, the privileged and the underprivileged. Following the script closely the state identifies and categorizes people along the cleavages, namely caste, designing social (read as developmental) interventions, like reservation policies, for the upliftment and emancipation of the disadvantaged, specifically the backward lower castes. Putting aside the immediate conflicts between the beneficiaries and the non-beneficiaries, the two interest groups, let us take a deeper look at the questions that are thrown up by such interventions – Is caste truly anti-modern? Does caste completely reject modern values and modernity itself? Or has caste acquired a modern form using the language of modernity and development to evolve new justifications of dominance and oppression that reiterate and legitimize the existing power relations, at least in some cases.

Acknowledgement

A part of this paper entitled 'De-politicizing Backwardness: Setting the Agenda for Discussion' was jointly presented with H. Ramachandran at a Round Table on 'De-politicizing Backwardness–Alternative Approaches', Department of Geography, Delhi School of Economics, University of Delhi. 29–30 August, 2006.

Notes

1. Mandal II, popularly refers to the reservation policy that introduces a 27 per cent quota of government jobs for Other Backward Classes (OBC) in educational institutes.
2. Delhi School of Economics in University of Delhi, which includes the Departments of Economics, Sociology and Geography, is commonly referred to as the D-School campus.
3. Interestingly, *Kayasthas* too had applied to the National Commission for Backward Classes for their inclusion in the backward class list but their plea was rejected on the basis that they were socially and educationally one of the most advanced communities of the country. See '*When Kayasthas Sought OBC tag'*, *The Times of India*, September 26, 2007, p. 11.
4. For details see comments made by Bedevilled. *Source*: http://groups.yahoo.com/group/noreservation/ (last accessed on September 11, 2007).
5. Internet posting made by Anonymous in Entrance to the Shrine: Anti-reservation Blogroll. *Source*: http://entrancetotheshrine.blogspot.com/2006/04/anti-reservations-blogroll.html (last accessed on August 01, 2008).
6. For details see The Constitution of India, Article 15(4).
7. Entrance to the Shrine: Anti-reservation Blogroll. *Source*: http://entrancetotheshrine. blogspot.com/2006/04/anti-reservations-blogroll.html (last accessed on August 01, 2008).
8. See 'It's Apartheid', *The Times of India*, New Delhi edition, May 25, 2006, p. 12.
9. Entrance to the Shrine: Anti-reservation Blogroll. *Source*: http://entrancetotheshrine. blogspot.com/2006/04/anti-reservations-blogroll.html (last accessed on August 01, 2008).
10. 'Arjun Singh Zindabad', Comments posted by dazedandconfused. *Source*: http://settingmeup.blogspot.com/2006_04_01_archive.html on April 12, 2006 (last accessed on August 01, 2008).
11. As quoted in Warrier, S., 'Education is the means of social mobility', May 30, 2006. *Source*: *http://www.rediff.com/news/2006/may/30spec.htm* (accessed on August 01, 2008).

12. Entrance to the Shrine: Anti-reservation Blogroll. *Source*: *http://entrance-totheshrine. blogspot.com/2006/04/anti-reservations-blogroll.html* (last accessed on August 01, 2008).
13. Elsewhere I have discussed the same in detail, See De, A., (2007). Also see Rudolph, L.I. and Rudolph, S.H., (1969) pp. 32–33 for a discussion on how aims of caste associations have been reformulated in keeping with liberal and democratic ideas and have pressed for action in welfare, educational and economic realms.
14. Here I have extended a similar logic to caste as Nandy does to religion. Nandy argues that religion in South Asia is split into two, faith and ideology. The latter represents the use of religion to protect or contest for non-religious interests, particularly political and socioeconomic interests. See Nandy, A., (1990), pp. 69–93.
15. Srinivas, M.N., (1960) observes that in case of the urban educated middle class in particular, caste is no longer an endogamous unit nor does it signify occupational homogeneity. Ghurye, G.S., (1961), too showed from a 1954 study of a village in Maharashtra that occupations were relatively free of caste restrictions and that cultivation, administration, military services and modern occupations were open to all castes.
16. For other complications regarding identification of backward classes and castes that include migration, marriage, adoption and religious conversions, which have not been dealt here, see Jenkins (2003).
17. Pratap Bhanu Mehta, former member of Knowledge Commission as quoted in Pandey, V., 'A case for excluding creamy layer', DNA, May 19, 2006, p. 12.
18. See Daydreamer, India's blog, "Mandal Commission". *Source*: *http://lifes-a-dream.blogspot.com/2006/04/mandal-commission.html*, April 8, 2006 (last accessed on August 01, 2008).
19. *Source*: http://www.obcreservation.net/ver1/content/view/48/9/1/3/ (last accessed on August 01, 2008)

References

Appadurai, A., 'Number in the Colonial Imagination', in Carole A. Breckinridge and Peter Van der Veer (eds.), *Orientalism and the Postcolonial Predicament: Perspectives on South Asia*, Philadelphia: University of Pennsylvania Press, 1993, pp. 314–339.

Bandyopadhyay, S., 'Caste, Class and Politics in Colonial Bengal: A Case Study of the Namasadra Movement of 1872–1937', in K. L. Sharma (ed.), *Caste and Class in India*, Jaipur: Rawat Publications, 1994, pp. 19–52.

Bandyopadhyay, S., *Caste, Culture and Hegemony: Social Domination in Colonial Bengal*, New Delhi: Sage Publications, 2004.

Bansal, R., 'Caste Vs Class'. *Source*: *http://youthcurry.blogspot.com*, posted on 11 April 2006 (last accessed on 1 August, 2008).

Bidwai, P., 'The anti-quota stir is misguided'. *Source*: http://www.rediff.com/news/2006/may/30bidwai.htm, 2006 (last accessed on 1 August, 2008).

De, A., 'Caste as Non-Western Civil Society: Narratives from Ahmedabad', *Occasional Paper Series 2007*, Bombay Geographical Association, 2007.

Deshpande, S., 'Merit, Caste and Discrimination in Higher Education Today', *Economic and Political Weekly*, Vol. 41, No. 24, 2006, pp. 2438–2444.

Dirks, N., 'Recasting Tamil Society: The Politics of Caste and Race in Contemporary Southern India', in C. J. Fuller (ed.), *Caste Today*, Delhi: Oxford University Press, 1997, pp. 263–295.

Ghurye, G. S., *Caste, Class and Occupation*, Bombay: Popular Book Depot, 1961.

Hamine, P., 'Ambedkar has Called for Measured Reservation Quotas', *Daily News and Analysis*, 17 May 2006.

Hasan, Z., 'Turning the Wheel', *Daily News and Analysis*, 18 May 2006.

Jenkins, L. D., *Identity and Identification in India: Defining the Disadvantaged*, London: Routledge, 2003.

Karanth, G. K., 'Reservation is Not the Solution', *Daily News and Analysis*, 25 May 2006.

Kolenda, P., *Caste in Contemporary India: Beyond Organic Solidarity*, Menlo Park, California: Benjamin and Cummings Publishing Company, 1978.

Kothari, R. (ed.), *Caste in Indian Politics*, New Delhi: Orient Longman, 1970.

Madan, T. N., 'Caste and the Ordering of Hindu Society', in F. Robinson (ed.), *The Cambridge Encyclopedia of India*, Cambridge: Cambridge University Press, 1989, pp. 364–366.

Mehta, P. B., 'Democracy, Disagreement and Merit', *Economic and Political Weekly*, Vol. XLI, No. 24, 2006, pp. 2425–2427.

Nandy, A., 'Evaluating Utopias: Considerations for a Dialogue of Cultures and Faith', in Ashis Nandy (ed.), *Traditions, Tyranny, and Utopias: Essays in the Politics of Awareness*, New Delhi: Oxford University Press, 1987, pp. 1–19.

Nandy, A., 'The Politics of Secularism and the Recovery of Religious Tolerance' in Veena Das (ed.), *Mirrors of Violence: Communities, Riots and Survivors in South Asia*, Delhi: Oxford University Press, 1990, pp. 69–93.

Nandy, A., 'Culture, Voice and Development: A Primer for the Unsuspecting', in Ashis Nandy (ed.), *Bonfire of Creeds: The Essential Ashis Nandy*, Delhi: Oxford University Press, 2004, pp. 304–323.

Omvedt, G., 'Beyond Quotas', *The Times of India*, 12 May 2006, p. 20.

Pandey, V., 'Why Medicos have Good Reason to Stir', *Daily News and Analysis*, 24 May 2006.

Pandit, S., 'Seat Hike will Crush Us: Colleges', *The Times of India*, 25 May 2006.

Raibagkar, S. J. and V. B. Pisharody, 'Strong Reservations', *The Hindustan Times*, 15 May 2006.

Rowe, W., 'Mobility in Nineteenth Century Caste System', in Milton Singer and Bernard S. Cohn (eds.), *Structure and Change in Indian Society*, New York: Viking Fund Publications, 1968, pp. 201–213.

Rudolph, L. I. and S. H. Rudolph, *The Modernity of Tradition: Political Development in India*, Hyderabad: Orient Longman, 1969.

Sinha, K., 'Rela, who used quota, slams it', *The Times of India*, 16 May, 2006.

Srinivas, M. N., 'The Indian Road to Equality', *Economic Weekly*, Vol. 12, Special issue, June 1960, pp. 867–872.

Srinivas, M. N., *Caste in Modern India and Other Essays*, Bombay: Asia Publishing House, 1962.

Srinivas, M. N., 'Mobility in the Caste System', in Milton Singer and Bernard S. Cohn (eds.), *Structure and Change in Indian Society*, New York: Viking Fund Publications, 1968, pp. 189–200.

Yadav, S., 'Promises to Keep', *The Hindustan Times*, 22 May 2006.

22

Spatial Patterns of Crime in India

Vandana Wadhwa and Ashok K. Dutt

No one is a born criminal; even if someone has the questionable 'crime-related gene', it is primarily one's environment and experiences that induce criminal conduct. Cruel and loveless upbringing, social and economic deprivation, a physically dilapidated and gang-infested neighborhood, hostile atmosphere in the house, crime-ridden historic traditions and suffocating population densities are some environmental conditions that contribute to the initiation and continuation of criminal activities (Dutt, Noble and Singh, 1979). Geographers first started to unravel the geography of crime in the 1970s. There were others who contributed to the study of spatial aspects of crime (Pyle *et al.*, 1974). In India, both criminologists and sociologists have researched different aspects of crime (Rao, 1981), but spatially-oriented crime studies started to appear only in the 1970s. Nayar (1975) provided a nationwide spatial analysis of crime. Indian crime studies with this spatial component followed from the 1970s through the earlier part of the twenty-first century. These studies may be grouped into three levels – city (micro), regional (meso) and national (macro). They have been reviewed here followed by an analysis of the relationship between crime and politics.

Review of City Scale Studies

The city has often been thought to be a good breeding ground for crime; possibly due to the contributing factors of anomie, congestion, heterogeneity, cultural and traditional breakdowns resulting from the processes of urbanization and industrialization; but also possibly because crime in rural areas is largely underreported. As a result, much of the literature on spatio-temporal patterns of crime has been done on a city scale, such as on Kolkata (Dutta, 1976), Chennai (Sivamurthy, 1981 and 1982), Ajmer

(Dutt, Noble and Sharma, 1985) and Delhi (Bhushan, 1997). Other scholars have studied patterns of crime in cities in order to contrast and compare national and regional patterns and trends, such as the study of the four metropolises of Delhi, Mumbai, Hyderabad and Vishakhapatnam by Rao (1981) and of Ahmedabad by Bhatnagar (1990).

Dutta (1976) attempted to delineate spatial patterns of crime in Kolkata based on ecological criteria. Although successful in this regard, the study could not relate these patterns to larger urban theories of structure. The absence of analyses regarding the places of occurrence of crime and the places of residence of criminals resulted in an incomplete understanding of crime.

Sivamurthy's Chennai Study

Sivamurthy (1981) incorporated factor analysis in his study on crime in Chennai. He combined eight crime variables with 22 physical, social, demographic and occupational characteristics to attempt an explanation of the city's crime pattern. There were several key findings. Property crime was found to be a function of physical characteristics (low housing density) and of economic prosperity, mostly concentrated south of the Central Business District and in the southern parts of the city. Residence of criminals was concentrated in the Central Business District and northern areas of Chennai, characterized by a high proportion of Scheduled Caste and Scheduled Tribe populations, low occupational status and slums, in direct contrast with the pattern and ecology of property crime, revealing that such crime was not committed in the same area where the criminals reside. Violent crime was most prevalent in the Central Business District and in the industrial areas of east and central Chennai. Sivamurthy, thus, demonstrated that occurrence of crime and place of residence of criminals vary highly over space and that this distribution was linked to physical, demographic, social and occupational characteristics of the area. However, Sivamurthy acknowledged that such a study was more useful for its methodology rather than results because a phenomenon as complex as crime does not lend itself readily to generalization (Wadhwa and Dutt, 2000).

A follow-up study on the spatio-temporal variation of theft in Chennai (Sivamurthy, 1982) employed correlation and regression techniques to identify spatial trends in the occurrence of theft over one long-term period (1965–75) and one short-term period (1970–75). Areas that displayed an increase in theft over both time periods were the affluent residential localities and commercial areas. Those areas that showed an increase in theft between 1965 and 1975, but a less than expected change over a five year period from 1970 to 1975 were those more attractive areas during the earlier period, that is out-migration of the higher income groups resulting in the residual congested low and middle-income areas becoming less attractive for theft.

The benefits of such a spatial study are that by understanding the link between crime, space and the area's ecology, more effective policing and prevention strategies may be framed. For example, if an area is an upcoming high-income residential locality, it may be wise to focus more attention on safety strategies than earlier.

Dutt et al. on Ajmer

Dutt *et al.*'s (1985) study of Ajmer, based on factor analysis, clustered 18 variables of crime along with five socio-demographic and ecological variables (total population, non-workers, occupied residential places, number of persons in Scheduled Castes and Scheduled Tribe populations, and literate population). Spatial plotting of the three major factors reveals – factor I (theft of motor parts, cheating) was predominant in the northern part of the city, which was characterized by low population density and a high standard of living, explaining the high incidence of theft of auto parts as a greater part of the population could afford automobiles; factor II (property crimes, murder) was predominant in the western section of the city, which was an old, congested, culturally diverse commercial area, a good breeding ground for property crimes and murder due to physical and social environment; factor III (receiving of stolen goods, death by poisoning) was predominant in the south and southeastern areas of the city, and was characterized by low standards of living, high Scheduled Castes and Scheduled Tribe populations. Lack of employment for these segments of society led to crimes related to receiving of stolen goods, and death by poisoning was mainly a result of deaths caused by illicit alcohol which the people drink in order to escape the frustrations of their daily life. A positive correlation was found between crimes in general and average density and maximum density, as also with total population and number of non-workers.

Rao's Four Metropolis Study

A study of four metropolitan cities and one medium city was conducted as part of a larger study by Rao (1981) investigating spatial patterns and factors affecting crime. The interest in studying cities is because, according to Rao (1981), crime rates in Indian metropolises are higher than the national or regional rates. Also, most crime (approximately 90 per cent) has economic roots (the motive of pecuniary gain), and is mainly the cause of a constant influx of population and the resultant congestion, familial disruption and the presence of opportunity. Interestingly, according to Rao's analysis, the size of the city had no effect on the volume of crime, but rate of growth of the city had a positive correlation with the level of crime.

Bhatnagar's Ahmedabad

Studying Ahmedabad within the context of its region (the state of Gujarat), Bhatnagar (1990) attempted to understand some of the bases of the commission of crime by examining the socioeconomic profile of 52 prisoners. Major crimes in Ahmedabad were murder, kidnapping and abduction, dacoity, robbery, home breakings, thefts, riots, breach of trust and cheating, which accounted for 75 per cent of the total crime in the city. The profile of the prisoners showed that a significant proportion (greater than 50 per cent) of them are non-Scheduled Castes or Scheduled Tribes, Hindu, married, lived in low income tenements (*chawls*) or in slums, had a low income of up to Rs 1000 per month and were rural migrants. Most of these perpetrators had their place of residence in the south zone (a mix of slums, lower and lower-middle class residences, *chawls*, small commercial ventures and traditional populations). The north (lower-middle class residential) and east (industrial areas) followed, with the west (middle and high income residential) having the least number of criminals residing there. Despite the utility of mapping the residence of criminals in order to understand the possible underlying socioeconomic causes of crime in Ahmedabad, two problems present themselves – the sample is too small to be representative of the population, and therefore limited in its usefulness in the making of any concrete generalizations.

Bhushan on Delhi

Bhushan (1997) probed the socioeconomic bases of the changing trends and patterns of crime in Delhi. Bhushan used a number of statistical techniques to understand and explain the patterns of crime in Delhi from 1971–91. Data analysis was done for the years 1971, 1981 and 1991 to provide a longitudinal cross-section, while keeping space consideration.

A moving average was taken of the years 1970, 1971 and 1972 to provide a more accurate picture for 1971, and similar steps were taken for 1981 and 1991 to remove data bias. Factor analysis was used to delineate socioeconomic patterns, using the nine variables of density, literacy, proportion of Scheduled Caste populations, number of persons per household, slum residence, unemployment, and proportions of primary, secondary and tertiary workers.

The factor analysis of crime variables for 1971 yielded six factors – violent crimes or crimes against a person (Trans-Yamuna and newly developed low-income colonies); property crime (the commercial and business districts); narco-threat, that is narcotics, excise, gambling and arms-related crimes, (slum colonies along the Yamuna and in the traditional communities of east-central Delhi); miscellaneous (in and around the walled city); heinous crimes, dacoity and armed robbery (rural fringes); and social crimes (near walled city and rural Alipur). The analysis for 1981 was as follows – violent crimes (Trans-Yamuna and newly developed colonies in the north); property crimes (in and around commercial and business districts); narco-threat (in and around the walled city and the Trans-Yamuna area); and social crime (walled city). For 1991, the factors and congruent spatial patterns were – violent crime (Trans-Yamuna area); property crimes (commercial and business districts, and south Trans-Yamuna area); social or institutional crime (northwest Delhi, extending from centre to fringe); narco-social (traditional area near the walled city); and pickpocketing (walled city).

Overall, single factor extraction revealed that in 1971, the highest loading was on burglary; in 1981, on other Indian Penal Code (IPC) crimes; and in 1991, on bodily injury, kidnapping and abduction, and other IPC crimes. There has been a rising trend in criminality, particularly in violent crime. All across the three points of time, the Trans-Yamuna area has always been an area of very high crime. High crime rates were found in the Central Business District (Connaught Place) in 1971, the northern area of new development (Kingsway Camp) in 1981 and Tilak Nagar in 1991. Fringe areas of the north and west, and areas southeast of the centre had consistently low crime rates.

An added dimension was given to this study by the analysis of data on the criminals themselves. Bhushan found that 98 per cent of the criminals were Indian (an element to be considered because Delhi is a fairly important hub of international connections). Of these, 70 per cent were from Delhi itself. Of the rest, half were from Uttar Pradesh, and more than 10 per cent each from Punjab and Haryana. Of the criminals hailing from Delhi, most were from the west, northwest, Trans-Yamuna, slum areas of south Delhi and the periphery of the walled city. Approximately 69 per cent were slum residents, 21 per cent from rural background and eight percent from a good socioeconomic background. In an analysis of distance of residence from place of crime committed, about 95 per cent committed crimes within a radius of less than 20 kilometres of their residence. The average distance was less for crimes against a person and more for property crimes.

Canonical correlation produced the following results – densely populated areas have the maximum users of narcotics and those engaged in immoral traffic; poverty indices are positively related with violent crime; and areas of high socioeconomic status were more vulnerable to property crime. Unemployment, number of persons per house, secondary workers and slum residence are positively correlated with crime; and literacy, primary workers and tertiary workers are negatively correlated. In the context of space, crime and criminal belts shifted from the core to the periphery between 1971 and 1991.

This study of Delhi has also revealed that during the two-decade period, cycle theft has declined because a large number of former cycle users have moved to scooter ownership, so the criminals are not interested in stealing bicycles. As people become more affluent, the nature of theft also changes.

Regional Scale Studies

Although the ecology of the local area (city) may heavily influence the magnitude and form of crime, its occurrence is often influenced by the larger context of the region. Studies on a regional scale, involving a number of districts, a state or a number of states, are not limited by purely local phenomena and thereby provide a broader picture of the occurrence of crime over space. Being, by definition, cohesive areas bound by physical or functional aspects, regions provide a scale of study that transcends insular influences while protecting against over generalization that may result from larger studies. Katare's (1972) study on dacoity in the ravine regions of Madhya Pradesh and Bhatnagar's (1990) study on Gujarat (part of a larger study) are examples of such studies.

Katare's Madhya Pradesh

Spatio-temporal patterns of dacoity (a form of robbery) in Madhya Pradesh were analysed by Katare (1972), wherein he found that this type of crime is concentrated in the transitional lowlands that are full of ravines and forests (which make for perfect cover). Dacoity decreases with distance from the ravine belts, and occurs mainly in the rural areas of the lowlands (where the population has sufficient means of sustenance) and in settlements that are away from major transport and communication links, and therefore away from organised resistance. The fewest dacoities are perpetuated during the monsoons (June to September). At this time the roads are muddy, the fields are soggy with low growing crop and the streams and gullies are flooded. Safe and quick escape for the dacoits is not guaranteed in this season.

There is a steady increase of dacoity during September through December. The conditions then are almost ideal for the dacoits in Madya Pradesh. It is also the marriage and festival season when wealth is displayed on every side.

Nights are long enough, offering cover for the dacoits to escape after committing the crimes. The main field crops are maize, jowar and bajra, all of considerable height which provide excellent cover.

After the harvest of these crops the dacoities drop in February, March and April, which also have few celebrations or marriages and, thus, little displayed wealth for the taking. The steep rise in dacoity in May is a response to the oncoming monsoon season. Dacoits must collect sufficient booty to tide themselves over the difficult monsoon period when they are least active.

Some suggestions made by Katare (1972) are directed towards preventing crimes. They are: (a) development of the Chambal basin through development projects that will result in greater connectivity of settlements, which will then provide less cover for the dacoits; and (b) the declaration of the Chambal basin as a single criminological unit in order to coordinate inter-jurisdictional efforts to combat the problem.

Bhatnagar's Gujarat Study

Bhatnagar's (1990) Gujarat study was an attempt to understand the interplay between crime and socioeconomic conditions in the context of a national picture, and also to understand intra-regional differentials. In the national context, Gujarat holds a relatively better socioeconomic status than many of the other states. It also does not figure in a high position in the state-wise list of volume of crime. The regression analysis of crime (the dependent variable including only the nine categories of murder, kidnapping and abduction, dacoity, robbery, house-breaking, theft, riots, breach of trust and cheating) and socioeconomic variables was performed. According to the analysis, low per capita income, low secondary sector population, low employment in the organised sector, high density, high primary sector population, high Scheduled Caste or Scheduled Tribes population and low literacy explained a large percentage of the variance in the dependent variable. Therefore, the backward districts characterized by these socioeconomic variables had higher rates of crime. On the whole as a state, Gujarat is subsumed by a larger regional context and displayed a particularly higher rate of riots, especially in areas where conflict populations (disadvantaged groups and traditional populations) reside.

National Scale Studies

Despite the danger of over-generalization, the depiction of crime in a larger areal context is necessary to achieve a holistic view of this complex phenomenon. Most of these macro-level studies concentrate on providing a national picture of crime by analysing only temporal trends and/or shifts (see national overviews of crime rates in Nayar, 1975; Rao, 1981; Bhatnagar, 1990; Sinha, 2000). But there is a genre of national-level crime analysis that has a spatial dimension. This includes the use of micro or meso-level data, that is city, district or state-level data, to produce a national picture of the patterns of crime over space at the national level. Examples of such studies are: Dutt and Venugopal (1983), and Pomeroy *et al.* (1999), where the city is used as the unit of analysis; Dutt *et al.* (1979), Deol (1996) and Banerjee-Guha (2000), where districts are the unit of analysis; and Nayar (1975), Rao (1981), Bhatnagar (1990) and Sinha (2000), where the national crime scenario is analysed by state.

Sinha's Culture of Oppression Concept

Sinha (2000) reasons that the prevalence of crime in India is related to a culture of oppression, which operates on the basis of hegemonic notions of superiority/inferiority or dominance/subordination. To him, oppression is culturally and economically nurtured in the caste-ridden social structure of India. Such social structure is characterized by: (a) a minimum economic dynamism, and (b) little upward mobility, within which established patterns of domination have lost their legitimacy, providing the context for growing conflicts. Presenting a radical view, Sinha (2000) states that the:

> ... story of crime in India is a story of ongoing struggle of the oppressed and marginalized people against age-old exploitation and victimization, aimed at liberation from the dual burden of class and caste exploitation. It is a desperate struggle for survival. It is about legitimate land rights, resolution of community rights and access to common property resources. It is about resistance against systematic dislocation of people from their native homes and from sources of traditional livelihood in the name of development. It is a denial to perform unpaid work against seizure of lands, crops, fishing rights in ponds, canals, rivers and coastal backwaters by the powerful social groups. The issues are not only agrarian or related to economic justice but also linked with non-economic coercion. All such forms of protests by the have nots have been reciprocated by violence and brutality unleashed by the hegemonic classes who desperately attempt to enforce subjugation and traditional order (Sinha, 2000, p. 260).

Sinha further asserts that 'conflicts should not be categorized as caste conflict, agrarian conflict, communalism, *harijan* atrocities or naxalism. These are all varied expressions of economic exploitation and social oppression which may be attributed as the root causes of all conflicts within which crime and violence take place.' (Sinha, 2000, p. 260).

He further analyses the question of types of crimes in India from 1950 to1995, revealing that the proportion of violent crimes has increased primarily because of accentuation of the culture of oppression. To justify Sinha's argument that criminal action in India takes place as a result of the culture of oppression, an index of such oppression, or indepth qualitative studies of particularly affected areas would be useful, whereas this study relies on substitute measures to display this relationship. However, the study's use of a robust theoretical framework furthers its potential for future research in order to develop a composite measure of oppression. This would help in answering questions pertinent to India, i.e., is there a greater prevalence of this culture of oppression in the north-central subculture of violence region than in the rest of India? How will this culture of contention concept relate to the existence of the southwestern coastal occurrence of counterfeiting?

While bringing out the spatial scenario of crime in India in the 1990s, Banerjee-Guha (2000) strengthens Sinha's concept. Her study attempts a regionalization of selected crimes that are of primary importance due to their high occurrence. These crimes are classified by a three-fold typology – offences against persons (murder, rape and cheating); offences against property (burglary, dacoity and theft); and group crime (rioting). In 1990, all of these together accounted for more than 70 per cent of total reported crime. In terms of national proportions of crime attributed to each state, states with high proportions of violent crimes, such as murder and rape, were Uttar Pradesh and Bihar for both and Madhya Pradesh as leader in the latter. Other violent acts termed as 'group crime' or rioting follows the same pattern, occurring most in Uttar Pradesh, Bihar, Rajasthan and West Bengal. Dacoity was found mostly in Bihar, but sometimes spilt over into isolated districts of states such as Andhra Pradesh. Thus, spatially, the major areas of crime emerged in the states of Uttar Pradesh, Bihar, Madhya Pradesh and Rajasthan (confirming the subculture of violence theory), with a second group of states with relatively high incidence of crime being Maharashtra, West Bengal, Andhra Pradesh and Tamil Nadu. Theft and burglary were not only the most diffuse crimes, they were also the most common. Therefore in the study, it was found that within the states themselves, the most common crimes were theft, burglary and riots. Banerjee-Guha suggests a high degree of negative association between socioeconomic conditions and violent crimes. Caste and class, the remnants of feudalism, and conservatism associated with illiteracy contribute to the socioeconomic deprivation of a society.

Examination of Nayar's 'System Perfomance' Concept

Nayar's (1975) state-wise analysis of national crime patterns from 1959 to 1968 examines two hypotheses – long-term trends are the functions of expansion or deterioration of economic and political capabilities of the nation; and short-term deviations are functions of either economic or political shifts in national capabilities. Violence and crime are responses to economic distress or progress and political discontent or satisfaction; therefore, trends in crime are a direct measure of system performance. This may also be applied to spatial patterns of crime. Certain crime types are more evident in particular areas of the nation and those reflect the socio-political culture of that state. The northern states (except Jammu and Kashmir) and southern states (except Tamil Nadu) enjoy greater levels of domestic security, while this level is low in the eastern states (except Orissa) and in the central region. The western region lies somewhere in between these two ends. In terms of specific crime, riots have the highest incidence in the eastern states (some of the following studies corroborate this), followed by the central region, then the south. Regression analysis showed that the East explained about 50 per cent of the variance in case of riots. Personal offences and fraud were found to be the function of areas with a high rate of growth of urbanization, while property offences and property offences with violence were found to be a function of areas with high proportion of Scheduled Caste or Scheduled Tribes. However, it should be noted that association does not imply causal relationships.

Socioeconomic Indicators of Crime

Rao's (1981) regional analysis of the nation's crime patterns are based on the hypothesis that five socioeconomic indicators (population density, illiteracy, per capita income, unemployment and proportion of Scheduled Caste or Scheduled Tribe populations) may bear some relationship to the spatial patterning of crime in India. In a correlation analysis, he found a significant positive correlation between unemployment and crime, and a weak inverse relationship with crime and the variables of per capita income and literacy. Low rates of crime were found in the northwest and south, and high rates in the central region, spreading from Madhya Pradesh to Uttar Pradesh and Maharashtra. Areas of moderate crime seem to be gradually merging into high crime areas due to industrialization, caste feuds and breakdown of traditional values, as in Bihar. As an example of intra-state differentials, Rao (1981) selected Rajasthan, wherein factor analysis revealed that spatial variations in crime reflected the cultural and economic development milieu of the areas, unemployment being a significant factor.

According to Bhatnagar (1990), certain social factors (proportion of rural population, density, proportion of Scheduled Caste or Scheduled Tribes and literacy) and economic factors (per capita income, proportion of primary sector and secondary sector workers, and proportion in industry) can explain variance in crime. A regression analysis revealed that economic factors accounted for 62.27 per cent and social factors accounted for 19.89 per cent of the variance in crime. Economic factors were responsible for kidnapping and abduction, riots, theft, house-breaking, breach of trust, robbery and murder, and social factors were responsible for dacoity and cheating. The volume of crime in 1967 was highest in Madhya Pradesh, Manipur, Maharashtra, West Bengal and Uttar Pradesh; while in 1977, it was highest in Madhya Pradesh, Maharashtra, Manipur and Uttar Pradesh. In 1960 and 1977, the leading crimes were thefts and house-breaking, followed by riots.

Dutt et al.'s North-Central Subculture of Violence

Dutt, Noble and Singh (1979), using varimax rotated factor analysis based on 12 crime variables, designated the north-central subculture of violent crimes in India covering an area from Assam all the way to Punjab, the southern limits being northern Madhya Pradesh and northeastern Rajasthan (Figs. 22.1 and 22.2). Violent crimes consisted of robbery, rape, murder, homicide and kidnapping. This study applied factor analysis using district-wise data of 1971. It found out that violent crimes were concentrated in north-central India. Factor 1 map indicates this very well (Fig. 22.1). Such concentration of violent crime is also evident from the incidence of dacoity (a kind of robbery) (Fig. 22.2). The authors ascribed the violence-related crime in this area to the historical and cultural roots associated with deeply entrenched caste divisions; the lack of village-based centralized religious organization; a sense of frontierism because of the action of the army invasions from the northwest, starting from Alexander in 326 BC and of plunderers like Tamerlane, and national and regional kings who fought with each other and experienced bloody dynastic changes and palace revolutions. Until the nineteenth century, this was a playground of roadside bandits called *thugs*. Thus, a regional subculture of violence is entrenched here, which has been thoroughly exploited by politicians of various parties and their henchmen since the 1960s.

Employing the same methodology of factor analysis as in Dutt, Noble and Singh (1979), Dutt and Venugopal (1983) studied the spatial pattern of crime in India on the city level (using 1971 official statistics for 153 Class I cities). Once again, the study confirmed the existence of a north-central subculture of violence region, but while the 1979 study had identified a broad area, the 1983 study shown in Figure 22.3 pointed out two distinct and separate ones. However, both lay within the subculture area identified in the 1979 study.

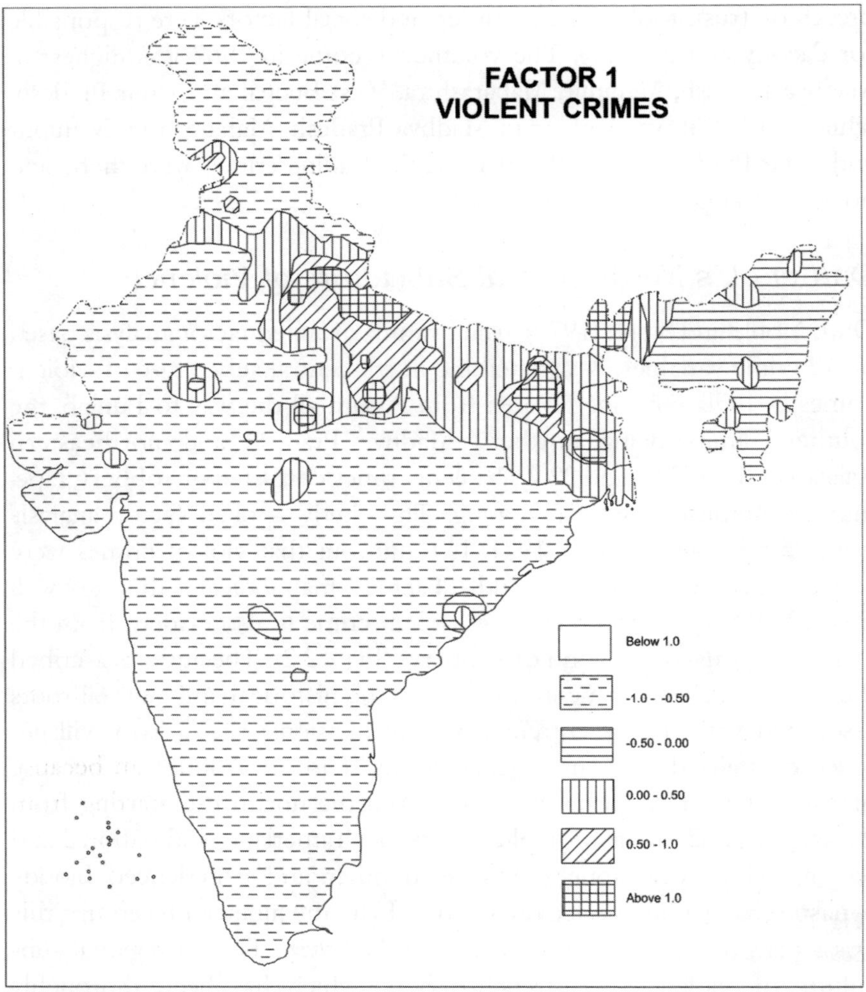

Fig. 22.1 Factor 1 map indicating the concentration of violent crimes in north-central India.
Source: Dutt *et al.*, 1979.

Attempting to understand the temporal element in crime patterns, a similar study was undertaken using the same methodology and city unit of analysis. Using 16 crime variables and data from 73 cities (most of them with populations in excess of 500,000 persons), Pomeroy *et al.*, (1999) performed a factor analysis in order to compare the situation after a lapse of 19 years (1971 – the base year for the preceding 1983 study, to 1990). They used GIS mapping techniques as well as computer-based statistical analysis. The factor analysis revealed that factor I (subculture of violence)

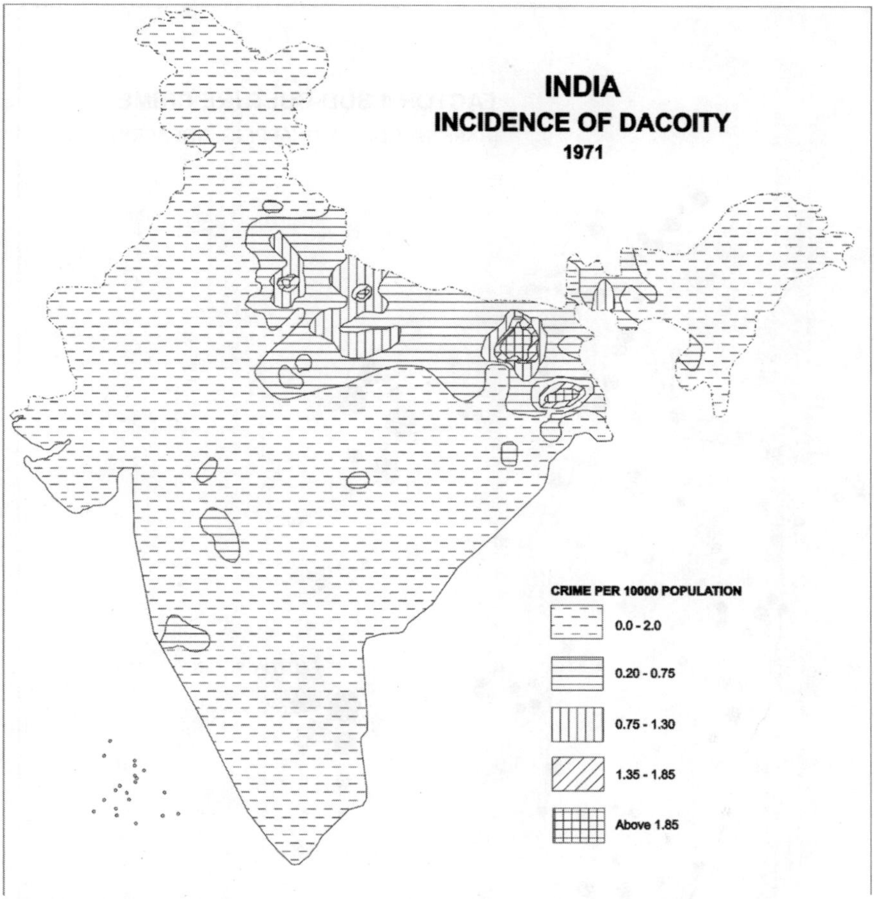

Fig. 22.2 Incidence of dacoity showing concentration in north-central India.
Source: Dutt *et al.*, 1979.

was still the most significant in that it explained the greatest variance. It includes crimes such as abductions, attempted murder, criminal breach of trust, homicide, dacoity, murder and robbery. Spatially, the subculture of violence region had spread, now stretching from the India–Pakistan border right up through to Assam, with a high concentration in Haryana, Uttar Pradesh and Bihar.

The Deadly Nexus: Crime and Politics[1]

As mentioned earlier in the paper, this study reveals that the north-central subculture of violence area has not only intensified, but has also spread

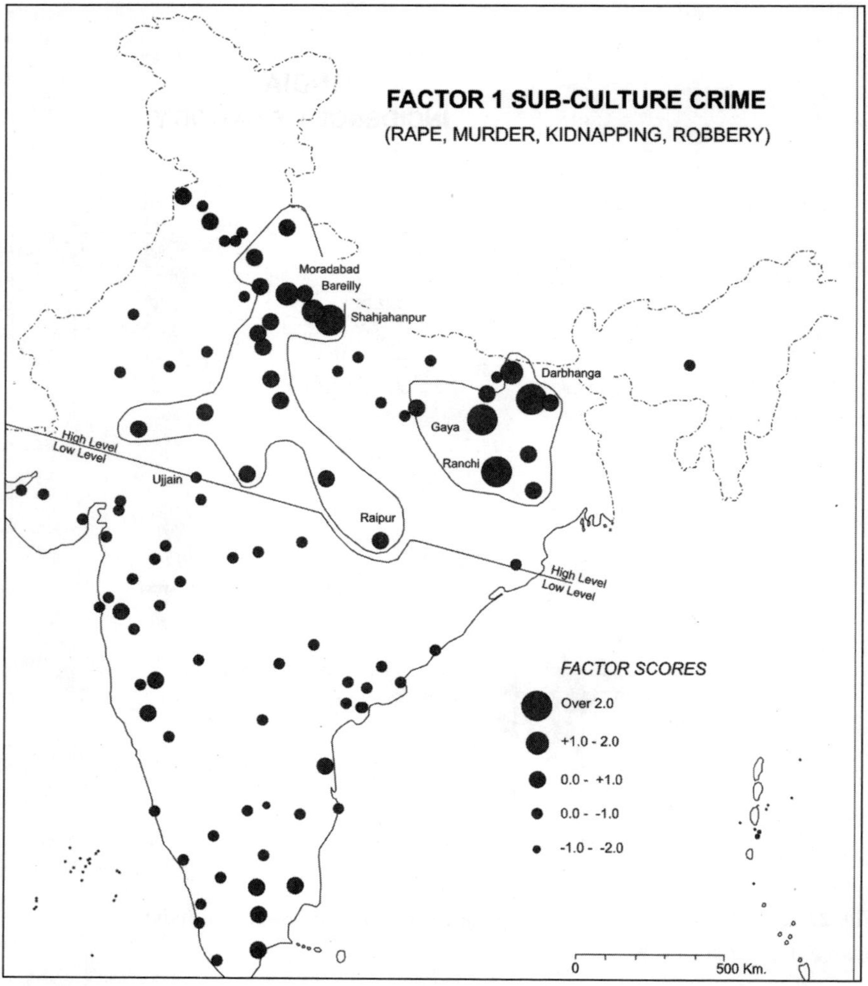

Fig. 22.3 Subculture of violence by cities of India showing the spread into two adjacent regions of north-central India.
Source: Dutt and Venugopal, 1983.

southwestwards, embracing parts of Rajasthan, Gujarat, Maharashtra and Madhya Pradesh. However, from 1971 to 1990, the time span of this study, the cause for the intensification and spread of violent crime in this area can be primarily attributed to political factors. Secondary factors, such as terrorist activities and communal conflicts involving religion and caste, operate under the umbrella of political manouevering and unrest.

In 1971, the post-war influx of Bangladeshi refugees into the Indian state of West Bengal caused great dissatisfaction among the local populace due to the increase in poverty and, subsequently, in crime. India's general elections in March 1971 became violent in West Bengal due to hostilities of the local leaders towards the then Prime Minister Mrs Indira Gandhi and the rise of the Maoist ultra-leftist group (Naxalites). This trend of violence and political instability continued throughout the years prior to the declaration of a General Emergency in 1975. Political elements were directly responsible for violent crimes, such as arson and murder in Assam and Uttar Pradesh in 1973. The same year saw a bloody revolt by the Provincial Armed Constabulary in Uttar Pradesh, a state that also experienced acts of violence due to student unrest. The students fervently opposed the tactics of the Congress Government and its leader, Mrs Indira Gandhi, resorting to violence as a sign of their displeasure. This started a tradition of student revolt and unrest in Bihar and Uttar Pradesh, a trend from which these states have still not recovered and which has only strengthened since then, contributing to violent crimes in all of north and central India. The severe drought conditions and resulting food shortages added fuel to the fire of unrest, and coupled with underlying communal conflicts, severe rioting broke out in the states of Bihar, Uttar Pradesh, Madhya Pradesh, Maharashtra and West Bengal, among others. There was immense loss of life and property. This continued into 1974, particularly in Bihar, one of the most underdeveloped and worst governed states of the time. Arson, sabotage and student demonstrations took a violent turn.

By 1975, a state of General Emergency was clapped on the nation in order to quell the 'divisive forces' within the country. It continued until 1977, a period of relative freedom from violent crime. However, within some months of the Emergency being lifted, there was a sharp increase in criminal activities, including violent communal and caste conflicts. There were repeated attacks on members of the lower castes in Bihar. By 1980, the country experienced widespread violence, particularly in northeast India and Uttar Pradesh, which saw a distinct deterioration of law and order. Political tensions and violence, along with ethnic warfare, contributed to the rise in violent crime in Assam and Tripura. Communal clashes characterized violence in Bihar, Gujarat and Uttar Pradesh, with the latter experiencing severe Hindu–Muslim rioting. In the last few years of the decade ending 1980, Gujarat, too became the scene of violence and bloodshed. The entire decade following the year 1980 was marred by terrorist and separatist violence. The politics of the caste system also came into play when the reserved positions in education and employment were almost doubled for the lower castes and others who had been traditionally discriminated against. The general populace was incensed to lose a large slice of the pie, leading to unruly demonstrations and needless deaths.

Sikh separatism had been gaining ground, but by 1981, the agitation became violent with the killing of a Hindu leader and an attempted hijacking of an aircraft. Hindu–Muslim riots broke out in the cities of Biharsharif (Bihar) and Aligarh (Uttar Pradesh). Student unrest turned violent in Gujarat over the issue of the impending increase in reservations for the backward castes. Political instability in Bihar, Uttar Pradesh and West Bengal fostered an atmosphere of crime. By the following year, Hindu–Sikh clashes were seen in Punjab, and Hindu–Muslim riots in Meerut (Uttar Pradesh) and Baroda (Gujarat). A large-scale dacoity (gang crime) claimed several lives in Uttar Pradesh and political unrest created a stir of violence in Assam. The latter escalated to a bloody election campaign in 1983 and more than 1300 persons were killed in Mangaldai and Nellie (Assam). Clashes between the Muslim refugees from Bangladesh and the native Hindus of West Bengal further strengthened the violent turn of events. Hindus found themselves the focus of violent activity, both here and in Punjab.

31 October 1984 marked yet another era of violence, with the assassination of Prime Minister Indira Gandhi by her Sikh bodyguards. Large-scale rioting in Delhi claimed more than 1000 lives (mostly Sikhs) and the Sikh agitation continued throughout the year, characterized by random killing, murders, assaults and hijackings, all of which were concentrated in Punjab and the neighbouring areas. The sabotage of an Air India jet over the Atlantic Ocean in 1985 took 329 lives, leaving no survivors. Other violent crimes killed 600 others. Some blame Sikh terrorists for this sabotage. Terrorist bombings and assassinations by Sikh separatists motivated by political gains and religious fundamentalism continued until the end of the decade (1990), and have abated only slightly since then. The demand for a separate Sikh nation of Khalistan is still the primary cause of violent activity, particularly in the states of Punjab, Haryana and Uttar Pradesh, and in the cities of Chandigarh, New Delhi and almost all the cities of Punjab. More communal strife, in the form of Hindu–Muslim riots, claimed several lives in Mumbai.

By mid-decade, the issue of reservations in education and employment for the traditionally backward castes had begun to turn violent. Cities in Gujarat saw violent demonstrations against this issue. The climax came in 1990, when the Mandal Commission report on this issue was to be implemented. The Mandal Commission report recommended that the existing reservation of education and employment opportunities for the backward castes and classes should be almost doubled, bringing the total reservations to 52 percent of all such opportunities. Indignant students of the general population protested by self-immolation (at least 160 students burned to death or suffered severe burns) and also displayed their displeasure to the Government by turning to arson and rioting. Affected areas were cities of Haryana, Uttar Pradesh, Gujarat and New Delhi (Basu, 1990).

Political interests continued to promote violence through fuelling of anti-nationalistic and separatist sentiments. Some examples of such movements which led to an increase in violent activities are the demand for a separate Gurkha state within West Bengal, which had severe repercussions in Darjeeling and surrounding cities (1986–87); the demand for Bodoland in northeast India (1989 onwards); and the demand for a separate state for the tribes of Bihar, West Bengal, and Orissa (1989 onwards). Politics also fanned the flames of communal fires, with resulting violent acts such as rioting, murder and arson. In 1986 and 1987, Gujarat (particularly the city of Ahmedabad) was the scene of ugly Hindu–Muslim clashes, and the latter year also saw similar violence in Meerut (Uttar Pradesh). In 1989, Laloo Prasad Yadav became the Chief Minister of Bihar, a state already torn apart by political, religious and caste-based turmoil. Under his rule, unruly elements were protected and able to carry on their agenda of terror and disruption. For political motives, he created a further rift among the various castes, unleashing a new spate of violent crime. The issue of Ayodhya, the birthplace of the Hindu epic hero Rama, which was built over (into a mosque, Babri Masjid) by the Muslim conqueror, Babar and subsequently destroyed by Hindu fundamentalists in 1992, pitched Hindus and Muslims against each other. The consequence was a rash of rioting in Jaipur (Rajasthan), Indore (Madhya Pradesh), Badaun (Uttar Pradesh), Mumbai (Maharashtra) and Bhagalpur (Bihar), among other cities all over the nation. Uttar Pradesh was more severely affected, not only because Ayodhya is located here, but also because in the same year, Urdu, the predominant language of Muslims in the Indian subcontinent, was declared the official language of the state.

The fundamentalist Hindus were incensed, leading to widespread rioting all over the state. Hindu fundamentalist leader Advani and his Bharatiya Janata further enflamed Muslims by declaring his intentions to tear down the mosque at Ayodhya, and to embark on a '*Rath Yatra*', a journey by chariot, like the epic hero Rama. He was arrested by the Bihar Government in Samastipur in 1990 before he could do so, but the damage had been done as severe Hindu–Muslim riots broke out across the nation.

The years 1989 and 1990 were politically unstable for the nation as well. The Congress Party, long the majority party of the legislature, could not retain its hold. A succession of alternative party leaders came into power, and each election brought bloodshed and mayhem with it, as in Haryana, West Bengal (over anti-Marxist demonstrations that turned violent, including acts of rape, arson and killing), Uttar Pradesh, and Bihar (*India Abroad*, 12 January, 89). (*The Britannica Book of the Year*, 1982–91).

These events, spanning the two decades 1970–90, have contributed to the intensification and spread of the north-central subculture of violence area. As is evident, political gain has been the prime cause for the occurrence of these violent acts and even secondary factors, such as terrorism, religion, and caste, are directly or indirectly related to the political agenda of the national or local leaders.

Conclusion

Crime geography studies in India have taken three approaches – descriptive, inductive and deductive. Most studies have taken recourse to the inductive method where generalizations have been made based on micro, meso or macro-level spatial analysis. Only one study (Sinha, 2000) has used a deductive method, where a broad theoretical framework of the 'culture of oppression' is positioned first, and an elucidation attempted after. This approach begets multiple questions. To sum the essence of the above studies from our perspective, it seems economic and social oppression, historical heritage, resistance to oppression, social divisions, economic necessities, and increasingly, politically motivated violence, all are responsible not only for breeding crime but for the continuation of the same. When such situation occurs in any area for a long period of time, there may develop a subculture of crime or a subculture of violence.

North-central India has clearly emerged as having a much higher incidence of crime than the rest of the country. Crimes that relate to poverty seem to be ubiquitous throughout the country, but violent crimes are undoubtedly concentrated in north-central India, designated as a region of sub-culture violence. The north-central subculture of violence zone had been the 'March Zone' of Indian history, across which the armies of conquest have swept and within which diverse cultures and rulers have clashed. It is in North India that the caste system appears to be less defined and village solidarity is much lower than in South India. All these combined factors–historical, cultural and geographical – have helped the emergence of regional subculture of violence in north-central India (Dutt *et al.*, 1979). During the late 1970s and 1980s, this region extended into Rajasthan, Madhya Pradesh, Gujarat and Maharashtra.

Note

1. This section is based on the chronology of events reported in: (a) *Britannica Book of the Year,* 1983–1990, Daume, D., and J. E. Davis (eds), Chicago: Encyclopedia Britannica and (b) *The Americana Annual*, 1979–82, United States: Americana Corporation.
2. The authors acknowledge with thanks the Annals of the National Geographical Association of India for use of an earlier work (see Wadhwa and Dutt, 2000), which is a partial basis for this current chapter.

References

Banerjee-Guha, S., 'Geography of Crime in India: The Scenario in the 1990s', in A.G. Noble, B. Thakur, A. B. Mukerji and F. J. Costa (eds.), *Geographic and Planning Research Themes for the New Millennium: Felicitations in Honor of Professor Ashok K. Dutt*, New Delhi: Vikas Publishing House Pvt. Ltd., 2000, pp. 263–282.

Basu, T., 'Job Reservation Program Brings Increased Fury', India Abroad, August 31, 1990, pp. 48–54.

Bhatnagar, R. R., *Crimes in India: Problems and Policy*, New Delhi: Ashish Publishing House, 1990.

Bhushan, P. S., *Crime, Criminals and Society: A Case Study of Delhi*, New Delhi: Manisha Publications, 1997.

Deol, G., 'Patterns of Criminal Breach of Trust, Cheating and Counterfeiting in India, 1981', *The National Geographical Journal of India*, Vol. 42, Nos. 1 and 2, 1996, pp. 19–27.

Dutt, A. K. and G. Venugopal, 'Spatial Patterns of Crime Among Indian Cities', *Geoforum*, Vol. 14, No. 2, 1983, pp. 223–233.

Dutt, A. K., A. G. Noble and K. K. Sharma, 'Variations of the Spatial Patterns of Crime in Ajmer, India', *Indian Journal of Criminology*, Vol. 13, No. 1, 1985, pp. 57–72.

Dutt, A. K., A. G. Noble and S. Singh, 'Is There a North-Central Sub-Culture of Violence in India?', *The National Geographical Journal of India*, Vol. 25, No. 2: 1979, pp. 101–111.

Dutta, M. K., *A Spatial Analysis of the Ecological Patterning to Crime in the Metropolis of Calcutta*, Unpublished PhD dissertation (Geography), University of Manitoba, 1976.

India Abroad, 'V. P. Singh Feels the Turmoil', Vol. 20, No. 9, 1 December 1989, p. 6.

Katare, S. S., *Patterns of Dacoity in India*, New Delhi: S. Chand and Company Pvt. Ltd., 1972.

Ministry of Home Affairs, *Crime in India*, New Delhi: Bureau of Police Research and Development, 1971.

Ministry of Home Affairs, *Crime in India*, New Delhi: Bureau of Police Research and Development, 1988.

Ministry of Home Affairs, *Crime in India*, New Delhi: Bureau of Police Research and Development, 1989.

Ministry of Home Affairs, *Crime in India*, New Delhi: Bureau of Police Research and Development, 1990.

Nayar, B. R., *Violence and Crime in India: A Quantitative Study*, Delhi: MacMillan Company of India, 1975.

Pyle, G. F., *The Spatial Dynamics of Crime*, Chicago: The University of Chicago, Department of Geography, Research Paper No. 159, 1974.

Pomeroy, G., A. K. Dutt and V. Wadhwa, 'Spatial Patterns of Crime in Indian Cities', in G. P. Chapman, A. K. Dutt and R. W. Bradnock (eds.), *Urban Growth and Development in Asia, Volume II: Living in the Cities*, Aldershot, England: Ashgate Publishing Ltd., 1999, pp. 292–302.

Rao, S. V., *Dynamics of Crime: Spatial and Socio-economic Aspects of Crime in India*, New Delhi: Indian Institute of Public Administration, 1981.

Sinha, S., 'Crime and Violence in India', in A. G. Noble, B. Thakur, A. B. Mukerji and F. J. Costa (eds.), *Geographic and Planning Research Themes for the New Millennium: Felicitations in Honor of Professor Ashok K. Dutt*, New Delhi: Vikas Publishing House Pvt. Ltd., 2000, pp. 243–262.

Sivamurthy, A., 'Urban Ecological Aspects of Crimes in Madras City', *Indian Journal of Criminology*, Vol. 9, No. 2, 1981, pp. 91–98.

Sivamurthy, A., 'The Spatio-Temporal Variation in the Incidence of Theft in Madras City', *Indian Journal of Criminology*, Vol. 10, No. 2, 1982, pp. 108–115.

Wadhwa, V. and Ashok K. Dutt, 'Crime Geography of India: A Review of Selected Contributions', *Annals, National Association of Geographers of India*, Vol. 20, No. 2, 2000, p. 124–136.

Rural Human Resource Development in India: A Spatio-Temporal Analysis

B. R. K. SINHA

Rural India, consisting of 72 per cent of the Indian population, is different from the urban segment of the country. The Indian village plays a very significant role in the progress of the whole nation; it is a source of art, culture, literature, religion, human values, philosophy, economic wealth and agricultural produce. It is also a storehouse of abundant human resources, though the majority of these resources are underdeveloped, undeveloped, unused, underused and overused, as well as inefficient and poor in quality. Rural India is also characterized by the presence of high birth, death, and infant mortality rates, low life expectancy, malnutrition, hunger, illiteracy, ignorance, unemployment, poverty, poor sanitation and housing conditions, water scarcity and many such stubborn problems of human resource development.

Human resource development is a continuous process of promoting quality of life for all people of an area. According to Gupta (1998), human resource development is the complete physical and mental growth of individuals. Rao (1999) emphasizes the importance of human resource development and states that it involves getting the right kind of people, creating a culture that nurtures and retains talent, providing avenues for competence development at all levels, ensuring utilization of talent and aiding in the renewal of various productive human processes. Nadler (1994) defined human resource development as a planned continuous effort by management to improve employee capacity levels and organizational performance through training, education and development programmes. Similarly, Kumar and Hansra (2000) define human resource development as an approach to facilitate the development of an individual's competence, environment and organization. Human resource development stresses upon the development of the individual, the family and the village community.

Human resource development relates to two aspects – human resource on-formation and human resource off-formation. The former is the continued addition of human resource formation through the process of acquiring knowledge, skills and abilities through formal and non-formal educational systems, on the job training or learning from some other source, with the integration of health, food and nutrition. However, those human resource values that are already achieved through the process of feedback, an existing stock of human resource, and are called 'off human resource formation.' According to Harbison and Myers (1964), the stock of human capital indicates the levels of human resource development already achieved. It is measured by levels of educational attainment, and net or gross addition (human capital formation) to the stock of human resources, indicates the rate of accumulation of human capital over a certain period of time as measured by the enrolment of students at various educational levels. In this way, human resource development builds people's capabilities and adds to the stock of human resources of an area. Thus, human resource development deals with the ongoing human capital formation as well as the existing condition of human resources already achieved as a stock. This chapter attempts to map out the spatial pattern of the stock of human resources in census years 1981 and 1991, and to note and interpret the distribution and changes that took place in human resource development.

Objectives and Methodology

The objectives of the present chapter are to: (i) delineate the spatio-temporal pattern of rural male human resource development, (ii) delineate the spatio-temporal pattern of rural female human resource development, (iii) calculate the rural male–female human resource development differential during two time periods along with their temporal change, and (iv) extend appropriate suggestions for bridging the male–female human resource development gap over space and time.

Since the concept of human resource development encompasses a variety of elements of both the mental and physical aspects of an individual, an adequate measurement of human resource development is difficult. Harbison (1973) admitted that to fix a yardstick to measure human resource development is a difficult task. No one has yet devised a comprehensive indicator of human resource development. If one was constructed, it should probably include at a minimum – a measure of educational achievements, school participation ratio, strategic skills, a measure of health by data on life expectancy, infant mortality, disease-burden, or critical measure of food and nutrition.

In their study, Harbison and Myers (1964) adopted various quantitative indicators and computed a composite index in measuring human resource development. Educational achievement, according to them, was the ideal indicator of human resource development. Schultz (as cited in Ghosh, 1998) also suggested education at elementary, secondary and higher levels for developing and measuring human resource development. Similarly, Singh (1982), Prodi (1996) and Kaur (1996) also considered educational achievements as an indicator of human resource development. Other scholars, such as Das and Karak (1988) and De (1988), considered and adopted decennial growth rate of population, density of population, literate and educated persons, proportion of urban population, working and non-working persons, as some of the indicators for measuring and mapping human resource development.

Harbison and Myers (1964) further considered the rate of literacy as an important indicator of human resource development. However, according to them it is relatively a poor indicator. Sinha (1999) employed a composite index technique in measuring human resource development. This was calculated using composite score values of individuals obtained by putting certain weights to several quantitative and qualitative parameters directly or indirectly related to physical and mental capability.

The present study is exclusively based on the human resource development index calculated by using total composite scores of all educational levels (very different from literacy rate) of the rural male and female population of respective states. For this, secondary data relating to all educational levels were collected from the 1981 and 1991 Census Series – India, Part IVA-C, Social and Cultural Tables. While calculating the composite scores, each educational level was given a certain weight, on the basis of its respective rank order. The weights assigned are as follows: Illiteracy–1, literacy–2, below primary–3, primary–4, middle–5, secondary/matriculation–6, higher secondary/intermediate–7, non-technical certificate or diploma not equal to degree–8, technical certificate or diploma not equal to degree–9, graduation and above (including post-graduation, teaching, veterinary, agriculture/dairying, medicine, engineering and technology and others–10. After putting the assigned weights to the respective educational levels, the composite scores of rural male and female human resources of 1981 and 1991 were calculated separately for each state employing the equation:

$$\text{Human resource development} = \frac{\text{Actual value} - \text{Minimum value}}{\text{Maximum value} - \text{Minimum value}}$$

Human Resource Development Indices (HRDIs) for rural male and female human resources of 1981 and 1991 of respective states were calculated. Actual value is meant for total composite score of male or female human resource of each state; minimum value considered was 100 (that is slightly less than the lowest composite score) and the maximum value selected was 500 (that is slightly more than the highest composite score). Finally, five levels of human resource development were demarcated depending upon the variation of human resource development indices – very high (more than 0.80 HDRI), high (between 0.60 and 0.80 HDRI), medium (between 0.40 to 0.60 HDRI), low (between (0.20 and 0.40 HDRI) and very low (less than 0.20 HDRI).

Analysis

This aspect deals with the spatio-temporal variation in the pattern of rural male and female human resource development in India.

Spatio-Temporal Pattern of Rural Male Human Resource Development

Table 23.1 and Fig. 23.1 depict the variation in the spatio-temporal pattern of rural male human resource development. Interestingly, we do not find the position of any state either in very high or in very low levels of human resource development in both the census years. Even in the high level human resource development range, Kerala was the only state that fell in this category in 1981, and even after ten years its position remained the same. However, some other states, such as Delhi, Lakshadweep, Pondicherry, and Goa showed good progress in human resource development, as their positions in 1981 were in medium and low level human

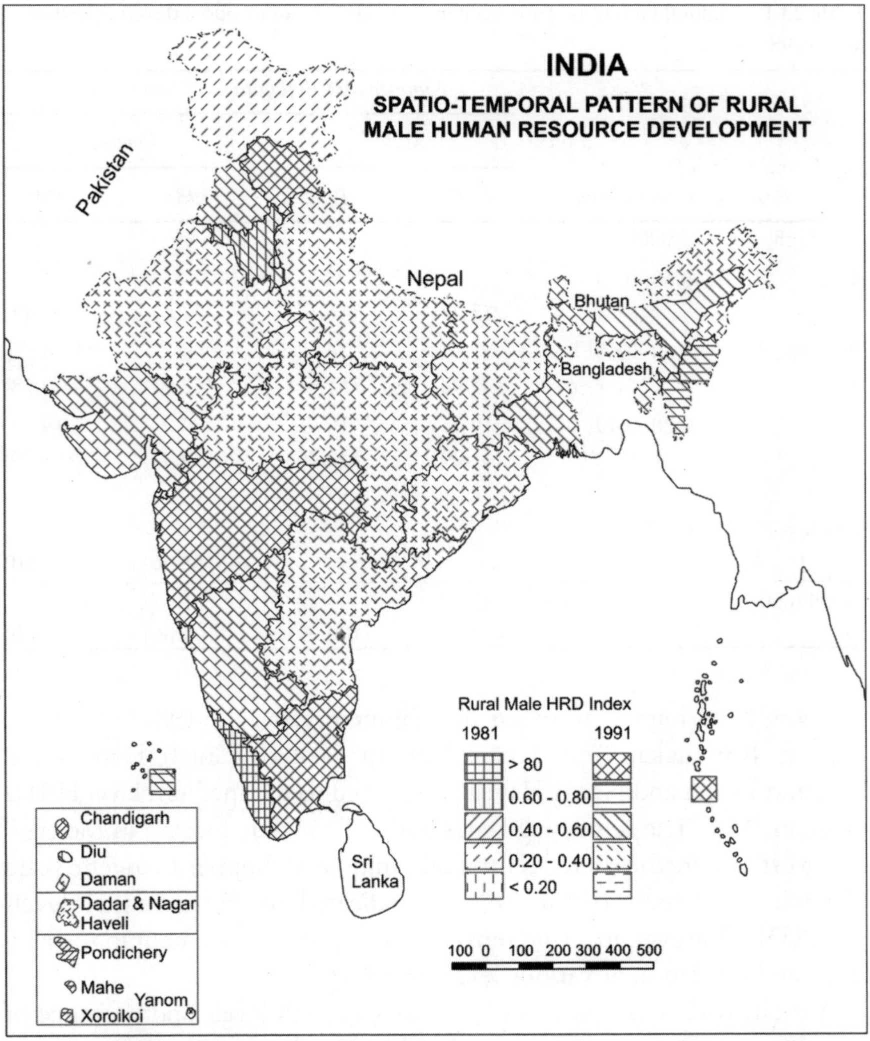

Fig. 23.1 India: Spatio-temoral pattern of rural male human resource development.

resource development range. Eleven (35.48 per cent) states and Union Territories (UTs) such as Maharashtra, Tamil Nadu, Pondicherry, Haryana, Himachal Pradesh, Manipur, Andaman and Nicobar Islands, Chandigarh, Delhi, Lakshadweep, and Mizoram were in medium level human resource development range in 1981.

Among these, Delhi, Lakshadweep, and Pondicherry went on to join a higher level human resource development range in 1991 and maintained that status in 1991. A majority (61.29 per cent) of the states and UTs were

Table 23.1 Temporal pattern of rural male and female human resource development in India, 1981–1991.

Levels and Index of Human Resource Development		*Number and Percentage of States for*			
		Male		*Female*	
		1981	*1991*	*1981*	*1991*
Very high	> 0.80	–	–	–	–
High	0.60–0.80	1 (3.23)	5 (16.13)	–	1 (3.23)
Medium	0.40–0.60	11 (35.48)	16 (51.61)	4 (12.91)	3 (9.68)
Low	0.20–0.40	19 (61.29)	10 (32.26)	9 (29.03)	19 (61.29)
Very low	< 0.20	–	–	18 (58.06)	8 (25.80)
Grand total		31 (100.00)	31 (100.00)	31 (100.00)	31 (100.00)

at a low level human resource development range in 1981. Of them, Gujarat, Karnataka, West Bengal, Tripura, Sikkim, Panjab, Daman and Diu, and Dadra and Nagar Haveli progressed to the medium level HRDI range in 1991. The remaining states and UTs, mainly located in the eastern, western, northeastern, central and middle and upper Gangetic plain maintained the status quo in 1991 and indicated no change in their levels of HRDI. However, in a true sense, a slow upward movement in their literacy and education at various levels is noted.

A total absence of states and UTs in very high levels and presence of very few in high human resource development levels in both the census years is indicative of poor development of male human resource in India. Secondly, a majority of the states and UTs in low and medium levels of human resource development in 1981, and a majority of them in medium and low levels of human resource development in 1991, in that order, also indicate poor development of male human resource in the country. Thirdly, Karnataka, Gujarat, Punjab, West Bengal, Tripura, Sikkim, Delhi, Lakshadweep, Pondicherry, Goa, and Daman and Diu are relatively progressive states and UTs in terms of male human resource development as they reached a high level of HRDI in 1991 as compared to 1981, and rose to medium levels of HRDI in 1991 as compared to 1981's low levels of human resource development.

Spatio-Temporal Pattern of Rural Female Human Resource Development

Table 23.1 shows the pattern of levels and index of rural female human resource development and Fig. 23.2 exhibits the variation in the pattern of rural female human resource development in space (across states and

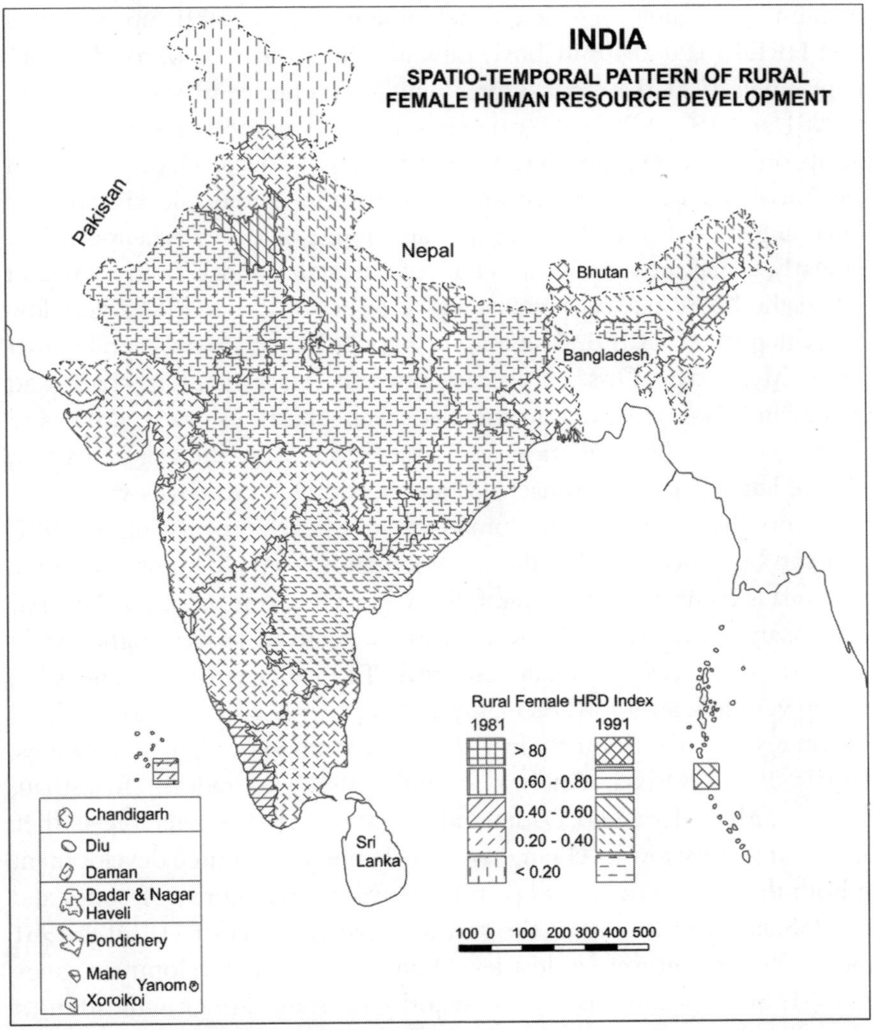

Fig. 23.2 India: Spatio-temporal pattern of rural female human resource development.

UTs) and time (span of ten years) in India. They show that there was no state or UT either in very high or in high level human resource development ranges, except for Kerala which was in the high level in 1991. Medium level (0.40–0.60) human resource development range includes only four (12.91 per cent) states in India in 1981. Out of these, only Kerala moved to the higher rung of the ladder of development in 1991 and Goa maintained its grade. Daman and Diu, and Manipur slumped to a low level (0.20–0.40) of female human resource development in 1991.

The Andaman and Nicobar Islands as well as Lakshadweep were in a medium level human resource development range in 1991, up from low level HRDI (0.20–0.40) in 1981. Low level of human resource development range (0.20–0.40) constitutes nine (29.03 per cent) states and UTs in 1981 and 19 (61.29 per cent) states and UTs in 1991. From the 1981 group, only Andhra Pradesh came down to a very low level, the Andaman and Nicobar Islands plus Lakshadweep rose to medium levels, and the remaining six states remained in the same range of development in 1991. Similarly, a majority (58.06 per cent) of the states and UTs in 1981 and only eight (25.80 per cent) states and UTs in 1991 were in the very low level category of HRDI. The map in Fig. 23.2 clearly demonstrates that Bihar, Meghalaya, Orissa, Madhya Pradesh, Haryana, Rajasthan, and Dadra and Nagar Haveli maintained their status in both years, and Gujarat, Karnataka, Maharashtra, Tamil Nadu, West Bengal, Nagaland, Sikkim, Uttar Pradesh, Arunachal Pradesh, and Delhi rose to low levels in 1991 from their very low level human resource development range in 1981.

It can be concluded that the development of female human resource in Kerala is comparatively better, followed by Goa, Andaman and Nicobar Islands, and Lakshadweep. These states are relatively more progressive in terms of their female human resources. The other ten states and UTs, having very low level HRDIs in 1981, also progressed a step to low level human resource development in 1991. The condition of eight major states, namely Bihar, Orissa, Andhra Pradesh, Madhya Pradesh, Rajasthan, Haryana, Meghalaya, and Dadra and Nagar Haveli, is vulnerable as they belonged to very low level range of female human resource development in both the years. The overall picture shows that a majority of states and UTs (58.06 per cent) were in the very low level category of HRDI in 1981 and 61.29 per cent were in low level human resource development range in 1991. Such conditions of the majority of states are an indication of very poor development of female human resources in India.

Rural Male–Female Human Resource Development Differential in India (1981)

Figs. 23.3 and 23.4 indicate the difference between India's rural male and female human resource development in 1981. A study of the situation of male human resource development (MHRD) reveals that Kerala, Goa, Daman and Diu, and Pondicherry were on the upper rung of the ladder, belonging to more than 0.50 HRDI, which may be because of greater awareness among the people towards education. Haryana, Himachal Pradesh, Maharashtra, Manipur, Tamil Nadu, Andaman and Nicobar Islands, Chandigarh, Delhi, and Lakshadweep, belonging to 0.40–0.50 HRDI, were on the middle crosspieces of the ladder. Other states, such as Bihar, Karnataka, Andhra Pradesh, Assam, Mizoram, Nagaland, Orissa (belonging to 0.30–0.40 HDRI), and Madhya Pradesh, Arunachal Pradesh, Meghalaya, Punjab, Rajasthan, Sikkim, Uttar Pradesh, Dadra and Nagar Haveli, and Jammu and Kashmir (belonging to 0.20–0.30 HRDI) were on the lower rungs of the ladder of human resource development.

Similarly, in the case of female human resource development, only Kerala was at par with its male human resource development level at more than 0.50. Manipur also remained at par with a female human resource development level of 0.40–0.50. Goa, and Daman and Diu also belonged to this HRDI but not at par with its male human resource development level. Other states and UTs, such as Himachal Pradesh, Mizoram, Punjab, Tripura, Andaman and Nicobar Islands, Chandigarh, Lakshadweep, and Pondicherry with figures in the range of 0.20–0.30 were at the low developmental level, whereas Andhra Pradesh, Gujarat, Haryana, Karnataka, Maharashtra, Meghalaya, Nagaland, Orissa, Sikkim, Tamil Nadu, West Bengal and Delhi belonging to 0.10–0.20 HRDI showed even lower levels. Arunachal Pradesh, Assam, Bihar, Madhya Pradesh, Rajasthan, Uttar Pradesh, Dadra and Nagar Haveli, and Jammu and Kashmir with less than 0.10 HRDI showed the lowest level in terms of female human resource development.

These figures indicate a clear-cut gap between the development of male and female human resources. The gap between male and female human resource development in Haryana, Delhi, Andhra Pradesh, Bihar, Goa, Assam, Gujarat, Himachal Pradesh, Karnataka, Madhya Pradesh, Orissa, Maharashtra, Rajasthan, Tamil Nadu, West Bengal, Chandigarh, Jammu and Kashmir, Lakshadweep, and Pondicherry was comparatively

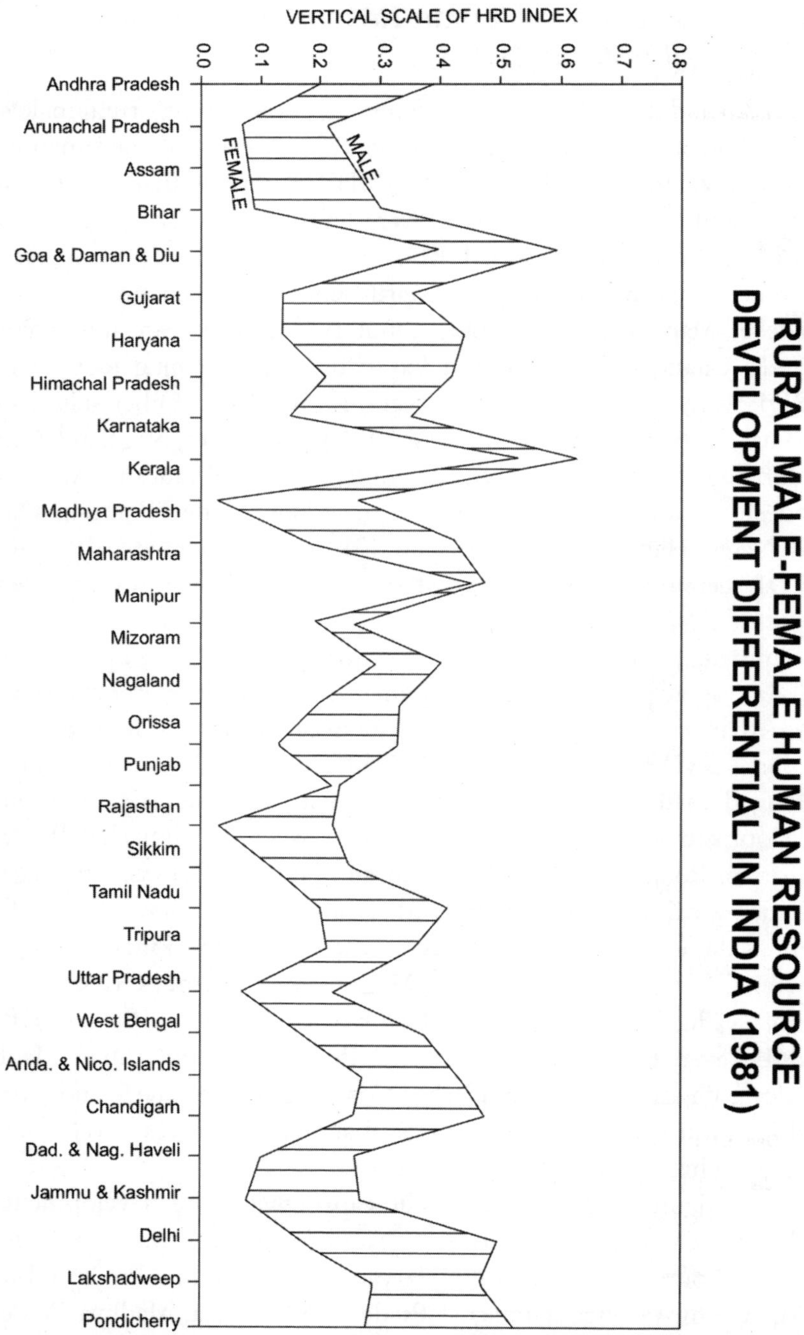

Fig. 23.3 Rural male–female human resource development differential in India (1981).

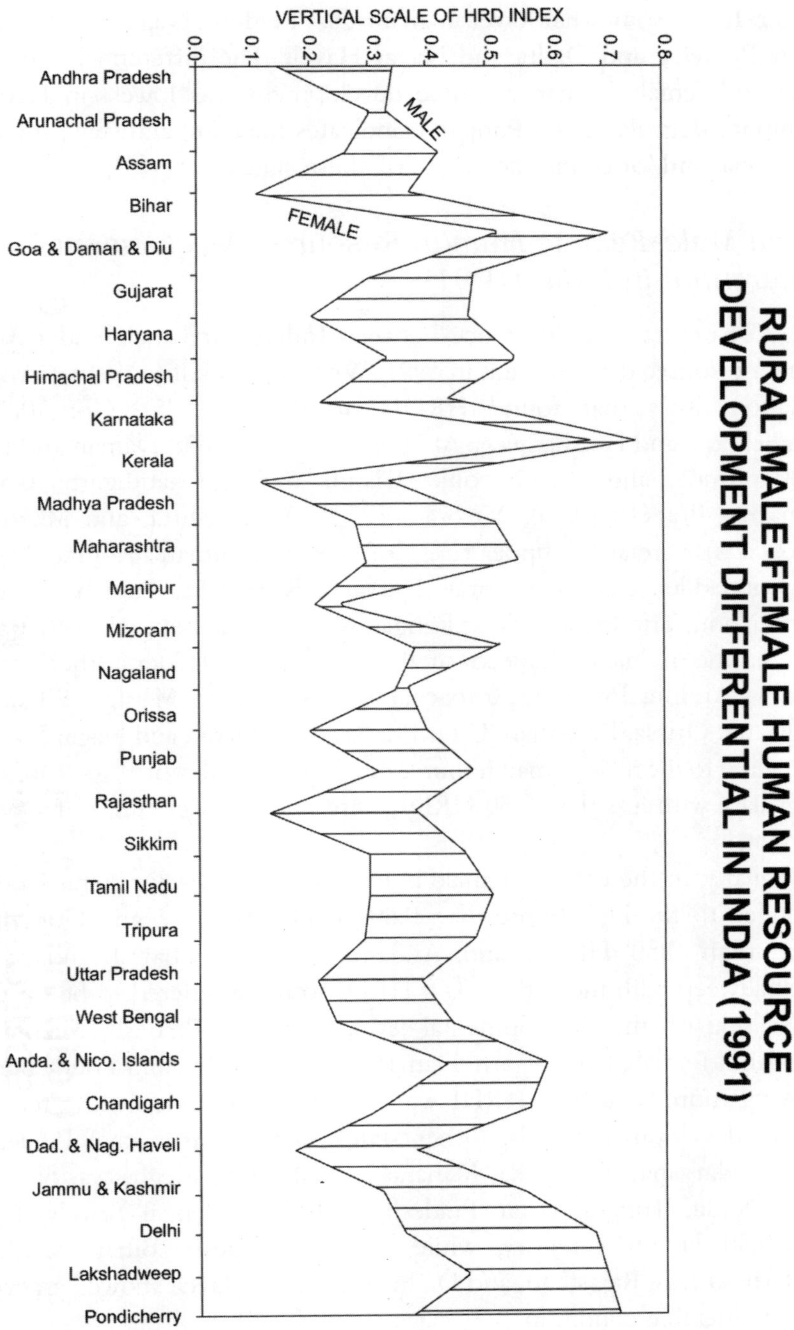

Fig. 23.4 Rural male–female human resource development differential in India (1991).

higher. It was somewhat lower in Arunachal Pradesh, Nagaland, Tripura, Uttar Pradesh, and Dadra and Nagar Haveli. The differential between male and female human resource development was lowest in Kerala, Manipur, Meghalaya, and Punjab. It indicates the comparatively progressive social and/or economic nature of these states.

Rural Male–Female Human Resource Development Differential in India (1991)

Fig. 23.4 depicts the difference between India's rural male and female human resource development in 1991. When we look into the pattern of variation, it is that found HRDIs of Kerala (0.75), Goa (0.72), Pondicherry, and Lakshadweep (0.71 each), Delhi (0.67), Daman and Diu (0.60), Andamand and Nicobar Islands (0.59), Chandigarh (0.57), Himachal Pradesh (0.55), Mizoram (0.53), Maharashtra, and Manipur (0.52 each) were at the upper rungs of the male human resource development ladder. Assam, Gujarat, Haryana, Karnataka, Punjab, Sikkim, Tamil Nadu, Tripura, and West Bengal, with HRDIs between 0.40–0.50, were on the middle crosspieces of the development ladder. Other states, such as Andhra Pradesh, Arunachal Pradesh, Bihar, Madhya Pradesh, Nagaland, Orissa, Rajasthan, Uttar Pradesh, and Dadra and Nagar Haveli belonging to the male human resource development index of 0.30–0.40, and Meghalaya with less than 0.30 HRDI, were on the lower rungs of development.

Similarly, in the case of female human resource development, Kerala belonged to the high (more than 0.60 HRDI) category, and Goa with more than 0.50 HRDI, and Andaman and Nicobar Islands and Lakshadweep with more than 0.40 HRDI were considered to be on the upper side of the developmental level. Himachal Pradesh, Mizoram, Nagaland, Punjab, Chandigarh, Daman and Diu, Delhi, and Pondicherry showing more than 0.30 HRDI were on the lower side of the female human development levels. Other states such as Arunachal Pradesh, Assam, Haryana, Karnataka, Maharashtra, Manipur, Meghalaya, Sikkim, Tamil Nadu, Tripura, Uttar Pradesh, and West Bengal belonged to 0.20–0.30 HRDI category, while Andhra Pradesh, Bihar, Madhya Pradesh, Orissa, Rajasthan, and Dadra and Nagar Haveli showed an even more vulnerable condition.

The gap between male and female human resources in 1991 was found to be greater in Bihar, Haryana, Manipur, Rajasthan, Chandigrah,

Pondicherry, Delhi, Daman and Diu, and Lakshadweep. The gap was less in Kerala, Nagaland, Maharashtra, and Arunachal Pradesh. Such a gap was moderate in Andhra Pradesh, Assam, Goa, Haryana, Himachal Pradesh, Karnataka, Madhya Pradesh, Maharashtra, Mizoram, Orissa, Punjab, Sikkim, Tamil Nadu, Tripura, Uttar Pradesh, West Bengal, Andaman and Nicobar Islands, and Dadra and Nagar Haveli. A similar gap was noticed in case of the development of both male and female human resources in 1981 as well.

Vertical Temporal Change in Male–Female Human Resource Development in India

A superimposition of the 1991 rural male–female human resource development differential on the 1981 male–female differential provides a clear picture of the temporal movement in the development of male and female human resources in India under the following heads: (i) All the states and UTs have shown upward movement in the development of both male and female human resources. Only Andhra Pradesh has shown a slight downward movement, which may be due to either less educational achievement or more out-migration of educated persons. Similarly, Manipur has shown much downward movement in female HRDI category, which may be due to greater drop-out of female students in comparison to male students during 1981–1991 because of political disturbance, (ii) The upward movement in HRDIs shows least progress in Meghalaya, Bihar, Karnataka, Madhya Pradesh, Haryana, Maharashtra, Nagaland, Orissa, West Bengal, and Chandigarh in case of both genders, and in Dadra and Nagar Haveli, and Rajasthan in the female HRDI category, (iii) More noticeable upward movement in male and female HRDIs is apparent in Pondicherry, Lakshadweep, Delhi, Daman and Diu, Arunachal Pradesh, Assam, Goa, Kerala, Gujarat, Himachal Pradesh, Mizoram, Punjab, Sikkim, Tamil Nadu, Tripura, Uttar Pradesh, and Andaman and Nicobar Islands, and (iv) Upward movement of female human resource development in Arunachal Pradesh in 1991 is even more than that of the male human resource development of 1981; a similar case is noticed with respect to female human resource development in Punjab, Sikkim and, Daman and Diu. This last may be due to more significant educational achievement among the women.

Conclusion

It can be concluded that there has been a very slow upward movement in rural male human resource development as the majority of states in 1981 were in low level and rose only to medium level human resource development in 1991. To be specific, a slow positive change took place only in Karnataka, Gujarat, Punjab, West Bengal, Sikkim, Tripura, Pondicherry, Daman and Diu, Delhi, Lakshadweep, and Goa. But in the rest of the 20 major states, no change in HRDI levels was noted. This is a poor sign in the development of rural male human development. Similar trends reflecting slow positive change were noted in the case of the development of rural female human resources as well. However, in comparison to the human resource development levels of rural males, the human resource development levels of rural females have consistently been lower. In the majority of states and UTs in 1981, female HRDIs were in very low level category, and in 1991 they were in low level category, which is not a significant improvement. The performance of Madhya Pradesh, Orissa, Andhra Pradesh, Rajasthan, Bihar, Haryana, Meghalaya, and Dadra and Nagar Haveli is notably very poor. Also, when we compare the development of rural male human resource with the development of rural female human resources in 1991, we find the quality of development of rural males to be better than that of rural females.

The one clear conclusion that appears to emerge is that most of the smaller states and UTs show better human resource development performance, leaving aside a few cases. It has also been found that Kerala and Goa were the only progressive states in the case of both male and female human resource development in 1991. But in the case of only male human resource development, some other states and UTs such as Pondicherry, Lakshadweep, Delhi, Daman and Diu, Chandigarh, Andaman and Nicobar Islands, Himachal Pradesh, Maharashtra, Manipur, and Mizoram were also of progressive nature. The position of some major states, such as Andhra Pradesh, Arunachal Pradesh, Meghalaya, Assam, Haryana, Karnataka, Maharashtra, Tamil Nadu, and West Bengal and of the BIMARU states (the least developed states of Bihar, Madhya Pradesh, Rajasthan, and Uttar Pradesh) was that of vulnerability in both male and female human resource development. After having gone through the variation of male–female human resource development in 1981 and 1991, we find that almost all states have shown upward movement at different levels of human resource development. However, in comparison to the development of male human resource, the progress in female human resource is found to be slower.

Almost all states except Andhra Pradesh and Manipur (in female HRDI only) have shown positive change from 1981 to 1991. However, such change is normally more in most of the UTs and in smaller states. Specifically in Arunachal Pradesh, Punjab, Sikkim, and Daman and Diu, the positive temporal change in the case of female human resource development was even faster than that of male human resource development.

These findings call for setting up adequate machinery for human resource development at both formal and non-formal educational levels by reaching down to the very grassroots of society. Also, there should be fair allocation and equitable distribution of adequate social, cultural, economic and political infrastructure or resources at all spatial levels in all the states and UTs. While doing this, special focus should be laid on the development of human resources of Scheduled Caste and Scheduled Tribes, and of the socioeconomically disadvantaged people from other sections of society. Women of all age groups and from all spatial units in rural areas should be given priority in utilizing the human resource development infrastructure. Thus, the required infrastructure should be established in spatial units of various types and at various levels, particularly relating to education, health, food, nutrition and shelter, for substantially reducing the rural male–female gap of human resource development, and in bringing about rapid progress in the nation.

References

Das, P. K. and Karak, 'Identification of Human Resources Development Zones and its Mapping', *Resource Mapping at District Level, Monograph 8*, Calcutta: NATMO, 1988.

De, N. K., 'Mapping of Human Resources in Bankura District, West Bengal', *Resource Mapping at District Level, Monograph 8*, Calcutta: NATMO, 1988.

Gupta, S. and P. Das, *Geographical Review of India*, Calcutta: The Geographical Society of India, Vol. 60, No. 4, December 1998.

Harbison, F. H., *Human Resource as the Wealth of Nation*, London: Oxford University Press, 1973.

Harbison, F. H. and Charls A. Myers, *Education, Manpower and Economic Growth: Strategies of Human Resources Development*, New York: McGraw-Hill Book Company, 1964.

Kaur, Parminder, *Human Resource Development for Rural Development*, New Delhi: Anmol Publications Pvt. Ltd., 1996.

Kumar, B. and B. S. Hansra, *Extension Education for Human Resource Development*, New Delhi: Concept Publishing Company, 2000.

Nalder, L., *The Handbook of Human Resources Development*, New York: John Wiley and Sons, 1994.

Prodi, R., 'The Evolution of Economic Organisation in Contemporary Societies', in C. Barnado, D. Paul and F. P. Max (eds.), *Resource and Population, New York: Clarendon Press*, Oxford University Press, 1996.

Rao, T. V., *HRD Audit: Evaluating the Human Resource Function for Business Improvement*, New Delhi: Response Books, A division of Sage Publications, 1999.

Schultz, T. W., 'Investment as Human Capital', *American Economic Review*, March 1961. (Quoted in B. N. Ghosh, *Fundamentals of Population Geography*, New Delhi: Sterling Publishers, 1985)

Singh, J. P., *Human Resources of North Eastern India*, New Delhi: Inter India Publications, 1982.

Sinha, B. R. K., 'Mapping of Human Resources Development in Rampurhat Block - 1 of Birbhum District, West Bengal', *Indian Journal of Landscape Systems and Ecological Studies*, Vol. 22, No. 2, 1999.

V
Indian Social Geography: City and State Context

Health Infrastructure and Healthcare Services in Uttar Pradesh

R. B. BHAGAT

Our healthcare and family welfare programmes are supposed to be demand driven under the new paradigm given in the post ICPD (International Conference on Population and Development, held in Cairo, 1994) era (United Nations Population Fund, 2004). But supply side issues are also considered equally important in terms of availability and quality of services. The network of Primary Health Centres (PHCs) and Sub-Centres (SCs) is the mode for providing healthcare services to the rural masses. The emphasis on family planning and immunization is obvious in view of the enormity of the population problem affecting the economic development and conditions of the poor in the country. The PHCs and SCs are also responsible for the prevention and eradication of major communicable and deficiency diseases such as malaria, filaria, tuberculosis, leprosy, blindness, and diarrhoea.

In rural areas, government health centres and government programmes play a key role in the provision of prenatal, natal, and postnatal services, including family planning services, immunization and treatment of common diseases. The implementation of the programme depends to a large extent on the availability and performance of doctors and Auxiliary Nurse Midwives (ANMs), Multi-Purpose Health Workers (MPHWs), trained birth attendants and village health guides. These grassroot level functionaries are the backbone of the health and family welfare programmes in the rural areas.

In the family welfare programmes, the Maternal and Child Health (MCH) care provisions are unbalanced, focussing on immunization and the provision of iron and folic acid rather than on sustained care of women and children, or on the detection and referral of high-risk cases.

On the other hand, the Pulse Polio Immunization (PPI) programme was launched in 1995–96. Till 1998–99, the PPI programme consisted of vaccination of children at fixed booths on two or three National Immunization Days (NID), six weeks apart, during the winter season. Although the coverage under the PPI programme since 1995–96 has been impressive, cases of polio continues to occur. The strategy to eradicate polio has been further intensified since 2000. In spite of very good coverage, several children are usually missed even in the PPI programme. A house-to-house search of missed children and their vaccination in the next 2–3 days following each NID is also practised.

Objectives and Methodology

The PPI programme is a new activity added in the overall family welfare and health programmes in the country. The grassroot functionaries are obviously increasingly burdened with new programmes. In such a situation, the availability of infrastructure, both physical and human, at the health centres in rural areas is critical to providing quality health services on a sustainable basis (Mishra *et al.*, 1982). Keeping this background in view, the present study focusses on two objectives: (i) to make an assessment of health and family welfare services at PHC and SC levels, and (ii) to study the clients' views about the availability and delivery of health and family welfare services.

The study was carried out in Uttar Pradesh, one of the states with high fertility. The state of Uttar Pradesh is also lagging behind in child immunization and family planning (Planning Commission, 2002). Since 1994, the State Innovations in Family Planning Services Agency (SIFPSA) has been promoting family planning in the state. As of 1 December 2003, SIFPSA covered 40 districts of the state. The state of Uttar Pradesh (UP) was divided into three geographical regions, namely western, central and south, and eastern Uttar Pradesh. Districts falling in each region were ranked according to their performance in the use of modern family planning, antenatal care, and complete immunization. Two districts with good and bad performance were selected from each geographical region. While selecting the districts, some districts like Kanpur Nagar, Lucknow, and Allahabad were excluded because they fall under the three metropolitan cities of Kanpur, Lucknow, and Allahabad respectively. Thus six districts were selected – Ghaziabad and Etah from western, Hardoi and Jhansi

Fig. 24.1 Location of study districts.

from central and southern, and Gonda and Pratapgarh from eastern Uttar Pradesh (Fig. 24.1). In the selected sample of districts, we find that Gonda from eastern, Jhansi from central and south, and Ghaziabad from western Uttar Pradesh also fall under the SIFPSA category. In each selected district, three block level PHCs (henceforth called PHCs) were covered based on their relative performance, as reported by the Chief Medical Officer's office, and their geographical distance. Altogether, 18 PHCs were visited. It was also thought that some exit interview of clients at the PHC level would help to increase our understanding of the problems of health and family welfare programmes and the quality of services provided at the grassroots level. Altogether, 265 exit interviews were carried out in 18 PHCs spread over six districts of Uttar Pradesh.

Data collection began in the last week of October 2004 and continued until the third week of December 2004. A team of four Assistant Research Officers, holding Masters' degrees and employed and trained at the International Institute for Population Sciences (IIPS), collected the data. It took nearly eight to ten days to complete the surveys in each district. The quantitative data were analysed through SPSS software.

Infrastructure and Quality of Health Care Services

This section presents an assessment of the availability of health infrastructure at the PHC and SC levels and the quality of health services as reported by the clients. In order to assess the availability of health infrastructure, information related to number of SCs, number of villages and population served, building conditions, staff positions, and availability of medicines and vaccines were collected. To know the quality of services at the PHC level, clients having received care were interviewed immediately after their exit and were asked to express their opinion about how they were treated at the health centres.

Infrastructure at the PHC Level

Table 24.1 shows that in all the selected districts, the size of the population served by each PHC ranged from about 150,000 to over 200,000. The number of villages covered by each PHC ranged from about 50 to over 300 villages. This shows that the difference in demographic and geographic coverage at the PHC level is significant. The size of population and the number of villages served by each SC has been acquired from the selected PHCs. Table 24.2 shows that all 18 PHCs have their own *pucca* (made of bricks or concrete cement) buildings, three of them needed major repairs and most of them needed some repair. Only three of the 18 PHC buildings were found to be in good condition. It was also found that quarters for staff were available in most of the PHCs, but doctors were seldom available at these quarters.

Water and sanitation facilities have an important influence on health. It may be observed from Table 24.3 that in almost all PHCs the sources

Table 24.1 Number of SCs, Number of Villages and Size of Population Covered by Selected Block Level PHCs in the Six Districts.

	Gonda	*Jhansi*	*Ghaziabad*	*Hardoi*	*Pratapgarh*	*Etah*
Average Number of SCs	18	32	24	24	23	19
Average Number of Villages	101	155	52	331	117	142
Average Population Served ('000)	162	163	235	154	192	155

Note: Such a large size of population served by a PHC is also found in an earlier study conducted by the Institute in the state of West Bengal (Verma, *et al.*, 1994, p. 41).

Table 24.2 Condition of Selected PHCs in the Six Districts.

	Gonda	*Jhansi*	*Ghaziabad*	*Hardoi*	*Pratapgarh*	*Etah*
Where PHC is functioning	Govt. B	Govt. B	Govt. B	Govt. B	Govt. B	Govt. B
Type of construction	*Pucca*	*Pucca*	*Pucca*	*Pucca*	*Pucca*	*Pucca*
Present condition of building						
Good	–	–	1	–	2	–
Needs minor repair	3	2	2	1	1	3
Needs major repair	–	1	–	2	–	–
Does the PHC have residential quarters for staff						
Yes	2	3	3	2	3	3
No	1	–	–	1	–	–

Note: Govt. B–Government Building.

of water supply were either through hand pumps or tubewells. Water supply was reported to be adequate in most of the PHCs. However, water supply was not connected through a pipe to the existing toilets. Due to this, though toilet facility was available in all PHCs, several of them were not cleaned everyday. When we looked at the electricity supply, it was found that all PHCs had electricity connections, though the supply of electricity was not regular at most of the PHCs. In most PHCs electricity supply was available for seven to eight hours everyday. In Etah district it was reported to be only four hours per day. However, it is important to note that each of the 18 PHCs had its own generator for supply of power. Also, we found that a majority of them had telephone facilities. Vehicles were available at most PHCs, but many were not in working condition. Similarly, it was also reported that drivers were available at a majority of the PHCs (Table 24.3).

Of the 18 PHCs, most had a labour room. Operation theatre was also available in most of them, but many of these were not fitted with an exhaust fan. A separate dispensary room was available in all of them. The survey of infrastructure in the selected PHCs showed that barring regular supply of electricity, all other facilities were more or less available. However, the proper use and maintenance of the exiting facilities need to be ensured.

Table 24.4 presents the staff position at the selected PHCs, both in terms of sanctioned posts as well as posts vacant. A large number of

Table 24.3 Infrastructural Facilities at PHCs of the Six Districts.

Facility	*Gonda*	*Jhansi*	*Ghaziabad*	*Hardoi*	*Pratapgarh*	*Etah*
What is the main source of water supply?						
Tap	–	–	–	–	–	–
Tubewell/Hand pump	3	3	3	3	3	3
Well	–	–	–	–	–	–
Is the water supply adequate?						
Yes	3	2	3	3	3	2
No	–	1	–	–	–	1
Is electricity available?						
Yes	3	3	3	3	3	3
No	–	–	–	–	–	–
Is a generator available?						
Yes	3	3	3	3	3	3
No	–	–	–	–	–	–
Is toilet facility available?						
Yes	3	3	3	3	3	3
No	–	–	–	–	–	–
Is the toilet cleaned everyday?						
Yes	2	3	3	1	3	2
No	1	–	–	2	–	1
Is telephone facility available?						
Yes	1	2	3	3	1	2
No	2	1	–	–	2	1
Is a vehicle available?						
Yes	2	3	3	2	2	1
No	1	–	–	1	1	2
How many vehicles are available?	2	3	3	2	2	1
How many vehicles are in working condition?	1	3	3	0	2	0
Is a driver available?						
Yes	2	3	–	1	2	2
No	1	–	3	2	1	1
Is a driver available for emergency duty?						
Yes	1	3	–	1	2	–
No	2	–	3	2	1	3

(Continued)

(*Continued*)

Facility	*Gonda*	*Jhansi*	*Ghaziabad*	*Hardoi*	*Pratapgarh*	*Etah*
Is an operation theatre available?						
Yes	3	3	3	3	3	2
No	–	–	–	–	–	1
Is there an exhaust fan in the operation theatre?						
Yes	–	2	3	–	1	1
No	3	1	–	3	2	2
Is a labour room available?						
Yes	3	3	3	1	3	3
No	–	–	–	2	–	–
Is a separate ANC* clinic room available?						
Yes	3	3	3	1	3	2
No	–	–	–	2	–	1
Is a dispensary room available?						
Yes	3	3	3	3	3	3
No	–	–	–	–	–	–

* Ante natal clinic

posts were lying unfilled both in the medical and paramedical staff categories. Several posts of medical officers were lying vacant. The shortfall in staff is most glaring in the case of male MPHWs. Many posts were lying vacant in all the districts. This proportion was more than half in the districts of Ghaziabad and Etah. Recently, some temporary ANMs, also known as RCH-ANMs (ANMs related to the Reproductive and Child Health Programme) have been appointed, but their numbers are few in each of the districts. There were also a large number of posts found unfilled belonging to the 'other employee' category, which includes drivers, peons, *chaukidars* (watchmen/security staff), *dais* (midwives), and sweepers. The declining trend in the regular appointment of these Class IV employees in the health sector is not something uncommon, but it reflects the wider policy of the Government to control expenditures in most government departments. This has some negative consequences in terms of cleanliness and maintenance of infrastructure at the PHC level.

Table 24.5 shows the availability of various equipment needed at the PHC level. It was observed that all the PHCs had oxygen cylinders,

Table 24.4 Staff Position in the Selected PHCs of the Six Districts.

Staff	*Gonda*	*Jhansi*	*Ghaziabad*	*Hardoi*	*Pratapgarh*	*Etah*
Medical Officer						
Sanctioned	6	9	14	6	6	6
Posted	5	7	12	6	5	6
Vacant	1	2	2	0	1	0
Health Education Officer						
Sanctioned	2	0	1	2	3	1
Posted	0	0	0	0	1	0
Vacant	2	0	1	2	2	1
Health Assistant						
Sanctioned	33	54	47	43	42	44
Posted	31	43	43	38	40	40
Vacant	2	11	4	5	2	4
MPW (male)						
Sanctioned	31	26	26	19	26	30
Posted	24	21	7	13	16	13
Vacant	7	5	19	6	10	17
MPW (female)						
Sanctioned	60	96	81	59	79	64
Posted	60	95	80	55	79	61
Vacant	0	1	1	4	0	3
RCH-ANM						
Sanctioned	6	0	0	2	2	3
Posted	6	0	0	2	2	3
Vacant	0	0	0	0	0	0
Clerk						
Sanctioned	7	11	8	7	7	5
Posted	7	8	7	7	6	5
Vacant	0	3	1	0	1	0
Other employees						
Sanctioned	23	22	16	25	13	18
Posted	15	22	11	16	12	16
Vacant	8	0	5	9	1	2

Note: MPW stands for Multi Purpose Worker, MO stands for Medical Officer, MOIC stands for Medical Officer In-Charge. Medical Officer as given above includes the MOIC and MO. Health assistant includes the Health Inspector, Health Visitor, Immunization Officer, Ophthalmic Officer, Lab Technician, Vaccinator and Pharmacist. RCH-ANMs are Auxillary Nurse Midwives affiliated with the Reproductive and Child Health Programme. Clerk includes computer operator/Upper Divisional Clerk and Lower Divisional Clerk. Other staff includes full-time and part-time driver, peon, *chaukidar, dai*, and sweeper.

Table 24.5 Availability of Equipment and Related Items at the PHCs of the Six Districts.

	Gonda	*Jhansi*	*Ghaziabad*	*Hardoi*	*Pratapgarh*	*Etah*
Oxygen cylinder	3	3	3	3	3	3
Labour room equipment	3	3	3	3	3	3
Cold chain equipment	3	3	3	3	3	2
Deep freezer	3	3	3	3	3	2
Thermo coal box	3	3	3	3	3	2
Ice pack	3	3	3	3	3	2
Refrigerator	1	2	2	0	0	0

labour room equipment, cold chain equipment, deep freezer, thermocol box and ice packs. The only difference observed was with respect to the availability of refrigerators. In the districts of Hardoi, Pratapgarh and Etah, none of the selected PHCs reported having a refrigerator.

Infrastructure at the SC Level

Information on 54 SCs belonging to the 18 PHCs in six districts of Uttar Pradesh was also collected from the respective ANMs. The results are presented in Table 24.6. It may be seen from the table that several SCs were serving populations of more than 10,000, much higher than the norm of 5000 per SC. Also, the number of villages served by SCs varied from less than five to 15 villages. Although a majority of SCs are located within a distance of 10 km from their respective villages, many are connected by only *kachcha* (non-permanent material) roads. Most of the SCs in Hardoi are not connected by *pucca* roads, as is the case with Gonda, whereas most the SCs selected from Ghaziabad are connected by *pucca* roads. Thus very few ANMs take a bus to reach their SCs. A majority of them reach SCs on foot. A few of them cycle to the SC. The time taken to reach SCs was mostly within the range of one hour.

Table 24.7 further illustrates that nearly two-fifth of the SCs are located in rented buildings. Most of the buildings require either minor or major repair and a few of them have '*kachcha*' structures. When questioned about where they live, nearly half of the ANMs replied that they lived in the nearby towns. Only one-fifth of them reported living at the SCs.

Nearly half of the SCs have only one room. As far as water supply is concerned, tap water was available in only two out of the 54 SCs. A

Table 24.6 Distribution of SCs by Background Characteristics in the Six Districts.

	Gonda	*Jhansi*	*Ghaziabad*	*Hardoi*	*Pratapgarh*	*Etah*
Number of villages covered						
Less than 5	5	7	7	2	5	1
6–10	4	2	2	5	4	5
11–15	–	–	–	2	–	3
Population size						
< 5000	–	4	–	1	3	–
5000–10000	8	5	3	7	4	7
10000–15000	–	–	4	1	1	1
15000–20000	1	–	1	–	–	1
> 20000	–	–	1	–	1	–
Distance from SC (in km)						
1–5	8	9	8	3	9	6
6–10	1	–	1	6	–	2
11–15	–	–	–	–	–	1
Connectivity to SC						
Pucca road	5	5	8	–	3	2
Semi-*pucca* road	1	3	1	2	4	6
Kachcha road	3	1	–	7	2	1
Mode of transportation						
Bus	–	–	2	–	–	1
Moped	–	3	–	3	1	3
Cycle	–	–	–	1	1	
On foot	9	6	7	5	7	5
Travelling time to SC						
< 30 Minutes	2	1	5	4	3	3
1 hours	6	8	4	1	6	4
1.5 hours	1	–	–	3	–	1
2 hours	–	–	–	–	–	1

majority of the SCs have no electricity supply. More than half of them do not have any toilet facility either. Table 24.8 shows that many SCs do not have Blood Pressure machines, stethoscopes or even weighing machines and sterilizers. In a nutshell, the data related to SCs show that large population size, lack of connectivity with the PHCs, lack of power supply and minimal equipment availability for daily work were some of the important impediments in the functioning of the SCs.

Table 24.7 Distribution of SC by Background Characteristics in the Six Districts.

	Gonda	*Jhansi*	*Ghaziabad*	*Hardoi*	*Pratapgarh*	*Etah*
Where is the SC located?						
Govt. building	8	6	6	4	6	4
Rented building	1	3	3	4	3	5
Other	–	–	–	1	–	–
Where does the ANM/MPHW reside?						
SC building	–	3	1	–	6	1
Another building in the same village	2	3	2	1	–	1
Another village of work area	1	–	1	3	–	2
Village outside her work area	–	–	1	3	–	1
Town/city	6	3	4	3	3	4
Where is the SC building located?						
Within the village	8	9	7	8	9	8
One km away from the village	1	–	2	–	–	–
One to two km away from the village	–	–	–	–	–	–
More than two km away from the village	–	–	–	1	–	1
Type of construction						
Pucca	9	5	6	6	7	7
Semi-*pucca*	–	4	1	3	2	1
Kachcha	–	–	2	–	–	1
Present condition of the building						
Good	3	1	3	2	–	–
Needs minor repair	3	6	6	3	5	8
Needs major repair	3	2	–	4	4	1
How many rooms are there in this SC?						
One	2	5	6	4	4	5
Two	4	3	–	4	3	1
More than two	3	1	3	1	2	3
What is the main source of water supply?						
Tap	–	–	1	–	1	–
Tubewell/Hand pump	7	9	8	8	8	8
Well	–	–	–	1	–	–
No facility	2	–	–	–	–	1

(Continued)

Table 24.7 (*Continued*)

	Gonda	*Jhansi*	*Ghaziabad*	*Hardoi*	*Pratapgarh*	*Etah*
Is electricity available?						
Yes	2	4	5	2	5	4
No	7	5	4	7	4	5
Is toilet facility available?						
Yes	7	4	7	4	5	4
No	2	5	2	5	4	5
Is toilet cleaned everyday?						
Yes	4	3	7	2	4	3

Table 24.8 Distribution of SCs by the Availability of Equipment in the Six Districts.

	Gonda	*Jhanshi*	*Ghaziabad*	*Hardoi*	*Pratapgarh*	*Etah*
Examination table						
Yes	7	7	7	7	7	7
No	2	2	2	2	2	2
Weighing machine (infant)						
Yes	6	7	6	8	7	6
No	3	2	3	1	2	3
Weighing machine (adult)						
Yes	5	7	8	8	6	8
No	4	2	1	1	3	1
BP Instrument						
Yes	5	7	6	5	7	7
No	4	2	3	4	2	2
Stethoscope						
Yes	2	5	1	2	3	4
No	7	4	8	7	6	5
Fetoscope						
Yes	7	7	7	6	7	7
No	2	2	2	3	2	2
Sterilizer						
Yes	7	7	8	6	7	5
No	2	2	1	3	2	4
Curtain						
Yes	1	1	1	2	3	–
No	8	8	8	7	6	9

Table 24.9 Socio-demographic Background of Clients and Who Advised Them to Visit PHC (Based on Exit interview).

Age	*Male*	*Female*	*Total*
< 20	(16.1) 19	(14.3) 21	15.1
20–35	(37.3) 44	(62.6) 92	51.3
35–55	(33.9) 40	(22.4) 33	27.5
55 and above	(12.7) 15	(0.7) 1	6.0
Education			
Primary	(16.9) 20	(7.5) 11	11.7
Secondary	(17.8) 21	(16.3) 24	17.0
Higher and above	(33.1) 39	(6.8) 10	18.5
Illiterate	(17.8) 21	(57.8) 85	40.0
Literate but no formal education	(14.4) 17	(11.6) 17	12.8
Occupation			
Household work	(5.9) 7	(72.1) 106	42.6
Agriculture and unskilled work	(59.3) 70	(16.3) 24	35.5
Professional and skilled work	(23.7) 28	(10.2) 15	16.2
Others	(11.0) 13	(1.4) 2	5.7
Household Size			
< 5	(11.0) 13	(27.2) 40	16.2
5–10	(73.7) 87	(59.9) 98	69.8
10–15	(13.6)16	(10.2) 15	11.7
15 and above	(1.7) 2	(2.7) 4	2.3
Who advised you to visit PHC?			
Self	(92.4) 109	(83.0) 122	87.2
Others	(7.6) 9	(17.0) 25	12.8

Note: Figures in parenthesis are in percentages.

Quality of Services: Clients' Opinion

Knowing the nature and the availability of facilities at PHCs is not adequate unless we also take into account the opinion of the clients. Keeping this in view, exit interviews of the clients were conducted at the PHCs. A total of 265 clients were interviewed from six districts and 18 PHCs of Uttar Pradesh. More than half of the clients were in age group 20–35. Females outnumbered males in all age groups. A large number of the clients were illiterate – this group too comprised of more females. Consequently, we find that a majority of the clients were either engaged in household work or worked in agriculture or had unskilled jobs. Further, most of them came from a large household. Male clients came from larger households than female clients. Interestingly, irrespective of their gender, a majority of them came to the PHCs to avail themselves of services of their own volition (Table 24.9).

When they were asked about the health problems for which they had come to seek treatment, most of them reported having general problems like fever, cough and cold, and diarrhoea. Most surprisingly, the least number of clients came to PHCs for family planning, ANC (ante natal clinic/care) and reproductive health services. However, more women came for family planning and child care than men, but there was little difference with respect to reproductive morbidities (Table 24.10).

The treatment-seeking behaviour and utilization of services at PHCs shows that family planning was not an important concern for clients who came to the PHCs to avail of the services. Furthermore, reproductive health-seeking is almost negligible at the PHC level. This shows that demand for family planning and reproductive health services from government sources is not high, which is a reflection of the overall low demand for family planning services in Uttar Pradesh.

An important fact emerging from Table 24.9 is that non-literate clients are in fact availing themselves of family planning, ANC and child care services more so than those who are literate or have higher levels of education. This is also true for the Scheduled Caste (SC) population as compared to Non-Scheduled Caste population. Thus, the education and caste pattern of utilization of family welfare services indicates that it is the poor who use such services from government sources more than the non-poor. Further, there was no difference in seeking family planning services between Hindus and Muslims in the study area. Nearly 15 per cent each of both of the Hindu and Muslim, clients used family planning services at the PHC level. It may be seen from Table 24.11 that more than half of the clients reached the health centres on foot. They received services like check-ups, medicines and injections, and more than one-third of them have been advised further diagnosis/tests or referred to specialists.

Most of those who came for treatment for health problems of a general nature have reported that doctors did not discuss with them any family planning matters. It seems obvious that in the minds of the doctors, family planning is not an important concern, or else they believe that it is a different area of concern, to be dealt exclusively either by ANMs at the SC or at the PHC during the time of the health camp.

Table 24.10 Percentage Distribution of Clients by Background Characteristics and Health-Seeking Behaviour (Based on Exit Interview).

Health-seeking behaviour	*General health*	*Family planning*	*Antenatal care*	*Reproductive health*	*Child care*	*Total*
Age group						
< 20	70.0	10.0	15.0	5.0	0.0	40
20–35	54.4	19.9	10.3	2.9	12.5	136
35–55	75.3	9.6	4.1	4.1	6.8	73
55 and above	75.0	6.3	6.3	0.0	12.5	16
Education						
Primary	67.7	12.9	6.5	9.7	3.2	31
Secondary	64.4	15.6	11.1	0.0	8.9	45
Higher and above	71.4	12.2	4.1	4.1	8.2	49
Illiterate	55.7	17.0	13.2	2.8	11.3	106
No formal education	73.5	11.8	2.9	2.9	8.8	34
Occupation						
Household work	56.6	20.4	14.2	1.8	7.1	113
Agriculture and unskilled work	62.8	10.6	6.4	6.4	13.8	94
Professional and skilled work	79.1	11.6	2.3	0.0	7.0	43
Others	80.0	6.7	6.7	6.7	0.0	15
Caste						
SC	59.6	19.1	10.6	4.3	6.4	47
Others	64.7	13.8	8.7	3.2	9.6	218
Religion						
Hindu	62.5	14.5	9.5	3.0	10.5	200
Muslim	67.7	15.4	7.7	4.6	4.6	65
District						
Hardoi	62.1	20.7	6.9	0.0	10.3	29
Gonda	56.3	20.8	10.4	4.2	8.3	48
Pratapgarh	52.2	17.4	6.5	8.7	15.2	46
Jhansi	66.7	17.8	11.1	0.0	4.4	45
Etah	58.0	10.0	14.0	4.0	14.0	50
Ghaziabad	87.2	4.3	4.3	2.1	2.1	47
Total	169	39	24	9	24	265

When asked about the quality of services or care received at the PHCs, more than half replied that they were not allowed to ask questions. Further, almost all said the doctors did not spend enough time with them and nearly two-fifth said waiting time was too long. Respondents also felt that there was a lack of doctors, particularly lady doctors, and paramedical staffs at the PHC (Table 24.12).

Table 24.11 Percentage Distribution of Clients by Mode of Transport Used and Type of Services Received (Based on Exit Interview).

	Numbers	*Percentages*
Mode of transport		
On foot	154	58.1
Other	111	41.9
Services received		
Check-up	218	82.3
Medicine and injections	256	96.6
Further diagnosis	99	37.4
Referred	2	0.8
Other matters discussed		
Family planning	15	5.7
Breast feeding	18	6.8
Immunization	36	13.6
Nutrition	33	12.5
ANC	16	6.0
Delivery care	12	4.5
Postpartum care	14	5.3
No discussion	229	86.4
Total	265	100.00

In a nutshell, clients' perspective on the availability and quality of services reveals that the PHCs acted as mini-hospitals, and the clients come there for seeking OPD (out-patient department) services for general health. Neither the seeking of family planning services by the clients, nor the provision of these services by doctors is considered to be important at the PHC level. The lack of quality services is aggravated by the rush of clients during the OPD hours as well as due to the lack of adequate number of doctors and para medical staff at the PHCs. This was also evident by the long waiting time and doctors not spending enough time with the clients.

Conclusion

The present study was carried out with the aim to understand the availability of healthcare infrastructure and quality of services as reported by the clients in 18 PHCs of the six districts of Uttar Pradesh. The state of Uttar Pradesh is divided into three geographical regions, namely western,

Table 24.12 Clients' Opinion Regarding PHC Staff and Quality of Services (Based on Exit Interview).

	Number	*Percentages*
Allowed to ask questions		
Yes	153	57.7
No	112	42.3
Problem in getting desired treatment		
Yes	25	9.4
No	240	90.6
Satisfied with available services at PHC		
Yes	242	91.3
No	23	8.7
Expectation from PHC staff		
Nothing	72	27.2
Good behaviour	64	24.2
Proper and responsible service	129	48.7
Facilities lacking		
Shortage of materials and drugs	8	3.0
Lack of skilled doctors and staff	142	53.6
Not lacking	115	43.4
Was waiting time very long?		
Yes	104	39.2
No	161	60.8
Did doctors spend enough time?		
Yes	15	5.7
No	250	94.3

central and south, and eastern Uttar Pradesh. Two districts were selected from each region in the study. Further, from each selected district, three PHCs were visited. Information was also collected for three SCs from each PHC. Altogether, 18 PHCs and 54 SCs were covered in this study. Two hundred and sixty-five exit clients who used the services at the PHCs were interviewed in order to know their health-seeking behaviour and their opinion about the quality of services. The state of affairs and main concerns emerging from the study are summarized below for the consideration of policy makers and managers of the health and family welfare programmes in Uttar Pradesh.

(i) Each PHC (block level) serves a very large size of population, ranging from about 150–200 thousand people. There is a shortage of doctors, particularly women doctors, and lab technicians for pathology tests. Clients also reported that this was one of the main hurdles they faced when visiting PHCs. They also reported long waiting time in view of the shortage of staff.

(ii) There was a large number of posts of male health workers lying vacant either due to retirement or promotion. This has resulted in the transfer of responsibilities of vertical programmes like malaria eradication, leprosy control and the DOTs (polio) programme for the control of tuberculosis to the ANMs.

(iii) Contractual appointments of ANMs known as RCH-ANMs have been in place for quite some time. They are neither properly trained nor provided with the supply of materials needed for their daily activities. They are also not paid on time, and backlog of salary mounts to several months.

(iv) The physical infrastructure issues in several PHCs and SCs was the lack of availability of electricity and regular supply of water. Due to lack of electricity it was difficult to maintain the cold chain for the upkeep of vaccines at the PHC level.

Recommendations

(i) All vacant posts should be filled at the earliest. The State Government must ensure at least one female doctor and a lab technician in each PHC. All PHCs should be provided with a generator for uninterrupted power supply and regular water supply must be ensured.

(ii) SC-based services are provided only for two days in a week. On other days health workers are required to visit their respective villages to provide services. While this is a good practice, SC-based services need to be strengthened and should be provided during all working days. This will require additional staffing at the SC level but will ensure greater reach of services to the people.

Acknowledgments

The author gratefully acknowledges the funds and support provided by the Indian institute for Population Studies (IIPS), Mumbai, in completing this research work. Thanks are also due to Dr S. K. Singh, Reader, IIPS, for his help in data collection.

References

Mishra, B. D., A. Ashraf, R. Simmons and G. B. Simmons, *Organization for Change: A Systematic Analysis of Family Planning in Rural India*, New Delhi: Radiant Publishers, 1982.

Planning Commission, *National Human Development Report 2001*, New Delhi: Government of India, 2002.

United Nations Population Fund, *State of World Population: the Cairo Consensus at Ten*, UNPF, 2004.

Verma, Ravi, T. K. Roy and P. C. Saxena, *Quality of Family Welfare Services and Care in Selected Indian States*, Mumbai International Institute for Population Sciences, 1994.

25

Status of Women in Aligarh Muslim University, India

NILOFAR IZHAR

The status of any population in a society is intimately connected with its economic position, which itself depends upon rights, roles and opportunities for participation in economic activities (Government of India, 1974, p. 148). Therefore, in addition to education, employment should also be considered as a variable measuring the status of women. Equal opportunity for economic participation is or should be the right of all men and women because discrimination against women is incompatible with human dignity and the welfare of the family and of society (United Nations, 1967).

The Constitution of India pledges equality of status and opportunity, justice, social, economic, political, and dignity of the individual to men and women equally. Despite the assurance of equal opportunity in employment, in reality women have less access to employment in services. The disparity in employment ratio is considered often attributed to the lower level of education of women. Moreover, in a patriarchal society these disparities are largely the result of several other factors, such as attitude of men towards women's role and employment, discrimination perceived by women in selection and promotion as well as due to their household duties and child care. A committee on the status of women in India stated that the 'image of Indian women is created by a few women holding high position or academic qualification', which serves to conceal rather than reveal the reality of the low status and educational levels of the average Indian woman (Government of India, 1974).

Objectives of the Study

In the light of the committee's comment, an attempt has been made to analyse the status of women academicians and researchers at the Aligarh Muslim University (AMU), Aligarh. The objective of the present study is to examine the status of women employees on the university campus. This study analyses the various problems faced by women academicians in the University, including health problems. An attempt has been made to uncover any gender disparity between male and female employees (both teaching and non-teaching) in the process of appointment, representation of women in different bodies of the University such as the Executive Council, Academic Council, and the University Court. It is hoped that the present study would reveal the status and conditions of women at Aligarh Muslim University.

Sources of Data

Data pertaining to employment have been obtained from the Council Section of the Registrar's Office, AMU, for the period 2001–02. In order to analyse the varied problems faced by women academicians and their health status, an exhaustive questionnaire was prepared and a field survey was carried out on the university campus. Questionnaire and interview were the methods adopted to obtain information and necessary data. Women academicians are either employed in the University or affiliated with the University for the purpose of doctoral and postdoctoral research. Samples were drawn of women belonging to different age groups in order to assess their problems at the workplace and their familial role that varies with their age as well as seniority. Significant numbers of them work and manage the household. One hundred respondents were chosen for the purpose of the study from different age groups and educational backgrounds using stratified random sampling. Information was obtained regarding the personal profile of respondents – their educational level, designation, size of family, nature of household duties, attitude of husband, problems in the workplace, opinion regarding harassment at the workplace, as well as the health problems from which they might suffer.

Women's Representation in Teaching Departments

The analysis of the data collected shows the gender-wise representation of teaching staff in various faculties of Aligarh Muslim University. Despite progress in the higher education of women over the decades (Abdullah, 1969), in none of these faculties is the ratio of women equal to that of men. In each faculty, men out-number women in all the three categories –

lecturership, readership, as well as professorship. In faculties of Agricultural Sciences, Commerce, Law, and Theology (both Sunni and Shia), women's representation is dismal. Women are also poorly represented in the faculties of Unani Medicine[1], and Business Administration. Astonishingly, women's representation is either nil or poor in important and prestigious departments such as Physics, Mathematics, Botany, Geology and Geography. In the faculty of Life Sciences, women are better represented only in Biochemistry. Fewer women academicians are employed in the largest professional field of Engineering and Technology. The bulk of the positions at all levels are occupied by men due to their advantageous position in this field. Whatever little representation of women is seen in the faculty of Engineering and Technology is mainly due to the higher proportion of women staff in the Women's Polytechnic. When compared to Science, Engineering and Technology, women are better represented in the faculties of Social Sciences, Medicine, and Arts. In the faculty of Social Sciences, women have faired reasonably well in disciplines such as Education, Psychology, and Sociology, while in Medicine, they are well represented in Gynaecology and Obstetrics, Anesthesiology, Microbiology, Paediatrics, Pathology, and Physiology. In the faculty of Arts, women are fairly represented in English, Persian, and History.

The gender inequality in the data for teaching positions (considering the University as a whole) reveals that female academicians account for only 19.25 per cent of the total staff strength. This figure also includes the female staff of the Women's College – a constituent college of the University. If the number of women academicians of the College is excluded, the percentage declines to 12.35. Gender disparity is also evident at the professorial level. Women constitute only 12.2 per cent of the professors (including the Women's College). If we exclude the figure for the Women's College, women's share in professorships further declines to 8.4 per cent. With regard to professorship, women are better represented in the faculties of Arts, Social Sciences, and Medicine. Thus, these figures confirm the findings of Norton Dodge who, while working on the problems of 'Women in Profession', has rightly pointed out that "the proportions of women have not increased significantly in many of the most attractive professions, such as enterprise directors or scientific research workers or teachers in higher education". (Dodge, 1977, p. 206).

Gender-wise representation of non-teaching staff in Central and Accounts Office in AMU during the period 2001–02 shows that women constitute only 4.4 per cent of non-teaching staff. They are poorly represented in these important offices and are mainly confined to certain jobs, such as stenographers, semi-professionals, assistants, and clerks. Even after promotion they could not reach higher administrative positions, such as Assistant Registrars or Deputy Registrars. Rarely was a woman appointed to a senior administrative position, such as Controller of Examinations, Finance Officer or Assistant Finance Officer. Women are largely excluded from positions of power in the 85 years of history of the institution. No woman has ever become vice-chancellor of AMU, nor has one ever been recommended by members of the Executive Council and the University Court. Even the posts of Pro-Vice-Chancellor and Registrar, which are appointed by the Vice-Chancellor, have never gone to a woman candidate. Again, even a career woman does not question the 'socially superior status of men' for these positions. Analysis of data shows that women's representation is far behind that of their male counterparts. They do not get elected to positions. While the researcher was interviewing participants for the present study, there was a general complaint on the part of women respondents that at the time of elections to the University Court, even the female staff of AMU (including the Women's College) do not vote for a 'woman candidate'. I could not get a satisfactory reply for this biased attitude of women against their own gender. It is because a woman does not trust another woman, or do the male condidates know the art of convincing voters better? In other words, does the competitive environment favour men more than women? From Evolutionary Biology to discrimination, to personal preferences, science and society have offered many reasons why men perform better relative to women.

Gender-wise Representation in the University Executive Council

The same pattern of gender inequality emerges in membership of the Executive Council, the University's highest body, where there was only one woman out of 25 members, that too the Principal of the Women's College, who is an *ex-officio* member. In addition to this, it is significant to mention that compared to women, men achieved a higher status in the field of research and technology. They received President's Awards as well as literary awards in Urdu, Arabic and Persian. Some of them received Padma

Shri, Padma Bhushan Awards for excellence and for their contribution to the field. Men of repute at AMU include Qazi Abdul Sattar, Mohammad Shafi, Moin Ahsan Jazbi, Aley Ahmad Suroor, Irfan Habib, Shaharyar; the list is long. These renowned academicians, who devoted their whole lives to academic pursuits and are well known in their particular fields, are all males. Enjoying the same benefits and same designations, the women academicians could not reach the stature of their male colleagues in their respective fields.

Women's role in higher administration and policy-making generally demonstrates the diminishing role of women academicians. As they move up the ladder, they are rarely on committees of importance, or editors of journal, and are yet to achieve the reputation of being international scholars.

However, senior women academicians do not agree with the reasons. They view the awards achieved by these male academicians not as manifestation of individual capabilities, but suggest that since the inception of the institution, distinguished women academicians are rare, invisible, unrewarded, and often belittled by their male colleagues. Thus, in their opinion there is a general prejudice against women, especially in the literary field.

Health Status of Women Academicians

While the phenomenon of women's inequality is universal, its magnitude and severity vary from country to country, and within a country from community to community, and within a community too (Shanthi, 1998, p. 1). This inequality manifests itself in several form, including gender disparity in employment and health. Gender discrimination and women's status are intricately entwined and together significantly influence the health of a woman (Price, 1994). Women academicians of AMU are no exceptions.

There is a general perception that employment empowers women. While there are undoubtedly some beneficial effects of employment on women's social and economic status, manifestations of negative implications for the health of women are also often seen.

This survey demonstrates that younger women academicians have greater problems in managing the dual role. Women's biological clock makes it imperative that important decisions regarding setting up a family are taken before it is too late. As a result, women academicians become burdened with two demanding full-time jobs – a young family and a budding career.

Some of them possess a brilliant academic record. This creates an imbalance at a crucial stage in their career. Both family and career require heavy investments in terms of time and energy. Usually women spend valuable time in caring for their children during the very years that demand commitment to research and teaching. Donald. E. Koshland, while discussing the subject in *Science*, writes, 'Society cannot afford to lose the potential of women's brainpower' (cited in Rastogi, 1996).

Problems increase further when the husband and the wife work at two different places. Women experience much stress in trying to maintain the balance between house and career. They have to look after the children and care for the elders in the family. Thus, when an individual is trying to perform two full-time jobs, the end result is often frustration and extreme exhaustion.

Gender gap is widely observed in appointments at entry levels, mainly due to the patriarchal outlook that women are suitable only for particular roles, the burden of reproductive health, personal preferences and the difference in the way men and women react to competition. There is a general feeling among the respondents that even if women have a much better academic record, men usually know 'how to get the position'. The majority of younger respondents held the view that in addition to personal preferences, there is clear-cut gender discrimination in the appointments made.

The research sample also included women academicians who are in the middle of their academic career; they seem comparatively comfortable. As their children grew, they seemed to adjust better to work-family demands. Thus, either they overcome issues, or learn to cope with their dual role.

In comparison, academicians belonging to the senior category face varied problems in various academic and biological phases of their life. In due course of time, their role at home reduces significantly. Their children become independent. Simultaneously, their aspirations also grow with academic seniority. Contrary to younger academicians for whom the home usually has priority, over time senior academicians begin to make sacrifices for their career. Thus, with the passage of time they realize why women rarely find the workplace environment favourable for long-term career growth. Usually, the most number of conflicts with male members of the faculty take place at the later stage of their academic seniority, either at the time of appointment or when holding an additional honorary position. At the same time, this phase often combines with degenerative diseases and other stress-related problems. The attitude of their male colleagues in a conservative society also makes their professional lives stressful. Almost 80 per cent of the respondents feel that mental harassment, which is mainly an outcome of verbal harassment women academicians face in the workplace, contributes greatly towards the stress and tension affecting their psycho-social well-being. In their opinion, a woman has to work at least twice as hard as a man in order to prove herself or to get the same position. Some 20 per cent of women academicians who were interviewed opined that 'even if a woman does not face injustice or discrimination at the workplace, the burden of the dual role itself is quite an exhausting experience for her'.

Gender discrimination is clearly observed in the conservative atmosphere of the institution. Some of the common instances of discrimination which women generally experience are: (i) less recognition and praise for women's intellectual ability and achievements, (ii) men's keenness to discuss women's age, physical appearance or family. Moreover, cases of sexual harassment also exist. These facts might be universal, but in a conservative society, the shock and trauma women face in the workplace might have a tremendous impact on their mental health. Thus, it is significant to study the diseases and illnesses that women suffer from at different stages of their life, and their position in varying environments (Table 25.1).

The analysis of the data collected reveals that women academicians who are in the beginning of their career mainly face reproductive and stress-related problems, as psychological and social burdens are often greater for them. Usually women academicians marry late and at the same time struggle for a permanent position. Unlike younger academicians, those in the senior category reported degenerative diseases as well as stress-related problems. Table 25.2 shows a positive correlation between higher educational level and the number of children, which is possibly reflective of stages of the life-course.

The crusade against gender discrimination is underway at the institution, and looking back through the 85-year long history of AMU, the male–female gap in employment should be reduced substantially. The deep-rooted gender superiority of men contributed much towards this discrimination. To sum up, the overall gender equality in employment in the institution is far from satisfactory. Women must realize that equality of employment and 'right to work' are their fundamental rights. They must come forward wherever they face any kind of discrimination. Moreover,

Table 25.1 Age-wise Classification of Women Academicions and Their Health Problems.

Age	*Commonly reported heath problem*
40 and below	Headache Fatigue Gynaecological problem Depression
41 to 50	High blood pressure Diabetes Migraine Hormonal problem Weight gain Gynaecological problem
51 to 62	Diabetes Osteoarthritis Heart ailments Liver problem Respiratory problem Ulcer Eye problem Cervical spondylitis

Data Source: Based on survey conducted by researcher, 2002–2003.

Table 25.2 Educational Level of Women Academicians and Number of Children.

Age group	*Academic qualification*	*Average number of children*
Below 40	MA, M Phil MS, MD, PhD, M Tech	1
41–62	PhD, MBBS, MD	2

Data Source: Based on the data collected by researcher, 2002–2003.

the time has come when we must consider women's health in terms of a holistic framework which is more significantly related to the psycho-social dimension.

Aknowledgments

I am grateful to the women respondents for their cooperation, without which this study would not have been completed. I am also thankful to the Council Section of the AMU for providing necessary data for this research. This study is dedicated to the Centre for Women's Studies, AMU, Aligarh.

Note

1. Unani Medicine is a holistic system of medicine that was developed in the Middle East at the juncture of Greek and Egyptian civiliztions with Chinese and Indian. It is therefore no wonder to find that the doctrine of Tibb Medicine encompasses many of the medicines and practices from these cultures.

References

Abdullah, S. M., *Mushahidat wa Ta'assurat*, Aligarh: Female Education Association, 1969.

Dodge, N., 'Women in Profession', in D. Atkinson, A. Dallin and G. Lipidus (eds.), *Women in Russia*, Stanford Press, 1977.

Government of India, *Towards Equality: Report of the Committee on the Status of Women in India*, Department of Social Welfare, Government of India, 1974.

Price, P., 'Maternal and child health care strategies', in D. R. Phillips and Y. Verhasselt (eds.), *Health and Development*, London: Routledge, 1994, pp. 138–155.

Rastogi, N., *The Hindustan Times*, 16 September 1996.

Shanthi, K., *Empowerment of Women*, New Delhi: Anmol Publication, 1998.

United Nations (UN), *Declaration on the Elimination of Discrimination Against Women*, New York: UN, 1967.

26

Social Geographies of Collective Action: A Case Study of India's Chipko Movement

SYA BURYN KEDZIOR

The Chipko movement is popularly recognized as the most famous and successful environmental movement in India's history. The term '*chipko*' is commonly translated from Hindi as 'hug' or 'embrace' and it refers to a method of protest in which one embraces a tree in order to prevent its felling (Right Livelihood Awards (RLA), 1987; Karan, 1994). The contemporary Chipko movement is best known for a string of protests that began in the 1970s, which most prominently involved an increasingly large number of peasant women. The majority of these protests occurred in the Himalayan foothills in the region of Uttarakhand (Fig. 26.1). A majority of the Indian Himalayas lie in this region, which borders both Nepal and Tibetan China. As two of the most heavily forested states in India, Uttarakhand (formerly Uttaranchal) and Uttar Pradesh have long been relied upon for their supplies of natural resources, which have been regarded as critical to national economic development (RLA, 1987). While organized resistance against restrictive and unjust economic development and environmental policies have occurred elsewhere in India, the materialization and manifestation of the Chipko movement reflects the specific multi-scalar social, political and ecological processes which constituted social life in the late 1960s Uttarakhand, and which was itself later reshaped by these distinctive patterns of struggle.

This case study examines Chipko movement activity at the specific regional scale of Uttarakhand in order to examine how social movements emerge from spatially-embedded power relations and social contexts. By analysing Uttarakhand[1] as the 'scaled space of resistance' in which Chipko movement activities literally 'took place', this study seeks to explore: (i) the dynamic interactions between social and ecological processes that constitute

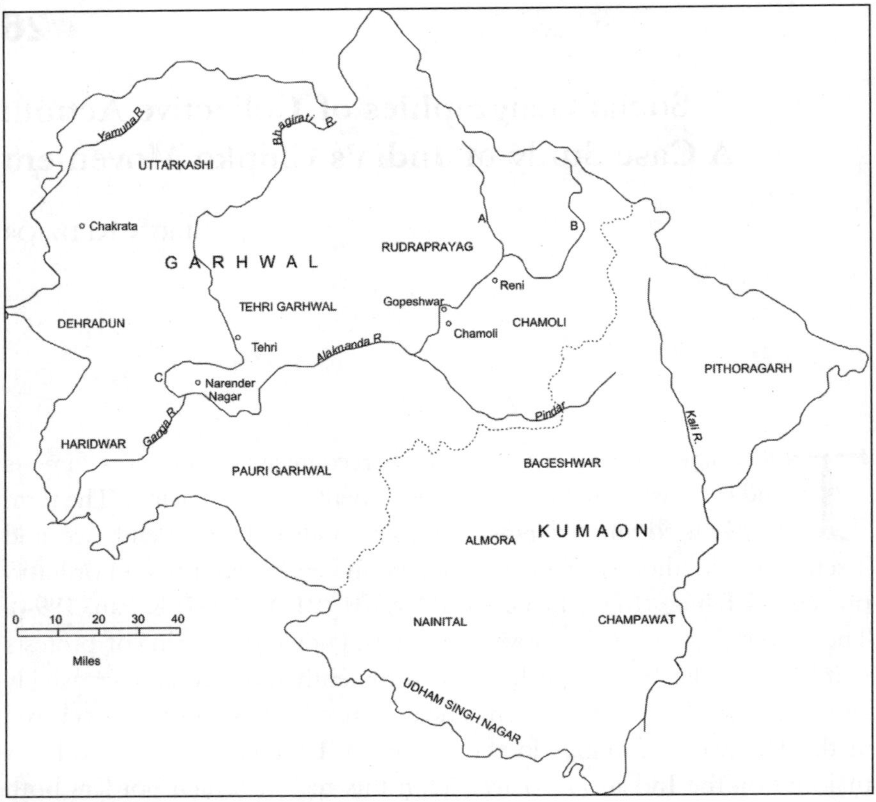

Fig. 26.1 Map of Uttarakhand (Uttaranchal).
(Map courtesy of Dick Gilbreath, Gyula Pauer, Center for Cartography and GIS, University of Kentucky)

the scaled nature of that space, and (ii) the productive power relations that shaped the Chipko movement as a distinct form of social action and organization. The application of a scalar analysis is particularly well-suited to Chipko, as the social and ecological processes that shaped the movement, to which it responded and that it aimed to influence, were focussed upon specific spaces that correspond to ecologically, politically and socially-formed scales, such as the nation, state, region, village, and household. For example, global-scale measures and theories of economic development in the mid-twentieth century influenced the ways in which forest policies were constructed at state and even national scales, leading to Uttarakhand's experience as an internal colony (Berreman, 1985); the creation of forest policy and management regimes at the state scale of

Uttar Pradesh influenced the terms on which local people were able to exercise their rights to local forests and their resources; the multi-regional ecological processes unique to the Himalayan foothills affected the impact of those state-scale forest policies, allowing them to manifest differently in that region than in others within the state of Uttar Pradesh; in Uttarakhand the household division of labour within homes influenced ideological divisions within the Chipko movement between women who were interested in alleviating forest scarcity and men who often aimed to strengthen local extractive industries. While each of these multi-scalar processes is examined in turn, the author nonetheless argues that they are overlapped. These processes were mediated at the regional scale of Uttarakhand, which the author examines as the primary 'scaled space' of the Chipko resistance.

Due to the importance of Himalayan timber resources to post-colonial development plans, increasing attention was paid to the ecology of the Himalayan foothills as the twentieth century progressed. As early as 1949, Mira *Behn* ('sister'), a disciple of Mahatma Gandhi, drew attention to the link between deforestation and the contemporary water crises. At the time, she concluded that 'unless the Ganga catchment area was replanted with broad-leaved trees, drought and floods would worsen' (Breton, 1998, p. 5). These predictions materialized in 1970, when the flooding of River Alaknanda and its tributaries destroyed villages, 500 acres of crops, and killed 55 people and 142 cattle (James, 2000). Since most of the destroyed areas were located beneath timber operations and deforested areas, people began to question forest policies more actively and to organize more frequently against unchecked tree felling (Hall, 1994). Still, few changes were made and the sale of local timber rights to extra-local contractors continued.

In the two years following the 1970 flood, numerous anti-logging demonstrations were held throughout Uttarakhand. The most important of these, in terms of the formation of the Chipko movement, were protests organized by the Dasholi Gram Swaraj Sangh (DGSS) forest cooperative in Tehri and Gopeshwar in 1971, and near Mandal in 1972. The DGSS had been established in Chamoli in 1964 by Gandhian sarvodaya workers whose 'aim was to organize village labourers and craftsmen to compete ... with private (outside) contractors and wholesalers' (Routledge, 1993, p. 83). Their 1971 protests, organized in response to governmental forestry meetings in Tehri during October, served as a forum for the DGSS to demand preference in the allotment of forest resources and the strengthening of local forest access. The 1972 protests were a reaction to the subsequent rejection of these demands and more specifically, to the Forest Department's reassignment of the DGSS' allotment of 12 ash trees from the local Mandal forest to the Symond Company, a sporting goods manufacturer in Allahabad, Uttar Pradesh. The auctioning of these 12 trees, along with 300 others, to Symond prompted the DGSS to take immediate action by organizing public meetings and demonstrations that aimed to educate local people about the Forest Department's action and the injustice of the contractor system (Chakraborty, 1999). By the time loggers arrived to fell the trees in the Mandal forest in March of 1973, they were met by a procession of villagers who successfully blockaded the forest and prevented the felling of even a single tree (Hall, 1994). The company's permit was quickly transferred and they were allotted trees in the forests near Phata Rampur. However, the protesters followed the contractor and used non-violent strategies to chase them away, successfully saving both forests while obtaining a logging permit for themselves (Chakraborty, 1999).

Following the Mandal protests, men serving as representatives of the DGSS negotiated with Forest Department officials with the aim of promoting local village forest industries. While they were successful in drawing attention to the ills of the timber allotment system, these men failed to represent the demands of women activists who supported the return of local forest management but not at the expense of continued forest scarcity. This conflict within the DGSS, 'between men, who wanted cash from commercial forest products, and women, who wanted to conserve the forests as local life-support systems', became more pronounced as the Chipko movement developed (Breton, 1998, p. 4). According to Somen Charaborty, an incident at Reni village in March of 1974 became 'the first occasion in which women participated in a major way independently of the male activists ... [and] defend[ed] their traditional forest rights against state encroachments' (1991, p. 31). The Reni demonstrations also marked the first documented use of Chipko 'tree-hugging' tactics and the articulation of ecological preservation demands.

The forests near Reni had been marked for felling the year before and the DGSS had organized protests, but they continued to be unsuccessful. On 26 March, state officials invited the men of Reni village to the District Administrative Centre in Chamoli to collect payments for lands lost to the Chinese military following a 1962 invasion. During this absence, timber contractors arrived at the forest near Reni to remove marked trees. Over two dozen women remaining in the village gathered under the leadership of Gaura Devi, President of a local women's organization, to confront the contractors and prevent any forest felling by embracing the trees. As Devi recounted:

> It was not a question of planned organization of the women for the movement, rather it happened spontaneously. Our men were out of the village so we had to come forward and protect the trees. We have no quarrel with anybody but we wanted to make the people understand that our existence is tied with the forests. (Guha, 1989, p. 159)

The Reni protests had a number of significant outcomes. Village women demonstrated that in the absence of male leadership they were able to organize a successful protest and advance a distinct agenda. These actions led to increased recognition of women's role in the movement, as well as a greater emphasis on female participation and representation in leadership (Sharma *et al.*, 1987). Media exposure gained from the Reni events also illustrated the efficacy of the tree-hugging method in preventing tree felling and calling attention to the interdependence of social and ecological welfare. Thereafter, members of the movement employed the tree-hugging strategy and adopted the 'Chipko' name. Finally, public concern sparked by the Reni uprising led to the creation of the Reni Investigation Committee (RIC), an agency consisting of both state officials and local representatives of the newly designated Chipko Movement. The RIC was charged with investigating the impacts of deforestation and its relationship to the 1970 floods, as well as other related ecological and economic concerns. The committee's findings, published in 1976, identified 'widespread deforestation' as one of the major causes of 'floods, unemployment and various economic problems in the mountain valleys' (Chakraborty, 1999, p. 4). Based on this report, the Uttar Pradesh State Government terminated the private contractor system in the Himalayan foothills and banned commercial logging of green trees in a 1200 sq mi area around River Alaknanda for the following decade (Sharma *et al.*, 1987; Chakraborty, 1999).

Over the next five years, Chipko mobilizations took place throughout Uttarakhand. In 1977 and 1978, Chipko demonstrations thwarted timber auctions in the Chakrata division forest of Dehradun, in the Chamyala forest near Silyara, at Loital and at Amarsar. In 1978, activists organized by the Uttarakhand Sangharsh Vahini (USV), a Marxist branch of the Chipko movement, organized protests against forest auctions in Chanchridhar, near Almore, in spite of recurrent local landslides. One of the most documented of these later mobilizations took place in 1977, following the sale of 640 trees from the Adwani forest and 273 trees from the Salet forest by the Uttar Pradesh State Government (Rawat, 1996). Chipko activists responded by occupying the forests for a week, while Sunderlal Bahuguna, a prominent Chipko leader fasted. A well-known and long-lasting slogan for the Chipko movement originated during the Adwani campaign, when a forest officer reportedly critiqued, 'You foolish village women! Do you know what the forests bear? Resin, timber and foreign exchange'. The famous reply he received became a chant, 'What do the forests bear? Soil, water and pure air! Soil, water and pure air are the very basis of life' (Weber, 1987, p. 53).

Through the course of the 1970s, twelve large-scale Chipko demonstrations were documented, along with various minor confrontations, involving an estimated total of 23,000 people in 175 villages (Hall, 1994). Chipko movement activities in Uttarakhand decreased rapidly following the passage of the 1980 Forest Conservation Act, which prevented state governments from reserving forests, from leasing forests to non-government entities and from clearing forests (Ministry of Environment and Forests, 1988). Activists began to spread the Chipko message beyond the Himalayas and to apply Chipko tactics in resistance to dams, mines, highways and State policies that would disrupt the ecosystem (Hall, 1994; Breton, 1998). Sunderlal Bahuguna is often credited for inspiring Chipko protests and raising environmental awareness throughout the Himalayas following his famous 4870 km march from 'Kashmir to Kohima' (Nagaland) from 1981 to 1983. Many former members of the movement also became active as leaders in smaller community development programmes, educational organizations and afforestation programmes in the region (Chakraborty, 1999). While Chipko methods continue to be employed in protests throughout India, a cohesive movement is no longer active in Uttarakhand.

Power and Representation in Indian Forest Governance (1947–1980)

The Constitution, adopted by India's Constituent Assembly in 1950, had granted state governments exclusive rights to formulate forest laws in the hope that the Central Government would be able to focus on more pressing post-Independence problems, such as those resulting from the Partition and the drawing of state boundaries (Khator, 1989). However, state governments often dismissed national policy recommendations and lowered environmental standards in order to keep forest industries operating profitably. This problem was partially addressed in the National Forest Policy Act of 1952, in which states' rights to exclusive control over forest protection, production and management was reinforced, but curbed by their need to serve the 'national interest' of fostering social stability and economic progress (Swain, 1997, p. 820). While these forest policies represented little real change from British colonial practices, especially for individual consumers, there were relatively fewer agitations against State-run activities in the first decades following Independence. This may be attributable to a widely-held belief that self-rule would translate into local governance or, as Haripriya Rangan has suggested, because of the 'considerable popular appeal' of 'the idea of a post-colonial state working toward national development, stability and progress' (1993, p. 169).

During the 1960s, State Forest Departments were called upon to produce the raw materials needed for industrial processing and were encouraged by the National Planning Commission to pursue afforestation programmes that managed the planting of rapid-growth species (Rangan and Lane, 2001). But few meaningful changes were made in national forest policy until the 1970s, when the Constitution was amended to increase Central control over forest policy formation and programme development, in order to address the non-availability of land for afforestation programmes following the growth of agricultural production during the 1960s. The Fifth Five Year Plan was drafted in 1973 as Chipko protests began to be organized in the Uttarakhand hills. In these protests, 'social forestry' was advocated as an alternative forest management approach in which local communities participated in the maintenance of forests. However, the Plan was terminated in 1978, after only two years of implementation, following the end of a 19-month state of emergency and the defeat of Indira Gandhi and the Congress party in an election that brought the Janata Party to power. During its brief, two-year period of control from 1978 to 1980, the Janata Party encouraged Gandhian economic policies that promoted the growth of village-based cottage industries. Indira Gandhi and the Congress party were re-elected in 1980, enabling Gandhi to serve her third and final term as Prime Minister until her assassination in 1984.

The centralization of forest governance continued into the 1980s, as the national legislature attempted to balance the demands of national economic development and increasing domestic consumption with the need to limit deforestation and related environmental destruction. The trend toward centralization culminated in the Forest Conservation Act of 1980, in which state governments were prohibited from allowing the use of forest lands for any non-forest purpose 'without the prior approval of the central government' (Khator, 1989, p. 16). While the Chipko movement helped to raise national awareness regarding Himalayan deforestation during the 1970s, its critiques had been levied primarily at Uttar Pradesh State Forest Department and were used to provide further support for the argument that national forest governance would result in more sustainable forest practices. Although these changes in forest governance had important national implications, forest access and control in individual villages of Uttarakhand experienced few meaningful changes in the 150 years from the beginning of British occupation to the start of Chipko protests in the 1970s. For Chipko activists, the forests of Uttarakhand had been continually exploited in the name of external growth – first for the British Empire, then for the independent nation and state that administered Uttarakhand until the end of the century. While changes in state forestry policy attempted to dictate local forest use practices, they were more influential in shaping how local people interacted with forest officials and policing authorities, who were sometimes treated as mere obstacles to be overcome by bribing or through the continuance of careful 'illegal' forest use.

Social Difference and Power Relations in Uttarakhand

As described above, both development programmes and forest policies implemented under-colonial and post-colonial rule tended to exploit the region for governmental benefit with little regard for peasant welfare. In many ways, it was the ecological uniqueness of this region that contributed to its exploitation. The glaciated peaks of the high mountains and the densely forested hills of the Uttarakhand Himalayas contrast with the plain terrain of most of India. In addition to serving as a critical resource for both the subsistence of local peasants and the material benefit of people throughout the country, the watershed system in the Himalayan hills also stabilizes soil and regulates drainage into the Indo-Gangetic plain, controlling both severe flooding and drought. The large and sacred Ganga and Yumuna rivers, which irrigate much of the plains downriver, both originate from glaciers in this region. In the years prior to the development of the Chipko movement, government contractors 'clear-cut large mountainside areas, inviting environmental and economic disaster' through practices that have been described as demonstrating ignorance of how the Himalayan watershed ecosystem functions (Breton, 1998, p. 4). After decades of this type of abuse, the level of environmental destruction became unavoidable and without adequate vegetative cover, the region began to suffer from devastating floods and landslides caused by soil erosion (Sharma *et al.*, 1987).

Historically, the designation Uttarakhand (Sanskrit for 'northern territory') was applied to the two kingdoms of Garhwal and Kumaon (Fig. 26.1), between the Himachal mountain range to the west and Tibetan China and Nepal to the east. The region is 53,483 sq km in area and is home to 8.5 million people (Census of India, 2001). Prior to 2000, Uttarakhand was a district within the larger state of Uttar Pradesh, of which it formed a small, but economically and strategically important area. Because the people of Uttarakhand constituted a small percentage of the population of Uttar Pradesh, the region was poorly represented in the State Government, whose administrative offices, including the State Forest Department, were located in the plains, hundreds of miles to the south at Lucknow. The successes of the Chipko movement helped to draw attention to regional independence efforts that materialized into an organized social movement in 1979, when the Uttarakhand Kranti Dal (Uttarakhand Revolutionary Party) was established (Mawdsley, 1998). After a prolonged struggle that involved a number of other social movement organizations, the region achieved separate statehood in 2000 under the name Uttaranchal, which was 'selected for its allegedly less separatist connotations' than Uttarakhand (Uttarakhand Support Committee, 2001). The state's name was officially changed to Uttrakhand in 2007 in response to political pressure and to reflect its continued popular usage.

Uttarakhand served as an important site for trans-Himalayan trade routes for hundreds of years prior to British annexation. However, the region's vast forest resources remained largely intact beyond the relatively accessible foothill areas and the few roads that transected the mountains. At Independence, forests still covered 60 per cent of the land area in the region, though they were controlled and administered almost entirely by the state (Rangan, 1993, p. 211). Geographical limitations on Himalayan forest accessibility began to be overcome in 1962, when India began construction of an extensive network of roads along the border with China in response to national security concerns following the Sino–Indian War (Rangan, 1993, p. 212). These actions opened the region to increased military traffic and expedited the extraction of forest resources and their transportation to the plains for processing and exportation (Karan, 1994). The war also contributed to an existing economic crisis that led to reforms in development policies throughout India. These policies placed emphasis upon the expansion of agricultural production and resulted in the redistribution of property in Uttarakhand. Although the region's '[m]ountainous terrain, lack of infrastructure, and fragmented land holding distributed across different ecological and altitudinal zones were hindrances to the introduction of Green Revolution techniques', the National Government intervened by annexing vast forest tracts and placing limits on the size of individual land holdings (Rangan, 1993, p. 212).

While national and extra-local state control over the Himalayan forests and their resources increased during this period, local access and decision-making rights were curtailed by new forest classifications that limited individual forest users' access to the forest for collection of fuelwood and fodder for personal consumption. The combination of restrictive forest access laws and the virtual decimation of trans-Himalayan trade networks following the war compounded the economic marginalization of the people of Uttarakhand. Many of the small forest-based industries that were established by local people since Independence failed because they were unable to secure the costly logging permits that were preferentially granted to large-scale extractive industries. Most households also failed to see any financial gains from the logging of local forests, as many logging companies preferred to hire migrant labourers from Nepal and then processed extracted forest materials outside of the region (Rangan, 1993). The revenue from Himalayan deforestation increasingly accrued at timber processing centres in the plains, forcing many male villagers to leave Uttarakhand in order to find cash employment. Gradually, more households in Uttarakhand became reliant upon remittances from these emigrated workers (Epsy, 1997). The absence of so many working-age males left women with the sole responsibility of 'running the home, looking after the children, bearing the drudgery of agricultural work, cattle care and bringing fuel, fodder and water from long distances' (Sharma *et al.*, 1987, p. 25).

As rates of deforestation worsened and forest policies became more restrictive, local women were forced to travel further afield in order to collect forest resources, such as food and fuel, and to adopt practices that were in direct violation of forest laws. In some areas of Uttarakhand, women spent up to seven hours per day collecting forest fuelwood in addition to their regular seven to eight hour workday (Sharma *et al.*, 1987; Karan, 1994). As Shubhra Gururani documented in an anonymous Kumaoni village she calls 'Bankhali', women travelled to the forest between two and three times each day, walking two to three hours each way, to collect a load of approximately 30 kilos of twigs and leaves (2000, p. 177). In order to maintain this degree of use, villagers monitored the activities and schedule of the local Forest Guard, timing their forest trips 'only after they have made sure that the forest guard has gone past their patch of the forest' (Gururani, 2000, pp. 177–178). Gururani interpreted this illegal use as a claim to property or ownership of the forest, but is careful to note that while the villagers of Bankhali describe their actions as illegal, they are justified by the 'demands of subsistence' (2000, p. 178). A similar refrain ran through Chipko movement literature, which argued that survival needs drove local people to break the law, commit suicide, or join the Chipko movement out of desperation and a need for meaningful change (CIC, 1987). As one Chipko activist described, 'When we could not obtain the wood to cook even the little grain we get, we had to resort to a movement' (Guha, 1989, p. 168).

Unfortunately, illegal use practiced by the villagers further served to fuel the Government's claim to exclusive control of the forests, based on the 'long-standing assumption that indigenous agriculturalists and herders caused deforestation by misuse and overuse' (Karan, 1994, p. 5). Local villagers continued to be blamed by the Government for deforestation, despite evidence that most peasants did not cut down entire trees, but rather used branches, dead trees and brush for fuel. Prior to the arrival of timber contractors, forests were managed as a communal resource by village *panchayats*, which Ramachandra Guha describes as the institutional expression of the solidarity among landowners and cultivators in Uttarakhand (1989, p. 21). Local governance allowed the largely homogeneous population[2] of Uttarakhand to meet subsistence requirements, despite the steep terrain, frequent floods, poorly developed irrigation systems and small-sized average land holding, all of which can make it difficult for local people to profit off their lands (Chakraborty, 1999). Even during periods of extra-local administration, *panchayats* remained powerful influences over social and political life in the villages by continuing to manage local internal affairs and to administer social and religious matters, as well as dealing with judicial issues that are 'technically under the jurisdiction of civil and criminal courts' (Guha, 1989, p. 21). Not surprisingly, the Chipko movement drew upon panchayat[3] leadership to organize many protests.

The development of the Chipko movement affected the socio-political and ecological processes of the region, and therefore contributed to a reshaping of Uttarakhand. As discussed earlier, the protests of Chipko activists against tree felling led to the establishment of the Reni Investigation Committee and subsequently to the series of bans against green tree felling in parts of the Himalayas. But whether these bans ultimately benefited people living in their enforcement areas is debated. Following the 1980 Forest Act, many Chipko members viewed the movement as a success, and began to disband campaigns and forest cooperatives at altitudes above 1000m. The political vacuum that resulted may have encouraged the growth of the 'timber mafia' in Garhwal and allowed for a general expansion of governmental bureaucracies at a number of scales (Rangan, 1993, p. 219). While the movement was credited with lessening women's workload in some areas, as forest health and abundance returned and women were able to spend a smaller portion of their working day collecting fuel and fodder, it has also been critiqued for encouraging conservationist policies that further restricted local forest access (Routledge, 1993). Importantly, the political struggle that constituted the Chipko movement served to reshape Uttarakhand by calling for greater self-determination and by reinforcing the tradition of political activism that has long characterized, and continues to distinguish, the region. Ultimately, the most long lasting-impact of the Chipko movement may be evidenced supra-regionally, as the movement today is best known for its critique of western economic development and its national impact as the 'first organized environmental movement in India' that served to raise national public awareness about environmental issues (Chakraborty, 1999, p. 26).

Internal Dynamics of the Chipko Movement

Just as the Chipko movement shaped social and ecological dynamics within Uttarakhand, the power relations expressed within the social organization of the Chipko movement were constituted by, and reflective of, local social dynamics. As with many social movements, the constitution of organizational membership, relationships between members, legitimization of leadership and representation of movement activities, each reflect the complex power relations embedded within the movement, as well as the socio-political context in which it develops (Pelling, 2003). Because of the diffused nature of the movement, its horizontal organization and communication network, and the spontaneous nature of many of its mobilizations, there is no membership list of the Chipko movement or of participants in various protests. However, information about its membership has been gathered from accounts of individual protests, the minutes of organizational and educational meetings, and accounts of former members and leaders.

As discussed earlier, many of the members of the Chipko movement were women from villages in Uttarakhand. In other respects, however, the movement's membership was notably diverse. Chipko protests 'bridge[d] gaps of age, class, region and social experience, and join[ed] … illiterate villagers and village elders in common cause' (Routledge, 1993, pp. 96–97). Guha theorizes that the general diversity of membership in the Chipko movement was attributable to the fact that all social groups 'were equally affected by deforestation' (1989, p. 167).

A prominent Chipko leader, Sunderlal Bahuguna, was a long-time sarvodaya worker and religious philosopher, who had been especially active in the post-Independence prohibition movement. There, Bahuguna networked with many women in the region who later became involved in the Chipko movement (Routledge, 1993). Along with these women and his wife Vimla, Bahuguna developed programmes later dubbed the 'Invisible Chipko', which focussed on reforestation schemes, the provision of forest guards and the establishment of women's organizations (Routledge, 1993). Through these social networks and his lengthy and well-publicized trans-Himalayan foot marches, Bahuguna was able to spread the Chipko message as a unique environmental ideology and was successful in recruiting new members throughout the region. Paul Routledge credits Bahuguna's marches for the prevalence of Chipko activity throughout Uttarakhand, noting that they 'brought people together across lines of traditional cleavages of misunderstanding, tension and conflict and also brought to their collective attention a wide range of issues otherwise recognized only by particular groups or categories of people' (1993, p. 97).

Bahuguna popularized the Chipko message and rallied much support for it, both within the region and internationally through his writings, speeches and other protest activities. This, of course, gave Bahuguna a unique influence over the ways in which different movement messages and goals were prioritized, and how the movement was represented in general, perhaps contributing to critiques that he was among other environmentalists who 'hijacked' the Chipko movement as early as 1978 (Weber, 1987). While both Bahuguna and DGSS founder C. P. Bhatt were inspired by Gandhian ideology, the village-based self-sufficiency valued by Bhatt was 'secondary to the major ecological objectives' of Bahuguna (Weber, 1987, p. 622). Although Bahuguna joined with Bhatt in identifying forestry policies and the contractor system as central to the problem of deforestation, Bahuguna saw them as manifestations of an anthropocentric worldview intrinsic to industrial civilization, rather than just misguided approaches to development (Guha, 1989). Bahuguna, therefore, articulated the goals of the Chipko movement as 'not simply to save a few trees in the Himalayas', but to alleviate the other ills inherent in 'our materialistic civilization' (CIC, 1987, p. 23). For Bahuguna, the Chipko message advocated a different view of nature, and therefore, an alternative way of life that idealized the village as a site of self-sufficient living with nature and not a space for extractive industries. Leading a Chipko lifestyle, therefore, required limiting individual consumption in order to promote ecological health, much as Gandhi had advocated a generation earlier. The success of the Chipko movement was, for Bahuguna and his followers, not measured in forest contracts or logging prohibitions, but in its ability to '[transform] the relationship between humans and nature … which would require also changing the nature of modern society' (Chakraborty, 1999, p. 44). As the Chipko movement waned, Bahuguna continued to be active in environmental campaigns against dam projects and mining, and to work closely with government officials to promote environmental conservation.

In the end, the successes of the Chipko movement reflect both Bhatt and Bahuguna's goals and their respective social justice and environmentalist agendas. Regionally, and even nationally, the Chipko movement is regarded as a victory over post-colonial forest policies. The logging bans that followed the 1976 RIC report reduced deforestation rates and led to further prohibitions on forest felling in Uttarakhand and throughout the Indian Himalayas (Sharma *et al.*, 1987; Chakraborty, 1999). The movement has also achieved an international reputation for raising environmental awareness in India (Epsy, 1997), for its members' tactic of 'hugging' trees, for its critique of Westernized developmental practices, and for serving as an example of 'a revolt … against the existing values, which regard nature as a commodity and the society only the society of human beings' (Sunderlal Bahuguna, quoted in CIC, 1987, p. 22). While few Chipko demonstrations were documented in Uttarakhand after 1981, many Chipko activists, including Bhatt and Bahuguna, remain active in struggles over the damming of rivers and other environmentally destructive practices, as well as in less confrontational forest-based activities, such as the educational workshops still run by the DGSS and the tree-planting programmes still managed by many village women's organizations. These activities continue to reshape Uttarakhand, and continue to contribute to debates over whether the changes wrought by the Chipko movement ultimately served to benefit or to harm the people of the region. In addition, the impact of the Chipko movement continues to be felt nationally, as a similar and related movement called 'Appiko' (the Kannada language equivalent to 'Chipko') has been active in Western Ghat regions of southern India. Chipko-inspired protests have also been held outside of India, in Switzerland, Japan, Malaysia, the Philippines, Indonesia, Thailand, and even New York, where 29 April has been officially designated as 'Chipko Day' (Hall, 1994).

The history of Chipko has shown that it stands out from other Indian forest struggles in that it achieved a higher degree of organization amongst a more geographically diverse population than before, and that:

> [c]ontrary to the earlier movements, Chipko, for the first time, combined the forest rights of people with the broader environmental questions (Chakraborty, 1999, p. 26).

The movement's success can be attributed, at least in part, to its adoption of a method of protest that resonated with a national tradition of non-violence, and that called attention to the dependence of human life on natural systems. Although the Chipko movement and a great number of its members were motivated by concerns over local livelihood and equitable access to forest resources, the movement's continuance in the form of educational workshops, environmental camps and involvement in other environmental movements shows that, regardless of critiques over the Chipko movement's inability to achieve universal environmental and economic justice for its members and the forest people it purports to represent, Chipko was not an economic movement that:

would subside once its demands were met. On the contrary, its main aim was the fostering of love towards trees in the hearts of its [members and the] re-establishment of a harmonious relationship between people and nature" (Sunderlal Bahuguna, as quoted in Chakraborty, 1999, p. 37).

Social Action and the Politics of Place

When it first emerged in Uttarakhand, the Chipko movement was 'criticized for being against the developmental interests of the nation and condemned as a narrow, regional movement' (Chakraborty, 1999, p. 41). Because of their demand that the forest rights of local peasants be considered before the economic development of the nation, the Chipko activists were seen as anti-development and looking to serve the needs of a few peasants over an entire country of people. In some ways, this critique was accurate, as many protesters were initially inspired by their need for immediate survival and identified the ongoing destruction of their environment caused by developmental policy as the source of their suffering. However, regarding Chipko as solely, or even primarily, a struggle for survival and livelihood fails to grasp the complexity of the movement, the diversity of its members, purposes and goals, as well as the complexity of the problems that sparked this movement. Thus clearly, the Chipko movement, like many other environmental and social movements, was multi-faceted, often joining a large and diverse membership with appeals for both ecological health and social justice.

The analytical framework, applied primarily at the regional scale in this study, helped to reveal the ways in which the social and ecological processes occurring within and involving Uttarakhand helped to produce not only the distinct socio-spatial configurations of resource use found in the region, but also the distinct characteristics of socio-political organization that shaped the Chipko movement. These characteristics include the movement members' choice of protest tactic, the constitutive makeup of that membership, the nature of the movement's struggle over material access to the space of the forests, as well as its goals in terms of a redefinition of development and nature–society interrelations. This analysis also revealed how the socio-ecological processes of the region influenced the ways in which the Chipko movement was ultimately able to affect change in the forest policies and patterns of natural resource use in Uttarakhand. Although the focus on regional scale adopted herein was particularly well-suited for a case study of the Chipko movement, aspects of the political struggle it entailed appeared at other scales, such as those of the village and household, that were only cursorily examined here. These deserve further exploration in order to reveal the nature of that struggle more fully. Finally, this analysis has illustrated the ways in which studies of social movements in general can benefit from geographical approaches that consider how socio-political struggles are 'constituted through space, place, and scale', rather than focussing solely on the ways in which individual choices or structures shape social movements at a single scale, as in conventional approaches to the study of social movements, such as resource mobilization theory, political process research and new social movement studies (Miller, 2000, p. 167). Geographical studies of social movements allow us to consider not only the ways in which geography shapes social movements by providing their spatial and temporal context, but also how social movements themselves entail struggles over space, place, power and scale.

Notes

1. Uttarakhand was a region within the larger state of Uttar Pradesh until 2000, when it gained independent statehood under the name 'Uttaranchal'. Its name was subsequently changed back to 'Uttarakhand' in 2007, in response to popular and political demands.
2. In Uttarakhand, between 80 and 92 per cent of the population is employed in agriculture, 85 per cent are members of the Brahmin and Rajput castes (compared to 11 per cent nationally), and 75 per cent belong to one of the two Hindu religious sects (Berreman, 1983; Mawdsley, 1998).
3. The term *panchayat* refers at once to a council of elected village representatives and an organization of five (*panch*) villages into an interdependent political system.
4. Other leaders of the Chipko movement are sometimes identified, including Dhoum Singh Negi, Gaura Devi, Mira and Sarala *Behn*, among others (Jain, 1985; Guha, 1989). The most contested of these are the stories of Reni organizer Gaura Devi and Mira *Behn*, a disciple of Gandhi and daughter of an English Admiral who's given name was Madeleine Slade. Although most accounts of the movement only credit her for helping to draw attention to the problem of Himalayan deforestation in the years before the Chipko movement organized, Shiva (1989) regards her as the 'real' leader of the movement, one who educated and inspired Bahuguna and Bhatt, and for whom they served only as 'runners' to spread the Chipko message (1970). Although Mira *Behn* was undoubtedly influential, most accounts of the movement do not identify her in a leadership position and there are few documented

accounts of her presence at Chipko protests. Similarly, Gaura Devi is usually only credited for her leadership role in the 1974 protest at Reni, which she adopted after serving as a representative on the local *panchayat* and as President of the Mahila Mangal Dal, a rural women's organization that later became associated with the Chipko movement (Lakshmi, 2000).

5. Bandyopadhyay (1999) recognizes, however, that the environmentalist face of the Chipko movement was the one that gained political support from urban environmentalists, who helped to draw attention to the struggle and ultimately led to the success of the movement.

References

Bandyopadhyay, J., 'Chipko Movement: Of Floated Myths and Flouted Realities', Mountain Forum E-Conference on 'Mountain People, Forests, and Trees', http://www.mtnforum.org/resources/library/bandj99a.htm, 7 November, 2005.

Berreman, G. D., 'Chipko: Nonviolent Direct Action to Save the Himalayas', South Asian Bulletin, Vol. 5, No. 2, 1985, pp. 8–13.

Breton, M. J., 'Women Pioneers for the Environment', Boston, MA: Northeastern University Press, 1998.

Census of India 2001, Primary Census Abstract: Basic Population Data, http://www.censusindia.net/t_00_005.html, 23 January 2006.

Chakraborty, S., 'A Critique of Social Movements in India: Experiences of Chipko, Uttarakhand and Fishworkers' Movement', New Delhi: Indian Social Institute, 1999.

Chipko Information Centre (CIC), *The Chipko Message*, Calcutta: Kayan Charitable Trust, 1987.

Epsy, C., 'Chipko Indian Movement', TED Case Studies, No. 236, *Source*: http://www.american.edu/TED/chipko.htm, 30 February, 2005.

Guha, R., *The Unquiet Woods: Ecological Change and Peasant Resistance*, Berkeley: University of California Press, 1989.

Gururani, S., 'Regimes of Control, Strategies of Access: Politics of Forest Use in the Uttarakhand Himalaya, India', in A. Agrawal and K. Sivaramakrishnan (eds.), *Agrarian Environments: Resources, Representations, and Rule in India*, Durham, NC: Duke University Press, 2000, pp. 170–189.

Hall, J., 'Eco-Feminism and Geography: The Case of Vandana Shiva and Chipko', Master's Thesis, Virginia Polytechnic Institute and State University, 1994.

Jain, S., 'Standing Up for Trees: Women's Role in the Chipko Movement', Unasylva, No. 146. *Source*: http://www.fao.org/documents/show_cdr.asp?url_file=/docrep/r0465e/ r0465e03.htm, 10 October, 2005.

James, G. A., 'Ethical and Religious Dimensions of Chipko Resistance', in C. K. Chapple & M. E. Tucker (eds.), *Hinduism and Ecology: The Intersection of Earth, Sky, and Water*, Cambridge, MA: Harvard University Press, 2000, pp. 499–530.

Karan, P. P., 'Environmental Movements in India', Geographical Review, Vol. 84, No. 1, pp. 32–41.

Khator, R., *Forests: The People and the Government*, New Delhi: National Book Organization, 1989.

Lakshmi, C. S., 'Lessons from the Mountains: The Story of Gaura Devi', *The Hindu*. *Source*: http://www.hinduonnet.com/2000/05/21/stories/13210414.htm, May 21, 2000 (last accessed 10 November 2005).

Mawdsley, E., 'After Chipko: From Environment to Region in Uttaranchal', Journal of Peasant Studies, Vol. 25, No. 4, 1998, pp. 36–54.

Miller, B. A., *Geography and Social Movements: Comparing Antinuclear Activism in the Boston Area*, Minneapolis: University of Minnesota Press, 2000.

Ministry of Environment and Forests, Forest Conservation Act, 1980, Amended in 1988. *Source*: http://envfor.nic.in/legis/forest/forest2.html, 25 January, 2006.

Pelling, M., 'Toward a Political Ecology of Urban Environmental Risk', in K. S. Zimmerer and T. J. Bassett (eds.), *Political Ecology: An Integrative Approach to Geography and Environment-Development Studies*, New York: The Guilford Press, 2003, pp. 73–93.

Rangan, H., 'Romancing the Environment: Popular Environmental Action in the Garhwal Himalayas', in J. Friedman and H. Rangan (eds.), *In Defense of Livelihood: Comparative Studies on Environmental Action*, West Hartford: Kumarian Press, 1993, pp. 155–181.

Rangan, H. and M. B. Lane, 'Indigenous Peoples and Forest Management: Comparative Analysis of Institutional Approaches in Australia and India', Society and Natural Resources, Vol. 14, 2001, pp. 145–160.

Rawat, R., 'Women of Uttarakhand: On the Frontiers of the Environmental Struggle', Uttarakhand Support Committee. *Source*: http://uttarakhand.prayaga.org/chipko.html, 1996 (last accessed 22 May, 2008).

RLA, 'The Chipko Movement', The Right Livelihood Reward Recipients. *Source*: http://www.rightlivelihood.org/recip/chipko.htm, 1987 (last accessed 12 November, 2005).

Routledge, P., *Terrains of Resistance: Nonviolent Social Movements and the Contestation of Place in India*, Westport, CN: Praeger Publishers, 1993.

Sharma, K., K. Nautiyal and B. Pandey, *Women in Struggle: The Role and Participation of Women in the Chipko Movement*, New Delhi: Centre for Women's Development Studies, 1987.

Shiva, V., *Staying Alive: Women, Ecology and Development*, London: Zed Books, 1989.

Swain, A., 'Democratic Consolidation? Environmental Movements in India', *Asian Survey*, Vol. 37, No. 9, 1997, pp. 818–832.

Uttarakhand Support Committee, 'Forging a New Destiny for Uttaranchal: Seminar Guide', Third Annual Convention of Uttaranchal Association of North America. *Source*: http://www.4dham.com/go2/Uttarakhand.html, 2001 (last accessed 17 October, 2005).

Weber, T., 'Is There Still a Chipko Andolan?', *Pacific Affairs*, Vol. 60, No. 4, 1987, pp. 615–628.

27

Sacredscape and Manescape: The Sacred Geography of Gaya, India

RANA P. B. SINGH

Mythology and Historical Geography

Gaya, a city in Bihar, is a famous pilgrimage centre. The literal meaning of 'Gaya', 'let's go to another place', refers to contact with the other realm; it symbolises a destination linking this world of humanity and the world of divinity (ancestral world). According to one of the most authoritative Sanskrit texts on pilgrimage and sacred places, the *Tristhalisetu* (TS), which means and dates back 'Bridge to the Three Holy Cities' circa sixteenth century, of the three pillars of the 'bridge to the realm of the soul', Gaya is the eastern most[1]. The others are Varanasi and Prayaga (Allahabad), both along River Ganga in the West. The name 'Gaya' was referred to in the earlier Vedic text, the *Rig Veda*, RV (10.63,10.64), as the name of a sage and writer, while later in the *Atharva Veda*, AV (1.14.4), Gaya was mentioned as a mystic and sorcerer. The first clear indication of Gaya as a holy place is when it is metaphorically eulogised in the RV (1.22.17)–'Vishnu crossed this and placed his first foot in three ways: the whole of it is encompassed in his steps'. The treatise *Nirukta*, NrT (12.19), circa eighth century BCE, explains this passage in two ways. The first, according to Shakapuni, refers to the three steps of Vishnu, viz. the earth, the firmament and the heavens. The second, according to Aurnavabha, refers to the three sacred places called Samarohana, Vishnupad and Gayashirsh. It is accepted that *Nirukta's* author Yaska was born long before the birth of the Buddha (Kane, 1973, p. 645). The *Mahabharata*, MbH (3.87.11; 3.95.9), and the *Vishnudharmasutra*, VdS (85.4), also mention Gaya as an altar (*vedi*). The 'Forest Retreat Canto' of the *Mahabharata* (3.85) described Gaya along with other holy places, and in another canto Gaya (MbH, 13.25.42) is mentioned with respect to *Ashmaprastha* (modern *Prestashila*) where one gets release even from the sin of killing a brahmin.

The vast corpus of *puranic* literature (Sanskrit encyclopaedic texts elaborating Hindu scripture and lore) of the sixth to the eleventh century consists of descriptions of Gaya (AgP, 114–116; PdP, I, 38.2–21; GdP, I, 62–86; NdP, II, 44–47). In many instances the same verse is cited at several places in different contexts. The most elaborate mythology of Gaya is recorded in the *Gaya Mahatmya*, GM, a part of the *Vayu Purana* (chapters 105–112; about 560 verses), dated circa the eighth to the ninth century (Kane, 1973, pp. 651–652). The GM also cites verses from the various *Puranas* and also the *Mahabharata* (for example, 13.25–42). Two other chapters of the *Vayu Purana* (70.97–108; 82.20–24) describe many sacred spots and sites of Gaya. The glory of Gaya was already accepted in the period of the *Mahabharata*, especially for ancestral rites. The *Mahabharata* (3.87.10–12) says:

> A man should aspire to have many sons; the reason is that one of them may go to Gaya (and liberate the ancestors by offering them *Pindas*, rice balls) or may perform an Ashvamedha (horse sacrifice) or may let loose a Nila bull. (Dave, I, 1970, p. 32)

Chinese traveller Hsuen-tsang (seventh century) has also mentioned Gaya as a sacred place for ritual bathing since it possesses the power to wash away sins (Beal, 1906, II, p. 113); similar accounts are given in the later Buddhist texts (Mahajan, 1996, p. 31).

The name Gaya is derived from a demon-king, Gayasur, who by his arduous austerity pleased the gods and obtained the blessing that the spirit of all the divinities would reside in his body – that is, the territory of Gaya is marked by the demon's reclining body (VyP, 106). By his power of great meditation the divine spirit met with the earth spirit, resulting in the formation of a very powerful holy place. To commemorate the glory and spiritual power of demon Gayasur, his city is called Gaya (AgP, 114.41). According to the *Vayu Purana* (105.16–18), liberation (*mukti*) is achieved by acquiring the supreme knowledge of *Brahman* (universe), or performing the ancestral rites at Gaya, or getting oneself killed while protecting a cow, or living a simple life at Kurukshetra; however, performing the ancestral rites at Gaya is considered the best. This view has also been supported by the other *Puranas* (for example, AgP, 115.3–4, 5–6; VmP, 33.8; NdP, II, 44.20). The *Buddhacharita* (12.87–88, edited and translated by Johnston, 1972) and *Uttaradhyayansutra* (46.86) narrate that the city was named after the sage-king Gaya, as in the case of the *Rig Veda* (10.63, 10.64). The story of the demon Gayasur seems to be an elaboration of this ancient tradition, one that probably arose during the period of struggle between Hindus and Buddhists.

Asher (1989, p. 46) suggests that the special sacred ritual of ancestral worship and pilgrimage to Gaya begun since the *Mahabharata* period 'probably drew *Sakyamuni* (another name for The Buddha) to the outskirts of Gaya where he engaged in meditation that resulted in the attainment of Buddhahood'. The *Mahabharata* (3.87.10–12) specially eulogises River Phalgu, *Gaya-shirsh/shir* and *Akshayavata* (the eternal Banyan) that give one never-ending merit by pleasing the ancestors.

Despite mythological evidence of the sanctity and glory of Gaya before eighth century BCE, the sculptural or inscriptional sources are not available for earlier periods. According to inscriptional sources, the antiquity of the site and the tradition of performing ancestral rites in and around the Vishnupad Temple goes back to the period of King Samudragupta (fifth century CE). A seal discovered at Basarh (Vaishali) mentions 'Sri Vishnupad Svaminarayan' (the patron deity of Gaya) in early Gupta characters (Archaeological Survey of India, 1903–04, pp. 10–11). The connection between Gaya and Vaishali is clearly apparent in *puranic* mythology (Mahajan, 1996, p. 32; AgP, 105.54, GdP, 84.32, VyP, 107.7–15), which describes the ancestral ceremony performed by King Vishala at Gaya. The Basarh seal is most likely to be a mark commemorating the event. A little later, the Mehrauli pillar inscription of King Chandra mentions a lofty installation of Vishnu on the Vishnupad Hill. This clearly indicates the historicity of Vishnupad dating back to circa fifth century CE (Mahajan, 1996, p. 32).

An inscription dated CE 872 of the Pala monarch Narayanapala commemorates the dedication of a house that was provided for ascetics (Asher, 1989, p. 46; Fleet, 1970). Another record of CE circa 1058 mentions a ruler of Gaya named Vishvarupa who built a temple of Gadadhara which today forms part of the Vishnupad complex (Banerji, 1915; Sircar, 1965). The construction of another temple by Vishvarupa is testified by another inscription of the same year, kept in the Krishna Dvaraka Temple (Chakravarti, 1901). Vishvarupa had also erected other temples (Asher, 1989, pp. 48–49). Later inscriptions, from the twelfth to the sixteenth centuries, attest to the tradition of continuous pilgrimage to Gaya, even from South India (Sircar, 1959; Sircar and Sarma, 1959). A major sculptural and architectural style is seen in the Vishnupad Temple and also in other temples made by Queen Ahilyabai Holkar of Indore in the late eighteenth century.

At the beginning of the present century, the town of Gaya recorded a population of 71,288 (Census of 1901), which declined by 29.97 per cent in 1911, on account of drought and epidemics. In 1921, the population had recorded a very high growth rate of 35.34 per cent. The town was declared a municipality in 1961 with an area extent of 30.51 km^2. It got a reconstituted boundary in 1971 with an area of 28.62 km^2 inhabited by 180,000 persons. During 1971–81, the growth rate was 37.35 per cent, the highest in the history of Census periods. In the decade of 1981–91, the growth rate at 18.98 per cent was below the national average and the population reached to 294,000 in 1991.

Bodh Gaya (10.98 km^2) was a declared town in 1961 when the population was only 6,299. By the 1970s the town was declared a heritage and pilgrimage site for Buddhists. This resulted in an accelerated growth of business and an influx of migrants. It led to the opening of the Magadh University, the establishment of monasteries and international institutions, and the consequent development of the supporting infrastructure. The period of 1971–81 recorded an unprecedented rate of growth of population, 125.66 per cent, and the population reached 15,724. In 1991, the town was declared a notified area, recording a population of 21,690 with a growth rate of 37.92 per cent during 1981–91.

The Context of the Sun

Visitors primarily come to Gaya on pilgrimage to perform ancestral rites. However, on two occasions in a year, that is in the Hindu months of *Chaitra* (March–April) and *Karttika* (October–November), a large mass of devotees visit sun-related sites, especially the sacred tanks (such as Suraj Kunda, Uttaramanasa, and the Sun Temple at Brahmani Ghat[2]. Pilgrims perform special rituals, taking holy dips and offering sacred items to the Sun god. In the Krishna Dvaraka Temple a record of Vishvarupa's son Yakshapala mentions the homage paid by him to the sun and 'draws upon solar imagery to convey a sense of the resplendent city that his father has built' (Asher, 1989, p. 54; Kielhorn, 1887). Most probably, Yakshapala installed the 1.5 m high image of the sun in mid-eleventh century. The figure stands by a black slab carved with flying figures and rarely found planets above his head. The biggest image of the Sun god (2.44 m) is located at the Brahmani Ghat, facing the east towards river Phalgu, like many of the images of *Surya* (Sun god) scattered all over Gaya; it is now cloaked in a Vaishnava[3] mantle. Asher rightly suggests that sun worship was once very important and dominant here:

> ... before Gaya became so closely linked with Vishnu's presence as manifest by his footprint in an ordinate number of slabs depicting the grahas. They may be seen at almost every vedi (stopping place) throughout the town (Asher, 1989, p. 54).

Before Vishnu and Shraddha gained importance in Gaya, sun worship may have been the dominant feature of the area. Widely scattered stone slabs depicting the nine *grahas* (planets) giving prominence to the sun support this possibility.

In the vicinity of the greater territory of Gaya (Gaya *Mandala*), there exist nine temples of the Sun god at Deo (Devarka), Madanpur (Umga), Hanspura (Deokunda), Madhusrava (Chyavanyashram), Ular, Belaur, Baragaon, Aungari and Pandarak (on the bank of River Ganga), all impressive in their grandeur and architectural finesse. In Bihar, the most popular festival involves worshipping the Sun god as 'mother' (*Chhatha*). These nine places with their historical monuments and settings associated with great tanks and folk mythologies attract devotees from all parts of Bihar during spring and autumn.

Sun Worship: The Chhatha (Shashthi) Festival

The worship of the Sun god is described as a fasting ritual and festival in the *Mahabharata* (3.16.31); people believe that this tradition has been maintained since then. Since the sun is the basis of all life on earth, the sun's energy might have been conceived as a motherly power in the animistic belief of the past. Most likely, the worship of the sun as a goddess started somewhere in the remote past because of this perception. It is also argued that fertility practices, like sun worship along with an offering of water, had been common earlier and was later on adopted by the brahminical tradition. With the passage of time, the textual recognition of the festive ritual honouring the goddess (Shashthi), believing to protect children, and the folk tradition of Chhatha became integrated with it. The most popular festival in Bihar is Chhatha – worship of the Sun god as 'mother' (*Chhathi Maiya*) – celebrated with great pomp and deep faith. This festival is held twice a year, that is in the *light half (moon cycle)* fortnights of *Chaitra* (March–April, spring), and *Karttika* (October–November, autumn). Gaya is one of the primary destinations for devout Hindus for celebrating the Chhatha festival. Gaya's Suraj Kunda ('sun's water pool') is the main site where over 50,000 devotees take part in the autumn festival and around 10,000 devotees participate in the spring festival.

The worship of *Chhatha* as 'mother' may be compared with the description of 16 mothers given in the *Brahmavaivarta Purana* (Prakriti section 1) that mentions Katyayini who takes care of children. The wife of Skanda is also referred to as Shashthi who protects children from sickness (SkP, Maheshvara Khanda) and the festival in her honour is called Skandashashthi. However, this festival is supposed to be celebrated in the month of *Karttika* and the main deity is Skanda. By this description it is obvious that the Skandashashthi has no direct association with Chhatha. According to the *Gadadhara Paddhati* (Kalasara, 83–84), Skandashashthi is celebrated on the 6th dark half of the Chaitra, which again never corresponds with the celebration of Chhatha in present times. The contemporary festival of Chhatha is close to the description presented in the *Hemadrivrata* (1.608–615) and *Nirnayasindhu* (134); both referring to the *Bhavisyaottara Purana.*

Another important motive of the Chhatha festival has been to get relief from skin diseases. The Sun god is believed to possess the power to grant relief from skin diseases, especially leprosy. Though protection of the child and relief from skin diseases are the primary motives, it is believed that attending these festivals also brings prosperity and progress to the whole family. The most popular Chhatha is of the autumn, whose initiation starts on the 4th light half of *Karttika* with a purificatory bath, taking of vows, taking simple food, cleaning the house, and preparing and arranging ritual items. The concluding ritual is performed on the seventh day by offering holy water to the sun and distributing fruits and special food items (*prasada*) among friends and family.

On the fourth day of the waxing fortnight in the Hindu month of *Karttika*, the passing of the sun through *Sagittarius* (*dhanu rashi*), results in an auspicious moment considered to be the best time for taking the vow (*sankalpa*) to perform the Chhatha. The vow is taken by offering holy water (of the Ganga, or in the name of the Ganga) six times to the sun god. Devotees eat only once in a day, and request the Sun god to give them vigour and energy for the successful completion of the Chhatha. On the fifth day these devotees fast the whole day, not even taking a drink of water. In the early evening they take a holy dip again and perform some rituals; finally take break the fast with plain *chapati* (Indian bread) and *khir* (rice cooked in milk), considered to be pure food. Many of the devotees never eat at all. They believe they receive more merit through this austerity. As the intensity of their hardship increases, the merit received also increases.

The sixth day is the hardest day of fasting with no food and no water allowed for 24 hours. Devotees and their family members are busy in making arrangements for the main *puja* (prayer rituals). In the evening they arrange sacred fruits (for example, coconut, banana, citrus, custard apple, apple, sugarcane, guava), sacred food items (made of hard bread fried in clarified butter) and colourful new clothes, especially *saris* and shawls, in baskets made of bamboo. At the *ghat* near the water site they draw small designs depicting the cosmos, using cow dung and holy water. Then begins the group song in honour of the Sun god as 'Mother' or *Chhathi Maiya*. The devotees take special vows (*manauti*), set the *koshi* lamps (elephant-shaped pot made of mud with 21 oil lamps on the top) and light them. Attached to these lamps are 14 other cups that are filled with germinated gram and fruits. After watching the sun set, the devotees return, carrying all these *puja* items with them. The devotees stay awake all through the night, slowly murmuring religious songs and listening to glorifying religious tales about *Chhathi Maiya.*

The seventh day of the ritual starts early in the morning, around 4'o clock, by rearranging all the items at the *ghat* that they had carried back the previous day, organizing them in their own mini-cosmic design. The Chhatha festival finally comes to end with the devotees and their families standing in the water, offering holy water to the rising sun, offering fruits and other *prasad* items, and chanting and singing religious songs together. In the last prayer the devotees request the Sun god 'Mother' to bless them with life and energy so that they can return next year to partake in the festival. In Bihar almost every Hindu celebrates this festival, irrespective of caste, creed, or social and economic status.

Sacred Topography

The Gaya *Kshetra* is generally a plain area, recording an average height of 100 metres. However there are four hills on which many holy sites exist.

These hills symbolise the interlinking ladders between the earth and the heavens through which the soul may attain final release. These hillocks play a major role in the spatial symbolism of transcendence – represented by their 'high appearance', 'vertical projection' and their seeming appearance of 'passing from the earth to other realm'. They are also the special domains of all the hierophanies of the atmosphere, and are therefore the dwellings of the divinities (Eliade, 1958, p. 99) – in case of Gaya, the resort of 'demigods' or 'associates of the God of Death, Yama'. Mythological literature mentions their roles in helping the departed soul settle down in the abodes of these divinities.

The three primal objects of nature symbolism described and given ritual connotations are the river Phalgu ('merit-endowing waters'), Akshayavata (the imperishable banyan) and Pretashila (the hill of ghosts). The river symbolizes fertility (living water) in which life, strength, and eternity are contained (Eliade, 1958, p. 193); the *Atharva Veda* (6.91.3) says, 'The waters are indeed healers; the waters drive away and cure all illness'.

Akshayavata represents the growth and expansion of the natural elements in the symbolic manifestation of the cosmos – 'Cosmos is a tree'. The sacred topography of the 'greater' Gaya *kshetra*, including Bodh Gaya, contains another manifestation of that *axis mundi* in the form of the north–south axis established by the eternal banyans in the North and the South, spaced at ten kilometers. The *Maitrayaniya Upanishad* (MtU, 6.7), says, 'Its branches are the ether, the air, fire, water, and earth'. The cosmic trees (like Akshayavata in Gaya and another in Prayaga/Allahabad) may have been elements of an ancient pillar cult, representing the mythical centre of the universe, where the earth and sky were pillared apart, and creation began (Irwin, 1983, pp. 253–257). That cosmogonic act of separation released the flowing river of time and gave birth to the sun and the moon, which had been imprisoned in the dark waters. It is suggested that the vertical arm of King Dasharatha in Sita Kunda may have been viewed as another variation of the pillar symbolism.

Hills and peaks are another cosmogonic representation symbolising the ladder linking the earth and the celestial sphere. Ascending hills for rituals is like 'following a ladder passing by a bridge for reaching the celestial world', says the *Taittiriya Samhita*, TaS (6.6.4.2). One among the three most important sacred places in Gaya mentioned in the Vedic period is '*Samarohana*' – literally meaning 'a retreat to the celestial world' (NrT, 12.19). It clearly refers to the hill of Pretashila.

The five hills marking the territory of *Gaya Kshetra* are Pretashila (northwest; VyP, 108.67), Ramashila (northeast; VyP, 110.15), Prabhas (also called Ramagaya Pahar), across the River Phalgu (east; VyP, 108.13, 16; 109.14), Brahmayoni (southeast; NdP, 2.47.54), and Griddhrakuta (southwest; VyP, 109.15). Except for Prabhas Hill (163 m) and Pretashila (266 m), the other three hill summits record a height of around 218 m. These hills are described with respect to the surrounding forests and specific trees, for example the banyan tree (*Ficus bengalensis*) close to Brahmayoni (MbH, 3.84.83; VyP, 105.45), the mango tree (*Magnifera indica*) close to Goprachar (VyP, 111.35–37), the holy Pipal tree (*Ficus religiosa*), that is the present Mahabodhi tree at Bodh Gaya (VyP, 111.26–27), and the thorny bushes (mostly *Karaunda, Amaranthus viridis*, and *Ber, Zizyphus jujuba*) around the Griddhrakuta (VyP, 108.63).

Territorial Layers

In Hindu tradition the earth is associated with powerful religious sentiments, most commonly as the terrestrial mother. Here spiritual magnetism linked to sacred geography is obvious at different scales, in different degrees and in different perspectives. Like most of the pan-Indian holy centres, Gaya also records the three-tier hierophanic expression comparable to macro (that is *Mandala*), meso (that is *kshetra*), and micro (that is *Puri*/city) cosmos, represented by concentric circles whose radii are fixed by the peaks of three hills. Respectively, they are Korambe Hill (south; 767 m) from where River Punpun originates, Pretashila (northwest) and Ramashila (northeast). The centre of this three-tier territorial extent is Vishnupad.

The triad division is comparable to the three cosmological divisions of shamanic landscape. By the specialised rituals of transcendence and complexity (that is, shamanism), a human being is attached to the departed but mobile soul, and either ascends to the sky or descends to the underworld with a view to travelling to other realms for an out-of-body experience – comparable to spiritual 'ecstasy' (Devereux, 1992, p. 55). Shamanism is to be considered as the primary experience of human consciousness. The triad divisions are the 'upper world' of spiritual beings (celestial world), the 'middle earth' of human reality (human world) and the 'underworld' of the shades (demonic world). These three worlds are linked, with the point of the highest state of manifestation of power serving as the world axis (the *axis mundi* or the *omphalos*), from where the Four Directions, the cardinal points, are marked. According to Devereux:

> Making the omphalos is the first great act of geomancy, or sacred geography, remembered today in the laying of a foundation stone for a building. The omphalos is the centre of a circle whose circumference is nowhere and everywhere. (Devereux, 1992, p. 56)

Vishnu's footprint in the centre of Vishnupad Temple of Gaya serves as an omphalos for the whole territory. Writes Eliade (1965: 12):

> being an axis mundi, the sacred city or temple is regarded as the meeting point of heaven, earth and hell. The earthly extension of cosmos is represented by *kshetra*, e.g., *Gaya Kshetra*, meaning the concentration of cosmic influence in the topography (cf. Devereux, 1996: 136).

The Gaya Mandala

The *Gaya Mandala* (Fig. 27.1) is marked by a radius of 25 *krosha* (80 km), delineated by three reference points – the banks of River Punpun in the north and in the southwest, and its source in the south from Korambe

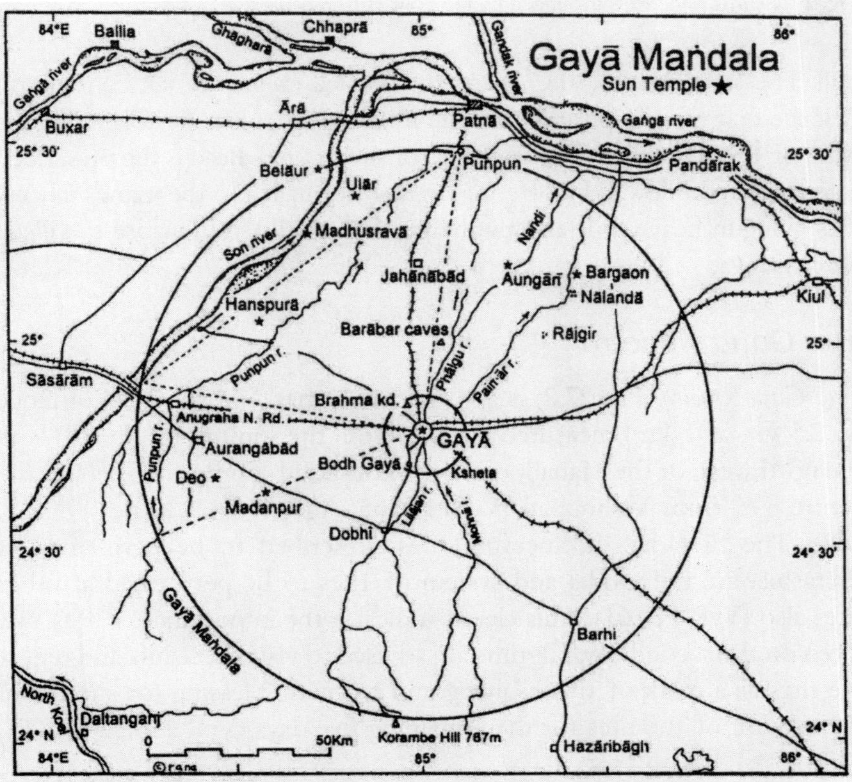

Fig. 27.1 *Gaya Mandala*–Gaya is the Centre and Belaur is the Radial Point.

Fig. 27.2 *Gaya Kshetra*, surrounded by the Four Hills.

Hill. The *Vayu Purana* (108.73) and the *Nardiya Purana* (II, 47.75) mention that the first rites of purification and initiation are to be performed at the bank of River Punpun ('Punapuna'). Tonsuring one's head is the prescribed standard rite, followed by offering *pindas* ('rice balls') to the manes (ancestors living in heaven). Presently there exists a sun temple close to village Madhusrava.

The Gaya Kshetra

The *Gaya Kshetra* (Fig. 27.2) is approximately marked by a radial distance of 2.5 *krosha* (8 km) measured roughly from the summit of Pretashila in the northwest, or the Mahabodhi tree in the south (in Bodh Gaya), to the centre, i.e., from Vishnupad (VyP, 106.65; AgP, 115.42; Kane, 1973, p. 667). The first day of ancestral rites prescribed to be performed at Pretashila are the model and system of rites to be performed at other sites also (VyP, 110.61). This clearly indicates the importance of this site. Even on the second day, pilgrims are advised to visit Pretashila and repeat the rites as a mark of thanksgiving and receiving blessing for successful completion of the rites for the remaining five days (VyP, 110.23–24; TS, 355).

The Gaya Puri

The *Gaya Puri* ('sacred abode') expands to a radial distance of 1.25 *krosha* (4 km) from Vishnupad, towards the summit of Ramashila (218 m) in the north (Fig. 27.3). On the third day of the ancestral rites, Ramashila is the prescribed central point. The core area of *Gaya Puri*, known as *Adi Gaya* ('the old Gaya'), is marked by a radial distance of 0.25 *krosha* (0.8 km) from Vishnupad to Sita Kunda across River Phalgu in the east, and skirting the edge of Prabhas Hill. *Gaya Puri* is identified closely with Gayashirsh (*shirsh* means head), conceived as the core area whose edges are marked by the Naga Hill in the east and the tank of Uttaramanas in the north (VyP, 111.22). Gaya and Gayashirsh were well known in ancient times and find frequent mention in ancient texts (Kane, 1973, p. 677). The *Gaya Puri* closely corresponds to the present city of Gaya.

Sacred Centres

According to various texts the number of holy spots in Gaya varies, and in many cases they are cited by different names too. The *Vayu Purana* mentions 324 holy spots and images that correspond with the numerical cosmogony, that is 12 zodiacs by 9 planets by 3 mythical realms. By taking the *Agni Purana*, *Garuda Purana* and *Vayu Purana* altogether, the total number of holy spots adds up to 432; this number may be compared with the numerical symbol of 12 zodiacs by 12 months by 3 mythical realms. According to the glorifying mythologies, all the sacred spots and holy images of the world are manifest in the holy territory of *Gaya Kshetra*. This is comparable to the cosmogonic frame of *Varanasi Mandala*, *Kshetra* and *Puri* where 324 forms of Shiva exist, and other holy numbers like 144, 108, 72, etc. also correspond to various systems of numerical symbolism (Singh, 1995a, pp. 59–60). Many of these holy spots have vanished and now only 45 remain. These spots are known as *vedis* (altars) where *pindas* (balls) are offered in a systematic order. The offering starts at the bank of River Punpun and closes at the holy banyan tree of Akshayavata. The final donation is given to the overseer priest at the Gayatri Ghat. The 45 active sites are easily arranged spatially into eight sacred clusters, where within each cluster, a sacred centre interlinks the associated images and also lends its name to the entire cluster. Usually such sacred clusters fall under the care of a single sect of priests although one cannot generalize that each sacred cluster is characterized by only a

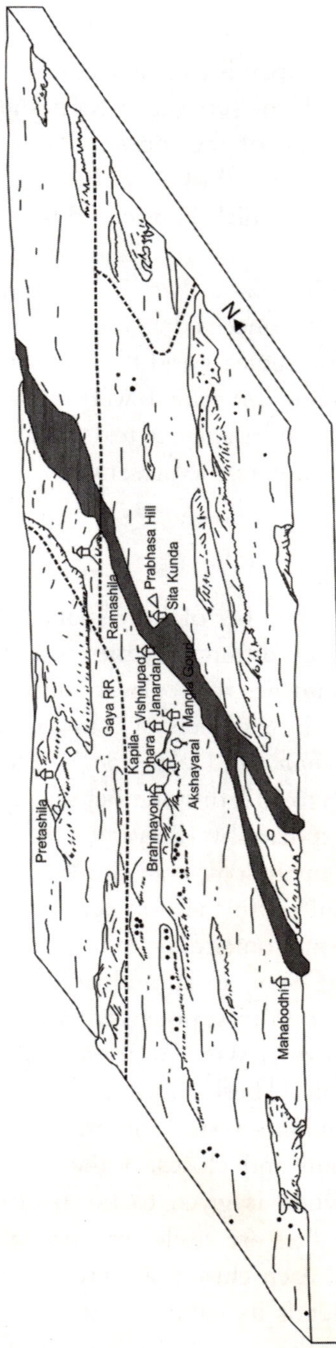

Fig. 27.3 *Gaya Puri*, Covering the Present City Area.

single set of sectarian deities (Vidyarthi, 1978, p. 7). Of the 324 sacred centres and spots described in the *Vayu Purana*, 84 are easily identified (see Table 27.1).

According to a recent survey conducted in 2008, out of the total number of pilgrims performing ancestral rites at present, about 60 per cent visit three places – River Phalgu, Vishnupad, and the associated sacred centres. Another 30 per cent perform rites at about five to seven places, and the remaining 10 per cent visit eight to ten places. The important sacred centres are described in the following sections.

Table 27.1 Gaya: Sacred Clusters and Sacred Centres.

Sacred Cluster	*No.*	*Sacred Centre*
1. Vishnupad	(14)	Vishnupad, Gayakupa, Gayashirsh, Gadadhar, Gayeshvari, Shamshan Ghat, Narasimha, Sakshi Shiva, Krishna Dvaraka, Partavi, Adi Gadadhar, Surya Kunda and the temple.
2. Uttaramanas	(11)	Uttaramanas (Gangatirtha; Sitala), Pitamaheshvara, Surya (Brahmani Ghat), Phalvishvara, Gayaditya Sun, Mahabir, Parvati, Gayatri Ghat(Kaleshvara, Kalabhairava).
3. Sita Kunda	(11)	Sita Kunda, Ramagaya, Rameshvara, Bharat Ashram (and Jagannatha), Brahma's foot, Hanstirtha, Nagakuta/Parvat, Amarakantak, Prabhas hill, Phalgu's bank.
4. Ramashila	(11)	Ramashila (images of Rama, Shiva, Yama), Rama Kunda, holy banyan at foothill, Kakabali (and Yamabali, Svanabali); and temples of Bageshvari and Baglamukhi.
5. Pretashila	(4)	Pretashila (and Pretabhairavi), Brahma Kunda, Brahmeshvara Shiva.
6. Griddhrakuta	(8)	Griddhreshvara, Griddhraghat, Akasha Ganga, Radha Kunda, Patal Kunda, Vaitarini, Godavari Kunda, Maha Kashi (Varanasi).
7. Akshayavata	(15)	Akshayavata (holy banyan), Manglagauri, Agasteshvara, Goprachar, Pundrikaksha, Janardan, Gadalol, Prapitamaheshvara, Brahmasara, Kapiladhara (Gangasagar), Brahmayoni, Savitri, Rukmini Kunda, Pushkarini.
8. Bodh Gaya	(2)	Mahabodhi Taru (tree), Mukhkand Kunda.
9. Punpun (scattered)	(8)	banks of the Punpun river in (a) the north and (b) the west: Madhusrava (Chyavanyashram); Deo; Deokunda(Hanspura); Surya-tirthas (may be Sun temples at Belaur and Ular); Kothagiri, 51 km southwest (probably Sun temple at Madanpur).

Vishnupad ('Vishnu's Footprint')

The mythology in the *Vayu Purana* (106) narrates the story of a demon Gayasur. His meditation and austerity endowed him with great strength and vigour. Later, Brahma and Vishnu requested him to provide his body to serve as an altar on which all the gods stood under Vishnu's direction. Vishnu's footprints commemorate this story. Vishnu's footprint (circa 40 cm) on a rock in an octagonal basin is the primary attraction of the temple. This sacred centre was also mentioned in the *Mahabharata* (3.87.10–12). The earliest inscriptional sources mentioning Vishnupad date back to the fifth century as mentioned in the Mehrauli pillar inscription of King Chandra (Mahajan, 1996, p. 32). Vishnupad is traditionally worshipped by citing the sacred verse from the *Rig Veda* (1.22.17): '[We bow] to this thou Vishnu's circular basement, *cakra*'. Vishnu is accepted as the patron deity of the city. Probably one of the oldest and most intriguing images in Gaya is a rock-cut Vishnu that is carved on a boulder in a shrine called Goprachar near Manglagauri Temple. This may be dated to the Kushan period, though such sculptures were also found in the Gupta period (Asher, 1989, p. 17), which would effectively date them between the first and fifth centuries.

River Phalgu (The Merit Giving River)

The *Agni Purana* (115.27) explains that the name 'Phalgu' is a combination of *phala* (merit) and *go* (wish-granting cow); by connotation it means that the river manifests the highest power of sacredness and merit. The *Vayu Purana* (111.16) says that River Phalgu is superior even to River Ganga because the former is the liquid form of *Adi-Gadadhar* Vishnu while the latter originates from Vishnu's foot. The *puranic* literature (for example *Agni Purana*, 115.25; *Vayu Purana*, 110.4–5) describe River Phalgu as Mahanadi (the great river). Among the sites where ancestral rites are performed, the bank of River Phalgu is given a special status in mythology (*Karma Purana*, 2.20.32).

Presently there are 11 *ghats* on the left bank of River Phalgu used for rituals, holy bathing and ancestral rites. The Shamshan (cremation) Ghat is the southern most *ghat* and is used only for cremation rituals. The area between Gadadhar and Sangat Ghats is the busiest as it is used for various types of rituals, oblations and festivities. On the right bank, facing west to Vishnupad, exists the Sita Kunda sacred cluster. The stairway to the bank is known as Ramagaya Ghat and is used for religious purposes associated with this cluster. For holy bathing in River Phalgu, devotees from a radial distance of c. 150 km visit this site on special occasions of full moon day (*purnima*) of Karttika (October–November), Bishua (close to the vernal equinox, 21st March) and during solar eclipses. These three occasions are believed to be the moments when the fire element of the sun or sky and the water element of the earth meet. The ancestral dark fortnight, *pitripaksha*, falling in Ashvina (September–October), close to the autumnal equinox (21st September) is the other period when hundreds of thousands of devotees from all parts of India come here for ancestral rites, and almost all perform various rites on the bank of River Phalgu.

Akshayavata (Imperishable Banyan Tree)

According to Hindu mythology, at the time of the cosmic flood (*pralaya*) when the earth was submerged under the ocean, Lord Vishnu (the Preserver) took the form of a child and went into deep sleep on a branch (or leaf) of a banyan tree (VyP, 111.79–82). *Puranic* literature describes this story in different ways, however they all indicate its location at Gaya (MbH, 3.84.83, 85.14; VyP, 105.45, 109.16; AgP, 115.70; PdP, I.38.2). The present banyan symbolises that mythic tree. Asher describes that:

> the size of the Banyan tree, enhanced by its many great prop roots and the contrast with the diminutive temple beneath it, suggests that it has been in place for a very long time. As the name of the place (*akshaya*) suggests, it appears to be undecaying, perpetual, an appropriate point of conclusion for a ceremony intended to propitiate the spirit of the deceased. (Asher, 1989, p. 58)

Pretashila (The Rock of Ghosts)

The Pretashila Hill, located at a distance of 2.5 *krosha* (8 km) northeast from Vishnupad, was perhaps, originally a site of spirit worship. A site of importance in folk religion transformed over time into a site for ancestral worship. The shrine of Pretabhairavi (the goddess of ghosts) and Vishnu were later additions. The *Mahabharata* (13.25.42) says that one can obtain release even from the sin of killing a brahmin by performing rituals at this site. The *Vayu Purana* (108.15) describes this hill as a part of a series of hills and prescribes (110.15) that after completing rituals on the bank of Phalgu, in the afternoon, the devotee should visit Pretashila. The *Vayu Purana* (110.10–12) also mentions that one has to offer *pindas* to ancestors on its summit and take a holy bath in the Brahma Kunda at the foothill, along with an offering of water to the divinities of the water pool. Close to this water pool, Brahma (the Creator) had performed his horse-sacrifice ritual.

Ramashila (The Rock of Rama)

The old name of this hill was Pretaparvata (the mountain of ghosts). Its location is identified by the *Tristhalisetu* (355). The *Vayu Purana* (110.61) suggests that all the rituals and oblations to be performed here are similar to other important sites in Gaya. It is uncertain when and how the name Pretaparvata changed to Ramashila. Based on Buchanan's (1811–12, p. 128) report, it is assumed that at the end of the eighteenth century when the temple of Rama was built there, the name would have changed and the folk stories were created to mythologize it. In course of time people have forgotten its original nomenclature. However, the age-old traditions of having a non-brahmin overseer at the shrine still exists, but close ties with brahmin priests are maintained.

Sita Kunda and Ramagaya

Prabhas Hill, about 800 m east of Vishnupad, is located on the right bank of River Phalgu. The meeting point of the hilly area and the waterfront is considered more holy for ritual baths. The Prabhas (light manifested) Shiva *linga* and Rama are worshipped by offering special rice balls (VyP, 108.22). The *Matsya Purana* (22.70) and *Agni Purana* (116.13) have described this area as Ramatirtha. The *Vayu Purana* (108.16–18) also mentions Ramatirtha and Bharatashram. Hindu mythology refers to how all the gods were standing on the body of the demon Gayasur; similarly, goddess Lakshmi in the form of Sita, Parvati as Manglagauri and Sarasvati as Gayatri also took their seats there (VyP, 106.77–98; Kane, 1973, p. 659). A tiny image of Sita exists is a small basin, known as Sita Kunda. Sita is described as Lakshmiangna (part of Lakshmi) in the *Mahabharata* (13.46). In this basin there is a stone image of a large hand carrying a ball, popularly believed to symbolize the right hand of Rama's father Dasharatha who put his hand out from the netherworld to receive the *pinda* offered by Sita (Rama's wife). The priest and assistants to the overseer narrate this story to any visitor with elaboration and justifications. According to mythology, Rama's brother Bharat lived here in a hermitage; the shrine and place is now known as Bharatashram (BdP, 3.13.105).

Uttaramanas

The holy tank of Uttaramanas is believed to be an ancient pool (MbH, 12.152.13; MtP, 121.69), which in course of time dried up and was filled with silt. However, by the mid-eleventh century it was renovated, and made broader and deeper by King Vishvarupa's son, Yakshapala, as mentioned in an inscription of verse 1040 (Kielhorn, 1887, p. 63). This was misinterpreted by Barua (1975, II, p. 67) who suggests that this water pool was made by Yakshapala. This misinterpretation was later on added in the *Gaya Mahatmya* (GM). Kane (1973, p. 651) opines that the spot was already famous as a site for ancestral rites by the eight century (AgP, 115.10; VyP, 82.21). At the water pool of Uttaramanas, three other holy spots are manifested, viz. Udichi in the northwest corner, Dakshinamanas in the southwest corner, and Kankhal at the centre. The devotees are advised to offer rice balls at these four sites, and then by the bank of River Phalgu. Altogether, these five sites are known as Panchatirthi (TS, 360; VyP, 111.1).

Mahabodhi Taru (Tree)

The Mahabodhi tree (*Ficus religiosa*) was already described in the *puranic* mythologies as a sacred spot for worship and ancestral rites (AgP, 115.34–37; MtP, 22–33; NdP, II.45.103–105; VyP, 111.26–29). This sacred Bodhi tree has a definite association with Buddhism as its locational affinity to Buddha Gaya also testifies (Barua, 1975, I: 234, II: 2–9). Gaya and Gayashirsh were well known sacred centres during the Buddhist period (for example, see *Mahavagga*, 1.21.1; *Anguttaranikaya*, IV.302). During the period of the seven-day ancestral rites, devotees visit the Mahabodhi tree on the fourth day. According to Vidyarthi (1978, p. 24) this tree was an object of worship for the Hindus as early as the seventh century, but around CE 600, the King Shashanka of Bengal, a devout adherent of Brahmanism, dug it up and burnt it to ashes. This view is supported by Hiuen Tsiang (CE 629, Book VIII, pp. 117–118). It is argued that the "... brahmin priests might have adopted the tree as a suitable object for veneration once Buddhism was on the decline and in this way they made a profitable use of the worship the Mahabodhi tree received from the Buddhists" (Vidyarthi, 1978, p. 24). It is also believed that in circa 620 King Purnaverma planted the sacred tree again. The *Vayu Purana* (111.24), while describing the Mahabodhi tree, mentions *yajna* (fire sacrifice), the *Bodhisattva* and the sacred fig on which Vishnu resides. The area was well known as the site of Shaiva and Vaishnavite worship. A relief dated with Dharmapala's 26th year (circa CE 807) depicting Surya, Lakulish and Vishnu supports this view (Asher, 1989, p. 56). Buchanan (1811–12, p. 126) also mentions this site as an active place for rituals. The *Padma Purana* (6.117.30) describes the Mahabodhi tree in respect to its association with the Buddha. Another of Dharmapala's reliefs dated in circa CE 850 also mentions the story of the Buddha (Cunningham, 1883, p. 3). Presently very few devotees visit this site. Muchkand Kunda, close to the water pool is also used as a ritual site.

Ritualscape: The Pilgrimage-cognitive Map

According to Devereux, 'Other people in other times and places have mapped the world quite differently from the way we have, and no less truthfully in their own terms' (1996, p. 158). The maps have the inherent quality of sensuous feeling and cognition. Such notional maps showing mythology and sacredness in space and pictorial symbolism are true representatives of the cultural system. When a deep sense of faith works in the formation of a spiritual–mental topography, fitting into the setting of a physical topography, it may be termed '*faithscape*' (Singh, 1995a, p. 97). Such maps produce a visual impression to make the pilgrim remember religious mythology and induce spiritual feeling. Like similar maps for other sacred cities of India, the pilgrimage-cognitive map of the holy city of Gaya is an example of cartography where 'faithscape' is portrayed through the means of pictorial signs and mythological support concerning sacred topography (Dubey and Singh, 1994, pp. 324–326). These pilgrimage-cognitive maps show visitors the mythical shape of the city and give them an image to help them remember the experience when they return home. These maps are also visual texts which can be read in order to gain a better understanding of the sacredscape of a holy place and, in a wider perspective, even of Hindu mythologies. By mapping the religious and mythological features of the holy city in the frame of cosmic design, these maps also help to expand the cosmogonic context leading to the emergence of 'pilgrimage *mandala*'.

Avoiding the sense of distance, the cognitive map of Gaya highlights various symbolic representations of mythology and topography. The bank of River Phalgu is prominently shown as the base on which Gayasur lay down; on his body a fire altar was made where the trinity of the Hindu pantheon, that is Brahma (Creator), Vishnu (Preserver), and Shiva (Destroyer) performed ritual sacrifice. All the important hills associated with ancestral rites are shown prominently when the divinities' images and devotees are marked. The directional and locational contexts are also given some consideration. All the important sacred centres visited during the course of ancestral rituals are well marked, including the centres at Bodh Gaya.

The mythical story of demon Gayasur and Vishnu is prominently shown with sketches that help the devotees understand the inherent meanings and messages. By performing ancestral rites at these sacred centres, devotees become a part of the communication between the worlds of humanity and divinity. Devotees and pilgrims seek to realize a sense of interconnectedness these two worlds. The map also suggests the procedures of pilgrimage followed for seven days and the cluster of holy centres to be visited on each days in the sequence of time and space, from north to south – starting at Prestashila and concluding at Akshayavata or the Mahabodhi Tree (Bodh Gaya).

Conclusion

The vitality and spiritual magnetism of a major pilgrimage centre such as Gaya may have fostered a transformation of the pilgrimage system to include ancestral rites, which have now overtaken solar symbolism and rituals. In the earlier phases of religious evolution, the fire element of the sun, the upward aspect of the hills, the liquid attribute of the river, and the pillar imputation of the tree, together linked to the cosmological frame resulted in the formation of sacred geography. Sacred geography is the basic frame of cosmic geometries and may be interpreted through locational alignments, interrelated correspondences and celestial occurrences like winter and solar solstices. These attributes are always awakened by sacred performances like ancestral rites and rituals held at the conjunction of a sacred time, a sacred place and a sacred spot. That is how a unique environment is evolved where sacredness, spatiality and temporality meet – this holistic environ is referred to as 'faithscape'. In Gaya the complexity of reference points for territorial delimitation, temporal phases of rituals, their locational association, and the sacred routes mobilizing the ritual functionality are altogether converged into an orderly system. Complexity becomes an order in the maintenance and continuity of a tradition.

Pilgrimage is a journey, and a place of pilgrimage is an archetype of universality of patterning whose holistic nature provides the power of transformation. In the context of Jungian thought, pilgrimage is a psychic reality of experience (Clift and Clift, 1996, p. 83). Pilgrimage is a way of healing the body and the soul by cleaning the body through exercise and rituals and revealing the soul through realisation and deep spiritual experiences inherent to the Mother Earth. For pilgrims the experience of pilgrimage is deep as it starts from the visual realm of exteriorisation and ultimately reaches the feeling of interiorisation. The visual landscape, the empowered sacred sites and spots, the associated rituals, the devout pilgrims (like at Gaya) – all speak for themselves in the silent voice of manifested sacredness, what Eliade calls 'hierophany' (1958).

By faith and rituals and by symbolic behaviour, a pilgrim is able to transform himself or herself. Pilgrimage is a process of faith-healing and soul mapping. The quest to know what happened at a sacred site: how is sacredness inherent there? Why do miracles happen there? Why do we pay our respects or give thanks? Why is the divine spirit more active there? etc., such questions awaken our inner call and kindle a desire to make a pilgrimage. With this curiosity many pilgrims follow the path on which their predecessors walked in search of wonder, miracle, peace and divine experience. Modern tourism often erodes the penitential dimension of pilgrimages (Preston, 1992, p. 36); it is our *dharma* (moral duty) to save our heritage where the spirit of humanity meets divinity (Singh, 1995b and 2000).

The very richness of solar symbolism at Gaya and the intensity and openness of the pilgrimage system may have provided the means for amplifying new energy and ideas by being part of the realm of the end of life. This realisation is a new beginning in itself. This dynamic aspect of Gaya lends the city a great vitality, making it a 'theosphere' that allows for self-transformation, as is the case in many self-organising systems.

Notes

1. All Sanskrit references cited in the text are elaborated upon below.

AgP – *Agni Purana*, Anandashram Sanskrit Series, No. 41, Poona: Anandashram Mudranalaya, 1957. (dated ca. ninth century CE).

AiB – 'Aitareya Brahmana', *Rigveda Brahmanas: The Aitareya and Kaushitaki Brahmanas of the Rigveda*, Arthur B. Keith (trans.), Harvard Oriental Series, Vol. 25, 1920, Delhi: Motilal Banarasidass, Second Indian Reprint, 1981, (dated ninth century BCE).

AV – *Atharva Veda*, (with commentary by Sayana), Bombay: Sri Venkatevara Press, 1895, (dated ca. tenth century BCE).

BdP – *Brahmanda Purana*, J. L.Shashtri (ed.), Delhi: Motilal Banarasidass Publishers, 1971, (dated ca. fourth century CE).

BvP – *Brahmavaivarta Puranam*, R. N. Sen (trans.), 2 Vols., 1920, New York: AMS Press, Reprinted 1974, (dated ca. sisteenth century CE).

Buddhacarita or *Acts of the Buddha*, of Ashvaghosa, E. H. Johnston (trans), 2 vols., Delhi: Motilal Banarasidass, Second edition, 1972, (dated ca. second century CE).

GdP – *Garuda Purana*, Varanasi: Chowkhamba Sanskrit Series, 1963, (dated c. ninth century CE).

GM – *Gaya Mahatmya*, (c. 560 verses from VyP, 105–112), Claude Jacque (ed. and trans.), Pondicherry: Auroville Ashram, 1962, (dated ca. eighth to ninth century CE).

KmP – *Kurma Purana*, A. S.Gupta (ed.), Varanasi: All-India Kashiraj Trust, 1972, (dated ca. eighth century CE).

MbH – *Mahabharata*, V. S. Sukthankar *et al.*, Baroda: Bhandarkar Oriental Research Institute, 19 vols., Critical edition, 1933–1959, (dated ca. fourth century BCE).

MtP – *Matsya Purana*, Anandashram Sanskrit Series, No. 54. Poona: Anandashram Mudranalaya, 1907, (dated ca. seventh century CE).

MtU – *Maitrayaniya Upanishada*, J. A. B. Van Buitan (ed. and trans.), the Hague: Mouton & Co., 1962, (dated ca. sixth century CE).

NdP – *Nardiya Purana*, Bombay: Sri Venkateshvara Press, Vol. 1 and 2, 1923, (dated ca. eighth century CE).

NrT – *Nirukta*, Yaska, Bombay: Sri Venkateshvara Press, *n.d.*, (dated ca. eighth century BCE).

PdP – *Padma Purana*, Vishvanath Nayayan Mandalika (ed.), Anandashram Sanskrit Series, No. 131, Poona: Anandashram Mudranalaya, 4 Vols., 1883–1894, (dated ca. 4th–5th century CE).

RV – *Rig Veda Samhita*, *The Sacred Hymns of the Brahmanas*, F. Max Muller (ed.), Varanasi: The Chowkhamba Sanskrit Series, Indian edition, 1966, (dated ca. fifteenth century BCE).

TaS – *Taittiriya Samhita*, Commentary by Sayana, Anandashram Sanskrit Series, No. 36, Poona: Anandashram Mudranalaya, 1897–1898, (dated ca. ninth century BCE).

TC – *Tirthacintamani*, Vachaspati Mishra, Kamalakrishna Smrititirtha (ed.), Calcutta: Bibliotheca Indica, 1912, *Gaya Mahatmya*: 268–328, (dated fifteenth century CE).

TS – *Tristhalisetu*, Narayana Bhatta, Anandashram Sanskrit Series, No.78, Poona: Anandashram Mudranalaya, 1915, (dated ca. sixteenth century CE), *Gaya Mahatmya*: 316–379.

Uttaradhyayansutra, Jan Charpenter (ed.), Archives d'etudes orientales, Vol. 18, *Uppsala*, 1922, (dated ca. fourth to fifth century CE)

VmP – *Vamana Purana*, A. S. Gupta (ed.), Varanasi: All-India Kashiraj Trust, 1975, (dated ca. eighth to ninth century CE).

VyP – *Vayu Purana*, Anandashram Sanskrit Series, No. 49, Poona: Anandashram Mudranalaya, 1860, (dated ca. seventh to eighth century CE).

VdS – *Vishnudharmasutra*, Bombay: Sri Venkateshvara Press, *n.d.*, (dated ca. fourth century CE).

2. In the context of this chapter, *ghat* refers to broad stair-landings built by the side of river banks, traditionally to facilitate access to the river, in this case for rites and rituals.
3. Vishnu is one entity of the Hindu holy trinitiy, and major diety of the Vaishnavite sect. The other two entities are Brahma the Creator, and Shiva the Destroyer. Vishnu is the Preserver.

References

Archaeological Survey of India, *Archaeological Survey of India, Reports*, Seal No. 31, Calcutta, 1903–04, pp. 10–11.

Asher, Fredrick M., 'Gaya: Monuments of the Pilgrimage Town', *Marg*, Bombay, Vol. 40, No. 1, 1989, pp. 45–60.

Banerji, R. D., 'The Palas of Bengal', *Memoirs of the Asiatic Society of Bengal, Calcutta*, Vol. V, 1915, pp. 78–79.

Barua, Benimadhab, *Gaya and Buddha Gaya: Early History of Holy Land*, 2 Vols., 1934, Varanasi: Indological Book House Organisation, Reprint, 1975.

Beal, Samuel, *Buddhist Records of the Western World. (Travels of Hiuen Tsang)*. London: Kegan Paul, Trench, Trubner & Company, Vols. 1 and 2, 1906.

Buchanan, Hamilton, *Patna-Gaya Report*, Patna: Bihar and Orissa Research Society, Vol. 1, 1811–12.

Chakravarti, M. M., 'Inscription of Nayapala Deva', *Journal of the Asiatic Society of Bengal*, Vol. 69, No. 1, 1901, pp. 190–195.

Clift, J. D. and W. B. Clift, *The Archetype of Pilgrimage. Outer Action with Inner Meaning*, Marwah, NJ: Paulist Press, 1996.

COI 1901, Census of India 1901, Bengal part 2, Vol. 6A, Imperial Tables. Government Press, Calcutta.

Cunningham, Alexander 1883. *Mahabodhi, or The Great Buddhist Temple under the Bodhi Tree at Bodh-Gaya*. Reprinted, Varanasi: Indological Book House (with 31 plates).

Dave, J. H., *Immortal India*, Bombay: Bhartiya Vidya Bhavan, Vol. 1, Gaya, 1970, pp. 32–40.

Devereux, Paul, *Symbolic Landscape*, Somerset, UK: Gothic Image Press, 1992.

Devereux, Paul, *Re-Visioning the Earth*, New York: Simon & Schuster, 1996.

Dubey, D. P. and Rana P. B. Singh, 1994. 'Chitrakut: The Frame and Network of the Faithscape and Sacred Geography of a Hindu Tirtha'. *National Geographical Jl. of India*, Vol. 41, pp. 307–332.

Eliade, Mircea, *Patterns in Comparative Religion*, London: Sheed & Ward, 1958.

Eliade, Mircea, *The Myth of Eternal Return*, Princeton: Princeton University Press, 1965.

Fleet, J. F., *Inscriptions of the Early Gupta Kings, Vol. III of Corpus Inscription Indicarum*, Varanasi: Indological Book House, 1970.

Gangadharan, N., *Garuna Purana: A Study*, Ramanagar, Varanasi: All India Kashiraj Trust, 1972.

Ghosh, J. C., 'The Antiquity of Gaya', *Journal of Bihar & Orissa Research Society*, Vol. 24, 1938, pp. 89–111.

Gode, P. K., 'The History of the Akshayavata (Undecaying Banyan Tree) at Prayaga and Gaya as Revealed by Some Sanskrit Texts – Between the First Century AD and 1900', *Annals of the Buddhist Oriental Research Institute*, Vol. 38, 1957, pp. 82–92.

Hopkins, Thomas J., 'Hindu views of death and afterlife', in Hiroshi Obayashi (ed.), *Death and Afterlife*, New York: Greenwood Press, 1992.

Irwin, John, 'The Ancient Pillar-Cult at Prayag (Allahabad): Its Pre-Asokan Origins', *Journal of the Royal Asiatic Society*, Vol. 2, 1983, pp. 253–280.

Kane, Pandurang Vaman, *History of Dharmasastra*, Government Oriental Series, Class B, No. 6; 5 Vols., Poona: Bhandarkar Oriental Research Institute, Vol. 5, Chapter 14, *Gaya*: 643–679, Second edition, 1973.

Keilhorn, F., 'A Gaya Inscription of Yakshapala', *The Indian Antiquary*, Vol. 16, 1887, pp. 63–66.

Kern, H., *Manual of Indian Buddhism*, Varanasi: Indological Book House Organisation, 1913, Reprinted, 1968.

Knipe, David M., 'One Fire, Three Fires, Five Fires: Vedic Symbols in Transition', *History of Religions*, Vol. 12, No. 1, 1972, pp. 28–40.

Mahajan, Arvind, 'Shraddhatirtha Gaya as Depicted in the North Indian Epigraphs', in D. P. Dubey (ed.), *Rays and Ways of Indian Culture*, New Delhi: M. D. Publications Pvt. Ltd., 1996, pp. 31–38.

Michaels, Axel, 'Ancestors, Demons and the Ritual Impossibility of Death in Brahmanical Hinduism', in E. Schömbucher and C. P. Zoller (eds.), *Ways of Dying*, New Delhi: Manohar Publishers, 1999, pp. 112–134.

Mitra, Rajendralal, *Buddha Gaya, the Hermitage of Sakya Muni*, (with 51 plates), Calcutta: Bengal Secretariat Press, 1878.

Paul, Debjani, 'Antiquity of the Vishnupad at Gaya', *East and West*, N. S., Vol. 35, Nos. 1–3, 1983, pp. 103–141.

Preston, James J. 1992. 'Spiritual Magnetism: an Organizing Principle for the Study of Pilgrimage.' In Morinis, Alan (ed.) *Sacred Journeys. The Anthropology of Pilgrimage*: pp. 31–46. Westport, CT: Greenwood Press.

Singh, Rana P. B. 1995a. 'Towards Deeper Understanding, Sacredscape and Faithscape: an Exploration in Pilgrimage Studies.' *National Geographical Jl. of India*, Vol. 41, No. 1, pp. 89–111.

Singh, Rana P. B. 1995b. 'Heritage ecology and caring for the Earth'. *National Geograpphical Jl. of India*, Vol. 41, No. 2, pp. 191–218.

Singh, Ravi S., *Goddesses in India: A Study in the Geography of Sacred Places*, Unpublished PhD dissertation in Geography, J. P. University, Chapra, Bihar.

Sircar, D. C. 1965. "Inscription of Visvaditya, Year 15 of Nayapala", *Epigraphia Indica*, Vol. 36, pp. 84–88.

Sircar, D. C. 1959. 'Inscription from Gaya'. *Epigraphia Indica*, 33(3), pp. 108–109.

Sircar, D. C. and K. H. V. Sarma, 1959. 'Inscription of Achyutaraya, V. S. 1588'. *Epigraphia Indica*, 33(3), pp. 113–116.

Tuan, Yi-Fu, *Landscapes of Fear*, Minneapolis: University of Minnesota Press, 1979.

Vidyarthi, L. P., *The Sacred Complex in Hindu Gaya*, New Delhi: Concept Publishing Company, Second edition, 1978.

Williams, Monier, 'Sraddha Ceremonies at Gaya', *The Indian Antiquary*, Vol. 5, 1876, pp. 200–204.

28

Madurai: A Holy City of Pilgrimage

MEERA CHATTERJEE AND ASHOK K. DUTT

A temple often becomes the focal point of history, culture and political supremacy in India. The southern part of India is speckled with many such temples that have made a distinctive contribution not only to the religious life of the people but also have served as the core around which the social and cultural life of the people revolved. Madurai is one such old temple city of India, although it has also become a major industrial city of South India. For the last two thousand years it has been a remarkable centre of South Indian culture and civilization. It is located on the banks of river Vaigai and derived its name from 'Mathura' of North India. Madurai is a brilliant instance of town and country planning of ancient India and has also been mentioned by the ancient Greek geographer Ptolemy as 'Modoura'. The Meenakshi temple in Madurai is one of the most significant centres of Hindu worship. Not only are pilgrims attracted to the site from all over India, but the temple also serves as a regional focus for worship and as a social centre for a large population. 'Madurai' in the local language means 'sweet place'. Myths are also attached to the name of the city. For instance, it is said that Lord Shiva was immensely pleased with the building of the city and sprinkled nectar (*madhu*) over it, hence the name Madurai. From ancient Tamil literature, nevertheless, it appears that 'Thirumarudam' was the initial name given to the city. 'Thirumarudam' refers to a place full of '*Maruda* trees' (*Kadamba* trees). Historical records show that thick *Maruda* forests bordered the original temple nucleus. The place came to be known as Marudai and then as Madura during the Chera, Chola and Pandya periods. Thus, the name Madurai may be a corrupt form of 'Marudai'.

The name of the city of Madurai has been changed several times in the past. The most recent change was in the 1960s, when the colonial name of Madura was changed to the earlier native name of Madurai.

During the British colonial time it was common for the British administrators to change the local native place-names to make them easier for the British to pronounce. These changed names were officially used and recorded in the gazetteers and censuses. Several pilgrimage cities underwent such changes. Varanasi became Benaras, Mathura became Muttra, Kanchipuram became Kanjeevarum, and Thanjavaur became Tanjore. Like Madurai, all five cities have reverted to their original native names after India gained independence in 1947.

The city has grown in importance as a seat of administration, a centre of higher education, a place of religious and cultural significance, a fascinating destination for national and international tourists and the focal point of trade, commerce and industry in the southern districts of Tamil Nadu. Numerous spinning mills manufacture a range of fibres for the handloom and industrial sectors – fine cottons, embroidery threads, and sophisticated blends for medical sutures, tyre cord, and fibres for parachutes. Additional engineering industries comprise sugar and chemicals.

Origin and History

Madurai is one of the few cities whose glorious history could easily be sketched back to primeval times. 'Sthalapuranas speaks of its hoary antiquity of when, it is said, Parvati and Shiva ruled over Madurai and Pandya territory' (Devakunjari, 1979, p. 1).

Pandya–Chola Period

The first Pandyas ruled over Madurai early in the Christian era. The Cholas, the other significant political power, controlled a large part of the Kaveri basin during the first five centuries CE; the first phase of Pandya–Chola rule concluded by about CE 300. Nevertheless, Pandyas effected an extraordinary revival during the last decade of the sixth century. In fact, Madurai city might have been built during the sovereignty of a great Pandyan King, Kadungkone. The Pandyan Empire later extended its control over almost all of peninsular India up to Nellore. However, the Cholas returned to rule in the late ninth century which was another period of magnificent rule in South India. They introduced an irrigation system, built monuments and structured the local administration. The ancient era in the history of Madurai was, therefore, an era of Pandya–Chola preeminence.

Vijayanagar Period

In 1311, Madurai was invaded by Malik Kafur, the general of Sultan Alauddin Khilji of Delhi. The entire city was deserted and the illustrious temple was mercilessly torn down, except for the inner shrine. Consequently, for a brief period it turned into a Sultanate. The eventual decline of the Delhi Sultanate by the first quarter of the fourteenth century offered an opportunity to Madurai to reinstate its independence. In 1364, it was captured by Hindu Vijayanagar kings, who retained power until 1565. Therefore, in the history of Madurai, the Afghan–Vijayanagar era is treated as a period of foreign rule. The Vijayanagar kings appointed Nayakas as their local governors. The decline of the Vijayanagar Empire during the second half of the sixteenth century facilitated the Nayakas to declare their independence. The Vijayanagar kings were great builders and they enriched and preserved the architectural legacy of the town. The present temple and the adjacent areas were designed and constructed during the rule of Nayaka dynasty.

Nayaka Period

Nayaka rule saw the transition of the region from a dependent to an independent political unit. 'During this time, the outlines of the city which persist to this day were established and the first directions of urban expansion were demarcated. Viswanath Nayaka, the first ruler of the Nayaka dynasty, constructed an extensive double-walled fortress around the city in order to check further Muslim invasions. Around the main temple the new city gradually came into existence with well planned roads forming a series of three squares [see Fig. 28.1], called the Chitrai (the inner square), the Avani (middle) and Masi (the largest and outer one). Each street forming the squares is named after the cardinal directions, (Ramesh and Noble, 1977, pp. 45–46). The four Veli streets – North, East, South and West – coincide with the walls of the old city. The Nayakas patronized arts and architecture, promoted Hinduism and attached great importance to the irrigation system.

Muslim Rule

In 1730, Madurai was invaded by Mysore-based Muslim rulers. The city came to be ruled by Hyder Ali and Tipu Sultan. A small number of mosques were built in the centre of the city, in the neighbourhood of the

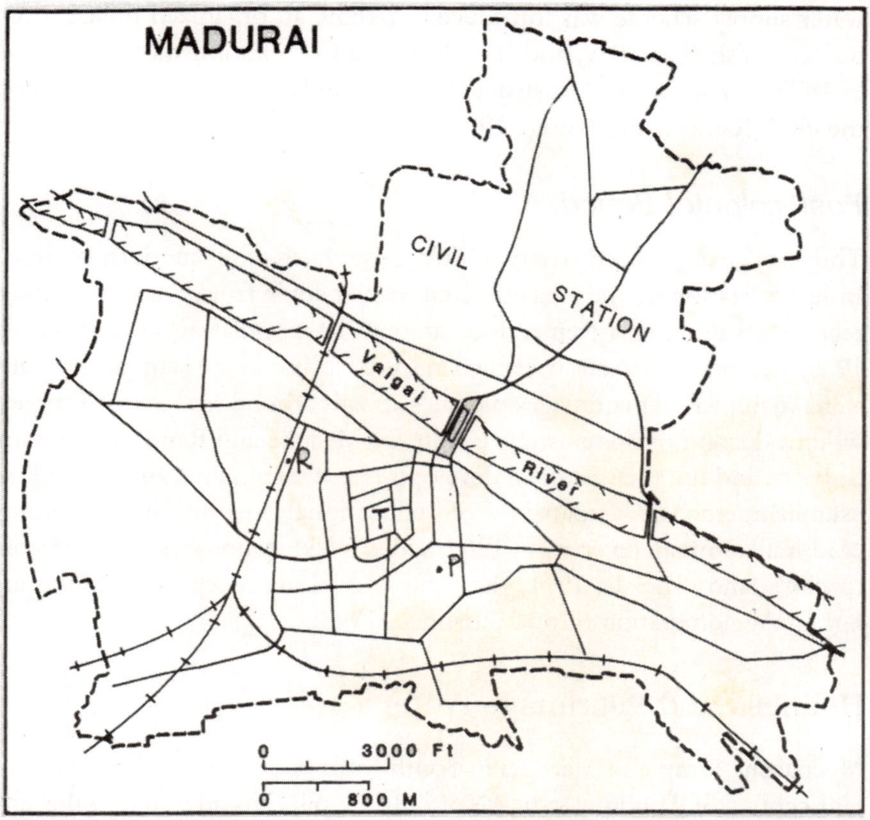

Fig. 28.1 Madurai City
T – Meenakshi Temple at the centre of the old town
P – Thirumalai Nayaka Palace near the southwestern edge of the old town (built in 1636)
R – Railway Station outside the old town
Source: Adapted from Noble, Dutt and Hasan, 1994.

Meenakshi temple. The latter half of the Muslim rule was not constructive for the growth of the city due to the regular skirmishes between the Muslim rulers and the British East India Company.

Colonial Period

This period in Madurai was to a substantial degree typical of the developments taking place elsewhere in the country under the East India Company's administration, which started in 1782. British troops were posted in the city for more than 20 years. During direct British rule after 1857, some attention was paid to urban facilities and supplies. 'The first water supply scheme was introduced in 1859, an organized police force was established in 1859, and the Municipal Corporation was constituted in 1875. A railway line constructed in 1875 induced westward growth of the city' (Ramesh and Noble, 1977, p. 48).

Post-colonial Period

The city experienced tremendous growth in the modern period. Industrialization of the area attracted many people from the surrounding regions resulting in a tremendous amount of population growth. After 1930, the other attractions which resulted in rapid growth of the city were: (i) improved pilgrimage amenities, mostly around Meenakshi Temple, (ii) introduction of administrative units for Madurai and Ramanathapuram districts, and (iii) the sustained development of commerce and trade. The establishment and expansion of educational institutions, including Madurai Kamraj University in 1966, added an education-based dimension to city's landscape. In 1971, the Census of India declared Madurai an Urban Agglomeration (Gopalakrishnan, 1998).

Holiness and Pilgrimage Pattern

Meenakshi Temple in Madurai in South India is one of the most important centres of Hindu worship. Not only are pilgrims attracted to the site from all over India, but the temple also serves as a regional focus for worship, and as a hub for weddings for a large local as well as regional population. The gates of the temple compound are opened at 4 a.m. and closed at 10 p.m., with a mid-day closure of three and a half hours. In the morning, up to about 9.30 a.m., the number of devotees streaming in steadily increases. Late afternoons and early evenings are busier times at the temple, with peak attendance between 7 and 8 p.m. According to a field survey, an average of 6,000 people enter and leave the temple at this hour, although numbers vary according to the day of the week (Noble, Dutt and Vishnukumari, 1987).

The great *gopurams* of the temple tower above the maze of the streets. The main entrance to the temple complex is through the *gopuram* and the gateway called Swami Sannathi, located on the eastern side of the structure and leading past the Thousand Pillared Hall directly to the shrine of Sundereswar. The survey also depicts that over 22,000 devotees pass through this gate daily, far more than any other portal, despite the fact that urban population density is highest to the south. This kind of distribution is attributed to the auspiciousness of the eastern gate and the location of city's central business district in the East. As might be expected from the population distribution, the western and southern gates rank next, probably because of the location of the railway station and the central bus stand in these respective areas. Both of these facilities are situated approximately three quarters of a mile west of the temple and pilgrims arriving by public transport would logically enter by the nearest gate (Noble, Dutt and Vishnukumari, 1987).

Gate number five (north gate) and two (a subsidiary eastern gate) have the lowest number of entrants. Entrance to the temple on Sundays and Mondays is roughly equal in the morning and afternoon. Tuesdays experience a much different pattern of attendance. Mornings are less popular than afternoons, and this disparity continues through the rest of the week to peak on Fridays, but declining on Saturday. The fluctuations in attendance are to an extent dependent upon astrological considerations. Certain days are considered to be auspicious. In the popular view, prayers offered or religious ceremonies undertaken on such days are most likely to be crowned with success. It is impossible to select a particular week which does not have such variables and these, of course, affect temple attendance. Therefore, it can be concluded that religious structures have impact on human activity and space (Noble, Dutt and Vishnukumari, 1987).

Socioeconomic Structure

Population Growth

Throughout the twentieth century Madurai's population has grown significantly every decade except between 1911–21. During these years, like every other place in the world, Madurai was also affected by the Spanish Flu that killed millions. Consequently, the population of Madurai remained stable during 1911–21. Starting from 1921, as with other Indian cities, Madurai's population registered a significant increase which culminated in a population explosion in the 1960s (Fig. 28.2). Consequently, for a decade (1960–70), the city experienced the maximum percentage increase of population in its history, leading to massive urban growth (Fig. 28.3). Although the rate of percentage change in population has now declined after a massive increase, the total population of the agglomeration has been increasing consistently.

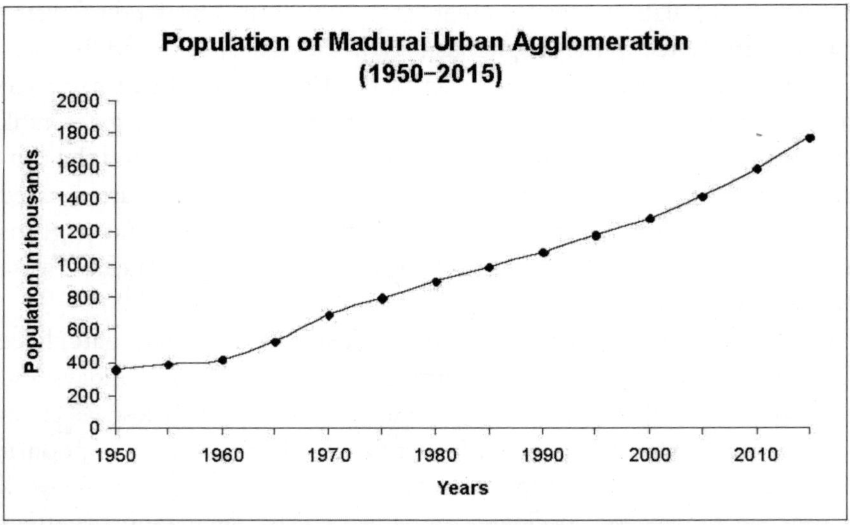

Fig. 28.2 Population of Madurai Urban Agglomeration (1950–2015).
Data Source: World Urbanization Prospects, UN, 2000.

Occupational Structure

Though the city of Madurai is a temple city with a huge concentration of temple-related activities, industries such as handloom and textiles are also important. Like many other urban agglomerations in India, Madurai includes a large tract of agricultural land within its urban jurisdiction (Census of India, 1991). As a result, over 54 per cent of the workers are either cultivators or agricultural workers. The agricultural activities are not solely devoted to rice cultivation, but also includes truck farming and floriculture (ritual flowers), both to meet the specific requirements of the city. Significant differences exist in the male/female distribution of the working population. Of the total female workforce, 56 per cent of the females are engaged in agricultural activities compared to 30 per cent of the males. On the contrary, the 'other workers' category that includes people employed in industry and services has a much greater proportion of the male workforce (51 per cent compared to 27 per cent of the females). The male population is more educated than the females though the differential in male/female literacy rates is not much. In this area of Tamil Nadu, the women stay at home and work in the farms, while men venture out for city jobs in industries and services.

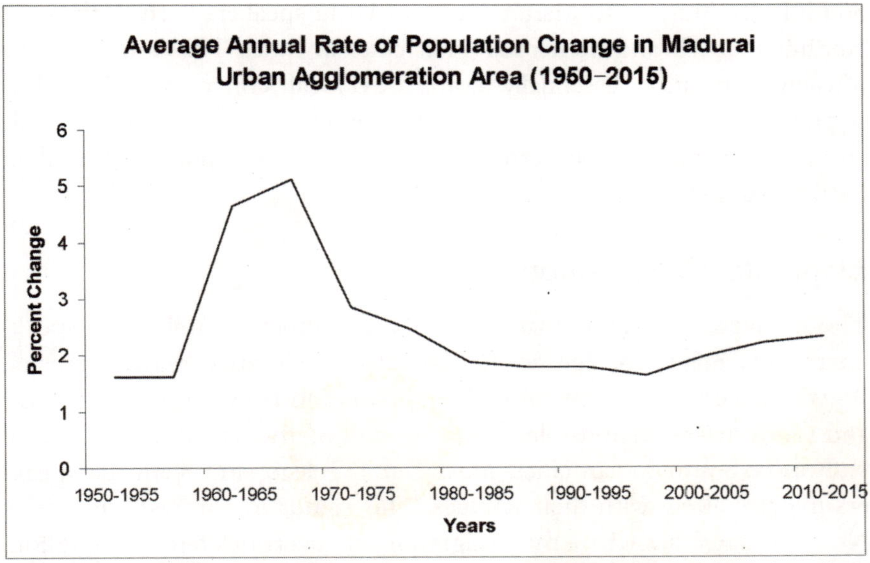

Fig. 28.3 Average Annual Rate of Population Change in Madurai Urban Agglomeration Area (1950–2015).
Data Source: World Urbanization Prospects, UN, 2000.

Religious Characteristics

Apparently, in the earlier part of the twentieth century, Madurai seems to have had a brahmin-controlled urban society, though it was estimated that 'only 18 in every 1000 population' were brahmins in Madurai (Francis, 2000, p. 85). Slowly non-brahmins, Christians, and Muslims started to migrate to the city in large numbers from other parts of Tamil Nadu, Karnataka, and Andhra Pradesh. Thus, there was a slackening of brahmin dominance which followed the dislodging of brahmin political power in the state and in the district of Madurai after 1947, particularly when the electoral system based on 'one person, one vote' was introduced. The brahmins, nonetheless, hold complete control over the Meenakshi Temple of Madurai.

Madurai consists of a predominantly Hindu population, amounting to 87 per cent of the total count. Christians and Muslims are six per cent and 7.5 per cent of the population, respectively. The relatively sizeable concentration of Christians is the result of the influence of Christian missionaries for the last three to four centuries. Once, Madurai and Goa were the only Catholic religious headquarters approved by the Church in all of

South India. Muslims in Madurai are not Urdu speakers such as those of Andhra Pradesh and numerous other cities in India. This is because the Muslim population essentially comprises local converts, rather than migrants from North India. As a matter of fact, in almost all of Kerala and in a large part of southern Tamil Nadu, Muslim residents speak their local languages, not Urdu.

Linguistic Composition

Though Kerala is adjacent to Madurai, the number of Malayalam speakers from Kerala is not significant. Malayalee immigrants are mainly males. As with other Indian cities, it is the immigration from adjoining districts and states that is responsible for the growth of the city. But, as is typical with most South Indian cities, most Tamil, Telegu, and Kannada speakers migrate along with their families. This stands in contrast with many North Indian cities where male migration still overrides female migration. Madurai maintains the status of a Tamil city, where four out of five people are Tamil speakers. Other major linguistic minorities are Telegu (15 per cent), and Kannada (five per cent). Urdu and Hindi speakers do not constitute a significant number.

Urban Characteristics and Structure

Madurai was declared a municipality (town) in 1856. It was given the rank of corporation in 1971. Such recognition brought about sanitary and purified water services for the city's residents. In 1991, as many as 825 out of every 1000 city dwellers had tap water facilities in their homes. Only a few depended on the river, canal, and tank as their source of water supply; these sources are likely to be contaminated and unsanitary.

Madurai is one of the most important pilgrimage centres in India. Its temple, called the Meenakshi Temple, was largely built in the seventeenth century by Hindu Nayaka kings. It is the temple and its accessory activities that dominate the landscape of the city. The city is bisected by the River Vaigai. The old city established on the southern bank of River Vaigai grew around the temple. In the South and the West there were well-marked physical boundaries in the form of the railroad lines and in the North the River Vaigai served as boundary. Meenakshi Temple is enclosed by high walls which are surrounded by streets called Veli streets.

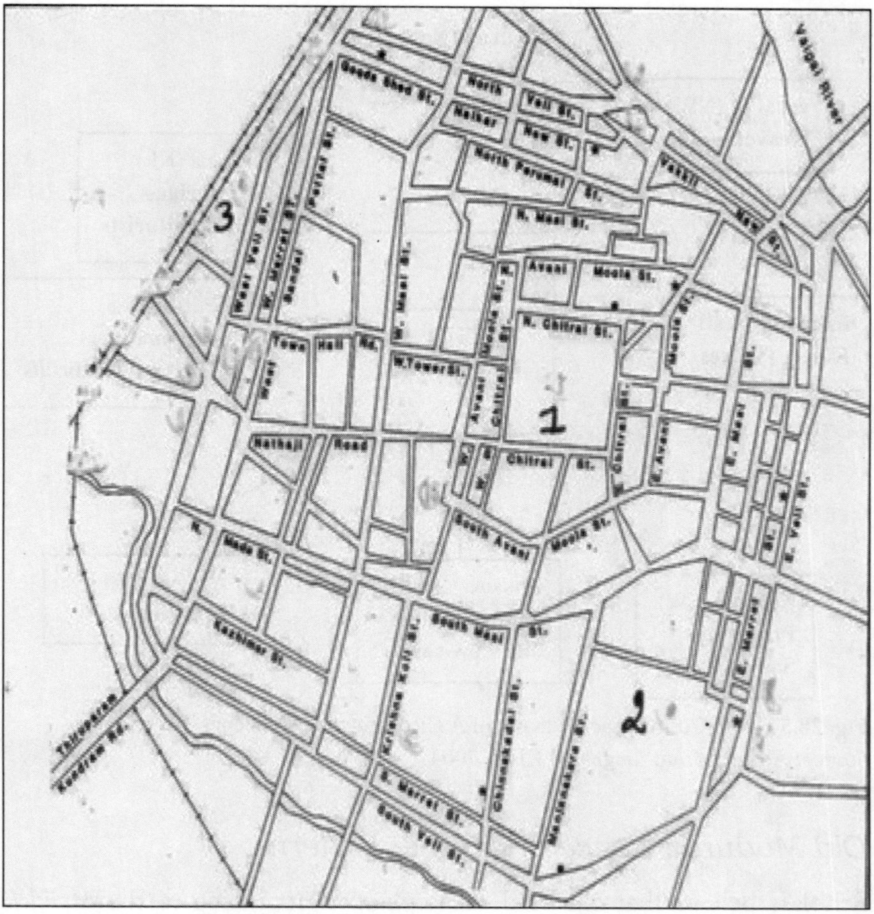

Fig. 28.4 Historic Madurai–*Mandala* Scheme.
1 – Meenakshi Temple 2 – Nayaka Palace 3 – Railway Station.
Source: Adapted from Noble, Dutt and Monroe, 1988.

The city also had walls occupying a seven-sided geometrical space. The Nayaka kings established their palace within the walls. The present-day city of Madurai has not only extended north of the River Vaigai, but also in the eastern and western directions from the old city walls, and to a limited extent towards the south of railroad lines as well (Fig. 28.4).

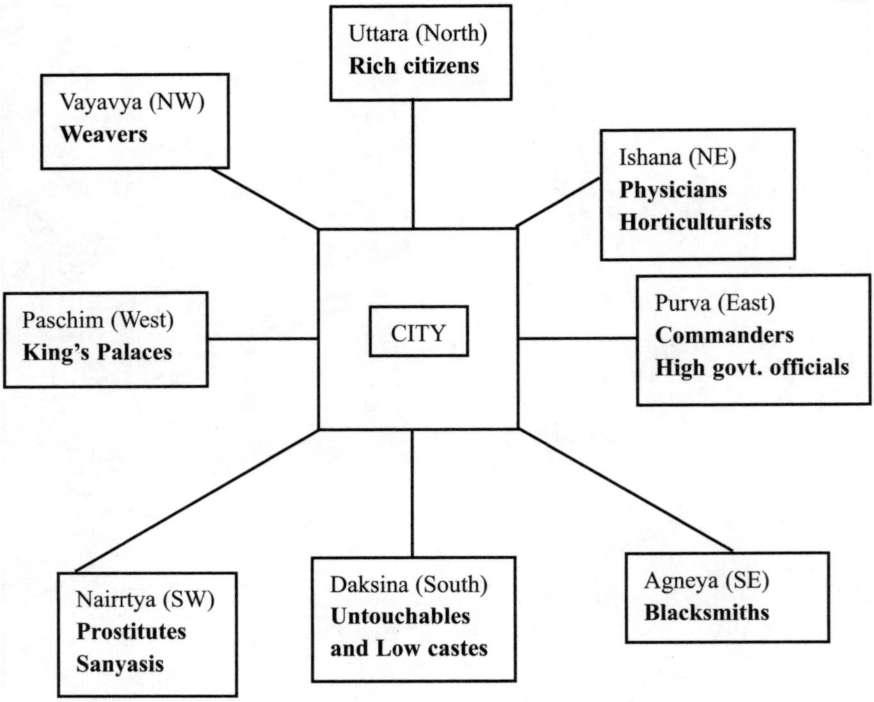

Fig. 28.5 Hindu Cosmological Layout of A City–*Mandala* Concept.
Source: Adapted from Singh and Khan, 2004.

Old Madurai: Concentric Street Patterns

Scholars believe that old Madurai is planned according to the *Mandala* scheme of Hindu cosmology. In a *Mandala* scheme, the city centre is at the centre of a geometrical space, while settlements spread in eight directions forming corridors of neighbourhood development (Fig. 28.5). Each direction has its own cosmological significance and place in the society. This layout provides a unique and organized character to an urban area.

Mandala

The *Mandala* concept also establishes separation of settlements or neighbourhoods by caste and status. The lower castes or the untouchables are always relegated to the most unfavourable direction or corridor, whereas the upper caste neighbourhoods are located in the corridors which are situated in the most favourable direction. Madurai did establish caste segregation in the past. Unfortunately, it still continues today to a great extent. Northwest India-based *Mandala* concept is not fully applicable to a South Indian city like Madurai. The king's palace (Nayaka Palace) is located in the eastern part of the old city, not in the west. The east side, according to the *Mandala* concept, is not a desirable location for such a palace. As there are variations in the direction of the wind between northwestern and southern India; the location of the palace in Madurai has been dictated to suit the local conditions. There are strong northeast retreating Monsoon winds in Madurai for three to four months, starting in October. This means that the king's palace was prevented from receiving polluted winds from lower caste settlements. Moreover, the *Mandala* concept also recommended specific geometrical shapes for the city – rectangle, square or circle. In the case of Madurai, the city walls were constructed in straight lines but had a seven-sided form, which can be traced from the layout of the Veli streets.

> Madurai has also spread across the river Vaigai. Initially, this was a result of the establishment of the British Civil Station in the 19th century. In the British view, the wide but easily bridged river provided a desirable boundary between the native Madurai settlement and the largely European station. The sparsely settled land of the Civil Station provided ample room for large bungalows set in spacious, walled compounds. The population density in the Civil Station remains much lower than south of the river, streets are often tree lined and there is far less congestion. Public, administrative and recreational facilities characterize the Civil Station. Among the more important are the Women's College, the Government Hospital, the American College, the Collector's Office, the Medical School, the Old Race Course, the English Club, Lady Doak College, the Cosmopolitan Club, the Government Tourist Bungalow, the Pandian Hotel and the Gandhi Museum (Noble, Dutt and Monroe, 1988, p. 143).

After Independence in 1947, Madurai has expanded into the peripheral areas like other cities of India. The most significant expansion is towards the northern part of the city, beyond the River Vaigai, adjacent to the old colonial settlement. This area has homes of wealthy people and high class hotels, making the area expensive. In totality, Madurai presents the characteristics of a densely populated centre around the walls of the Meenakshi Temple with lesser density around the peripheral areas. The commercial area primarily lies in the city centre. Today, there are three distinct physical barriers – River Vaigai to the northwest, and the railway lines to the south and the west of the old city. These are important physical barriers for regular transport. Only three bridges have been built across River Vaigai. Present-day Madurai conforms to the traditional bazaar city model (Dutt and Pomeroy, 2003). Madurai has grown from the temple location, from where main roads lead towards the railway station in the south and towards the river bank in the north.

> The bazaar, or the city centre, consists of an amalgam of land uses that cater to the central-place functions of the city. The commercial land use, dominating the centre, consists of both retail and wholesale activities. As the greater portion of family income is spent for the basic necessities of life–food, clothing, and shelter–most streets are related to the retail sale of foodstuffs and clothes. Perishable goods, such as vegetables, meat, and fish–which consumers buy fresh daily because of lack of refrigeration facilities in most homes–are sold in specific areas of the bazaar, which often lack enclosed walls but have a common roof. In the process of bazaar evolution, functional separation of retail business occurs: textile shops stay together, attracting tailors; grain shops cluster together near the perishable goods markets; and pawnshops are adjacent to jewellry shops. Sidewalk vendors are present almost everywhere in the bazaar.
>
> Wholesale business establishments also form part of the bazaar landscape. Situated near an accessible location, they tend to separate according to the commodities they deal in, such as vegetables, grains, and cloth, depending on the size of the city the bazaar serves. Traditionally, the public or nonprofit inns provide modest overnight accommodation in the bazaar for a nominal fee (Dutt and Pomeroy, 2003, pp. 343–344).

In the case of Madurai, temple and tourism-related businesses add to its commercial landscape. Businesses have grown around the temple particularly to the east which is the main commercial hub, where the rich merchants' houses are also located. These merchants usually reside on the upper floors or at back of their shops. The peripheral areas have lesser density of population, including the Civil Lines area towards the north which was added to the old city during the British colonial times.

One handbook (Bradnock, 1996) has identified 10 hotels within the old city, which are mostly budget hotels, located between the railway station in the West and the Meenakshi Temple. Three bus terminals are situated near the railroad station. The tourists, who primarily come to visit the temple, arrive mostly by train or by long-distance buses or coaches. Hence, the hotels are located near transport terminals.

Conclusion

Madurai is an ancient city of South India. It has an administrative and religious basis. The layout of the ancient city basically follows a *Mandala* concept, but the modern city structure is explained by a traditional bazaar city model. Though the city structure has components that are entrenched in retail trade, manufacturing, education and administration, it is the Meenakshi temple and temple-related activities that are the main bases of the city's economic activities. The temple is not only Madurai's principal cultural or religious hub; its influence has spread all over the country.

References

Bradnock, Robert, *India Handbook*, Bath, England: Footprint Handbooks, 1996.

Census of India, 1991. Government of India, available from http://www.censusindia.net/accessed

Devakunjari, D., *Madurai Through the Ages from the Earliest Times to 1801 AD*, Madras: Society for Historical and Epigraphical Research, 1979.

Dutt, Ashok K. and George M. Pomeroy, 'Cities of South Asia', in Stanley D. Brunn, Jack, F. Williams and Donald J Zeigler (eds.), *Cities of the World: World Regional Urban Development*, Oxford: Rowman and Littlefield Publishers, Third edition, 2003, pp. 331–371.

Francis, W., *Madura Gazetteer*, New Delhi: Cosmo Publications, Reprint, 2000.

Gopalakrishnan, K. S., 'Madurai: The Temple Town of India', in R. P. Misra and Kamlesh Misra (eds.), *Million Cities of India, Growth Dynamics, Internal Structure, Quality of Life and Planning Perspectives*, Volume 2, New Delhi: Sustainable Development Foundation, 1998, pp. 658–669.

Noble, Allen, Ashok K. Dutt and P. Vishnukumari, 'Daily and Diurnal Fluctuations in the Attendance Patterns of the Meenakshi Temple, Madurai, India', in V. S. Datye, Jaymala Diddee, S. R. Jog, Charulata Patil (eds.), *Explorations in the Tropics*, Pune: Professor K. R. Dikshit Felicitation Volume Committee, 1987, pp. 290–294.

Noble, Allen, Ashok K. Dutt and Charles B. Monroe, 'The Morphology of a Temple Town Center: Madurai, India, 1975', in Frank J. Costa, Ashok K. Dutt, Laurence J. C. Ma and Allen G. Noble (eds.), *Asian Urbanization: Problems and Processes*, Berlin: Gerbruder Borntraeger, 1988, pp. 221–249.

Noble, Allen, Ashok K. Dutt and Zeenat Hasan, 'The Spatial of Commercial Establishment in Two South Asian City Centers: Rajshahi and Madurai', in Ashok Dutt, Frank J. Costa, Surinder Aggarwal and Allen G. Noble (eds.), *The Asian City: Processes of Development, Characteristics and Planning*, Boston and Dordrecht: Kluwer Academic Publishers, 1994, pp. 99–117.

Rajayya, K., *History of Madurai: 1736–1801*, Madurai: Madurai Kamraj University, 1974.

Ramesh, Atur and Allen G. Noble, 'Pattern and Process in South Indian Cities', in Allen G. Noble and Ashok K. Dutt (eds.), *Indian Urbanization and Planning*, New Delhi: Tata McGraw-Hill Publishing Company, 1977, pp. 41–63.

Singh, Jai Pal and Mumtaz Khan, 'Hindu Cosmology and the Orientation and Segregation of Social Groups in Villages in Northwestern India', in Neelam Grover and Kashi Nath Singh (eds.), *Cultural Geography: Form and Process*, New Delhi: Concept Publishing Company, 2004, pp. 143–164.

United Nations, *World Urbanization Prospects*, New York: United Nations, 2000.

World Bank, *World Development Report, 2000/2001*, New York: Oxford University Press, 2000.

29

Assessment and Dynamics of Urban Growth in the City of Kolkata

CHANDANA MITRA, J. MARSHALL SHEPHERD
AND THOMAS R. JORDAN

The world has seen, and is still seeing the rapid development and spread of urban areas. Cities and towns have sprouted up everywhere around the globe. Villages are transforming into towns and towns into cities, attracting more and more people, and adding to urban expansion. Population increase and industrialization are the key factors behind such a phenomenal change in spatial structure.

India, the second most populated country in the world, has experienced large-scale development in and around its urban areas. The city of Kolkata (formerly Calcutta until 2001) in eastern India, the focus herein, has being aggressively multiplying in size over the last three decades. However, the real population explosion took place between 1940 and 1950, during the Indian independence phase, although growth as such is still continuing (Chakraborty, 1990).

Closely associated with the morphology of any city are its past and present populations that have adhered to certain social and economic customs and followed distinctive occupations (Dutt *et al.*, 1989, 151). Kolkata was the first major city developed by the British East India Company in the early 1700s. The East India Company built their first fortified construction, Fort William, to protect them from the other colonial aspirants. It was around this same fortified structure that the city of Kolkata grew and nurtured itself. It was a garrison town first, then the Company's town, next a provincial city, and later the headquarters of the British India government (National Atlas and Thematic Mapping Organisation (NATMO), 1996). This established a level of importance for the city and stimulated significant growth in its size over the years.

The Kolkata megalopolis began with a population of 100,000 in 1735 and grew to 15 million (KMDA Report, 2005), reflecting largely uncontrolled growth over the past 300 years.

This article assesses the extent of urban sprawl of Kolkata over the years and characterizes its growth pattern using historical maps and satellite images. To the best of our knowledge, this study represents possibly the most thorough spatial as well as temporal evaluation of Kolkata's urban dynamics, spanning several centuries. Also presented is a detailed assessment of the political and natural dynamics and influences governing urban growth in Kolkata. Specific methods used are historical cartographic analysis and more recent technological advancements in remote sensing and modelling. Particular attention is also paid to future studies as to how environmental factors such as urban heat island and pollution will affect climatic patterns as Kolkata transforms from Dominique Lapierre's 'City of Joy' into a 'City of Concrete'. This study also paves the way for further research in other similar cities, especially coastal cities that have similar terrain. The local government can also benefit from this study as policies and decentralization techniques can be moulded depending on the findings of the study.

Study Area

Kolkata is located in the eastern part of India at 22°82′N 88°20′E. This 300 year old city has witnessed great development over the centuries, spreading linearly along the banks of the river Hooghly (Fig. 29.1). Kolkata still retains many of its former attributes as the first major city of India – the magnitude of its population, its volume of trade and commerce, the avenues of employment that it offers, the variety of its inhabitants speaking diverse languages that give it a cosmopolitan character, and its continued importance as a centre of art and culture (Roy, 1996).

The Kolkata Municipal Corporation administers an area of 185 square kilometres or 71.43 square miles (Metropolis, 2005). The city is at sea level, the average elevation being 1.5 to 9 metres (approximately 5 to 30 feet), although there are some natural depressions in the area (likely remnants of dead river channels). The whole area falls in the Ganges Delta (Survey of India, Topographical maps, No. 79 B/6, B/7).

However, the city has continuously expanded, and today the urban agglomeration (Kolkata Metropolitan District or KMD) comprises 157

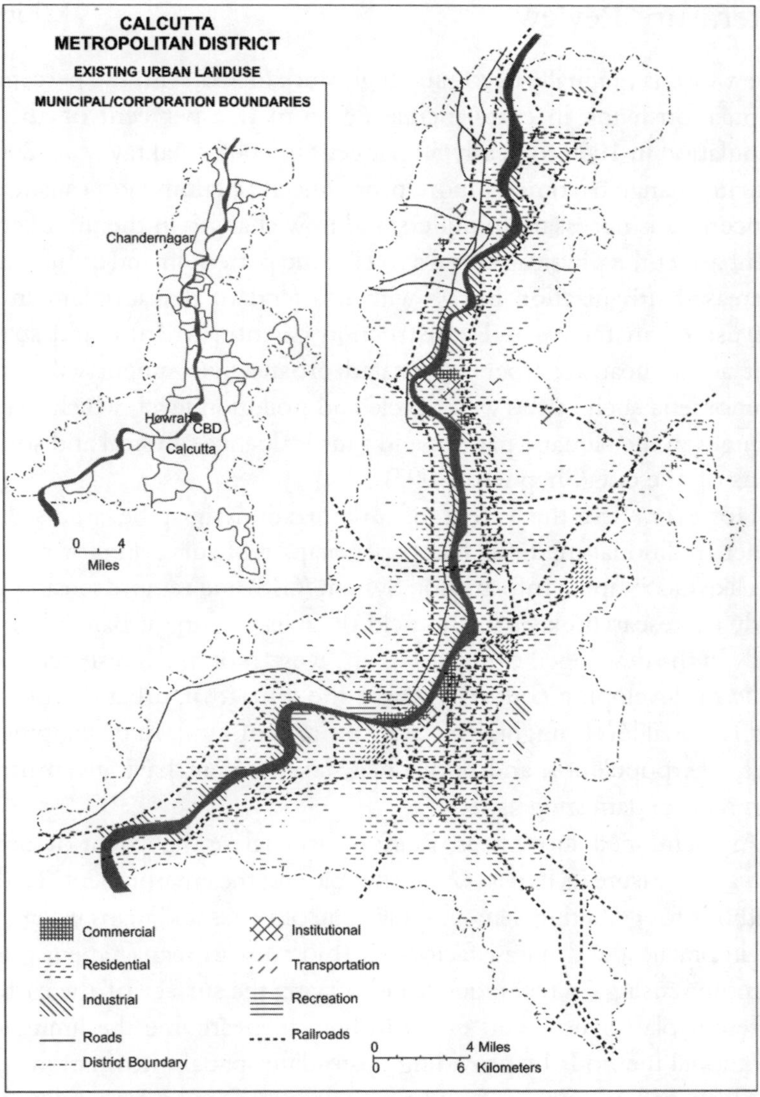

Fig. 29.1 Calcutta Metropolitan Area.
Source: Dutt and Geib (1987, p. 133).

postal areas and is formally administered by several local governments, including 38 local municipalities, 72 cities and 527 towns and villages (Kolkata Postal Codes, 2007). The suburban areas of KMD incorporate parts of the districts of North 24 Parganas, South 24 Parganas, Howrah, Hooghly and Nadia (World Association of Metropolises, 2005).

Literature Review

The world is gradually becoming highly urbanized, with the percentage of population living in cities increasing from five per cent of the global population in 1900 to nearly 50 per cent in 2005 (Maktav *et al.*, 2005). As climate change becomes a more pronounced phenomenon causing global concern, it is necessary to understand how changes in the urban environment affect the physical, social and climatic pattern in and around the city. Increased urbanization brings with it attendant development involving the use of materials, and construction of infrastructure and structures that act as heat absorbers. A heated urban environment will influence phenomena such as the water cycle and pollution level, which may bring changes in the climatic pattern and thus influence physical and social patterns of the city (Shepherd, 2005).

However, first the extent of urbanization must be assessed, using either traditional methods like paper maps and surveying, or new methods like Geographic Information System (GIS) and remote sensing. A large body of research exists in the field of assessing the urban extent, especially in the developed countries of the west. Not much research has been done in developing countries where the impact of urbanization at local and regional levels might, in fact, be more profound. In developing countries, overpopulation and unplanned development have given urbanization a more damaging aspect.

As mentioned above, it is necessary to analyse the extent of urbanization and measure its impact on the people and the environment. Traditional methods for gathering demographic data, censuses and maps using samples are impractical and unsatisfactory for most urban management purposes. Remote sensing – a technique for observing the surface of the earth from different platforms – and GIS can help to overcome the limitations of traditional methods by providing up-to-date spatial information.

This trend of using GIS and remote sensing for understanding growth patterns of cities in developing countries began in the 1970s (Maktav *et al.*, 2005). Since 1972, numerous technical improvements have led to the second generation of Earth observation satellites, such as Landsat[1], SPOT[2] and IRS[3]. From 1999 onwards, one can distinguish a third generation of Earth observation satellites with very high geometric resolution (IKONOS-2, Quickbird-2, etc.) (Maktav *et al.*, 2005). The convergence of GIS, remote sensing and database management systems has helped in quantifying, monitoring, modelling and subsequently predicting this dynamic phenomenon of urban sprawl (Sudhira *et al.*, 2004).

Small (2002) performed a comparative Spectral Mixture Analysis (SMA) of Landsat 7 Enhanced Thematic Mapper (ETM+) imagery for a collection of 28 urban areas worldwide to provide a physical basis for a spectral characterization of urban reflectance properties.

In 2002, Paul C. Sutton of the University of Denver used night-time satellite imagery to delineate urban areas. Maktav, Erbek and Jurgens (2005) attempted to highlight the importance of remote sensing as one of the most reliable mechanisms to assess the consequences of urbanization quickly and effectively in developed and developing countries. Different sensors on different platforms (HRSC-A[4], aerial cameras, LIDAR[5], satellite sensors) acquire high resolution 3-D surface information that is needed to model air movement within a city (Maktav. *et al.*, 2005).

It is evident that monitoring of urban land use change using techniques of remote sensing and GIS, and its subsequent modelling is lacking in the context of India (Sudhira *et al.*, 2004), although a few instances of such work do exist. Sudhira, Ramachandra and Jagadish (2003) used remote sensing and GIS to understand the pattern and sprawl of the city of Udipi in the Mangalore region of India. They used standard image processing techniques such as image extraction, rectification, restoration, and classification in the study. They found that the rate of development of land in Udipi was outstripping the rate of population growth, which implied that the land was being consumed at excessive rates. Between 1972 and 1999, population in the region grew by about 54 per cent (Census of India, 1971, 1981, 1991), while the amount of developed land grew by about 146 per cent (Sudhira *et al.*, 2004).

Venugopal and Turcotte (1993) used IRS-1AISS1 satellite data transformed through principal component analysis to classify what was then the Calcutta Metropolitan District into five generalised land use/land cover (LULC) categories. They mapped high, medium and low density built-up areas for the district. Two other studies in 2009 (Taubenbock *et al.*, 2009; Bhatta 2009) used Landsat and Indian Remote Sensing images to perform spatiotemporal analyses and divide Kolkata city into density zones.

Some of the other cities of India that have been the focus of studies employing GIS techniques and remote sensing include Ahmedabad, Surat and Vadodara (Jothimani, 1997), Vadodara (Bhatt *et al.*, 2006), Dhanbad

(Srivastava, 2000), Hyderabad (Lata *et al.*, 2001), Bhopal (Saxena, 2003), and Allahabad (Srivastava and Gupta, 2003). This review highlights the value of using cartographic and geographic information sciences in studying urban growth and sprawl, eventually aiding in policy-framing exercises. It also highlights the need for an objective and quantitative study of Kolkata, a fast-developing city with historical evidence of incessant unplanned growth of populace due to various political and social issues. This study can be an ideal case study for future studies with similar conditions.

Research Objectives

The overarching objective of this study is to quantify the extent of urban sprawl in the city of Kolkata and to reveal how the city has developed in the past 300 years, despite natural and human induced barriers. The first objective is to delineate the growth of the city and the extent of urban sprawl through an analysis of historical maps and satellite images. The second objective is to place Kolkata's urban growth within the context of different factors that have contributed to this population explosion and moulded its growth – the natural and political factors that have profoundly influenced the sprawl in the twentieth century will be highlighted. The third objective is to analyse the short-term and long-term impact of uncontrolled urban growth on the local and regional climatic patterns of Kolkata. This would also aid future studies on the subject. The article also features some examples showing how LULC changes have occurred over the decades due to population pressure.

Data Sets

The maps and images used to delineate the urban growth of Kolkata are historical paper maps, Landsat images (1990 and 2000) and topographical maps. Of the Landsat images, the first is a Landsat TM image dated 14th November 1990. It is a World Reference System 2 (WRS 2) image and the path and row are 138 and 044, respectively. The second image is a Landsat ETM satellite image dated 17th November 2000. It is also a WRS 2 image and the path and row are 138 and 044, respectively.

In addition to these two images, a historical paper map (scale 1:100,000) of Kolkata city showing the growth of the city from before 1756 to 1990 was used (NATMO, 1996). Two topographical maps accessed from

Survey of India (scale 1:50,000, Nos. 79 B/6 and 79 B/7), showing Kolkata city and adjoining areas were also used.

Methodology

In this study, traditional cartographic sources like paper maps were employed because no existing digitized historical maps of Kolkata were available. The results from digitization were validated by remotely sensed images from recent years. The topographical maps and the city growth map were both paper maps, so the first step was to scan the maps and obtain them in digital form. The scanned topographical maps were then rectified with the base paper maps using latitude/longitude coordinates found along the margins of the maps. The two topographical maps were mosaiced together to have a larger view of the area.

The Kolkata urban sprawl map did not have any coordinates, so it had to be georeferenced to the topographical map. For this process, 16 ground control points were chosen on both maps to georeference one to the other using Leica Geosystems Imagine 9.1 software. To facilitate further analysis, all data sets had to be precisely registered and transformed into the same coordinate system. The historical growth map was based on geographic coordinates and was transformed to Universal Transverse Mercator (UTM) grid-system coordinates. The growth map and the Landsat images could not be overlaid to compare urban growth without the same coordinates, therefore the images were also transformed from geographic coordinates to UTM coordinates using the ArcGIS 9.1 software. After all the transformations were complete, the study area lay in the UTM system, Zone 45 N and was cast on the World Geodetic System (WGS)-84 datum.

All the maps used in the analysis were published as paper products, so none of the features of interest had been previously digitized. The extent of growth in the city was delineated using heads-up digitizing methods from the urban growth map and Landsat images using the ArcGIS 9.1 software. Although the process of digitization was very time-consuming and difficult, it was necessary to reveal the phases of growth in different time frames, beginning from before 1756 to 1990. The result was a unique view of the growth history of Kolkata over this time period (Figs. 29.2A,B,C).

The next step was to overlay the digitized maps onto the satellite images to further digitize the map and detect the changes in the growth

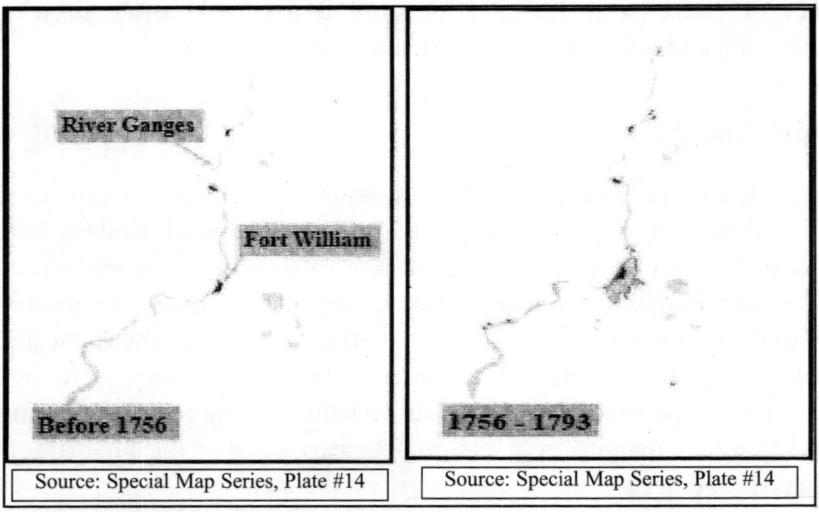

Fig. 29.2A Digitized Map of Kolkata Showing Urban Growth: Before 1756–1793.

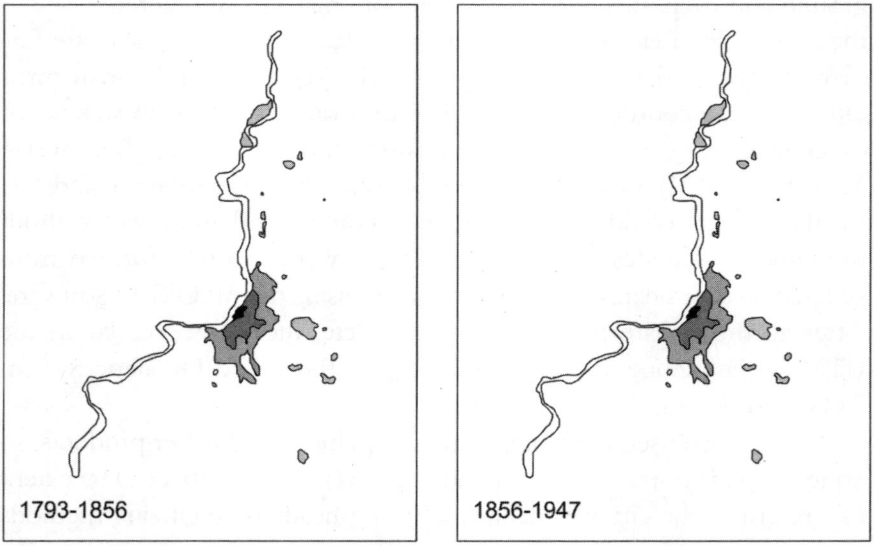

Fig. 29.2B Digitized Map of Kolkata Showing Urban Growth: 1793–1947.

pattern between 1990 and 2000. The overlaying of the digitized growth map over the 2000 satellite image showed an extension in area from the 1990 urban sprawl. An unsupervised classification of the image was done on the 2000 image, but the results were not completely satisfactory. Since the unsupervised classification did not yield the desired result, a portion

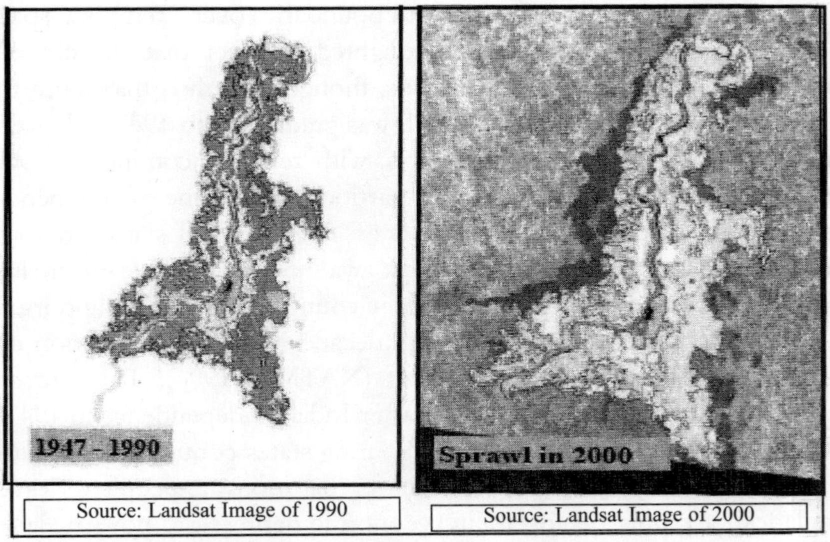

Fig. 29.2C Digitized Map of Kolkata Showing Urban Growth: 1947–2000.

of the digitization was done based on visual interpretation. The areal extent of the city in different phases was calculated post-digitization, using the attribute table of ArcGIS 9.1 software.

Results and Discussion: Growth Factors and Patterns

A major factor contributing to the influx of millions of refugees across the border was India's independence from British colonial rule in 1947. Many refugees from East Pakistan settled in the Calcutta Metropolitan area on whichever plots of land were available, without regard to planning or other regulations. Another factor contributing to the urban sprawl was the influx of people from the surrounding non-urban and less developed areas into the city (Roy, 2003). Kolkata is the most important city as compared to other cities in eastern India. It has become the target city for east India and a source of financial advancement for many people. Population growth and the drive for economic development have led to unplanned and sporadic expansion of the mega city. Kolkata, from the days of its inception, was never a planned city. It grew haphazardly around the port, the old fort and the ancient *Barabazar* market by the river (Dutta, 2003). However, little research has been done to measure the extent of damage done by the unprecedented urban sprawl.

The digitization of the urban growth boundaries over a temporal span of approximately 300 years has highlighted the fact that the city of Kolkata has spread out in all directions, though growth is maximum to the east of River Hooghly. The growth was gradual up to 1947, followed immediately by a population explosion, with refugees coming in from Bangladesh due to the India-Pakistan partition at the time of independence of the two countries. The influx of migrants had started before independence, as people were somewhat aware of the possible aftermath of the post-independence partition of the country. This fact is supported by the census data for the 1931–1941 decade when the population of Kolkata city increased by 77 per cent (NATMO, 1996). The rate of increase of population became faster after India's independence in 1947.

People from Bangladesh and neighbouring states continue to settle in Kolkata even today. The economic factors that motivate people to leave Bangladesh are political instability, economic depression, poverty, lack of employment opportunities, struggle for livelihood, forced grabbing of landed property from minority groups, social insecurity, and lack of industrialization (Datta, 2004).

The city grew more or less naturally and gradually till 1947, though the influx of refugees had already started from the 1930s. After 1947 the city suddenly burst out in all directions, reflecting the sudden increase in the population and thus, in the city limits.

Table 29.1 shows the growth in area from the beginning of the 1700s to the year 2000. The striking feature to be seen in the calculations is the change in area after 1947. This agrees with the previous findings regarding the influx of refugees in huge numbers just before and after Indian independence in 1947. There was a threefold increase in the area of the city during this time span around Indian independence. The yearly spatial growth was also high (23.30 square kilometres or approximately 9.0

Table 29.1 Change in area of Kolkata over years in sq. km.

Year	*Total Area (sq. km)*	*Change in Area (sq. km)*	*Area Change/Year (sq.km)*
Before 1756	3.46		
1756–1793	33.57	30.11	0.8137
1793–1856	135.88	102.31	1.6239
1856–1947	361.27	225.39	2.4768
1947–1990	1363.36	1002.09	23.3044
1990–2000	1658.12	294.76	29.476

square miles) up to 1990. Further, it can be seen that the yearly growth of the city limits did not slow down even in the next decade (1990–2000) – it was a high 29.47 square kilometres (11.38 square miles) each year. This demonstrates that the city continued to grow fairly rapidly, in fact, at an even higher rate than before. Figures 29.2 A, B and C are a graphical representation of Table 29.1.

During the last two decades, the population of the city of Kolkata has only been growing at the slow rate of 2 per cent per decade. In contrast, the Kolkata Metropolitan District (KMD), which includes the rural tracts and townships that ring the city, has been expanding spatially at a decadal rate of over 18 per cent (Census of India, 1991; Roy, 2003). This information is alarming enough for the government and planners to think and rethink the magnitude of damage such a high rate of expansion could have on the overall environment of the city.

The authorities have overlooked the possible environmental degradation that might set in due to the gradual filling up of the city's wetlands in the east. Some of the fastest growth is occurring on the eastern fringes of the KMD. This involves state-controlled developments, such as Salt Lake City and the proposed New Kolkata at Rajarhat, as well as a flurry of private building activities, especially in the sphere of middle-class housing (Roy, 2003). The Salt Lake City (India), a satellite town east of Kolkata developed by the government in 1960s, was a 15 sq. km. (5.8 sq. mile) stretch of wetland that is now being transformed into a concrete jungle. It took approximately seven years to fill this wet zone with sand. Five-mile long pipes were laid down to transport the sand and silt from Ghushuri to Salt Lake. It now supports a population of 167,848 (Census of India, 2001). Additionally, unplanned development in the southeastern part of Kolkata is expanding, gradually drying the wetland areas.

Future Research

The buildings, concrete, asphalt, and the human and industrial activity in urban areas cause cities to maintain higher temperatures than their surrounding countryside. This phenomenon of increased heat is known as an urban heat island. It is known that the air in an urban heat island can be as much as two to ten degrees higher than rural areas surrounding the city (Shepherd, 2005). The roughness of the urban buildings and urban pollution also contribute to the higher temperatures in the cities. The urban heat island effect, in turn, affects the microclimate of the city and causes the intensity of rainfall to change in and around the city (Shepherd, 2005).

It is apparent that as unplanned and unrestrained development occurs in cities, the environmental health of the cities will deteriorate. But, unless appropriate steps are taken, there will be no other option left but to continue living in those deleterious conditions. The prospect of continued growth in Kolkata raises a number of serious questions about urban growth in general and Kolkata in particular as related to environment. For example, what happens to city micro-climates when built-up areas increase in a city? What will happen to Kolkata in the future? Will urban growth (spread) affect the environment? Will the uncontrolled growth and land use change of Kolkata have any impact on the precipitation in and around the city?

Further research can help answer these questions and also improve the general living conditions of the city of Kolkata. Our ongoing research will encompass the projection of the future growth of Kolkata in the next 25 years, using the CA-Markov model, a cellular automata model inbuilt in Idrisi Taiga software (see Eastman 2003). The model charts urban growth through the analysis of rasterized maps representing land use/cover change. This will help to foresee the areas where the pressure of growth will be greater. Planning of the city can be done on the lines of this projection, so that there is uniformity in development.

The results from the CA-Markov model will then be fed into the Weather Research and Forecasting (WRF) model to see if climate variables such as precipitation will increase or decrease around the city due to this undaunted urban growth. The study will involve an analysis of hundred years of rainfall data from weather stations in and around Kolkata. The results from this study will examine how urban growth affects climate, and will contribute to original research in this area.

Abbreviations

1. Landsat – Derived from Land Satellite.
2. SPOT – Satellite Pour l'Observation de la Terre
3. IRS – Indian Remote Sensing Satellite
4. HRSC-A – High Resolution Stereo Camera Airborne
5. LIDAR – Light Detection and Ranging

References

Barba, C. V. C. and L. B. Rabuco, 'Overview of Ageing, Urbanization, and Nutrition in Developing Countries and the Development of the Reconnaissance Project', *Food and Nutrition Bulletin*, Vol. 18, No. 3, 1997. *Source*: http://www.unu.edu/unupress/food/V183e/ch03.htm, (last accessed on 25 August, 2007).

Bhatt, B., A. K. Gupta and G. Gogoi, 'Application of Remote Sensing and GIS for Detecting Land Use Changes: A Case Study of Vadodara' 2006. *Source*: http://www.gisdevelopment.net/application/urban/sprawl/remotesensing.htm, (last accessed on 14 September, 2007).

Bhatta, B., Analysis of urban growth pattern using remote sensing and GIS: a case study of Kolkata, India. *International Journal of Remote Sensing*, Vol. 30, No. 18, 2009, 4733–4746.

Chakraborty, S. C., 'The growth of Calcutta in the Twentieth Century', in S. Chaudhuri (ed.), *Calcutta: The Living City*, Calcutta: Oxford University Press, 1990, pp. 1–14.

Chatterjee, M., 'Town Planning in Calcutta: Past, Present and Future' in S. Chaudhuri (ed.), *Calcutta: The Living City*, Calcutta: Oxford University Press, 1990, pp. 137–147.

Datta, P. 'Push-pull Factors of Undocumented Migration from Bangladesh to West Bengal: A Perception Study', *The Qualitative Report*, Vol. 9, No. 2, 2004, pp. 335–358.

De Almeida, C. M., A. M. V. Monteiro, G. Câmara, B. S. Soares-Filho, G. C. Cerqueira, C. L. Pennachin and M. Batty, 'GIS and Remote Sensing as Tools for the Simulation of Urban Land-use Change', *International Journal of Remote Sensing*, Vol. 26, 2005, pp. 759–774.

Dutt, Ashok K. and M. Margaret Geib, *Fully Annotated Atlas of South Asia*, Boulder and London: Westview Press, Inc., 1987.

Dutt, A. K., D'Sa Gerardine and C. B. Monroe, 'Factorial Ecology of Calcutta (1981) Revisited', *Geo Journal*, Vol. 18, No. 2, 1989, pp. 151–162.

Dutta, K., *Calcutta: A Cultural and Literal History*, New York: Interlink Books, 2003.

Eastman, J. R., Idrisi Kilimanjaro. Clark University. Massachusetts, 2003.

Elvidge, C. D., K. E. Baugh, J. B. Dietz, T. Bland, P. C. Sutton and H. W. Kroehl, 'Radiance Calibration of DMSP-OLS Low Light Imaging Data of Human Settlements', *Remote Sensing of Environment*, Vol. 68, No. 1, 1998, pp. 77–88.

Heiden, U., S. Rossner and K. Segl, 'Potential of Hyperspectral HYMAP Data for Material Oriented Identification of Urban Surfaces', in the Proceedings of the *Second International Symposium on Remote Sensing of Urban Areas, Regensburg, Germany*, 22–23 June, 2001 CD ROM, C. Jurgens (ed.), Regensburger Geographische Schriften, 35, (Regensburg: Selbstverlag), pp. 69–77.

Jothimani, P., 'Operational Urban Sprawl Monitoring Using Satellite Remote Sensing: Excerpts from the Studies of Ahmedabad, Vadodara and Surat, India', *Eighteenth Asian Conference on Remote Sensing*, Malaysia, 20–24 October, 1997.

Kolkata postal codes. *Source*: http://www.bloom9.com/info/postal_codes.asp, (last accessed on 28 August, 2007).

KMDA Annual Report 2005. *Source*: http://www.cmdaonline.com/profile.html, (last accessed on 14 January, 2008).

Lata, K. M., C. H. Sankar Rao, V. Krishna Prasad, K. V. S. Badrinath and V. Raghavaswamy, 'Measuring Urban Sprawl: A Case Study of Hyderabad', *GIS Development*, Vol. 5, No. 12, 2001.

Maktav, D., F. S. Erbek and C. Jurgens, 'Remote Sensing of Urban Areas', *International Journal of Remote Sensing*, Vol. 26, 2005, pp. 655–659.

Meij, H., 'Integrated Datasets for the USA', Consortium for International Earth, Science Information Network, 1995.

National Atlas and Thematic Mapping Organisation (NATMO), *Kolkata: Atlas of the City of Calcutta and its Environs*, NATMO, Ministry of Science and Technology, Government of India. Second edition, 1996.

Roy, A. C., *Calcutta and Environs; A Comprehensive Guidebook of the City of Calcutta & its Suburbs*, Calcutta: Lake Publishers, 1996.

Roy, A., *City Requiem, Calcutta: Gender and the Politics of Poverty*, University of Minneapolis Press, 2003.

Saxena, A., 'Remote Sensing & GIS in Assessing Physical Transformation of Bhopal City, India', Map Asia 2003, Kuala Lumpur, Malaysia, 13–15 October 2003.

Shepherd, J. M., 'A Review of Current Investigations of Urban-induced Rainfall and Recommendations for the Future', *Earth Interactions*, Vol. 9, No. 12, 2005, pp. 1–27.

Small, C., 'A Global Analysis of Urban Reflectance', *International Journal of Remote Sensing*, Vol. 26, 2005, pp. 661–681.

Srivastava, S. K. and R. D. Gupta, 'Monitoring of Changes in Land Use/land Cover using Multi-sensor Satellite Data', 2003. *Source*: http://www.gisdevelopment.net/technology/rs/mi03109.htm, (last accessed on 10 September, 2007).

Srivastava, V. K., 'Application of Remote Sensing and GIS Techniques in Monitoring of Urban Sprawl in and around Jharia Coalfields (Dhanbad)', 2000. *Source*: http://www.gisdevelopment.net/application/urban/sprawl/urbans0002.htm, (last accessed on 14 September, 2007).

Sudhira, H. S., T. V. Ramachandra and K. S. Jagadish, 'Urban Sprawl: Metrics and Modelling Using GIS', *International Journal of Applied Earth Observation and Geoinformation*, Vol. 5, 2004, pp. 29–39.

Survey of India, Surveyor General's Office, Post Box No. 37, Dehra Dun – 248001. *Source*: http://www.surveyofindia.gov.in, (last accessed on 9 September, 2007).

Sutton, C. P., 'A Scale Adjusted Measure of "Urban Sprawl" Using Nighttime Satellite Imagery', *Remote Sensing of Environment*, Vol. 86, 2003, pp. 353–369.

Taubenböck, H., Wegmann, M., Roth, A., Mehl, H.,Dech, S., Urbanization in India – Spatiotemporal analysis using remote sensing data. *Computers, Environment and Urban Systems*. 3(33), 2009, 179–188.

The Weather Research and Forecasting Mode. *Source*: http://www.wrf-model.org/index.php, (last accessed on 14 September, 2007).

Venugopal, G. and Kevin M. Turcotte, 'Land Use/Cover Classification Using Enhanced IRS-1ALISS1 Data – A Case Study of Calcutta Metropolitan District, India – 1989', *GeoJournal*, Special issue, guest edited by Ashok K. Dutt, *et al.*, Vol. 29, No. 2, 1993, pp. 139–141.

World Association of Metropolises, 'Metropolis', 2005. *Source*: http://www.metropolis.org/ upload/file/438_007_kolkata_eng.pdf, (last accessed on 7 September, 2007).

Zhou, G. and M. Kafatos. Future intelligent earth observing satellites, Pecora 15/Land Satellite Information IV/ISPRS Commission I/FIEOS 2002 Conference Proceedings.

30

Socioeconomic and Demographic Conditions of the Slums of Hyderabad[1]

KALPANA MARKANDEY, V. VIJAY KUMAR AND KAVITA TORAN

Slums and squatter settlements are an essential facet of the urban landscape of most countries, more so that of the developing countries. They are also somewhat of a paradox in themselves. They are both: (i) a manifestation of urban poverty, and (ii) a reflection of the economic pull of urban areas. The definition of a slum varies from country to country, depending on the cultural mores and economic conditions. Slums are residential areas of least choice, characterized by dilapidated houses, poor ventilation, inadequate lighting, poor sanitation, lack of clean drinking water, overcrowding, convoluted street patterns, fire and flood hazards, poor facilities for education and health, unhygienic living conditions causing air and waterborne diseases. Socially, they are characterized by drug abuse, alcoholism, crime, vandalism, escapism, apathy and social isolation (Haggett *et al.*, 1981; Census of India, 2001). In India, slums have been defined under Section 3 of the Slum Areas (Improvement and Clearance) Act, 1956, as areas where buildings are unfit for human habitation by reason of dilapidation, overcrowding, faulty arrangement and design of such buildings, narrowness or faulty arrangement of streets, lack of ventilation, light, sanitation facilities or any combination of these factors which are detrimental to safety, health and morals.

Census of India 2001 has adopted the definition of 'Slum' areas as follows: (i) All areas notified as 'Slum' by State/Local Government or Union Territory Administration under any Act, (ii) All areas recognized as 'Slum' by State/Local Government or Union Territory Administration which have not been formally notified as slum under any Act, and (iii) A compact area inhibited by at least 300 people or about 60–70 households inhabiting poorly built congested tenements in an unhygienic environment, usually with inadequate infrastructure, and lacking in proper sanitary and drinking water facilities (Census of India, 2001).

Squatter settlements, which are often similar to slums in their physical appearance, lack basic amenities and are a concentration of dwellings built on land neither owned nor rented by the squatters (builders). These settlements develop by organized invasion, by gradual accretion or by government initiation. They are a dominant feature in urban areas of Asia, Latin America, and Africa and have high rates of in-migration from traditional inner-city dwellings and from rural areas. They are, therefore, regarded as transitional urban settlements. The United Nations has suggested that they should be encouraged as architecture that works, as it is cheaper to provide services to the squatters *in situ* rather than to initiate clearance and public housing construction programmes (Haggett, *et al.*, 1981). Thus, while the term 'slum' refers to the environmental aspects of an area, 'squatter' refers to the legality of land ownership and infrastructure. While slums take up the old settled central city locations, squatters are usually found on the periphery of the city. Squatters are also known as spontaneous settlements or shanty towns as they come up without notice and grow in an uncontrolled way. They also lack in service provision. They are the transitional areas at the fringe of urban areas that act as reception zones for the migrants where they find a semblance of both the rural and urban life and hence ease in adaptation. They are perceived as 'slums of hope' rather than of 'despair' as they can develop social and communal organization and services through self-help and government action (Yeates and Garner, 1971; Haggett *et al.*, 1981).

According to Srinivas (n.d.). the "Encyclopaedia Britannica defines slums as '... residential areas that are physically and socially deteriorated and in which satisfactory family life is impossible. Bad housing is a major index of slum conditions. By bad housing is meant dwellings that have inadequate light, air, toilet and bathing facilities; that are in bad repair, damp and improperly heated; that do not afford opportunity for family privacy; that are subject to fire hazard and that overcrowd the land, leaving no space for recreational use...'. Therefore, while a slum settlement refers to the condition of a settlement; squatter settlement would refer to the legal position of the settlement. There are a number of names by which various authors describe squatter settlements. These names highlight the attitudes and approaches towards them, ranging from a positive to neutral to negative outlook. These are – informal settlements, low-income settlements, semi-permanent settlements, shanty towns, spontaneous settlements, unauthorized settlements, unplanned settlements and uncontrolled settlements."

Literature Review on Slum Research in India

Dutt, Mitra and Halder (1997) while studying slums of Calcutta have reviewed a number of slum studies of India. The following quotation is taken from their study (p. 413–414):

> Literature on the growth, general situation and the nature of Indian slums are many. Housing shortage caused by poverty, under employment, mismanagement and financial constraints, lead to slum formation (Dewit and Schenk, 1989, p. 8). Slums are places of greatest deprivation in urban areas; about '90% of the structures in all size classes of Indian cities do not have separate latrines' and '34% in large cities are exposed to flooding during monsoon period' (Nangia, 1988, pp. 135–136). It is the constant flow of migrants from the rural areas that adds to the rapid swelling of urban slum population. To Yadav it is the perceived differences between places that are important rather than 'pull' mechanism because as long as rural migrants perceived that urban places have more opportunities, there will be 'a greater volume of migration from rural to urban areas' (Yadav, 1989, p. 228). To Nath, however, the cause of rural/urban migration is 'large differences in productivity and income between the rural and urban workers' (Nath, 1994, p. 305.). The rural workers are enmeshed in low productivity agriculture while the urban workforce is engaged either in secondary or tertiary activities, where the earnings are relatively higher. Katyal concurs with Nath as he argues that the phenomenal growth of Delhi slums in the recent years is the result of better employment and infrastructural facilities (Katyal, 1988). Religion, language, caste and kinship (relatives in particular) ties form the bases of attraction for slum settlement and community formation (Dutt, Tripathi and Mukhopadhyay, 1994, p. 210).

Slum dwellers in India are constrained by lack of upward or vertical economic mobility. This, however, was not the case with the European migrants to the cities in the United States as a large number of these migrants settled in the central cities, primarily in the poor slum-like habitat. With the subsequent improvement in economic status, they moved to the peripheries and suburbs for better housing. In terms of horizontal or spatial mobility, in a study of the activity patterns of slum dwellers of

Kolkata and Delhi, it was found that daily shopping for perishable goods results in the least distance travelled, whereas slum dwellers travel much longer distances for occasional recreation. For daily work they travel greater distances than daily shopping but lesser distance than occasional recreation. There is always an overall critical distance limit for each activity because a slum dweller doesn't travel beyond this limit (Dutt, Tripathi and Mukhopadhyay, 1994).

Sita points out that the slums of Mumbai are growing rapidly because the conventional supply of housing is so low that it is unaffordable to a very large number of people. She points out that as a consequence:

> 40,000–50,000 new temporary structures tend to spring up annually on available land [in Mumbai]. This has resulted in the proliferation of slums. By 1991, fifty percent of the population of the city resided in slums. The squatter settlement became a very visible symbol of a major problem facing the city (Sita, 2007, pp. 430–431).

Multi-Dimensionality of Slums

Slums are multi-dimensional entities, and the socioeconomic and demographic facets are parts of this complex multi-faceted mosaic; the following dimensions are taken from Markandey (2007). They have a *structural dimension*, where they are out of harmony with the surrounding areas from a structural viewpoint. While on the one hand cities boast of mansions and skyscrapers, on the other side there are the densely packed, low-built, single room, tin-roofed tenements that constitute the slums. They have the cheapest available building materials and the houses are usually put together by the residents themselves, giving them a disorganized and irregular look so far as the juxtaposition of the structures is concerned. They have distinct physical problems, like open drainage system, apathy in disposal of garbage, unsanitary conditions, washing clothes and vessels in open places, narrow lanes and by-lanes, innumerable dead-ends, etc.

Slums are quite crowded and display a distinct *demographic dimension* of (i) in-migration and consequent over-crowding, with implicit high densities, (ii) low dependency ratios as even the children are engaged in gainful employment, (iii) low sex ratios, as the immigrants to the slums are mainly males who have left their families in the rural areas, and (iv) a youthful population as most of the migrants are in the working age group. Migrants to slums may be from other slums, rural areas, and other urban areas.

Social or human problems associated with this demographic dimension include lack of privacy, almost impinging on the space of each other, and a related sense of insecurity. The occasional brawls that ensue may lead to law and order problems at times. The fragile socioeconomic conditions can lead to a higher vulnerability of slum population to indulge in petty crimes and take refuge in the 'politically secure' environment of the dense, impenetrable population clusters of almost homogenous groups of people.

This reflects the not so concealed *social dimension* of the slums, where they are often known as havens for criminals who can take refuge in the anonymity and size of the population. They can also become the breeding ground for criminals, as those who are out of employment may resort to petty crimes and gradually graduate to bigger ones. The residents are also supposed to constitute the underdogs of society and socially ostracized groups. They are the shadow zones of urban existence where poverty and crime, aesthetic pollution, apart from other types of pollution, disease and deprivation co-exist.

Slums also have an unmistakable *spatial or locational dimension* and are in close proximity to such land-uses as industries, contact zones with commercial land use, quarry pits, river beds and banks, tank beds, lakes and other water bodies, ill-drained hollows, railway sidings, workshops, cemeteries, slaughter houses, wholesale markets, timber yards, etc. They are thus areas of least choice in a locational context. They also exert pressure on the amenities and facilities in the city like water, sewage disposal, garbage disposal, electricity, and roads.

The slums also have an *economic dimension.* They provide the essential labour pool for the industrial and commercial sectors of the cities, not to speak of the service sector, which includes working as domestic help. While slums provide the essential labour requirements of the city, they also strain the employment potential and available sources of employment in the city. Thus, they also prompt the growth of the informal sector of the economy when the formal sector is not able to accommodate the employment requirements of the immigrants. Reliance of slum dwellers on informal retail (street vending), informal industry (home-based crafts), and informal finance (money lending) is not uncommon. The slum population is also the most marginalized on the economic front. Some of them survive on a shoe-string budget and live a hand-to-mouth existence, though cases of relative prosperity hidden in an ocean of poverty cannot be ruled out. However, generally the slum population lives close to, or below the poverty line.

The *political dimension* of the slums should not be overlooked also as they are an effective vote bank, and hence of interest to politicians. They also provide a grooming arena for petty political leaders.

Slums also have a typical *behavioural dimension.* Slum dwellers have certain distinguishable habits and traits like chewing tobacco, smoking, drinking, and gambling. It does not mean that these traits are absent in the rest of the population. However, they seem more manifest in the slum population as the slum dwellers need some form of relaxation after a hard day at work. Slum dwellers are a more cohesive society compared to the rest of the population of the city. They are far removed from the 'anonymity and transiency syndrome' associated with the behavioural pattern of the urban population. The very concept of a slum, however, is an evaluative one rather than an analytical one. Hence, what is considered a slum in one cultural setting is just an adequate housing facility in another.

So far as the semantics are concerned, slums have positive as well as negative connotations. The negative bias in the definition of slums regards them as a rash on the landscape, a blot on civilization or a cancer of the cityscape. Positive exemplification of slums is where they are regarded as a component of a city's evolution, an element of the urban complex, a transitional settlement or a facet of subsistence urbanization.

Methodology

An attempt is made in this study to sieve out the demographic profile of the slum dwellers of Hyderabad – a city teeming with a population of 6.14 million. There are 811 notified slums in Hyderabad apart from about 450 squatter settlements. Data for this study were acquired through a detailed questionnaire. The field surveyors visited all the 811 notified slums of Hyderabad and acquired data pertaining to the historical aspects of slums, their demographic profile, economic profile, infrastructure facilities, and the developmental schemes being implemented. These data were acquired from community elders, non-governmental organization workers, as also the slum leaders. All three categories of respondents are well acquainted with the conditions in their respective slum. The response of each one of them more or less matched with the others. In case of ambiguous responses, the ground reality was obtained from the slum dwellers. However, such instances were very rare. Some of the demographic variables obtained by this method were compared with demographic data obtained from the Municipal Corporation of Hyderabad and a total synchrony was found between the two sets of data.

The data for individual slums were aggregated at the municipal block level. Values of certain variables reflect the computed conditions of slums. There have, however, been gaps in the data since information for some variables for some slums could not be collected. The raw data for each slum was entered in a set format in MS Excel and aggregated on the basis of the Municipal Ward and Block in which it was located. The values of the chosen variables were computed and converted to DBF (database file) format to link it with the coverage prepared in Arc Info 3.5.1, and eventually converted to shape files in Arc GIS Arc View 9.0.

The data from the slum survey, which was tabulated in an Excel format, was attached to the ESRI shape files of Municipal Wards and Blocks in order to generate choropleth maps pertaining to this data. This brought certain demographic and economic characteristics of the slum dwellers in focus and had spatial connotations which made it fit within the various theoretical models.

Findings

Slum residents are found in pockets all over the city (Fig. 30.1). A large chunk of such areas in the northwestern part of the city is associated with the presence of upper class residences, specifically in the Banjara and Jubilee Hills localities. The slum dwellers obviously find employment doing all manner of jobs for the people of these localities.

The southern part of the city also has a large slum population in these old residential quarters of the city, an area largely steeped in poverty where people eke out a living by engaging in the informal service or retail sector as roadside motor mechanics, pushcart vendors, etc. The part to the east of Hussain Sagar Lake in north Hyderabad is an area with a large concentration of middle and upper middle class residences as also the main commercial quarters of the city, where a majority of the slum dwellers find ready employment in the informal sector in commercial establishments as well as homes.

A study of the growth rates of slum population based on the formula given below shows the average annual per cent increase or decrease in population:

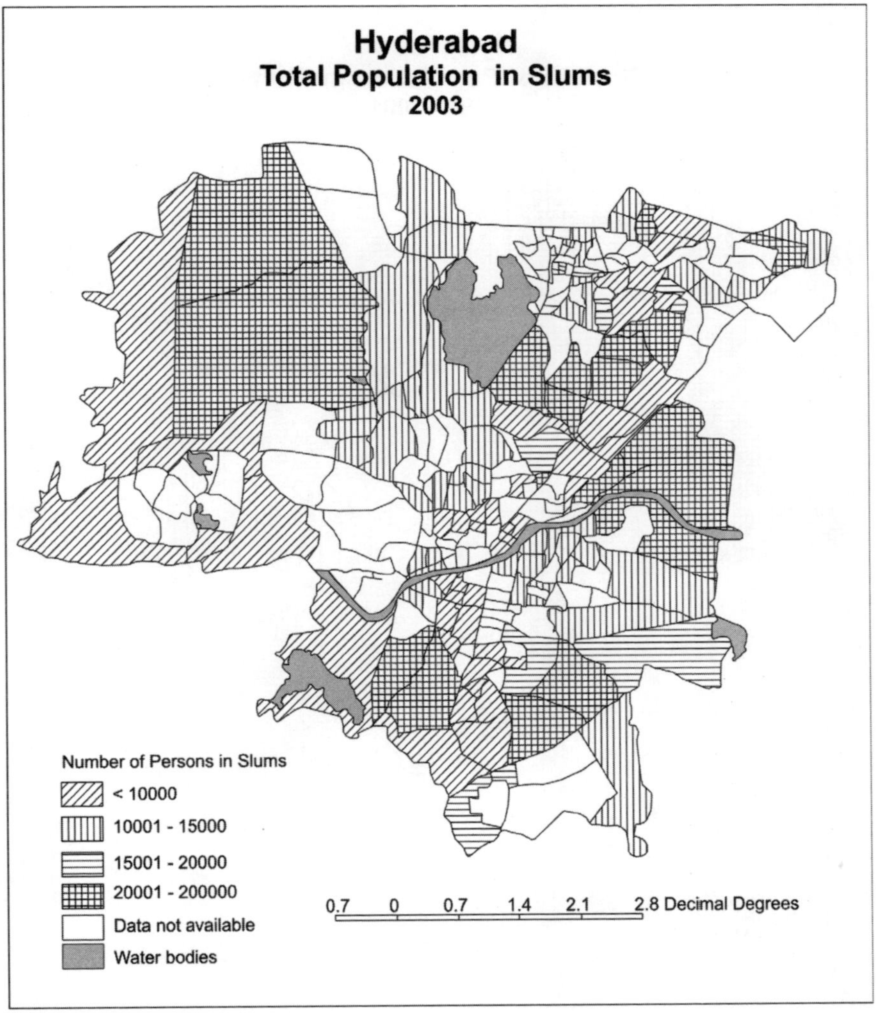

Fig. 30.1 Total Population in the Slums of Hyderabad, 2003.

$$\text{Growth Rate} = \frac{P2 - P1/t}{P2 + P1/t} \times 100 \quad \text{where}$$

P1 is population at 1st time period and P2 is population at 2nd time period

The growth rates are categorized on the basis of natural breaks in the data and has been represented in Figure 30.2. While negative growth (a decrease in population) is witnessed in some pockets in close proximity to the Central Business Distinct of Hyderabad and Secunderabad in

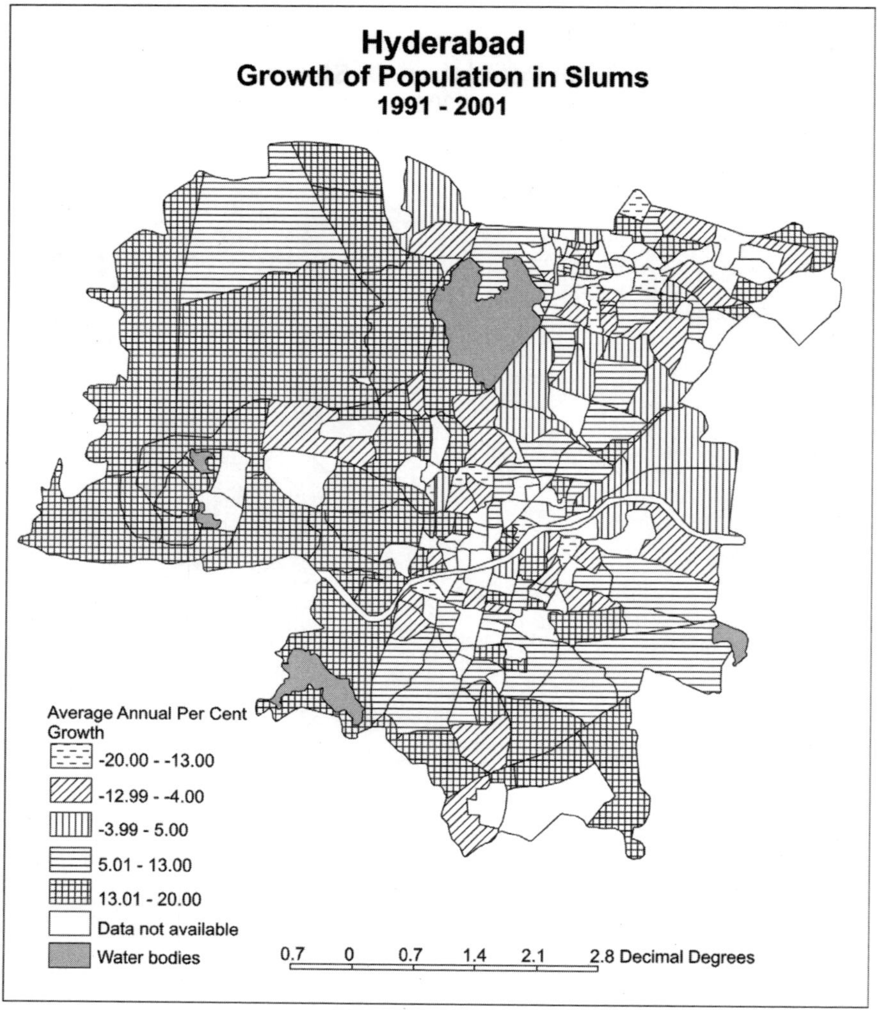

Fig. 30.2 Growth of Population in the Slums of Hyderabad, 1991–2001.

1981–1991, these pockets seem to have grown in number and spread far and wide all over the city in 1991–2001. This spatial pattern of the slum population may be a reflection of the larger pattern that prevails in the city in its entirety. This is a reflection of the development of an 'urban crater' effect, that is a decline in the central city population due to lack of migration to those areas, as they are already saturated and display high population densities. On the other hand, the areas of highest growth rate of slum population spanned a wide stretch in the western part of the city in 1981–91; in 1991–2001 the 'very high' category with regard to growth rate seemed to have retracted to smaller pockets spread all over the city. Density of slum population is either high in areas of low growth rate, as for example, Golconda on the extreme western tip of Hyderabad, where a pre-existing high density masks any increase in population, which is registered as a miniscule proportion in relation to an existing high base of population; or density is also high in areas in the core of the city, in close proximity to the commercial establishments, where the slum dwellers find employment in the informal sector.

The density of slum population is also high in the upcoming commercial areas – Somajiguda to the west of Hussain Sagar Lake, Sanatnagar in the northwest which is an industrial area, and Lalapet and Lalaguda in the northeast, which are railway colonies (Fig. 30.3). High slum densities are thus found to be coterminous with sources and places of employment.

The proportion of males is less and hence by implication females outnumber males in some of the old settled traditional parts of the city like Saidabad and Madannapet in the southeast, Red Hills and Mallepally in the central western part, and Himayatnagar, Narayanguda, Nallakunta, etc. in the central eastern part of the city. Gandhinagar and Bholakpur to the northeast of Hussain Sagar Tank also display this tendency. These areas also display a high to very high sex ratio. On the other hand, sex ratio is very low in Mehdipatnam in the southwest and in small quarters spread all over the rest of the city. Although the distribution of low sex ratio defies a spatial pattern, it is clearly not found in South Hyderabad, which is a more tradition-bound society. A low sex ratio, which is related to male dominant immigrant streams, is almost absent in South Hyderabad where the slums seem to represent a balanced distribution.

A look at Figure 30.4 reveals that in most instances a majority of the slum dwellers are workers. This is the dominant trend in the western, central, and southeastern parts of the city. A high proportion of workers is also a reflection of a lower dependency ratio. In some pockets of South Hyderabad the proportion of male workers is inordinately high in comparision to the pattern of distribution of female workers. Though large parts of the city seem to have a proportion of female workers in the range of 0 to 20 per cent, their proportion is 40 to 60 per cent of the total female population in slums in the western area of the city (Fig. 30.5). This is an upcoming area of the city. A lot of construction activity is taking place in and around this area as new residential colonies are coming

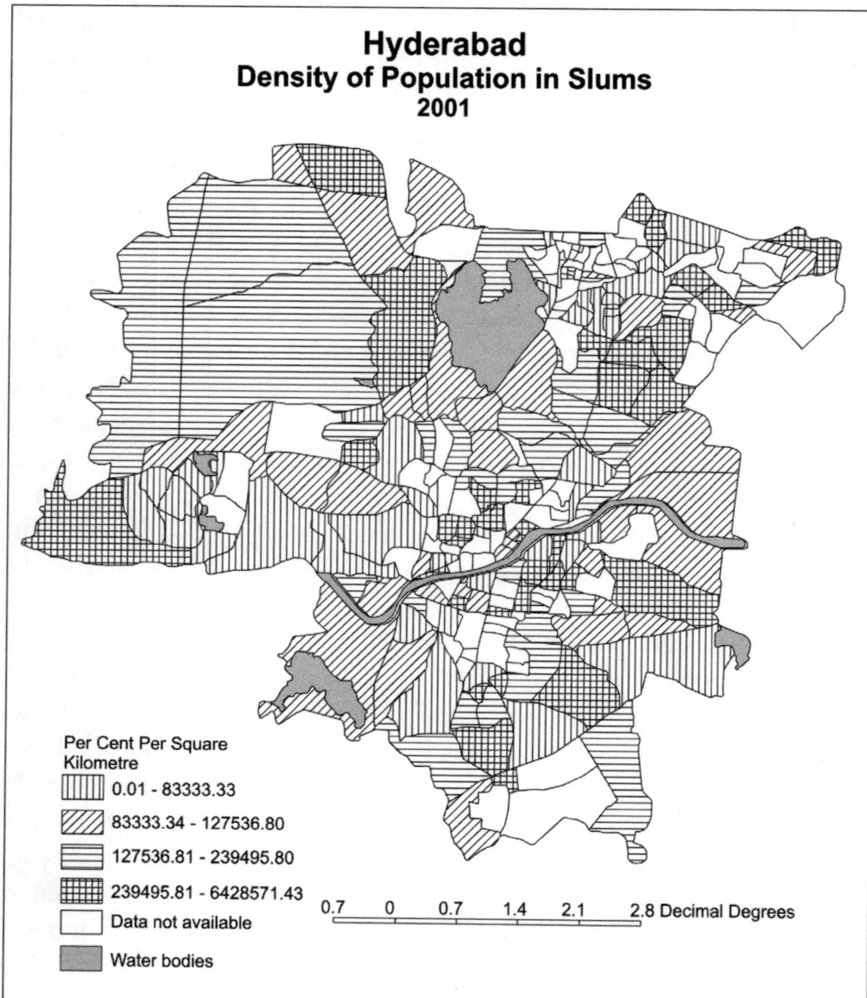

Fig. 30.3 Density of Population in the Slums of Hyderabad, 2001.

up in this quarter. Also, industrial areas are close to this area which explains the high workforce participation rate of both males as well as females among the slum dwellers in the western and northwestern parts of the city.

Close to eight per cent of the child population is part of the workforce in certain quarters of the city (Fig. 30.6). These sections include slums in places like Malakpet, Musheerabad, Asifnagar, Narayanguda, and Kachiguda. A verbal enquiry in the course of the survey had revealed that

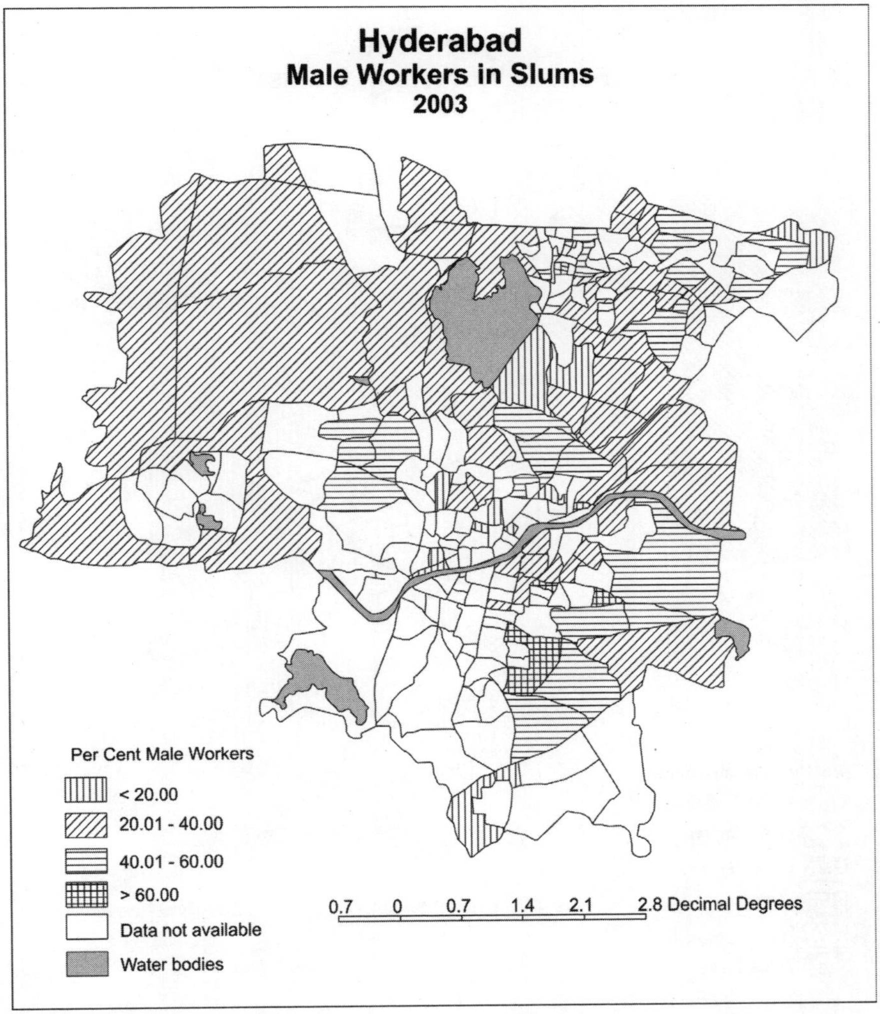

Fig. 30.4 Male Workers in the Slums of Hyderabad, 2003.

most of the children work as mechanics in garages or run petty errands for traders. A further probe into the raw data revealed that this was also true in the slums of Parvathinagar, Khan Agar (Talab Katta), and Galbalguda.

Figure 30.7 showing patterns of literacy among the slum population reveals that literacy among slum dwellers is high in the central part of the city in places like Domalguda, Ashoknagar, Narayanguda, Barkatpura, and Gunfoundry, in one continuous stretch to the north of the River

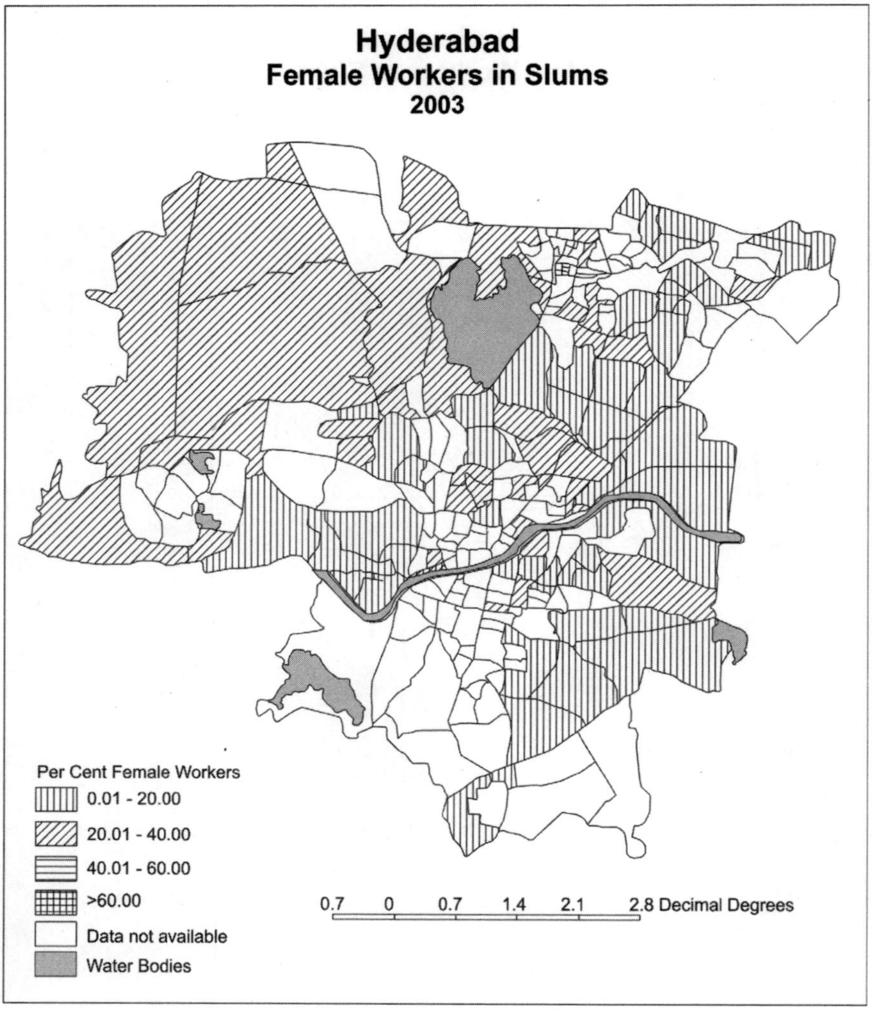

Fig. 30.5 Female Workers in the Slums of Hyderabad, 2003.

Musi, besides other isolated pockets. It is also high in Saidabad, Old Malakpet, and tiny pockets spread to the south of the Musi. This pattern is more or less repeated when one looks at literacy patterns for males in the slums. These are also the areas where female literacy is high in the slums of Hyderabad. A literacy rate of less than 20 per cent in the general slum population, however, is clearly noticeable only in South Hyderabad, reflecting the overall resistance of this area as far as upliftment on any count is concerned. Also this area offers ready jobs for slum dwellers in

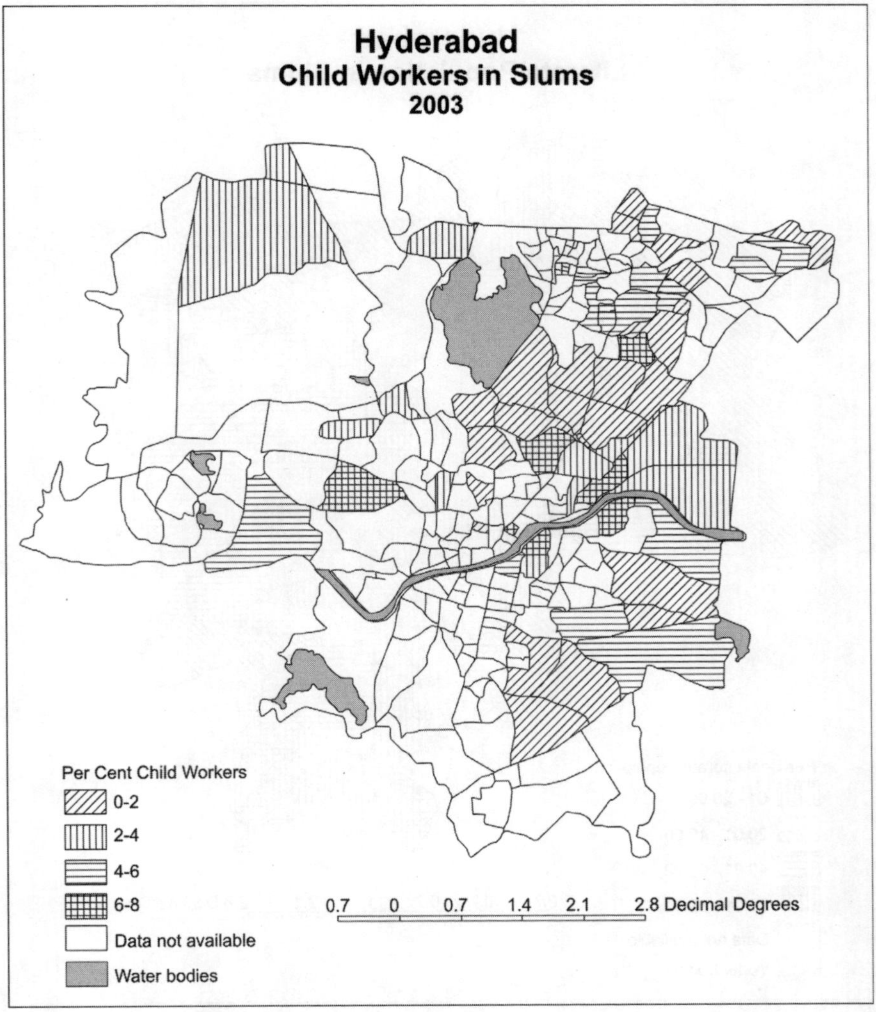

Fig. 30.6 Child Workers in the Slums of Hyderabad, 2003.

occupations that do not require educational skills or qualifications, such as motor mechanics or helpers in small shops. In contra-distinction to this, the jobs for even slum dwellers in areas to the north of River Musi require them to be educated. It is the educated among the migrants who settle in these slums. The organized-sector commerce in this area requires a minimal level of education from its employees, which explains the different composition of the slum population on the count of literacy. The pattern is more or less the same for the male and female slum

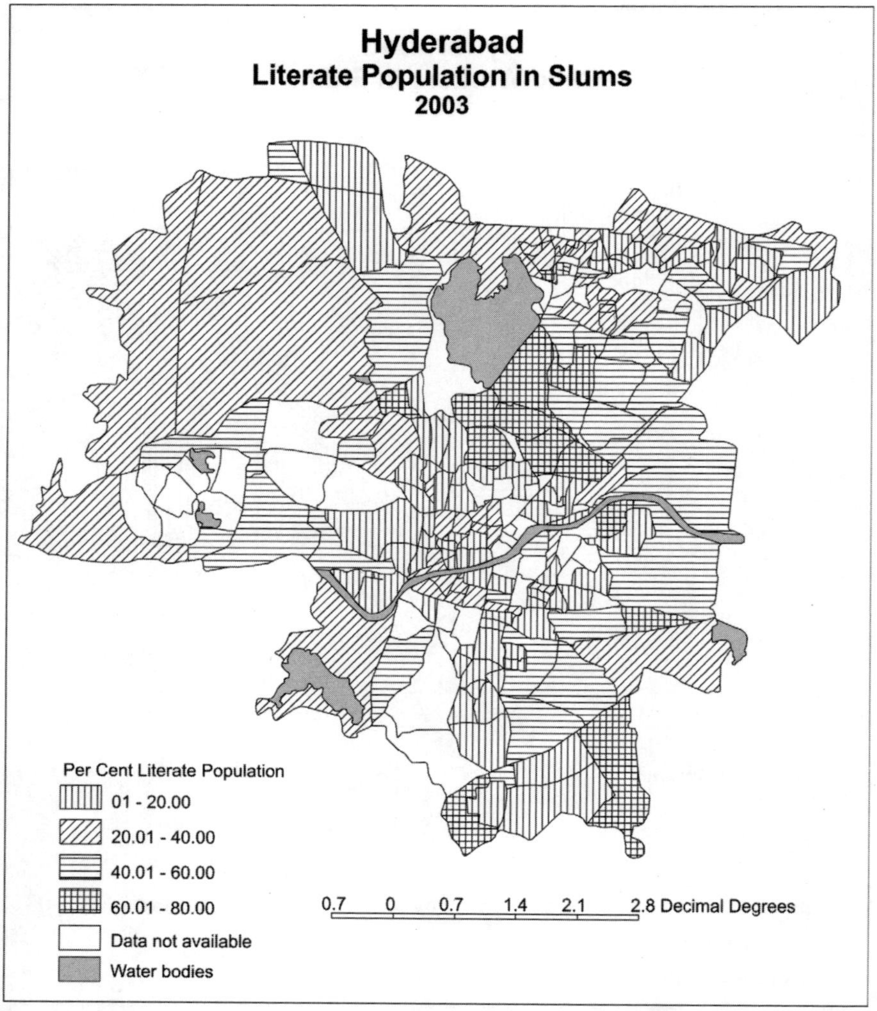

Fig. 30.7 Literate Populations in the Slums of Hyderabad, 2003.

dwellers, with the only distinction being that the overall proportion of literate female slum dwellers is much less than that of the males.

The distribution pattern of community halls in the slums in the different blocks of the city reveals that eight to 12 halls are found in the slums in Nallakunta, Amberpet, Kachiguda, and Domalguda in the central and eastern parts of the city, Erragadda, Yellareddyguda, and Yusufguda in the northeastern part of the city, and in the vicinity of Falaknuma in South

Hyderabad. Areas adjacent to these pockets have four to seven community halls. Yet there are large parts of the city where a lesser number or no halls at all may be found in the slums.

These choropleth maps portray some of the demographic, and by implication, socioeconomic conditions prevailing in the slums in the municipal blocks of Hyderabad. It was found that the slum population is greater in those parts of the city where there is heavy construction activity. These are distinctly the western pockets of the city. Even the growth rate registered in 1981–91 has been phenomenal in these pockets. A study of the density of population among the slum dwellers reveals that population density is high close to the commercial areas of the city, more so the upcoming commercial areas, and close to the industrial areas. This confirms what was stated earlier with regard to the residential choice of slum dwellers, that their first priority is proximity to the workplace. From the workforce participation rate, it has been found that levels of dependency are relatively low in the slums as a large majority of the people are employed. Workforce participation rate is very high in the upcoming areas in the western part of the city where construction activity is taking place. The patterns of literacy among slum dwellers show that literacy is high close to the central parts of the city, which reflects the varying nature of occupations among the slum dwellers in different parts of the city. The central city locations with jobs in organized-sector commerce require their workforce to be literate, whereas the peripheral areas – more specifically the western periphery with ongoing construction activity – can make do with a non-literate workforce. Incidentally literacy is low in South Hyderabad, reflecting the type of occupations available to the slum dwellers residing in this area, as also the general socioeconomic conditions in this part of Hyderabad. Also, female and male population is found in a more or less balanced proportion in the slums in South Hyderabad, which is more traditional in nature.

Conclusion

Though the city of Hyderabad has a long history and is experiencing a fast pace of growth, development, spread and sprawl, it is not without the growth of slums. These slums have distinct locational characteristics. They began to grow and develop on vacant plots of land more than 40 years ago. They are found in the center of densely populated residential areas in the center of the city. The more recent slums began to develop near upcoming residential and industrial areas, especially in the west, northwest, north, and northeast. Slums are also found close to water bodies, sometimes encroaching on their dry beds, and hence are susceptible to flooding. They are also found in other floodable low-lying areas. Slums are mostly found close to upscale neighbourhoods and commercial areas of Hyderabad, which provide employment opportunities to the slum dwellers. Thus, it is not surprising to find islands of poverty in the midst of an ocean of opulence.

Note

1. This study is the product of a project sponsored by IRSO called 'Urban Squalor as a Facet of Urban Landscape: Environmental Issues from Hyderabad'.

Select Bibliography

Census of India 2001, Series 29, A. P. Provisional Population Totals, Paper 2 of 2001, *Rural and Urban Distribution of Population*, Controller of Publications, New Delhi, 2001.

Corbley, K. P. 'Image Processing and Analysis Empowering Users with New Tools'. *Source*: http://www.imagingnotes.com/mayjun00/mayjun1/htm.

Dial, Gene and Jacek Grodecki, 'Applications of IKONOS Imagery', *ASPRS 2003 Annual Conference Proceedings*, Anchorage, Alaska, May 2003.

Dutt, Ashok K., Chandreyee Mitra, and Animesh Halder, 'Slum Location and Cycle of Poverty: Calcutta Case', *Asian Profile*, Vol. 25, No. 5, 1997, pp. 413–425.

Dutt, Ashok K., Suprabha Tripathi and Anupa Mukhopadhyay, 'Spatial Spread of Daily Activity Patterns of Slum Dwellers in Calcutta and Delhi', in Ashok K. Dutt, Frank J. Costa, Surinder Aggarwal and Allen, G. Noble (eds.), *The Asian City: Processes of Development, Characteristics and Planning*, Dordrech/Boston/ London: Kluwer Academic Publishers, 1994, pp. 309–326.

Dwit, Micheal and Hans Shenck, *Shelter for the Poor in India*, Delhi: Manohar Publications, 1989.

Hagget, P, R. J. Johnston, D. R. Stoddart, D. M. Stoddart, D. M. Smith and D. Gregory, *Blackwell Dictionary of Human Geography*, Oxford: Basil Blackwell, 1981.

8http://www.censusindia.net/results/slumnote.html

Hyderabad Urban Development Authority, Hyderabad 2020, A Plan for Sustainable Development, 2003.

Lohmann, P, et al., 'Land Cover Classification using IKONOS Data'. *Source*: http://www.geo.ucl.ac.be.

Markandey, K., 'Hyderabad: A city of Contrasts', in Baleshwar Thakur, George Pomeroy, Chris Cusack and Sudhir K. Thakur (eds.), *City, Society and Planning*.

Essays in Honour of Professor A. K. Dutt, Vol. 1: City, New Delhi: Concept Publishing Company, 2007, pp. 381–394.

Mukhopadhyay, Anupa, '*Spatial Analysis of Daily Activity Pattern of a City Slum in Calcutta*', Master of Arts Thesis, University of Akron, 1990.

Nangia, Sudesh, 'Slums of Urban India', in Frank, J. Costa, Ashok K. Dutt, Lawrence J. Ma and Allen G. Noble (eds.), *Asian Urbanization Problems and Processes*, Berlin: Gebruder Borntreager, 1988, pp. 131–142.

Nath, V., 'Poverty in Metropolitan Cities in India', in Ashok, K. Dutt, Frank J. Costa, Surinder Aggarwal and Allen G. Noble, *The Asian City: Processes of Development, Characteristics and Planning*, Dordrech/Boston/London: Kluwer Academic Publishers, 1994, pp. 295–308.

Prasada Raju PVSP, et al., 'The Role of Satellite Derived Maps in National Spatial DataInfrastructure'. *Source*: http://www.gisdevelopment.net/policy/India/Technology/mi03157.htm.

Singh, Tara and Girishwar Misra, 'Human Response to Population Growth and Environmental Challenges, The Indian Experience', *Newsletter of the International Human Dimensions Programme on Global Environmental Change*, April 2004.

Sita, K., 'The Cityscape of Mumbai: Continuity and Change', in Baleshwar Thakur, George Pomeroy, Chris Cusack and Sudhir K. Thakur (eds.), *City, Society and Planning*. Essays in Honour of Professor A. K. Dutt, Vol. 1: City, New Delhi: Concept Publishing Company, 2007, pp. 419–438.

Srinivas, H., 'Urban Squatters and Slums: Adopting a Rational Approach'. Source: http://www.gdrc.org/uem/squatters/define-squatter.html

Yadav, C. S., '*Migration and Urbanization in India: A Case Study of Delhi*', in Frank J. Costa, Ashok K. Dutt, Lawrence J. C. Ma and Allen G. Noble, Urbanization in Asia, Honolulu: University of Hawaii Press, 1989, pp. 227–244.

Yeates M. H. and B. J. Garner, *The North American City*, New York: Harper and Row, 1971.

31

Writings of Mirza Ghalib: A Study in Literary Geography

NILOFAR IZHAR AND RAIS AKHTAR

Yi-Fu Tuan, an American geographer, propounded the concept of Literary Geography. 'Literature is a source material for geographers, and literature provides a perspective for how people experience their world. In geography, it includes the topographical poem and the regional novel as well as the works of academic geographers' (Tuan, 1978). Creative literature profoundly reflects the temporal and experiential dimensions of the space it portrays. In this aspect imaginative literature and its sources are ideal for studies focussing on the environment and socio-cultural dimensions of the landscape of a region.

> It makes direct use of literary works of recognised quality input data to achieve understanding of the feelings, attitudes, and values of people in relation to their environment. (Dhussa, 1990)

Literature serves the geographer by throwing light on: (i) possible modes of human experience and relationship, (ii) overview of social space, and (iii) environmental perceptions and values of a culture.

India is a vast country with a wide variety of physical and cultural landscapes. Poets and writers in various languages have described the unique regional structure of the different areas in the country. Geographers can discover this uniqueness of the region and the description of such unique features which, as Richard Hartshorne emphasizes, is the fundamental core of geographical research.

Hardly any attempt was made by geographers in India to learn geography from poetry and the regional novels. A significant contribution was made by Ramesh Dhussa whose PhD thesis was on the geographical perspective of Premchand's writings. The basic objective of Dhussa's study was to reconstruct and express the environmental images of eastern

Uttar Pradesh, and to present a description of its diverse spatial phenomena, that is physical environment, climate, agricultural activities, taboos, glimpses of rural life, etc. (Dhussa, 1990). The first chapter of E. M. Forster's *A Passage to India* contains a vivid description of the physical and social setting of the country. Ashok K. Dutt and R. C. Dhussa's work on novelist Sarat Chandra's perception of Bengalis in *probash* (foreign lands) is a significant effort in Literary Geography (Dutt and Dhussa, 1983).

Literary geography may leave some room for subjectivity and even bias on the part of the author in interpreting some phenomena, but one great advantage is that there will be vividness and penetration in the writings.

> What a writer feels about life or observes in the society he depicts in his creation, written in the form of novel or poem, and this is especially true with the modern writers who are becoming objective in their writings. The writer being sensitive, perceives not only the change in the environment but also the reaction to it (Apte, 1970).

Similar expressions were noted by Duncan.

> Novelists are often astute observers of landscape and geographers should, therefore, be able to read novels as a rich source of new data (Duncan, 1974).

However, Allen G. Noble regretted that literature as a subject for professional scrutiny by geographers, although not a recent percept, has never been given the attention which the variety and scope of available fictional material warrants (Noble, 1976). Since the last several decades, much more work has been seen in this sub-discipline (see Hones, 2008 for review).

The inspiration for writing this paper, however, stems from the pioneering research on health, society, and environment in Victorian Manchester by Marilyn and Colin Pooley. The study focusses on the conditions in the city of Manchester (England) and the relationship between the characteristics of the social, cultural, economic, political, physical, and disease environments of urban areas (Pooley and Pooley, 1984).

Objectives

The objective of this study is to demonstrate the use of literature as an important source for geographic enquiry into socioeconomic and environmental conditions of Delhi, and the occurrence of cholera and availability of healthcare during the latter half of the nineteenth century, based on the letters and poetry written by Ghalib[1], the great Urdu poet and writer of the Indian subcontinent. The information contained in the writings of Ghalib, especially his letters have been utilized for the reconstruction and the expression of environmental conditions and dimensions of health and healthcare in and around Delhi. Ghalib's perception about the environment, and his description of cholera and fever outbreaks in the urban setting of Delhi at a time when the city was under the siege of British troops, especially during the revolt of 1857, have been very vivid. Ghalib stayed in Delhi for most of his life and had seen the various facets of Delhi, which was in the words of Percival Spear:

> ... a great imperial city with anything between one and two million inhabitants. It was the largest and most renowned city, not only of India, but of the entire East, from Constantinople to Canton. (Spear, 1945)

Meanwhile the Empire itself was disintegrating, weakend by a fierce succession struggle and the continued dominant role of the East India Company. Ghalib saw the last days of the crumbling Mughal Empire in early nineteenth century followed by the formal takeover of Delhi by the British after the 1857 Revolt, then the subsequent expulsion of the population of Delhi – both Hindus and Muslims – and the deterioration of urban Delhi. For example, historian Narayani Gupta quoted from Ghalib who witnessed the terror stricken population of Delhi in 1857.

> When angry lions entered the town, they killed the helpless ... and burned houses. Hordes of men and women, common men and noblemen, poured out of Delhi from the three gates and took shelter in small communities and tombs outside the city. Ghalib wrote these lines from the deserted city of Delhi... (Gupta, 1992).

The Revolt of 1857

It was on 11 May 1857 that the Meerut rebels crossed the Yamuna at Delhi by a bridge made of boats. To quote the contemporary poet Mirza Ghalib:

> On the 11th of May the walls and ramparts of the Red Fort shook with such force that the vibrations were felt in the four corners of the city (Indian History Congress, 1990).

In a letter written to his contemporary, the poet Sarur 18 months later on 18 November 1858, Ghalib narrated the account of the destruction of Delhi. His account of the Revolt of 1857 was also cited by historians.

> On May 11, 1857 the disorder began here. On that same day I shut the doors and gave up going out. One cannot pass the days without something to do, and I began to write my experiences, appending also such news as I heard from time to time (Russell and Islam, 1969, p. 132).

In September, 1860 he wrote to Sarur about the demolition in Delhi and the soaring prices of food items.

> Here it seemed as though the whole city is being demolished. Some of the biggest and most famous bazars – Khas Bazar, Urdu Bazar and Khanam Ka Bazar each of which was practically a small town, have gone without a trace. You cannot even tell where they were. Householders and shopkeepers cannot point out to you their houses and shops used to stand. It is the rainy season, but there has been practically no rain, and it is under the rain of picks and shovels that houses are collapsing. Food is dear, and death is cheap, and grain sells so dear that you would think that each was a fruit. *Mash* [lentils] sell at sixteen pounds to the rupee, millet at thirty-two pounds, and wheat at twenty-four pounds; gram at thirty-two, *Ghi* [clarified butter] at three. Vegetables too are expensive. And to crown it all, the month of *Kunwar* (September–October), which they call the threshold of the cold season, is as hot as *Jeth* and *Asarh* [May and June] the water is warm and the sun fierce, and the hot wind is blowing ... (Russell and Islam, 1969, pp. 244–45)

Descriptions of Urban Environment

Ghalib visited a number of places, especially in northern India. In October 1827, he went to Calcutta, passing through Banda, Allahabad and Varanasi on his way, and finally reached Calcutta (now Kolkata) on 20 February 1828 – nearly one year after his departure from Delhi. Varanasi particularly enchanted him. He wrote a poem in Persian in its praise which he titled *The Lamp of the Temple,* alluding to its fame as a holy city of the Hindus. More than 30 years later he still remembered Varanasi with pleasure, writing on 12 February 1861 to his friend Sayyah:

> What praise is too high for Banaras[Varanasi]? Where else is there a city to equal it? The days of my youth were almost over when I went there.

> Had I been young in those days I would have settled down there and never come back this way. (Russell and Islam, 1969, p. 47)

Calcutta he liked too, a city he used to visit in connection with his pension from the British Government. Ghalib arrived in Calcutta on 20 February 1828. In his short Persian poem, Ghalib gives an imaginary dialogue between himself and an unnamed advisor. Clearly he admired the greenery everywhere, and less understandably, according to Russell and Islam, seemed even to have liked its climate[2].

> I said to him, 'So tell me, then what is Calcutta like?' He said, 'You cannot find its like in all the seven climes: Ah me, my friend! The mention of Calcutta's name has loosed a shaft that pierces to my soul. Its greenery and verdure take away your breath; All freshness and all sweetness are its luscious fruits; its mellow wines are pleasing beyond all compare'.

This was in contrast to what Rabindranath Tagore had said about Calcutta in the early twentieth century, revealing its changing landscape.

> Calcutta sits on brick pavement with a brick-cap on her head. (Dutt and Dhussa, 1976)

To Tagore, Calcutta was a brick and mortar complex. This is similar to the description of Calcutta in 1782 by MacIntosh who viewed the city of Calcutta as 'an undistinguished mass of filth and corruption'.

Lucknow was another important urban centre visited by Ghalib. According to Ghalib:

> What praise was too high for Lucknow? It was the Baghdad of India, and its Court – may God be praised! – a mint of rich men. A man could come there penniless and become wealthy. Alas that autumn should come to such a Garden. (Russell and Islam, 1969, p. 241)

Ghalib was quoted by historian Robinson.

> 'Lucknow – the fate of Lucknow was little better. It was the largest pre-colonial city in South Asia. With a population of 400,000, the Baghdad of India as Ghalib called it, whose buildings were much admired by European visitors. (Robinson, 1993)

Since Ghalib's milieu was urban Delhi of the British period, he gave graphic descriptions of the socio-cultural life and environmental conditions of Delhi and threw light on sanitation, sources of water supply, and the outbreaks of cholera and fever. We will discuss these aspects in detail in the context of Delhi.

Description of Hot Summer Months

Delhi and surrounding areas experience dust storms during the hot season, sometimes so intense as to make the day quite dark. In a letter written in the month of June 1867, Ghalib writes:

> How can I describe what things are like here? In the words of Sadi – God's mercy be upon him – there is no water left except the lustre that gleans upon the unmatched pearl.
>
> Night and day it rains fire or dust, and one can neither see the sun by day nor the moon by night. Flames leap up from the earth and sparks fall from the sky. I wanted to describe something of the heat, but my reason said, see here foolish man, your pen, like an English match, will burst into flames and burn up the paper. My brother, the hot wind is a torment, and when from time to time it ceases, that is even harder to endure. (Russell and Islam, 1969, p. 352)

In another letter written on 5 July 1855, Ghalib described the torrential rains in Delhi.

> The air is very pleasant now, and it rains every day.

Ghalib complained about the disruption of normal life as a result of heavy rains.

> This time I had to wait a long while for a letter from you, and several days ago I felt like writing to complain. But the rain made it impossible for me to send my man out to post, and after that your letter came two days ago. Yesterday it still rained, but today it's cleared up; that is, the rain has stopped.

The impact of heavy rains was described in a letter written on 26 July 1855.

> It's rained until there's a river wherever you look, and the sun appears as briefly as the lightning flash – that is, it only shows its face very occasionally. Many houses in the city have collapsed. It's still raining as I write this. I am writing the letter, but let's see when it can be taken to the post office. I'll tell my man to wrap a blanket round him and go ... the mangoes this year have been ruined (Russell and Islam, 1969, p. 126).

On the Purity of River Water

While in Rampur city in western Uttar Pradesh, Ghalib wrote a letter to Hakim Ghulam Najaf Khan on 3 February 1860.

> There's a river here called the Kosi. God be praised! Its water is so sweet that you would think it was diluted *sherbet* – clear, light, refreshing and quickly assimilated. For these eight days I have been safe from attacks of constipation. I develop a really good appetite in the morning.

The same River Kosi is threatened by pollution these days as the large number of small-scale sugarcane factories that are located around it discharge effluents into the river. More importantly, methane producing factories and breweries are also located along the river. Almost 130 years after Ghalib's description of the water of River Kosi, it is now one of the most contaminated water bodies in India. A study conducted in the upper reaches of River Kosi shows the changes in the physico-chemical properties of the water (Pande *et al.*, 1990).

Prevalence of Fever in Epidemic Form

Delhi and some districts of northern India were under the grip of a fever epidemic during the nineteenth century. Fever was the dominant cause of death in all the provinces of British India (Indian Medical Gazette, 1872, p. 264). W. Geddes' *Report on Fever* (1927), Day's *Tropical Fever* (1863), J. Fayrer's *Climate and Fevers of India* (1882), W. J. Moore's paper on fever published in the *Indian Medical Gazette* (1886), and Ronald Ross' paper on Indian fevers published in the *Indian Medical Gazette* (1892) are important contributions on the ecology of fevers in India (see Moore, 1886; Fayrer, 1882; Harrison, 1994). In a letter written on 6 September 1851 to Haqir from Delhi, Ghalib writes:

> I read in the papers that epidemics are raging in Agra and in Patna. There was nothing about Aligarh, but now I have learned of the situation from your letter.... All is well here, except that, as usual with the changes that take place at the beginning of this season, there's a wave of fevers and agues and colds. But there's no epidemic. It's been very hot, but for the last two days there's been a cool breeze. The clouds are gathering, but there has been no rain. (Russell and Islam, 1969, p. 115)

In the same letter, Ghalib discusses the intensity and expansion of fevers in different districts. He relates the fever outbreak to the hot and humid climatic conditions.

The occurrence of famines and the outbreak of fever in Delhi date back to the last half of eighteenth century. Spear explains the reasons for the fever outbreak.

> First the canal system broke down. Water ceased to flow into Delhi after 1761 and the canals became a series of stagnant pools which witnessed the past glories and present mosquitoes. The whole northern district [of Delhi] fell back upon the uncertain rains for their annual crops. The second was the great famine of 1785 which was far more destructive than all the wars put together. From a half to a third of the rural population died. (*Asiatic Annual Register*, 1800, Vol, II, p. 3, quoted from Spear, 1945)

The vivid description of poverty-induced diseases by Ghalib such as malnutrition as well as environmentally-induced diseases such as cholera and malaria was unparalleled. In the following letter written in early July 1860, Ghalib reviews the political scenario in Delhi and the outbreak of cholera.

> Five invading armies have fallen upon this city one after another: the first was that of rebel soldiers [mutineers], which robbed the city of its good name. The second was that of the British, when life and property and honours and dwellings and those who dwelt in them and heaven and earth and all the visible signs of existence were stripped from it. The third was that of famine, where thousands of people died of hunger. The fourth was that of cholera, in which many whose bellies were full lost their lives. The fifth was the fever, which took general plunder of men's strength and powers of resistance. There were not many deaths, but a man who has had fever, feels that all the strength has been drained from his limbs. And this invading army has not yet left the city. (Russell and Islam, 1969, p. 243)

In a letter dated simply July 1861, Ghalib writes about the severe epidemic of cholera in Delhi.

> The epidemic has died down somewhat. For six or seven days it raged everywhere. Two days ago Kwaja Mirza (son of Kwaja Aman) came to Delhi with his wife and children. Yesterday night his nine year old boy contracted cholera and died ... The epidemic affects Alwar too. Alexander Heatherly, known as Alec Sahib, has died. I tell you truly and sincerely, he was very dear to me, a man who wished to advance my interests and as a link between me and the Raj. And it was for this crime that death has taken him. Well, this is the world of causes and effects. What are its workings to us? (Russell and Islam, 1969, p. 258)

It is evident that Ghalib applies the mechanical explanation, that is the cause and effect relationship, in the foregoing lines, which is a reflection of the dominant theory of the origin of species propounded by Charles

Darwin in 1859. It should be noted here that Ghalib lived in a period which was significant for the development of new scientific ideas. Alexander von Humboldt, Charles Darwin and Ghalib – all lived during the same period. There is a possibility that Ghalib was influenced by the idea of the cause and effect relationship originally explained by Humboldt and later incorporated by Darwin in the development of his theory. There was a tremendous flow of information between England and India, and newspapers in India routinely reported various scientific developments taking place in Europe during the nineteenth century.

The diseases prevalent in Delhi – cholera, malaria, and the 'Delhi Sore' – were thought to be caused entirely by waterborne contagion, transmitted through running water, brackish well-water, and water-logged pools. *The Moffussilite* reported in 1863 that Delhi was unprotected because it was unhealthy, which was why Europeans could not survive the Delhi climate for long. The river and its miasma, proximity to certain polluted areas in old Delhi, and brackish well-water were the causes of ill-health in general and of the Delhi Sore specifically. The city's water supply was also found to be inadequate.

Description of Medical Practitioners in Delhi

In a letter written to Alai dated 15 February 1862, Ghalib discusses the treatment of his father's illness. He goes on to list some of the famous *hakims* (indigenous medicine practitioners), remarking that though some of them were no longer in Delhi, there were still some excellent *hakims* in the city who would attend to him.

'And what more does he want? True there are one or two doctors, who have a reputation because they are of the same race as our rulers, and an obscure vaid or two [Vaid – a man who practises the ancient Hindu system of medicine] lurking in holes and corners'.

Ghalib was a strong supporter of the *Unani*[3] system of medicine, and was against spiritual medicine. In the same letter, he writes:

> The *Hakims* will take care of the treatment, and I will not fail in companionship or sympathy, or I shall stand convicted.... The names of God and the verses of the Holy Quran used in effecting recovery, breaking spells, and driving out spirits are all established, and may be expected to exercise their due effect. (True, the maulvis and reciters know nothing and introduce all sorts of complications to impress people).

He further adds in his letter of 16 February 1862:

> It has been settled that he is to be treated as Hakim Mahmud Khan prescribes – that is, he has written the prescription, the pills have been made up, and the materials for the medicines sent for so that they can be put in soak today ready for use tomorrow immediately after he has taken the pills. But it looks to me as though the noble patient and his well-wishers are in two minds about going through with the cure. (Russell and Islam, 1969, pp. 268–269)

The analysis of the above two letters of 15 and 16 February 1862 reveals the following dimensions: (i) There were one or two English doctors who were practising in Delhi in 1862, (ii) The ancient Hindu medical system of *Ayurveda* was not popular, and only one or two practitioners of *Ayurveda* had their clinics in obscure parts of Delhi, and (iii) It is evident from the second letter that *Unani* medicines are prepared each time they are required for the patients.

In another letter dated 21 June 1863, Ghalib writes about his own illness and about the treatment by *hakims*:

> The swelling on my leg has increased beyond all measure. It turned out that it had not reached the stage where the matter can be drawn off, and inflammation set in. Two or three *Hakims* are attending me, and on their advice a poultice of neem leaves will be applied from tomorrow. (Russell and Islam, 1969, p. 287)

Ghalib's Knowledge of Unani Medicine

In Ghalib's time *Unani* medicine was so widely practised that even laymen knew names of some of the drugs. 'Ghalib fully represented his age and implied the traits of the prevalent culture' (Siddiqi, 1979). In May 1848 Ghalib wrote to Hargopal Tufta.

> What's wrong with our good friend Munshi Nabi Baksh Haqir that you write that even goat's whey couldn't cure it? There is a recipe given in *Tibb-i-Muhammad Husain Khani* which has no harmful effects and does you good, though it takes a long time for its effects to show. This is it. Take six or seven quarts of water, and in the proportion of half an ounce to each quart, put in it crushed China-root. Boil it until a quarter of the water has evaporated. Strain the remainder into a fresh, unglazed earthenware vessel. Leave it to stand some hour and then drink it.

> Follow your normal diet, but whenever you feel thirsty, either by day or at night, drink only this. Make a fresh supply every day. After a full year its beneficial effects will be evident. Give him this recipe (Russell and Islam, 1969, p. 115).

According to Tazimuddin Siddiqi:

> Ghalib used well-known medical terms in some of his verses. The texture of Ghazals like lyrics being very delicate and fine generally does not admit technical terms, medical or otherwise, but Ghalib has employed them so superbly that instead of tottering under their weight, they enrich the verses and enlarge their scope and meaning.

The following verse, in which Ghalib has used terms of *Unani* medicine, shows his familiarity with this medical system.

> O Ghalib, drink in moon-lit night as much wine as you can get. This hot thing alone will suit you since you have a phlegmy temperament.

Siddiqi provides a basis for *Unani* medicine. For more than a millennium ancient physicists believed that there were four primary elements or four humours, namely blood, phlegm, yellow bile and black bile. From this theory of four humours was deduced the principle of human temperament. On this theory of humours and temperament rested the edifice of *Unani* medicine. A person having an excess of phelgm is said to be of phlegmy temperament which is cold. Hot drugs are given to treat a patient with such a temperament. Wine being hot is supposed to help people of phlegmy temperament and Ghalib very imaginatively finds an excuse for his excessive drinking in his phlegmy temperament. Ghalib stated that, 'My limbs have grown weak. No longer is there a balance in my elements (Humours)' (Siddiqi, 1979).

The verse is based on the concept of humours. Under modern medicine the weakness of human organs and faculties or their slow movement and functioning is attributed to loss of energy or impairment of immunity or to anaemia. But according to the principles of *Unani* medicine the unbalanced humours bring about the weakness of the organs. Taking a cue from this principle, Ghalib means to say that he is weak and feeble, because the elements of his body or humours have lost their equilibrium. (Siddiqi, 1979, pp. 185–186)

Scholars and physicians of *Unani* medicine had a knowledge of the circulation of blood according to Siddiqi.

> Much before William Harvey, it was Ibn Nafis who presented his theory of blood circulation. Ghalib too believed in the theory but prescribes a more exacting test, that eyes should shed blood instead of the ordinary tears.
>
> Blood circulates through veins in the body, but for us it is not enough. We won't take blood as blood if its drops are not shed by eyes (Siddiqi, 1979, p. 195).

It is evident from the last verse quoted that Ghalib uses his poetic skill in revealing his knowledge of *Unani* medicine.

Conclusion

The assessment of Ghalib's writings in the framework of geography does provide a glimpse of the rich source material pertaining to socioeconomic and environmental dimensions of society during the latter half of the nineteenth century. The description of socio-political and urban conditions, particularly in Delhi, Calcutta, and Vanarasi, highlight the quality of life of the population. Vivid descriptions of the political disturbances in Delhi, demolition of houses and shifting of population after the Revolt of 1857 are of great historical value. It is also evident that Ghalib's writings throw light on the practice of medical systems in Delhi. The study shows that Ghalib had a deep knowledge of *Unani* medicine.

Historical geographers will find Ghalib's writings a good source material on environmental conditions, outbreaks of epidemics, and health care provision in Delhi during the latter half of nineteenth century. There is a need to further assess regional literature in order to study the social and environmental issues, epidemics, and healthcare of a region in the historical context.

Notes

1. Mirza Asadullah Khan Ghalib (1797–1869), noble, poet, and wit of Mughal Delhi, the doyen of Indian poetry in Urdu, was born in Agra. The writings of Ghalib have been translated into German, Czech, Russian, Chinese, Japanese, Korean, and even into many African languages. He was in the Court of the last Mughal Emperor, Bahadurshah Zafar, as his *ustad* (teacher). Delhi in the period of Bahadurshah Zafar was an Indian Weimar, with Ghalib for its Goethe. Ghalib also received pension from the British, and wrote a poem in honour of Queen Victoria, but was later punished by the British who stopped the pension as they suspected Ghalib was a

revolutionary and an important force behind the Revolt of 1857. When Ghalib was born the Mughal Empire was dying and indeed it was already in full decline when his grandfather came to India from the Central Asian region of Transoxiana, north of River Amu (presently Uzbekistan), inhabited by Seljuk Turkish stock (Russel and Islam, 1969).

2. It must be mentioned that Calcutta being on the coast of the Bay of Bengal has a moderate climate in comparison to extremely hot and humid as well as cold climate of Delhi. Ghalib used to complain about the harsh climate of Delhi, which was why Ghalib liked Calcutta. This geographical fact was not understood by Russell and Islam.
3. Unani medicine is a holistic system of medicine developed in the Middle East at the juncture of Greek and Egyptian civilizations, and is highly consonant with with Chinese and Indian medicine systems.

References

Apte, M. L., 'Reflection of Urban Life in Marathi Literature', in R. G. Fox (ed.), *Urban India: Society, Space and Image*, Durham, NC: Duke University, 1970, p. 199.

Dhussa, R. C., 'Premchand's Writings: A Gold Mine of Geographic Images', *National Geographical Journal of India*, Vol. 36, Nos. 1 and 2, 1990, pp. 95–108.

Duncan, J. S., 'The Urban Novel in the Study of Landscape Perception', *Seventieth Annual Meeting of the Association of American Geographers*, Seattle, April 1974.

Dutt, A. K. and R. C. Dhussa, 'The Contrasting Image and Landscape of Calcutta through Literature', *Proceedings Annals, AAG*, 1976, pp. 102–103.

Dutt, A. K. and R. C. Dhussa, 'Novelist Sarat Chandra's perception of Bengalis in Probash (foreign lands): A Literary Geographic Study', *National Geographical Journal of India*, Vol. 29, Parts 3 and 4, 1983, pp. 188–206.

Fayrer, J. On the Climate and Fevers of India, London, J&A Churchill, 1882.

Gupta, N., *Delhi Between Two Empires*, New Delhi: Oxford University Press, 1992.

Harrison, M. *Public Health and British India: Anglo-Indian Preventive Medicine 1859–1914*, Cambridge, Cambridge University Press, 1994.

Hones, S., 'Text as it Happens: Literary Geography', Geography Compass, Vol. 2, No. 5, 2008, pp. 1301–1317, DOI 10.1111/j.1749-8198.2008.00143.x

Indian History Congress, *Historic Delhi*, New Delhi, 1990, p. 32.

Moore, W.J., Fever, Indian Medical Gazette, Vol. 21, 1886, p. 129.

Noble, A. G., 'The Emergence and Evolution of Malgudi: An Interpretation of South Indian Townscapes from Fictional Writing of R. K. Narayan', *Proceedings of A.A.G.*, 1976, p. 106.

Pande, R. K., D. S. Rawat and A. Pant, 'Seasonal Rhythm in the Physico-chemical Properties of Nana Kosi River (Kumaon Himalaya)', in R. K. Trivedi (ed.), *Ecology and Pollution of Indian Rivers*, New Delhi: APH, 1990, pp. 209–218.

Pooley, M. E. and C. G. Pooley, 'Health, Society and Environment in Victorian Manchester', in Robert Woods and John Woodward (eds.), *Urban Disease and Mortality in Nineteenth-Century England*, London: Batsford Academy, 1984, pp. 148–9.

Robinson, F., 'The Muslims of Upper India and the Shock of the Mutiny', in M. Hasan and N. Gupta (eds.), *India's Colonial Encounter: Essay in Memory of Eric Stokes*, New Delhi: Manohar Publishers, 1993, p. 194.

Russell, R. and K. Islam, *Ghalib 1797–1869: Life and Letters*, Delhi: Oxford University Press, 1969.

Siddiqi, T., 'Ghalib and Unani Medicine', *Studies in History of Medicine*, Vol. 3, No. 3, 1979, pp. 181–198.

Spear, P., *Delhi: A Historical Sketch*, Bombay, Oxford University Press, 1945.

Tuan, Yi-Fu, 'Literature and Geography: Implications for Geographical Research', in David Ley and M. S. Samuels (eds.), *Humanistic Geography: Prospects and Problems*, London: Croom Helm, 1978, pp. 194–206.

32

Geographic Images of Old Delhi through Literature

RAMESH C. DHUSSA

'Literature represents a source of geographical data and perceptions that are mostly untapped by geographers. Among Indian writers of fiction in both English and Hindi, the city of Delhi, the capital of India, is 'an idea with physical boundaries.'[1] Both Hindu and Muslim authors regard the capital city with mixed emotions of reverence and resentment. The urban environment of Delhi presents sharply contrasting images of security, retreat, familiarity, noise, crowds and filth. Authors carefully describe both the city's physical frame and the quality of its communal life. This essay is intended to examine the 'idea' of Old Delhi (Shahjahanabad, the walled city) in its contrasting facets across the writings of representative Indian authors. Old Delhi has been a living city since the seventeenth century and forms a part of the much larger Delhi Metropolitan Area.

Old Delhi: The Traditional City

The crowded world of Old Delhi is vividly portrayed in numerous novels and short stories including Jhabvala's *The Householder* (1960), Yadav's *Andekhe Anjan Pul* ('Unseen, Unknown Bridges') (1963), Ali's *Twilight in Delhi* (1966), Rakesh's *Lingering Shadows* (1970), Chopra's *Jaren* ('The Roots') (1972), Vaid's *A Blind Alley* (1972), Bista's *Beete Din* ('Bygone Days') (1974), Nahal's *My True Faces* (1978), and many others.

The city of Old Delhi, which now spreads even beyond the old walls of Shahjahanabad, mainly towards its west and northwest with the traditional settlement pattern, was developed largely after the Revolt of 1857. The images of Old Delhi, both inside and outside the city walls, reflected in literature emphasize certain common features found throughout the city. These are: over crowding, both inside houses and out on the streets; narrow and dirty lanes; congested traffic, which includes all types of vehicles such as trucks, buses, cars, scooters, three wheelers, bicycles, *tongas*, *ekkas* (types of horse carts), bullock carts, and *rickshaw's* or *thelas* (carriages pulled by men to transport goods over short distances); the stench of drains; stray dogs fighting among themselves; whining beggars, etc.

In spite of an seemingly uncomfortable and unhygienic environment, the natives of Old Delhi remain emotionally attached to their district's environment, especially within the walled city area of Shahjahanabad. Ali's characters, who interact with each other in that environment, extol such sentiments frequently. The native residents' intense attachment with Old Delhi has also been witnessed historically. After the suppression of the Revolt of 1857, the British made some major modifications in urban Delhi. When they brought railroad lines into the city, they had to demolish some old structures. The British offered cheap plots of land to the owners of those houses elsewhere. However, '... many of the people of Delhi opted to lose themselves in the familiar environment rather than seek a new life outside' (Gupta, 1981, p. 39). These *Delhiwalas* wanted to stay inside the city walls and remain amidst the Old Delhi culture which was distinctly different from that of other parts of India, for example Punjabi culture of Lahore or Bengali culture of Calcutta. The cities of Delhi, Lahore and Agra were capital cities of the Mughal Empire at different times. While Lahore was characterized by Punjabi culture, Agra on the other hand, exhibited 'Braj Bhasha' and Hindi culture.

Finally, Delhi had evolved its distinct culture, characterized by the Urdu language and a rich Urdu literature. Narayani Gupta mentions that many of the so-called *Delhiwalas* preferred to do manual labour and even accepted charity in order to stay inside the city walls. Most of them preferred to stay because Old Delhi's unique culture was much more important to them than a higher standard of living elsewhere. In spite of suffering economic loss, many inhabitants of the city of Shahjahanabad preferred to stay because they viewed themselves as an integral part of the exclusive Delhi culture. Psychologically, they felt safe and secure (Gupta, 1981). Such was the importance of Delhi and its culture in the eyes of the natives who lived there for several generations. Among the people who stayed in Delhi are some of the characters of Ali's *Twilight in Delhi* who do manual labour or beg for a living. Some of these descended from

Muslim noble families or were even distantly related with the Mughal dynasty. One could see them begging in the alleys of Old Delhi or even driving a *tonga* in the streets of this part of the city. They relished the security of their familiar setting. Such feelings, however, are not commonly found among residents of present day Old Delhi, at least as revealed in those novels and short stories that are set in modern times. Except for those few characters who have been living there for several generations, most characters are less attached to their districts.

Many Muslim characters, after leaving Delhi for Pakistan, decided to return to Delhi because they felt Delhi was their home and they could not live outside the city. Ibadat Ali in *Lingering Shadows* is a good example of this. Ibadat lived in a 'predominantly Muslim locality' called Qassabpura. This locality, according to the description in the novel, is situated west of the city wall. Ibadat Ali's home was a gift to his forefathers by the Mughal court. During communal riots at the time of the Partition in 1947, he left for Pakistan. After the situation settled down, however, the attachment with Delhi impelled him to return 'home' (Rakesh, 1970).

As stated earlier, such examples are not found in abundance in literature depicting Old Delhi in the post-Partition period. The lack of emotional attachment to the place can also be found in *Lingering Shadows*. In the same lane and neighbourhood of Qassabpura, so dear to Ibadat Ali, was a 'dingy lane', as viewed by the author of the novel, where Harbans lived in one room of Ibadat Ali's house (Rakesh, 1970). For Nilima, who lives in a modern house on Hanuman Road near Connaught Place, Qassabpura is so repulsive that it took some time for her to get over the stench of the environment.[2] Therefore, in a novel like *Lingering Shadows* various characters exhibit emotions widely divergent regarding the same district. Ibadat's character displayed love and feelings of nostalgia, but both Harbans and Nilima detested the crowds, dirt, traffic, poverty and stench.

Subzi Mandi

Subzi Mandi, literally meaning 'vegetable market', reflects the fact that the area contains the largest vegetable market in Delhi. Kamal's parents in *My True Faces* lived in Subzi Mandi. Kamal, who lived in a place called Matahari in South Delhi, often visited his parents there. What can one expect to see in such a market? Kamal saw from the balcony of his parents' house,

'Trucks and horse carts rumbled in the streets below, loaded with tons of fresh food' (Nahal, 1978, p. 206). Subzi Mandi is characterized by narrow lanes through which vehicular traffic cannot easily pass. These lanes, therefore, were less noisy than broad avenues and were also cooler than wider streets which received more direct sunlight. During the summer season, families would spread their beds on the streets in the evening. Doors of the small houses would remain open and family possessions would be visible from the outside. Nothing was hidden from the passers-by. The belongings of these lower middle-class houses were, of course, modest. 'Tin suitcases, cooking pots and pictures on the walls – pictures of Krishna, of Shiva, of Kali (Nahal, 1978, p. 220). Delhi's summer heat is so uncomfortable that in crowded middle-class areas such as Subzi Mandi, families can be seen in the evening '... huddled on the cots in the lanes' (Nahal, 1978, p. 220). Members of the family quarrel and eat publicly. Kamal feels if there is anything which is severely lacking here, it is privacy. Do they ever get privacy, these men and women? "Didn't they ever wish to be alone?" (Nahal, 1978, p. 220).

Qutub Road Bridge

The Qutub Road runs parallel to the western city wall, and the railroad track links Old Delhi and New Delhi. The road generally runs in a north-south direction. There is a bridge in the northern section of this road over the railway tracks. Nahal finds this bridge, especially its surrounding area, the '... most bizarre place in the city' (Nahal, 1978, p. 184). According to the author, this is the place where the two cities meet 'with a bang.' From the place one can view the characteristic crowds and filth of Old Delhi existing side by side with the spaciousness and cleanliness of New Delhi. The bridge symbolizes the transition from one world to another newer world. But Nahal is more attracted to the filthy side of the bridge than to its spacious, clean side. Below the bridge, by the side of the railway tracks, is the area with Delhi's worst slums. Seen from the bridge, these mud houses, whose roofs mingle with one another, give an impression of 'one squalid mass'. The hovels extend so close to the railway lines that the trains could barely pass through the gap between them. The entire length of the railway lines passing through this slum is covered with human waste, mostly excreta of the children who can be seen playing there.

The top of the bridge itself is not less strange. It is a one-way bridge. To Nahal perhaps this symbolizes a transition from the older to the newer world, from a traditional to a more modern culture. The traffic mostly consists of horse-driven *tongas*. Horses look exhausted because of their heavy load and the tropical heat. The strangeness of the bridge lies in the market which spreads over the bridge, similar to Ponte Vecchio in Florence. The bazaar, '... a nameless, roofless, shapeless bazaar, spread on the ground or on rickety benches or stood up against the wall, the parapet of the bridge' (Nahal, 1978, p. 185). Any imaginable type of commodity can be found there and at a much lower price than elsewhere. Services also abound – locksmiths, dentists and even doctors, all have their place in the bazaar, while on one side a mesmerizing show is in progress. Nahal feels forlorn seeing such an area in the midst of the capital of India. Krishna Baldev Vaid's story 'A Blind Alley' also summons up an image of an alley in Old Delhi, perhaps somewhere near Subzi Mandi, which is so full of filth, stench and unsightly scenes that even before going into details he advises his readers in the first line of the story, 'You had better have your handkerchief on your nose, for the lane stinks awfully' (Vaid, 1972, pp. 13–21).

Old Delhi *Mohallas* ('Neighborhoods')

Ali's Old Delhi *mohallas* are not so malodorous and dirty as those previously described. His *mohallas* have narrow, labyrinthine lanes, dark vestibules leading to the houses, and small courtyards, but not reeking lanes. Ali's characters love this environment. Such type of houses and alleypatterns provide coolness during the summer. The other environmental attributes of Old Delhi Ali describes are people setting pigeons in flight, flying kites, and spending time in leisure and relaxation. Such scenes recur frequently throughout *Twilight in Delhi*. The milieu of *Twilight in Delhi* reflects the eastern and central parts of the walled city in the vicinity of the Jama Masjid.

The area south of Jama Masjid has been vividly described in the story *Beete Din* ('Bygone Days'), a Hindi story by Pankaj Bista. This largely Muslim section of Shahjahanabad still exhibits a medieval appearance. One will commonly see Muslim girls in *burqua* (veils), *bhistis* (water-carriers) carrying water in a goatskin satchel and an occasional group of *hijras* (eunuchs) in the lanes of this area. A main street runs southward starting from the southern gate of Jama Masjid. Although this street is not very narrow, few cars are seen there. More common modes of transportation are *tongas, rehras* (hand-driven cart), rickshaws and bicycles (Bista, 1974, p. 21).

Bista is so overwhelmed by the environment of this area that he has devoted a good deal of time to describing it. It appears that he is surprised to find and experience the old, traditional Delhi, so close to New Delhi where an altogether different world is thriving. There is a sense of pride and satisfaction within his descriptions of New Delhi still being linked with its past.

Pahari Dhiraj: A Rural Enclave

Sudarshan Chopra's stories *Jaren* ('The Roots') and *Oob* ('Disgust') depict a relatively unexplored environment of Old Delhi, portraying the life and environment of migrant labourers from neighbouring states. The entire environment in the story *Jaren* gives an impression of a rural area. The locale of these stories is Pahari Dhiraj and its vicinity in Delhi. The characters of both of these stories still speak their native dialect, which seems to be Hariyanavi. One can see from the stories that people who speak this dialect tend to live together in this small area and maintain their native rural cultural traditions. People do not mind accommodating a new member from their native village. As a result, the area is very crowded, and a character such as Jangi even lives in a *miani* (mezzanine). The inhabitants of this neighborhood are content and 'enjoy' the transferred flavour of their native region. Characters in these stories neither praise nor despise the dirty, crowded, lesser developed rural-like environment. They just live there among their own people and work in different places scattered throughout the city, such as Modi Mills and the Delhi Cloth Mills (Chopra, 1972a). It seems that when they are at their workplace they are physically and spiritually in the city of Delhi; but when they return to their neighbourhood, they retreat to their native rural environment. The metropolis does not linger in their minds. Such dichotomy gives the fulfilment of living in the best of both worlds.

Katra: Traditional Old Delhi Business and Residential Area

Although Jhabvala does not explicitly use the word 'katra' while describing a specific mixed residential and commercial area in the central part of Shahjahanabad in her novel *The Householder*, she is most probably talking about a *katra* in Chandni Chowk when describing how Prem and his friend Sohan Lal rode a bicycle from their college '... a long way, right into the heart of the old city' (Jhavbala, 1960, p. 72). After reaching this part of the old city they stopped by '... a narrow lane running off the main bazaar, then both of them entered into an arched gateway, and eventually proceeded through another arch leading off that one' (Jhavbala, 1960, p. 72). All these details reveal that she was talking about *katras* in the Chandni Chowk area.

Katras are a unique characteristic of old Delhi. These are a traditional mixed residential and commercial urban formation in the heart of Old Delhi, found in and around the central part of the old city, Chandni Chowk. Here people live on the upper floors and businesses are run on the ground or first floor. If traders had to commute they would waste hours of valuable time. Rory Fonseca defines a *katra* as 'a market with residential quarters and storage facilities enclosed by walls and entered through a gate (Fonseca, 1971, p. 74).

Jhabvala's *The Householder* offers a reader glimpses of the environment of a typical *katra* visited by Prem and his friend Sohan Lal. After entering the arched gateway, they noticed rich cloth shops. Even the merchants within appeared rich. They sat cross-legged, smoking *hookahs* (water pipes) and chewing *paan* (betel). It looked as if they were not eager to sell their commodity. Apparently they were relaxing and gossiping (Jhavbala, 1960, p. 72).

On passing the narrow lane bordered by these shops, Prem and Sohan Lal found themselves in a 'paved courtyard.' They noticed a cobbler repairing a shoe as he sat under a tree in the courtyard and a horse 'being led out of the gateway'. They even noticed a cook running into a house carrying a chicken (Jhavbala, 1960, p. 72). The *katra* seemed a world in itself where commerce, transport, manufacturing and domestic chores all coexisted.

Katras featured a variety of economic activities and are inhabited by people of different economic levels. For example, when Prem was looking for the *katra* where he hoped to find a Swamji (Swamji is a title for a holy person), he entered several outwardly similar looking arched gateways and lanes and observed different types of activities and residents. In one courtyard he even found a 'disused mosque', indicating that this *katra* was once inhabited by Muslims who had since moved elsewhere. While looking into one *katra* after another in search of Swamiji's place, Prem noticed a large carpenters' workshop and a nest of squatters who had settled down in the 'niches' of an old house, occupying the entire courtyard with their cooking items, washing and battered tins and several other household articles. Prem found such quarters altogether different from those of other parts of Delhi. He had come to Delhi from another town only a few years before. One common feature he experienced was that all these *katras* were not as clean and spacious as he had seen in some recently constructed areas of New Delhi. Prem was yet to see the 'surprise' of this ugly looking area. During his second visit when he climbed the narrow and dark stairs after crossing the dirty courtyard, where this time too he noticed a cobbler sitting under a tree and 'hammering nails into a shoe', Prem was confronted with the roof of the house which suddenly appeared like 'a charming garden'. Swamiji was staying in one of the rooms situated on the roof. Beside the room, on the rooftop, was a large open area. Although the *katras* looked untidy from the outside, they were beautifully decorated. When Prem came to the rooftop, people were gathering there to see the Swamiji and listen to his sermon. The rooftop was appropriately decorated for the occasion. Its parapet was covered with clusters of red creepers and flower pots were arranged all around. There was a garlanded image of Lord Vishnu. Prem even noticed a small crystal clear pond built with stones where many colourful fish were swimming. The entire environment was soothing. The Swamiji was walking slowly and his devotees were following him. The sky was tinted with the orange glow of an approaching sunset. The environment differed in every aspect from what Prem had encountered on the way. Consequently the *katra* offered contrasting experiences for its visitor, the celestial atmosphere on the rooftop and the crowded city below. People were asking religious and philosophical questions, and Swamiji was replying to them one by one in a gracious and calm voice. The room in which Swamiji was sitting 'was sweet and heavy with incense. The temple bells began to ring, and there was chanting and clashing of cymbals in the temples in the city below' (Jhabvala, 1960, pp. 72, 128, 129, 1631).

Thus, the *katra* evokes an image of physical contrasts and a complex way of life. Only yards from the crowded, busy streets with intense commercial activity, the *katra* provided a retreat where one could reflect about religious and spiritual thoughts.

Chandni Chowk: The Moonlit Square

Tuan maintains that 'Naming is power – the creative power to call something into being, to render the invisible visible, to impart a certain character to things' (Tuan, 1991, p. 688). The very name Chandni Chowk evokes a powerful image of a glittering market of Mughal Shahjahanabad. Chandni Chowk extends westward from the famous Mughal Red Fort. During the eighteenth and nineteenth centuries it was one of the world's most beautiful bazaars. However, it no longer fits the descriptions of historians. The traditional view, however, is so deeply embedded in the minds of the people throughout India that a romantic image of the area is instantly triggered by the words 'Chandni Chowk'.

Shahjahanabad (1638–48), capital of the last Mughals, was planned by the Emperor Shah Jahan; the city is the true reflection of Mughal architecture (Dutt and Geib, 1987, p. 141). When the capital was built there were two main roads, Chandni Chowk and Khas Road. One of the visitors from Europe in 1656–68, Bernier, described the city in the following words, paraphrased by Dutt and Geib (1987, p 143):

> Many streets had arcades but except for the Chandni Chowk and Khas Raod, they were asymmetrical. On both sides of the streets lived officers and merchants. Most houses were made of clay and staw, few were brick or stone-built. A large number of common troopers, servants and camp followers lived in much smaller houses with thatched roofs, susceptible to fire. In one summer three fires were recorded which consumed 60,000 roofs because they occurred during the gusty summer winds that are known as loo. The Omrahs and the exalted men lived in the suburbs and on the banks of Jumna. The Chandni Chowk (Silver Market) was 150 feet wide with a canal in the middle and was considered the 'Great Bazaar of the Orient'. Even there the costly merchandise was not displayed, but were kept in warehouses and the shops were 'seldom decked with rich or showy articles'. On the other hand, one could see pots of oil or butter, baskets of rice, barley, chick-peas, wheat and other grains and lentils, as they were always displayed.

Once the heart of the old city of Shahjahanabad, Chadni Chowk maintains its glamorous image as one of the two major shopping centres of greater Delhi, the other being Connaught Place. The lively streets of Chandni Chawk are world famous. Several types of commercial endeavours are carried on here. Even for those who have not seen Chandni Chowk or who have never visited Delhi, Chandni Chowk summons up an image of a glittering, scented bazaar with Mughal splendor. One commonly envisions well-behaved crowds of shoppers strolling on the sidewalks or merely relaxing and chatting with fellow visitors. An area of business activity as well as relaxation, Chandni Chowk can be thought of as a traditional Indian version of Piccadilly Circus of London or Times

Square of New York. When one thinks of Delhi, Chandni Chowk automatically comes to mind. Various persons have differently translated the words 'Chandni Chowk' as 'Moonlit Square', 'Silver Street', 'Moonlight Street', and 'Moonlight Square'. Indeed 'Moonlit Square' is the closest translation, though Chandni Chowk is, in fact, more of a street than a square.

Much has been said in praise of Chandni Chowk in history books, very little of which is a negative. Rory Fonseca provides an example of an image of pre-British Chandni Chowk.

> Chandni Chowk, before its reconstruction in 1860, had many chattas across it but present building by-laws forbid such construction. This architectural feature, together with the canal and shade trees must have made it a remarkable street (Fonseca, 1971, pp. 74–75).

Shaded boulevards, a central running canal, *chattas* across the street, grandeur, royal elegance and an ambiance of glamour must have surrounded Chandni Chowk during those days. Besides its historical fame, its present-day attractions account for its important position in the minds of characters of contemporary fiction. The character of Chandni Chowk is distinguished and different from other areas of the city. Vibrant crowds, bright lights, decorated shops, sidewalk vendors, historically famous shopping spots such as *Ghantewala's* sweetmeat shop or *Parathewala's* lane, and well-known religious edifices such as the Sikh temple, Gurudwara Sisganj, the Muslim mosque, Fatehpuri Masjid, or the Jain Temple, all come to mind when one thinks of the place.

> The two main thoroughfares, which connected the city with the fortress and the outside world, were lined with merchant shops. One of these thoroughfares, Chandni Chowk ('silver market'), ran straight westward from the Red Fort toward the Lahore Gate of the city. The Chandni Chowk was one of the great bazaars of the Orient.
>
> Chandni Chowk continues to be a traditional, busy bazaar where motorized vehicles are prohibited. It is very densely populated with a mixture of Hindus and Muslims. Large parts of Old Delhi are gradually being transformed into commercial and small workshop uses (Dutt and Pomeroy, 2003, p. 338).

A Contrasting Image

Kamal's experience of Chandni Chowk, in the novel *My True Faces* by Chaman Nahal, is very different from the images previously described. Gurudwara Sisganj is one sacred place which stirs a feeling of reverence in him. But with the passage of time that sense has become much feebler than during his childhood days when he used to go there with his grandmother. During those visits his grandmother (whom he addressed as *Bebé*) used to clean the marble steps of the *gurudwara* before entering the sacred structure. The boy was accustomed to repeat what his *Bebé* used to do. Later in life religion had little significance for Kamal. In Chandni Chowk he saw several religious places (some small, some big), but they no longer stirred any religious feelings in his heart. He could not justify cleaning the marble steps of the Gurudwara Sisganj. Kamal thought that although there were many sacred places all around, there still existed misery and suffering for human beings.

For Kamal, Chandni Chowk looked like 'The broad, funnel-like passageway' (Nahal, 1978, p. 83). He found the bricks used in the construction of houses were of odd kinds. For him these bricks '... had no special spectrum, no distinct identity; a curious mud mixture, it was not even properly fired'. There were glittering shops on either side of the street, full of electric bulbs and neon lights, but the apartments were narrow and small. There was a large number of such houses on either side of the street. Kamal visualized these houses like 'scarred faces' which had only 'sockets' and not eyes. The area of Chandni Chowk is crowded, dirty, disorderly, and full of noise and bustle. Even its traffic did not maintain any discipline. He noticed a beautiful car trying to pass through the crowd on the road. The driver was honking the horn of his car to disperse the crowd to make a path for his car, but nobody was paying attention. Besides the unmanageable crowd, Kamal saw 'battered buses', cycle rickshaws and *tongas*, all jumbled together. Obese *sethjees* (rich merchants) were sitting lazily inside their shops. Pedestrians found it extremely difficult to walk on the sidewalks as the hawkers and vendors occupied most of the space to anchor their carts (Nahal, 1978, p. 83). Besides them, numerous small sidewalk vendors were selling a wide variety of commodities. Kamal thought that they might be earning only a rupee a day (about 25 cents at the time when the novel was written, that is the 1970s. Now equivalent to about 4 cents). He found that in Chandni Chowk one could see merchants of every status, ranging from very rich to the very poor.

Most of the customers and pedestrians Kamal saw in Chandni Chowk were clad in *dhotis* (traditional dress for men in India) and caps. Other types of dress such as pants, bush shirts, *kurta* (traditional upper garments for both men and women in India) and *shalwar* (traditional lower garments for both men and women in India) could also be seen. Women were mostly in *saris*. Although one could see *saris* of many colours, most wore *saris* in varying degrees of whiteness, ranging from spotlessly clean white to dull and soiled. Kamal's picture of the area indicates that Chandni Chowk is a traditional Indian market or dwelling place in structure and function.

Kamal went a step further in thinking that if there was any single identity of Chandni Chowk, it was in its 'uniform drabness'. Unlike the glamorous images of Chandni Chowk conveyed by various historical accounts, Kamal's Chandni Chowk surprisingly appeared untidy and dull. The entire environment – every object, street, sidewalk and buildings, trees, leaves – seemed to have been covered with a thin veneer of 'soot' and 'smut'. Kamal became so philosophical seeing such an environment in the area that he visualized drabness and gloomy surroundings as 'Brahman' (the all pervading supreme spirit).

Nahal notes that as one proceeds on the main street of Chandni Chowk, one sees narrow lanes meeting the main street from both sides. At their corners one finds crowds and noise. Humidity, heat, and stenches such as that of burning shellac, ooze from the lanes and strike the main thoroughfare. Sarcastically, Nahal observes that this is the 'bullion market' of Delhi, the 'legendary Chandni Chowk'. It is possible that bullion, gold, and silver might be hidden in the iron safes but what pedestrians experience is unsightly scenes and stench. Nahal is obsessed by the dirty surroundings. The picture he evokes is full of:

> '... murky greyness, a brownish, blackish line of horses and carriages and people flowing on through the drain of overhanging buildings and trees and wires, flowing on like an open sewer, this mess of poverty and dirt, swelling in strength as each small lane came and joined it, swelling in stink, and in gloom and in drabness (Nahal, 1978, p. 84).

Eventually, Kamal reaches his cousin Mukut's house located on a narrow lane near Fatehpuri Masjid (the mosque). Upon entering the lane, Kamal encounters a large number of children on the street. During summer evenings and nights, it is common to sleep on rooftops. Mukut and Kamal sleep there and Kamal notices that people have also gathered on a neighbouring rooftop. Some are even eating their dinner there. During the summer evenings, rooms are very hot and uncomfortable. Rooftops then provide very soothing breezes. Ahmed Ali's *Twilight in Delhi* includes several descriptions of family members coming up to the rooftops in the evenings.

In present times, both male and female members can be seen enjoying the cool breeze. Kamal observes that these men and women were partially or casually dressed. Male members are in *dhotis* and females in their 'petticoats'. Men had even rolled up their *dhotis* so that they could feel the cool breeze over their entire body. They had left the pain of the oppressive heat of the day behind them. Some were even laughing and singing in a low voice.

Since it was not yet dark, many kite-flyers came upon the rooftops and started flying their kites. They were deeply engrossed in defeating their competitors. They tried to fly their kites higher than others and also to cut the threads of the kite of their opponents. This created a picturesque scene in the evening sky. In *Twilight in Delhi* there are numerous depictions of such scenes (Ali, 1966, pp. 28, 62). Kamal observed from the rooftops during the evening hours that the city streets did not seem to be emitting the stench that he had experienced on his way to Mukut's house. The world of the rooftop seemed a world away from what he had encountered earlier on the street. People were relaxed, enjoying the moment, happy and oblivious to what transpired in the streets below (Nahal, 1978, p. 88).

Conclusion

We have seen through examples in literature that Old Delhi (the walled city, Shahjahanabad) is presented in a variety of images. Knowledge of such experiential dimensions of geographic environment could be gathered only from reading literary pieces written by perspicacious, reflective and powerfully creative writers. Scarcely changed since the British occupation is the area of the *katras* with their kaleidoscopic combination of shops, storage areas and private residences with contrasting views of littered courtyards and attractive rooftop gardens. Readers of literature note diametrically opposed images of the area that remains the heart not only of Old Delhi, but of the entire city. Chandni Chowk, despite its romantic and legendary aura as the silvery moonlit square is shown by realistic writers to be crowded, dirty and even repulsive. From the view of fictional characters in novels and short stories as well as from the observations in reports, Old Delhi, while maintaining the vitality of its bustling streets, has gradually lost the romantic splendour of the Mughal Shahjahanabad and the romance of the silver street.

References

Aiken S., Charles, 'Faulkner's Yoknapatawpha County', *The Geographical Review*, No. 67, 1977, pp. 1–21.

Ali, Ahmed, *Twilight in Delhi*, Bombay: Oxford University Press, 1966.

Bista, Pankaj, *Beete Din* ('Bygone Days'), Kahani, February, 1974.

Chopra, Sudarshan, 'Jaren' ('Roots'), 'Sarak Durghatna' ('Road Accident'), Allahabad: Nilabh Prakashan, 1972a, pp. 11–33.

Chopra, Sudarshan, Oob ('Disgust'), *Sarak Durghatna* ('Road Accident'), Allahabad: Nilabh Prakashan, 1972b.

Dayal Maheshwar, *Dilli Meri Dilli* ('Delhi, My Delhi'), New Delhi: Hindustan Times Prakashan, 1978.

Dutt, Ashok, K. and Margaret M. Geib, *Fully Annotated Atlas of South Asia*, Boulder: Westview Press, 1987.

Dutt, Ashok, K. and George, M. Pomeroy, 'Cities of South Asia', in Stanley D. Brunn, Jack F. Williams and Donald J. Zeigler (eds.), *Cities of the World: World Regional Urban Development*, Lanham/Boulder/New York/Oxford: Rowman & Littlefield Publishing, Inc., 2003, pp. 330–371.

Fonseca, Rory, 'The Walled City of Old Delhi', Ekistics, No. 31, 1971.

Gupta, Narayani. 'Delhi Between Two Empires 1803–1931: Society, Government and Urban Growth'. Delhi: Oxford University Press, 1981.

Jagmohan, *Rebuilding Shahjahanabad: The Walled City of Delhi*, Delhi: Vikas Publishing House Pvt. Ltd., 1975.

Jhabvala, Ruth Prawer, *The Householder*, New York: W. W. Norton and Co. Inc., 1960.

Nahal, Chaman, *My True Faces*, New Delhi: Vision Books Private Ltd., 1978.

Rakesh, Mohan, 'Lingering Shadows', Delhi: Hind Pocket Books (P.) Ltd., 1970.

Tuan, Yi-Fu, 'Language and the Making of Place: Narrative–Descriptive Approach', *Annals, Association of American Geographers*, No. 81, December 1991, pp. 684–696.

Vaid, Krishna Baldev, *A Blind Alley: Silence and Other Stories*, Calcutta: A Writer's Workshop Publication, 1972.

Yadav, Rajendra. *Andekha Anjan Pul* (Unseen, Unknown Bridges) Delhi: Rajpal and Sons, 1963.

33

Spatial and Temporal Characteristics of Elite Residential Colonies in Delhi, 1982–2004

BALESHWAR THAKUR AND MUKESH YADAV

Nature of Problem

Land in Delhi is used for a variety of purposes among which residential land use is most important. It accounts for a large part of built-up area of the city with varying patterns of population density and housing quality. Being the largest user of space, residential houses are heterogeneous, immobile, complicated and expensive. The houses are occupied by households belonging to different social and economic classes, depending on their capacity to pay the housing market. Therefore, in Indian cities, the segregation of people into different neighbourhoods on the basis of social characteristics, such as ethnicity, occupation or income is a fairly common feature. The spatial distribution of housing characteristics, the nature of housing markets and the neighbourhood communities within cities have become one of the major research foci of urban social geography (Cadwallader, 1996, p. 241).

Over the last three decades, most cities in India, including Delhi, have experienced residential and social polarization in the built-environment and social space resulting into slums and squatter settlements and high-status residential areas. The net result has been massive inequality and increasing intolerance. Our cities are becoming more divided, increasingly segregated and differentiated across the lines of race, ethnicity, gender, sexuality, ability, class and power (Del Casino, 2009, p. 1). Social geographers are interested in these issues because they deal with organization and contestation of space (Del Casino, 2009, p. 2). However, study of intra-urban residential patterns has largely focused on ethnic segregation, slum identification and eradication (Dutt and Halder, 2008), gentrification, renewal, housing markets and patterns, homogenous social areas, fringe development and residential mobility. Dutt and Halder (2008, p. 117) made the following observation:

> The non-slum dwellers, [a considerable section falling in the elites colonies] ..., consist primarily of the middle class with a section of the lower middle class and all of the rich.... Non-slum dwellers' exclusive housing characteristics include living in flats, multi- and two storey dwellings, roofs made from permanent materials, household living space over 200 sq feet, household with three or more rooms, owned bathrooms, separate kitchens and toilets, and tap water. Again, the exclusive asset ownership of non-slum dwellers includes ownership of color TV, telephones and automobiles.

Various studies on urban land use indicate that the high income group plays a major role in shaping the internal structure of the city (Thakur and Parai, 1992; Knox, 1994; Cadwallader, 1996). This is the segment of society that monopolizes power, holds status and wealth, and makes meaningful decisions about the development of infrastructures, in the process of fostering efficient democratic governance at the local level and examines the activities and values of urban managers. The action of specific urban elites will have a powerful, if not determining, influence on the course of urban development (Moffett and Freund, 2004, p. 134). Thus, the structure and dynamics of social status in a city control urban structural change, especially residential segregation. Here social status means earning good educational qualifications, engaged in lucrative occupation and income. Viewed in this light, the elitists and representative groups from civil society attempt to shape their cities by developing comprehensive infrastructures. It is therefore essential that key roles played by elitists must be recognized, as they work to improve living conditions, not just for themselves, but also for the communities. Elites are the most distinguished and powerful groups of the society and are important constituents of the class system (Bottomore, 1964; Thakur and Chauhan, 2005, p. 100). They generally occupy strategically sound urban land on good sites with higher intensities of basic services, transportation and communication linkage (Thakur and Chauhan, 2005, p. 100). They are affluent households and occupy desirable sites on well-drained high land away from nuisances, such as noise, odours, smoke, industry and flooding (Harris and Ullman, 1945).

Cities are dynamic and evolve with time. With the continued expansion of the urban area, the high-status areas also expand and their location and characteristics change fast in response to physical, economic, social and political forces operating in the city (Thakur and Chauhan, 2005, p. 100). The urban limits of the city have expanded four-fold and incorporated the green grasslands as well as the fertile agricultural lands under it's fold. The rapid growth of the city owes much to industrialization. With the growth of industries and transport technologies, the elite area expands sectorally along transportation lines in response to a desire among the elites to combine accessibility with fringe living to a desire among the almost-as-affluent to acquire the social cachet of living in the same neighbourhood as the rich (Knox, 1994, p. 101). It may also develop in a leapfrog manner in any part of the city. The result of this process is the growth and development of single-family home in the fringe, especially on a large farm land called 'farm house'. This is the vehicle for maximizing capitalist consumption. Thus, with the development of transport technologies, significant rearrangements in high-status residential areas have occurred, such as proliferation in the number of areas, vertical and horizontal expansion, and growth of new bourgeois consisting of public administrators, scientists, private sector executives, financial analysis, management consultants, designers, marketing experts, technicians, people directly involved in cultural production (e.g., authors, editors, radio and TV producers and presenters) and journalists (Knox, 1994, p. 218). Taken together, the residential landscape in big cities over the last four decades has changed tremendously. Thus, it is important to study the pattern and the spatial location of the residences of high status group.

Background

Research on elite colonies has not attracted much attention in spite being an important segment of residential ecology across the world. However, a few studies are available which have identified, measured and analyzed the locational characteristics of elite colonies.

Burgess (1925) concentric zone theory is an initial attempt to conceptualize the location of highest status group on the city's periphery. His zonal model became popular as a device for describing and explaining urban structure. It has become a benchmark in urban studies. Hoyt's (1939) theory of spatial pattern of socioeconomic status also places high class residential areas radiating from the CBD in sectors following the transportation lines. The multiple nuclei theory of Harris and Ullman (1945) identifies a series of nuclei rather than the single central core. According to them, the high class residential areas were found to be located at well-drained highlands close to the outlying business district, away from low class residential areas. The above classical models of urban structure reflect some broad patterns of residential mosaic that the socioeconomic status of an area increases as one moves away from the city centre towards the periphery.

A different picture emerged in an analysis on Philadelphia (Blumenfeld, 1940) where the economically-privileged area of the city was intermediate between the CBD and not fully urbanized fringe of the outer zone of the city. In another study on Oxford (Collin and Magey, 1959), the concentration of high class residential areas was found closest to the city centre. The same pattern has been identified in Puerto Rico with the highest status group residentially congregated in the city centre, while the low status group in the fringe (Schwirian and Ri-Velaso, 1971).

A few attempts have been made to measure the status of areas using the indices as possession of telephones, renting values, property values, entries in *Who's Who*, etc. The locational pattern of high-status areas in Melbourne for 1913, 1922, 1933, 1941, 1950 and 1962 was delineated (Johnston, 1966). It is revealed that the area dominated by the elitists is within 6.5 kms of CBD. The obtained pattern confirms sectoral theory as the majority of the elitists are concentrated in just two sectors. On the contrary, Robson (1966) finds the concentration of high status areas in the outskirts of Sunderland and poor in the city core by plotting rating values. The high class residential areas in Edinburgh are found to be centrally located while using property values as an index by Gordon (1966). Houghton (1987) study on Melbourne for a period of fifteen years concluded that the higher income occupation groups were spread out towards the periphery. In consonance with Burgess theory, a positive relationship between social status and distance from the city centre has been found in a study on 318 American cities (Schwirian, Hankins and Ventrescas, 1991). Thus, the above review brought into focus the difference in location of elites in industrial and non-industrial cities. The study of Chicago by Burgess is an example of industrial city where the location of elites has been shown towards the periphery, whereas Sjoberg (1960) studied non-industrial cities selecting examples from contemporary Third World, historical Europe and ancient Mesopotamia. Of particular interest is the fact that the pattern of location of elites in a non-industrial city is completely reversed to that of an industrial city.

A few studies on Indian cities have appeared during the post-independence phase. In the pre-industrial cities, such as Delhi and Mumbai, the centres were mainly occupied by the high status and high income groups, while in colonial times they were occupied by the merchants, businessman and their business establishments (Thakur and Chauhan, 2005, pp. 103–104). Studies dealing with urban residential structure in India have ignored the fact that the cities are the outcome of historical circumstances which are in no way similar to the European and American history. Here, caste is one of the oldest bases of residential segregation and people belonging to similar racial, cultural, religious and economic backgrounds tend to segregate. Residential deconcentration and segregation are more based on caste and religion than on ecological or economic factors (Gandhi 1983, p. 58). In Bangalore, the best buildings were inhabited by Brahmins and, usually, the best buildings of residences are in or near the inner core (Gist, 1958). By contrast, in Banaras the location of good residential houses with great open space is found in the outer zone (Singh, 1955). However, in Hyderabad-Secunderabad, there is no graded pattern in the distribution of income groups (Alam, 1965). The high rental areas in Pune are located close to the city centre (Mehta, 1968); but in Kanpur, the elite residential location has been found to be confined to the river front sector in the north, due to its higher ground, pleasant river view and fresh air (Singh, 1972). The concentration of industries in inner core has shifted the elites to the fringe. It has been competently argued by Singh (1977) that in Shillong, the pattern of high status areas conforms to combinations of both sector and multiple nuclei theories. In the linear city Patna, which is located on the southern bank of Ganga, the high status residential areas including power, business and professional elites are found in the western and southern fringe of the city along the transportation axis (Yadav, 1987).

In reality, the Indian city is more complex than many cities in the world, and is characterized by a discontinuous telescoping of political, cultural and economic structures belonging to different historic periods (Tewari, Weinstein and Prakasa Rao, 1986, p. 5). Brush (1977) study revealed that the central bazaar is still regarded as prestigious which inhabits high status people. New housing colonies of high status groups are coming up in the fringe areas. Another study on the socioeconomic structure of Mumbai and Delhi, Brush (1986) demonstrates that there are inner parts of both urban areas with high status population and people of low rank living farther from the centre. Accordingly, old cores of both cities retain features of traditional social ranking, while the current growth parallels the ecology of economic classes observed in Western civilization. In addition, it is stated that new elite residential colonies are found in well-defined sectors of the outer zones in Mumbai and Delhi. There is also a recent tendency of the upper classes to move to the outskirts in Delhi, in farm houses and posh residential complexes (Dupont, 2004, p. 163). Berry and Rees (1969) study on Kolkata and Berry and Spodek (1971) study on Ahmedabad, Mumbai, Kanpur, Chennai, Pune and Sholapur confirmed similar theories on centrality of white collar occupational groups. Dutt and Noble's (1977) study on Kolkata again confirmed that most desirably residential location factor in the city is centrality, but high rent and cost factor limit residential land use which consist of high rise apartments and older buildings. Bangalore's ecological structure is found to be not simple "rich centre and poor periphery" of the classical model, but a middle class city core and both high status and low status periphery (Prakasa Rao and Tewari, 1986). Cities are in constant flux. One of the best examples is the development of Koramangla area in Bengaluru on the model of the industrial metropolis. Kalra (2007) has recently documented the emergence of new elite residential colonies in Bengaluru consisting of recreational sites, shopping malls, tech-culture, state-of-the-art architecture, quality building and luxurious residential theme-based apartments by world class builders in the high-tech zone.

Thakur and Sagu (2007) studied the locational patterns of elite colonies in Delhi and developed elite typology. It has been concluded that the spatial distribution of elite colonies makes a belt south of the CBD, i.e. Connaught Place. It is found that the colonies close to the core have administrative and political elites and industrial and business elites in the periphery. In another study, Thakur and Chauhan (2005) compared the growth characteristics of elite colonies in Mumbai and Delhi and found that status of elites increases with distance from the core in Delhi, but it is totally different in Mumbai.

Scope of Study

The purpose of the present study is to identify elites, examine the change in the levels of elite residential colonies and analyze the changing patterns of their distribution in Delhi between the period of 1982 to 2004. Such dynamic study may throw light on the changing patterns and processes operating in the city system of Delhi, and may contribute towards a theory development on urban residential differentiation.

Study Area

Delhi has been selected for the present study because it is the most important centre of political and economic power. Secondly, the authors have a deep familiarity with the study area. Thirdly, this research work is an extension of the previous studies conducted by the authors (Thakur and Chauhan, 2005; Thakur and Sagu, 2007).

Delhi is located in northern India on the banks of the river Yamuna, a tributary of the Ganga, 23 meters above the sea level. It is bounded by the states of Uttar Pradesh on the east and Haryana on the south, west and north. It is one of the oldest cities in India and has served as the capital city for a succession of empires and kingdoms, as well as for modern India. Historical evidences seem to indicate that the city has an antiquity of at least three thousand years (Dayal, 2003, p. 2). Its timeless glory can be seen in its magnificent monuments, great ruins, centuries old settlements and ancient paths (Dayal, 2003, p. 2). The architectural monuments of Delhi include all periods of Indian history which include Qutab Minar, Red Fort, Jama Masjid, Old Secretariat building, Parliament House, India Gate and its environs, Lutyen's Delhi, Connaught Place, Pragati Maidan, Asian Games Sports complexes, University of Delhi, Jamia Millia Islamia, Jawaharlal Nehru University, All India Institute of Medical Sciences, Rashtrapati Bhawan, Pusa Institute, numerous forts, Indian Institute of Technology, Akhshardham Temple, palaces and gardens, and Delhi Metro Rail. The most prominent non-architectural feature of New Delhi is the Raj Path, the main east-west axis, along which are located governmental buildings, research centres, National Art Gallery and Museum. Thus, Delhi presents a very interesting picture, blending the ancient with the modern. Two prominent features of the geography of Delhi are the Yamuna floodplains and the northern extension of Aravalli range called the Delhi ridge. Today, Delhi is not just a major regional metropolitan centre, but it is the national capital of the Indian Republic since 1912, when the British Government of India constructed its new capital.

Delhi is the largest city in north India (15.3 m) and second largest in the country after Mumbai (18.3 m), Kolkata having 14.3 m (Weeks, 2005,

p. 471). In the last six decades, Delhi has experienced phenomenal growth in population. Its population has increased from 1.4 m in 1951 to 5.7 m in 1981, 9.7 m in 1991, 13.7 m in 2001 and 15.3 m in 2005 (Dayal, 2003, p. 3; Weeks, 2005, p. 471). The combination of the demographic transition, political independence and the migrants and refugees after country's partition in 1947 triggered an explosive growth of population. The city has always attracted people of diverse cultural settings from other states, resulting millions of people migrating to the city in search of jobs. They mostly crowd around the outer zone of the city in the shanty settlements. Consequently, the urban area has increased from 46 km^2 in 1901 to 648 km^2 in 2001. Densities in Delhi increase with distance from the central area and continue to do so even at the urban fringe (Kumar, 2000, p. 156).

Delhi consists of three contrasting landscapes: Old Delhi is the former Muslim capital and is a crowded city with many narrow streets and slum dwellings. New Delhi, in contrast, possesses orderly and diagonal traffic pattern with wide boulevards, modern buildings and expansive residential areas, which exude a feeling of openness and quiet. The unplanned form constitutes about 35 per cent of the total city landscape which is a loose coalition of urban villages (Tyagi, 1982). It is an inverted compact city, which has low gross residential densities in the inner areas and high gross densities in the outer areas (Kumar, 2000, p. 153). There are single or double-storey residential buildings in most of the inner city areas, while four to eight storey residential buildings are quite common in the outer areas (Kumar, 2000, p. 153). The busiest street in Delhi is Chandni Chowk, which is lined with tiny commercial shops. Connaught Place is the city centre and central business district which was built by the British in 1931, just south of the old city of Delhi. South of the government area is more expansive residential area focused on expansive parks and ornamental gardens. Located in New Delhi are the embassies, luxury hotels, government office buildings and airline offices necessary for a vibrant political capital.

Delhi has been the important commercial, cultural, industrial, financial, trading and transportation centre of northern India for centuries. It has become an important manufacturing centre producing electronics and engineering goods, automobile parts and electrical appliances, equipment and metal products. Also, Delhi is the home of 90 Colleges and half a dozen universities, making a good centre of learning and education. The global market economy, evident across the nation, is visible in Delhi, where swanky clubs, restaurants, department stores, boutiques, cinemas and video parlours share space with traditional businesses.

Delhi reflects the imprint of globalization (Shrivastava, 2005). Economic globalization is reflected in the offices of transnational corporations and international hotels and cultural globalization is visible in the advertisements for Western popular culture. It has become the important centre for the flows of information, global markets for commodities, investment capital, foreign exchange, advertising, major national and foreign firms, international headquarters of trade, leading non-governmental organizations, for example, WHO, UNESCO, UNDP, etc., and cultural industries including art and design, fashion, film and television.

Data and Methods

This study attempts to identify and analyze the nature and characteristics of the elite residential colonies for 2004 and compare the results with those of 1982. The colonies which are most preferred by the high status group are identified as the elite residential colonies. Elites were identified on the basis of positional and reputational approaches. According to the positional approach, the study identified five stratas of elites, namely: civil, defense, foreign, political and business, and according to the reputational approach, academic, humanities and others including religious leaders, feudal groups, etc. The study, thus, formulated eight stratas of elite occupational groups. The study uses India's *Who's Who* and the Telephone Directory of Delhi to identify important personalities residing in Delhi. Those considered as elites are the top-class political leaders, Members of Parliament, high officials, top lawyers, industrialists, Ambassadors in India, defense, civil services, academics, business, and top post holder of various firms. A sample of about 700 persons for 1982 and about 980 samples for 2004 have been collected from the above-mentioned secondary data sources (Satyajit, 1982; Inderjit, 2004). India's *Who's Who* is an authentic collection of elites which is published annually and can be considered as the best available published data for this study. Seventy-six colonies are thus listed and the number of important personalities residing in each of them ranges from one to fifty-four for 1982 and 196 colonies for 2004 are listed and the number of important personalities ranges from as low as one to as high as fifty-one. This difference suggests that not all the colonies are equally preferred. The one with higher number of elites show higher degree of preferability and recording low preference indicates very low degree of preferability.

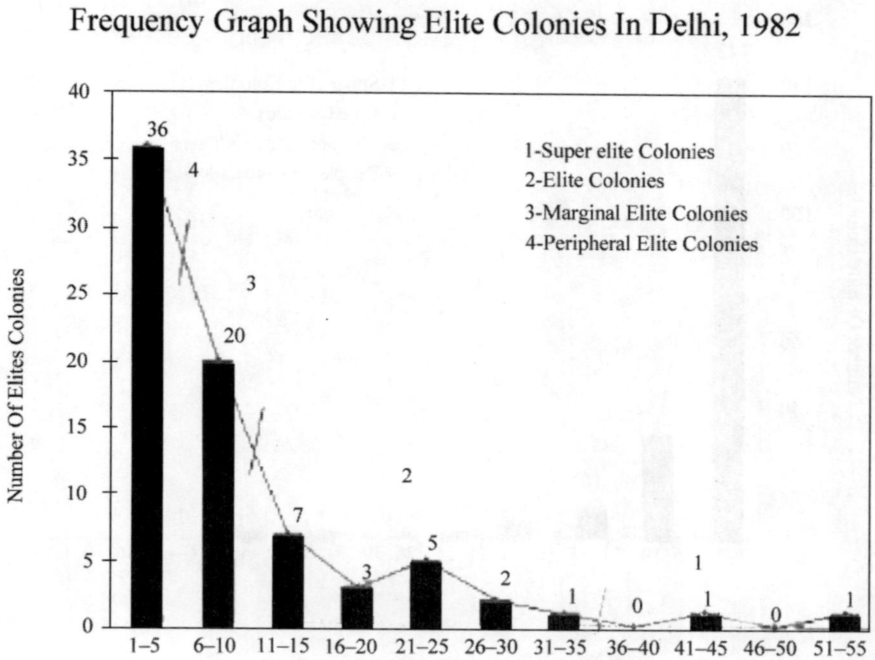

Fig. 33.1 Frequency Graph Showing Elite Colonies in Delhi, 1982.

Thereafter, the colonies are grouped with the help of a frequency graph (Figures 33.1 and 33.2). These groups represent a set of histograms and polygons, which have been drawn to show the concentration of colonies in each group for 1982 and 2004. Since the graph reveals four clear breaks, the colonies are grouped into four categories: first are super elite colonies, second are elite colonies, third are marginal elite colonies and fourth are peripheral elite colonies.

Results and Discussion

Elite Colonies in 1982

The first group includes "super elite colonies" which were two in number, each of which contained thirty-six to fifty-four important personalities; the second group including eighteen colonies, termed as "elite colonies", recorded eleven to thirty-five personalities each; the third group of twenty colonies is termed as the "marginal elite colonies", in which each colony contained between six to ten personalities; lastly, there were thirty-six

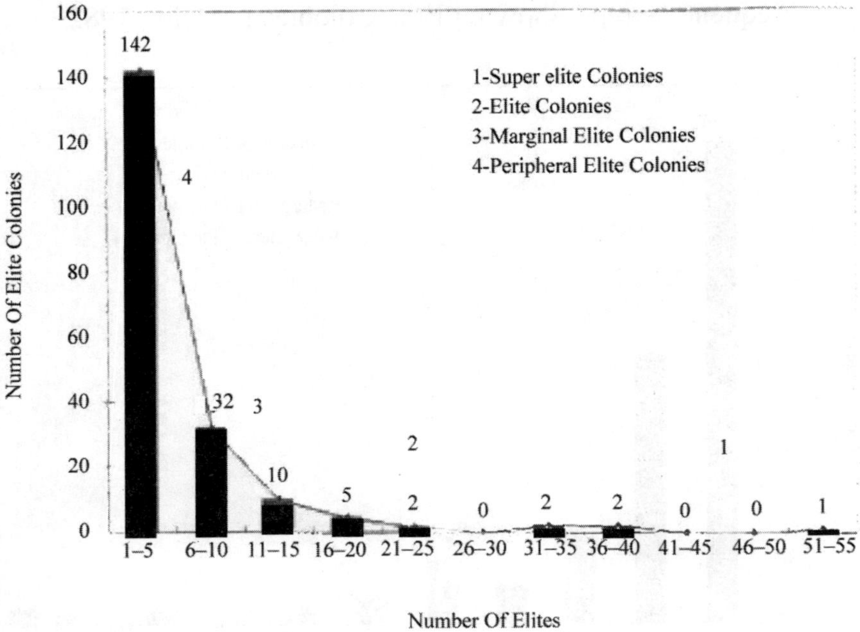

Fig. 33.2 Frequency Graph Showing Elite Colonies in Delhi, 2004.

colonies termed as "peripheral elite colonies", each containing less than five personalities.

The general location of these four groups shows that the higher the standard, the greater is the distance from the core and those high-grade, elite colonies were located closer to major communication lines. Nearly all the elite residential colonies were located on the "Kohi" region because the area is not prone to floods. The spatial distribution of elite residential colonies was not random but indicated a sectional pattern as the major concentration was in just two sectors of the city showing an outward expansion of the same sectors in which the elite had first located themselves. The distribution pattern of the elite shows a concentration of particular occupation groups in certain colonies. The two "super elite' colonies show a concentration of diplomats in one and elite industrial or business persons in the other. Most of the "elite colonies" show a dominance of industrial or business persons, some colonies like Kaka Nagar, Lodhi Colony, Tilak Marg and Pandara Road, show the dominance of elite government offices. All the "marginal elite colonies" do not show similar characteristics. Some display a dominance of industrial or business persons, some others that of government officials, whereas a few represent a much diversified character.

The small sample size of the "peripheral elite colonies" does not permit any generalization. The colonies closer to the core have an administrative character and those towards the periphery show a greater industrial character. Because of the diverse character of elites in the city, the colonies are classified as international, national, state and city level elite residential colonies. Of all the colonies, Chanakyapuri is the only one which reveals a very high concentration of the international elite.

Elite Residential Colonies in 2004

Figure 33.2 indicates the persistence of four groups of elites in 2004 also. The location of the identified elite residential colonies shows that most of these colonies are located to the south of CBD. From the 196 identified colonies, only 42 fall to the north of CBD. This implies that the residents of about 78 per cent of identified elite colonies favour the southern locations. These colonies are spread from the core to the periphery in the south of the CBD with the river Yamuna acting as the eastern boundary and the cantonment area on the western side. It forms a triangular zone with Gurgaon-Badarpur Road in the base and Connaught Place as its apex. The general trend of the elite colonies shows that with time, the elitists started moving away from the congested core and slowly more and more elite colonies came to be located towards the periphery.

The absolute pattern of the elite colony is analyzed by taking the total figures of showing the concentration of the elitists in the colonies and the percentage of the occupational categories of each of the colonies to show the dominant occupational structure in the form of identified elite groups.

Super Elite Colonies

The three colonies – Chanakyapuri, Vasant Vihar, and Safdarjung Enclave – classified as super elite colonies, are located to the south of the CBD. Chanakyapuri, also known as Diplomat's colony came into existence in 1953. Vasant Vihar is located further and came into existence in 1955. It is about 9 kms. to the south of CBD and is very close to Anand Niketan, West End, R.K. Puram, and Munirka. Safdarjung Enclave located east of Vasant Vihar and R.K. Puram is about 8.4 kms south of the CBD. It is occupied mainly by public and defense elites.

Elite Colonies

All the colonies under this group are located south of the CBD except Mayur Vihar Phase I. More than 55 per cent of them are located in the Southern triangle between CBD and Ring Road and Panchsheel Marg. They are along major roads and have easy connections not only with CBD but other parts of Delhi. In 1982, twenty colonies were identified which have now decreased to 19 in 2004 due to movement of Safdarjung Enclave to super elite colonies. Some of the colonies like Sundernagar, Panchsheel, Malviya Nagar, Lajpat Nagar, and Defence Colony have been developed after independence by the Ministry of Rehabilitation. Large number of elite samples is from Tughlak Road, Tilak Marg, Haus Khas Enclave, Greater Kailash I, Defence Colony, Lodi Road, etc. Multi-functional elites live in this group.

Marginal Elite Colonies

Under this group, eighteen colonies were included in 1982, which rose to thirty-two in 2004. Colonies of higher number of samples are Motibagh, Dr. Rajinder Prasad Road, Bapa Nagar, Janpath, New Friends Colony, Prithviraj Road, Rajouri Garden and Jangpura Extension. Fifty per cent of these colonies came into existence either before independence or after to house the refugees. These colonies are closer to CBD than the first two groups. They are at an average distance of about 7 km from the CBD but little away from the Ring Road.

Peripheral Elite Colonies

This group consists of varied nature of development. This is occupied by low grade elites consisting of varied class and creed with different education and social background. They account for large share of percentage of elite colonies. In 1982, they were 36 in number, which jumped to 142 in 2004, accounting for 70 per cent of the total elite residential colonies. They are located close to the core and towards the periphery. Some of them developed before 1947 and some after 1965. The peripheral colonies are of two kinds: the older and the newer elites. The older elites are located very close to the core and the newer have developed towards the periphery. The majority of the colonies are located in south and northwestern sectors and a few are elsewhere.

Relative Pattern

The relative analysis is completed by taking the percentage of each occupational group and analyzing its distribution in the city. Fifty-four colonies consist of industrial and business elites. Sadarjung Enclave, Vasant Vihar, and Maharani Bagh have the highest percentage of industrial elites as they are closely located to Mehrauli, Naraina and Okhla industrial area. The maximum percentage of diplomats is located in Chanakyapuri, Parliament Street, Vasant Vihar, Jor Bagh, Greater Kailash I, Haus Khas Enclave and Friends Colony. The major concentration of civil elites is in Moti Nagar, Chanakya Puri and Kaka Nagar. The major concentration of public sector elite is in Safdarjung Enclave, Greater Kailash I, South Extension I, Defence Colony, Barakhambha Road, and Tees January Marg. The South Extension and Greater Kailash I are the private freehold colonies. Power elites dealing with public affairs, like the government, ministries etc., show the highest number of samples, i.e., 197. They are mostly concentrated in Central and Southern part of the city in Lodi Road, R.K. Puram, Dr. Rajinder Prasad Road, South Avenue Lane, etc. The trend of distribution shows that power elites are less concentrated. Tughlak Road, Safdarjang Enclave, Jor Bagh, Defence Colony, Chanakyapuri, Rafi Marg, Greater Kailash I, Lodhi Colony and South Block specialize in defence elites being closer to Defence Headquarters. The elites in the field of humanities are spread over eighty-eight colonies including Hauz Khas, Defence Colony, Golf Link, Gulmohar Park, Kalkaji, Vasant Vihar, and Vikas Marg. Similarly, academic elites are also scattered over seventy colonies as the institutions are also dispersed in the city. Other elites include astrologers, sportspersons, etc., which contain small part of the total.

Changes in Spatial Locations

The number of elite colonies in 1982 were seventy-six, while in 2004, they increased to one hundred ninety-six (increase by two and a half times). The number of super elites was two in 1982 and three in 2004, elites twenty in 1982 and nineteen in 2004, marginal elites eighteen in 1982 and thirty-two in 2004, and peripheral elites thirty-six in 1982 and one hundred forty-two in 2004. The change in number is most obvious at the marginal and peripheral levels indicating five-fold increase in the latter. This process of spatial change can be termed as peripheralisation or suburbanization of elite colonies. Two broad classes of explanation can be suggested for this phenomenon. The first is natural evolution emphasizing change in transportation technology and the construction of new housing at the urban fringe in Delhi. The second is flight from MIG colonies emphasizing the migration of high income households to avoid the social problems of central parts (Mieszkowski and Mills, 1993). The first suggests a laissez-faire approach and the second an interventionist strategy indicating that richer people will move from the central city towards more remote fringe (Bogart, 1998, p. 181)

Thus, it is important from the above that center and fringe is contrasting with respect to the number and size of elite colonies. During 1982–2004, the upper level elite colonies have shown stability and size has not changed due to restricted expansion. The colonies are fully built and are occupied only by elites. In case of vacancy, the houses are occupied only by elites. Therefore, a balance is maintained. On the other hand, the lower level elite colonies are accommodative particularly in the fringe making size of the elite colony dynamic.

The zonal analysis has shown increasing concentration of the elite colonies in the fringe and the sectoral analysis has revealed heavy concentration in the southern sector. The concentration has been influenced by the local site conditions as well as relief features. The sector has also been influenced by the Aravalli ridge (Delhi ridge) and dense networks of roads making the area environmentally suitable. On the other hand, the northern sector has not been attractive to the elites, except growth of farm houses along the G.T. Road. Thus, a decentralization of elite residence has been common in the last two decades, which is discernible in Rohini, Dwarka, Patparganj, and Mayur Vihar. Surprisingly, east Delhi is devoid of elite colonies, except for Patparganj, Mayur Vihar and Vivek Vihar due to environmental constraints.

The pattern of occupational groups among elites reflects many changes. Most of the super and high status colonies inhabited a specialized occupational group, whereas lower status colonies did not show any pattern of occupational concentration. In 2004, business, defense, and humanities elite groups moved outwards towards the periphery, whereas political and civil elites stayed back at the core. Political and civil elites were largely located closer to the CBD, whereas business and industrial elites were located at a distance from the CBD. Delhi being the seat of political power and a center of commerce pulls people of higher strata in the city. With growing population, many elite residential colonies are mushrooming in the city lured by fascinating malls, multiplexes, real estates, entertainment centers, and hip-hop lifestyles. If the pattern of their expansion continues, soon Delhi can justifiably earn the title of "Elite Island".

Conclusion

The following conclusions are obtained from the foregoing analysis: (i) there has been significant changes in spatial locations of elite colonies between the period 1982 and 2004 (ii) the study has demonstrated that the number, size-distribution and functional characteristics of elite colonies have variations across the city, reflecting stability in the core and instability in the periphery (iii) the study has also revealed the process of peripheralization and suburbanization in the location of elite colonies due to natural evolution of the city, migration of high income households from LIG and MIG areas and DDA policy (iv) it is evident that industrial, business and humanities elites have moved to peripheral elite colonies in the hope of acquiring large urban space (v) the analysis also found that the acute measurement and identification of changing elite colonies is a challenging exercise, methodologically. Therefore, of particular interest would be an updated study of identification of elite colonies, focusing on income of households, land values, and area covered by the house.

References

Alam, S. M. *Hyderabad and Secunderabad (Twin Cities): A Study in Urban Geography*, Bombay: Allied Publishing, 1965.

Berry, B. J. L. and Rees, P. H. 'The Factorial Ecology of Calcutta', *American Journal of Sociology*, 74(5): 445–491, 1969.

Berry, B. J. L. and Spodek, H. 'Comparative Ecologies of Large Indian Cities', *Economic Geography*, 47(2): 266–285, 1971.

Bogart, W.T. *The Economics of Cities and Suburbs*, Upper Saddle River, N.J.: Prentice Hall, 1998.

Blumenfeld, H. 'On the Concentric Circle Theory of Urban Growth', *Land Economics*, 25: 209–212, 1949.

Bottomore, T. B. *Elites and Society*, London: Penguin Books, 1964.

Brush, J. E. 'Growth and Spatial Structure of Indian Cities', in A. K. Dutt and A. G. Noble (eds.) *Indian Urbanization and Planning: Vehicles of Modernization*, New Delhi: Tata McGraw Hill, 64–82, 1977.

Brush, J. E. 'Recent Changes in Ecological Patterns of Metropolitan Bombay and Delhi', in V. K. Tewari, J. A. Weinstein and V.L.S. Prakasa Rao (eds.) *Indian Cities: Ecological Perspectives*, New Delhi: Concept, 121–149, 1986.

Burgess, E. W. 'The Growth of the City' in R. E. Park, E. W. Burgess and R. D. McKenzie (eds) *The City*, Chicago: University of Chicago Press, 47–52, 1925.

Cadwallader, M. *Urban Geography: An Analytical Approach*, Upper Saddle River, N. J.: Prentice Hall, 1996.

Collision, P. and Mogey, J. 'Residence and Social Class in Oxford', *American Journal of Sociology*, 64: 599–605, 1959.

Dayal, A. *A Dream Revisited: An Archival Journey Into the Making of the Delhi Metro Rail*, New Delhi: Delhi Metro Rail Corporation Ltd, 2003.

Del Casino Jr., V. J. *Social Geography: A Critical Introduction*, Chichester: John Wiley and Sons, 2009.

Dupont, V. 'Socio-Spatial Differentiation and Residential Segregation in Delhi: A Question of Scale?' *Geoforum*, 35: 157–175, 2004.

Dutt, A. K. and Pomeroy, G. 'South Asian Cities', in S. D. Brunn, J. Williams and D. J. Zeigler (eds.) *Cities of the World: World regional Urban Development*, Lanham: Roland and Littlefield, 331–372, 2003.

Dutt, A. K. and Noble, A. G. 'Urban Development of South Asia', in A. K. Dutt, A. G. Noble, G. Venugopal and S. Subbiah (eds.) *Challenges to Asian Urbanization in the 21st Century*, Dordrecht: Kluwer Academic Press, 255–272, 2003.

Dutt, A. K. and Noble, A. G. 'Growing and Changing of Cities and the Spread of Urbanization in South Asia', in A. K. Dutt, H. N. Misra and M. Chatterjee (eds.) *Explorations in Applied Geography*, New Delhi: Prentice-Hall of India, 275–307, 2008.

Dutt, A.K. and Halder, A. 'Rich and Poor in Kolkata', in G. Pomeroy and Gerald Webster (eds.) *Global Perspectives on Urbanization*, Washington D.C.: American University Press, 151–179, 2008.

Gandhi, R. 'Social Structure of Urban India: Continuities and Change', in G. R. Gupta (ed.) *Urban India, Main Currents in Indian Sociology*, Vol. 6, New Delhi: Vikar, 3–85, 1983.

Gist, N. P. 'The Ecology of Bangalore, India; an East-west Comparison', *Social Forces*, 35: 356–365, 1957.

Gordon, G. 'The Evolution of Status Areas in Edinburgh", Institute of British Geographers Study Group in Urban geography. *The Social Structure of Cities*, Liverpool, 27–37, 1966.

Hoyt, H. *The Structure and Growth of Residential Neighborhoods in American Cities*: Washington, D. C.: Federal Housing Administration, 1939.

Inderjit (ed.) *India's Who's Who*, New Delhi: Infa Publications, 2004.

Johnston, R. J. 'The Location of High Status Residential Areas', *Geografiska* Annaler, 48 B: 23–35, 1966.

Kalra. R. 'High Technology and Urban Transformation in Bengaluru, India, Ph. D. Dissertation, Department of Geography, Kent State University, Kent, Ohio, U. S. A., 2007.

Kaushik, S. P. 'Farm Houses and Land: A Study of Peri-urban Space of Delhi', in B. Thakur, G. Pomeroy, C. Cusak and S. K. Thakur (eds.) *City, Society and Planning*, Vol. 1, New Delhi: Concept, 572–581, 2007.

Knox, P. L. *Urbanization: An Introduction to Urban Geography*, Englewood Cliffs, N. J.: Prentice Hall, 1994.

Kumar, A. 'The Inverted Compact City of Delhi', in M. Jenks and R. Burgess (eds.) *Compact Cities: Sustainable Urban Forms for Developing Countries*, London and New York: Spon Press, 153–166, 2000.

Mehta, S. K. 'Patterns of Residence in Poona', *American Journal of Sociology*, 74: 469–508, 1968.

Mieszkowski, P. and Mills, E. ' The Causes of Metropolitan Suburbanization', *Journal of Economic Perspectives*, 7:135–147, 1993.

Moffett, A. and Freund, B. 'Elite Formation and Elite Bonding: Social Structure and Development in Durban", *Urban Forum*, 15(2): 134–161, 2004.

Prakasa Rao, V. L. S. and Tewari, V. K. 'The Ecological Structure of Bangalore City', in V. K. Tewari, J. A. Weinstein and V. L. S. Prakasa Rao (eds.) *Indian Cities: Ecological Perspectives*, New Delhi: Concept, 221–242, 1986.

Robson, B. T. 'An Ecological Analysis of the Evolution of Residential Areas in Sunderland', *Urban Studies*, 3:120–142, 1966.

Satyajit (ed.). *India's Who's Who*, New Delhi: Infa Publications, 1980–1981.

Schewirian, K. P., Hankins, F. M. and Ventresca, C. A. 'Residential Decentralization of Social Status Groups in American Metropolitan Communities, 1950–1980', *Social Forces*, 68: 1143–1163, 1990.

Shrivastava, V. K. 'Globalization of Urban Regional Conflicts in the Retailing Structure of Delhi Metropolis', in B. Thakur, V. N. P. Sinha, M. Prasad, N. Sharma, R. Pratap, R. B. Mandal and R. B. P. Singh (eds.) *Urban and Regional Development in India*, New Delhi: concept, 141–149, 2005.

Singh, H. H. *Kanpur: A Study in Urban Geography*, Varanasi: Indrani Devi, 1972.

Singh, J. P. 'Residential Land Use in Shillong', *Geographical Review of India*, 39: 232–240, 1977.

Singh, R. L. *Banaras: A Study in Urban Geography*, Varanasi: Nand Kishore and Bros., 1955.

Sjoberg, G. *The Pre-industrial City: Past and Present*, New York: The Free Press, 1970.

Thakur, B. and Parai, A. 'A Review of Recent Urban Geographic Studies in India', *GeoJournal*, 29(2): 187–196, 1992.

Thakur, B. and Chauhan, S. B. S. 'Growth and Characteristics of Elite Residential Colonies in Mumbai and Delhi', in B. Thakur, V. N. P. Sinha, M. Prasad, N. Sharma, R. Pratap, R. B. Mandal, and R. B. P. Singh (eds.) *Urban and Regional Development in India*, New Delhi: Concept, 99–118, 2005.

Thakur, B. and Sagu, A. K. 'Locational Analysis of Elite Colonies in Delhi':, in B. Thakur, G Pomeroy, C. Cusak and S. K. Thakur (eds.) *City, Society and Planning*, Vol. 1, New Delhi: Concept, 494–522, 2007.

Tewari, V. K., Weinstein, J. A. and Prakasa Rao, V. L. S. 'Introduction: An Overview', in V. K. Tewari, J. A. Weinstein and V. L. S. Prakasa Rao (eds.), *Indian Cities: Ecological Perspectives*, New Delhi: Concept, 1–13, 1986.

Tyagi, V. K. *Urban Growth and Urban Village: A Case Study of Delhi*, Delhi: Kalyani, 1982.

Yadav, S. K. *Residential Structure and Social Patterns in Patna: A Study in Social Geography*, New Delhi: Inter-India Publications, 1987.

Weeks, J. R. *Population: An Introduction to Concepts and Issues*, Belmont, CA: Wadsworth/Thomson Learning, 2005.

Index

Pondicherry, 347